EMPIRE OF THE DEEP

EMPIRE OF THE DEEP

The Rise and Fall of the British Navy

BEN WILSON

Weidenfeld & Nicolson

LONDON

First published in Great Britain in 2013
by Weidenfeld & Nicolson

3 5 7 9 10 8 6 4 2

A CIP catalogue record for this book
is available from the British Library.

ISBN: 978 0 2978 6408 0

Typeset by Input Data Services Ltd, Bridgwater, Somerset

Printed and bound by CPI Group (UK) Ltd, Croydon CR0 4YY

Weidenfeld & Nicolson

The Orion Publishing Group Ltd
Orion House
5 Upper Saint Martin's Lane
London, WC2H 9EA
www.orionbooks.co.uk

The Orion Publishing Group's policy is to use papers
that are natural, renewable and recyclable products and
made from wood grown in sustainable forests. The logging
and manufacturing processes are expected to conform to
the environmental regulations of the country of origin.

There must be a beginning of any great matter, but the continuing unto the end until it be thoroughly finished yields the true glory

Francis Drake

For Conrad,
who was born, narratively speaking,
during the Battle of Barfleur-La Hogue

And in loving memory of
Jamie Brigstocke

CONTENTS

CONTENTS

II STATE NAVY: 1603–1748

IV DOMINANCE, DEFIANCE
AND DECLINE: 1805–2013

Part 12 Power

Part 13 Götterdämmerung

Part 14 Last Stand

Part 15 Decline

ILLUSTRATIONS AND MAPS

ILLUSTRATIONS

Section one

Admiral Beatty *(Author's collection)*

The Grand Fleet's dreadnoughts and escorts en route to Scapa Flow in 1914

HMS *Repulse* during exercises in the 1920s *(US Navy 2013)*

HMS *Queen Mary* blowing up at the Battle of Jutland, 31 May 1916 at or shortly after 4.26 p.m. *(IWM SP 1708)*

HMS *Ark Royal* c.1930 *(Author's collection)*

HMS *Ark Royal* during an attack by Italian aircraft *(IWM A 2298)*

HMS *Ark Royal* under fire from enemy bombers *(IWM A 2325)*

Captain Walker and his men dropping a pattern of depth charges over a submerged U-boat from the stern of Walker's sloop HMS *Starling* *(IWM A 22031)*

Captain Walker takes a bearing on a submerged U-boat *(IWM A 21986)*

Statue of Captain Frederic John Walker, CB DSO*** by Tom Murphy at Pier Head, Liverpool *(Stephen Wallace)*

HMS *Victorious*, HMS *Ark Royal* and HMS *Hermes* *(IWM MH 33794)*

A Harrier jump jet landing on *Atlantic Conveyor* during the Falklands War *(IWM/Getty Images)*

Ships involved in Operation Enduring Freedom *(US Navy 2013)*

MAPS

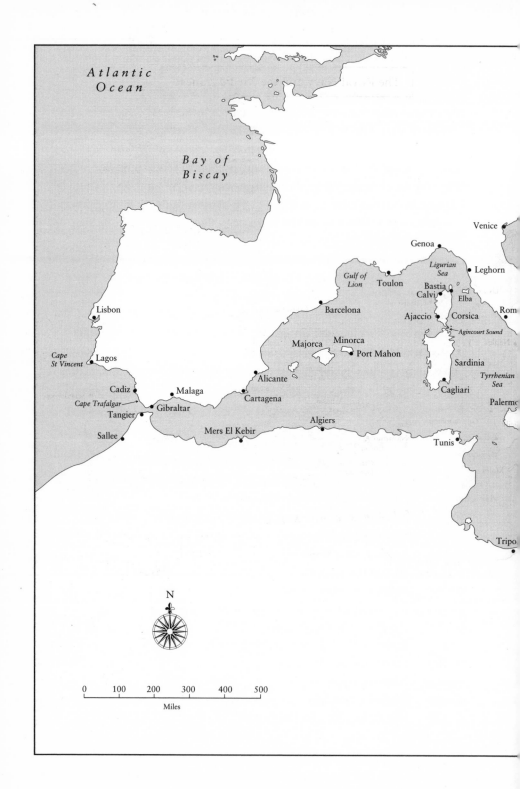

Atlantic Ocean

Bay of Biscay

Venice

Genoa

Ligurian Sea

Leghorn

Gulf of Lion

Toulon

Bastia

Calvi

Elba

Barcelona

Ajaccio

Corsica

Rom

Lisbon

Majorca

Minorca

Port Mahon

Agincourt Sound

Cape St Vincent

Lagos

Sardinia

Tyrrhenian Sea

Alicante

Cadiz

Malaga

Cartagena

Cagliari

Palermo

Cape Trafalgar

Gibraltar

Tangier

Mers El Kebir

Algiers

Sallee

Tunis

Tripo

N

```
0    100   200   300   400   500
Miles
```

The Royal Navy and the Mediterranean

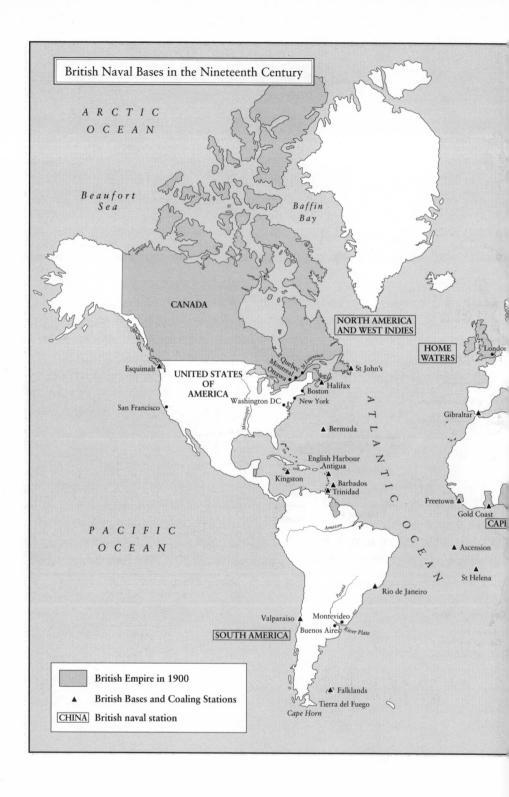

British Naval Bases in the Nineteenth Century

ARCTIC OCEAN

Beaufort Sea

Baffin Bay

CANADA

NORTH AMERICA AND WEST INDIES

HOME WATERS

London

Esquimalt

UNITED STATES OF AMERICA

Quebec St Lawrence
Montreal
Ottawa

St John's

Halifax
Boston
New York

Washington DC

San Francisco

Mississippi

Gibraltar

Bermuda

English Harbour
Antigua

Kingston

Barbados
Trinidad

Freetown

Gold Coast

CAPE

Amazon

ATLANTIC OCEAN

PACIFIC OCEAN

Ascension

St Helena

Rio de Janeiro

Paraná

Valparaiso

Montevideo

Buenos Aires River Plate

SOUTH AMERICA

British Empire in 1900

▲ British Bases and Coaling Stations

CHINA British naval station

Falklands

Tierra del Fuego

Cape Horn

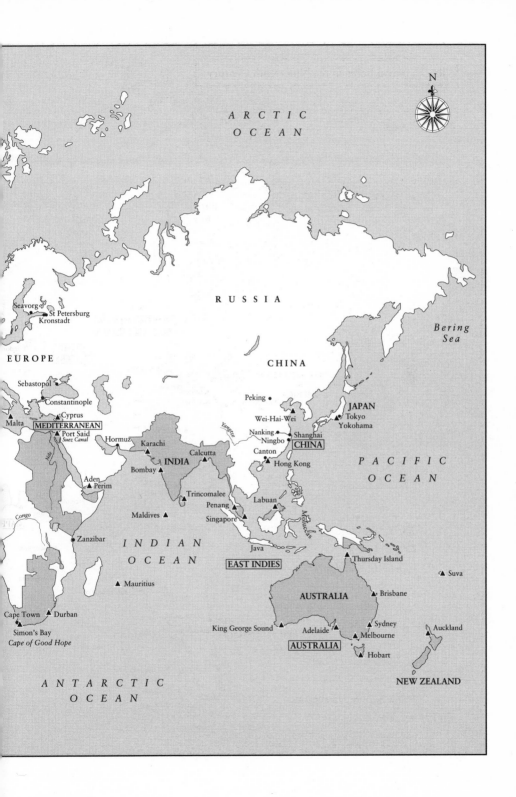

N

ARCTIC
OCEAN

RUSSIA

Bering
Sea

EUROPE

Seavorg
St Petersburg
Kronstadt

CHINA

Sebastopol
Constantinople
Cyprus
Malta
MEDITERRANEAN
Port Said
Suez Canal
Nile

Peking
Wei-Hai-Wei
Nanking
Ningbo
Shanghai
Canton
CHINA
Hong Kong

JAPAN
Tokyo
Yokohama

Hormuz
Karachi
INDIA
Bombay
Calcutta

PACIFIC
OCEAN

Aden
Perim

Trincomalee
Penang
Maldives
Singapore
Labuan
Moluccas

Congo

Zanzibar

INDIAN
OCEAN

Java
EAST INDIES

Thursday Island

Suva

Mauritius

AUSTRALIA

Brisbane

Cape Town
Durban
Simon's Bay
Cape of Good Hope

King George Sound
Adelaide
AUSTRALIA

Sydney
Melbourne
Hobart

Auckland

ANTARCTIC
OCEAN

NEW ZEALAND

PREFACE

The passenger described the captain of the ship: 'he is a very extraordinary person. I never before came across a man whom I could fancy being a Napoleon or Nelson ... His ascendancy over everybody is quite curious: the extent to which every officer and man feels the slightest praise or rebuke would have been before seeing him incomprehensible.'[1]

The passenger was Charles Darwin, who was twenty-two years old when the *Beagle* set sail at the end of 1831; the captain was Robert Fitzroy, then aged twenty-six. Darwin witnessed the Royal Navy at its zenith. Before the *Beagle* departed he was shown HMS *Caledonia*, a leviathan 120-gun ship of the line. 'So large a vessel is an astonishing sight, one wonders by what contrivance everything is governed with such regularity and how amongst such numbers such order prevails. On coming near her the hum is like that of a town heard at some distance in the evening.'[2] At another time he remarked of HMS *Beagle* that below decks, where the men messed and slept, everything was so clean that it put to shame many a gentleman's house.

Regularity, order, cleanliness – these were the hallmarks of the Royal Navy. Its ships purred like lubricated machines. Its men were trained and drilled to work in teams, the cogs that turned the complex mechanism of a fighting ship. The discipline, efficiency and health of British sailors, the professionalism of their officers and the smooth operation of the ships in which they served propelled the Navy to dominate the world's seas.

Sixteen years before, another giant of the nineteenth century had boarded a British warship. On 15 July 1815 Napoleon surrendered for the final time to the captain of HMS *Bellerophon*. 'What I admire most in your ship,' he told the captain as the ship's crew raised the boats, turned the capstan and hoisted the topsail yards, 'is the extreme silence and orderly conduct of your men; on board a French ship everyone calls and gives orders, and they gabble like so many geese.'[3] The same clockwork routine and unquestioning obedience to orders with which British sailors went about their daily shipboard tasks allowed them to fire their broadsides again and again in the heat of bloody, frenzied battles such as Quiberon Bay, the Saintes, the Nile and Trafalgar, with withering regularity. The success of the Royal Navy consisted in stamping order onto chaos.

Captain Fitzroy was born in July 1805, three months before the Battle of Trafalgar. When he became a midshipman at the age of fourteen and acting commander of HMS *Beagle* at twenty-three he joined a brotherhood of officers acutely aware that they inherited exacting standards of leadership and seamanship. Fitzroy promised to be among the best of his generation. He embodied what were seen as the virtues of a nineteenth-century naval officer. He was the scion of an aristocratic family; his grandfather, the Duke of Grafton, had been prime minister and his uncle, Lord Castlereagh, was foreign secretary from 1812 until 1822.

Fitzroy might have had impeccable connections, but the Navy demanded more than inherited qualities of nobility. Exceptional as he seemed to Darwin, Fitzroy's qualities were expected of all captains in the service. Since the seventeenth century the Navy had taken the sons of gentlemen and nobles and introduced them to life at sea from a tender age, sometimes as young as nine, to learn practical seamanship – how to splice, tie knots, haul on ropes, fire guns, for instance – as well as the technicalities of navigation and battle tactics. They were schooled to the sea as surely as a Grimsby fisherman. From 1677 they even had to take examinations to qualify as commissioned officers – a radically meritocratic idea in an age when military leadership was seen as the preserve of the aristocracy. But it created a Navy led by men of status who had spent their lives at sea. Fitzroy was awarded the mathematics prize at the Royal Naval College and scored an unprecedented 100 per cent at his examination to qualify as a lieutenant. He was considered one of the best seamen of his day.

But his courage and leadership would not be tried by battle. Instead they were tested by the elements. Robert Fitzroy took command of the brig *Beagle* in 1828 when her captain committed suicide off the unforgiving coast of Tierra del Fuego, the southernmost tip of South America. *Beagle* was one of two vessels conducting hydrographical surveys in South America. The expedition's leader, Captain Philip Parker King, in HMS *Adventure*, had already distinguished himself exploring and surveying the coast of Australia. Tierra del Fuego was a tough proposition. The purpose of such hydrographical surveys was to gather navigational information that would be used to produce detailed nautical charts for the Admiralty. King and Fitzroy led their surveying teams in subzero conditions and stormy seas.

These expeditions pushed the endurance and seamanship of officers and men to the limits. Officers on the frontline of exploration such as Fitzroy were driven by passion for science. It was something shared by officials at the Admiralty as well. In 1831 the Hydrographer of the Navy, Captain Francis Beaufort, suggested that Charles Darwin accompany Fitzroy on the second voyage of the *Beagle*. Darwin was to make geological observations in the lands the expedition encountered as it circumnavigated the globe. Fitzroy's task was to use astronomical observations made across the Pacific and Indian Oceans to establish the meridian distance between set points on the same longitude.

The aim was to add vital information to the store of knowledge being gathered by the Admiralty. After 1815 many of the hundreds of smaller vessels called into service to defend Britain from Napoleon were converted into survey ships to map the seas of the world, to make them safe for commerce. Between 1815 and 1817 the fighting officer Captain William Fitzwilliam Owen surveyed the Great Lakes and upper St Lawrence River. Captain King charted the coast of Australia and gathered information on topography, flora, fauna, climate and the native population. Between 1821 and 1826 Captain Owen surveyed 20,000 miles of the African coast. It was one of the most arduous surveying expeditions of all times. Owen lost half his crew and thirty-one out of forty-four officers to malaria and yellow fever. He returned home with three hundred charts for the Admiralty; they were invaluable in the Navy's war against slavery, a crusade that had spurred Owen on during his years of pain. By 1850 the entire coastline bounding the Indian Ocean had been charted, completing the work begun by Captain Owen.

Voyages of discovery under the naval officers John Franklin, Edward Parry and John Ross endured wretched Arctic winters charting the seas and searching for the North-West Passage. Between 1839 and 1843 John Clark Ross charted the coastline of Antarctica. In happier climes Navy hydrographers surveyed the coasts and archipelagos of the Mediterranean. Captain Thomas Graves spent ten years in the eastern Mediterranean, mapping the area and revealing important archaeological discoveries to the world.

All expeditions brought back information and sketches on the geology, botany, fauna and archaeology of the places they surveyed. It was not just what was visible on the surface or in shallow coastal water. In 1857–58 HMS *Agamemnon* and USS *Niagara* conducted the heroic first attempt to lay a telegraph cable almost 2,000 miles across the Atlantic. When the cable snapped – as it often did during the first attempts – it had to be grappled at depths of 3,200 metres. The venture was the beginning of a revolution in global communications; the side-effect was the revelation of a new world miles below the waves. In 1868 the Navy dispatched the first oceanographic expedition. But it was between 1872 and 1876 that the first great breakthrough in oceanography took place when HMS *Challenger* undertook a 70,000-mile, three-and-a-half-year voyage. *Challenger* surveyed the seabed of the world's oceans, making numerous deep-sea soundings, temperature observations, trawls and dredges. About 4,700 new marine species were discovered. The Challenger Office in Edinburgh published scientific reports that filled fifty volumes.

But no naval expedition was as important to the history of science as that of the *Beagle*. Darwin and Fitzroy's voyage took five years. The result of Darwin's observations was the basis for his theory of evolution. The time at sea was a trial for Darwin, who hated life on the ocean waves in the confines of a small ship. Compared with the Arctic ventures of Franklin and Parry it was not particularly gruelling; Darwin's discomfort is a reminder of how trying these surveying voyages were at the best of times. The Navy did not get much of a chance to fight between 1815 and 1914. The officers and men who did the most to uphold the service's traditions of courage and seafaring excellence were the surveyors. They added scientific research to that tradition. The resilience and qualities of leadership ingrained in the officers of the Royal Navy reached their apogee with the expeditions of Robert Falcon Scott.

The nineteenth-century scientific voyages show the Royal Navy at the peak of its capabilities. They are also emblematic of Britain at the summit of its power. There are many expressions of power and many uses for it, but the map is one of its most potent symbols. Maps imply ownership. Sea charts were needed for strategic and tactical ends. The greatest surveyor of them all, Captain James Cook, began his career as a hydrographer in the Gulf of St Lawrence in 1758, during the fight with France for the control of Canada. William Owen learnt the arts of surveying off the coast of Brest during the wars against Napoleon. This was the most important area of coast in the world for the Royal Navy. It was here that British warships patrolled incessantly, bottling up the French navy in its Atlantic ports. The Biscayan coast, with its lurking rocks, strong tides and hidden shoals, is highly dangerous. It had been the nursery of British sailors since the Middle Ages. It was also the key to British global power. By knowing intimately every one of its barely concealed, incisor-like rocks and its maze of channels, the Navy could lock up the French fleet in a tight blockade and enjoy the freedom to range the world with impunity.

After the conclusion of the Napoleonic wars the hydrographers were not just a symbol of power; they were its instrument. The surveyors and their crews were trained fighting men and their vessels were often gunboats. They policed the edge of empire as they went about their work. They fought slavers and chased pirates; British traders and diplomats called upon their help to tilt the scales in their favour during local disputes; and they imposed treaties on local rulers. Knowledge is power. By revealing the mysteries of the world the Navy opened up blanks on the map to traders. Surveys of Africa and South America were followed by expeditions sent to China, Japan, Malaya, Indonesia and Borneo. These were areas that were being forced to trade with the West in the middle part of the nineteenth century. In 1841, for instance, hydrographic surveyors brought a naval expeditionary force 170 miles up the Yangtze. The Navy's surveying teams made Asian waters safe for trade in two ways – by making charts and by turning their guns on pirates and unhelpful local officials. Hydrographers were harbingers of traders, consuls and colonists.

The resulting charts were the Navy's gift to the world: they were not kept top-secret, but made available so that the seas could be safely navigated by traders and warships of any country. The Admiralty also issued invaluable sailing instructions, lists of lighthouses and tide tables.

Mapping the world was a luxury that could only be enjoyed by a nation that was supremely confident of its own security, at home and abroad. The Royal Navy was, after Trafalgar, an unassailable world force. Ships and men that might otherwise have been needed to defend the realm or defeat an enemy were dispatched to distant oceans or to the frozen wastes of the poles. The Navy existed to defend trade. It had done it in battle; now it was doing it by science.

The Navy was able to send its surveyors to every nook and corner of the globe for the same reason that it was able to establish colonies and extend its trade with the force of the gunboat. This global clout was possible only because Britain had suppressed the myriad seaborne threats that had assailed her for millennia.

This book is the story of that epic struggle to overcome the dangers that emerged from the deep. It is about the unique authority Britain wielded over the seas and the equally epic story of the loss of that power in the twentieth century. Throughout the book I concentrate on two themes developed in this preface. The first is the accumulation of centuries of training, fighting and tradition by which the Royal Navy became a honed, war-winning machine. The second is the series of hurdles Britain overcame to become the predominant global maritime power. For most of their existence the kingdoms on the British Isles were the victims of the sea. The rise to greatness at sea was never automatic for those states that eventually became Great Britain. England was, for long periods of its history, economically weak and a third-rate maritime power. It was only by a tremendous effort of political will that England, and then Britain, developed a Navy that was feared around the world. That is why I reach back further into the past than most naval historians who have attempted a history of the Royal Navy. It is impossible to appreciate fully the Navy of Nelson, for instance, or indeed the state in which we find ourselves today, without understanding the prehistory of the Royal Navy.

Few other countries had fallen so deeply in love with a branch of the armed forces as the British did with the Royal Navy. It is an effort for us now to appreciate the extent to which the Navy was at the heart of national political, economic and cultural life. It was in large part the firmly implanted conviction that Britain's destiny was to rule the waves – a tradition that went back into the mists of time – that made that prophecy self-fulfilling. The British sense of national identity was in large part forged at sea. British history is inexplicable without reference to this fact.

We forget that at our peril. We have lived without the sense of the sea's danger since 1945. Even our identity as islanders dissipated in the age of air travel and the Channel Tunnel. But the sea has a way of intruding, in one way or another, on our nation's life.

ACKNOWLEDGEMENTS

The last few decades have seen a golden age of writing about British naval history. I am indebted to numerous scholars working today, whose works I recommend to readers of *Empire of the Deep*; a few of whom I name here. For the early period, up to the later seventeenth century, Kenneth Andrews, Bernard Capp, J. D. Davies, David Loades and Susan Rose. Our knowledge of the Royal Navy of the eighteenth century has been enlarged in recent years by, among others, Jeremy Black, Daniel Baugh, Michael Duffy, Richard Harding, John Hattendorf and Brian Lavery. Sam Willis's valuable new book, *In the Hour of Victory*, which brings to life an important cache of dispatches discovered in the British Library, appeared too late, alas, for my purposes. The study of Nelson has also been transformed in recent years with several biographies and specialist studies, most notably by Roger Knight, Colin White and John Sugden, whose two-volume biography is unlikely to be superseded. Andrew Lambert has made the Royal Navy of the nineteenth century his own in a series of recent works. Undoubtedly the historian who has revolutionised the field the most in recent years is N. A. M. Rodger, whose two- (soon to be three-) volume naval history of Britain is required reading.

On a more personal note, I would like to lavish praise on my agent, Clare Conville, and her assistant, Alexander Cochran. Thanks and gratitude for their hard work to all at Weidenfeld & Nicolson, especially Holly Harley, Jess Gulliver and Alan Samson. Bea Hemming has been an incomparable editor. This book could not have been finished without the love and support of my mother Marney and my wife Claire.

I

LAWLESS WATERS

to 1603

INTRODUCTION

The boat that bore him was no more than a skiff, and it had but eight rowers. The passenger, who took it upon himself to steer the vessel, was neither old nor young at twenty-nine years old. It was no doubt an even-keeled, straightforward pleasure cruise up and down the river Dee that summer's day in AD 973.

Edgar, the passenger and helmsman, could look with satisfaction on his crew who worked the oars. One was Kenneth, king of Alba. Another Magnus Haroldson, king of Man and the Isles. Also set to work on the oars were King Malcolm of Cumbria, King Donald of Strathclyde and King Iago ab Idwal Foel of Gwynedd. Indeed, all eight were rulers of, or heirs to, British kingdoms. They had obeyed Edgar's summons to Chester; they had given him their pledge to 'be his allies on sea and on land'; and they had made public their subordination by rowing their overlord, the king of England. As Edgar disembarked to make his way to his palace he observed to the courtiers following him that 'each of his successors would be able to boast that he was king of the English, and would enjoy the pomp of such honour with so many kings at his command'.

It was his fleet, and its ability to project power as far as the Hebrides and defend the realms of Britain, that gave Edgar the right to demand homage from his brother rulers. Ships were the key to power. Edgar was known as 'the Peaceful', but it was peace that came from continual watchfulness over the lawless seas. As the *Anglo-Saxon Chronicle* had it: 'nor was there fleet so proud nor host so strong that it got itself prey in England'.[1] Every year, to reinforce this boast, Edgar divided his fleet into four, stationed off each coast, so that it encircled Britain.

Half a millennium later another young English king put himself in command of a ship. Henry VIII was inordinately fond of visiting his warships and he was fonder still of showing off their size, state-of-the-art technology and gunnery to foreign dignitaries (who could be expected to report back to their rulers the awe-inspiring sight of England's defences).

In June 1514 Henry commissioned his pride and joy, the monstrous *Henry Grace à Dieu*, in the company of ambassadors from countries that might think of allying with or invading England. It was decked out like a flashy pleasure barge. The sails were of cloth of gold; at the tip of the bowsprit was a golden pinnacle topped with an orb and crown; enormous pendants, as long as fifty-six yards, flowed from the masts along with at least a hundred smaller flags bearing crosses of St George and Tudor roses; and everywhere were richly painted decorations.

Ships, the performance screamed aloud, were no mere workaday wooden hulks or (as they had been through much of the Middle Ages) unfashionable, unaristocratic and beneath the dignity of *real* warriors. Henry wanted all Europe to know that the English monarchy and sea power were synonymous. The ships of war were *royal* and the king was father of the navy, giving law to other nations and projecting power throughout Europe. To reinforce this point, and to remind the world that the *Henry Grace à Dieu* was no royal yacht, the visitors were honoured with a salute comprising every gun on board as they disembarked.

A year later Henry went further when he launched a new warship in front of the ambassadors. 'Henry acted as pilot,' wrote the French ambassador, 'and wore a sailor's coat and trousers made of cloth of gold, and a gold chain with the inscription *Dieu et mon Droit*, to which was suspended a whistle, which he blew nearly as loud as a trumpet.'[2]

The ship of state, the monarch as the pilot who weathered the storm: these were ancient metaphors even in Edgar's day. And so too was the self-proclaimed duty of an English king to safeguard the seas. But behind every performance lies reality. The northern seas of Europe were brutish, lawless waters. They would remain so for centuries. The struggle to keep the seas would plague every monarch. Maintaining a fleet of warships, bringing enemies to battle on the seas, even defending the coastline and estuaries – these were beyond the capabilities of the medieval and early modern state. The Royal Navy has had many fathers foisted upon it – Alfred the Great, Richard I, John, Henry VII or Henry VIII, according to taste. All have plausible claims on paternity, to be sure, but what can be lost in the search for a definitive origin of the Navy is the fact that sea power and kingship are intertwined in the history of the British Isles.

So when Anglo-Saxon chroniclers or the ceremonies of Henry VIII boast of fleets guarding the coast and monarchs giving law to the seas we should be aware that these were expressions of how things should be rather than what they were. The legend of Edgar, his immense fleet and his claim to sovereignty over the British seas reverberated down the centuries, transfixing kings and patriots. English kings, it was believed, had a moral right to the seas and a military obligation to secure that right. Charles I venerated Edgar; Cromwell flaunted Edgar's example in the face of the Dutch; James II had a short-lived son named Edgar. This legend was powerful. Kingship, in England, was bound up with control of the sea. More often than not it was a taunt to Edgar's successors, an impossible dream.

For Britain was not secure behind a defensive moat, but highly vulnerable to invasion from the sea. She stood a tempting prospect to anyone with a warship or a fleet. The sea was a thing of danger, not of security.

The harsh world of the North Atlantic was hard to subdue; but in time the British would come to specialise in the piratical conflict associated with this region, and even to export its peculiar form of violence to the rest of the world.

PART 1: INVASION ISLAND

Anglo-Saxon England and the Vikings:
the Situation in AD 878

0   50   100   150
Miles

N

*Atlantic
Ocean*

*North
Sea*

STRATHCLYDE

NORTHUMBERLAND

• Lindisfarne

Tyne

• Durham

Tees

Isle of
Man

*Irish
Sea*

Lune

Ribble

Ouse

Wharfe • York

Derwent

Aire

Mersey

Humber

Dee • Chester

Derwent

DANISH
MERCIA • Lincoln

Trent • Nottingham

Witham

Buttington • Bridgnorth

Severn

Nene

Great Ouse

Thetford

Yare

WALES

ENGLISH
MERCIA

KINGDOM OF
GUTHRUM

Deben

Ipswich

• Sutton Hoo

Oxford •

*Sashes
Island*

Lea

Hertford •

Maldon •

Shoebury

Wallingford •

London •

Isle of Sheppey

Chippenham •

Wantage •

Thames

Rochester •

Isle of Thanet

Reading •

Sittingbourne •

Sandwich

Ethandun •

The Weald

Downs

WESSEX AND ITS DEPENDENCIES

Appledore •

Folkstone

Athelney •

Winchester •

Hastings

Tone

Wareham •

Exe

Avon

Exeter •

Tamar

Poole •

Isle of Wight

English Channel

Jutland

Frisia?

Jumièges

Rouen

Seine

Rhine

Dives

Rhone

CHAPTER 1

ENGLAND
793–878

Near where I was brought up, at Cookham lock, willow-strewn Sashes Island breaks up the course of the Thames. All is peace and tranquillity, especially on a summer's day as pleasure boats meander towards the lock. But at the beginning of the tenth century Alfred the Great chose it as a fortification against the Vikings. The inhabitants of this pretty, fertile part of the interior of England found themselves on the frontline against seaborne attack. Then as now the sea seemed far away. But its menace loomed closer as the fortifications went up on the small island.

When we look at a map of Britain today we see a land slashed with ribbons of roads, some marked in thick blue, some in green and fainter traces of red. They seemingly divide the country into road-bound regions; they determine how we see Britain on our travels. For early mapmakers, however, it is the rivers that were accentuated; modern maps barely show them. In Matthew Paris's famous map from the thirteenth century, for example, big blue tentacles reach into the heart of Britain, so that the mainland looks less like an island than an archipelago. These blue cables don't look like rivers but inlets from the seas.

In the ninth and tenth centuries this sense of Britain as a land of rivers must have been acute, even without the aid of maps. For settled people like the Anglo-Saxons rivers were boundary markers, often disputed, between kingdoms. They could be a thing of safety in troubled times and a conduit of trade and commerce. For the Anglo-Saxons, long established in England, the interior of their island was a peaceful and prosperous place far removed from the wild and dangerous seas.

But with predatory, land-hungry, migratory warriors on the prowl in northern waters the rivers of Britain ceased to be highways of trade and became highways of violence. Living inland was then a false security. Shallow-draught Viking longships were highly developed: under sail they were strong enough to withstand open seas; under oar they could navigate far inland. And if a river ran out the light vessel could be carried to the next stretch of water. An estuary, howsoever small, was sufficient to bring a war boat within the network of British rivers.

The shock of attack came on the coast, at the monastery on Lindisfarne, an island off the coast of Northumbria, in AD 793. 'It is nearly 350 years that we and our forefathers have inhabited this most lovely land,' wrote Alcuin in the aftermath of the raid, 'and never before has such a terror appeared in Britain as we have now suffered from a pagan race, nor was it thought possible that such an inroad from the sea could be made.'[1] Attacks had occurred in southern Britain; a surprise attack on an island in the North Sea had been thought impossible. But if the sea had once defended 'this most lovely land' it was henceforth a channel of invasion. For the Vikings had the ultimate adaptable weapon: ships strong enough to withstand rough waters and light enough to penetrate deep into the interior. They could appear without warning. They came as isolated bands of roving warriors, not tied to anywhere in particular and prepared to cover large distances for a hefty reward or land. In time they would swarm together in co-ordinated fleets.

The tactics of the Vikings made defence very hard. Their priority, strange as it seems, was to avoid fighting. Once they had manoeuvred their ships into the right location they would fortify a strategic site from where they could conduct raids and withstand sieges from local forces. From this position of strength they could menace the countryside and demand payment to leave.

Early Viking raiders targeted the rich areas of northern Europe: Frisia and the coast of modern-day Germany. But the glittering prize was Charlemagne's Frankish empire. The key to naval defence, as Charlemagne perceived, was not to engage Vikings in warfare at sea. That would have been impractical on a large coastline: the enemy was large, flexible and mobile enough to simply bypass any defending forces and raid elsewhere. The art of defeating such a foe was to guard their *exit*. Coastal forts were erected, watches kept and bridges built to defend rivers. Estuaries and rivers from Germany and Flanders to northern France were defended by specially constructed ships. Smash-and-grab raiders need an escape route, and by bottling up estuaries and river mouths with boats and bridges the Franks made pillaging too hard.

This defensive system was maintained by Charlemagne's heir, Louis the Pious, but when that king died in 840 Francia fell into disarray as his son Charles the Bald and his brothers squabbled over the inheritance of an empire. The Viking raiders took full advantage as the defences crumbled into neglect. In 841 they rowed up the Seine, attacked the abbey at

Jumièges and sacked Rouen. In 845 an attack on Paris was headed off by payment of 7,000 lb of silver. In the following years Vikings were active on the Seine, Rhône and Loire, looting and destroying settlements and monasteries. The rivers of Francia were happy hunting grounds for many years; they went as far as the Camargue and raided along the Rhine. It was only when Charles the Bald got a grip over his fractious kingdom and began to revive his grandfather Charlemagne's defensive network that the Vikings looked for a softer target.

Viking raiders had harried the English coast sporadically during the years when Francia was the favoured target. The long south coast of the kingdoms of Wessex and Kent bore the brunt, and on several occasions royal ships went out to take on the Vikings at sea. In 851 Æthelstan, son of Egbert king of Wessex and himself king of Kent and Surrey, encountered Viking ships off Sandwich 'and slew a great host ... and captured nine ships and put the others to flight'.[2]

It was great for propaganda and great for Wessex: the Kentish nobility looked to the only real Anglo-Saxon naval power for protection against the threat to their coast. But such a victory was actually a trap. Æthelstan's ships had no doubt fought off a force of Viking ships, but it could have been no more than a small raiding party.

Gathered together, a Viking fleet was huge. In 850 a sizeable group wintered on the Isle of Thanet and in 854 on the Isle of Sheppey. The 865 winter encampment on Thanet was no passing annoyance however. Now the Viking collective numbered between 300 and 400 longships. When winter gave way, the Great Heathen Army entered East Anglia. This was a co-ordinated attack, aiming at the conquest and colonisation of England. Northumbria fell first in 866, East Anglia in 870. From here fresh forces from Scandinavia really could strike at the heart of England. The Trent took them to Nottingham, which was occupied in 868, and further into Mercian territory. The Great Ouse, the Nene, the Avon, the Derwent and other waterways invited them to fresh fields of conflict and conquest. The centre of their activity was the market at York, from where their raiding parties ravaged England in co-ordinated armies.

One by one the kingdoms north of the Thames fell under Scandinavian control – under the so-called Danelaw.

That is why the Wessex boast of naval supremacy on the south coast was a delusion. This would not be a war at sea. The real threat came from the north and from Viking ships on the Thames. The great emporium of London lay in Mercia. And so the Vikings had free access to the principal English river and the heartlands of the last free English kingdom, Wessex.

In 870 the Vikings were on the upper Thames and had set up camp at Reading. There followed a series of battles early in 871 in the area between Berkshire and Dorset. Neither side prevailed. At the last battle, however, King Æthelred was slain. His younger brother Alfred came to the throne of beleaguered Wessex. Another defeat followed and Alfred brought the war to an end, probably by paying off the Vikings, who departed to London.

Five years later the Vikings, led by Guthrum, king of the Danelaw, were back. Guthrum attacked Wessex from Poole harbour, joining another Viking raiding party at work on the Frome and Piddle rivers. They besieged Wareham, which stands between those two waterways. They failed to take it and Alfred was able to negotiate a truce. It was a dangerous deal, however. The Vikings broke their oaths, killed their hostages and took Exeter, where they awaited a fresh invasion fleet. This time the sea came to Alfred's defence. A storm scattered the relieving Viking ships, leaving the Danes in Exeter no choice but to strike a deal and retreat to Mercia.

They were soon back. At the feast of the Epiphany in 878 Guthrum launched a lightning strike on Alfred and his retinue at Chippenham. Most of the West Saxons were killed, but Alfred fled with a small band. They found refuge on Athelney, an island hidden away in the swampy fens on the Somerset Levels. The Vikings' subjugation of Anglo-Saxon England was almost complete. Only Alfred and his small group of followers hidden away in the marshes offered any real resistance.

CHAPTER 2

SEA ROVERS
878–901

> ... hither came
> The Angles and the Saxons from the east
> Over the broad sea sought the land of Britain,
> Proud warmakers, victorious warriors,
> Conquered the Welsh, and so attained this land.
>
> From *The Battle of Brunanburh* (AD 937)

One of the iconic artefacts of British history is the masked ceremonial helmet found at Sutton Hoo near Ipswich. When the mound was excavated in 1939 it yielded invaluable archaeological information. The earth covered an enormous longship, some ninety feet in length with a high prow and room for forty oarsmen. No timbers remained of this kingly vessel; but its decomposition created a photographic image. The sand was stained where the hull was interred, leaving a remarkable, ghostly impression of the outline and details of the vessel.

The helmet was found in a specially constructed wooden chamber inside the ship with the trappings of a great ruler: coins minted all over Europe, silver and gold jewellery from east Europe and the eastern Mediterranean, Celtic bowls, Germanic drinking horns, richly decorated weapons and much more beside. No body was found, but soil analysis suggested that one may have been buried inside the longship.

The Sutton Hoo ship had not been constructed specially for burial; all the signs were that it was of excellent quality and had been repaired during an active service life. The find made real the famous description of a ship burial in *Beowulf* in which a deceased king is placed amidships of his princely vessel, with his treasure and weapons piled over him, and sent out into the eternal waters. The Sutton Hoo longship was not pushed out into the tide as in *Beowulf*; it was dragged up onto the ridge overlooking the tideway of the river Debden. But the symbolic gesture is the same: this ship will carry the mighty king and his treasure into the afterlife.

The man for whom all this was done is believed to have been Rædwald, king of the East Angles in the early seventh century AD and *Bretwalda*, overlord, of the Anglo-Saxon kingdoms. His ships allowed him to project his power out of modern-day Suffolk and Essex throughout most of England; they made him feared and respected.

The Sutton Hoo ship burial bespeaks a people with a keen sense of maritime power. Two centuries before Rædwald's funeral the Germanic tribes, known to us as the Anglo-Saxons, had, like the Vikings of the ninth century, invaded Britain from the sea and conquered the land by taking their longboats up the same rivers.

The northern waters of Europe had always been a home to pirates and raiders emanating from Germany and Scandinavia. The Romans had been plagued by seafaring Germanic tribes who came out of the Rhine delta and the fens and wetlands of the North Sea coast. In AD 82 a cohort of the Roman army stationed in Britain made up of the Usipi tribe mutinied. The Usipi were accomplished seamen. The mutineers stole three large Roman ships and conducted the earliest known circumnavigation of Britain on a pillaging raid that ended when they were shipwrecked in Jutland.

Germanic piracy increased in the third century AD when the Romans pulled back from the Rhine and their power began to collapse in northern Europe. This coincided with rising waters on the North Sea coast which devastated the agriculture of the tribes who lived there. This is when we first hear of the Angles, Saxons and Jutes as pirates. Pliny had identified the Saxons as living between the Elbe and Jutland. The Angles came from modern-day Schleswig and the Jutes from Jutland. As the sea levels rose and Roman power ebbed they became land-hungry raiders. By the middle of the fourth century Germanic raids were frequent, and they had begun to push out the Britons and settle their land; a century on, England was under Anglo-Saxon control.

The Anglo-Saxons had entered Britain as sporadic raiders. They had harried the coast, then pushed up river and conducted surprise attacks. Then they had begun to settle and colonise. And then they had established political control. What the Vikings were doing five hundred years later was in a pattern long established in northern waters. The memory of men leaving their homes and setting out on a boat to find new lands was preserved in the poem *The Husband's Message*, which is a summons from a warrior to his wife for her to follow him over the sea and join him in his newly conquered estate:

... my lord
Compelled by need pushed out his boat and left
And had to cross the rolling waves alone,
Sail on the sea, and, anxious to depart,
Stir up the water ways. Now has this man
Conquered his woes; he lacks not what he wants,
Horses or treasure in this world,
O, prince's daughter, if he may have you.

By Rædwald's heyday, in the seventh century, the Anglo-Saxons had carved out kingdoms in England; they were prosperous and cultured communities, with a powerful aristocracy, trading links with Europe and a growing Christian presence. The finds at Sutton Hoo are testament to that flourishing culture.

This lavish ceremony was perhaps a last hurrah of Anglo-Saxon maritime dominance. Now war at sea became a part of folk memory. By Alfred's day, over 200 years since the death of Rædwald, the once mighty sea warriors were impotent against the Vikings. During centuries of peace the inhabitants of England had let their maritime traditions and prowess fade away.

And for good reason. The Anglo-Saxons felt secure in their rich and pleasant land. They had done the hard work. Once established, the ships could rot; with conquest once achieved, they were redundant. If there was any doubt that a life as a settled agriculturalist was far and away preferable to that of a migratory warrior the poem *The Seafarer* (dating from at least the tenth century) was a reminder of the terrible rigours of the sea:

... He knows not,
Who lives most easily on land, how I
Have spent my winter on the ice-cold sea,
Wretched and anxious, in the paths of exile,
Lacking dear friends, hung round by icicles,
While hail flew past in showers. There heard I nothing
But the resounding sea, the ice-cold waves.

The sea was something to be escaped; that was what made joining a longboat and crossing the waters to fight worthwhile in the first place. There were many Danes in England in Alfred's day who had exchanged the ship for the plough – and many more who wanted to do likewise. The portion of the Great Heathen Army that conquered Northumbria, for instance, 'were engaged in ploughing and making a living for themselves' at the time when Guthrum was turning his eyes to Wessex. Other Vikings favoured Britain because it stood within the maritime trade network that linked markets stretching from Dublin to York, Thetford and Lincoln to the Rhine, Scandinavia, Novgorod and Kiev. They were active in trade that connected the Atlantic world to the Muslim Mediterranean and the Black Sea.

Britain stood as a temptation for migratory warriors from tribes in Scandinavia and Germany. She was not defended by the seas, but a plum target for those who could master their waters. From Scandinavia the Norwegian Vikings targeted Shetland, Scotland, the Hebrides, Man, Ireland and, eventually, the north-west coast of England, while the Danes had easy access to the Narrow Seas and the Channel. The Anglo-Saxon period seemed to be a lull in a history of invasion and colonisation – a history of which they of course were part. No one who settled, it appeared, could be safe for long before more land-hungry tribes arose in the east, took to the sea, and another wave of seaborne invasion crashed over the isles.

That was the situation that faced Alfred on Athelney Island. He was acutely aware of his maritime heritage. But he also knew the dangers that came from the sea in his own time.

The first step in defending England from the sea was an inside-out strategy. From Athelney Island and the marshes of Somerset, Alfred summoned an army from his scattered people. Guthrum and his Vikings were defeated at the Battle of Ethandun in Wiltshire and starved to surrender at Chippenham. Guthrum converted to Christianity and became Alfred's godson. The boundary between Wessex and Guthrum's East Mercia was pushed back to the river Lea and Watling Street west of Bedford. Alfred gained London and western Mercia. Underemployed Vikings mustered an enormous fleet on the Thames at Fulham and headed to fresh fields of violence in Flanders. It was a stunning reversal of fortune. Alfred was without doubt the leader of Anglo-Saxon resistance to the Vikings not just in his own kingdoms but in England as a whole.

'Defence in depth'[1] is the term used to describe Alfred's strategy in the following years. The Viking threat had faded but not vanished. Alfred borrowed from the tactics of Charlemagne and the Vikings themselves. Garrison towns, known as *burhs*, were set up throughout Wessex and English Mercia as a way of countering the Vikings' own tactic of throwing up fortifications and terrorising a region. Rivers were defended by bridges and twin *burhs* on each bank or an island. On the all-important Thames these were at London, Sashes Island, Wallingford, Oxford and

Cricklade. The old Roman roads and other highways were guarded. Ports were given better defences and watch was kept on the coast to prevent the Vikings beaching their longboats. These strongholds were to be linked by a mobile field army, which could march or ride to relieve the *burhs* when the Vikings appeared.

Areas of England under Alfred's control would therefore be harder to plunder. The rivers lost their attraction as highways of invasion. Mobility, which the Vikings relied upon, was impeded by the defence-in-depth strategy. And, strange as it may sound, these land- and river-based military reforms had profound implications for the development of England's navy.

To fight the Vikings at sea was a perilous venture. One of the reasons the Anglo-Saxons abandoned their warships was that they could not be adapted to the needs of a settled agricultural people. Ship-based warfare in the Dark Ages was biased sharply in the favour of attackers, not defenders. Ship-to-ship combat was possible only in calm waters and if both sides desired it. The Greeks, Romans and other peoples of the Mediterranean developed high-sided, oar-driven ships that could be brought alongside enemy vessels. Fighting at sea was like fighting on land. An opponent had to be grappled and boarded and overwhelmed by swords and spears and other conventional weapons. Fighting ships, then, were platforms for combat. It differed from fighting on land only by the confined space, a timbered floor and a higher risk of drowning.

In the Atlantic region, however, the seas were too rough for this kind of action. Longboats were troop carriers that propelled warriors to their targets. They relied on surprise, speed and secrecy. Fighting was done on dry land, the ships left hidden or under guard. Using naval means to contain this threat was impossible. Viking raiding parties were flexible in their objectives. Their attacks came without warning, out of a vast and dangerous sea that no king could patrol. A defensive navy was, in these conditions and with these kinds of ships, an impossibility.

The only way to neutralise this way of war was to deprive the Vikings of mobility, surprise and terror – which was exactly what Alfred did with his reforms. A Viking force, on land or on sea, could not be headed off, but it could be brought to pitched battle or forced to abandon its plunder – two things the Vikings hated. By garrisoning somewhere like Sashes, deep in the interior, Alfred was undermining the premise of Viking warcraft, conceding them maritime supremacy but denying its advantages.

In 885 the success of the policy was demonstrated when a Viking raiding party entered Kent and besieged Rochester. Alfred led his standing field army to battle. Instead of fighting, the Vikings returned to their boats and made sail.

Alfred did have naval ambitions. After the defeat of Guthrum the situation in Anglo-Saxon England in the 880s was comparable to what it had been in the years before the Great Heathen Army entered East Anglia. There were plenty of raids, but no organised Viking army. In 881 Alfred fought a sea battle against four Viking ships and destroyed two of them. In 885 he took his ships to the river Stour in Essex, on the boundary of the Danelaw, where he encountered a band of some sixteen Viking longboats. Alfred beat the Danes, recovered their spoil and killed the crews. But as he was leaving the river estuary his ships were intercepted by a large fleet of Vikings and defeated.

This shows Alfred's activity as *Bretwalda* of Anglo-Saxon England. He was on the move, defending different parts of England against raiders, showing his intent to eliminate the Viking threat. This was, as we have seen, within the traditions of Wessex kings, who possessed royal ships and were eager to use them. But his range of activity was limited. In the right situation – during a surprise attack on a river or against a tiny group of Vikings – he could fight on equal terms; faced with a larger fleet in wider waters he was hopelessly outmatched.

Resistance was all very well against small raiding parties who were not bent on invasion. In 892–93 a massive force of Vikings converged on Wessex and Mercia. The larger group, which came on 250 ships, based themselves at Appledore in Kent; the others, under the legendary Hastein, with eighty ships, fortified Milton, near Sittingbourne on the Thames Estuary. Hastein had been on campaign since the 860s, mainly in Flanders and Francia; he had terrorised the Mediterranean in his younger days. In the early 890s he had suffered a series of reverses in Francia. It was an ominous sign that in 892–93 he was, like his fellow Vikings, accompanied by his wife and children.

This was no raid, but a full-scale migratory conquest.

Once again the vulnerability of England had been exposed. A force landing by sea in Kent would be protected by the Weald, an enormous forest that cut off the south-easterly tip of England from a defending army. Faced with hundreds of ships that could pounce anywhere along the coast, Alfred was forced to negotiate. The Anglo-Saxon sources are reticent about this, but it is clear that Alfred tried to deal with Hastein, standing godfather to one of his sons and paying geld. But it was a forlorn strategy.

The Vikings based at Appledore raided southern England, but were eventually defeated by Alfred's son Edward at Farnham in Surrey. They were forced to cross the Thames and then onto the river Colne. They were besieged at Thorney Island near the modern-day intersection of the M4 and M25. The rest of the Appledore contingent took their ships to the Essex coast. From the safety of the Danelaw the Vikings began a huge and concerted attack on Wessex using the coastline and rivers. There were 470 ships off the coast of Wessex attacking from the east and from Devon. Alfred and his army hardly knew which way to turn.

Alfred went west and it proved futile, as the Vikings could evade him by returning to sea to continue their raids elsewhere. The real action happened in the Thames Estuary and the river Severn. The Londoners marched out and took Hastein's camp at Benfleet and captured his wife and children. Hastein moved on, set up a *burh* at Shoebury and was reinforced by Vikings from East Anglia and Northumbria. He proceeded up the Thames, moved on to the Severn and continued up to Buttington near Welshpool. There the Vikings were besieged and defeated as they tried to break out. The survivors fled back to Essex, regrouped, and dashed back across England and took Chester. Alfred's troops simply destroyed all available food stocks nearby, so the Vikings could not survive the winter and limped back to Shoebury via the Danelaw.

Hastein, it seems, was trying to establish a new Viking kingdom in the west Midlands. The last bid for such a prize was a Viking attack up the river Lea. They established a base near Hertford. Alfred marched to the scene and established a double *burh* on the lower reaches of the Lea. The Vikings went from attackers to defenders. They abandoned their ships and fled across land, reaching Bridgnorth on the Severn. The once-mighty fleet was reduced to five vessels which left the Severn to raid the Seine.

It was a long, involving victory, expensive in lives and treasure. Persistence played off. The policy of a standing army, fortified towns and bottling up rivers proved a tactical success. It made Alfred's England a much less attractive place for soldiers of fortune such as Hastein. After the defeat of the Vikings Alfred embarked upon a new strategy to safeguard Wessex and make good his claim to overlordship of Anglo-Saxon England. He began to build new longships. They were 'swifter and steadier and also higher'[2] than the Danes' longships and were constructed according to Alfred's own design.

Clearly these ships were intended to fight at sea – their size ruled out riverine conflict. They were probably built in partial imitation of classical Mediterranean ships, high enough to provide a platform for a boarding operation and big enough to intimidate invaders.

Alfred's ships got their first outing in 896 on an unidentified estuary against six Viking ships which had been attacking the south coast. The Vikings had beached three of their ships to plunder inland, leaving three afloat. These latter ships tried to break out of the river mouth when they saw the English ships. Only one escaped, and that with a crew of just five. The other two ships were taken and their crews slain. The English then beached their ships to pursue the Vikings who were on shore. Three of Alfred's ships were on the side of the estuary chosen by the Vikings; the other six waited to pounce from the opposite side. As the Vikings tried to board their ships there was a furious battle by the shore. Alfred lost sixty-two men, the Vikings 120. The surviving Vikings managed to put to sea as the tide rose and rowed out of the estuary.

The English in their state-of-the-art ships could only watch, for the shallow-draught Viking ships could get out much faster – Alfred's were larger and needed the tide to come in a bit more before they could float. It was the sea that finished the Vikings off. Their ships were damaged and their crews decimated; two were forced ashore on the Sussex coast and their men hanged on Alfred's orders.

Alfred's fleet was, it seems, intended for just such an action – to trap small groups of raiders in river mouths and estuaries. The first battle was far from a success. English casualties were high for little gain. The ships themselves were damned by their imposing size, allowing the Vikings to use the tide to outmanoeuvre them. As with the Vikings, his ships were intended primarily to bring troops to conflict in the quickest possible time. The main part of the fighting was done on land; the battle on water was against a skeleton crew waiting for their fellows to return with their plunder.

Alfred was once called the father of the navy. It is clear, however, that he stood in a tradition of West Saxon monarchs who had used ships as one of many weapons in their armoury. It was not a navy as we would understand it. In any case, ships as an offensive and defensive instrument of war had a completely different meaning in the Dark Ages. Alfred's achievements lie elsewhere. For the first time there was an idea of England. And it coalesced around defence against a common enemy. Alfred gave it the means to survive.

CHAPTER 3

THE KEY
901–1066

The key to England is an area of sea off the south-east coast between North Foreland and South Foreland in Kent. For centuries the roadstead known as the Downs would be of vital strategic importance to England and her enemies. It lies near the closest point between the mainland of Britain and continental Europe. To the south and west are the Channel and the northern coast of France; to the east the North Sea and the coasts of Flanders, Jutland and Scandinavia. It is close to the ports of the south coast and to the Thames Estuary.

But what makes the Downs so valuable to seafarers is their safe anchorage during stormy weather. They are protected to the east by the Goodwin Sands, a shifting sandbank ten miles long, and to the north and west by the Kent coast. The Goodwin Sands have lured many ships to destruction, but a good pilot with local knowledge can get a ship into the safety of the roadstead. Vessels coming from London, the North Sea ports and the Baltic waited here for a wind to carry them down the Channel.

The Downs were a place of muster for English fleets coming out of the Thames. They are also the perfect base from which to invade the soft underbelly of England or to gather ships prior to battle. They have been the site of battles and shipwrecks. The Downs make many appearances in this book.

The Downs are a haven ideal for large ships to ride at anchor protected from the sea. In the eleventh century shallow-draught longships would be able to use the part of the Downs called Sandwich Bay. It must have been a welcome sight for seafarers. The shingle Sandwich Beach, the five miles of mud and sand known as the Sandwich Flats and the estuary of the river Stour were perfect for beaching a longship. The ships could also be anchored in the bay, ready for use.

Again and again in the eleventh century chroniclers mentioned Sandwich Bay. It was the most strategically important part of England. Here a defending squadron could keep watch on the North Sea and the Channel, standing ready to deliver troops to the site of enemy incursion. It was vital for an invading force, which could gather here before striking at the most vulnerable part of the south and east coasts or the Thames. Whoever commanded Sandwich had the possibility of controlling England.

Alfred's England continued to expand in the decades after his death in 901. When Edward, his son and heir, died, England south of the Humber was under the control of the Wessex dynasty. His grandson, Æthelstan, gained the north of England and had coins minted with the legend *rex totius Britanniae*, king of all Britain.

The imperial authority commanded by Edward and Æthelstan was backed by a formidable land army and an administrative system that grew in complexity as the territory of the West Saxons increased; it also rested on royal ships. Edward had 100 ships that he used in his conflict with the Northumbrians. By the time of Æthelstan, England had become a major European force. His ships fought as far away as Caithness (against the Norse) and the Flanders coast (in support of Louis IV). He received the gift of a state-of-the-art Viking longship, complete with golden beak, purple sail and gilded shields, from Harald Fairhair of Norway. And it was said that one of the most famous and successful of all the Vikings, Rollo, the conqueror and first duke of Normandy, recruited sailors and had ships repaired in England.

Æthelstan had been born when Alfred faced marauding Viking ships and armies. A few decades on here was a Viking ruler honouring an Anglo-Saxon with a ceremonial ship. The tables were turned. England was a maritime power in the north Atlantic.

Fleets brought prestige. Even if they were never used they intimidated would-be raiders and invaders. They made foreign kings desirous of peace and eager for help. They made England the dominant power in Britain. No Anglo-Saxon king knew this better than Edgar, who made a great show of his naval strength. 'It was widely known throughout many nations across the gannet's bath [the sea] that kings honoured ... [Edgar] far and wide ...'

The naval strength of England depended on its monarch's will and ambition to keep it alive. When Edgar died in 975 the country fell into deep divisions. The succession was disputed between his sons Edward and Æthelred. England had been strong, secure and peaceful for a long time. Now it was riven with internal divisions and weak leadership. The Vikings, who had been kept out for decades, scented an opportunity.

Raids began in 980. In 991 the situation became much worse. A Danish fleet of ninety-three ships gathered off Sandwich, attacked Folkestone and worked its way up the coast to Ipswich. It then turned back south, entered the Blackwater estuary and encountered Ealdorman Byrhtnoth and a small English army at Maldon in Essex. They sent the English a messenger demanding gold in return for protection.

The English refused this opportunity and chose to fight. They lost, and it was decided that England should pay tribute of 10,000 pounds. It did not stop the Viking raids. They continued until 994, when a fleet led by Olaf Tryggvason and Swein Forkbeard attacked London from the sea. This time Æthelred paid 22,000 pounds of gold and silver. He had tried to raise a navy, calling upon 'all the ships that were of any use'.[1] The tribute only put a temporary stop to the raids. After decades of peace the defensive system built up by Alfred and Edward and maintained by their successors had been neglected and allowed to collapse.

This was a different kind of Viking attack to the one Alfred had faced a century before. The raiders were after plunder for a specific purpose. They were not after territory this time. Instead Viking fleets remained on England's coasts more or less permanently, raiding and demanding protection money.

Æthelred continued to stump up large sums. In 1002 the Viking fleet was paid 24,000 pounds 'on condition that they should cease their evil-doing'.[2] The evil did not stop however. Later that year the king ordered the murder of all Danes in Britain. One of those massacred was the sister of Swein Forkbeard, king of Denmark. Now he was back at the head of the fleet, attacking the West Country and then East Anglia. This time the Danes met resistance, but it was ineffectual and it was only famine in 1005 that secured the retreat of the Vikings.

They were back the next year, this time in a 'great fleet' that appeared at Sandwich, based itself on the Isle of Wight and proceeded inland to ravage, burn and slay in 'every shire of Wessex'. They left for Scandinavia upon receipt of 36,000 pounds.

Æthelred had to revive England's naval power if his kingdom was to survive. In 1008 the king 'ordered that ships should be built unremittingly over all England'. The unit of administration was the Hundred, made up of 100 hides – a hide was the area needed to feed a family. Under the policy 310 hides made up a 'ship soke', which had to provide a ship and a crew of sixty sokesmen.

They were ready within a year: 'there were so many of them as never were in England before'. The ships and their levies came from all over England and mustered at Sandwich Bay. Maritime England had been revived.

Æthelred is known as the 'the Unready'. This is a mistranslation. It comes from his contemporary nickname *Unræd*. It was a pun on his name. *Æthel* meant 'noble' and *ræd* meant 'council', but seeing how his reign turned out, *Unræd* – 'ill-advised council' – seemed more appropriate. *Unræd* became 'unready', a completely different but seemingly apt meaning. Throughout his reign he was certainly ill-advised – and ill-served. At Sandwich Brithric, the brother of a noble, accused another commander, Wulfnoth, of treason. Wulfnoth went on the run with twenty ships and began to plunder the south coast. Brithric went in pursuit with eighty ships, which were driven aground in a storm. Wulfnoth took advantage, burning his pursuers' ships.

When he heard of the disaster Æthelred abandoned the remaining ships and went home, and so did his nobles. It was a terrible, humiliating disaster. The *Anglo-Saxon Chronicle* says of the king and his nobles' departure: 'thus lightly did they forsake the ships; whilst the men that were in them brought them back to London. Thus lightly did they suffer the labour of the people to be in vain.'

The English fleet was replaced off Sandwich by an enormous Viking fleet led by Thorkell the Tall. His invasion of England was one of the most horrific yet seen. Little resistance was offered as Thorkell ravaged the country. Back in Denmark Swein saw that England was defenceless. Thorkell – his subject after all – had it at his mercy. Why not simply conquer the whole kingdom? But there *was* still defence, and it came from the unlikely source of Thorkell. In 1012 he undertook the defence of England and demanded a tax, the Danegeld, in return.

Swein's fleet mustered at Sandwich Bay and then went up the coast and entered the Humber and then the Trent. The Danes swept south, forcing Æthelred and Thorkell out of the kingdom. Swein reigned as king of England and Denmark until his death in 1014. He was succeeded by his son, Cnut.

Once again England had strong naval protection. In 1018, for instance, Cnut 'put to sword – thank God – the crew of thirty ships of pirates and thus he, who had earlier been an invader together with his father, and a sworn destroyer of the country, now became its sole defender.'

A Danish king was able to prevent further invasion. And indeed English and Danish ships fought on the same side as Cnut pressed his claims against Norway and brought Scotland to heel. He was dominant in the Irish Sea as well, bringing various Gallic regions under his sway, defending England from Vikings from the Orkneys and Hebrides. English taxation paid for a permanent fleet – comprising forty ships – with which Cnut built and maintained a mighty North Sea empire. It was perhaps an irony that England – defeated England – stood at the centre of this empire and indeed that invasions of Scandinavia originated in a country that had suffered so much at the hands of Scandinavia.

Cnut died in 1035 and was succeeded by his brutal son Harthacnut. He was the last of the line of Danish kings who ruled England. Under him the English fleet expanded from forty to ninety-four ships. Sea power was achieved by stringent taxes imposed on the English. Harthacnut lived until 1042; his death brought Edward of Wessex to the throne.

Edward was indisputably English. He was the son of Æthelred, a king infamous for his failures at sea. But in the mid-eleventh century England was a formidable naval power. Edward was determined to keep it that way. In 1044 he commanded a fleet of thirty-five ships off Sandwich in defence against the predatory moves of Magnus I, king of Norway and would-be successor to Cnut and Harthacnut's North Sea empire.

Now it was the Danes who were desirous of England's maritime strength. Edward was asked to send fifty heavily manned ships to aid them, but he decided against it. His ships were best kept off Sandwich, where they could dictate terms to England's enemies and aid her friends. In 1047 the Holy Roman Emperor sent an army against Count Baldwin of Flanders who was in revolt and requested that Edward guard the seas to prevent Baldwin taking to ship. 'In consequence, the king went with a great fleet to the port of Sandwich, and remained there until the emperor had obtained from Baldwin all he desired.'

But a large navy was a dangerous, perfidious beast in the eleventh century. At the heart of the English fleet were ships crewed by Danish mercenaries. Edward gradually paid them off. By 1051 they were all gone. Edward was able to abolish the detested Danegeld, the tax that had given England naval power.

Yet the country's naval forces also represented a domestic danger. The Goodwin Sands are named after Edward's mightiest subject, Godwin, the earl of Wessex. Godwin was a living embodiment of English sea power. His father was Wulfnoth, the pirate who had wrecked Æthelred's navy in 1009. Cnut had given Godwin lands in eastern Wessex. He controlled the southern coast of England, including the vital Sandwich Bay, and he contributed forty-three ships to the navy. He was also King Edward's father-in-law.

After 1050, however, the king was ready to shake off the influence of one so powerful. Edward offended his in-laws by appointing Normans to positions in church and state. In 1051 he confronted the power of the Godwin family and forced it into exile. In order to shore up his position

Edward sought a closer alliance with William, duke of Normandy. Later it was said that Edward had made William his heir in return.

Godwin and his sons would not take this humiliation. They were powerful at sea and, like the founder of their clan, Wulfnoth, they had the loyalty of the seafarers of the south coast. Edward tried to cobble together a fleet to seal off Sandwich Bay and the Downs. But it was a fiasco. English sea power belonged to Godwin. He and his sons took a mighty fleet from Portland Bill all the way to the Thames. Edward awaited them at London with fifty ships.

He could offer no resistance. Edward was forced to welcome back Godwin and his family and dismiss the Normans he had brought over. But Godwin did not live long to enjoy his return to power. He was succeeded as earl of Wessex by his eldest son, Harold Godwinson.

The return of Godwin was a reminder, if one was needed, that England's fortunes were inextricably linked with the sea. Godwin and his family had mastered the Channel in a crucial moment and it allowed them to strike at London. From 1052 Edward ceased to have control over the military. He was a puppet king. Harold took command of the navy, which he used to invade Wales in 1063. Harold was the most powerful man in England, monarch in all but name. It caused little surprise that he was crowned king as soon as the childless Edward died in 1066.

Harold would need the formidable navy that he had built up in England. For there were challengers to his authority. The first came from his brother Tostig, who was trying to raise forces in Flanders. The second came from William of Normandy. William believed that he was Edward's heir and had plans to invade England. It was a risky undertaking, as his barons warned him. Harold, they said, 'had a great fleet and highly skilled sailors'. Could the Normans compete against the massive sea power built up by Wulfnoth, Godwin and Harold?

It was a good point. Normandy had no navy to speak of. William needed 700 ships at least to transport an army of about 7,000. The Bayeux Tapestry captures something of the frenetic activity in constructing a huge fleet at short notice.

Meanwhile Tostig secured ships and raided the English coast. Harold correctly saw this as the prelude to greater trouble. He gathered together the largest fleet yet seen in England. Its destination, as so often, was Sandwich, where it could guard England's east and south coasts. This mobilisation forced Tostig north.

By this time Harold knew that William was preparing a large invasion fleet on the Dives estuary. Throughout the summer the south of England

Building the invasion fleet, from the Bayeux Tapestry.

was well guarded. Troops were stationed on the shore and the navy based itself on the Isle of Wight.

They waited and waited. William did not stir. Harold's forces on land and sea had nothing much to do but eat their way through all available supplies. On 8 September the ships were forced to return to London for fresh provisions and men. Once again the Channel was unguarded. William took out his fleet, but it was forced into St Valéry on the Somme. The same storms did great damage to Harold's navy as it headed back to London.

And Harold had another threat to deal with. Harald Hardrader of

The size of the men is exaggerated in the Bayeux Tapestry (note the size of the horse in the middle ship for a truer sense of scale). Also of note is the helmsman, who steers the ship and gives direction to the sailor setting the sail.

Norway had led a huge force of ships and linked up with Tostig on the Humber. Just as William's fleet was ready to sail, Harold was forced to march his army north to fight off this invasion. Hardrader and Tostig were both killed at the battle of Stamford Bridge and their armies defeated. Meanwhile William's army had crossed the Channel unopposed in over 700 invasion ships and landed at Pevensey. They fortified the area to protect their ships from Harold's navy.

Harold sped back to London. His plan was to attack as soon as possible. It was a risky move as his army had been weakened in the fight against Hardrader and it would take time to raise reinforcements. Harold's plan, however, was to fight as close to the sea as possible. He would launch an attack down Senlac Hill, trapping the Normans on the Hastings peninsula. Their retreat would be sealed off by seventy ships sent from London.

Harold came from a family with long associations with the sea and naval warfare. He was a seafaring warrior himself. And in 1066 he was fighting on his home turf – the coastline dominated for decades by the sons of the pirate Wulfnoth. No doubt he believed a combination of land and sea warfare would bring success as it had done before. But it was not to be. It was the naval upstart William who defeated Harold in 1066.

CHAPTER 4

CHAPTER 4

CROSS CHANNEL
1066–1221

At one moment the king of England is in Ireland, the next in
England, the next in Normandy; he must fly rather than travel
by horse or ship.

Louis VII on Henry II

History might have been very different had England remained a maritime
empire on the Scandinavian model. The Norman Conquest made England face in a different direction.

The high point of English naval power in the Middle Ages was during
the reigns of Edward the Confessor and Harold. England was a powerful
maritime force in large part thanks to the Danish connection. It had the
potential to dominate the British Isles by the force of its ships and it was
orientated towards the maritime networks that stretched from Ireland to
the Baltic.

Instead it became part of another empire, one that did not rely upon
sea power. The gravitational pull of Normandy and France meant that
traditional spheres of activity, such as the Irish Sea, were neglected. These
areas were ceded to nascent naval powers in the British Isles with strong
Viking and Celtic connections: the Dublin Vikings, Man, Galloway, the
Scottish isles and Wales.

Britain, which had on occasion accepted English hegemony, frag-
mented. And indeed William took a different approach to naval defence:
one of slash and burn. According to the *Anglo-Saxon Chronicle* he filled
the country with troops 'and had the land near the sea laid waste, so that
if his enemies landed, they should have nothing to seize on so quickly'.[1]

The sea that mattered was the Channel. And with Norman control
of both sides it became a highway connecting the king's two realms. It
ceased to be a barrier. For early Norman kings Channel crossings were
a normal function of government. William I travelled between England
and Normandy seventeen times in twenty-one years, William II ten times

in thirteen years and Henry I twenty-one times in thirty-five years. In addition there was a regular transfer of money, dispatches and administrative commands from wherever the court was based. There was a speedy royal ship, known as an *esnecca*, on permanent standby to ferry royal personages or their representatives from one side to the other. On numerous royal documents Henry I wrote 'transitus' – in transit – instead of giving a place name.

By the twelfth century Viking raids had become a part of history, the threat ended by internal disputes in Scandinavia and a strong network of forts and castles in England itself. With the accession of Henry II in 1154 the seas could not have been calmer. Henry's empire, at its height, therefore extended from the Firth of Forth in the north to the Pyrenees in the south. He controlled the Narrow Seas, the Channel and the Bay of Biscay. He was the greatest king in Christendom.

Ports could once again flourish now that the seas had been tamed. By the twelfth century the waterfront of the old Roman port of London was extended and improved with timber revetments jutting out into the river so that goods could be unloaded directly from ships. At the end of the century wooden cranes were being used. Other key port towns, such as King's Lynn, Southampton and Bristol, were similarly improved with quays, warehouses and cranes. When Matthew Paris drew his map of Britain in the middle of the thirteenth century, with its conspicuous ribbons of blue, the rivers had become highways of trade, not of war. The twelfth century saw the beginning of a highly significant and enduring network of trade that linked the Baltic to south-west Europe, with England guarding the route.

In time these emerging links would dictate the pattern of war at sea in northern Europe. Another factor in the development of naval warfare was the revolution in northern European shipping that started in the eleventh century. Before then the only ship that mattered in this part of the world was the Viking longship. This type of ship was highly mobile on the high seas and on rivers. It could be replicated in great numbers by relatively inexperienced shipwrights along the shores of northern Europe.

The basis of its design was the long curved keel. The hull was built around it. The first plank was fitted along the length of the keel, and the rest followed, built up one after the other and fastened into place with iron clench nails so that they overlapped at their edges. Most workaday modern rowing boats are still constructed in this way, with distinctive rows of curved overlapping planks along their lengths.

This was known as a clinker-built vessel. It was strong enough to withstand the force of northern winds and waters. In the placid Mediterranean the frame of the ship was built first and the planks fitted to them to construct the hull. The sides of the ship were therefore smoother, with none of the characteristic step outline of a clinker vessel. They were larger and easier to handle than clinker-built ships, but not as able to withstand Atlantic rollers. They were called carvel ships.

The Viking-type ship that was widely used in northern waters was light, fast and adaptable. It carried migrants and warriors as far as Greenland and Newfoundland, the Mediterranean and the Black Sea. But it had drawbacks. It did not perform well when sailing into the wind. It did not have much in the way of hold space. This determined the Vikings' penchant for high-value lightweight goods. In an age of bulk transit its deficiencies were shown up.

From the ninth century a variation on the Viking ship called the cog was pioneered by Frisian shipwrights. It retained the clinker design, but the hold capacity was increased by a flat bottom and a more rounded hull. By the thirteenth century the cog had become the dominant trading and war vessel in northern Europe. It had grown to such a size that it could hold five times more cargo than the largest Viking ships. As such the cost per ton of transporting cargo fell, as did the size of the crew. It represented a breakthrough in ship design that transformed the European economy.

As a bulk carrier the cog's advantages during a time of flourishing trade are readily apparent. As a warship it was revolutionary. It heralded the advent of fighting at sea. Wooden castles, with battlements and arrowslits, were constructed fore and aft. These, and the crow's nest on the mast, allowed warriors to project arrows, spears, iron bars or whatever was to hand down on to the decks of enemy ships. Such a vessel offered a platform for defensive and offensive operations at sea that the Viking longship simply did not have. Height mattered. It made all the difference in short, sharp, vicious contests at sea. Size mattered too: cogs were also ideal for transporting large invading armies, their horses and supplies.

The first king after Harold to use ships as a major instrument of war was Richard I. He had been impressed by oared galleys he had seen while on crusade in the Mediterranean. On his return to his European empire he found a rejuvenated France and a French king with territorial ambitions. While he had been on crusade, Philippe Auguste of France had intrigued with Richard's brother, John, and launched an offensive against Normandy. The first stage was the invasion of the Vexin, which lay along the Seine valley and was the borderland between France and Normandy.

From there Philippe was able to raid Normandy and push towards his goal – access to the Channel.

Richard was to spend the rest of his life fighting to reclaim Henry II's great empire. And warships were at the heart of his strategy. Contrary to the trend for larger ships, Richard reverted to light-draught, oar- and sail-powered vessels. And for good reason. He was fighting for the Seine valley, and his galleys, despite their expense, limited range and high crew levels, were the perfect weapon. Richard took a special interest in Portsmouth as a naval base. The intent is clear: an offensive chain that linked the south coast of England with the Seine and its tributaries and pushed deep into the Vexin. Richard's fast-moving ships could transport men to where they were most needed at short notice; they could resupply castles and troops in hostile territory; they could distribute cash to seduce men of influence. Richard's mastery of riverine warfare recalled the Vikings.

John, king of England after the death of Richard in 1199, inherited a substantial fleet of galleys. By 1204, however, their original purpose had been frustrated. Philippe Auguste had achieved the unthinkable and cleared John out of all his ancestral lands in France with the exception of Gascony and Poitou. Now the Channel was crucial for England's survival. It had an enemy across the water; that enemy was in possession of a long coastline and key ports and had the potential to control the Channel. Once more the sea became a place of conflict and lawlessness.

John lost his French possessions in part because he failed utterly in the joint naval and land operations perfected by his brother Richard. The land forces and the galleys did not work together well enough and control over the Seine valley was lost; the rest of the empire soon fell. John assembled fleets to try and regain his lost territories. In February 1205 writs were issued to stay all ships in port so that they could be used for the reconquest. During the spring and summer the fleets were mustered at Portsmouth, Northumberland and Dartmouth. Work was done to transform merchant cogs into ships of war and crews were recruited to man them. The supplies and naval stores needed for the invasion were assembled in Kent. These are the first records for the mustering and equipping of a royal fleet. The expense was daunting: £2,222 19s 4d spent at Portsmouth and £1,049 2s 6d on the other squadrons. But in June the plan was called off.

At this time we also get the earliest surviving records of naval administration. The galley fleet sucked up money. In charge of it was the royal administrator William de Wrotham. He was a proven manager and he oversaw work on the galley fleet, commissioning twenty new galleys and thirty-four other ships. But in the long run it was not possible to maintain a force of this size. Although John had a navy he had no clear strategy for its use. Galleys were ideal for raiding and reconnaissance; they were not suited to moving a large invasion army. That was a job for cogs, with their generous hold space. As things turned out his offensive force would be put on the defensive.

In 1206 John had fifty-one galleys stationed around the shores of England. There was no invasion of Normandy in these years, but the galleys and other ships were used against Wales and Ireland. As John tightened his grip on England and wrung tax out of his people, the galleys were also used on customs operations. For now that the southern shore of the Channel was in enemy hands, the seas' overall authority had crumbled. Piracy made a comeback.

Foremost among the new generation of sea rovers was the mysterious, brutal sea commander Eustace the Monk. In time he would enjoy a romanticised biography similar to Robin Hood. He was the son of Baudoin Busket, a lord from the neighbourhood of Boulogne. Eustace went to Toledo to study black magic and returned to become a monk in an abbey near Calais. He left around 1190 to avenge the murder of his father, then entered the service of Renaud de Dammartin, count of Boulogne. He fell out with his master, however, and hid out in the forest with a band of merry men and played out a series of humiliating tricks on Renaud.

That's the story anyway. In 1205 it is clear that he was in the service of King John, in command of thirty ships defending the Channel Islands against Philippe. This did not stop him from preying on merchant shipping passing along the Channel. He was a dangerous, useful sort of man, hated by the Channel merchants and fisherman but prized for his depredations on French shipping. Like many a seafaring man he profited from anarchy.

But Eustace was a man for hire. In 1215, John's *annus horribilis*, when he was compelled to sign Magna Carta, the Monk switched sides and joined the more formidable navy of Philippe Auguste. England was in disarray after the financial exactions and humiliations of John's reign.

From having no navy at all in the first years of the thirteenth century, the French had an imposing force by 1213. It was aimed at Flanders and England. At the same time John had assembled his own fleet to attack France via Flanders. The men and ships converged on Dover and then split into three squadrons, one remaining at Dover while one went to Faversham and the last to Ipswich. Meanwhile Philippe's enormous fleet was working its way down the Flanders coast, attacking Ypres, Cassel and Bruges. At the last site of pillage, Philippe left his ships at anchor at Damme, Bruges's port on the estuary of the river Zwyn. By great good luck an English fleet came across these defenceless ships. By the time they had finished their work it 'seemed as though the sea were ablaze'.

It was a rare success for an English fleet. Philippe's fleet was decimated and the few survivors scattered. But naval victory or not, the decisive battle was on land. John was comprehensively beaten by Philippe at Bouvines. In 1216 a new French fleet had been assembled and placed under the control of Eustace the Monk. By now John was faced with the dissatisfaction of his barons, who were in revolt against the king's oppressive policies, his military disasters and his disregard of Magna Carta. Even a French conqueror was better than the tyrannical John, they reasoned, and they invited Louis, son and heir of Philippe Auguste, to join them in dethroning John.

At first it seemed as though John would prevail. His fleet – purchased with the wealth of England exacted by stringent taxes – was still a significant force. He also secured naval support from Flanders. But the English weather intervened. His most important ally from Flanders was shipwrecked off Dunwich. John's own fleet was driven apart by the storms.

The gateway to England was wide open. Since the middle of the twelfth century the five key coastal towns in Kent and Sussex known as the Cinque Ports – Sandwich, Dover, Hythe, New Romney and Hastings – had been at the centre of national naval defence. They were obliged by royal charter to provide ships for royal service in return for tax breaks and the right to police the seas. Now the Cinque Ports defected to Louis and the rebellious barons. Eustace's newly enlarged fleet was sent to secure English ports from Southampton round to the Wash. The nightmare had happened: another sovereign had the potential to control the Channel and the Narrow Seas.

In their fight against John the barons had chosen the lesser evil and turned to the French. Help, however, soon turned to invasion. The barons' problem ended in November 1216 when John died, leaving a son, Henry III. The nine-year-old boy was preferable to a French king, and the arch-royalist William Marshal succeeded in winning back most of the barons to their ancestral monarchy. Most importantly, he committed Henry III to Magna Carta. But Louis had been proclaimed king in the bad days of John, and he was in no hurry to leave.

Louis was in control of over half the kingdom and could call upon reinforcements from France. What he did not have was Dover Castle. Its defender, Hubert de Burgh, rightly called it 'the key of England'. He defended it against waves of attack. In 1217 Louis was defeated at Lincoln. He went to London and called upon reinforcements from France.

The English royalists had fought hard to recapture the Cinque Ports throughout the spring of 1217. The ports had gone over to Louis because they had been hard pressed – enslaved they said – by John. But they had no great love for Eustace the Monk either, who had preyed upon their shipping. One by one they switched allegiance to Henry III.

Meanwhile Eustace was preparing a fleet that would bring fresh forces, siege equipment, money and supplies to Louis at London. It was sighted off Dover on 24 August. It seems that a squadron of English ships refused to go out to engage so powerful a force, but another squadron under Hugh de Burgh came out of Sandwich and sailed past the French. Louis's men could see no armed knights on board the ships. Eustace exclaimed that 'he knew those wretches think to seize Calais, but it is well defended'. The French jeered at the English sailors as they went by. But as soon as they were past, the English gained the wind and turned back on the French.

This tactic – the first we hear of it in a battle fought between sailing ships at war – was called taking or seizing the weather gage. The English had manoeuvred into a position where they had the wind while the French would have to turn back and attempt to sail into the wind or carry on with the English at their heels.

Eustace might have thought to press on to London, but his ship was weighed down with a heavy siege catapult (a trebuchet) and the English were soon upon him: he had no choice but to fight. But his ships were smaller than the English cogs. From this height advantage the English could fire down crossbow bolts and other missiles. It was said that they also threw quicklime to blind the French, again making use of the wind to carry the powder. The English then grappled their enemy, brought down their sails and masts, so that the French sailors were caught 'like birds in net', and boarded.

It must have been a bloody and confusing tangle of rigging, sails, masts and men. The English showed no mercy as they put their opponents to the sword there and then. Thanks to superior tactics, good fortune and the advantage of larger ships, the English were able to capture most of Louis's fleet. Eustace managed to escape in the flagship and continued towards London with his valuable cargo – the trebuchet – and a company of knights, but the English were still in pursuit. Eustace hove to off Sandwich in order to allow the rest of his ships to reach Louis. Fifteen French ships escaped, but some were so badly damaged from the two battles that they sank. Eustace's ship was surrounded by four English vessels. In the melee he tried to ward off the attackers with an oar. He then crept off to hide in the bowels of the ship while many of the knights jumped overboard in their armour to avoid their fate at the hands of the English.

The boarding party at last found Eustace hiding in the bilges. He tried to bribe his way out, but by now English seafarers were heartily sick of him. He was offered a choice. He could either be beheaded on the bulwark of his ship or on the trebuchet. 'He had little desire for either, but anyhow they cut off his head.'

Louis had no chance of fighting on and gave up his ambitions in England. The Battle of Dover had had a decisive effect on the war. But England had not secured control of the seas for long, despite two major naval victories. Sea power was an ephemeral thing unless a country maintained a strong navy and suppressed all external threats, including piracy.

But the truth was that England could not afford a navy. As a result the waters round England were turbulent and uncontrollable. Henry III, John's son and heir, lost La Rochelle to the French in 1224. Now Henry II's continental empire had been reduced to Gascony, which lay far beyond hostile waters.

England was surrounded by powerful navies. For the first time in well over a century a Scandinavian force was active in British waters. In the 1220s the Norwegians intervened to secure their lordship over Man and the Western Isles. Alan, lord of Galloway, raised a fleet of 200 ships in a failed attempt to construct a maritime empire stretching from Western Scotland to Ulster. King Alexander II of Scotland had ambitions over the isles and in 1249 he 'made it plain to his men that he intended not to turn back until he had acquired all the Norwegian king's dominion to the west of the Solunder sea'. Alexander died during this attempted naval conquest, and Norway held on to its empire.

In contrast England barely counted as a naval power. In the thirteenth century it was a reduced kingdom, haunted by its lost empire and riven by divisions. France, the emerging force in Western Europe, seemed likely to dominate the seas.

PART 2: WINE AND WOOL

England and the Angevin Empire

Stirling

Largs
2 October
1263

Edinburgh
Berwick

North Sea

N

Beaumaris
Conway
Caernafon
Rhuddian
Harlech
Criccieth
Aberyswyth

King's Lynn

Dunwich
Ipswich
Aldeburgh
R. Orwell
Harwich

Sluys
24 June
1340

Bristol

London

Sandwich
Dover
1217
Damme
30-31 May
1213
Brugge
Antwerp
Ghent

Southampton
Poole
Portsmouth
Winchelsea
Calais
1346
Ypres
Boulogne
29 August
1350

Plymouth
Dartmouth
Isle of Wight

Agincourt
25 October
1415

Falmouth

English Channel

Dieppe

Crécy
26 August
1345

The Scillies

Harfleur
Honfleur
Rouen

NORMANDY

Paris

Brest
Saint Mathieu

BRITTANY

MAINE

Seine

ANJOU

Loire

TOURAINE

Bay of Bourgneuf

POITOU
Poitiers

Ile d'Oleron
La Rochelle
22/23 June
1372

LA MARCHE

Bay of Biscay

DUCHY OF
AQUITAINE

Gironde

LIMOGES

AUVERGNE

PERIGORD

Bordeaux
Garonne

TOULOUSE

GASCONY

Toulouse

CHAPTER 5

MERCHANT WARRIORS
1221–1335

The voyage was long, perilous and uncomfortable. The rewards were handsome. The ships left Southampton and travelled together for mutual protection against the manifold dangers lurking in one of the most dangerous waters of Europe. They stuck together out of courtesy and for business reasons; in times of war it was a legal requirement to travel in convoy and there may have been warships to 'waft' or escort them. For these ships were engaged in vital work.

The bobbing cogs awaited a favourable wind and hugged the English south coast, keeping familiar landmarks in sight at all times. They looked out for church towers, monasteries, cliffs, trees and anything prominent and permanent to guide their way. This sequence of features, which marked the way and warned of dangers, came from the accumulated experience of generations of seafarers. The only other help might be a magnetised needle attached to a twig or straw which, when floated in a bowl of water, pointed north.

The prevailing wind in the Channel blows from the south-west. The ships were heading in the opposite direction, and the men in the unwieldy cogs were in constant danger of being driven onto rocks. Ships leaving Southampton might have to seek shelter in havens such as Dartmouth, Plymouth and Falmouth as they hopped west. When conditions favoured it they would attempt to cross the Channel to seek shelter on the alien coast. As Chaucer said of his Shipman, a character in the *Canterbury Tales*:

> He knew all the havens, as they were,
> From Gottland to the Cape of Finisterre,
> And every creek in Brittany and Spain.

Such knowledge of havens and creeks, large and small, was indispensable on the perilous trading routes. It was a stop–start journey. Ships would have to ride at anchor for lengthy periods waiting for a kind wind. A favoured spot to pause, regroup and revictual was at St Mathieu's Point on the Brittany coast. Here they were entering the most dangerous part of the voyage. The Bretons were notorious pirates who did not discriminate between the nationalities or owners of the ships they plundered. There was no question of heading out to sea, for now the ship was on the Atlantic, the roughest of the world's oceans. Meeting pirates was many times better than venturing out into the ocean. The ship would continue to cling to the coast of the Bay of Biscay.

Those who manned these ships and risked their lives on these long voyages were a hard-bitten bunch. There was a rough sort of democracy among them. When a ship was awaiting the right wind the master was required by law to say to his crew: 'Gentlemen, you have this weather.'[1] He would then listen to the advice of his sailors and only set sail when the majority agreed that the 'weather is fair and good'. The master had an obligation to feed and shelter his men and bring them safely home. But in other cases discipline was tight. A drunken sailor forfeited his right to be fed and sheltered by the master, and could be dropped off at any port. If a dispute blew up between a shipmaster and a member of the crew the master had the right to deprive the recalcitrant sailor of his place at the mess table. If the insubordination continued the sailor could be dropped off on land at any stage of the voyage, but the crew would have to make that decision. If any member of the crew denigrated another he would have to forfeit a day's wage (4d); if the shipmaster denigrated a sailor he would lose 8d. If a member of the crew was struck by the master he had to take the first blow passively; he could fight back if the master continued to strike him. However, if the sailor struck the first blow the crew would decide whether he should be fined 100s or lose a fist.

The food would be of poor quality – bread when it could be obtained, salt fish and preserved meat if you were lucky, and beer, which was liable to spoil. Provisions ran out on voyages when ships were forced to anchor and wait for the wind. The men could expect no living quarters on the voyage and sanitary conditions were appalling. One voyager described the bucket hanging over the side that was used for sailors to relieve themselves – 'the perilous perch and the splashing of the sea are both discouraging to your purpose and your only hope is to dose yourself with purgatives'.

The sight of Bordeaux, at the end of the Gironde estuary, must have been welcome. Every year, at spring and autumn, ships would arrive to trade. Here the sailors would unload their cargo – grain, salt fish, meat, cheese, butter, leatherware and so on. But the return cargo was the prize that made the voyage worthwhile.

Medieval England had an extraordinary appetite for wine. In 1308–9 a staggering 102,724 tons of wine[2] were exported from Gascony to England. Customs accounts show that between 20 January 1303 and 18 August 1304 about 1,000 ships, most of them under 100 tons, sailed from Bordeaux to England. So important was this trade that the unit of weight called the ton derives from the container that held the wine – the tun. A ship that was rated as having a capacity of 100 tons could carry 25,000 gallons of wine stored in 100 wine tuns in its hold. The foodstuffs and wares brought from England could not pay for this quantity. These commodities were necessary for the people of Gascony, who had given up most of the available land to vines to satisfy the thirst of the English. The wine was purchased from the wealth of England: the wool that was sold in the markets of Flanders, the white gold of the Middle Ages.

This trade began with the loss of Normandy. Before then the wine of choice came from Burgundy and was transported down the Seine and across the Channel. Then the white wine of the Poitou found favour. But after John and Henry III lost their French possessions all that was left was Gascony and its light red wine known as claret. The last vestige of a once mighty empire was a source of pleasure for the people and profit for the Crown. Most significantly, from the point of view of naval history, this holy grail of English trade lay at the end of a dangerous voyage. This was the nursery of English sailors in the Middle Ages. Ships used on this route formed the navies of English kings. And most importantly, the fortunes earned in the wine and wool trades paid for England's wars.

The wool and wine trades were at the heart of England's economy and were the lifeblood of the monarchy. This interconnection can be charted in the life of Walter le Fleming, one of the men who made Southampton great.[3] Walter died a wealthy man in 1258, a major shipowner and landowner in Southampton, Chichester, Portsmouth and Winchester. He was at the centre of civic life in Southampton: bailiff in 1129 and 1242, chief officer in 1249 and a major benefactor of religious houses in and around the port. His wealth rested on the ownership of trading vessels – large cogs that plied the Bay of Biscay from the 1210s – but his great fortune came because he made his ships, his commodities and the sea lanes he travelled useful for the king.

Henry III was bent on winning back the great empire lost by his father, King John. He was hampered by lack of money, but merchants like Walter le Fleming offered a way out of the financial mess. In 1224, the year Henry lost Poitou, Walter was given safe conduct to trade with the enemy, and his cog *La Heitee* went to La Rochelle to obtain wine, salt and other goods.

In 1229 the favour was returned: *La Heitee* was pressed into royal service, taking war supplies to Gascony. Walter did well from the deal. He stepped into the role of bailiff of Southampton in that year. In 1230 Henry III ordered him and his business partner to purchase the best Gascon wine and sell it directly to the royal cellars. In the 1230s the Crown granted licences to Walter permitting him to trade between the king's lands; best of all he was given the lucrative contract to replenish the king's wine cellars in London. Walter retained his power base in Southampton – he was bailiff again in 1243, the year in which he sent his cog *La Jonette* to Bordeaux laden with royal treasure; it returned with the best of the vintage, destined for the king's cellars. In 1253 one of his ships carried the bishop of Bath to Spain on royal business.

Walter le Fleming was one of many merchants who made considerable sums of money by entering into partnership with the Crown. In return for offering their services to the state they were given the chance to participate in overseas trade. Walter sold his wines to the most important and highest-spending customer in the land – the king – because he made his ships available as transports and for courier duty. Walter's son Henry inherited the business, was appointed keeper of the customs at Southampton and died a member of the gentry. Henry's son, Richard le Fleming, was parliamentary burgess for the town seven times between 1298 and 1330. Like his father and grandfather he prospered by combining business with royal service, the one supporting the other. It was an arrangement that would persist for centuries. Such traders provided the foundations for a navy.

Flourishing trade meant that kings could afford ships of their own. Customs receipts from the export of wool and the import of wine were mainstays of royal finance. During the thirteenth century English wool exports were in thriving health: 30,000 sacks of wool were exported annually. This was a vast amount given that a single sack contained the clip of 250 sheep.

Economic activity such as this was the precondition for naval greatness. In the Middle Ages a king's 'navy' was the sum of the nation's shipping. The Crown had the right to requisition all the ships in his country's ports in time of war. What royal ships there were formed the nucleus of a massive armada assembled from all the vessels and sailors that could be mustered by royal officials. Apart from galleys there was no such thing as a distinct warship. All ships were equipped to fight in the lawless waters and all could be equipped for war.

Until the seventeenth century it was impossible to distinguish between a nation's private merchant marine and its ships of war. The more private ships there were, therefore, the larger the fleet the king could muster to control the sea, win glory abroad and suppress piracy.

But England in the later Middle Ages was decidedly not a great maritime power.

English kings needed lots of men like Walter le Fleming, who could advance the economy and furnish ships for war. Walter was a rarity however. Wealthy families and institutions in England invested in land, not in shipping. The result was that foreign shippers stepped in to export England's wool. It was exported by foreigners on foreign ships to be turned into cloth in the textile centres in Flanders. England in the Middle Ages and into the sixteenth century had handed over the seaways and the profits to be made from them to more skilled and astute foreign traders.

But the most important reason was that the Crown was massively indebted to foreign bankers. Henry III borrowed £54,000 in the 1250s while his son Edward I borrowed £200,000 in the first years of his reign, 1270–77, from the Riccardi banking family and other Italian houses. The debt was paid by exempting these firms from tolls and duties and granting them freedom of trade and export licences. The lucrative task of collecting customs duties was also granted to the Italians. Foreign shippers thus started with an overwhelming advantage over hard-pressed locals.

Henry III and Edward I also granted privileges to traders from German towns such as Lübeck, Bremen, Gotland, Rostock, Riga, Danzig and Cologne.[4] It was this group of north German trading centres that came to be known as the Hanse, and in time it would become a great maritime trading empire, eclipsing mere nations such as England. It would use its financial clout to influence policy in weak states like England and its ships would have sufficient coercive power to lay down the law on the seaways and to nations. The Hanse was particularly prominent on the east coast, taking a large share of imports and exports to and from ports such as Boston, Lynn, Hull and Ravenser. It also dominated North Sea and Baltic fishing, a highly valuable trade given that the religious obligation was to eat fish on Fridays, during Lent and on other days throughout the calendar. The chief export was wool, destined for Flanders and further afield, and it was carried on the Hanse's improved, enlarged cogs.

But even these ships looked small when a massive Mediterranean ship rowed into Southampton in 1278. It must have been quite a sight for the merchants and seafarers. Suddenly their ships seemed puny and primitive. This kind of ship had more than one mast and had a large number of rowers. It was built as a defensive merchantman that could ward off the pirates who infested the Mediterranean. Unlike the cog, it could make a relatively easy passage out of the Mediterranean and into the Atlantic. There was nothing like it in northern waters.

This was the first of the annual voyages of the Genoese great galley, which would make the long trip from the Middle East to Bruges and then Southampton, where it would winter. A century later one of these Genoese ships was blown by a storm into Sandwich: 'It was of astonishing size, full of treasures, which might easily have supplied the needs of all the country.' These great galleys must have looked like arrivals from another world. In a sense they were. Mediterranean ships were technologically superior to the single-masted clinker-built ships that plied the Baltic, North Sea and Channel. The Genoese galley also carried exotic cargoes from the Far East: fruits, dyes, silks and spices. It carried back English wool and finished cloths from Flanders.

The dominance of the Hanse and the Italian city states rubs in just how backward England was as a European maritime nation. Under Henry III England was a third-rate naval power even in the British Isles. In 1262, for instance, Håkon Håkonsson of Norway began negotiating an anti-English alliance with the rulers of Connaught, Hebrides and Man. In 1263 he brought his fleet of enormous warships, led by a colossal flagship 260 feet long, into the Irish Sea to attack Scotland. The Scottish, however, defeated this force at the Battle of Largs.

It was Edward I who began to rebuild England's fortunes in the British Isles. And it was money loaned from foreign businesses, with the wine trade as security, that enabled him to construct an army and a navy large enough to restore England's prestige.

Like Richard I, Edward had been on crusade before becoming king. He no doubt studied the Mediterranean way of war. In his campaigns against Wales and Scotland he made use of ships to augment land power – the best use of naval forces in the thirteenth century. In Wales ships delivered and supplied armies. They also cut the Welsh off from their allies over the water in Ireland. Most important, they supplied the powerful castles that Edward constructed along the coast of Wales. The king secured large numbers of ships from the port towns, which established crucial supply lines emanating from the central base at Chester as his armies advanced along north Wales. Just as importantly they helped cut off the grain that came from Anglesey to supply the Welsh fastness of Snowdonia.

It was an expensive way to wage war and not, in the end, completely successful. Keeping relatively small garrisons in coastal castles supplied and reinforced required a large number of ships. War against Scotland was also dependent on ships providing the logistical support for troops. The castles on Scotland's south-east coast and on the Firth of Forth were the key to control of the kingdom, and both sides knew that victory was dependent on the seaborne supply lines that proved decisive during sieges.

Edward I fought in Wales, Scotland, Flanders and Gascony. It was a serious military commitment and ruinously expensive. Between 1294 and 1298 he spent £750,000, much of it raised from exactions on 'the sovereign merchandise and jewel of this realm of England': wool.[5] He had placed customs duties on the export of wool from the beginning of his reign. His debts to the Italian banking firms were so great that they were forced into bankruptcy, allowing Edward to reclaim his income from the customs. But it was never enough. In 1294, when he was in dire need of cash, he proposed that the Crown should seize all the wool in England as a compulsory loan, export it, reap the profit and collect the customs. The merchants resisted this move and instead a tax of 40 shillings, known as the maltote, was placed on every sack of wool. In 1297 however the Crown seized large stocks of wool. Responsibility was given to the great wool magnate Lawrence of Ludlow to manage the seizure. Export was delayed to drive up prices.

When the time was ripe the wool fleet set sail from London for the Low Countries under the protection of ten heavily armed warships. Lawrence's ship was wrecked off Aldeburgh with an immense cargo of wool. It was, to the hard-pressed people of England, divine justice: 'because he sinned against the wool mongers he was drowned in a ship laden with wool.'

Throughout the thirteenth century English kings undermined the foundations of English naval strength. They sought short-term solutions, such as bartering away trading rights or seizing wool. The result was a downward spiral. Foreign traders got more business, English shippers suffered, which meant that the Crown had to rely on foreigners even more. The cost of war increased as the Crown had to hire non-English ships for maritime ventures such as the wars against Wales and Scotland.

All the same, this did not dampen the English enthusiasm for ruling the waves. Kings were happy to look back at the apparent golden age of the reign of Edgar and make some extravagant claims.

In May 1293 sailors from Gascony, the Cinque Ports and Ireland fought sailors from Normandy in a sea battle. This had come at the end of months of minor conflict between sailors plying the Bay of Biscay. Edward's subjects won and the men of Bordeaux went on to attack the rival port of La Rochelle. This was a striking and early example of something that would become all too common in northern waters: private wars between sailors of different ports and countries. In time it would have a significant impact on European history, but in 1293 Edward was summoned to appear before a Parisian court of his feudal lord, the king of France.

This was humiliating for an English king. To prevent it, Edward's lawyers had the audacity to come up with a piece of legal fiction. It was not, they said, a dispute between Edward's Gascon subjects and subjects of the king of France, but something that took place *outside* the realm, at sea. And English kings, they claimed, 'time out of mind had been in peaceable possession of the sovereign lordship of the English sea and the islands therein'.

This was a wild boast, utterly untrue, and it would have serious repercussions. Edward was saying that he had sovereignty over the sea, and hence sole legal responsibility. At a time when the waves were infested with pirates, he would have to accept responsibility for the lawless water. In effect this meant paying compensation to aggrieved parties because Edward had no ability to police the seas.

For the truth was that the English Crown was far too weak to establish any kind of authority over the deep. Navies were ruinously expensive, far beyond the reach of most monarchs. And so the burden was placed on private merchants who, like it or not, were sucked into conflict. Merchant ships were obliged to arm themselves when they ventured out, even in times of peace. During war many seafarers considered the ships belonging to the opposing country to be legitimate prey on the high seas. War meant anarchy beyond the shores. And for some – those who were not squeamish about legal niceties – anarchy was profitable.

In the early decades of the fourteenth century the seas around Britain lapsed into chaos. Edward II was in dispute with Flanders. The Low Countries were dependent on English wool, so when Edward placed an embargo on the export of wool the traders were forced to become pirates.

By 1310 there was an undeclared war going on in the North Sea, with reprisals committed on both sides. The most notorious Flemish pirate, John Crabbe, seized upon valuable English cargoes of wine, wool and other goods carried in ships everywhere from the Bay of Biscay round to the coast of Northumbria. His depredations on English shipping, inflicted at first in the name of war, greatly angered Edward II, who complained to the count of Flanders and sent out warships to protect shipping. It was in vain. The Bordeaux wine that Crabbe seized en route to London in the Downs went to the count's cellars. The response of the English traders was to play the same game. In December 1310, for instance, English sailors attacked Flemish ships in the bay of Graunzon in Brittany, burnt them and made off with their cargoes.

Men like Crabbe prolonged wars. When England and Flanders settled their differences, private wars between aggrieved merchants and shippers raged unabated. Sometimes piracy could be of help to monarchs, for it at least encouraged an armed merchant marine that could be used in time of war. In 1322 the king of France complained to Edward II that English sailors who attacked French ships 'described themselves as custodians of the sea on your behalf'. Edward replied that he was sovereign of the seas and therefore had unlimited jurisdiction.

It was another wild claim. In truth, the king of England had little control over the sea and the violence was doing him harm. The men of the Cinque Ports took advantage of Edward's weakness to raid and burn Southampton in 1321. The Flemish were taking stolen English wool to Scotland to be re-exported to the Continent; they also brought much-needed food and weapons to help the Scots in their struggle against England. This was particularly damaging to Edwards I and II. Only when they dominated the English and Scottish seaboard could they prosper in their war to control Scotland. But with someone as dangerous as John Crabbe at large on the North Sea, smuggling wool and carrying supplies to Robert the Bruce, the English lost control of the seas. It became harder to keep the Scottish castles, which lay at the heart of their strategy. Berwick was lost to the Scots in 1318. In return for his services against the English John Crabbe was made a burgess of Berwick. It proved an ideal base from which to raid English shipping and supply the Scots.

John Crabbe was one of those people who seem to prosper whichever way the wind blows. In 1333 his fleet of ten ships was destroyed by a force sent by Edward III in his war against Scotland. Crabbe was at last in English hands and his many enemies south of the border were after his blood.

But the ageing pirate managed to get permission to meet the young king. Edward III was impressed with the artful brigand who had defied, at one time or another, rulers and powerful commercial interests along the coasts of the Bay of Biscay, the Channel, the Narrow Seas and the North Sea. He certainly saw that Crabbe had talents that could prove very useful. Crabbe, to the chagrin of his many victims, was once again a free man, and he used his experiences as a sea commander and former confidant of Robert the Bruce to advise the English in their recapture of Berwick and advance up the east coast of Scotland. Crabbe was pardoned all his felonies, including murder, made constable of Somerton Castle in Lincolnshire and given other offices and financial rewards for services to the

Crown. In 1335 he was given joint responsibility to raise a force of ten ships and 1,000 men from the east coast and take charge of them at sea. He was also given responsibility to fortify ports on the North Sea coast.

This was poacher turned gamekeeper – who could be better than the man who had terrorised the waters around England to secure its defences? Edward III was determined to become a great European monarch. For that he needed to make real his father and his grandfather's claims to sovereignty of the sea. He was prepared to cut cards with the devil.

CHAPTER 6

KEEPING THE SEAS
1336–1399

Edward III, with the accustomed bombast of an English king, said that his ancestors had 'ever been sovereigns of the English seas on every side'. That claim echoed through history. Only rarely had it reality. In 1336 Edward had huge ambitions to conquer France. He had just three cogs to accomplish it.

The route to victory over France, he reasoned, lay through the Low Countries. This region had recently revolted from French control. It lay just across the Narrow Seas and gave access to France's north-east border. The cities and fiefdoms of the region were prosperous and powerful, but they had a vulnerability that Edward could manipulate: they were dependent upon English wool for their economic survival. And England's wealth, which Edward needed to harness, came from the textile towns of the Low Countries. Once again, the Crown aimed at control of England's wool.[1] It could be used as a diplomatic lever and as the source of the fortune that was needed to conquer France. As a wool trader and warrior, Edward III needed a navy.

When northern European monarchs wanted to strengthen their naval resources they looked to the Mediterranean, where fighting at sea had become a fine art. The great trading city of Venice relied upon its state navy, which was kept in readiness by the state-owned dockyard, the Arsenal. Venice had become immensely wealthy because its ships had given it the ability to monopolise lucrative trading routes. By the fourteenth century it had a regular naval force that guarded its routes, colonies and merchant shipping.

Venice's rival, Genoa, did not share its centralised efficiency in naval organisation. As it had been for the Vikings, and would be for the English in the sixteenth century, the driving force behind exploration and commercial and military might was individualistic rather than state-directed. Genoa's military prowess in the later Middle Ages was owing to the zeal of its aristocracy and commercial class, who armed their ships and fought for Genoa's interests.

In northern waters the country most successful at emulating the Mediterranean navies was France. In 1293 Philip the Fair had determined to build a permanent navy to challenge the English in the Channel and the Bay of Biscay. He ordered the construction of the Clos des Galées in Rouen, now therefore the only naval arsenal in northern Europe. England had nothing like it. The Clos des Galées built and maintained a fleet of galleys. The labour force and crews were recruited from the Mediterranean regions of France and the officers came from the maritime powerhouse of Genoa. Other port towns, such as La Rochelle and Marseille, also had smaller arsenals and permanent warships. In 1336 Philip VI ordered thirty galleys to muster in the Channel. They were joined by 300 requisitioned merchant ships that would carry 26,000 men to invade England.

Edward's England did not enjoy the flourishing trade of Venice or the tax base of France. Under the serious threat of invasion, every ship and thousands of sailors were pressed into service. A large scratch fleet was stationed in the Downs. It was poorly co-ordinated and badly disciplined; some crews took the opportunity to engage in piracy and the men of Great Yarmouth settled some scores against the Cinque Ports. The requisitioned ships could not stay on station indefinitely, and they were powerless to stop French raids on Suffolk and the Isle of Wight, where valuable cargoes and ships were carried away. On the seas as well, English merchant shipping was attacked and merchant ships and property were arrested in French and Flemish ports. But the French muffed their chance to invade, and the English were confident enough to send the wine ships to Gascony, though this year they had to sail in convoy.

The English got their wine that year, but there was a fear that it might be the last vintage. The French turned their attention to Gascony. They entered the Garonne valley and pressed on to the Dordogne and St Émilion, destroying the vines as they went. In March 1337 Edward ordered every single one of his subjects' ships to join his service for three months. The royal fleet may have been in poor shape, but the levy of the merchant marine showed its shortcomings as well.

Thanks to the economic weakness of England and its ceding of the carrying trade to the Hanse and the Italians, English ships were very small. As Edward found, requisitioning such a diverse and scattered force was no easy task. His officials had to travel from port to port pressing men and ships into service and somehow finding supplies, victuals and armaments to convert these elements into a navy. It took two months to assemble. It always caused resentment, even at the best of times.

Now, in 1337, the ports, seafarers and merchants were squeezed even harder. Their ships were taken and they had to build new ones, barges and galleys for the king's navy. The wine and wool trades were in disarray. There was some respite when the wine ships were permitted to sail. They were ordered to travel in convoy and search ports and roadsteads along the way and engage enemy ships. No vessel was permitted to carry more than half a load of wine to make them more manoeuvrable and provide room for archers and soldiers. The total tonnage declined from 74,053 in 1335–36 to 16,577 the following year. It was a miserable situation, made worse by the plundering of English ships on the seas.

French ships stationed off the island of Oléron in Brittany compounded the situation. Not only did wine ships coming out of Bordeaux suffer but food convoys travelling in the opposite direction were harried. Gascony was under attack from the French and dependent on English deliveries of money, materiel and food. When these were reduced to a trickle by French piracy Gascony headed towards mutiny.

And at the same time Edward had put a stop to wool exports to the Low Countries. This was the most densely populated area in the world and its thousands of textile workers could only work when English wool came in. It sparked rioting in the cities as the textile industry ground to a halt. Parliament and the English wool merchants had agreed to loan the king almost the entire stock of English wool – 30,000 sacks in all, or 90 per cent of the total, purchased from the growers on credit at rock-bottom prices and sold at a single staple (market) at Dordrecht. After a year of embargo it was assumed that the king could sell the wool at the highest prices to desperate weavers.

This was the end of free trade. Wine imports were regulated with military objectives in mind. Foreigners were forbidden to export English wool and the weavers of the Low Countries could only buy the wool at a single staple. In a few short years Edward had set about radicalising the whole of the English economy, attempting to resolve every problem that had retarded England's development as a maritime economy. Now English ships carried English wool and traded it at an English market in the Low Countries.

The wool was to be transported with the army on the newly mustered fleets. The navy, therefore, would be at once an invasion fleet and a merchant convoy. The military operation would pay for itself. And the Low Countries, hungry for wool, would be forced into alliance. That was the plan. In practice it was much more complex. A glut after a famine does not necessarily mean high prices. The logistics of transporting wool and

troops were hampered by the lack of ships, the onset of winter and marauding French vessels. But the principalities of the Low Countries did
enter into an anti-French alliance led by Edward III.

The policy also depended upon control of the seas between England
and Flanders. Edward had fleets at sea. The infamous John Crabbe was
sent back to the waters he knew so well between England's east coast
and Flanders, this time using his well honed expertise to defy the French.
The makeshift navy was not up to this task. In 1338 a convoy en route to
Gascony was badly mauled off Talmont, a settlement on the Gironde. The
French raided the south coast again. The Genoese galleys and barges from
Normandy, flying English colours, attacked Portsmouth in March. Southampton was taken by surprise in October by the enemy galleys when
the townsfolk were at mass. The invaders killed many of the burgesses,
raped women and burnt down buildings. They also struck at Edward's war
machine: a great stock of wool ready to be exported was burnt and wine
and spices spoiled or looted. This was part of a deliberate French strategy.
They were hitting at Edward's means to fight the war before he had a
chance to deploy them.

Even more disturbing to Edward's plan was the French attack on five of
the largest English cogs – including the king's best ships, the *Christopher*
and the *Cog Edward* – which were delivering wool to the count of Flanders. After a long battle in the Scheldt estuary the Englishmen were killed
and the ships taken into the French fleet. The next year Carlo Grimaldi
took a fleet of Genoese galleys, French ships and, most humiliatingly for
Edward, the *Christopher* and attacked the Channel Islands and then made
for Gascony, where they took Blaye and Bourg, which guarded the Gironde estuary – the approach to Bordeaux.

The other Genoese galleys entered the North Sea and raided the coast
from Harwich to Bristol. That summer wool exports to the staple at Dordrecht were again banned because too much was being lost at sea to pirates and the French were gathering a large naval force on the Flanders
coast. In the battle for control of the seas the French were prevailing. The
raids, the devastating onslaught on English trade and shipping and the
build-up of the French navy were clearly the prelude to an invasion. The
English could not safeguard their key commodities, even on the short
crossing to Flanders. Edward's plan of fostering a self-sustaining navy on
the model of Venice was heading for disaster.

There was a rare success in April when an English fleet under Lord
Morley and his subordinate John Crabbe attacked a French convoy in the
Scheldt estuary and took a good number of ships, but this victory only

exposed the shady character of the English naval forces. Having defeated the legitimate enemy the English sailors then plundered all the ships they could see, including Edward's allies. They then fell out over the booty and part of the fleet deserted. Like Crabbe, many of these men must have made their careers in piracy, and their patriotic instincts did not override their desire for loot.

The only glimmer of hope was the withdrawal of the Genoese from French service in 1339 over a pay dispute, depriving the French of their Mediterranean galleys. It allowed the English galleys to hit back at France, raiding the Channel coast and attacking Boulogne and destroying eighteen out of twenty-two of the Channel galley fleet and twenty-four merchantmen along with valuable naval supplies. The English also terrorised French coastal towns. The Flemish burnt Dieppe.

It was a blow to the French navy, but in 1340 they were back in force on the Flanders coast ready to make trouble for the wool ships and prevent Edward landing troops. There were over 202 French ships, six galleys and twenty-two barges in June in the roadstead off Sluys, an area now silted up but which in the fourteenth century provided a large anchorage in the Scheldt estuary between Walcheren and West Flanders. The position guarded the way to Dordrecht, Antwerp and Bruges. It was also the ideal base from which to invade England.

Edward meanwhile was in Suffolk with a fleet in the Orwell roadstead and an army camped nearby. His councillors advised caution, as did prominent naval advisers such as John Crabbe. They urged the king to wait until his fleet and army were reinforced. But Edward was determined to attack the French at once with what he had – between 120 and 160 ships. The fleet set sail on 22 June and sighted the French on the 23rd, at about noon, outside Sluys. In 1340 the geography was very different. The town of Sluys (now known as Sluis) is today inland, but in the fourteenth century it was on the coast; between it and Walcheren lay a number of small islands, such as Cadzand and Wulpen, which were submerged in the sixteenth century. The French were anchored off Sluys and had fortified Cadzand. They saw the English approach in the afternoon and the order was given to draw up the ships and chain them together in three ranks. The English, when they approached, saw so many masts that they said it looked like a forest. This unwieldy mass of ships was intended to deny the English entry to the estuary. They got a nasty surprise the next morning.

The tide and wind rushed the English ships into the estuary. Edward's fleet was organised with the strongest cogs in the centre and the ships carrying archers on the flanks. Every two ships carrying archers were accompanied by one bearing men at arms.

The French fleet was the larger and should have used this advantage to outmanoeuvre the enemy. Instead the mass of stationary ships provided a large and compact target for the English archers and crossbowmen. The Genoese galley commander urged the French to disentangle their ships before the battle, but the French were determined to block Edward's way to Bruges. The folly was all too apparent, and the Genoese forces slipped away before battle commenced.

Confidence on the French side remained high, however, and they blew trumpets in defiance as the English appeared to tack out of the way. In reality Edward's ships were manoeuvring for advantage. Then missiles rained down from the summer sun. The French ships were stuck fast, unable to dodge the onslaught; the troops on the open decks could find no respite from the arrows and bolts. Then the English grappled the enemy ships and the men-at-arms boarded. 'This battle was very murderous and horrible,' wrote Jean Froissart. Edward III said the French fought valiantly until night fell, but despite their greater numbers and superior naval experience they were fighting for their lives. As Froissart wrote, fights at sea were worse than those on land because there was no chance of retreat or surrender. The mighty *Christopher* was recaptured, to Edward's joy, and its crew killed and thrown overboard before the English used it to chase the hated Genoese. Indeed, Edward and his countrymen were elated to have the chance to punish the French–Genoese navy which had made such a mockery of them at sea for so long.

Fighting continued from ship to ship: arrow attack followed by boarding actions. Some French ships managed to escape, but Crabbe was sent in pursuit. By the end the English had captured 190 ships and killed 18,000 men. Mutilated corpses littered the Flanders coastline. Now it was the turn of the English to blow trumpets and other instruments, which they did all night long.

It was the largest naval battle of the Middle Ages in northern waters and an impressive achievement for England. French shipping suffered and the planned invasion of England was called off. Yet Edward did not achieve command over the seas. France made use of Castilian and Portuguese galleys to disrupt English communications with Gascony. Within a month French ships attacked an English wool convoy to Flanders. The south coast again suffered raids. On the debit side, the English managed to capture Brest Castle, which gave the convoys to and from Gascony some protection. But as long as the French could procure the superior ships of southern Europe for use in the Bay of Biscay and English waters, Edward would suffer at sea. In 1346 it was the presence of Carlo Grimaldi off La Rochelle with a large force of Mediterranean galleys that put Edward off sending his army to Gascony. Instead his ships and men headed for Normandy. While they raided the coast Edward moved south and inflicted a crushing defeat on the French at Crécy.

This victory allowed Edward to besiege Calais from land and sea. Calais was like an island, protected from the north by the Channel and to the south by large marshes. The key to taking it was to starve it into surrender by cutting its seaborne supply lines. England used 738 ships manned by 9,300 men to supply its besieging forces and blockade Calais. Grimaldi's galleys managed to smash through the English blockade, but his squadron was paid off in due course and its Castilian replacements did not arrive at the agreed time. The French relieved Calais with their own galley and barge fleet. The English solution was simple. They attacked Boulogne and destroyed the enemy boats. Now Calais really was an island. The town that would give England command of both sides of the Dover Strait for over two hundred years was in Edward's hands from August 1347.

It was in this strait that the next great naval battle of the Middle Ages occurred in 1350. The year before, a Castilian fleet had helped France in the Bay of Biscay by attacking English convoys. In 1350 the fleet went to Flanders to sell Spanish wool and raid English ships on the way. Edward was angry enough to lead a squadron of English ships to intercept the Castilians as they returned. Battles at sea and pre-planned interceptions of enemy fleets were all but unheard of in the Middle Ages. Edward, his son the Black Prince and other nobles were at anchor off Winchelsea. The king was being entertained on deck by a troupe of minstrels when the Castilians were spotted. Trumpets sounded and the fleet went out to meet them. The enemy could simply have sailed on down the Channel without troubling themselves. Instead they chose to give battle, perhaps when they saw the English king was leading the charge.

'Steer towards that ship for I want to joust at her,'[2] Edward shouted at his steersman, pointing out the leading enemy vessel. The ships collided at speed, producing a sound like thunder. The masts entangled and the Castilian ship's topcastle broke off and fell into the sea. Edward's ship began to let in water and his knights set about bailing it out without informing the king of the peril he was in.

Edward indicated the ship he had just rammed and said: 'Grapple my ship to that one; I must have her!' But his knights managed to convince him to go for a bigger ship. The English found a suitable ship, grappled it, and the fight for the king's life began in earnest. The Castilians had a height advantage and were able to fire arrows and hurl metal bars down at the English, but Edward and his knights forced their way on to the ship and threw the remaining Castilians overboard. Only then was Edward told of the danger he had been in and his original ship was jettisoned.

The Black Prince's ship had got into worse trouble; it had been badly holed and was letting in water, but the prince's knights could not force their way onto the enemy ship they had grappled. It was only when the duke of Lancaster's ship came up against their opponent that the Black Prince and his men could board the enemy. As they did, their ship began to sink. By now it was dark and the rest of the English fleet could not see that the ship carrying the king's household was being towed away by an enemy galley. It was saved when someone had the presence of mind to creep on to the Castilian ship and cut the halyard, bringing the sail down and immobilising the ship.

It was a much-celebrated triumph for Edward III and capped his reputation as a sailor king. But it was a reputation won through luck rather than strategic vision. Indeed, it was the French and their Mediterranean allies who had the clearest concept of how a naval campaign should be conducted. Edward was bold and impulsive at sea, characteristics better suited to cavalry charges.

The Battle of Winchelsea, or Les Espagnols sur Mer as it is known, was an example of why battles at sea were so rare. It was a risky business fighting there, and so unpredictable that advantage of ships often counted for little. This battle only took place by, as it were, mutual agreement; in other situations enemy ships could sail for long periods undetected and the English navy was too ponderous to respond to hostile fleets. Patrolling the seas or remaining on station was a stretch too far for medieval ships. A running battle on the high seas, as in 1350, was almost unknown, and beyond the capabilities of contemporary ships; closely fought encounters where archers and men-at-arms could replicate land battles in calm waters, like Sluys, were more viable.

It made better sense to raid undefended ships and ports than to seek out battle; in other words, to practise what we would call piracy. A good use of a navy was to protect merchant shipping and establish local, temporary zones of dominance prior to an invasion. Hence its work would be essentially negative: preventing piracy, picking out enemy vessels and aiding sieges rather than seeking out battle. Judging from Edward's zeal at the Battle of Winchelsea, it seems he was eager for showy victories. This might have impressed chroniclers and the public who stumped up vast sums for ships but had nothing tangible in return; it did not amount to a strategy. A crushing victory like Sluys or an adventure like Les Espagnols sur Mer was never decisive enough to make the risks worth it: ships were easily replaced but victories guaranteed nothing in the long term.

During the Hundred Years War both England and France had periods of success at sea and times of weakness. France was at its best when it could call upon the expertise of southern European sailors, England when it could muster vast invasion flotillas. In the 1350s the French were deprived of their Castilian allies not because of Edward II's victory off Winchelsea but because there was a civil war in Castile. The Black Prince was able to invade France from Gascony and won a major victory at Poitiers. England recovered Poitou in 1360, along with its strategically invaluable port, La Rochelle.

In 1372 parliament declared that 'every nation acknowledged our lord king of the sea'. It spoke too soon: La Rochelle was lost that year and an English fleet carrying £20,000 was attacked and burnt by Castilian galleys in French service at the Battle of Oléron. Parliament petitioned the king,[3] saying that the 'navy' – meaning the kingdom's shipping – was in crisis. Merchants and shipowners were going out of business because their vessels had been in royal service for too long and English seafarers were seeking new occupations. By this time Edward III was old and mentally infirm and the country was drained by decades of war. France, in contrast, was rediscovering its élan.

Days after Edward III died in June 1377 a force of galleys from France, Castile, Portugal and Monaco raided the coast of England and destroyed a number of towns. They came back for more two months later and England was hopelessly outmatched at sea in the following years. England faced invasion and its coastal regions and trade suffered greatly.

Richard II was accused of failing in the primary task of an English king, that of keeping the seas. The rot had set in before he came to the throne, however, when the permanent fleet of royal ships had been neglected. It was one of Richard's domestic opponents, Lord Arundel, who achieved a rare success when in 1387 he intercepted and chased a Castilian fleet in the Strait of Dover. He ran it into the Swyn estuary and took 70 ships and 19,000 tons of wine. It was a rare victory.

English successes at sea, spectacular as they may have been, were few. Moments of dominance were followed by years of weakness. And the latter were calamitous. The southern and East Anglian coasts and ports were repeatedly ravaged by French forces. England's weakness as a maritime nation stemmed from its retarded economy. She simply could not afford to defend herself. As so often in history, the sea brought danger.

CHAPTER 7

DEFENCE OF THE REALM
1399–1509

The sea is lost, France is lost.

Jack Cade, 1450

England stood well placed to become a great seafaring nation in the later Middle Ages. The gap between Dover and Calais was small; through it passed cargoes of immense value. Surely if England could exert its power over just this small but vital area of sea everything else would fall into place. It could control the affairs of Europe by threatening to cut off trade. With this lever it would ensure the defence of its entire coastline, making the sea 'the wall of England' rather than its curse.

That was the point made in the poem *The Libelle of Englyshe Polycye* ('The Little Book of English Policy') of the late 1430s. It was a vision of England as a great maritime nation, fulfilling its destiny as the keeper of the seas. What made it all the more galling for the author of the *Libelle* was that within recent memory England had had this very kind of dominance. Henry V's 'great ships' held sway over the Channel and the Narrow Seas in the 1410s; it had been one of the greatest and most innovative navies of its time.

When the *Libelle* was penned the mightiest of northern medieval warships, Henry's 1,400-ton *Grace Dieu*, had lain useless for almost two decades on the mudbanks of the river Hamble near Southampton; in 1439 it burnt to the waterline. Its surviving timbers, which can still be seen at low tide, provided a sorry reminder of vanished greatness. The rest of Henry V's ships rotted on riverbanks or at anchor. And, as if to mirror the fate of the ships, England had declined from the apogee of power; it was weak, humiliated and divided. Again.

Henry V had a fleet of thirty-six ships. He was not bequeathed a glittering inheritance. Richard II (king from 1377 to 1399) had, late in his reign, taken an interest in ships and commissioned four new vessels. Henry IV, who seized the throne from Richard in 1399, tried to find ways to make up for England's naval deficiencies. The seas were particularly anarchic during his reign. The cure was in many respects worse than the disease.

Henry IV granted licences to individuals to 'provide for the destruction of the king's enemies'. These seafaring men were not exactly pirates in the strictest definition, but they defined their orders very generously to themselves and made their commissions highly profitable.

One of those who took the commission was Harry Pay of Poole, who in 1405 was at sea fighting off the French. He also took an active, and profitable, role in attacking Henry's enemies. He pillaged Bilbao's iron trade, sacked Gijón on the north coast of Castile, stole a crucifix from the church of St Mary of Finisterre and plundered Spanish ships as he found them. Others jumped at the chance of fighting at sea. This brought England into conflict with the Low Countries and the Hanse, both of whose ships were stolen or plundered by English sailors. Pero Niño,[1] the half-brother of Henry III of Castile, was given authority to suppress robbery at sea and one of his targets was the notorious 'Arripay' of Poole. This was a lucrative command for Niño; he raided the south coast and attacked English ships at sea in the first years of the fifteenth century.

Men like Niño and Pay had status and, most importantly, authority. Licensing seafarers to carry out war at sea might have seemed cheap, but they did discriminate between friends and enemies in their 'keeping of the seas'. Chaucer said of his Shipman: 'Of nice conscience took he no keep'. While piracy flourished, trade suffered.

One man who made money in these troubled times was William Soper. He came to Southampton as an apprentice and, like Walter le Fleming two centuries before, made himself a fortune as a trader and servant of the city. Southampton was the main port for Italian ships and Soper developed strong links with Mediterranean traders, acting as an agent for them and trading to the south on his own account when relations with the Italians broke down over piracy in 1412. He helped the Crown as well, and in 1413 – the year Henry V came to the throne – he was MP for Southampton and collected customs and the wool subsidy for the Exchequer. Later that year one of the ships he jointly owned captured *Santa Clara*, an enormous Castilian carrack.

The Castilians were furious, claiming that they had a letter of safe conduct from the Crown; Soper, it seemed, had gone too far. He did a deal to save his skin. He was obliged to return *Santa Clara*'s royal standards, armour, weapons and its dog. He kept the ship and its cargo. The Crown had helped Soper out; now he had to repay the favour. The *Santa Clara* was refitted and renamed *Holighost de la Tour*, a two-masted royal warship of 740 tons burden. From now on Soper would be at the centre of royal shipbuilding and administration. The Crown benefited from an experienced shipper; Soper was well rewarded for his services.

This marked the beginning of a royal fleet with ships built on a new model. The start of the fifteenth century saw a breakthrough in ship design. Once again it was the Genoese who made it. Their carrack was

'orrible, grete and stoute': a fifteenth-century carrack.

a fusion of Mediterranean and northern European ship designs. It took the Hanseatic cog and enlarged it with the Mediterranean technique of frame-first, carvel-hull construction. It had a sail plan based on northern and southern traditions. Its two or three masts carried the square sails found on northern ships and the triangular fore-and-aft lateen sails that had propelled Mediterranean galleys for centuries. This heterogeneous sail plan allowed the carrack to sail in all sorts of winds and made handling it more manageable. The carrack was a bulk carrier, capable by mid-century of holding 2,000 tons of cargo. It was a huge ship that carried valuable goods from the Middle East to northern Europe.

The so-called 'full-rigged ship' ranks among the most significant inventions in medieval Europe. It changed everything, from trade to war, exploration and, eventually, domination of hitherto unseen portions of the world.

Opponents were terrified by its size alone. The carrack towered above other ships and had a particularly enlarged prow. The author of the *Libelle* called them 'orrible, grete and stoute'. Its bulk and height provided the ideal platform for raining missiles on smaller vessels. It revolutionised trade and exploration, for it was the first large oceangoing ship that could carry stores for long voyages.

Its drawback was that it could only put into deep harbours. The favoured port in England was Southampton, where valuable cargoes were traded by men like William Soper. It was little wonder that Soper was chosen to reform the royal fleet. Henry V, if he was to master the Channel and invade France, must not be outclassed by foreign vessels, for the French were once again in alliance with Genoa and Henry's ships and men would be likely to encounter their monster ships. Soper was commissioned to help build Henry's 'great ships'. They were the first sailing ships designed exclusively for war.

The moving force behind the new fleet was William Catton, clerk of the king's ships from July 1413.[2] While Soper turned the *Santa Clara* into a great ship, Catton rebuilt the old *Trinity de la Tour* as the *Trinity Royal*, a ship of 540 tons burden. Also of great importance to the royal fleet was the ballinger. This vessel was originally a Biscayan whaling boat. It was hardy and manoeuvrable, powered by oars and a single square sail and had a carrying capacity of between 20 and 120 tons. Ballingers were used as companion boats for the larger ships, for patrols, guard duty and transporting troops. These ships were built and repaired under Catton's supervision at Winchelsea and under Soper's at Southampton. All of them were brightly coloured and festooned with coats of arms and religious symbols.

Henry V had a strong understanding of sea power. He invaded France in 1415 with a fleet of 1,500 requisitioned merchant ships (many of them were foreign-owned – testament to the decline of English sea power in the fourteenth and fifteenth centuries) that landed his army at Harfleur. He won his famous victory at Agincourt that year. In 1416 the French were in the Channel in force, attempting to reverse Henry's successes. The English were dependent on mastering the sea and securing French ports. Places like Harfleur had to be held as bases for Henry's war of conquest.

The French held the advantage in 1416. Their Genoese allies had eight carracks and a galley fleet commanded by Gioanni de' Grimaldi. These ships raided the south coast of England and were active in the campaign to recover Harfleur by cutting off English supplies. In August Henry's brother, the duke of Bedford, was in charge of a fleet of 300 ships, including Soper's recently constructed *Holighost*.

Luck was with the English. The galleys withdrew when Grimaldi was killed attacking an English wine convoy. A Spanish squadron deserted when it saw the size of Bedford's fleet. The French ships did not dare venture out of Honfleur. After a day of vicious fighting the smaller English ships had captured three carracks, driven one aground, sunk a German hulk and forced the rest of the Genoese ships to flee. It seems that the large carracks were caught in a falling tide, allowing the smaller English ships to harry them until they could be boarded. Overcoming a carrack was a serious challenge. At another time the earl of Warwick, captain of Calais, had led six ballingers with 1,500 men against a carrack with a crew of just sixty-two. The ballingers matched the carrack for speed, but every time they raised ladders to board they had been beaten off with missiles thrown from the massive ship.

But under Bedford the English had prevailed over carracks. The fight must have been desperate as English soldiers tried repeatedly to raise ladders and swarm on to the towering vessels. It was well worth the effort. These were highly valuable ships, and the addition of three genuine Mediterranean carracks was a great victory for the English.

In 1417 there were three squadrons at sea made up of Henry's great ships and merchantmen. Between them they captured four carracks and several Castilian ships. In the following years the patrols were kept up and the navy supported Henry's conquest of Normandy. At the same time the building programme continued. In 1417 the gigantic *Jesus* (1,000 tons) entered the king's service. Now England was more than a match for the great navies of Europe. It was in complete control of the Channel. In 1418 Soper's masterpiece, the *Grace Dieu*, was launched.

The remains of the greatest of Henry V's great ships suggest that it was built in a hurry. It was certainly not made to look good: some of the planks and ribs are roughly finished. Most likely the deficiencies in the aesthetics of the ship were covered up with a lick of bright paint. It was a vast ship. In all 2,735 oak, 1,145 beech, fourteen ash and twelve elm trees were felled to build it. It carried over 250 men and had three cannon. The prow rose 50 feet above the waterline, providing a large and high platform for archers to rain death on smaller ships. It was 218 feet long and 50 feet wide, making it comparable in size to HMS *Victory* and twice the size of *Mary Rose*. Carracks were carvel-built, but the *Grace Dieu* retained the clinker technique. This ship was triple clinker – three planks were nailed together with long iron rivets to provide a thick, reinforced hull waterproofed with tar and moss sandwiched between the planks. The shipwrights and carpenters who worked on her between 1416 and 1418 were experimenting in ship design, taking a Genoese ship and applying northern principles to the construction. It must have been a work of trial and error, which explains the crudeness of its timbers.

Grace Dieu was celebrated in Europe as one of the greatest ships ever launched. The only problem with her was that by the time she was operational in 1420 the aims that had given birth to her were no longer relevant. England had control of the Channel and Castile was no longer in France's service. The Treaty of Troyes of that year provided that Henry's heirs should succeed Charles VI as king of France. *Grace Dieu* served as a useful reminder to foreign visitors that England possessed the technology and political will to claim sovereignty over the seas.

When Henry V died in 1422 his ships were treated as his private property rather than as part of a royal navy. Many were sold off to pay his debts. The four great ships were taken into the anchorage on the river Hamble. After a few years at anchor they were laid up in mud berths near the port of Bursledon. They were perhaps intended for a future use, but if so it was an optimistic or sentimental hope; they were rotting away. In 1430 William Soper, by now in charge of the administration of the entire navy, dined the commander of the Florentine merchant fleet on board *Grace Dieu*. The distinguished guest had never seen a larger, better constructed or more beautiful ship. High praise indeed from an Italian of the fifteenth century.

Not much of Henry V's navy was left when in 1439 lightning struck *Grace Dieu* and everything above the waterline was burnt. William Soper had no ships left to look after when he retired three years later.

When he inherited the thrones of England and, shortly after, France,

Henry VI was an infant. His government was in financial difficulty and his council's military strategy involved land operations in France supported by an alliance with Burgundy. By the 1430s the Burgundians had turned against England. In 1436 Philip le Bon of Burgundy raised a fleet of ducal ships and merchant vessels to take Calais; it was thwarted by storms at sea. The French won back their ports one by one. England's military woes were compounded by the complete rundown of the navy. Land operations in France and diplomatic leverage over Burgundy were all but impossible without domination of the seas. Gascony was once more in a parlous situation, its supply route from England under threat. In 1449 France retook Rouen. In 1452 the unthinkable happened and France conquered Gascony. All that remained of the empire was Calais. England lost control of the Channel thanks to the greatest enemy of the navy: the indebtedness of the Crown.

Once again the Crown was reduced to licensing private interests to 'keep the seas'. In 1436 thirty ships belonging to private interests in various English ports elected two admirals and formed a single fleet. Such a contracting scheme solved very little. It was expensive and there was a risk that these armed merchants would seek to profit from their commission and terrorize the seas. This was especially so since the Burgundians had closed their markets to English wool, putting a stop to legitimate trade. In 1442 the Crown was forced to hand over control of the seas to parliament. It had a grandiose scheme to keep a patrol of eight ships, attended by barges and ballingers, on the seas at all times between March and November. That was a sensible solution to what was the lowest point in English naval power, but it was too expensive to work, and the Crown once again issued licences to enthusiastic individuals.

Under Henry V piracy had been stamped out. Under his son it made a big comeback. One of the men who took part in 'keeping the seas' for the king was Robert Wenyngton, former mayor of Dartmouth. Traders like him had plenty of scores to settle in the near-permanent private wars that engulfed the shipping lanes. In 1449 he captured two ships from Brest returning home from Flanders. The Bretons raised a fleet, which included great ships and carried 3,000 men. Wenyngton prepared to meet this force, but instead he came across 130 hulks returning from the Bay of Bourgneuf laden with salt. Many of the ships belonged to the Hanse. Wenyngton demanded that the ships strike their colours in acknowledgement of England's sovereignty of the sea. The Hanse admiral refused. Wenyngton 'bade them strike [the sails] in the name of the King of England, and they bade me shit in the name of the King of

England.'[3] So Wenyngton ordered his ships to attack.

The Hanse admiral was not concerned because the English had so few ships. But Wenyngton had the weather gage and he ordered his ships to 'sail over', or ram, the merchantmen. It was a crazy move, but it worked. Rather than risk a kamikaze attack, the salt fleet surrendered, probably trusting that someone with greater authority and a cooler head would release them. Wenyngton took the Hanseatic ships because, he said, they had fired at him first. The ships were escorted to the Isle of Wight and then taken up the Thames to London; so great was the quantity of salt that it was warehoused in every available space, including a royal palace.

Wenyngton had far exceeded his orders, but salt was a valuable commodity. Much of the Hanse's wealth came from the trade in salt fish, and suddenly they lacked the preserving ingredient. The Hanse was unpopular with English traders. Citizens of the German cities had extensive trading rights and privileges in England, but they consistently refused to grant English merchants reciprocity in Germany and the Baltic. Wenyngton became something of a hero. The Hanse punished England by closing the sound of Denmark to its traders and committing acts of reprisal against its merchants. The king might have made the right noises of indignation, but members of the council profited from Wenyngton's piracy.

So much for keeping the seas; so much for England's sovereignty over them. Rather than policing the seas the English were the most rapacious seafarers and the greatest disrupters of trade. It was not just small-time pirates acting on their own initiative; it was also men in authority who had an interest in keeping the seas beyond the law.

In 1458 the earl of Warwick, acting in his capacity as captain of Calais, seized eighteen ships from the Hanse city of Lübeck when they did not salute the English flag.[4] His command of the Narrow Seas reflected the breakdown in authority in England after the loss of empire and the descent of Henry VI into madness. Richard Neville, sixteenth earl of Warwick, was thirty in the year he attacked the Hanse ships. He was the richest landowner in England and he had a grievance against the Crown and the men who ruled in Henry's name. They blocked his smooth inheritance to a vast conglomeration of lands. He supported Richard of York's opposition to Henry's government and in 1455, during York's guardianship of England, he became captain of Calais.

When the Lancastrians reasserted their power they were eager to dislodge Warwick from his position of strength. They attempted to starve him out, but the people of Kent continued to send supplies. In 1457 the French raided Sandwich. This attack was aimed against Warwick, and he put it about that Queen Margaret, Henry's consort, had encouraged the French. The raid caused great indignation in England, and the Lancastrians were forced to pay Warwick to keep the seas. In 1458 he pillaged a Castilian fleet. A few weeks later he took the Hanse ships. The following year he made a successful and profitable attack on a fleet of Spanish and Genoese ships.

The Hanse could wait for its revenge. Warwick the Kingmaker helped Richard of York's son dislodge Henry and become King Edward IV. In 1469 Warwick turned back to Henry VI and used his massive naval clout to restore the Lancastrians. But Edward IV was able to win over the many nations Warwick had offended in his madcap career of piracy. The Hanse helped restore Edward. Warwick was killed at the Battle of Barnet. It resumed its privileges and trading dominance in England. The Hanse was not an organisation one could slight with impunity.

Edward IV was more a merchant king than a warrior king. In the late fifteenth century England was a diminished power with limited ambitions abroad. Edward IV, Richard III and Henry VII were cautious in their dealings with foreign powers, beset as they were by internal threats and financial worries.

Edward IV had had to respond to the mercantile community who were angry that they paid taxes for protection at sea but got nothing in return. Royal ships 'wafted' or escorted the ships of the Merchant Adventurers trading to the wool staple at Calais and Zeeland. They also accompanied the fishing fleet to Iceland. A ship owned by Henry VII was chartered by private business interests to trade as far as the Mediterranean. Trade was of vital importance to these kings and to England. It is significant that the Lord Admiral chosen by Richard III was John Howard, a landowner who made a fortune as a shipowner, trader and naval commander. He was an early supporter of the House of York and his ships were often chartered to act as armed guards for merchant fleets. Howard served in the navy as deputy admiral of Norfolk and Suffolk in the 1460s; he victualled the east coast fleet in 1468; and he commanded patrols in the Channel. He was also enlisted as an envoy to foreign courts, using his trading links to further England's diplomacy. In 1481 he led a successful naval expedition against Scotland. Richard III made him Lord Admiral and duke of Norfolk; he died with his king at the Battle of Bosworth.

The Howard dynasty would dominate the English navy for over a century. It was this partnership between the Crown and shipowners like the Howards that gave the country a degree of naval strength.

What royal ships could not do was prevent attacks on England. Henry

VII was able to land his forces in Wales to take the throne from Richard, and Henry in turn was harassed by pretenders who arrived by sea. The first Tudor was determined to deter invaders with large, imposing ships. Within two years of winning the Crown at Bosworth, Henry VII had large carracks on the seas – the first purpose-built warships since the days of Henry V. By the end of the century such ships were laden with small breech-loaded cannon fastened to the sides of the castles. Henry VII's *Sovereign* bristled with 141 serpentines and his *Regent* with 225. These guns were small weapons designed to rake an opposing ship's decks with shot, killing as many soldiers and sailors as possible and wreaking mayhem with billowing smoke, flashes of fire and explosions. The tactic remained the same as ever: gain the weather gage, come alongside, open fire with serpentines and arrows and then board once the enemy's decks had been cleared. The aim was to overwhelm the enemy; it was not to cause fatal structural damage to another ship.

Henry VII's new great ships may have been impressive enough, but in technology and size they lagged behind more substantial naval powers. Mediterranean galleys at this time mounted heavy ship-killing guns called basilisks in the prow. Nearer to home Scotland was an expanding naval power. By 1449 James II had a carvel-constructed ship. The English navy would have to wait till the 1460s for such a breakthrough, and then the Crown had only a part share in a carvel ship built at Dunwich by Howard. James IV's *Margaret* of 1504–7 was 700 tons burden and *Michael*, begun in 1506, was 1,000 tons and mounted twelve heavy guns on each side. In addition two bronze basilisks protruded from the bows and one from the stern. The guns were cast in Scotland, and they were so heavy that each required six wagons to bring them to the dry dock. The basilisk was the largest contemporary gun, with a barrel of twenty feet or more. Most worryingly for England, the assurgent Scottish navy was at the disposal of the king of France.

By the end of the fifteenth century England was a second-rate naval power. English seafarers were adept at fighting at sea, even if in less than noble causes. It was an offensive power key to national sea power and it had to be harnessed. Henry VII introduced an important innovation. He paid bounties to shipowners who built ships over a certain size. It made the Crown part-owner of the nation's largest ships, binding the merchant marine ever closer to the monarchy.

As ever, it was a double-edged weapon. Weak kings were dependent on insatiable seafarers. Partnerships with shipowners worked best when the Crown could draw upon loyal, dependable magnates like Howard. But as for England's private naval capabilities, it was the same variation on a familiar theme. By the fifteenth century English shippers now carried most of their country's wool and cloth abroad. But the route to the Low Countries was too short to call upon sufficient and large enough ships to form a powerful national sea force.

What England lacked so palpably were the funds and the organisation to provide consistent naval protection. The rises of English sea power in the Middle Ages – always brief and occasionally glorious – were enough to implant a sense that England's right and destiny was maritime supremacy; its falls were predictable and melancholy reminders of the country's weakness, internal divisions and economic backwardness.

PART 3: ATLANTIC

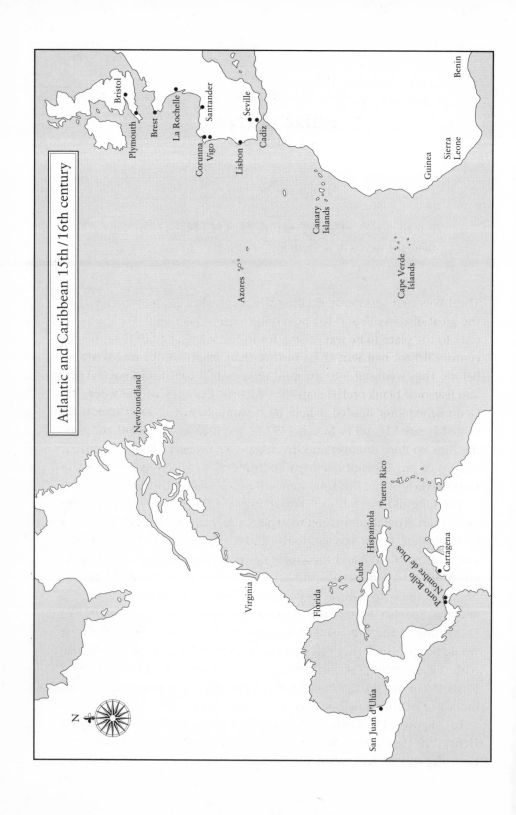

Atlantic and Caribbean 15th/16th century

N

Bristol
Plymouth
Brest
La Rochelle
Corunna
Vigo
Santander
Seville
Lisbon
Cadiz

Benin
Guinea
Sierra
Leone

Canary
Islands

Azores

Cape Verde
Islands

Newfoundland

Virginia

Florida

Cuba
Hispaniola
Puerto Rico

Porto Bello
Nombre de Dios
Cartagena

San Juan d'Ulúa

CHAPTER 8

HOME WATERS
1509–1530

It is the long voyages ... that harden seamen and open unto
them the secrets of navigation.

Hakluyt

The 1490s were gloriously exciting times – if, that is, you were aware of
the great discoveries and the possibilities they opened up. For Giovanni
Caboto the place to be was Bristol, for in the second half of the fifteenth
century Bristol had sent ships further than English ships had ventured
before. They went out into the great unknown, into the midst of the vast
and fearsome blank on the map – the Atlantic Ocean. That was where the
Genoese explorer headed, where he became known as John Cabot. He
visited Henry VII and in March 1497 he received letters patent authoris-
ing him 'to find, discover and investigate whatsoever islands, countries,
regions or provinces of heathens and infidels, in whatsoever part of the
world, which before this time were unknown to all Christians'.

The king did not advance any money, or indeed any practical help
other than general permission to explore parts of the world undiscovered
by Christians. Henry was cautious – and for good reason. The papal bull
Inter Caetera of 1493 and the Treaty of Tordesillas the following year divided the extra-European world between Portugal and Spain. A line was
drawn in the map halfway between the Portuguese Cape Verde Islands
and the Spanish islands of Cipangu (Cuba) and Antilia (Hispaniola).
Everything to the east would belong to Portugal; the lands to the west
would be Spanish. Henry was in the process of seeking a marriage alliance
with the assurgent power in Europe, Spain. He was wary about offending
Fernando of Aragon and Isabella of Castile; he was not prepared to lavish
money or help on a risky voyage.

In August 1497 Cabot rode from the docks of Bristol directly to
Henry VII. He reported his startling news. He had set sail in May on a
tiny fifty-ton caravel called the *Matthew* with a crew of twenty. After

thirty-five days' sailing west into the Atlantic they sighted land. Cabot and his crew stepped ashore onto this new world. They did not advance further than the shooting distance of a crossbow. In that time they found nets, wooden tools, footprints and the remains of a fire, but saw no actual humans. They raised English and papal banners and claimed this 'New Found Land' for Henry VII. Back on the *Matthew* and continuing their journey they sighted yet more land. And, most significantly, they saw seas teeming with cod.

Cabot believed he had found the eastern fringes of the great empire of Cathay – China. Henry gave him patents to continue exploring the far side of the Atlantic, and merchandise to carry to the New Found Land on five ships, one of which was funded by the king himself. The fleet left Bristol in 1498.

And that was the last that was ever heard of John Cabot. Neither he nor his ships ever returned.

Cabot's voyages came during the crowning years of late medieval discovery. Christopher Columbus reached mainland South America in 1498 and the following year Vasco da Gama returned to Portugal from a gruelling voyage round the Cape of Good Hope to India.

Spain and Portugal were perfectly placed for exploring the Atlantic. The Castilians conquered the Canaries in 1402. The Portuguese reached Madeira in 1419 and the Azores in 1427. Before the middle of the century they had pressed on to Cape Verde and Sierra Leone. In 1488 Bartolomeu Dias rounded the southern tip of Africa.

The Portuguese had, during their burst of exploration, developed a new ship. The caravel took its inspiration from deep-sea Atlantic fishing boats. It was lighter and had a shallower draught than the carrack; it had much reduced upperworks and a lower prow. What it lacked in size it more than made up for in speed, manoeuvrability and stability. The caravel could sail into the wind better than any previous European ship, making the deep ocean navigable. The *Matthew* on which John Cabot sailed was a caravel that had a mixed plan of square and lateen sails. Unlike other medieval ships, it was the kind of vessel you could trust to take you into the ocean and back.

It was this ship that made the breakthrough of exploring the Atlantic, for the Portuguese had discovered that there were good following winds from Iberia on the journey out to the Atlantic islands and south down the African coast. Returning home was just as straightforward if the sailor headed into the ocean and picked up a following westerly at 35° north off the (then undiscovered) North American coast. The Portuguese thus needed to determine latitude. The age of discovery prompted a revolution in oceanic navigation – techniques that were simply not needed by medieval seafarers who relied on hugging coastlines and on observation and experience. This was the breakaway moment for Western Europe.

England was not blessed by geography to join this push out into the tropics. Iberian sailors benefited from the Atlantic wind system that carried ships in a clockwise pattern to the Canaries, across to the West Indies with the trade winds behind them and home again, with the added propulsion of the Gulf Stream, via North America. Sailors from the British Isles could not benefit in this way. The prevailing winds in the Channel and Bay of Biscay were against them and they had no friendly islands en route to resupply them.

But seafarers from England and Scotland did begin to venture out into the northern Atlantic. From the end of the fourteenth century Englishmen were fishing off Iceland. That island had long been cut off from Scandinavia; 'No news from Norway' its Chronicle repeated dismally year after year. In 1412 there was still no news from Norway, but something broke the accustomed solitude: an English ship had arrived in search of food. The next year more than thirty English doggers put in and various traders appeared to supply the Icelanders with goods. The locals were forbidden to trade with aliens, but their need was great, and if they didn't want to trade their new visitors were prepared to bully, fight, steal, smash up boats and kidnap until the Icelanders complied. Some traders and fishermen appeared in armour.

The violence and lawlessness of English waters had been exported.

This was an important moment for English seafaring. After centuries plying the same routes along coastlines to Iberia, Gascony and the Baltic, all of a sudden English sailors seemed perfectly at home sailing the ocean. Somehow navigational expertise had been absorbed, perhaps from contact with more sophisticated foreign sailors.

By the second third of the century, ships from Bristol traded and fished in Iceland during the spring and summer and journeyed to Iberia, Gascony or the Netherlands in the autumn and winter. These ships went via the west coast of Ireland, where the Bristolians had good trading links as well. Iceland was the source of great wealth. The demand for salt fish was acute throughout Europe, and the traders of Bristol did well out of exporting Icelandic fish to Portugal (along with English cloth). Bristol merchants went further afield. Robert Sturmy (d. 1457), a sometime 'keeper of the sea', ventured into the Mediterranean, taking pilgrims out and returning with spices. William Canynges (d. 1474) sent his merchant fleet of ten ships to Iceland, the Baltic, Iberia, France and the Netherlands.

Men such as Sturmy and Canynges made Bristol the most important port in England; they pushed into new markets and developed links throughout Europe and even the Middle East. By the end of the century ships from Bristol were plying the Mediterranean regularly.

Men of the next generation were more ambitious still. They were also rich enough to risk longer, exploratory voyages to places like North Africa. From 1480 we get tantalising hints that a group of Bristol merchants were sponsoring voyages into the Atlantic to search for the island of Brasil.* This island, along with various others including the island of the Seven Cities, appeared on contemporary maps in the great blank of the Atlantic Ocean to the west of Ireland; they were the focus of stories about what lay beyond the horizon. We know about this because Thomas Croft, a customs official of Bristol, had an eighth share in an Atlantic voyage of 1481. He was accused of engaging in trade, an activity forbidden by his office, but the jury – made up of a tight-knit group of Bristol's trading grandees – found that the ships had been sent out 'to the intent to reach and find a certain isle called the Isle of Brasil'. Croft was exonerated on the grounds that the ships were exploring, not trading.

In fact the expeditions westward were not simply voyages of explora-tion. English traders had been forced out of Iceland by the Hanse at this time. They needed a fresh source of fish with which to trade in Iberia and elsewhere. The search for Brasil was a pretext. They went for fish, which they found in staggering abundance on what would become known as the Newfoundland Banks. They did not want anyone muscling in on their find, so they hushed up the aim of their voyages. 'The island of Brasil' was a convenient pretext; these men had no interest in exploration, just money. That's why the ship on the voyage of 1481 carried great quantities of salt – hardly a must-have item for exploration but indispensable for preserving cod.

The accidental 'discovery' of Newfoundland years before Cabot came back and described it probably stemmed from just one of many secretive voyages. The English were banned from Iceland and Greenland by the king of Denmark, but they went anyway and left few records. It is possible that an English fishing vessel illicitly working in Greenland strayed off course, got to Newfoundland and returned to Bristol by working out the latitude. All this was kept a secret, but news of 'Brasil' might have

---

* The name Brasil comes from Old Irish. Its eerie similarity to Brazil, which got its name from brazilwood, is coincidental.

leaked out in Iberia, which is why John Cabot made straight for Bristol. In a letter by John Day, trader of Bristol, to Christopher Columbus describing Cabot's voyage he says that 'as you [Columbus] are already aware' the men of Bristol had 'at another time' discovered the island of Brasil. In a dispatch to Fernando and Isabella in 1498, the ambassador reported that the people of Bristol had been sending out caravels in search of Brasil. Might these have been clandestine fishing fleets masquerading as hapless explorers? Certainly the men of Bristol were not given to investing in romantic voyages of exploration. Tellingly, they did not invest much money in Cabot, perhaps because they knew enough about Newfoundland already – enough at least to know it was not Cathay (China) or a land suitable for cultivating sugar or brazilwood. Furthermore, they would have known that Cathay was a lot further than Columbus and Cabot were suggesting.

Cabot's disastrous voyage of 1498 did not put a stop to Atlantic exploration. In the early sixteenth century Henry VII continued to shower favours on Bristolians who made or sponsored voyages to the New Found Land. In 1502 he rewarded a mariner who brought him back hawks and another who gave him an eagle. In 1505 he received mountain cats and popinjays and met three North American natives. A Company of Adventurers to the New Found Lands was founded by merchants from Bristol and London. However, by the second half of the decade it was clear that North America was not worth the effort. It did not generate anything like the returns that the Caribbean and South and Central America brought to Spain and Asia to Portugal. The Company of Adventurers fizzled out. Moreover, the English were intruding on the Spanish zone of monopoly, and neither Henry VII nor Henry VIII wanted to offend the new superpower of Europe. Interest in the New Found Land ended.

When he came to the throne in 1509 Henry VIII was ambitious, vigorous and youthful. He was also deeply traditional. His concept of kingship and of England's destiny was derived from romance and history – particularly that of his more illustrious ancestors, Edward III and Henry V. His charisma, the wealth hoarded by his father, and the lustre of his court helped to gloss over – for a time – the fact that England had declined to become an irrelevant country confined to Europe's margins, cut off from the main currents of exploration and trade.

Imbued as he was with new Erasmian learning, and well versed in modern geography, Henry's style and outlook were all the same medieval, nostalgic and Anglocentric. This extended to the sea as well. The naval capacity of the nation was geared, as ever, towards home waters.

Henry favoured ships that were symbolic of majesty and boasted sovereignty over the seas. In his early years he created an impressive-looking navy, with big new intimidating ships. *Mary Rose* at 500 tons and *Peter Pomegranate* at 450 were comparable in size to James IV's *Margaret*; the gigantic *Henry Grace à Dieu*, built from 1512 and known as the *Great Harry*, matched the 1,000-ton Scottish warship *Michael*.

Mary Rose and *Peter Pomegranate* certainly looked the part. They were named after saints and emblems: the Virgin was known as 'the mystic rose' while the pomegranate (also associated with the Virgin) was the personal emblem of Queen Catherine. The leading English warships were resplendent with religious iconography and royal insignia; the great streamer on *Mary Rose* measured 150 yards and was coloured green and white, the Tudor colours. *Mary Rose* was much favoured by Henry and by his admiral Sir Edward Howard (grandson of John Howard, first duke of Norfolk), who called her 'the noblest ship of sail ... at this hour that I trow be in Christendom'.[1]

The two new ships and the older *Regent* were sent out under Howard in 1512 as Henry began his first war against France. The fleet of seventeen, mainly requisitioned merchantmen, 'kept the seas' without much opposition, harassing French fishing boats, seizing merchant shipping and harrying coastal regions. Two towns and numerous villages in Brittany were burnt to the ground.

But before Henry VIII could spend too long congratulating himself as the new Henry V, the sixteenth century caught up with the English navy. Over the winter Louis XII reinforced his fleet. As so often before, the French turned to the Mediterranean for the latest in maritime warfare. Six galleys under the fearsome Prégent de Bidoux joined the French fleet at Brest.

Howard was facing a problem that would beset every naval commander in the sixteenth century. Here he was, ready to strike a blow against the French navy, but he was paralysed for want of food and beer. He begged for supplies 'or else we shall be driven to come again into the Downs and let the Frenchmen take their pleasure'.[2]

Howard got his supplies and put out; again he forced the French fleet to retreat to Brest. So far, so good. Then, a few days later, Prégent arrived with the galleys. On 22 April 1513 the English sailors got a violent and traumatic taste of a fearsome new weapon. Their ships were bombarded from close quarters with heavy shot hurled out of enormous basilisk cannon mounted on the prow of the French galleys. One ship was sunk and another crippled, but that was nothing compared with the terror that engulfed the English mariners as cannonballs ripped through their ships, splintering timbers, tearing rigging and sails and reducing their comrades to tangled heaps. Their light, breech-loaded guns could not match this onslaught at close quarters. No one had experienced an attack like this.

The galleys took up station in a nearby bay. Howard was running out of food; his men were hungry and scared; and Henry was taunting him for failing to fight. There was only one solution. He ordered every light boat lowered and filled with men.

Sir Edward Howard's boat made for Prégent's galley. The Lord Admiral leapt aboard, but his boat was pushed away, and his men could only watch as he waved his arms and shouted: 'Come aboard again! Come aboard again!'[3] When he saw this was impossible he wrapped up his gold admiral's whistle and threw it in the sea to deprive the enemy of so symbolic a trophy. The French speared Howard with their pikes and tossed him into the sea; weighed down by his armour he drowned. The fleet limped back to Dartmouth, where the men rampaged round the countryside in search of food. Thomas Howard, Sir Edward's brother, took charge and restored order and prepared to return to Brest on receipt of Henry's orders. Then the king changed his mind, and lucky he did so. The sailors and soldiers of the fleet would rather go to purgatory, Thomas Howard reported, than go back to meet the galleys and their new, terrifying way of war.

Henry's naval expedition was the last hurrah for medieval naval warfare. Naval artillery had upset the traditional means of fighting whereby a large ship would get close to an enemy ship as a prelude for a contest between archers and knights.

The problem in the early sixteenth century was that while artillery had improved, no sailing ship had been designed that could carry or deploy it effectively. The huge basilisks mounted on the French galleys in 1513 might have terrified English sailors, but the sheer size and weight of the gun slowed the galley down and deprived it of the manoeuvrability that had made it such an effective warship. Carracks were no better placed to take advantage. Heavy guns placed high in the upperworks made them unstable.

The great breakthrough was the gunport. The first ports, holes cut into the hull of a ship with lids that could be shut and waterproofed, appeared on the stern, where the heavy cannon did not destabilise the ships. A continuous gun deck was not possible in the early sixteenth century. The main weapon continued to be the small breech-loading anti-personnel gun. These were not 'ship-killing' vessels. Shipboard artillery was not good enough to sink an opponent. Henry's great ships were floating castles in home waters, designed as much for prestige as for military capability.

Henry VIII cared deeply about ships, perhaps more so than any other monarch since the Anglo-Saxons. He took a personal interest in his navy royal and he identified his kingship with naval strength. The launching of a royal ship was a state occasion. In part such displays were a chance to show off new techniques in ship design and advanced gunnery technologies. They were also about kingship and England's traditional claim to sovereignty over the seas. The close connection made between the Tudors and naval power was intended to recall the best of English kings, from Arthur to Alfred, from Edgar to Edward III. In the context of the 1510s and 1520s it was also to remind, or inform, foreign princes that although England might be small, poor and geographically distant from the foci of European power politics, her clout derived from the sea. Hence she was strong out of all proportion to her ostensible means. Or at least that was what Henry wanted the world to believe. For he believed it himself.

Henry was genuinely enthusiastic about the navy. But after he had blown the cash he inherited from his father it became harder to afford a large prestige navy. By 1524 the great ships were laid up for want of cash.

If Henry had a passion for the sea, it was for mastering home waters with his massive floating fortresses and bridging the gap between England and France. In other words, trying to achieve what his ancestors had failed to do. During this golden age of Spanish and Portuguese exploration, Henry remained impressively unadventurous when it came to extra-European ventures. This marks him out from contemporary monarchs in maritime countries. Spain and Portugal were adding to their knowledge of America and Asia and the French were exploring the east coast of North America. In 1509, the year he came to the throne, the Portuguese navy beat a coalition of Ottoman, Indian, Venetian and Ragusan ships in a sea battle off Diu, on the west coast of India. It added to their conquests in the Indian Ocean, which included Socotra and Muscat, and gave them control over the Indian Ocean and Red Sea. Two years later they captured Malacca.

Henry was jolted out of inactivity once more in 1527. It was thanks to his arch-enemy François I, who sponsored Giovanni da Verrazano's exploration of the coast between the Carolinas and Newfoundland. In response Henry sent one of his own ships, captained by an experienced officer called John Rut, to search for a north-west passage to Asia. Rut was forced back by icebergs off Labrador. He then headed for the West Indies, probably to report to Henry on the huge amounts of gold that the Spanish were carting home from the recently discovered Inca Empire. The Spanish were displeased to find a foreigner intruding on their new world.

The mission was an expensive and somewhat embarrassing failure. Henry was in no position to take on Charles V in 1527. This was when he was pressing the pope to investigate and annul his marriage to Catherine, and Charles, the Holy Roman emperor and Catherine's nephew, had to be kept on side. Charles was also at the apogee of his powers, rich beyond the dreams of avarice with gold and silver from the New World. As it was, the coast of North America was devoid of gold. It seemed bleak and inhospitable and the natives strong and hostile. There was no trade to be had; no quick returns on investments that would have made colonisation attractive for private interests or the Crown.

Where there was a handy profit to be made was in trade with Iberia. Englishmen who made the journey to Lisbon or Cadiz, the Azores, Cape Verde or the Canaries stood the chance of importing a rich array of exotic goods, for which there was high demand. Such sailors, mainly from the south-west, were fully part of the new Atlantic world, trading in Iberian produce such as olive oil and wine – always in high demand – and also the spoils of the Americas, the Caribbean and Asia: fruits, pepper, spices, sugar, brazilwood and 'Newland' fish. They made contacts with foreign merchants, heard of far-flung places and, most important of all, learnt the arts of oceanic navigation and combat. It was an experience of seafaring unobtainable in royal service.

It was a rough world in the Atlantic, where trading links and sources of supply were jealously guarded and fought over. You had to have a strong head to thrive. Very few Englishmen joined in. The man who ventured furthest and made the most money was William Hawkins of Plymouth. By the 1520s he was one of the richest merchants in Plymouth and an agent of the Crown. Much of his trade was in Iberian products purchased through middlemen or in the Atlantic islands. He did not get where he was by being nice. He was in trouble locally and nationally for violence and faction fighting in his home town. By the 1530s he had fought, cajoled, bullied and bribed his way to power, serving two terms as mayor.

His bravado and bullying stood him in good stead for intruding into other people's waters. In 1530 he took his 250-ton ship the *Paul* to Upper Guinea, where he purchased ivory and pepper. He then crossed the Atlantic to Brazil and obtained brazilwood, which produced a highly valuable dye. He was the first Englishman to trade directly with Africa and South America, in defiance of the Portuguese monopoly. He became immensely wealthy and famous as a result. On a second voyage to Brazil he brought back a local chief to meet Henry VIII. The king praised Hawkins 'for his wisdom, valour, experience and skill in sea causes'.

The praise was deserved, but Hawkins was an exception, and Henry did little to encourage such ventures. He was preoccupied with his prestige navy. The age of discovery passed him by. This was to have serious implications for the development of the navy. As had been the case throughout the Middle Ages, English traders lost out on new opportunities for trade and the navy – in the wider sense of the word – was the loser. The pioneering spirit of the Bristolians had been stifled by royal indifference. English mariners did not develop the skills taught by long-distance exploration.

The merchant navy remained underdeveloped and orientated almost entirely towards the Low Countries. England remained a backward European power, an irrelevant presence in the world's seas, and barely able to control the waters that swirled round her coastline. Henry's showy navy was a white elephant.

CHAPTER 9

BRAVE NEW WORLDS
1530–1556

The sheen had worn off Henry's glamour by the late 1520s. He was frustrated in his ambitions abroad and frustrated in his attempts to annul his marriage to Catherine and marry Anne Boleyn. While the *Mary Rose* and other of Henry's crack ships lay in docks with minimal repairs, Henry had to face his weakness as a European monarch and the strength of Charles V, king of Spain, ruler of mighty empires in Europe and the New World. Henry was unable to influence the papacy, just as he was powerless to dictate terms to his fellow sovereigns.

The end point of his long intellectual evolution was to come to understand, first, that England was an empire entire unto itself, which did not acknowledge the superiority of any foreigner, even the pope; and second that kings had a special spiritual duty and authority over their own people. Such radical positions – an agonising time in the making – put him at odds with much of the rest of Europe, particularly the nephew of the spurned Catherine, Charles V, who believed he had a special responsibility for upholding the true faith against heresy. Spain was an oceanic naval power and Charles ruled the Netherlands – with its formidable naval resources – as well; in alliance with France and Scotland he could seriously menace England from the sea.

It would seem logical for an island country in so parlous a position to rely upon the navy to back up its claim to separateness. But this did not happen, not at once. The process of Reformation took a long time, and the implications were only slowly grasped. In 1533 the imperial ambassador Eustace Chapuys reported to Charles that none of Henry's great ships were serviceable and it would take eighteen months to restore them to full strength. This was meant to encourage the emperor to invade a much-reduced and powerless England – Chapuys was an ardent partisan of Catherine – but Charles was preoccupied with more important business: war at sea against Muslims and on land against the Turks.

Chapuys was in part correct. Henry's great ships had been laid up for a long time. But the king did have warships at his disposal. By 1536, Henry's *annus horribilis*, when he faced rebellion at home in the form of the Pilgrimage of Grace and the threat of invasion from abroad, eight of the largest ships, including *Mary Rose* and *Peter Pomegranate*, had been rebuilt and the *Great Harry* and the *Great Galley* had been 'new made'. (A ship that was rebuilt was reconstructed, enlarged and improved using its existing timbers; one that was 'new made' was started again from scratch.) In addition, new ships were added to the fleet.

The ambitious programme – a sure sign of war – was paid from Henry's second great fortune. From 1534 the Crown dissolved the monasteries, bringing in the money needed to maintain a proper navy.

In 1539 England faced the threat of invasion, this time from an alliance between Charles and François; but when it materialised the navy had never been stronger. The French ambassador reported that Henry's entire fleet numbered 150, including requisitioned merchantmen and ships hired from Venice, Ragusa and Florence.

It might not be the largest navy in Europe, but it had become the most technologically advanced, particularly in its weaponry. *Mary Rose*, along with the other great ships, was rebuilt with a main gun deck lined with gunports. According to Walter Raleigh the maindeck gunports on the *Mary Rose* were just eighteen inches above the waterline. This allowed her guns to fire at the hull of an enemy ship, where the greatest structural damage could be wrought.

The floating fortresses were the core of the navy. Around them clustered smaller warships of various shapes and sizes. There were galleys that carried guns below the oars and galleasses that carried them on platforms above the rowers. There were barges, carracks and caravels. There were also pinnaces – small, swift companion vessels to the ships, powered by oars and sails and carrying light guns. It was a heterodox navy, consciously experimental in its search for the ultimate sailing ship of war and deliberately varied so that it had a ship for every circumstance.

By this time an administrative structure had come into place. During Henry's early years as king an ad hoc system had built up around one man. William Gonson was one of those brilliant men who flourished in the early Tudor government machine. He amassed a fortune in the City as a man of business and a shipowner, but he had another foot planted at the heart of royal and political power – he was one of Henry's gentlemen ushers and he was a teller of the Exchequer. He used his experience in shipping to command naval squadrons made up of royal ships and hired merchantmen. The navy had always been directed by men who regarded trade and royal service as interchangeable. Gonson was the latest incarnation.

He owed his advancement to his usefulness to men in power, and his personal power rested on control of the purse strings rather than formal authority. Gonson held the unpromising-sounding post of Keeper of the Storehouses at Erith and Deptford. As so often in Henry's reign, men with humble job-descriptions found their way to the levers of power. Gonson was Thomas Wolsey's (and later Thomas Cromwell's) man in the navy, and in return for loyal service he received money directly from the Exchequer to hire, as he saw fit, contractors to supply, repair and victual the navy royal. It gave him power in the maritime community and access to reservoirs of cash.

Gonson ran the navy single-handed for twenty years. He led it at sea as an admiral and he maintained the fleet in dock. But in 1541 his son was executed as a traitor, and whether as a result of this, or of the strain of running a navy alone with England at war, in 1544 Gonson committed suicide. The whole system came crashing down.

It was a terrible blow for the king, and one that took two years to repair. William Gonson was replaced by the Council for Maritime Causes, known to history as the Navy Board. Three permanent posts already existed: Clerk of the Ships, Clerk Comptroller and Keeper of the Storehouse. To these were added four new posts: Lieutenant (or Vice Admiral), Treasurer, Surveyor and Rigger, and Master of Naval Ordnance. The members were known as the 'Principal Officers' of the navy.

It was the first step in the professionalisation of a system that had been centred on ministers and their appointees. The officials received a proper salary for their services. James Baker became the first shipwright to be employed directly by the navy. Three other shipwrights and an anchor-smith were on the payroll by 1548, along with clerks, purveyors, storemen, guards, shipkeepers, labourers and chaplains.

It did not mark the end of the ad hoc system that had governed the navy through the Middle Ages. The key task of victualling still went to others: Stephen Gardiner, bishop of Winchester, was saddled with it, and with the nickname Stephen Stockfish. When war came, in time-honoured fashion, the navy would be commanded by members of the nobility and merchant-masters and crewed by ordinary seamen conscripted from their fishing boats and merchant ships.

But for all the strength of Henry's navy in the 1540s it was not big or strong enough to match the king's ambitions. In 1544 he issued a proclamation to his seafaring subjects. In it he empowered them to attack his enemies with no legal restrictions. English piracy had reached a high point a century before, but it had been restrained for decades under strong Tudor government. Now it was unleashed once more.

The seafaring men of England jumped at this chance. William Hawkins gave up his burgeoning Atlantic trade to take part in the much more profitable business of privateering in home waters. Many more traders switched their operations to take part. It was a critical moment in the history of the sixteenth century.

For the seaborne war was not confined to England's enemies. Hawkins had scores to settle. Such men had traded with the Iberian powers quite happily for years. Henry's divorce and the Reformation changed everything. Englishmen who ventured abroad faced hostility from the Spanish. Men like Hawkins were not content any more to tolerate Spanish and Portuguese monopoly of extra-European trade. For, after all, their pretensions to carve up the world between them were based on nothing more than the authority of the pope, an authority not just rejected by the English but now regarded as heretical.

For ambitious traders the Iberians seemed impossibly arrogant in their dreams of world empire; the emperor Charles seemed bent on world domination, using the riches of the New World to subdue the Old and reimpose Catholicism. Now, in 1544 and 1545, Henry's desperate appeal to these seafarers offered a golden opportunity. They attacked Spanish ships with the same enthusiasm they attacked French and Scottish ships, on the grounds that the Spanish were, or might be, trading with the enemy.

This free-for-all proved a disaster for Henry. The Channel had become a key zone for Charles V. In the beginning of his reign he had been preoccupied with Italy; now, in the 1540s, the Netherlands commanded his attention. It was the most important part of Charles's empire, and the most troublesome. It had become the economic powerhouse of Europe, but it was slipping towards Protestantism, which the emperor had vowed to stamp out. Therefore the Channel and Narrow Seas were more vital than ever for Spain's economic well-being and Charles's imperial vision. This was put in jeopardy by marauding English sailors.

Charles turned his back on Henry in the middle of the war. He retaliated against piracy by arresting English shipping and goods in the Low Countries. That only egged on the traders-turned-pirates. One of the most prominent participants in the private war was Robert Reneger who, like Hawkins, had made a sizeable fortune trading with Iberia and Brazil. He had become caught up in the religious passions of the time and saw his livelihood under threat from Spanish bigotry and French piracy. In 1545 he pulled off a real coup and sparked a major diplomatic incident when he captured the *San Salvador*, a Spanish treasure ship returning from San Domingo. Suddenly the Spanish empire did not seem so mighty after all. In fact it was revealed as being highly vulnerable. Reneger's four ships easily overpowered the lightly armed and complacent Spaniards off Cape St Vincent.

Robert Reneger caused Henry real discomfort and brought him to the brink of war with Charles's empire at a time when he was engrossed in war with France. But Reneger had also brought great riches; he had twitted the great Catholic empire, augmented England's seafaring reputation. Ministers and courtiers egged him on and shared the profits. He was a hero to the great and the humble alike.

Many West Country seafarers and London traders vied to be the next Robert Reneger. Aristocrats, City merchants and members of the West Country gentry led or funded privateering in hope of a fast profit and everlasting glory. One of them, Thomas Wyndham, had learnt his military skills working for Cromwell in Ireland and serving Henry at sea against Scotland. He was one of many well-to-do respectable men who turned to piracy. Lord Admiral Lisle wrote: 'Every Spaniard, Portugalle or Fleming that comes from the south is robbed by our adventurers, some calling themselves Scots, some wearing visors'.[1]

The Crown was powerless to rein in what it had let slip. The City of Antwerp complained: 'Not a ship is allowed to pass without the English pillaging something from her.'[2] Some high-profile transgressors were punished. William Hawkins for example spent a short amount of time in prison as a token punishment to appease Spain. Thomas Wyndham was fined for taking a Spanish ship. But not Robert Reneger. Shortly after his return with *San Salvador* he was serving in Henry's fleet stationed off Southampton.

The Crown had need of experienced sea warriors like Reneger. In 1545 its warships and privateers had command of the Channel, but the French were not idle. A large invasion force was being assembled in the Seine. There were between 150 and 200 ships there, of which thirty were warships and twenty-five were Mediterranean galleys. The fleet carried a vast army of between 30,000 and 50,000 men. Their objective was to destroy Southampton and Portsmouth and as much of the English fleet as they could.

The main ports for Henry's navy were in the Thames Estuary, but a favourable wind for the French (the prevailing south-westerly) would bottle the English navy in the Thames, leaving the southern rump undefended.

In the spring, summer and autumn months Portsmouth and Southampton were crucial for the defence of England, as the only bases capable of keeping the navy in the Channel. If the French could destroy these two harbours, they could throw the English out of Boulogne and make the Channel safe for French merchantmen.

Against the massive French invasion force Lord Lisle, the English admiral, had eighty ships. On 19 July they were at anchor in Portsmouth harbour and the king himself had come down to admire his glorious navy primed for action. He was dining on the *Great Harry* when news reached him that the French were a short distance from Portsmouth. Henry ordered a man to climb up to get a better view. Sure enough the lookout espied numerous sail off the Isle of Wight. The king hurriedly departed his great flagship and joined a great throng for a grandstand view of the coming battle from the safety of the shore fortifications.

The French fleet took up position off St Helens on the east coast of the Isle of Wight in view of the entrance to Portsmouth Harbour. The galleys took advantage of a calm sea and windless day to row round into the Solent so that the English ships leaving the harbour into the narrow channel would be in range of their gigantic basilisk cannons.

Despite their haste, the English navy could not make headway. There was no wind. At last, in the late afternoon, a slight breeze got up which allowed the ships to leave harbour. The priority was to attack the galleys before they could damage the English ships and dart back to the main French fleet. Leading the attack was *Mary Rose*, whose formidable broadside could be brought to bear against the lurking galleys. As she came out and bore towards the French galleys she was seen to be heeling over in the wind. *Mary Rose* fired off a starboard broadside and then, as she was coming about to loosen off a volley from the other side, she was caught by a gust of wind that heeled her over again.

The gunports were still open on her starboard side and water gushed through them. *Mary Rose* sank with terrifying swiftness. Nets that had been spread over the deck to prevent the enemy boarding prevented the sailors from abandoning ship. Only thirty men survived from a complement of 415. In later recriminations the crew was blamed for drunkenness and insubordination. The French claimed a direct hit, but that was unlikely given the poor record of shipboard artillery in sinking ships. Most probably the refit of the *Mary Rose* and the desire to pack her with guns had destabilised her so that she was likely to cant dangerously in strong winds. The open gunports made it a fatal flaw. 'Oh my gentlemen! Oh my gallant my gallant men!,' the king exclaimed as he took in the disaster.

The breeze died down after that. The English used their knowledge of the tides to work the rest of the fleet out of harbour and the galleys scrambled to withdraw when they saw the English ships unexpectedly emerge. The French landed men on the Isle of Wight, but the situation resolved into stalemate. The French admiral Claude d'Annebault botched any attempt to press home the unexpected advantage given to him by the sinking of *Mary Rose*. After a few days the calm weather, lack of supplies and disease forced the French to concede that a landing was impossible and they abandoned the invasion.

D'Annebault was a reluctant commander; the pressure to complete the invasion by France came from François, who repeatedly ordered his admiral to engage the English. D'Annebault, sick with the gout and desperate to be on dry land, took his mighty fleet back to the Sussex coast. Lord Lisle reorganised his fleet, which had swollen to 104 with the addition of ships from the West Country. There were three ranks of ships. First came some large merchantmen hired from the Hanse. These would soak up the initial shock of battle. Then came the major warships and then, in the third wave, a mixture of warships and requisitioned merchantmen. The formation was flanked by the oared ships of war – galleys, galleasses and rowbarges.

The English navy set out and sighted the French off Shoreham. Then, as before, the wind died away. The opposing fleets were left in sight of each other but unable to do anything about it. At last the French galleys broke the calm by rowing into attack. Their volleys did little damage and the English galleasses did good work seeing them off. Night fell and the two fleets anchored close by each other.

When the sun rose the next morning the French were nowhere to be seen. Eventually lookouts on *Great Harry* spotted them to seaward, but the wind had fallen once more. When conditions improved it was discovered that d'Annebault had taken his fleet back to the Seine. François was furious; Lisle and the English commanders felt cheated of a good fight; and the French naval officers fell to bickering over their half-hearted campaign.

The navy did little more than shadow-box in Henry's wars. But the service had transformed in the sixteenth century. When Henry died in 1547 he left a navy of fifty-four ships administered by a group of seasoned commanders who in turn could call upon the services of officers who were experienced alike in private warfare and royal service. The navy now had permanent bases and storehouses, shipwrights and a domestic iron industry supplying its guns. The operational base was at Portsmouth, where ships could menace the French coast and sweep the Channel. Repairs were conducted in the Thames Estuary, out of striking distance by the French fleet. The navy royal was supported by coastal forts and a system of warning beacons. It was recognisably a modern navy.

It cost a fortune to maintain. The navy had a million pounds lavished on it during the 1540s. Henry's child heir Edward VI governed a country bankrupted by war against France and Scotland.

But a new generation of courtiers, naval officers, merchants, seafarers and members of the gentry were not prepared to turn their backs on the extraordinary opportunities for enrichment and glory on the high seas. Henry's ill-fated attempt to privatise war at sea had opened people's eyes to the staggering wealth that criss-crossed the oceans. The appetite for loot could not be restrained, although the navy was supposed to police it.

Edward VI's first Lord Admiral, his uncle Thomas Seymour, commanded a nest of pirates on the Scillies and undermined the navy's efforts to subdue lawlessness at sea. The new Master of the Ordnance, in charge of munitions, was none other than the pirate Thomas Wyndham. Explorers, pirates, courtiers and naval officers were an interchangeable bunch.

With recession in Antwerp from 1550, merchants were forced to seek out new markets further afield. Overseas exploration was given a fillip by the death of Henry VIII. John Cabot's son, the explorer Sebastian, was recalled after years away from his adopted homeland in 1547. He was an old man, his days of active exploring far behind him, but he represented a skein linking the ambitious men of Edwardian England with an earlier generation that sponsored and sailed with John Cabot. Sebastian was supported by the leading figures of the Council, including Lord Protector Somerset and the earl of Northumberland, who, as Lord Lisle, had commanded the English navy. He also attracted the attention of City merchants and seafarers who were desperate to widen their horizons.

Cabot brought with him the excitement of foreign adventures and also a wealth of knowledge of the world outside England's narrow compass. He was pressed for information by would-be adventurers. For the first time in decades there was a buzz about exploration in England. Attention focused in three directions: on the Levant, on Portuguese West Africa, and on a northern route to East Asia. First came the Levant: a good school for long-distance ventures to parts of the world where Englishmen were not really wanted. Thomas Wyndham, sometime pirate and vice admiral, opened up regular trade with North-West Africa. On his first voyage from Bristol in 1551 his ship the *Lion* left 'laden with merchandise, so and in like manner with munitions, as Morris pikes in great number, with hand guns, shirts of mail, with other great artillery meet for the war'. Englishmen, late to discovery, had need of arms. Wyndham had honed his skills preying on foreign shipping in home waters; now he was preying on other countries' colonies far away. He led two successful voyages to the Barbary Coast and Guinea in defiance of the Portuguese, but he died on his third in the Bight of Benin. Most of his crew shared his fate; even so the venture returned a handsome profit.

On 10 May 1553 an English expedition left Radcliffe on the Thames rowed by mariners in sky-blue uniforms. Thousands of Londoners cheered as the ships passed. At Greenwich the squadron fired a salute to Edward VI, who was watching from his sickbed. This was a voyage of exploration much discussed in Europe. It was funded by courtiers and City magnates. If the English managed to exploit a new route to the East the world order carved out by the Iberian powers, with the blessing of the pope, would be upset. The imperial ambassador wrote to Charles V that the English were searching out the north-east passage to the Far East: 'they believe the route to be a short one, and very convenient for the kingdom of England, for distributing kerseys [woollen cloth] in these countries, bringing back spices and other merchandise in exchange'.

A different fate awaited. The route to China was not found; the explorers froze to death. But the voyage reawakened the desire to join the age of discovery. England, it seemed, was on the road to naval greatness.

But just when it seemed as if English explorers and merchant adventurers might compete with the established oceanic powers, the energy was bottled up again. Edward died at the age of fifteen in 1553. His sister Mary was determined to return England to the Catholic Church. She married Philip, son and heir of Charles V, already king of Naples and soon to inherit much of the sprawling Habsburg empire. To the horror of many in England, Philip became king-consort. During Mary's reign the prohibition against intruding on or competing with the Iberian empires was enforced.

The ban was an affront to Protestant adventurers. The papal bull that had divided the Atlantic between Spain and Portugal had, in the age of Reformation, become a touchstone for conflict. The right of Spain to dominate the Atlantic had been called into question. The Spanish saw it as a divine right; to a new generation of Englishmen – greedy for trade and zealously Protestant – it was a heretical presumption that had to be challenged.

And the English had the means to do so. Most armies, navies and privately owned ships used cannon cast in bronze, which made them extremely expensive and put them out of reach of most private individuals. Yet in England there was a thriving iron industry that was producing in abundance guns that cost a fifth of the price of European cannon. They were inferior to bronze armaments, but their extraordinarily low cost meant that even bit-part shippers could afford to turn their mean ships into fearsome instruments of piracy. The combination of cheap weaponry and aggressive English seafarers was a dangerous prospect for the world's shipping lanes. English sea rovers were never shy about taking on richly laden ships; now that they packed heat their relatively small ships were more than a match for larger foreign vessels and colonial settlements that were prohibited by cost and scarcity from matching the belligerent English gun for gun. A new chapter was about to be opened in maritime history – and it was made possible by the forges and furnaces in the foundries of the Kentish Weald.

The Atlantic was now a place of lawlessness and war – a lawlessness nurtured for centuries in the waters round the British Isles and now exported by seafarers who had never recognised the concept of private property at sea and who now had the chance to extend their depredations far into the Atlantic with their improved ships and cheap guns. And there, deep in the ocean, English sailors would learn a new way to wage war.

CHAPTER 10

ENGLISH GUNS
1556–1568

This gold that comes from the Indies does fall on Spain as rain
does on a roof – it pours on her and it flows off.[1]

Venetian ambassador

John Hawkins was a violent young man – he needed to be in his line of
work. But much more than preceding generations of sea rovers he was a
gentleman and politician, something of a dandy and a charmer.

He came from a notorious seafaring dynasty. His father was William
Hawkins, the first Englishman to venture to Brazil. The son took after the
father: at the age of twenty-one he became a murderer. He walked free
because William, a man of wealth and political power in Plymouth and
Westminster, where he sat as an MP, was able to secure a royal pardon.
John followed his father into local politics and into the rough and tumble
of Atlantic trade. In the late 1550s he was trading to the Canaries where,
through hours of conversation and listening to Spanish seamen, he
gained a good understanding of the Caribbean, its amazing wealth and its
weaknesses. No English ship had been there since 1527.

In 1559 John Hawkins moved to London, where he married into the
naval aristocracy, wedding the daughter of Benjamin Gonson, treasurer of
the navy and son of the famous William Gonson. By 1562 he had drawn
together a syndicate – which included Gonson, the Surveyor of the navy
Sir William Winter and wealthy City merchants – to fund a foray into the
Spanish empire.

He led three small ships to the coast of Guinea and then to Sierra Leone.
Here he took by force, it was later claimed, six Portuguese ships and their
cargoes, which included luxury goods and 900 slaves worth in excess of
32,000 ducats. The strange thing was that no one was killed in these raids.
Hawkins claimed, probably truthfully, that he had purchased the ships
and their contents. He further claimed that he had taken only 300 slaves
and returned five of the ships. The Portuguese in Africa no doubt traded

Sir John Hawkins

willingly with Hawkins, but if they did they had broken the law. Later they claimed to be victims in order to avoid punishment.

Hawkins, his three ships and a large Portuguese ship crossed the Atlantic to Hispaniola. In his long conversations with Spanish traders he had learnt that there was a high demand for slave labour in the Caribbean, a demand that the Spanish could not meet. Accordingly John Hawkins arrived with, he said, 300 slaves – or 400 if you believe the Spanish and 900 if the Portuguese were correct – and began to sell them in Hispaniola. He was welcomed by Spanish colonists who had been badly neglected. They paid him in gold, ginger, hides, sugar and pearls. To show his good faith, Hawkins paid local customs and sent part of his cargo to Seville and another load to Lisbon, where they would certify their goods with local customs officials.

His aim was to act like a regular merchant – albeit one who had broken into the trade. But the ships were seized and their cargoes treated as contraband. Hawkins was accused of piracy by both Spain and Portugal. Luckily for his investors, Hawkins had sent most of his cargo directly to England and, despite losing £20,000 in Seville and Lisbon, the venture made a handsome profit.

The voyage was an experiment. Hawkins had believed his actions would be tolerated, or else he would not have sent two valuable ships to Iberia. After all, he was *helping* the Portuguese and Spanish in their horrendous trade, shoring up the deficiencies in both empires. Not only that, he managed to sell slaves at cheaper prices despite setting out from England.

But Philip of Spain was not prepared to let foreigners trespass upon the hallowed Spanish empire, the gift of God, least of all heretical foreigners. In the resulting furore Elizabeth took the side of Hawkins. He had, she believed, every right to trade as he saw fit.

Elizabeth's accession at the end of 1558 signalled a new and assertive England. Within a few months of coming to the throne she had contributed two royal ships, the *Minion* and the *Christopher*, to a squadron that went to Guinea and Benin. This was done with the approval of the Lord Admiral and in the face of furious protests from the Portuguese, who claimed all of West Africa as their own. Elizabeth simply refused to acknowledge that Portugal – or any other country for that matter – had the right to circumscribe England.

The feeling was that England had subordinated her interests to other more powerful nations. She had, for decades, put up with unequal alliances with the giants of Europe. While other powers traded around the world, England was as dependent as ever upon exporting her wool and cloth to the Netherlands. With the accession of Elizabeth came a fierce bid for independence on the European and world stages. England would break into the trades denied her by the titans of Europe.

Generations of English seafarers had plundered the waters around the British Isles. In the 1560s the violence had spread. It was not so much that the English saw themselves as breaking the law. They had come to regard the Atlantic as literally lawless – beyond the sovereignty of any monarch.

John Hawkins personified the new spirit. He did not believe that anyone had the right to stop him engaging in peaceful trade. When he set sail again in 1564 on another slave-trading expedition he did so with the financial backing of his cronies in the Navy Board, the City, leading courtiers, the Lord Admiral and the queen herself. Elizabeth contributed the ageing warship, the *Jesus of Lübeck*, which had been purchased from the Hanse by Henry VIII in 1544. Not only that, but Hawkins was honoured with a private interview and given the authority to raise the royal standard and the cross of St George. The Spanish ambassador's protests were brushed aside.

Hawkins left with a crew of just 150. He returned with 130, a quite extraordinary success. A light crew helped prevent disease. Hawkins was no doubt a brilliant sailor. What marked him out from his contemporaries was his meticulous gathering of intelligence and his skills as a negotiator in all kinds of different settings around the world. Above all he was a first-class leader of men, made evident by his concern for the welfare of his crew. His instructions for the second voyage remain famous: 'Serve God daily, love one another, preserve your victuals, beware of fire and keep good company.'[2]

Most importantly his second triangular voyage to West Africa and then the West Indies netted a spectacular profit for his queen and her courtiers, his investors.

Philip recognised the danger to his empire from brilliant interlopers like Hawkins. A report from the New World pointed out: 'The colonists' needs are great and neither penalties nor punishments suffice to prevent them from buying secretly what they want'.[3] The emperor had little sympathy; larger things were at stake. Officials who had traded with the English were punished. Philip's ambassador in England, Don Guzman de Silva, invited Hawkins to dinner to sound him out. Hawkins, as he always was in the company of Spaniards, was solicitous for the health and welfare of Philip. He assured de Silva he would never return to the Caribbean without the emperor's permission. He even offered to lead a group of English privateers to help Philip fight the Turks in the Mediterranean. Don't believe a word of it, wrote de Silva to Philip; it was best to keep Hawkins and his band of English rovers away from the Spanish empire 'so that he may not teach others, for they have good ships and are greedy folk with more liberty than is good for them'.[4]

Why was the queen antagonising the mighty Philip? Hawkins was not by nature a secretive man and his voyages were hardly clandestine. And Elizabeth made no secret of her desire to make inroads into the Spanish New World. On the other hand the last thing she wanted was war with the Habsburg Empire. In fact, throughout her reign thus far she had been in alliance with Philip against France. England was also as economically dependent as ever upon the northern portion of Philip's empire, the Netherlands. Philip for his part regarded belligerent England as a nuisance. It nurtured pirates and heretics. But he needed English friendship to allow his ships to travel between Spain and the Netherlands. He had good reason to fear an Anglo-French alliance.

Throughout the 1560s the Anglo-Spanish relationship deteriorated. France was embroiled in civil war, which removed the threat that glued Tudor and Habsburg. Most importantly, the Netherlands was engulfed in Calvinistic fury against the Catholic Church, a heresy Philip was determined to stamp out. In August 1566 the duke of Alba invaded the

Netherlands. It was a disaster for the English wool and cloth trades. But worse than that, if Alba was successful it would be the first major victory against Protestantism. England would be next in the firing line. The heir to the throne, Mary Stuart, was Catholic and, with the exception of the rebellious Netherlands, so were all her neighbours. Elizabeth could not intervene with much force in the Old World. The New World was something different. It was a weak spot in Philip's armour which Elizabeth was beginning to probe. And men like Hawkins – brilliant nuisances – were a resource that belied England's military weakness.

John Hawkins reflected this equivocal relationship with Philip. He was deliberately ambiguous in all his ventures. Was he a friend of Spain or its worst enemy? Was he a trader or a pirate? Did he represent England or just himself? Nor was it entirely clear, either, whether he was in the Caribbean to make money or to scope out its weaknesses. But a squadron flying the royal colours and led by the queen's ships looked suspiciously like an official naval expedition. This was even more apparent in 1567, when the *Jesus of Lübeck* was joined by another royal warship, the *Minion*.

In August the ships were being prepared in Plymouth Sound. As well as the two royal ships, Hawkins had four others, including a bark called the *Judith* which was commanded by a young man called Francis Drake. All was going smoothly when an imperial fleet entered the harbour claiming refuge, they said, from bad weather. They did not dip their flags and lower their topsails in salute – a hostile act in itself – and made for Hawkins's ships. They might have been hoping they were not armed, but Hawkins was prepared. He ordered the guns to open fire, and they continued to fire at the imperial ships until they saluted and changed course.

The voyage did not get off to a good start. The *Jesus* was a ship from another generation. It was a high-charged carrack built for short-range summer cruises in home waters. Large ships like this pitched and rolled to an alarming degree in bad weather, causing their planks to strain and 'spew out' their caulking. The *Jesus* met a fierce storm off Finisterre. Hawkins called upon his men to pray. The master did not think the old ship would survive. She did pull through, even though her crew had to plug leaks with their own cloth.

Trading in the Spanish Indies was hard work this time. Governors of towns were under orders to resist alien incursions; Hawkins and Drake had to coerce the Spanish colonists to trade with them. Only at Cartagena were the Spanish powerful enough to resist them. By the time Hawkins amassed enough gold and cargo he had tarried too long. The hurricane season was approaching and the *Jesus* was in poor shape. The planks at the stern opened and shut with the waves and 'the living fish did swim upon the ballast as in the sea'. The bad weather started off the western end of Cuba. The *Jesus* was unable to sail into the strengthening winds. She was forced to turn about and sail with the wind. The other ships kept company with her as she hurtled on, powerless against the force of a hurricane.

The terrifying winds abated at last, but Hawkins and his men faced disaster. They were running low on provisions. They did not know where they were or where they could stop to repair and find supplies. A Spanish ship pointed them in the direction of San Juan d'Ulúa, a safe haven, but warned Hawkins that it was where the *flota* – the Spanish treasure fleet – loaded gold and silver bound for Spain. It was expected at any moment. Hawkins took a gamble and approached San Juan. He took down the flags of St George, but kept up the royal standard, which looked like the Spanish flag. His men stood ready at their guns. As he neared he saw twelve ships and guns of the shore battery trained on the *Jesus*. They opened fire.

It was a salute for Martin Enríquez de Almanza, the new viceroy of Mexico, who was a passenger on the *flota*. The Spanish garrison, in their remote corner of the empire, had never encountered alien intruders. They assumed the ships were the *flota*. When they realised it was 'Juan Aquínes', the scourge of their empire, they panicked. 'The Lutherans are here!' someone cried out. The Spanish soldiers abandoned the island in haste, leaving their commander alone to face the heretical pirates.

Hawkins told the commander that these were the ships of the queen of England in need of victuals. He promised to pay for repairs and supplies and assured the Spanish officials that this was not an act of war. His plan was to get under way again before the *flota* arrived.

But when the sun rose next morning the *flota* was in sight. Hawkins was in a position of apparent strength. He had control of the shore battery. However he knew he could only go so far. Denying the Spanish entry to their own port would be a virtual declaration of war. It would have far exceeded his orders from Elizabeth and, as her officer, Hawkins had a higher responsibility. He decided to negotiate: the Spanish could enter the harbour on condition they allowed Hawkins to complete his repairs.

The viceroy was incandescent. To his mind Hawkins was a pirate – nothing more, nothing less. He had heard of the Englishman's most recent violations of the sacred empire. Now here he was, in the most vital of all Spanish New World ports, dictating terms as if he were the equal of an imperial viceroy. Enríquez sent word to Hawkins that he was the viceroy of the king of Spain and he could enter the harbour when he wanted; what was more, he added, he had a thousand men.

Hawkins laughed. He was, he said, also a viceroy, and thousand men or no, he had enough powder and shot to look after himself. While he was saying this, the messenger saw that the *Jesus* was being cleared for action and sawdust was being scattered on deck. He noted with surprise, and disdain, that Hawkins was helping out with the dirty work.

Enríquez had to sign a truce. The Spanish fleet was allowed to enter and Hawkins could finish his repairs in peace. However, while this was being worked out, the viceroy had secretly packed his ships with armed men from nearby Veracruz.

After two days of bad weather the *flota* entered harbour. San Juan was a small shingle island, just 450 yards long and 200 wide. There were a few buildings for the garrison and not much else, but the inlet between it and the mainland was the safest place for large ships on the coast. It was a complex business squeezing all the ships into the harbour, and when it was complete it looked as though a wooden bridge had appeared. You could walk the length of the harbour from ship's deck to ship's deck. Separating the Spanish *flota* from the English ships was a large disused hulk. Then came the English in a row: the *Minion* next to the hulk, the *Jesus* next to her, the *Grace of God*, then Drake's *Judith*, next to him the *Angel* and lastly the *Swallow*.

Sailors from both sides fraternised on the beach; some indulged in private trade. Everyone was watchful and suspicious, not least Hawkins. At night he heard strange sounds coming from the hulk. It was, as he suspected, being filled with men and arms ready for an attack on his ships. The next morning he asked the Spanish viceroy what was happening. He was fobbed off. Hawkins sent his second in command, a brilliant sailor called Robert Barrett, who was fluent in Spanish and Portuguese, to ask the viceroy bluntly one last time if there were soldiers on board the hulk. Then he settled down for dinner (a mid-morning repast for Elizabethan officers) knowing that the inevitable battle was not far off.

As the officers were sitting down to eat one of the Spanish hostages was caught with a knife up his sleeve, apparently intended for Hawkins. Hawkins was not prepared to play along any more. He stomped up on deck, crossbow in hand. There he saw the Spanish preparing to attack from the hulk. He shouted at the Spanish vice admiral that these were not the actions of a gentleman; the man replied that it was his duty as a fighting man. Hawkins shouted back that he was right, and then fired a bolt at him.

The Spanish were ready for action. They rounded on Hawkins's men on the beach and overwhelmed the shore battery. The soldiers on the hulk poured on to the *Minion*. Hawkins was watching from the forecastle of the *Jesus*, which towered alongside the other royal warship. He called out to his men to protect the consort ship. There was a melee on board the *Minion* as sailors from both sides clashed. The battle spread to the decks on the *Jesus*.

This was battle on Spanish terms. They had superiority of numbers, and a boarding action in a home port was exactly to their taste. But Hawkins had expected this all along. The English were ready to go. The cables were cut and the ships began to warp out of harbour.

It was a slow business warping out. A boat carried out a ship's anchor, which was thrown into the water. Sailors on the ship then heaved the ship towards the submerged anchor. Then the men on the boat must raise the anchor, row out, and repeat the procedure until tide and wind could carry the ship out of harbour. It was hard enough at the best of times; now Hawkins's men were doing it in the middle of a battle.

Laborious work it may have been, but it tipped the balance of the fight. The English guns were now in play. The *Judith* got out first. The *Minion* made slower progress. But as it made its tortuously slow movement out in the harbour the hulk moved into the vacated berth and the *Minion*'s guns had the Spanish vice admiral's ship, the *Almirante*, in their sights. They opened fire. Then the *Jesus* had a clear sighting, and its mighty cannonade roared, pounding the *Almirante* with its large culverins. One of the shots got lucky, igniting the Spanish ship's magazine. A huge explosion tore the ship apart.

What was left of the *Almirante* drifted into the harbour and began to capsize. Now the English could train their guns on the next ship in the line, the viceroy's ship, *Capitana*, which was almost empty, as its soldiers and sailors were fighting on the *Jesus*. Again the English guns had a devastating effect, firing point-blank at the Spanish flagship. Cannonballs ripped into its hull. The haughty viceroy himself, who must have thought at dawn that he had the English in an inescapable trap, had to hide behind the mainmast as his ship was bombarded and his crew were decimated by shot and flying splinters. In a short while *Capitana* began to sink.

It was clear to Hawkins that the *Jesus* was not going to make it. The queen's ship was a wreck in any case; now it was being pummelled by the shore battery. Job Hortop, a young lad on the expedition, later remembered Hawkins cheering on his soldiers and gunners before calling to his page for a cup of beer. The silver tankard was brought up to Hawkins, who drank it down and 'willed the gunners to stand by their ordnance lustily like men'.[5] He put down his empty tankard, and as soon as he did so a Spanish cannonball blew it away. 'Fear nothing,' Hawkins shouted, 'for God, who hath preserved me from this shot, will also deliver us from these traitors and villains.'[6]

The *Jesus* was only partially out, and Hawkins used it as a screen to protect the *Minion* as the bulk of the treasure was loaded onto that ship and the *Judith*. The mighty old carrack, which had served four Tudor monarchs, was being blasted to pieces. Down came the foremast. Then the mainmast. But still the English guns fired and still the men carried hides, spices, sugar, gold and silver to the smaller ships. The narrow harbour was crowded with capsized and burning ships, small boats and men swimming for shore or floundering in their armour. At last the Spanish sent in fireships and, in great fear, the sailors on the *Minion* and the *Judith* raised sail. Hawkins, at the last possible moment, jumped free of the *Jesus* onto the *Minion*.

Of Hawkins's squadron of six, only *Minion* and *Judith* survived the battle at San Juan. It was a terrible day for the English. But the Spanish had fared little better. Thanks to English guns and the abilities of Hawkins's sailors, they could not prevent their great tormentor leaving with the bulk of the treasure. What was more, the *flota* had been immobilised. What had started as a snare for the English had trapped the Spanish. They could only watch as the *Minion* and the *Judith* dropped anchor and remained in front of their noses off shore, waiting for a gale to die down.

It was a terrible humiliation. It augured an age when foreign ships would ply the Caribbean without fear of the Spanish navy.

But far worse than fears for the future was the actual situation facing Hawkins. In the night Drake had set sail and disappeared for home. *Minion* was laden with treasure but hardly any food. It was in no position to take on the Spanish again and loot victuals. It was a death ship facing a difficult passage home with bad leaks and no supplies. Francis Drake had clearly decided that he only stood a chance of survival alone and had deserted his commander and fellows. Hawkins was furious. He had little choice but to give his men permission to desert. Over a hundred men out of two hundred chose the hostile shore of northern Mexico rather than the doomed voyage home. As they made their way through the jungle they were attacked by natives. The survivors handed themselves over to the Spanish authorities at Tampico. Some were sent to Spain, but the rest were left to their own devices and some prospered.

But then came the Inquisition. The boys were sent to do menial work in monasteries. Some of the men were strangled and burnt; others were lashed and sentenced to work as galley slaves. The few survivors left on San Juan were sent to Spain. Robert Barrett had been captured in his capacity as Hawkins's messenger. He was tortured and burnt alive for, it was alleged, mistranslating Jesuit preachers to his fellow prisoners, ridiculing their religion. His fellow prisoners were also burnt or sent to the galleys. Job Hortop made it back to England after twenty-two years as a Spanish prisoner. He was one of only a few survivors to make it out of a Spanish prison.

The *Minion* took three months to reach England. During that time the men were reduced to eating rats, parrots, oxhides and leather gloves. The crew were starving and suffering from scurvy. They put into Vigo in Spain and purchased food. Eating excessively after starvation is very dangerous, and forty-five men died from their apparent deliverance. Several Spanish thought to take advantage and capture Hawkins. He put on his velvet jacket and silk cloak over his weakened body to confront them. Even at his lowest point he was able to put on sufficient show to scare them off. *Minion* limped back to England with, it was said, just fifteen men of the two hundred or so who had departed San Juan. He wrote to the Queen: 'All is lost, save only honour.'

San Juan d'Ulúa was never forgotten. The story of betrayal reverberated among the English seafaring community for decades. Suddenly the Spanish empire did not seem impregnable. The queen's own ships had fought in foreign waters. The men and the guns, if not the ships, had acquitted themselves well. The incident at San Juan d'Ulúa pointed to a future where English ships penetrated the wealth of the Americas.

English seafarers also had a reason for arming ships and going in search of fabulous wealth. The maritime community burned with anger for what had happened at San Juan and for the terrible fate that befell the prisoners. It set many on a course of enrichment and revenge against the Spanish. And most eager to settle scores was Francis Drake. Hawkins's third slaving voyage marked a turning point for the navy and, most important, for seafaring England. Private wars between English and Spanish sailors spread around the globe.

CHAPTER 11

REVOLUTION
1568–1585

When he was sixteen Philip II was given Spain to rule. That was back in 1543. He inherited the kingdom of Naples in 1554, the year in which he became king of England by virtue of his marriage to Mary Tudor. The dukedom of Burgundy became his in 1555 and the kingdom of Spain in 1556. He also ruled New Spain (Mexico), the West Indies, Peru, Chile and the Philippines. From the New World came the money needed to defend the vast European empire. But the jewel in his crown, the richest, most productive territory in Europe, was the Netherlands.

In 1568 all was not well. The threat did not come from the Indies; the incident at San Juan d'Ulúa was deeply irritating, but in the scheme of things it was inconsequential. While Hawkins was violating his empire in the New World a bigger crisis blew up in the English Channel. Some of Philip's ships were chased by French Huguenot privateers into Plymouth. They were met by William Hawkins, John's elder brother. William Hawkins persuaded the Spanish officials to move their cargo into the shore defences for safe keeping. The Spanish agreed; their cargo was an immense amount of silver coin.

Once the money was safely under English protection the Queen cast her beady eyes on it. The silver was on loan to Philip from Genoese bankers. Its destination was the imperial army in the Netherlands, to pay the troops who were putting down a serious rebellion. Elizabeth decided she would like to borrow the money herself.

Philip was enraged. The Spanish Netherlands were vital for the economic well-being of his entire empire. And worse than that, the Dutch rebels were motivated by Calvinism. Philip believed he was on a mission from God to protect the true Catholic religion. The political and religious rebellion had to be stamped out at all costs. Unfortunately the sea route between Spain and the Netherlands was blocked by a pugnacious, rowdy, anarchic, *Protestant* island.

It had once been a virtual irrelevance, languishing on the margins of

Europe. A succession of kings and queens – from Henry VII to Elizabeth – had feared the might of the Spanish empire and preferred to mollify rather than antagonise the Habsburgs. But now England was making itself a nuisance at sea. Behind his woes Philip saw the hand of Elizabeth. She was goading on the Dutch Calvinists and she was aiding Protestant rebels – the Huguenots – against the French king as well. It looked to Philip like a Protestant conspiracy, at whose centre sat Elizabeth. The last straw, for him, was the seizure of his silver. Now his offensive in the Netherlands would grind to a halt. He retaliated by seizing English property in Spain.

The Dutch Calvinists, the French Huguenots and Elizabethan England had one thing in common: the only way they could harm Philip's mighty global empire was at sea. The brilliant admiral Gaspard de Coligny led French Huguenot expeditions to colonise parts of the New World in defiance of the ban. The centre of his maritime power was La Rochelle. The Breton port was also the base for the Dutch Sea Beggars, a confederation of privateers from the Netherlands, which plundered Spanish shipping between Iberia and the Netherlands. English seafarers joined their Protestant colleagues in an undeclared war at sea in 1568 in retaliation at Philip's confiscation of English goods.

John Hawkins got in on the act when he led a naval expedition to Brittany. Like all his previous operations it looked like a trading voyage. In reality he was bringing food, weapons and money to the Hugenot base at La Rochelle. He brought back wine, salt and bronze bells looted from Catholic churches. The great bells would be melted down and turned into guns, to be used against Catholic ships.

Rich Spanish merchantmen were attacked by Protestant pirates in the narrow waters of the Channel. The southern coast of England had become a rookery of pirates and their loot was unloaded and sold in the safety of English ports. The resumption of anarchy in English waters meant that some enterprising men got very rich, but it served a strategic purpose as well. The wealth of the Indies used by Philip to pay armies in Europe was enriching his enemies.

Most of the depredations were carried out by men operating out of small vessels close to shore. A few privateers went as far as the Canaries or the Azores in search of Spanish cargoes. Francis Drake went further still.

He struck at the weakest link in the imperial system that connected the silver mines of Peru with the battlefields of Europe: the Isthmus of Panama. There lightly guarded mule trains carried staggering wealth from Peru to the waiting treasure ships. Drake launched a series of spectacularly lucrative raids on ships and settlements around the Isthmus of Panama.

He brought home several staggering fortunes. He grew rich. And very, very famous.

For the Dutch Sea Beggars and the French Huguenots, war against Philip at sea was a matter of survival. Things were not as desperate for the English. Queen Elizabeth was an astute strategist. She knew she could never defeat Philip. She did not even want to be an imperial rival in the New World. What she wanted was stability in the Netherlands: Spanish lordship over autonomous cities and provinces, not domination. For if Philip was pushed out of the Netherlands the French could step in, and that would be disastrous for England. But if Philip grew too strong in the Netherlands he could use the provinces as a base for invading England. The heir to the throne of England was Mary, Queen of Scots, a Catholic. There was evidence that the king of Spain was plotting to assassinate Elizabeth and place Mary on the throne. Protestant England feared the swelling power of Philip, even if it was not on the front line. As Lord Burghley maintained, England's first line of defence was the Dutch rebels: 'The nearer their end, the nearer is the peril come to England.'[1]

Unleashing adventurers of the high seas such as Hawkins and Drake to prey on the outposts of the Spanish empire was risky but worth it. Any precious metal or cargo of spices seized at sea chipped away at Philip's European war machine, in particular the oceans of cash he lavished on suppressing the Dutch. Hawkins had revealed the weakness of the Spanish at sea. It was Philip's weak spot and Elizabeth's more bellicose ministers enjoyed probing it.

Soldiers of fortune like Hawkins and Drake were ideal weapons. For a start they were flexible. If they brought home treasure it filled Elizabeth's coffers and diminished the imperial war chest. If they failed or provoked hostility they could be written off as common criminals who acted without any kind of authority. And their hostility could be turned on and off like a tap, depending on England's relationship with Spain. In 1572 Elizabeth needed Spain as a counterweight to France, so the Sea Beggars were denied entry to English ports and sea captains such as Hawkins were converted from poachers to gamekeepers and sent to suppress piracy.

By 1577 Spain was a threat in the Netherlands again. Elizabeth had to respond without overt force. In that year John Hawkins was made Treasurer of the Navy and Francis Drake took command of a squadron bound for some mysterious destination.

Hawkins inherited the position of Treasurer of the Navy Board from his father-in-law, Benjamin Gonson. The Gonson family had dominated the running of the Navy since the second decade of the century; Hawkins was carrying on the family business. Other members of the Board were as long-serving and nepotistic. William Winter had served as the Board's Surveyor of the Ships since 1549 and Master of the Ordnance since 1557. His brother George was Clerk of the Queen's Ships from 1560 to 1582. The Board's Comptroller, William Holstocke, had begun his career in ships owned by William Gonson which traded with the Levant. All these men had combined shore-based administration with active service in royal warships.

They were also active participants in the unofficial wars in the Atlantic and privateering in the Channel. All of them owned and invested in privateering ships. Gonson and the Winters had sponsored Hawkins's earliest voyages. They were also zealous Protestants and fanatically anti-Spanish. William Winter had supported Lady Jane Grey in her attempt to seize the throne from Mary Tudor in 1554 and he had been involved in Thomas Wyatt's rebellion in the same year. The Board's weekly meetings were presided over by the Lord Admiral, Lord Clinton. Like the members of the Board, he was an old lag: he had first been made Lord Admiral in 1550. Like his subordinates he sponsored private warships and he had seized the Tower in support of Jane Grey.

John Hawkins was in good company with these aggressive men. There was very little to distinguish the aims and methods of England's lawless seafaring community and the Queen's Navy. All the same, the Navy Board had become one of the most important and professional institutions in Elizabethan England. It had its permanent members, but it also employed or retained the services of numerous other people. Most important were the master shipwrights, who managed business in the dockyards. There were mariners employed to keep the ships when they were laid up. There were messengers, shipwrights, carpenters, wheelwrights, smiths and, at Deptford, there was the Keeper of the Plug, employed to maintain the plug in the dry dock. The supplies and victuals that lubricated the working of the naval machine were put in better order, with a paid official in charge of stockpiling and allocating essential naval stores, food and beer. Separate from the Navy Board, but inextricably tied to it, was the Ordnance Board, an older but just as sophisticated institution charged with making, purchasing and maintaining guns and materiel. It provided the ships and coastal fortresses with guns and ammunition.

At the time of Henry VIII's death in 1547 there were fifty ships in the Navy. Not many of them survived when Elizabeth came to the throne in 1558. William Winter produced a report – the first of its kind – which aimed to lay out a strategic plan for the Navy. It should have a permanent force of twenty-four ships between 200 and 800 tons, the majority comprising galleons of the middling sort of up to 600 tons. This small force would be the core of a bigger navy when it came to war. Winter identified forty-five privately owned ships that could be used as warships.

There was, in the late 1550s and early 1560s, a surge of energy and enthusiasm for the Navy evinced by those who had to pay for it: parliament and the Treasury. The rasp of saws and clatter of nails was nigh constant at Deptford, Woolwich, Portsmouth and Gillingham. It was an unprecedented programme of shipbuilding. And not only that, it was an unprecedented state enterprise. In 1559 there were 520 shipwrights and 100 labourers at work in the dockyards, a huge workforce for the time. Old ships dropped out and new ones were added, maintaining the agreed optimal level of around twenty-four warships. By 1564 fourteen ships had been built for the young queen. High-charged great ships such as *Great Harry* and *Peter Pomegranate* were no longer on the lists. The Navy Board still favoured large ships to protect the shores of England, but they were smaller and sleeker than the enormous Henrician warships. Typical of the new ships were the *Elizabeth Jonas* (680 tons), *Triumph* (740), and the converted merchantmen *Victory* (800) and *Elizabeth Bonaventure* (600).

Continuity and experience counted for a lot in the Elizabethan Navy. The members of the Board were fully attuned to the needs of modern naval warfare because of their participation in privateering. In the 1560s and 1570s the Navy was charged with developing a new kind of warship, one that was powerful but cost-effective for a small, cash-strapped country. Gonson and William Winter had reformed naval gunnery, arming the queen's ships with culverins – guns with better accuracy over a longer range than their predecessors.

But key to the evolution of the Navy were the master shipwrights Peter Pett, Matthew Baker and Richard Chapman. Pett had worked in royal dockyards since he was a boy in 1523. He had trained Baker, who had served since the later days of Henry VIII. He had also trained Chapman. The royal shipwrights, like the members of the Navy Board, had a collective memory and wealth of experience that extended far back into the sixteenth century. They had worked on great ships and galleasses, galleys and rowbarges. In 1570 they had built the *Foresight* as a new type of galleon. In 1573 the brand-new *Dreadnought* showed what a modern warship should be. It displaced 700 tons and carried guns weighing a total of thirty-one tons. That meant that 4.43 per cent of the ship's displacement came from its artillery. This was a significant improvement. There was no other ship that carried so many heavy guns in relation to its size. The

The *Golden Lion*: an example of an English galleon.

mighty *Revenge* launched in 1577 was only 400 tons, but carried a deadly array of forty-two heavy guns.

The new ships were known as 'race-built galleons'. They are among the most important ships ever built by the Navy. The word 'race' gives the impression of speedy ships. That was certainly true of them, but in fact the word comes from 'raze' – the new breed of warship had its upperworks razed, or reduced, especially at the bow, and had a much lower freeboard at the waist. Its profile above the waterline was like a tilted crescent moon or a melon slice, with the stern upperworks sloping downwards to the waist, and the bow, with its distinctive beak, appearing to plunge into the water. It had fine underwater lines, modelled on the Mediterranean galley. It was wider amidships, and tapered upwards towards the stern, where the ship was much narrower and the aftercastle rose higher into the air on a sharp curve.

Compared with other European ships, the English galleon had a greater length-to-beam ratio, sometimes exceeding 3:1. It was a longer and thinner ship. It had greater stability and mounted more and heavier guns along the broadside. Its bow was modelled on the beak of the Mediterranean galley and its stern and sail-plan conformed to the northern sailing-ship type. This meant that it solved the conundrum that had baffled shipwrights for generations. The galley was such a dangerous ship because it could fire ahead from heavy guns mounted in its bows. Sailing ships could not fire directly forward, making them vulnerable to galleys and unsatisfactory as an offensive weapon. The wave-cutting beaked bow of the galleon was a breakthrough in warship design: it combined the forward-firing capabilities of the galley with the manoeuvrability and heavy broadside of the sailing ship. It was designed to fight at a distance, using speed and firepower to outpace and outgun opponents.

The race-built galleon was favoured by privateers, for all those reasons. Private individuals began to build galleons on the model of the Navy's new ships. An outstanding example was Walter Raleigh's *Ark Raleigh*. She was a fast, agile galleon designed to further Raleigh's ambitions to found colonies in Virginia and best the Spanish. The Navy had a number of state-of-the-art private galleons like this to call upon in the event of a war.

Such ships were smaller than their predecessors and the size of the fleet was modest, compared with its peak under Henry VIII and to other navies. But the Navy had the best warships of its time – swift, high-performing and bristling with heavy, long-range weapons. It was in great part due to the poverty of the Crown that the race-built galleon was constructed at all. They were the children of necessity and financial austerity. The country could not afford vast floating fortresses.

Lord Burghley, the Lord Treasurer and the queen's chief minister, believed that one day England would have to fight the might of Spain. Only by having a powerful Navy could England hope to hold off Philip's forces. His choice of Hawkins – the scourge of the Spanish empire – as the Navy's Treasurer reflected his hostility to Philip. The appointment of the most famous ocean-roving English sailor to the most important job on the Board symbolised the connection between England's privateering seafarers and the Navy. Hawkins had, after all, led naval operations that not only paid for themselves but returned a profit for the Crown and its investors. He was also the only member of the Board to have commanded royal ships outside European waters.

John Hawkins was Burghley's man in the Navy. In order to achieve ultimate control over the service they would have to displace the old hands on the Board. Just before he took over as Treasurer of the Navy Hawkins submitted a report detailing how the Crown was systematically ripped off by the members of the Navy Board. William Winter, he alleged, conducted naval business in his own private books; he overcharged for ship construction, over-ordered materials, got the Crown to pay for timber it already owned, built ships for himself on the Navy's account and so on.

A lot of it was true in essence. The Board could not hope to micromanage so vast and complex an institution. The administration of the Navy was decentralised, each member of the Board taking charge of different functions. These areas became personal fiefdoms – and very valuable ones at that. Members of the Board and the master shipwrights contracted work out to favoured suppliers. They received money from the Treasury to build and maintain ships and kept any money left over.

The result was a mysterious system – one that no one person could understand or control. The Navy was the sum of its parts. Those who ran it made vast profits. That way of working was perfectly normal in Elizabethan England. But it gave Hawkins the chance to level charges of corruption at his colleagues. He wanted Winter out of the way.

He had a plan to run the Navy much more efficiently – and more cheaply. His proposal was that the Exchequer should pay him for all 'Ordinary' naval expenditure – that is the cost of ship repairs, the upkeep of storehouses, wages for shipkeepers and all the other routine expenses. (The 'Extraordinary' expenditure, as opposed to the 'Ordinary', was for new buildings, new ships, major repairs to dry docks and war materiel.) The Ordinary expenditure was £7,000 a year; Hawkins said he could do it for £4,000. The proposal was accepted. Hawkins became responsible for designing and equipping the queen's ships. He elbowed Winter and the others out of the way in as brutal and complete a way as he could manage. In effect John Hawkins had, with Burghley's connivance, centralised the whole machinery of the Navy.

Hawkins had proved himself a master of organisation on his voyages. He brought the same energy and attention to detail to the Navy Royal. Under the terms of the so-called 'First Bargain' made between the Crown and Hawkins in 1579, Hawkins undertook to supply equipment to the Navy for £1,200 a year, money he did not have to account for as long as the job was done properly. Under similar terms, Pett and Baker agreed to overhaul the Navy's five largest ships every three years and the next five in order of size every two years. Every year all the ships had to be recaulked and repaired. For this the two royal shipwrights received £1,000 per year, from which they had to procure material and pay and lodge the workmen.

In addition to keeping the fleet battle-ready, Hawkins worked on the infrastructure of the Navy. The Board got a permanent headquarters and lodgings at Chatham. He built a sluice gate at the drydock at Deptford – previously drydocks had been closed in with earthen barriers and it took twenty men one month to remove the earth to flood the dock when a ship was launched. He had a mast pond – used for seasoning timbers and poles to prevent them drying and splitting – dug at Chatham. In 1579 he repaired the fort at Sheerness, which guarded the entry to the Medway, where the work of keeping the Navy fighting fit took place. He also had a boom made to defend the Medway at Upnor Castle. An iron chain could be drawn across the river, pulled by winding machinery and lighters to protect the dockyards against attacks from Philip's ships operating out of the Netherlands. Large warships could base themselves at the strategically vital port of Dover once again after Hawkins added a sluice gate to prevent the harbour from becoming silted up. On board ships there were minor but vital alterations. Hawkins had them fitted with a chain pump and a capstan for raising the anchor. Most importantly, he ensured that ships he commanded carried livestock and fresh fruit to feed the mariners.

Under Hawkins the pace of updating the Navy increased. In his first year six Navy ships – *Triumph*, *Victory*, *White Bear*, *Hope*, *Philip and Mary* and *Antelope* – were converted into race-built galleons. By 1585 half the Navy's ships conformed to the new design.

Hawkins was a brilliant administrator. He took control of the Navy by ruthless means and he used his power to transform it into the fighting force he believed was necessary to fight Spain. Over the previous four decades the Navy Board had worked a quiet revolution in administration. It might look chaotic to modern eyes, but the achievement of the Gonsons, the Winters, Pett, Baker and Chapman was outstanding. They had provided their queen with a Navy that was ready for war. These men bridged the gap between the worlds of privateering and national defence, making the two virtually indistinguishable. Above all they had made the queen's Navy the backbone of a strong national Navy.

But it was a thuggish world, even in the queen's service. Hawkins had to exhibit the ruthlessness and bombast he had displayed against the Spanish to work his way to the top.

Hawkins saw a showdown coming. He hurried through the programme of converting the royal ships and keeping the fleet ready for war. The English race-built galleon was an oceangoing warship, extending the Navy's range out onto the high seas and to distant shores. And the intent was signalled when Hawkins brought in a new method of hull construction that protected it against wood-boring beetles. These beetles were only present in the tropics – places the Navy Royal had no business. The Navy was equipped to penetrate the Portuguese and Spanish empires if that was what was required of it.

While Hawkins was beginning to revolutionise the Navy news began to filter back of Drake's spectacular voyage around the world. After a battering passage through the Magellan Strait, Drake's *Golden Hind* was, at 150 tons and with eighteen guns, the most heavily armed ship in the Pacific. It terrorised the coasts of Chile, Peru, Panama and Mexico, raiding settlements and taking lightly armed but richly laden treasure ships. Of equal value at least to the treasure captured were maps of the coasts and the charts of the galleon route across the Pacific to Manila. Using this he navigated across the Pacific to the Moluccas – the fabled Spice Islands, which had tantalised traders for centuries but which no Englishman had seen before – where he obtained a cargo of spices. After that he sailed the Indian Ocean, cleared the Cape of Good Hope, and returned home via Guinea.

Drake and Elizabeth made staggering fortunes from the voyage. So too did his investors – Hawkins among them. And for the English seafaring community the way seemed open to the Americas, the Moluccas and the Pacific. The Spanish were clearly no match for the English at sea.

For Philip it was a major irritation. Drake had scythed through his world. But the king of Spain had bigger concerns than the heretical pirate he viewed as a squalid nuisance. He was on the brink of fulfilling the divine plan.

In 1580 Philip II seized the throne of Portugal, uniting two mighty global empires that encompassed the Atlantic, Pacific and Indian oceans.

And not only that, he now had at his disposal a mighty navy. Throughout the 1560s he had built up his Mediterranean galley fleet. Its size peaked at 140 vessels. In 1571 it joined other Christian powers in the Mediterranean and comprehensively beat the Ottomans at the Battle of Lepanto, the largest naval battle thus far in history. In 1582 a veteran of Lepanto, the marquis of Santa Cruz, ventured out into the Atlantic. His target was the Azores. Don Antonio, the nephew of the previous king of Portugal, claimed to be the rightful monarch of Portugal. He was holding out against Philip on the Azores, with the help of eager French and English privateers. For many an Englishman, service under the flag of Don Antonio was their first taste of war on the high seas. They would later bring this experience to Elizabeth's Navy.

Santa Cruz's fleet sent to the Azores was the largest navy ever seen on the Atlantic. What was more, it achieved the impossible. Spanish ships operating hundreds of miles from home in the Atlantic Ocean sustained a joint land and seaborne attack on enemy territory. Don Antonio's Anglo-French fleet was defeated at the Battle of Terceira. The Azores fell to Philip.

'After the taking of Terceira,' wrote one Spaniard, 'the captains who accompanied the Marquis of Santa Cruz ... said openly that now we have Portugal, England is ours; and little by little we shall gain France also.'[2] Santa Cruz was convinced that Spain had become the world's greatest naval power. He advised Philip that the time was ripe for an invasion of England that would, at a stroke, remove the threat to the empire from the Netherlands to the West Indies, from the Strait of Magellan to the Moluccas. The king was coming to the same opinion: 'In order to terminate [the Dutch revolt] once and for all it might be advisable to take steps to ensure that the war is not sustained from England.'[3]

For Philip, as for Elizabeth, the future of Europe – and of England – would be decided in the Netherlands.

By 1584 Elizabeth's ministers were aware that war with Spain was inevitable. In that year Drake had prepared yet another fleet to rampage through Philip's world. The king of Spain ordered a close watch kept on the English pirate. Rumours of his destination were many and various. Some said he was bound for the Moluccas to establish an English presence in the Far East. Others said that Drake was after the Spanish treasure fleet. It was clear, however, that whatever the plan it was backed by the queen and had a strategic aim.

It had not yet sailed when an English merchant arrived from Spain. The story he told changed everything. He had fought his way out of Bilbao after being approached by Spanish officials. He had kidnapped one of them and found letters ordering an embargo of Dutch, German and English ships. Four days later the Privy Council interrogated Spanish captives. They ascertained that Philip had ordered that foreign ships be requisitioned to join the Spanish fleet to defend the empire against Francis Drake.

It marked the beginning of an undeclared war that would last until 1604. Elizabeth responded by giving affronted English merchants the right to compensate themselves by attacking Spanish ships. Drake's planned voyage got a clear strategic purpose: to reduce Spain's ability to wage war and to bring back a handsome profit. The objective was to capture the *flota* itself, the prize of the oceans. The strategy was to so weaken Philip's empire that his ships would be diverted from Europe. As Drake advised the queen, by despoiling his empire and ships Philip 'may best be withstanded and most endamaged with least charge to the Queen's Majesty'.[4] By this policy 'the king of Spain may be brought to know that any kind of peace shall be better for him than wars with England'.[5]

Drake failed to capture the *flota*, but his voyage of mayhem took him from the coast of Spain, where he pillaged Bayona to the Cape Verdes, then across the Atlantic to raid Santo Domingo, Cartagena, Cuba and Florida. Once again Spanish officials and colonists trembled throughout the empire. It seemed that nowhere was safe from Drake and his blood-thirsty men. Meanwhile thousands of other English seafarers took to the seas to hunt down Spanish ships in retaliation for Philip's arrest of English shipping. English soldiers were sent to stiffen the Dutch resistance to Philip. Burghley wrote that England was about 'to sustain a greater war than ever in any memory of man it hath done'.[6]

He was right. Philip ordered Santa Cruz to go ahead with his plans to invade England.

PART 4: ARMADA

CHAPTER 12

THE GREAT ENTERPRISE
1585–1588

The advantage of time and place in all martial actions is half a
victory; which being lost is irrecoverable.

Francis Drake, 1588

Philip II governed his empire from his study. He did not like face-to-face
interviews; business was done by correspondence. He pored over maps
and charts, read reports on anchorages and coastlines. The king took personal control over everything, hearing advice but making up his own
mind. This included the great enterprise against England. Once Philip
had decided on a plan he convinced himself it was at God's dictation.

Santa Cruz, Philip's leading admiral, had envisaged a naval campaign,
with a mighty fleet carrying an army to Ireland and then England. The
most experienced naval officer in Philip's service, Juan Martínez de Recalde, believed that an invasion was only possible once the English Navy
had been defeated or worn down; he advocated capturing a West Country
port, taking control of the seas prior to disembarking the army. Recalde
had the advantage of knowing the seas around England well; he had led
ships to Flanders in 1572 and 1575 and he had been to the west coast
of Ireland. The duke of Parma, the commander of Philip's armies in the
Netherlands, wrote from the north. He believed that an armada sent from
Spain was not necessary. If it was all kept a secret, he could launch a lightning strike across the Narrow Seas, capture Elizabeth and take London.

There were thus two strategies, one naval, one military. There was also
a division between commanders who knew only the Iberian and Atlantic world and those whose careers had been spent in the Netherlands.
The Atlantic worldview had visions of a repeat of the conquest of the
Azores: first establish local naval control in the western Channel, set up
supply lines to Spain, then start a land campaign that was bound to be
long and slow. The advantage above all else was that England would be
destroyed as an Atlantic power and its dreaded sea rovers confounded.

For those whose orientation was westwards, the most vulnerable part of England was the West Country. The Navy Royal would almost be fighting in foreign territory, inasmuch as all its bases, victualling depots and brewhouses were east of Portsmouth and it was hard to supply a fleet any distance from London.

The Flanders men fought and thought in a different way. Speed and surprise were what counted. They were not used to including warships in their strategies: to rely on lumbering ships that were dependent on wind, tides and anchorages seemed to them to be impossibly slow and complicated. Moreover, their mental map of England showed its key vulnerability to be its south-eastern rump, Kent. But to Philip, busy over his maps and reports, neither strategy appeared workable.

The problem was Elizabeth's Navy. It was stronger than ever. Once the war began John Hawkins swung into action. The policy of keeping a defensive Navy of twenty-four ships had been appropriate when Spain was primarily a Mediterranean naval power. Now she was an Atlantic power as well, England suddenly looked weak. A survey of the Navy conducted by the Solicitor General, Lord Ellesmere, found that the fleet was in a good state. In 1585 Hawkins made his Second Bargain with the Crown, which included a rolling plan for annual repairs of ships, the conversion of older ships into race-built galleons and the construction of new galleons. Hawkins wrote to Burghley that 'we shall be able to go forward with the works of those apt and nimble vessels which shall mightily strengthen the navy and be most fit and forcible to offend the enemy'.[1]

In the summer of 1586 Hawkins displayed the operational finesse of the Navy Royal when he took a squadron of the queen's galleons to the Iberian coast and remained there for three months, lying in wait for the treasure fleet. Hawkins served as admiral in *Nonpareil*; William Borough, the Clerk of the Queen's Ships, was vice admiral in the *Lion*; Thomas Fenner commanded the *Hope*, Edward Berkeley the *Revenge* and Benjamin Gonson the brand-new *Tramontana*.

It was an unprecedented show of maritime strength. Hawkins failed to capture the *flota*, but he showed that the Navy Royal was, for the first time, capable of operating far from home for considerable periods. Hawkins took the opportunity to demonstrate to high-ranking Spaniards just how advanced the English Navy was. A prisoner reported that the *Nonpareil* was clean, fast, and had a plentiful supply of food, including live animals and fresh fruit. It was heavily armed – forty-four bronze guns and 300 men. Another prisoner in Fenner's *Hope* said it was larger than the *Nonpareil*, perhaps as big as the *San Martín*, a 1,000-ton Spanish galleon. It had fifty-four bronze guns and 350 men. These ships were clearly formidable and their crews were tough and disciplined.

In 1587 the intention to invade England was given fresh impetus when Mary, Queen of Scots was executed. It shocked and sickened Catholic Europe. Philip was more convinced than ever that a decisive blow had to be struck against England.

But Elizabeth got in first. Early in the year a private fleet gathered by English traders to rob Spanish treasure in compensation for the stoppage of trade was detained in the Thames. It was added to a fleet being gathered by Drake. As ever with Drake the plans were vague and changed over time. He originally went into partnership with some disgruntled traders who would share the booty from a raid with the queen. Then he said he was going to aid Don António; finally he claimed to be going to attack the Spanish coast. He left Plymouth in April 1587 with a fleet of twenty privately owned warships and oceangoing pinnaces. Drake was in command of four galleons from the Navy Royal. He was also given orders from Elizabeth. He was

> to prevent the joining together of the King of Spain's fleet out of their different ports. To keep victuals from them. To follow them in case they should come out towards England or Ireland. To cut off as many of them as he could, and prevent their landing. To set upon the West Indian ships as they came or went.

A week after the fleet set sail, fresh orders were sent after Drake ordering him not to enter any Spanish port. He never received them. Perhaps he was not meant to.

Drake sailed in the Navy ship *Elizabeth Bonaventure*; his trusted friend Thomas Fenner commanded *Dreadnought*. The rear admiral was Robert Flick, admiral of the Levant Company fleet, which had contributed a number of its galleons. The vice admiral, Drake's second in command, was William Borough, Clerk of the Queen's Ships, in the *Golden Lion*. All four royal ships on the expedition were of the new type, including the *Rainbow*, launched in the previous year.

The fleet was off the Iberian coast when it received intelligence that there was an enormous merchant fleet gathering at Cadiz. The Spanish Armada would be mustered at Lisbon, but the news Drake gleaned was that the fleet was being equipped at Cadiz. Spain had to work hard to be a naval power, let alone mount an invasion of England. It did not have the resources for naval supplies or victuals. Pitch, cordage, timber, sailcloth and cheeses had to be obtained in the Baltic and the Netherlands, and they had to be transported the 'north about' route, around the north coast of Scotland, to avoid English ships in the Narrow Seas and Channel. Trading vessels had been embargoed from England, Scotland, Venice, Genoa, Naples, the Baltic and Ragusa. Provisions and supplies also came from the Mediterranean, and troops from every corner of the empire. This complex business was co-ordinated in Cadiz, under the protection of shore batteries and a squadron of galleys.

Drake approached Cadiz without showing any colours. A galley ventured out to ascertain where these strange ships came from. When it reached cannon-shot range the English opened fire. The galley fled and the alarm was given in the town – Drake had arrived. The women and children ran to the citadel; twenty-seven died in the press to reach safety. The men were ordered to defend any point where the English might try to land. Cadiz had an inner and outer harbour, with the great assemblage of ships crowded in the inner; Drake's ships had no trouble entering. William Borough was left in the outer harbour.

Drake was in his element. The English boarded ship after ship, looting them and then setting them on fire. They sank a Biscayan merchantman of 1,200 tons and burnt a 1,500-ton ship owned by Santa Cruz. They were in Cadiz for three days, during which time thirty-one ships were destroyed and four laden with provisions were taken away. They contained enough victuals to prolong Drake's voyage of destruction for three months. In all the damage was said to have cost 172,000 ducats. When darkness fell on the first night in Cadiz, the harbour was a scene of chaos and the Spanish were in a 'marvellous panic', Thomas Fenner reported with relish: 'the sight of which terrible fires were to us very pleasant, and mitigated the burdens of our continual travail, wherein we were busied two nights and one day'.[2]

The Spanish could only watch. Their shore batteries did no harm. The galleys were kept at bay by the long-range guns favoured by the English. Fenner reported to Walsingham how inferior the long-feared galleys were to the new English galleons: 'We have now tried by experience the galleys' fight, and I assure you that these her Majesty's 4 ships will make no account of 20 of them.'[3]

For the first time the English had seen the sheer scale of the Spanish preparations. They were able to report back to Walsingham that Philip was in deadly earnest. In return they wrought terrible destruction. They had dented Santa Cruz's honour by burning 'his own princely bark'. But they had 'singed the King of Spain's beard', not destroyed his navy. Drake and his officers knew that this victory had to be followed up. Drake wrote to Walsingham: 'Prepare in England, and most by sea. Stop him now, and stop him ever. Look well to the coast of Sussex.'[4]

Drake was equipped to continue for much longer, able to harry Spanish shipping and destroy or divert the precious supplies. For several weeks his fleet hovered off Cape St Vincent, where it was free to prey on Spanish shipping. On 17 May Drake wrote to Walsingham that since the raid on Cadiz he had captured or destroyed 'forts, ships, barks, caravels, and divers other vessels more than a hundred, most laden, some with oars for galleys, planks and timber for ships and pinnaces, hoops and pipe-staves for casks, with many other provisions for this great army'.[5]

By the end of the month, however, the fleet was weakened by disease and most of the ships had to make for home. Drake begged Walsingham for six more royal warships so that he could keep the pressure on Philip. They were not forthcoming, so he and the few remaining ships headed for the Azores. There they captured the greatest prize yet: Philip's own treasure ship the *San Felipe*. The capture of this ship alone paid for the entire voyage *and* made a profit for the Crown and the investors. Its looted cargo was worth 10 per cent of England's total imports that year.

Drake returned home a hero. Investors may have grumbled that he had concealed the true extent of the profit, but the expedition had been an outstanding military success. There would be no invasion in 1587, as had been widely expected.

Pope Sixtus V, when he heard that the Armada would not sail in 1587, said that Philip II was 'a coward that had suffered his nose to be held in the Low Countries by a woman, braved and spoiled at his own nose in Spain by a mariner'. Even after Drake had returned home, the effects of his raids lived on. Santa Cruz had to abandon his preparations and take to the sea to escort the incoming treasure fleets.

Drake's success had been a blow to the invasion plans, but Philip was keener than ever that the Armada should strike. As soon as Santa Cruz returned he was ordering that the Armada set sail, even though it was not ready and the winter was coming on.

Philip had settled on his plan. He was influenced by a close adviser, Don Juan de Zúñiga, a man who had co-ordinated land and seaborne campaigns in the Mediterranean.[6] The same could be done against England: the Atlantic/naval strategy and Parma's army plan would be combined. The plan – worked out in 1587 and retained throughout the campaign – was for the Armada to head for Flanders in the hope that by then they would have defeated or scared away the English naval forces. Once in place the ships would await word from Parma. His army could then cross to England under the protection of a vast escort. The Armada would also carry more men, the siege train and supplies necessary for the invasion.

As far as Philip was concerned, September 1587 was the optimal time for the Enterprise. The diplomatic situation had swung to Spain's advantage. Catholic Europe craved revenge against England for the execution of the queen of Scots. France would not intervene to prevent Spain's invasion. Elizabeth was even in bad odour with the Dutch, who felt she had let them down with a botched campaign in the Netherlands. Philip gave orders for the Armada to sail. But after Drake's raids had delayed it, Santa Cruz was in no position to go. Throughout the winter, morale among the Spanish plummeted and the hordes of soldiers and sailors ate their way through the supplies.

And then illness struck. First Philip was ill over Christmas and the New Year. Then Santa Cruz, in common with many of the idle sailors, caught typhus. He died at the beginning of February 1588 with the Armada still not ready to sail. In his place was appointed the duke of Medina Sidonia. Santa Cruz had managed to resist pressure from the king. Medina Sidonia was unfailingly obedient to Philip. He was thirty-seven years old and lacked military experience, but the combination of his high rank – which would overawe critical officers – and his unconditional loyalty – which would mean that Philip's orders would be executed to the letter – recommended him to Philip. Under Medina Sidonia preparations were stepped up.

The delay was of great help to the English who, surprisingly, were under-prepared in the late summer of 1587, when everyone knew of the scale and imminence of the Spanish Enterprise. Not until October did the Privy Council meet to discuss the strategy to defend England. The agenda, written by Burghley, included keeping pinnaces off the coast of Spain to monitor Spanish activities; putting the Navy into readiness; and staying all shipping so that private ships and sailors could be included in the naval defences.

Later in the month a report written by the master shipwrights Pett and Baker gave the alarming news that the Navy Royal was in a serious state of decay. All the vessels that went to Cadiz were in need of work; three of the four 'great ships' were in a poor state; and five other ships had to be repaired. They blamed John Hawkins for the 'havoc'.

Since 1585 the dockyards had burst into activity again. The Navy Royal possessed thirty-four ships, of which twelve were under 250 tons. It was a Navy of very different ships; there was no English 'type'. Each ship's design revealed the experimental nature of the previous years. They were of various sizes and each had a different keel-to-beam ratio. It was a small, powerful fleet, but in the early winter of 1587 it appeared that it was too small and badly kept to counter the massive force concentrated against it.

When Lord Admiral Howard of Effingham inspected the fleet in December he could report: 'I have been aboard every ship that goeth out with me, and in every place where any may creep, and I do thank God that they be in the estate they be in; and there is never a one of them that knows what a leak means.' As it turned out, despite the panic in the shipwrights' report, the repairs were completed within a few months.

During the winter Martin Frobisher patrolled the Narrow Seas with seven of the ships. In January twenty-three privately owned warships were added to the fleet, including ships owned by the earl of Leicester, Walter Raleigh, Fenner and the great City of London trading companies. Drake and Fenner were in Plymouth with about thirty ships; Howard and Hawkins remained at Queenborough with the rest of the fleet. All ships, apart from those on patrol, were kept in port (to Drake's irritation – he was eager to go to Spain) and many of the sailors were demobilised.

The cost of keeping ships in battle readiness and victualling a large body of sailors placed an immense strain on the Exchequer. All the commanders worried that the partial demobilisation had lost the Navy some of its best men. Howard wrote to Walsingham in February: 'I have a good company here with me, and so good willers to her Majesty's service, that if the Queen's Majesty will not spare her purse, they will not spare their lives and that which they have.'[7]

The English commanders could not bear the long wait. John Hawkins knew more than anyone the way a fleet soaked up money: 'Our treasure doth consume infinitely with these uncertain wars, and nothing assured to us but new and continual charge'.[8] England could not go on long like this. The Spanish could defeat the Navy by merely keeping the threat of invasion dangling. Pretty soon the money would be gone, the supplies exhausted and the men would starve or desert. 'Therefore,' Hawkins advised Walsingham, 'in my mind, our profit and best assurance is to seek our peace by determined and resolute war.'[9] It should be Spain that was on the back foot, not England. He wanted six royal warships and six pinnaces to menace the Spanish coast for four months at a time. These ships would then be replaced by new ones. It would cost £2,700 a month in wages, but the costs would be recouped by taking Spanish ships.

The plan was not acted upon, but Hawkins's frustrations were shared by most of the officers. They champed at the bit, worn down by inactivity and aroused by rumours of the immense Armada sitting in Spanish ports. Once the battle drew close, like fighting men at all times, they could not bear the hiatus. It was agonising, and exacerbated by niggling problems of logistics and discipline.

Howard's fleet made for Plymouth on 21 May, parting company with the squadron led by Lord Henry Seymour, which was to patrol the Netherlands coast to prevent Parma taking the opportunity to dash across the Narrow Seas.

Charles, Lord Howard of Effingham, Lord High Admiral of England, was a very different naval commander from the stars in the national maritime firmament. He was a calm, authoritative man, not particularly gifted, but an inspired choice to lead the Navy during a national crisis. He came from the country's foremost aristocratic naval family. His uncle had died fighting the French galleys in 1513; his father had been Lord Admiral under Mary. Charles had served on ships in his youth and he owned private warships. As a Howard he understood the security of the Tudor monarchy to be his personal responsibility. The Howard dynasty was, as they saw it, the pillar of the realm. Leading the defence of the country against the Spanish was therefore his moment of destiny. The queen trusted his judgement. In comparison with Philip, who micromanaged his forces from a distance, Elizabeth gave Howard a large measure of discretion.

The Navy he led in 1588 was commanded by officers who were burning with animosities against each other. They were a bunch of men with monstrous egos and contempt for their fellows. Howard stood above these petty disputes. He alone had sufficient authority and status to keep them in line, even if Drake, Hawkins, Frobisher and Fenner believed they knew best. He was prepared to listen to his senior officers, but he was obedient to the queen and would not be shaken from doing his duty.

Fittingly, Howard was on board the *Ark Royal*, the fastest and most manoeuvrable of the large English ships. He could therefore move with ease around the fleet, keeping his eye on his brilliant but wayward admirals. His leading officers, who formed his council of war, commanded the largest and best of the new race-built galleons. Drake, second in command, was in *Revenge*; John Hawkins, third in command, was in the *Victory*. The Lord Admiral's cousin, Lord Thomas Howard, was in the *Golden Lion* and Lord Sheffield, his nephew, in the *White Bear*. Also on his advisory council were Frobisher, commanding the *Triumph*, the largest warship on either side, and Thomas Fenner in the *Nonpareil*. In the smaller eastern squadron patrolling the Narrow Seas, Lord Henry Seymour was in the *Rainbow* and Sir William Winter in the *Vanguard*. Rather forlornly and on his own,

William Borough had a squadron numbering just one (the *Galley Bonavolia*) on the Thames to make a last stand if everything went wrong.

As soon as he arrived in Plymouth the council convinced Howard to sail for Spain, even though the supply ships had not arrived. They had news that the Armada was ready to sail with the first wind. 'God send us a wind to put us out,' Howard wrote to Burghley; 'for go we will, though we starve.'[10]

The English got the news that the Armada was about to leave on 28 May. That was the day Medina Sidonia did put to sea from Lisbon. But the Armada made poor progress in stormy seas. Much of the fleet's supplies had been badly stored and he had to lead it back into harbour to revictual. Back in Plymouth, captains such as Thomas Fenner laughed at the Spanish who had prepared so long and failed to clear their own coast. But the English were in little better case.

The same bad weather also prevented Howard from sailing to Iberia to attack the invasion force. For close to a month the English, so eager to fight, were frustrated by summer storms that made the ships cavort in harbour 'as lustily as the gallantest dancers in the Court'.[11] Howard could only watch as his great fleet was weakened by ennui, disease and lack of food. 'My good Lord,' he wrote to Burghley, 'there is here the gallantest company of captains, soldiers and mariners that I think ever was seen in England. It were a pity they should lack meat, when they are so desirous to spend their lives in Her Majesty's service.'[12]

During the hiatus Howard, Burghley and Walsingham argued by correspondence about the best plan. The Council ordered Howard *not* to go to the Iberian coast. The Lord Admiral replied that the best seafarers in England disagreed. They believed that the Spanish were teasing them, forcing them to keep in a constant state of mobilisation: 'when our victuals be consumed in gazing for them,' asked Howard, 'what shall become of us?'[13] The best policy was to wait for the Spanish on their own coast. If the Armada then risked making the passage they would gift the English the weather gage and have them on their backs all the way. The closer the Spanish got, warned Drake, Frobisher, Hawkins and Fenner, the harder it would be to defeat them in the rougher waters around England. The coast of Spain was the ideal place for a battle. However the queen was adamant that the fleet should stay close to England. Howard was vocal in disagreement. 'But I must and will obey'.[14]

When the winds calmed Howard found himself with too little food and beer to put out. At the same time the officers were driven frantic by news that the Armada had been scattered by the storms and its ships were sitting targets. When he was assured that supply ships were on their way he wrote to Walsingham: 'I will not tarry one hour after our victuals do come to us.'[15] He did not exaggerate; as soon as the supplies arrived at Plymouth his underfed men worked through the night to load their ships. Then, at last, they were at sea.

For two and a half weeks the fleet that had lusted for so long to go into battle tried its best to hold station at the Sleeve, or the mouth of the Channel between the Scillies and Ushant. Howard was under orders to wait until he had definite intelligence of the position, formation, size and course of the Armada. Drake's ships were on the flank off Ushant; Howard was in the centre; Hawkins lay off the Scillies. The seas were ominously empty. Now a new fear wormed its way into Howard's mind. Perhaps the Spanish had evaded him, and the invasion had begun. It was a terrible thing to contemplate.

Then news began to arrive that the Armada had not even sailed and was in fact scattered around Spanish ports. Drake and the others whispered in Howard's ears: this was the moment and it must be seized. Howard was sorely tempted. He fought the temptation to break his orders. At last the wind answered his dilemma. He allowed the fleet to be carried south. The English were almost in sight of Spain.

Then the wind changed to a southerly.

It was an invasion wind. Suddenly the Navy Royal really was in the wrong place. The Spanish could race north, perhaps unseen by Howard, leaving the hapless English fighting the wind in the Bay of Biscay. Besides, the curse of the English Navy had struck again, and the fleet was short of provisions. Howard ordered the fleet back to Plymouth. He wrote to Walsingham: 'the southerly wind that brought us back from the coast of Spain brought them out'.[16]

They had waited for months. They had prepared every last detail. They had imagined defeating the Armada before it even sighted England. Now, when news came that a great swarm of ships had been seen off the Lizard on 19 July, the English were trapped in Plymouth by an incoming tide.

CHAPTER 13

BATTLE
1588

When the Armada reached sight of the Lizard on 20 July the duke of Medina Sidonia ordered the sails of his flagship, the *San Martín de Portugal*, to be taken in and his flag to be raised. It was a signal to his admirals. They took in sail and made their way to the *San Martín* on small boats for a council of war.

The wind was from the south-west. The English were trapped in Plymouth. Conditions seemed eminently favourable. Medina Sidonia had experienced senior officers, veterans of naval warfare from the Mediterranean to the southern Atlantic, from the Caribbean to the coast of Flanders. They had fought against the Ottomans at Lepanto, the French in Florida and the English everywhere; many had led ships in the conquest of the Azores. This was the cream of the Spanish warrior nobility. At the council, the duke's second in command Don Alonso Martínez de Leiva said that the best course of action was to attack Plymouth. There they could destroy the English fleet and begin the conquest of England.

Whatever Medina Sidonia thought, he would not countenance this course of action. He had not summoned his officers to ask their opinion. They were there to be told the plan worked out by the king, a plan that must be followed to the letter.

The Armada was not in English waters to wreak havoc in the West Country, as many of the Atlantic veterans hoped. It was not there to destroy the English Navy. The Armada was to move into a formation known as *en lúnula*, the crescent moon. It was then to proceed towards Flanders without engaging the English in battle. Once there it would escort Parma's army to Sandwich. While Parma marched on London the Spanish warships would head into the estuary and attack the capital.

At each *cuerno* – the horns of the crescent – would be placed the fast-moving ships – galleons, galleasses and galleys. The stronger, best-armed vessels would guard the rear of the formation, with the bulky and lightly armed transport ships screened behind the warships. It was a formation that had served Spain well in other campaigns. When the fleet came under attack the *cuernos* would close in on the enemy, trapping them in a pincer. On the way to England, Leiva had led the vanguard, Medina Sidonia's warships and troop transports were in the middle, and the rearguard was commanded by Recalde. On 31 July the line of travel formed into the line of battle. Leiva's vanguard fell back to form the left *cuerno*; Recalde's warships came forward to Medina Sidonia's right, to become the other horn. The distance from horn to horn was seven miles.

The Armada's *en lúnula* was below par in this campaign. The ease with which Drake's fleet had put the galleys to flight at Cadiz had meant that all but four of the fifty galleys earmarked for the Enterprise had been stood down. This loss did not only weaken the mobility of the *cuernos*. The supreme advantage of galleys was defending ships anchored in deep-water ports, particularly during calm periods. Galleys could use their oars to move swiftly into position to fight off opponents, hiding behind the larger warships and darting out to inflict crippling blows on the enemy before disappearing again into cover. Galleys were ideal for amphibious operations. When troops were being landed on shore in small boats, the best sight they could see would be these oared warships screening them from the enemy. The four that did join the Enterprise were forced back by the summer storms.

The emphasis of Philip's chosen formation was defensive. The job of the Armada was to link up with Parma and escort him across the Narrow Sea. The king had studied the ships and tactics of the English Navy and he had decided that a sea battle would be disastrous. His instructions read:

> In particular I must warn you that the enemy's intention will be to fight at long distance, on account of his advantage in artillery ... The aim of our men, on the contrary, must be to bring him to close quarters and grapple with the weapons they hold in their hands; and you will have to be very careful to carry this out. So that you will be well informed, I am sending you some reports from which you will see the way in which the enemy employs his artillery to fire low and sink his opponent's ships; and you will have to take such precautions as you consider necessary in this respect.

The duke of Medina Sidonia thought that the whole Enterprise was ill-conceived. The Armada consisted of lumbering troop transports, fighting galleons, galleasses, carracks and caravels. The king's orders were explicit: the sole objective of the first phase of the invasion was to link up with Parma. He could not give battle to the English until the army of Flanders was safely on board or under escort. Instead he would have to defend himself as best he could against the Navy Royal. It had been assumed that Elizabeth's fleets would be stationed somewhere between the Thames Estuary and Southampton. The definitive sea battle would take place in the Downs or on the coast of Flanders, in calmer waters where Philip's fighting instructions to grapple with the English and overwhelm them by force of numbers would become relevant. But Howard, Drake and the others were ready and waiting in the west.

More worryingly, no one knew where Parma was or when he would be ready. As the Armada entered the Channel Medina Sidonia was getting nervous. Until he had definite word from Parma, he said, 'to a large extent we are navigating in the dark'.[1] But he was honour-bound to obey Philip's instructions to the letter and the last man.

The naval commanders at the Duke's council of war were apprehensive about these inflexible orders. Some fishermen from Falmouth had been captured and revealed that the English were already under sail. The Armada would have to withstand attack for as long as it took to find Parma. Philip trusted that God would see to it that all went well. Martín de Bertendona, commander of the Levant squadron, agreed that divine help was necessary:

> Unless God helps us by a miracle the English, who have faster and handier ships than ours, and many more long-range guns, and who know their advantage just as well as we do, will never close with us at all, but stand aloof and knock us to pieces with their culverins, without our being able to do them any serious hurt. And so we are sailing against England in the confident hope of a miracle![2]

Howard knew that his ships and guns outclassed the Spanish. He boasted that one English ship was worth five Spanish. The men who had been on the Cadiz expedition would have agreed. By no means should English ships get close to the Spanish. Instead they should use their manoeuvrability, speed and guns to inflict damage on the enemy. The plan, according to Howard, was to 'course' the enemy as if they were greyhounds hunting a hare, so 'they shall have no leisure to land'.

The first challenge was to get to sea against the tide and the wind. All night long on Friday 19 July the ships warped out of harbour as quickly as the men could work. The *Ark Royal* and six other ships were out of Plymouth Sound and lying off Reme Head; by Saturday morning between fifty and sixty ships (out of ninety at Plymouth) were at sea, beating westward against the wind and rain. At three that afternoon the Armada was sighted westwards of Fowey. Howard led his fleet through the night against the wind. The rest of the fleet meanwhile warped out of Plymouth and sailed on to join Howard.

When dawn broke on Sunday the sailors on the Armada could see some eighty English ships to windward of them (that is to say, astern of them) and eleven more beating westwards on their lee, the shore side. These ships fell in with the main fleet. Warping the ships out of harbour in a summer gale and beating down the Channel was a complex, strenuous manoeuvre and a considerable achievement, and yet Howard said it was accomplished 'with such diligence and good will, that many of them [the ships] got abroad as though it had been a fair wind'. At 09.00 the Lord Admiral's pinnace *Defiance* sailed alone into the middle of the crescent to 'give defiance' – fire a symbolic shot – at Medina Sidonia's *San Martín*. The battle had begun.

Ark Royal led the attack on the left *cuerno*, Drake and Hawkins on the right. In his report to Walsingham that evening Howard wrote that 'we durst not adventure to put in among them, their fleet being so strong'.[3] The English had to be flexible in their strategy. This was the first sight of the Armada and its formation. None of the captains, gunners and mariners, in all their long experience of fighting at sea, had ever encountered anything like it. They had never fought as part of a fleet and they had no fleet tactics with which to confront a defensive crescent of ships that refused to give battle. When English sailors took on a Spanish ship on the high seas they would 'charge' the enemy, firing off the bow chasers, turn to give it the broadside, then turn again to fire the stern chasers. Other ships in the squadron would follow suit until the enemy surrendered or it could be boarded.

Now, on 21 July, this tactic could not be adopted. As Howard noted, no English ship could risk getting too close to a Spanish ship or finding herself in the midst of the crescent. Most of the men on board the English ships were there to sail or fire the heavy guns. The Spanish, by contrast, had ships full of armed men who wanted nothing more than to grapple and board English ships.

The English captains therefore had to suppress their instincts to engage in individual ship-to-ship duels with the enemy. This is what they were best at, but they were under orders to stand off and use their heavy guns to wreak carnage on the Spanish, who were unable to answer in kind. *Ark Royal* attacked the outermost ships on the left horn, followed by the other ships in her column, intending to keep them under constant cannon fire as each ship came in to fire off its ordnance before retiring to reload and reform the line.

Over on the right wing, Recalde found himself abandoned by many of the rearguard, the ships moving into the main body of the Armada. Recalde 'determined to await the fight' and a queue of English ships led by Drake and Hawkins took it in turns to pummel his *San Juan*. After two hours the ship had been pounded with 300 rounds of shot and had sustained serious damage to its foremast, stays and rigging before the Biscayan squadron and *San Martín* dropped back to defend it. Medina Sidonia regrouped the Armada. As he said, this was all he was able to do 'as the enemy had gained the wind, the English ships being swift and well handled, so that they could do as they liked with them'. Drake and Hawkins prudently retired and that day's fighting was over by two in the afternoon. The English pursued, or rather followed, the Spanish eastwards.

The tactic to which the English were trusting was the power of their guns. Hawkins had shown at San Juan d'Ulúa and Drake at Cadiz how effective English cannon were when deployed against enemy ships. It was an advantage Philip II was well aware of and every Spanish sailor feared. But in the first battle the damage inflicted on Recalde's *San Juan*, notwithstanding two hours' bombardment, was slight and easily repaired. What was apparent was that the Spanish advantages in manpower and the English advantages in gunpower were cancelling each other out. The English did not dare sail close enough to make the best of their guns, which was at point-blank range. And the Spanish were not going to make things easier by turning round and fighting. If the Armada was going to keep its tight formation, refusing battle all the while, the best the English could do was to try and use their firepower to prevent the Armada from making a landing. The only problem was that after only a few hours' fighting many of the ships were low on shot and powder. It must have been a rude shock to English seafarers who had long grown complacent. 'There was little harm done,' Don Pedro de Valdes reported to Philip, 'because the fight was far off.'⁴

The only cheer the English got on the first day was when the powder magazine on *San Salvador* exploded and *Nuestra Señora del Rosario* lost her bowsprit in a collision. The significance of this may not have been known to the English, but it was to the Spanish. These two ships alone carried 10 per cent of the Armada's ordnance.

Things did not look good to Howard and his council when it convened that evening. The mood can be gleaned from Howard's note to

Walsingham: 'Sir, for the love of God and our country, let us have with some speed some great shot sent us of all bigness ... and some powder with it.'⁵ The Armada had passed Plymouth. But where was it bound for? Perhaps it would try and secure a beachhead at Torbay, or Lyme or Portland; it might even take the most vulnerable part of England, the Isle of Wight. The Spanish could, unless the Navy Royal was vigilant and fast-moving, make landfall within a day or so. As far as the English were concerned, the crisis was approaching. Howard appointed his best officer, Francis Drake, to lead the fleet by the light of the great stern lantern on *Revenge*, during the night.

When the sun rose the next morning Howard got a nasty surprise. His *Ark Royal* along with *Bear* and *Mary Rose* were right behind the Armada. They were on their own.

During the night, the rest of the English fleet had halted when they lost sight of the *Revenge*'s stern light. Howard and the rest had to fall back as fast as they could and wait for the rest of the fleet. During the night Drake had deserted his post and gone off in pursuit of the damaged *Rosario*. At daybreak, *Rosario* found itself facing the big guns of the *Revenge* just three cables' length away; after a token defence the Spanish ship surrendered. Drake was not a natural Navy man; he had done what he did best and disappeared on a personal adventure.

As it was, the Armada kept plodding on and did not seek to make a sudden landfall. And with his accustomed luck, Drake had turned an act of recklessness into something of a triumph. *Rosario* had forty-six guns, 2,000 rounds of shot and 50,000 ducats on board. The extra ammunition was invaluable for the English. There was another gift from the Spanish. Medina Sidonia had ordered the damaged *San Salvador* to be scuttled during the night, but it had drifted into English hands and 2,246 rounds of shot were recovered.

Had Philip given Medina Sidonia more discretion it might have been a fatal adventure on Drake's part. The English were able to spend Monday regrouping. On Tuesday the wind shifted to north-west and the Armada now had the weather gage. The English were beating against the wind to seaward of them. Howard watched with horror as the Armada took up a new formation in Lyme Bay. The two *cuernos* fell back to form a rearguard. *San Martín* moved forward to lead a small vanguard, and the transports were between the warships. This rearrangement of the squadrons was to prevent the English stealing past the Armada and impeding its link-up with Parma.

To Howard's nervous mind, however, it was an invasion formation.

The rearguard, he believed, was in place to screen the disembarkation of the Spanish army on Chesil Beach. Howard had to act fast to prevent this catastrophe. He led his ships to get past the leeward Spanish ships in order to regain the gage. They were headed off by the Spanish vanguard – *San Martín* and the galleasses. Then Howard led an outflanking manoeuvre, taking the opposite tack out to seaward. To do this he had to run the gauntlet of the Armada's powerful rearguard. It came about, forming into a crescent, and began to close in on Howard and the largest English ships, *Victory*, *Elizabeth Jonas*, *Golden Lion*, *White Bear*, *Nonpareil* and their accompanying ships and pinnaces. Recalde's inshore squadron attacked the rearmost English ships. For the first time, the Spanish came into attack, endeavouring to use the weather gage to get close enough to the English to grapple and board. As the crescent began to encircle the English a furious battle began. 'But it was all useless,' Medina Sidonia reported to the king, 'for when the enemy saw that our intention was to come to close quarters with him, he sheered off to seaward, his great advantage being in the swiftness of his ships.'

While this battle raged in Lyme Bay, Martin Frobisher in the *Triumph* led *Mary Rose*, *Merchant Royal*, *Margaret and John* and *Centurion* on the original lee tack, round to Portland Bill, where they dropped anchor. It was a tempting sight for Medina Sidonia. These were the perfect conditions for his galleasses: stationary English ships in calm waters, with the shore behind them. The four galleasses detached themselves from the vanguard and rowed furiously to corner them.

But local knowledge outweighed all the advantages the Spanish enjoyed. The strong current at Portland Bill and the north-east wind meant that the galleasses could not outflank Frobisher's squadron. They were forced into a head-on attack. Frobisher ordered the guns to be loaded with chainshot. They opened fire on the enemy ships' oars. For ninety minutes Frobisher's galleons held the galleasses at bay. Then the wind changed. Now the English had the weather gage. Howard brought his ships north, engulfing the squadrons led by Recalde and Leiva.

Medina Sidonia, once the galleasses had been sent to attack Frobisher, turned about *San Martín*, which made its way through the body of the Armada. As he worked through his fleet, the duke saw that his rearguard had broken away from the main fleet and was surrounded by the English rearguard. He sailed in to rescue his warships, bravely lowering his topsails to make himself a juicy target for the ambitious English admirals and captains. As soon as *San Martín* was seen to be on her own, the English broke away from their battles. Led by Howard, the English fleet sailed past the *San Martín*, each firing in turn at the Spanish flagship. The Spanish returned fire, keeping the English outside their optimal range so that by the time half the Navy had passed, its line had been forced further away and out of range. Meanwhile Recalde and Leiva had regrouped and were taking up formation with *San Martín*, 'although by the time they came up the hottest fury was passed'. The English withdrew, to seaward, to avoid being entrapped and to husband their diminishing stocks of ammunition.

At the close of the third day, things had resolved into a stalemate. Even when they enjoyed the best conditions possible, the Spanish had still been outmanoeuvred and outgunned by the English. The Navy's bombardments prevented the Spanish from closing in and boarding. But all the same, the English could not find a way to bring their guns to bear as they would like. They had no fleet tactics. Howard would lead his best ships into battle where he saw fit, then it was every ship for itself in a melee. Every time they tried to close in, the Spanish Armada remained disciplined. It was able to get back into formation too quickly for the English to isolate and bombard individual warships. In these conditions, no side could fight the kind of decisive action it wanted.

As the day's fighting revealed, however, the advantage lay with the English. They could use their superior ships to dictate terms. The Armada's options for fighting were essentially negative. They could hold off the Navy, but it was now clear that without destroying Howard's fleet they would find it hard to choose an anchorage from where they could co-ordinate with Parma.

Howard and his men had expected to have destroyed or chased away the Spanish by now. The kind of fighting they were forced to adopt was ruinously expensive. For very little tangible gain they had spent most of the ammunition intended to sustain them for the entire campaign. On Wednesday the English kept close to the Spanish rearguard, sometimes close enough to exchange fire. With no new insight into co-ordinating his fleet, Howard split the ships into four groups. From now on the Lord Admiral, Francis Drake, John Hawkins and Martin Frobisher would lead their ships as they saw fit. Howard was forced to concede to Walsingham: 'Their force is wonderful great and strong; and yet we pluck their feathers little by little.'[6]

CHAPTER 14

CRISIS
July–August 1588

When the sun rose on 25 July the English fleet saw three stragglers from the Armada. The sea was calm; the wind had dropped away; it seemed a golden opportunity. Hawkins made for the *Duquesta Santa Ana*; Howard chose the *San Luis*; and Drake's ships moved in on the *Donella*. Now, at last, they could sink or take a Spanish ship.

This was what Medina Sidonia had intended. He could see the Great Enterprise unravelling. He had sent small, speedy ships to Flanders to inform Parma of his whereabouts. But answer came there none. 'I have constantly written to Your Excellency,' wrote an exasperated Medina Sidonia to Parma, 'and not only have I received no reply to my letters, but no acknowledgement of your receipt.'[1] The only solution was to seek a safe anchorage and await accurate information as to Parma's whereabouts and state of readiness.

The obvious choice was the Solent, the last haven before the Calais Roads. Philip's detailed instructions gave Medina Sidonia permission to enter the Solent and take the Isle of Wight if something went awry. The three Spanish stragglers were bait to tempt the English away and allow him to enter the Solent.

The three seemingly isolated ships were in reality being watched by nearby Spanish warships. When Hawkins moved in the galleasses were ready to fly out in defence. Drake found himself facing Recalde's squadron. *Ark Royal* was being towed by its boats towards *San Luis*, but found itself facing Leiva's *Rata Encoronada*, which was being towed by a galleass. It looked as if Medina Sidonia's plan was working.

But Martin Frobisher had a diversion of his own to play. Once again he drew on his local knowledge. An eastward inshore current propelled the *Triumph* and the rest of Frobisher's squadron past the Armada's leeward flank. Now they were off the Isle of Wight, facing the Spanish admiral. *San Martín* came under attack from *Triumph*'s guns, which inflicted damage to the Spanish ship's mainmast. Frobisher had brought his ships

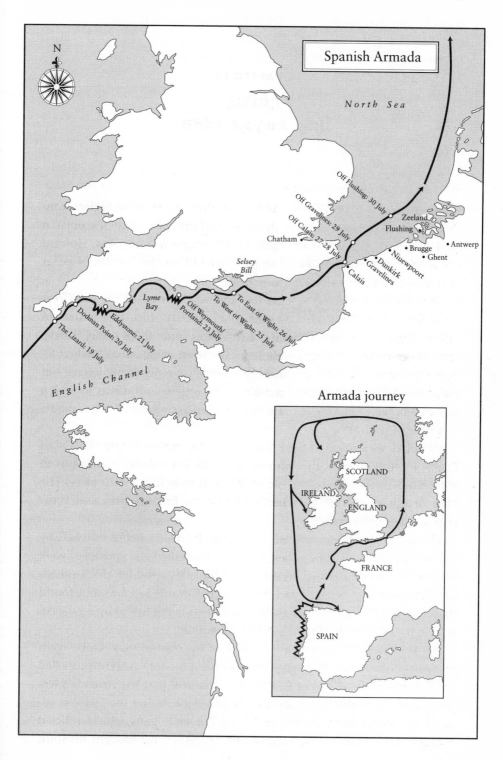

Spanish Armada

North Sea

Off Flushing: 30 July

Off Gravelines: 29 July

Off Calais: 27-28 July

Chatham

Zeeland
Flushing

• Antwerp

• Brugge
Niuewpoort • Ghent
Dunkirk
Gravelines

Calais

Selsey Bill

To East of Wight: 26 July

Lyme Bay

To West of Wight: 25 July

Off Weymouth/
Portland: 23 July

Eddystone: 21 July

Dodman Point: 20 July

The Lizard: 19 July

English Channel

Armada journey

SCOTLAND

IRELAND

ENGLAND

FRANCE

SPAIN

closer to the Spanish than any English ship had done hitherto. Now his guns began to tell.

It was a brilliant move on Frobisher's part. Under this assault, the Armada's vanguard could be halted, and the whole Spanish formation would bunch up, disrupting the rearguard that was closing with the Navy's leading warships. But at the crucial moment the wind picked up from the south-west and *San Martín* was reinforced. Recalde broke away and moved north to block the rest of the English fleet from joining Frobisher. Suddenly *Triumph* and her companions seemed to be about to be sacrificed. Some of the ships managed to get back to the main fleet, but the large and relatively unwieldy *Triumph* was becalmed. *Bear* and *Elizabeth Jonas* dropped their boats in an effort to tow Frobisher's ship to safety, but by now the enemy was bearing down on *Triumph* to finish her off.

The English fleet saw imminent disaster. Fenner and Fenton lowered their ships' topsails in an effort to tempt some of the Spanish to attack. It failed. Howard and Hawkins charged the Armada's rearguard, forcing the enemy ships to reform and some to break away from the attack on Frobisher. But nothing seemed able to save Frobisher, who now had five warships closing in on him.

But then the *Triumph* disappeared. That is an exaggeration; but it might as well have done for the astonishment expressed then and long after by the Spanish. A fortuitous change in the wind allowed the *Triumph* to evade the best galleons of the Armada and rejoin the English fleet. The Spanish were left standing as *Triumph* sped away. This marvellous display of the qualities of English race-built galleons and the skills of the men who handled them came as a hard lesson to the Spanish, and a demoralising one. They had been cheated of what would have been a significant victory, their ships exposed as markedly inferior to their enemy's.

The sudden escape of Frobisher's squadron left the Armada in confusion. Howard, Hawkins and Frobisher were inshore of the Spanish, to the left of the formation. Drake had earlier disappeared from the battle, working his way to seaward. At the crucial moment his ships surprised the Spanish right wing. He sailed in so close that he was able to fire at close range. *San Martín* and the principal fighting ships had to come back again to protect the Armada. The effect of the surprise attack, and its close-quarters ferocity, drove the Armada towards the Outer Owers shoals off Selsey Bill. Medina Sidonia was forced to signal to the Armada to change course and sail out to sea.

As the Armada headed south and east away from Selsey Bill the English were elated. It was the most welcome sight of the campaign thus far. They had headed Medina Sidonia away from the Solent and the Isle of Wight. Now the Spanish had no deep-water port available to them until they reached Flanders. The English coast was safe. It was clear for the first time that the sole objective of the enemy was to link up with Parma. Howard could now join forces with the Narrow Seas fleet led by Seymour and Winter.

The defence of England came down to this single aim: keep Parma where he was.

The next day, 26 July, Howard knighted Frobisher on board *Ark Royal*. He deserved it for his heroism and strategic foresight. John Hawkins was also knighted, his ships at last vindicated. It was a moment of respite. As ever, problems of supply began to nag. The Cinque Ports were ordered to brew beer and get it to the Navy. The fleet had expended most of its shot and powder. The coastal forts and ports had to be emptied of their stocks, which were transferred to the ships. The Lord Mayor of London was busy requisitioning private ammunition. This was a crisis of supply not just for the Navy, but for the nation. Three days of battle were enough to exhaust the country's stocks of gunpowder. Howard wrote: 'Forasmuch as our powder and shot was well wasted, the Lord Admiral thought it was not good in policy to assail them any more until their coming near unto Dover.'[2] On Friday and Saturday (26 and 27 July) 'the Spaniards went always before the English army [fleet] like sheep, during which time the justices of peace near the seacoast, The Earl of Sussex, Sir George Carey, and the captains of the forts and castles alongst the coast, sent us men, powder, shot, victuals and ships to aid and assist us'.[3]

Howard needed a decisive encounter before his powder ran out. The danger was now that the Armada would arrive off Calais, where he would find Parma's invasion flotilla awaiting him, ready to be escorted to Dover.

That was what Medina Sidonia thought as well. The reason he had not heard from Parma was that exchanging messages in a timely way between a mobile fleet and a land army was next to impossible. Getting a dispatch to Parma was complicated. He was not simply waiting on a beach. The Dutch were at sea, in cromsters, small coastal warships, which nonetheless were capable of damaging his transport barges. He had to keep his army safe from Dutch attacks, and his invasion boats were dispersed across several Low Countries ports. Part of his army had made a feint towards Zeeland, and Parma himself moved between Antwerp, Ghent and Bruges in an attempt to confuse the Dutch and the English. It worked – perhaps too well. It certainly confused Medina Sidonia.

Parma's strategy made perfect military sense. Medina Sidonia had done well to keep his fleet together and get it to Flanders. The problem was that these manoeuvres and stratagems worked independently and in complete ignorance of each other. Messengers from the Armada had to evade English and Dutch ships, then find Parma on his journeys round Flanders. Any message going back to the Armada would first have to locate it on the high seas – a task hard enough at the best of times, fraught with danger in a theatre of war.

The failure of communication was the weakest thing in the whole plan. Neither commander knew what the other needed, or even where he was, until they were almost within sight of each other. Parma wrote: 'Medina seems to believe that I should set out to meet him with my small ships, which is simply impossible. These vessels cannot run the gauntlet of warships; they cannot even withstand large waves!'[4]

And so at Calais Roads on 27 July Medina Sidonia received the crushing news that Parma would need six days to embark his army. That was six days of riding at anchor with the English Navy playing merry hell with his Armada. In an angry council of war, Recalde pointed out the danger of waiting in this exposed roadstead. It would be far safer to seek a secure anchorage in the Downs. The English fleet, now reinforced to bring its strength to 140, lay to windward; to the lee of the Armada were dangerous and unknown shoals. And because the Armada had no shallow-draught galleys, Parma's little barges would be unprotected by warships. They would be blown to pieces by the Dutch boats before they could get to the warm embrace of the Armada. It was a trap of Spain's own making.

The short distance between the Armada and the army of Flanders must have seemed like the widest stretch of water in the world.

The Spanish admiral knew what Howard would do. Fireships would be sent in to panic and disperse the Armada. Once dislodged from their positions, the Armada ships would have no choice but to drift towards the shoals. So Medina Sidonia ordered the pinnaces to shield the Armada and head off or bear the brunt of the fireships. And most importantly he sent firm orders to his captains. If a fireship got too close they were to weigh anchor (on no account must they cut their cables), then they were to take evasive action before returning to their stations.

Medina Sidonia had a technique of seeing his orders obeyed. They were delivered in writing by his sergeant majors, who each took a patache, or dispatch boat, to the ships. 'Orders were also given to them [the sergeant majors], in writing, to immediately hang any captain whose ship left her place, and they took with them the Provost Marshals and hangmen necessary for carrying out this order.'

And so on the night of 29 July the Spanish were ready as the English fireships, sailed by small crews of brave men, approached. The first ship was successfully grappled and sent clear of the main fleet, but the other seven drifted in. They did not represent much of a threat to the Armada. This was psychological warfare.

Just three years earlier, Spanish ships lashed together to form a bridge besieging Antwerp had come under attack from fireships packed with gunpowder and shrapnel, detonated by a clockwork time bomb. The explosion could be heard fifty miles away and the immediate devastation was horrifying. The earth shook like a volcano; the sky was lit up for a second before darkness closed in again. Nearby houses were toppled and people in a wide vicinity were thrown off their feet. Slabs of granite 'vomited by the flaming ship' were embedded in the earth three miles away. 'The air was filled with a rain of plough-shares, grave-stones, and marble balls, intermixed with the heads, limbs and bodies of what had been human beings ... a thousand soldiers were destroyed in a second of time; many of them torn to shreds beyond even the semblance of humanity.'[5]

The Antwerp 'hellburners' put the fear of God into the Spanish. They had been designed by the Italian engineer Frederigo Giambelli, who was now living in England. Howard knew of the hold that fireships had over the Spanish military imagination; he knew that the Spanish knew that Giambelli was in the pay of Elizabeth. And so when the fireships appeared a blind terror spread through the Armada. In fact, the fireships were eight ordinary ships hastily purchased for £5,000. There was not enough gunpowder left to turn them into hellburners.

The Spanish were not to know this. Some of the ships obeyed orders and weighed anchor or held station; most of them cut their cables and fled into the night, their anchors lost for ever in the Channel. Some ships regrouped round *San Martín*; the rest refused to obey orders and drifted eastwards towards Dunkirk.

For the first time the Armada had broken its sturdy formation. Its ships were scattered in the dark seas, its sailors crippled by fear. They were drifting towards the Dunkirk shoals, and Medina Sidonia was obliged to weigh anchor and sail east to extricate his ships from the dangers and regroup them.

Howard held off the attack till morning. At first light he was diverted from his plan to lead the Navy against Medina Sidonia's *San Martín*, and went in to attack the galleass *San Lorenzo* instead, which had foundered on the sands. It was his first serious mistake of the campaign and a terrible misjudgement. The time was perfect to inflict a major defeat upon the Spanish, for now the English fleet, which had reached its maximum strength of some 140 ships, faced *San Martín* and just five galleons. Instead it turned into a free-for-all. Howard and his ships went after the stricken *San Lorenzo*. Drake and Fenner meanwhile led the attack on *San Martín*. Drake and Fenner sailed in, firing a broadside each on the Spanish admiral. They then set about the other Spanish ships. Drake and Fenner were followed by Hawkins, then Beeston, Frobisher and other Navy ships. They were rejoined in the afternoon by Howard and *Ark Royal*.

The battle off Gravelines that morning was the fiercest of the whole campaign. For the first time the English were fighting as they desired, sailing in among the Spanish ships at close enough range that words could be exchanged between the enemies. *San Martín* took 200 hits. Some penetrated the hull at the waterline, letting in water, and the ship had to be saved by two courageous divers who repaired the damage with oakum and lead patches. The *San Mateo* was 'riddled with shot like a sieve'. Notwithstanding this attack the Armada was able to reform, with *San Martín* and other warships acting as a rearguard.

This was not a fleet action. It was a melee in which the Navy ships tried as best they could to prevent the Spanish reorganising their formation and to pick off and damage as many ships as they could. The privately owned ships kept out of the fighting. In the midst of the Spanish ships, Elizabeth's ships put up a fierce fight, but it was a series of duels, not a co-ordinated battle.

Even so, these were conditions entirely favourable to the English. Medina Sidonia needed to bring the Armada back to Parma's waiting army; the English priority was to drive the Armada east, away from Calais and towards the Flanders shoals, inflicting damage along the way. The Battle of Gravelines that day was fought over many hours in rough seas and amid a thick pall of smoke and much confusion on both sides. The purser on the hulk *San Salvador* described a moment in the conflict:

> The enemy inflicted such damage upon the galleons *San Mateo* and *San Felipe* that the latter had five guns on the starboard side and a big gun on the poop put out of action ... In view of this and seeing that his upper deck was destroyed, both his pumps broken, his rigging in shreds, and his ship almost a wreck, Don Francisco de Toledo [captain of *San Felipe*] ordered the grappling hooks to be got out, and shouted to the enemy to come to close quarters. They replied, summoning him to surrender in a fair fight; and one Englishman, standing in the maintop with sword and buckler, called out 'Good soldiers that you are, surrender to the fair

terms we offer you.' But the only answer he got was a musketball which brought him down in sight of everyone and [Don Francisco] then ordered the muskets and arquebuses to be brought into action. The enemy therefore retired, whilst our men shouted to them that they were cowards, and with opprobrious words reproached them for their want of spirit, calling them chicken ... and daring them to return to the fight.[6]

At last the English had discovered a way to engage the Armada. Hitherto Howard had been afraid to take the risk of sailing too close to the enemy formation and had stood off and fought. But after days of experimenting and observing it was clear that the Spanish guns were far inferior to the English. The heavy guns they carried could not be fired fast enough to make them tell. Recalde estimated that while the English blasted 1,000 rounds at him at Gravelines, he replied with only 300. And these were mainly shot fired from smaller guns. The meticulous inventories kept by the Spanish, and the evidence gleaned from shipwrecks off Ireland, show that while the Spanish gunners had made serious inroads into their small-shot stocks, they had not had the opportunity to use much of their heavy shot. As long as the queen's galleons could keep the weather gage they could come close enough to pound Philip's ships and veer away from the deadly small-arms fire and grappling hooks. William Winter in *Vanguard* was never more than fifty yards away and often 'within speech' of enemy ships as his men discharged 500 cannonballs from their thirty-seven guns. The *Maria Juan*, which carried twenty-four guns, was sunk by English cannonballs. *Felipe* and *Mateo* were crippled and abandoned on the shore. Many other ships were so badly damaged that they would never see Spain again. At Gravelines the English had the courage, and by now the experience, to fight at close quarters and make the best use of their technical advantages.

It was too late. Between four and five in the afternoon the Navy began to break off the attack. They had run out of ammunition. But without destroying many enemy ships, victory was theirs. Medina Sidonia needed to bring the Armada back west, because once he left the Channel it would be hard to re-enter. However the Armada had been forced along the coast of Flanders and a pilot had to warn Medina Sidonia 'that not one ship in the fleet would be saved. They were drifting towards the shallow waters of Zeeland, and nothing could be done ... only God could save them'.[7] Their only hope was to get away from the shoals and enter the North Sea.

A Spanish shipmaster recalled that this was the moment of defeat: 'by dawn we were scattered among the shoals. As we knew so little of those shallows, and they [the English] were so familiar with them, being (as it were) their homeland, they were able to profit so well from our dispersal that despite refusing to board us, and fleeing every time we attacked, yet they defeated us'.[8]

Philip's battle plans had counted on divine help. Only at dawn the day after the Battle of Gravelines were Spanish prayers answered when the wind changed and took them out into the North Sea. Medina Sidonia wanted to return to Calais to complete the job, but by now his Armada was a defeated rabble. Many of his captains refused his order to continue fighting. The south-westerly carried the Armada north, away from Parma and out of the Channel, with the English, as ever, nipping at their heels. Medina Sidonia could not now lead the Armada from the vanguard; he was forced to bring *San Martín*, damaged as she was, into the rearguard to protect his ailing fleet. Three times in the North Sea Howard's fleet formed up to attack again, but then refused to fight. As Howard admitted: 'notwithstanding that our powder and shot was well near spent, we set on a brag countenance and gave chase, as though we wanted nothing'.[9]

Howard had to return to port for want of victuals when they reached the Firth of Forth on 2 August, leaving only some pinnaces to 'dog' the Armada and report on its progress. Howard's plan was to take on more supplies at the Downs and continue the battle when Medina Sidonia returned. But things began to go terribly wrong for the English. *Ark Royal* made it to Harwich. Many of the other ships were almost wrecked off Norfolk and limped to join Howard at Harwich and later Margate. The exhausted, starving men were unfit for further action. Things got worse when the supply ships got lost trying to find the fleet.

Meanwhile Parma continued to embark his men. Throughout August there were 10,000 men on board barges at Nieuwpoort and 8,000 men at Dunkirk. Howard's council of war put their minds to Medina Sidonia's intentions. Francis Drake told the Lord Admiral that the Armada was most likely in Norway or Denmark, where they could get 'great anchors, ropes and victuals; and what the king of Spain's hot crowns will do in cold countries for mariners and men, I leave to your good lordship'. And, in his opinion, the Spanish would be eager to put right their humiliation: 'The Prince of Parma, I take him to be as a bear robbed of her whelps.'[10]

The Navy's galleons were remarkably unscathed and they were ready to fight again. But who was to man them? Few English sailors had died in battle, but from the moment they disembarked in eastern ports after eight months in service the rate of mortality soared. This was when Howard showed his virtues as a military leader. He wrote to Burghley: 'My good

Lord: Sickness and mortality begins wonderfully to grow amongst us; and it is a most pitiful sight to see, here at Margate, how the men having no place to receive them into here, die in the streets.'[11]

Howard saw to it that any building, be it barn or outhouse, was used for lodging in and around Margate, but the men had no money and there was not much food to be found. After months on their ships their clothes hung in rags from their wasted bodies. Disease swept through the fleet. It had been present on *Elizabeth Jonas* from the beginning, and she had fewer than 300 men alive of the 500 who had sailed from Plymouth. 'It would grieve any man's heart,' wrote Howard, 'to see them that have served so valiantly to die so miserably.'[12]

Burghley hardened his heart to the plight of the Navy's heroes. He was anxious to save money after so much expense. Dead sailors did not claim pay. And so the men continued to weaken and die throughout August. By the 22nd seven or eight ships were left stranded in Margate, without enough fit men to weigh their anchors to take them to Dover to defend the country. The maritime strength of England was so depleted that it represented a greater loss than a Spanish victory at sea.

'Sir,' Howard wrote to Burghley, 'for my own part I know not which way to deal with mariners to make them rest contented with sour beer, for nothing doth displease them more.'[13] The survivors were bitter and growing restless. In all 5,000 English sailors, or half the fleet's manpower, would succumb to disease. Many of the rest had to try and find their way back to their home in the West Country, and the Lord Admiral was reduced to issuing them with tickets permitting them to beg along the way. New recruits were particularly prone to the typhus and dysentery that were rife in the ships. Howard dug into his own pocket to try and relieve the distress. He was not inordinately wealthy, 'but before God, I had rather never a penny in the world than they should lack'.[14]

Burghley's callousness was vindicated when news began to come in that the Armada would not return. A bark came from Shetland reporting that some fishermen had 'described a very great fleet of monstrous great ships, to their seeing being about 100 in number'[15] sailing in a westerly direction. The east wind had continued for some days, making it impossible that the Armada would return. The Spanish chose the 'north-about' route home. It was off the coasts of Scotland and Ireland that the Armada met its doom. Many of the ships, weakened by a long campaign, battered by English cannonades and without their anchors, were driven ashore in Atlantic storms.

When news of the disaster reached him Philip was plunged into a deep spiritual crisis. Inexplicably, his God had turned against him. Philip's empire was not, after all, invincible. As for the English, not only had the realm been saved but God had clearly shown his favour. The medal commemorating the defeat of the Armada had the motto 'He blew and they were scattered'.

It appeared that God, not the Navy, deserved the credit. It was a miracle, victory by the greatest good luck. English superiority at sea had not been established; if anything, the ships and guns had fallen far short of expectations, and after the campaign England was a weaker naval power than she had been at the beginning. The Navy contemplated something of a defeat, with its manpower drastically reduced and its inherent supply problems revealed. That mood, however, would soon change.

CHAPTER 15

AFTERMATH
1588–1603

A myth was born and grew up very quickly after the summer of 1588. It is one of the most potent and important myths in English history.

The belief that England ruled – or had the right to rule – the seas around the British Isles went back into the mists of time. This much-trumpeted sovereignty over the seas had more often than not been exposed as a sham. The idea of Britain as an island set in a silver sea, defended against barbarous foreigners and standing aloof and independent from the tangled affairs of the Continent, was always dreamt about but often the reverse of the truth – the lawless waters round Britain were highways bringing invading armies, plunderers and rapacious merchants. For centuries the sea made England poor and weak, not strong and independent.

The events of 1588 appeared to change all that. The Spanish Armada had been deflected by a formidable English Navy, poor planning and the weather; it had not been defeated. But in official propaganda and the popular imagination, it was the greatest victory in English history. Memories and myths concerning the defeat of the Armada would nourish and sustain England's sense of itself for centuries.

Central to that self-definition was England as a great maritime power. England was destined to rule the waves – and national survival meant she *had* to rule them. God had spoken in 1588. It was up to the English to make good their advantage.

England's rise to power had been due in large measure to the seamanship and fighting prowess of its seafaring community. The men who crewed and commanded the ships in 1588 had learnt their skills in the rough school of private warfare in the West Indies, West Africa and the Atlantic. They were the best sailors in the world and the backbone of England's considerable strength at sea. The English Navy had emerged from nothing to become the most feared force on the water thanks to the enterprise of a generation of explorers, traders, privateers and pirates.

After the defeat of the Armada there was a high demand for private men-of-war – boom time in the docks. There were more shipwrights; they were ambitious and ever more technologically advanced. In 1582 there had been just twenty private ships of 200 tons and more; by 1597 seventy-two more had been built. And these ships travelled further and for longer than their predecessors. Although they preferred the eastern Atlantic as a hunting ground, 235 expeditions raided the West Indies. English merchants and adventurers pushed further and further in their search for trade and plunder.

The Navy Royal was strong and professional, the best-organised and handled in Europe. But, as in the days of Edward III, it was just one part of England's total strength at sea. England was becoming a major maritime power, but the source of its strength, the collaboration between Crown and people, dictated the way it fought. It meant that the fight could be taken to the Spanish all around the world and it allowed the state, poorly financed as it was, to punch far above its weight. It also imposed limitations. The English waged war as a profit-making enterprise, picking off ships and raiding colonies as and when the opportunity allowed. It was economically devastating, but it fell short of the lofty dreams of co-ordinating a systematic destruction of Spain by seizing strategic bases, blockading Iberia and capturing the treasure fleets. The Crown was too poor to undertake operations on its own. It therefore had to organise military expeditions on a joint-stock basis with commercial interests.

This meant that the wildly inflated hopes whipped up by the defeat of the Armada could never be fulfilled. In 1589 Elizabeth ordered Drake to destroy the lightly defended and half-repaired survivors of the Armada that were lying at Santander and San Sebastían. Drake set sail with six Navy ships, sixty merchantmen, sixty Dutch flyboats and twenty pinnaces. The balance was tilted far in favour of the private investors. As such strategy was pushed to one side. Drake sailed past Santander and Philip's warships were left unmolested because attacking the ships would have taken too long and returned no profit. Instead the force raided Lisbon and went off to the Azores in search of loot. The queen was furious.

John Hawkins and Martin Frobisher went in search of the *flota* in the years after 1589, with scant success. Meanwhile Spain recovered as a naval power. New galleons of over 1,000 tons were constructed immediately after the defeat of the Armada – the so-called 'Twelve Apostles'. Another twelve were commissioned straight after. Within ten years of the defeat Philip had sixty or seventy warships constructed for service in the Atlantic. That was not the only bad news for Elizabeth. In 1590 Parma campaigned in northern France and captured a string of Channel ports. While

Hawkins and Frobisher searched for the elusive *flota* in the vastness of the Atlantic the Spanish sent a fleet to Brittany. It captured the fort at Blavet, giving the Spanish control over Brest. It was the ideal place to launch an invasion of England. In 1595 Spanish ships raided the West Country.

On 28 January 1596 a lead coffin plunged into the harbour waters of Porto Bello, Panama. The last orders of Sir Francis Drake had been disobeyed; in the days before, as he lay dying of dysentery in his cabin, he had told his officers that he wished to be buried on land. His officers had suffered a gruelling, disorderly and frustrating voyage and the body of their leader was dumped into the sea as they strove to reorganise the fleet. Drake's last hurrah occurred when he was fifty-five. A few months earlier the venture's other commander, Sir John Hawkins, had died at the age of sixty-three and been buried at sea off Puerto Rico.

The English ships had left Plymouth in August 1595 to avenge the Spanish attack on the West Country. They departed with ambitious hopes of repeating the glory days when Hawkins and Drake had terrorised the West Indies and made a fortune. This time they intended to land at Nombre de Dios, capture Panama and cut off Spain's supply of silver from the Peruvian mines. The dual goal of advancing England's interests abroad and making a fresh fortune would thus be served. But Drake had been disorganised as ever, and Hawkins just as prickly. They had quarrelled about strategy from the very start. Hawkins did not want to attack the Canaries, but Drake prevailed. The disastrous attack delayed things and gave the Spanish time to reinforce Central America. The subsequent loss of one of the ships gave the game away to the Spanish. The English were repulsed at San Juan de Puerto Rico and Nombre de Dios, both of which had been forewarned of Drake and Hawkins's plan. The whole thing descended into a shambles; many men perished of disease; and the fleet returned home with a paltry haul, worth just £5,000.

Small-scale, privately funded privateering voyages did much better than grand operations that attempted to further the national interest and make a profit. In the three years following the defeat of the Armada there were 236 ships engaged in this activity and they took over 300 prizes at sea. To put this in context, over the same span of time exactly a decade earlier a handful of English private warships captured just ten Spanish ships.

Fortune favoured the opportunistic professional seaman with his eye solely on the main chance. The proliferation of predatory English ships in the Atlantic and Caribbean put the Spanish and Portuguese empires under the greatest strain they had faced. English corsairs terrorised the

Caribbean, putting a virtual stop to legitimate trade in places like Santo Domingo. Philip's revenues took a painful hit. Cuba was under virtual blockade. As the general in command of New Spain put it: 'The shameless-ness of these English ships has reached such a point that they come very close to the harbour, even pursuing the barges which bring water from a league away'.[1] The archbishop of Santo Domingo wrote in the early 1600s that 'the defence of this city now consists of its poverty' after years of English pillaging.[2]

For the earl of Essex the English effort amounted to 'idle wanderings upon the sea'. In 1596 he was ready to take the war by the scruff of its neck and weld the forces of the Crown and the mass of private shipping to become a devastating military force. Robert Devereux, the second earl of Essex, was a brilliant man, a handsome, smooth talker and an adept prac-titioner of the art of courtly love. He was a dashing soldier, who fought in the Netherlands, Ireland and Normandy. The 63-year-old Elizabeth doted upon Essex, who was half her age, craving his company and showering him with intense maternal love. Queen and courtier were already inter-twined. Essex's great-grandmother was Mary Boleyn, Elizabeth's aunt, he was a ward of Lord Burghley, and his stepfather was the earl of Leicester, the queen's great love, who died in 1588. When Essex ran away to join Drake's attack on Cadiz in 1589 it was against the queen's direct orders and she was furious, but Essex was not content to be royal favourite. He chaffed at the petty intrigues and politicking at court, desiring only to be a great military leader and a substantial statesman.

His plan was to lead an Anglo-Dutch naval and army force to Spain, where they would destroy Philip's fleet, capture a port and use it as a base to seize treasure from the New World. All this went contrary to the queen's policy, which was to disengage from continental affairs. The only way to get her backing was if the Spanish were shown to be preparing an-other Armada. Essex manipulated and distorted the evidence to show that this was likely. The Spanish raid on Cornwall in 1595 and their capture of Calais in 1596 seemed to confirm his warnings. Still Elizabeth vacillated. The expedition was cancelled in May 1596 to Essex's intense frustration. 'I know I shall never do her service,' he moaned, 'but against her will.' Finally he sailed in June, determined to carry out his plan even though Elizabeth had ordered him not to capture and hold a Spanish port.

The Anglo-Dutch fleet was led by Lord Howard. It comprised 150 ships, seventeen of which were Navy warships. They carried over 6,000 soldiers and 1,000 volunteers led by Essex. Their orders were to destroy Philip's fleet before it could be used against England or Ireland. Essex had other ideas: he was determined to capture a port and stop Spanish trade, 'whereby we shall cut his sinews and make war upon him with his own money'. Unfortunately the other commanders were not in on the plan, and in any case were duty-bound to obey the queen. Lord Admiral Howard led the fleet exceptionally well. It sailed in secrecy, as fast as possible, away from land, seizing any ship that crossed its path to prevent news reaching the Spanish. Not even the officers knew where they were bound. Only when Howard anchored off Cadiz did it become clear what the English were intending.

Bad weather prevented an immediate attack. It gave the Spanish time to bring the outgoing *flota* into Puerto Real, the inner harbour, for safety. The Spanish galleys and galleons moved to bar access to the richly laden *flota*. At five the next morning the English and Dutch warships launched their attack. Once again Howard displayed his strengths as a commander. The English ships made mincemeat of the enemy, concentrating their fire and reloading rapidly. It was a better performance than in 1588. The English guns roared out, expending most of their shot and powder in just two days' fighting. That meant up to 500 rounds fired from the largest English warships. It was a devastating rate of fire. Two Spanish galleons were captured; two more were set ablaze by their own crew to avoid the same fate.

There was no answer from the Spanish navy. English and Dutch soldiers were disembarked, captured Cadiz and set about looting. The men were noted, however, for their good treatment of civilians, particularly women and children. The next day the duke of Medina Sidonia arrived, but by then he could not prevent the English remaining at Cadiz for another fortnight, living as comfortably, it was said, 'as if we had been in Cheapside'. Howard wrote to Medina Sidonia: 'As I was entrusted with the command of my lady the Queen's Majesty in the year 1588, I suppose I may not be unknown to you ...'

The duke needed no such introduction. He knew the skills and ruthlessness of the English. And so he ordered all the Spanish ships in the inner harbour to be burnt. It amounted to thirty-two ships, which included warships and the entire *flota*.

The fires that engulfed them destroyed cargoes worth £3,500,000 – at least ten times Elizabeth's annual revenue. From a naval point of view the operation was the greatest success of the war. After two weeks the English left, having burnt Cadiz to the ground and taken two brand-new galleons and 1,200 guns. Essex was overruled: he had wanted to keep hold of Cadiz. It was an absolute disaster for Philip, but he was spared a further body blow when, to Essex's added frustration, Howard decided to obey orders rather than go in pursuit of the incoming *flota* (which carried treasures worth £4,000,000).

The fleet returned home with news of a significant victory but very little booty for the queen – although many men came back very rich. They were followed a few months later by an avenging Armada, as big as the one that had sailed in 1588. It would have found a weakened England, one that could no longer afford to mobilise a defensive fleet for any period of time. Disaster was averted when autumn storms scattered the Armada.

The queen was extremely angry that so little loot had come her way as a result of the raid on Cadiz. In 1597 Essex led a force of seventeen royal ships to capture Ferrol and use it as a base to bring back enormous wealth to Elizabeth. His fleet was forced home by storms. He sailed again, but the ships were scattered and by the time he reached Lisbon he did not have enough troops to take and hold Ferrol. Instead he decided to blockade the Iberian cost, but then abandoned this in a madcap pursuit of the *flota*. Essex was a poor admiral. He quarrelled with his second in command, Walter Raleigh, and, like every other English commander on a similar mission, completely missed the *flota*. Part of the problem was that he was desperate: he needed cash to fund another invasion of Spain. Talk about 'idle wanderings upon the sea': finding a treasure fleet in the Atlantic was pot luck. Essex was as unlucky as anyone else who tried.

The fiasco was compounded when Essex's fleet reached England. A massive Spanish Armada had put to sea to intercept him and capture Falmouth as a prelude to invasion. Essex had left England undefended. Luckily the weather came to the country's aid yet again, and storms headed the Spanish off. Essex was in disgrace, exposed as a poor naval commander and strategist. The day his fleet crept into Plymouth Howard was made earl of Nottingham, putting him second in order of precedence of the nobility. To Essex it was a sign that Elizabeth had given all the credit for the victory at Cadiz to the Lord Admiral. He felt cheated of what he saw as his major achievement and his only claim on greatness. He had lost the esteem of the queen and the respect of his peers. He would never recover. Essex's fall meant that a great force of energy that was driving England's war effort in an aggressive direction was taken away.

The poverty of the Crown and the dependence on private ships to conduct offensive operations against Spain shaped strategy. It also had an economic impact. In 1592 a joint-stock expedition with ships contributed by the queen, Raleigh, Howard, Hawkins and others had taken the gigantic Portuguese carrack *Madre de Dios* after a long fight. *Madre de Dios* was the largest ship afloat in the world, and she was homeward-bound from the East Indies. Her cargo was breathtaking. There were hundreds of pearls, over a thousand rubies and 847 diamonds. The pepper alone netted the Queen £80,000. The cargo also included valuable scents; so much was looted that when the discharged sailors left Plymouth they wafted trails of amber and musk into the countryside.

Such conspicuous successes lured thousands of men to venture to sea to join the war against Spain. They encouraged wealthy individuals and City syndicates to invest in privateering. The amount of wealth tied up in private warfare distorted the economy. Wool and cloth exports to the Low Countries were severely disrupted. A lot of City money was diverted to piracy. It allowed some to prosper in the short term, but pillaging the Spanish at sea was not more profitable than trading in a legitimate way. While privateers cruised the oceans in search of easy prey close to home, long-distance trading and colonisation were neglected. There was very little reason to engage in risky voyages to the Indian Ocean when Asian goods could be stolen at sea. The few English attempts to venture to the Pacific and Indian Ocean in the 1580s and 1590s were poorly planned and financed and as a consequence failed. By the end of the war there were plenty of ships built specially to fight and pillage. These kinds of ships gave up a lot of room to guns, so they could carry only high-value, low-volume luxury goods looted on the high seas. As such they were un-suited for long-distance bulk trade. A realisation in the late 1590s that the war might not last for ever encouraged a number of merchants, who had grown rich on privateering and the Levant trade, to found the East India Company in 1600 to insure themselves against the risk of peace breaking out.

When James VI of Scotland came to the English throne as James I in 1603 he ended the long, unwinnable war with Spain. His accession marked an important moment in the history of Britain and maritime his-tory. Before 1066 there had been periods when Anglo-Saxon or Viking kings had achieved supremacy in the British Isles by ruthless displays of naval power. The Norman Conquest diverted England's attention to con-tinental Europe and away from hegemony of the islands. It left England exposed on its northern and western flanks and hampered its potential as a serious maritime power. In 1603 the picture was very different because one man now sat on the thrones of England, Scotland and Ireland.

Navy ships now flew a new flag – the Union Jack, which combined the English cross of St George and the Scottish saltire. That meant that one major part of the Navy's role – guarding England's back door from

Scottish attack – had come to an end. Up until the coming of the Stuarts the English could never truly think of themselves as an island people because they shared their landmass with an inveterate enemy. But now England was without question the dominant power in its archipelago. This hardened the island mentality and freed its ambitions to become a global, rather than a regional power.

James was a unifier, but also a man committed to peace. That too had a major impact on England's future. After 1604 pugnacious seafarers and City investors had to seek their fortunes in legitimate trade and colonisation. It was a painful adjustment. While England had been plundering the wealth of the world from Spanish ships, other nations had made giant strides in world trade, leaving the English trailing in their wake.

Peace between England and Spain brings this part of Britain's naval history to a close. From the age of Alfred the Great to that of Elizabeth, England's fortunes at sea varied from abject weakness to stunning success. The country had risen to greatness on the waves in a few short years at the end of the sixteenth century by harnessing the lawlessness of the seas – a lawlessness that had, for most of England's existence, more commonly brought terrible dangers. Competing on the anarchic waves had bred tough, skilled and resourceful generations of seafarers, men who learned the arts of naval warfare by barging into other people's trades and colonies. The Crown's partnership with these sailors gave the country a taste of independence and power.

The defeat of the Armada in 1588 was the crowning moment in English naval history, not so much for what happened but for what it represented. The English came to identify themselves with the sea and to believe in their vocation to rule it. National destiny and the Navy became intertwined. The victory over the Armada had a profound impact on the national character.

The country took its Navy to its heart. It represented England's defiance of foreign superpowers. In 1599 news came of a new Armada being assembled at Corunna. It was like 1588 all over again, with the same level of panic. The Navy raced to get a fleet together at Plymouth. Although in the end the Spanish diverted to take on the rebellious Dutch, the Navy Board had shown how professional and formidable English defences were in mobilising eighteen warships in twelve days. It was a signal to foreign powers that the walls of England were stoutly defended. The Navy was a highly organised fighting force, capable of providing continuous defence for the country. The compact fleet of powerful warships depended upon the infrastructure of shipwrights, dockyards, storehouses, suppliers and victuallers that had been built up over the years.

There was no other navy like it in the world. William Monson wrote of the speedy mobilisation in 1599 that 'the Queen was never more dreaded abroad for anything she ever did'.[3]

II
STATE NAVY
1603–1748

INTRODUCTION

A boy looked down from above Portsmouth and glimpsed the sea for the first time. The boy in question, William Cobbett, had an additional thrill that day. 'I had heard of the wooden walls of Old England: I had formed my ideas of a ship, and of a fleet; but what I now beheld, so far surpassed what I had ever been able to form a conception of, that I stood lost between astonishment and admiration.'

Cobbett was looking at the British fleet riding at anchor at Spithead in all its glory. His memories were from 1783, but they express an emotional attachment to the Navy held by Britons through the ages. Cobbett wrote that he had been fed, like every other British boy, on the stories of famous admirals and sailors. 'The sight of the fleet brought all these into my mind in confused order, it is true, but with irresistible force. My heart was inflated with national pride. The sailors were my countrymen; the fleet belonged to my country, and surely I had my part in it, and in all its honours.'

That sense of ownership and belonging seems strange to us now. The Navy, and the sea, have retreated to a small corner of our collective consciousness. It is hard for us now to fully comprehend the extent to which the Royal Navy was once at the heart of Britain's political, economic and cultural life. This next part of the story is about the emergence of the Navy into public life in the seventeenth and eighteenth centuries. It tells how the British fell in love with their Navy.

Key to that love affair was the image of the ship. Until the twentieth century the ship was the most technologically advanced system that the human mind had created. But it was not just a highly sophisticated weapon; it was a thing of seductive splendour, perhaps the most beautiful engine of war ever invented.

A pamphleteer at the start of the eighteenth century remarked that not even a humble frigate or sloop could be launched without paintings and engravings of it being disseminated around the country. There is a faint echo of that passion today: a painting of a wooden ship of the line is still the British public's favourite painting. J. M. W. Turner's *Fighting Temeraire* heads a mighty gallery of maritime art.

The seductive power of a wooden warship consists in a paradox; it looks beautifully simple yet at the same time wondrously complex. The skill of the maritime artist – like the skill of a good ship's company – is to transform what the landlubber knows in his heart to be inordinate complexity into grace and flow. The ship's progress through the water or into the storm of battle represents the sum total of thousands of unseen individuals, from the shipwrights who designed her and the labourers who toiled on her, to the crew who haul on ropes and the officers who direct the myriad cogs that work the great machine.

Like most key developments in the seventeenth century the British pilfered the tradition of maritime art from the Dutch. The epic paintings of the Anglo-Dutch wars of the mid- to late seventeenth century, with their big skies, wind-whipped flags, smoke billowing from broadsides and fairy-tale ships, were the works of Dutch artists, the most important and prolific of whom were Willem van de Velde and his son of the same name. Between them they depicted the key moments of the wars. Van de Velde the Elder was the official Dutch artist during the Second Dutch War (1665–67). He sketched the battles as they were happening from Dutch warships; later some of them became the great canvases we know today. His series of sketches of the marathon Four Days' Battle of 1666 are blow-by-blow accounts.

The van de Veldes moved to Greenwich in 1673, where they received the patronage of Charles II, the duke of York and the nobility. Maritime art entered English culture. The Dutch father and son produced paintings of the great battles fought by the Royal Navy. Willem the Younger also made hundreds of portrait sketches of English warships, bequeathing a rich database of visual evidence about the Stuart Navy. Both artists were able to capture the technical details of ships and their complicated rigging, not to say the glittering gold of their stern decorations.

Never has war looked so beautiful. Sea battles took on the quality of earth-shattering world events, epic contests that would grace the history books on equal terms with the battles of classical times. British and Dutch warships looked stately and impossibly grand.

And this is why art mattered in the history of the Royal Navy. It had the power to elevate naval contests to heroic status. The Navy had become a service fit for a prince or a peer; the ships themselves were aristocratic in their bearing. The patronage given to the van de Veldes and native artists was a sure sign of the status the Navy now had in British life. Great moments in battle were commemorated, but so too were individual ships going about their business. Even apparently inconsequential skirmishes were transformed by artists into momentous events. This was clearly a nation that was smitten with its maritime traditions and contemporary Navy.

Nor was it just the aristocratic patron and his cronies who enjoyed the spectacle. The work of maritime painters such as Peter Monamy (1681–1749) was exhibited at Vauxhall Pleasure Gardens to entertain the London crowds. Through the eighteenth century and into the nineteenth, paintings of naval battles and officers captured the public imagination. The canvases of (among others) H. Vane, John Cleveley (1712–77), Nicholas Pocock (1740–1821), Thomas Buttersworth (1768–1842), J. M. W. Turner (1775–1851) and Clarkson Stanfield (1793–1867) popularised and perfected the genre.* The depiction of ships and battles helped create a truly national culture, with the Navy at its centre. The ships became the physical representation of national prestige and self-confidence.

A warship cost a fortune to build; each ship took a slice out of the country's budget. The battleships, frigates, sloops and yachts of the Royal Navy were national assets, prized and cherished by the people. The physical beauty of the vessels and the art that they spawned from the late seventeenth century helped rivet public attention. These, after all, were ships that they had paid for. Art brought them close to the action. Like Cobbett, people felt that they were in some way bound up with the Navy. That was good public relations, but it was better politics, as the delicious cocktail of romance and patriotism sweetened the pill for taxpayers who funded the service.

On canvas, even in the heat of battle, the ships remain stately. Indeed a dismasted ship with a tangle of rigging and a vast canvas sail riddled with holes draped over it still looks grand when rendered by an artist with the power of Turner. Very few works of marine art before the nineteenth century spare much attention on the horrors of battle or the conditions in which the sailors lived and worked. Reality would have ruined the illusion. The public wanted romance, and they got it. The stirring paintings put the Navy at the very centre of national life. And public enthusiasm and affection filled the Navy's sails.

* Pocock, Buttersworth and Stanfield all served in the Navy.

PART 5: FLOUNDERING

CHAPTER 16

FALLEN COLOSSUS
1603–1628

I know not any enemy so terrible as want of money.

Viscount Conway, 1640

Sir John Coke, the Secretary of State, sat in despair in an inn in Portsmouth. It was, he said, more like being in a 'hospital amongst multitudes of sick men'[1] than an improvised military headquarters. From this stinking, overcrowded, miserable tavern in the summer of 1628 he was trying, almost single-handedly, to launch the fleet to attack France.

Many of the sailors had not been paid for months, even years, and they were gnawed by fears for their families. These starving men were selling their ships' provisions, so desperate were they for money. Ships lay idle for want of repairs; men began to mutiny; supply ships were captured by pirates. The Navy was on the point of disintegration. Illness swept uncontrolled through the raggedy fleet. One captain said of his crew that 'their toes and feet miserably rot and fall away piecemeal'.[2] Every time Coke made progress, a fresh regiment of disasters sprang up; 'the longer I stay here,' he moaned, 'I shall every day see the fleet and voyage go further backward.'[3]

England had been the pre-eminent naval power at the beginning of the century. By the 1620s its decline was obvious. The fleet arrived home on 12 November, having achieved nothing and cost a fortune. Two weeks later six Spanish galleons and thirteen ships containing gold and treasure were escorted under guard into Falmouth. It was the Spanish *flota* – which had defied, Drake, Hawkins and countless other heroes – captured at long last.

That it was a Dutch admiral, Piet Heyn, who had pulled off the feat only served to show which way the tide was flowing. The Dutch had spread their sea power around the world, and they made a mockery of England's claims to sovereignty over the British seas. The Spanish were resurgent as a maritime nation. The French, so long hampered by civil war, challenged England's naval pretensions.

Added to that, the coasts, ports and even estuaries of England were being harried by a deadly new threat. Pirates from North Africa – the Barbary Coast as it was known – seized English ships and raided ports, capturing men and boys to be sold into slavery.

Although the sight of foreign sea rovers raiding English coastal towns and carrying away its folk was not unknown, it seemed to belong to history. Now it had made a comeback, as vicious as in the days of the Vikings. Sailors rioted in the streets of London and mobbed ministers, demanding years' worth of pay still owed to them for service in the Navy. A procession of keening women dogged Charles I's court, the wives of men enslaved by African pirates, begging for their king's help.

England had fallen a long way from the glorious days of Good Queen Bess; the myth of 1588 was a distant memory. Back then English seafarers made the world tremble; now the country could hardly raise a naval force and it was the helpless victim of a new generation of pirates. What had gone so wrong?

No one knew more about the reduced state of the Navy than Sir John Coke. Twenty years before, back in the last days of Queen Elizabeth, he had served as deputy to the Treasurer of the Navy Board. Very quickly he saw that there was something badly wrong with the Navy, even in its years of pomp. The Lord High Admiral, Lord Nottingham (the victor of the Armada), was in partnership with the Surveyor of the Navy, John Trevor. Anyone who wanted a job or a contract – down to the humblest workman – had to pay them a hefty bribe. In order to justify this 'investment' those who worked in the dockyards found ways to enrich themselves. They sold naval stores and routinely overcharged the Treasury. Trevor was a dab hand at this. The best timber purchased in Norway or collected from the royal forests was sold at favourable prices to Trevor's business partners. The inferior, less desirable timber left over was then sold to the Navy at exorbitant prices.

Officers in the Navy filled their pockets by claiming pay and victual allowances for a full complement of sailors when their ships sailed at 70 per cent capacity. The phantom 30 per cent of men drew what was called 'dead pay' and victual allowances, money that went straight into the pockets of the captain and his cronies.

Coke believed that the only answer was to have Nottingham dismissed. He hoped that the new king, James I, would support him when his eyes were opened to the sewer of corruption. Like many a whistleblower, it was Coke who was thrown out.

Nottingham and Trevor got a new Treasurer, Robert Mansell, an unpleasant, forceful character. He was Nottingham and Trevor's tool for closing their grasp on the Navy. Money flowed from the Treasury to the Navy and into the pockets of Nottingham, Trevor and Mansell. This triumvirate survived an official inquiry in 1608, even though all their crimes became public knowledge.

It was accepted that servants of the Crown used their office for self-enrichment. Members of the Navy Board had always blurred the lines between state and private business, striking bargains with contractors and making a profit with every transaction. It was tolerable while the naval administration provided the nation's defence, but now, as the Venetian ambassador noted, the ships were mainly 'old and rotten, and barely fit for service'.

Just as the Commission began its work, the keel was laid at Woolwich by the master shipwright Phineas Pett for the largest warship yet built – the *Prince Royal*. Reports were not encouraging. Other shipwrights alleged that Pett was making money by billing the Treasury for the best materials but using cheap unseasoned timber. James travelled to Woolwich in 1610 to see *Prince Royal*. The sight that greeted him was breathtaking. The new warship was gigantic at 1,200 tons burden. Even more impressively, she was the first warship to have guns mounted on three tiers of continuous deck. She represented a move away from the nimble galleons of Elizabeth's reign in favour of prestige warships designed to overawe foreign powers.

James went aboard *Prince Royal* and 'spent almost two hours in great content in surveying the ship, both within and without'. The king was no expert on ships. *Prince Royal* cost £20,000 to build. Just eleven years later the Navy needed £500 just to get her afloat and £6,000, or the cost of a new warship, to make her serviceable.

In 1615 the Venetian ambassador journeyed to the Thames, where he saw '24 first-raters, each like a fallen colossus, shut up in a ditch of stagnant water, disarmed and abandoned, a prey to the rage and injuries of the weather'.[4] There was nothing new in the state's largest ships being kept in 'ordinary', or mothballed, during peacetime, but in the first two decades of the seventeenth century they were left to rot at their moorings.

It was not just the state of the ships that had weakened the Navy. King James detested war. And in any case conflict was unlikely: Scotland was no longer a threat to England; the Dutch had wrested de facto independence from Spain, giving England security across the Narrow Seas for once; and France was torn apart by civil war in her maritime regions. In this weak piping time of peace the Navy was left to its own devices, with neither the pressure nor even the rumour of war to sharpen its reflexes, no enemy – notional or real – against which to measure itself and no leader inspired enough to purge it of evil and hone it for use.

James's hatred of war was matched by his horror of piracy. It disrupted the peaceful intercourse and concord of nations, he believed; it was deeply immoral and dangerously destabilising. When the Venetian ambassador alleged that Nottingham was helping pirates James began to display 'extreme impatience, twisting his body, striking his hands together, and tapping with his feet'. His first years on the throne saw a flurry of proclamations aimed against the sea rover. In 1608 nineteen pirates were hanged in a row at Wapping, and many others were punished or compelled to serve in the Navy throughout his reign.

If the Navy had been used to further James's campaign against piracy things might have been different, but Nottingham was on the wrong side. He owned privateering ships, and under his control the Navy's fight against piracy was half-hearted.

Many English pirates switched their operations to places like Algiers, Tunis and Sallee (near modern-day Rabat, on the Atlantic coast of Morocco). They brought with them tactics long honed in English waters. The Newfoundland fishing fleet came under attack, as did the City's Levant Company, which traded as far as Aleppo. Piracy was spreading into home waters as well. James had tried to deal directly with the Barbary regencies in North Africa, using diplomacy to suppress the worst excesses of pirates. In 1617, however, there were proposals afoot for an international effort to deal directly with the Algerine pirates.

King James at last confronted the reality of years of neglecting the Royal Navy. It was incapable of action.

The inquiry held into the Navy in 1618, unlike previous attempts, had teeth. It was not simply that the king had realised that the Navy had slipped into decrepitude. There was a new mood for reform. The courtier George Villiers had captivated James and had risen to prominence as marquis of Buckingham and a Privy Councillor. Buckingham was eager to do some good, to show himself a statesman as well as a good-looking young favourite. He believed that he could mend the tense relationship between king and people. The profligate court and wasteful departments had to be reined in. The Navy was next on the list.

The inquiry found that the Royal Navy consisted of forty-one vessels, of which twelve were completely unserviceable and twenty-three in need of major repairs. The report of the Commission gave the accounts of the Navy's expenditures during the previous years, concluding acidly: 'So the whole yearly charge of his Majesty's navy that could not keep it from decay is ... £53,004'.[5]

In 1618 Buckingham became Lord High Admiral. The Commission showed how it could reduce naval expenditure from £53,000 a year to £30,000 while restoring the Navy to operational strength. Out went the Navy Board that had milked the Navy for its own profit. In came a commission of twelve officials. It was headed by John Coke, the man whose warning about the state of the Navy had been ignored over a decade before.

Coke's priority was to build a Navy suitable for the times – one that befitted a nation that had been at peace for fourteen years. The Commission committed itself to repairing the ships that could be salvaged and to building ten new large ships. The emphasis was on a cheap, prestigious Navy, not a workaday one. It would exist as a national asset, capable of being mothballed for long periods of time, the mere fact of its existence enough to cow other nations and scare away pirates. As ever, the private shipping of the realm would be pressed to fill the gaps.

But just as the Navy was being reconstructed the international situation changed.

James I died in 1625. His son Charles, egged on by Buckingham, was determined to be a great warlike king. That meant using the country's beloved Navy to win glory and immortality. In the year before James died parliament showed itself eager to revive Elizabethan glories in a war against Spain. It dreamed of a return to the days of Gloriana. Private warships would pick the Spanish empire to its bones, while the Navy secured home waters.

But parliament was horrified when it heard Buckingham's proposals. For a start he proposed to take personal control of the war. MPs did not believe the courtier was cut out to be a military leader. They detested his strategy. Buckingham wanted to take the Navy to Spain, secure a port and capture the legendary *flota*. Members of parliament questioned the state of the Navy. There were loud complaints that the Narrow Seas had been left unprotected, allowing pirates from Dunkirk and the Barbary states to pillage English merchant ships, fishing fleets and ports. An MP from Plymouth complained 'that the King's ships do nothing, going up and down feasting in every good port'.

The type of war most MPs had in mind was a kind of fantasy of an Elizabethan campaign. Captured Spanish treasure would flow into English coffers and the taxpayer need not be bothered. But the reality was that the costs of war had rocketed. There was uproar among MPs when they heard the bill. Coke told parliament that the Crown had already spent £280,000 on military preparations and needed another £293,000 for the expedition. Parliament was not prepared to lavish money on a war it neither approved of nor could control. 'This fleet must then proceed whatsoever it shall cost,'[6] Coke told them. Parliament called his bluff and voted a paltry £160,000.

Coke pressed ahead, grimly determined to equip a war fleet with dribs and drabs of money. Only with great difficulty and expense was the fleet victualled. Once that happened, funds were released to purchase ammunition. While this was being done, the fleet consumed its food and beer and a fresh search for supplies had to begin.

Captains on the ships complained of the 'beggarliness' of the fleet.[7] The commander of the expedition, Sir Edward Cecil, wrote that 'more ignorant captains and officers can hardly be found' and said that the sailors were 'so stupefied that punish them or beat them they will scarce stir'.[8] His fleet consisted of fourteen royal ships, thirty merchant ships, forty Newcastle colliers, and twenty Dutch ships.

It set sail in October, far too late in the year, and after so much fuss and palaver that the Spanish knew it was coming. But things had gone too far and cost too much to stop.

Coke looked on with relief as his fleet left Plymouth on 5 October 1625, even though he had to order the last fourteen reluctant merchant ships 'upon pain of death to weigh anchor'.[9] But a day later the Navy returned, to Coke's utter dismay. Cecil was worried about the state of the ships and their ability to weather autumn gales. Coke was tart in his reply: 'wars require hazard ... if the safety of your ships had been most respected, the way had been to have kept them at Chatham'.[10] Perhaps it would have been better if they had. When Cecil set out again he still had no definite strategy.

The expedition bungled a raid on Cadiz and failed to locate the *flota*. The ill-fated adventure merely revealed how weak the Navy was. English monarchs had always relied upon the consent of the people and the enthusiasm of the seafaring community to wage war. When that broke down, as it so plainly had in 1625, the result was chaos. When he tried to capture Cadiz Cecil found the masters of the private ships reluctant to put their employers' ships in danger; he had to cudgel them to do his bidding. It was a far cry from the blood-curdling enthusiasm evinced by mariners little more than a quarter-century before.

The other problem was that after three decades of peace there were few people able to manage the logistics for a massive amphibious landing.

When the troops were ready to be landed it was found that the ships had been stowed without thought to military requirements. The ladders were only found at the last minute; the grenades could not be located at all. Food and beer ran out; illness spread through the fleet; and the leaky ships performed badly. Sailors died in the streets when they finally disembarked from their rotten ships; the rest sought a way home, emaciated, stinking and barely covered by their rags. It was poor value for half a million pounds.

Sir John Coke warned Buckingham that the Cadiz fleet had to be paid off before a new one could be raised. If this was not done disaster would strike and 'expose all our actions to the scorn of the world'.[11] But Buckingham was already planning another invasion of Spain.

Parliament fumed. The Cadiz disaster was a blow to national pride. Sir John Eliot, MP and vice admiral of Devon, saw with his own eyes the state of the fleet on its return from Cadiz and the wasted state of the sailors. That sight stayed with him. He told parliament: 'our honour is ruined, our ships are sunk, our men perished, not by the sword, not by an enemy, not by chance, but ... by those we trust'.[12] But there were plenty of other complaints. The Narrows had been left unguarded because there was no money to procure provisions. Piracy was worse than ever.

If Buckingham was removed and punished, parliament said, it would grant Charles money. Charles chose to dissolve parliament. In 1627 he ordered a forced loan from his subjects.

Even as parliament was attacking Buckingham rumours abounded that a Spanish Armada greater than that of 1588 was being prepared. When a traditional ship levy from the ports was ordered, rather than rush to defend their country the local authorities pleaded that they had been ruined by the disruption to trade caused by the war. The Navy Commissioners at Portsmouth simply could not procure any food. The Victualler was buying what he could on his own credit. As he was preparing ships to meet the Spanish Armada, the men began to mutiny, planning to march to London to petition Charles for eighteen months' worth of pay. When the officers urged them to stay the sailors replied that 'their wives and children were like to starve at home and themselves to perish abroad for want of clothes and other necessaries'.[13]

In August Buckingham's coach was halted by a mob of sailors who would not let him continue till he promised to pay them. A couple of months later the mob smashed his coach to pieces.

The fleet led by Lords Willoughby and Denbigh was intended to sail once again to capture the *flota*. Throughout a summer of chaos and repeated mutinies, supplies were assembled at Portsmouth. But there was no co-ordination within the Navy. When the Victualler managed to start supplying the fleet it was found that the ships lacked anchors, rigging, sails and other vital equipment. The Victualler then had to find more food while the fleet waited for its equipment.

When Buckingham asked the Navy Commissioners why these were not ready he was told that they would get the job done only by 'forcing men to work with threatening, having no money to pay them'.[14] Willoughby had to sail in September without fireships and pinnaces. Once again, it was a case of getting the fleet to sea at all costs, in hope rather any anticipation of success. Rear Admiral John Pennington wrote to Buckingham's secretary, Edward Nicholas: 'I must confess I have no hope of the voyage, the time of year being so far spent and we being victualled but for ten weeks'. Everyone shared this view. The Navy met storms in the Bay of Biscay and turned back.

News reached the Privy Council of a new threat. Cardinal Richelieu had purchased the office of Admiral of France. His plan was to build up the French navy and crush the Huguenot rebellion in La Rochelle. He purchased twelve warships in Amsterdam, which would be used, Charles's Council said, 'for the usurping of an absolute or equal dominion with His Majesty upon the British Ocean, to the great prejudice of His Majesty's regality and the ancient inheritance of his imperial crown'.[15]

This was a real threat. But could the Navy counter it after two financially crippling sallies against Spain? The Navy had to fall back on its traditional source of power. The Council demanded twenty ships from the City of London.

At the beginning of September the ships should have been in Portsmouth. A month later the City told the Council that the ships were still not ready. They were to serve for three months, and when they did set sail the City was eager that they eat a massive chunk out of the allotted time. It took them a month to get to the mouth of the Thames.

Pennington was waiting for them at the Downs. He was shocked at what he saw. The crews consisted of 'landsmen and boys who are able to do little service'.[16] The ships were 'very mean things', poorly armed, with only enough gunpowder for a two-hour fight. Pennington's job was to search for and destroy Richelieu's new ships. Already the London fleet was hinting that its time was nearly up; the men, and even the officers, were mutinous.

Pennington led the London fleet across the Channel to search for the French ships. On 14 January he discovered them at St Malo. But the

Londoners said their time had expired and they returned home without engaging the enemy.

This fresh debacle represented a turning point in naval history. Since the days of Æthelred at least, English naval power had relied on levying private shipping. Now it was clear that a divergence had taken place between the Royal Navy and the merchant marine. Private shipping was no longer willing or able to serve in naval wars. There were a number of reasons for this. Since the heyday of the collaboration in the late sixteenth century ships had become more specialised. The large warships favoured by the Stuarts were very different from ships designed for trade. The system of bounties instituted by Henry VII, which paid money to shipowners who built large ships suited for war, had been abandoned in 1618.

But more importantly, the nature of war at sea had changed. It no longer offered the chance of mutual profit for Crown and people. Even the anarchy unleashed on the seas by war no longer enticed traders as it had done for centuries: the greater value of trade meant that shippers had more to lose than to gain. Charles's wars were unpopular with parliament, people and merchants. Private owners resisted service, and when it was forced upon them they undermined operations.

The dawning realisation that merchant auxiliaries were no longer up to the job increased the burden on the Crown to defend the realm. In an era of financial and constitutional crisis this was becoming a serious challenge.

In the early part of 1627 Pennington swept the Channel, capturing prizes worth £128,600. This windfall helped Buckingham to mount his campaign for the summer: a naval operation to aid the Huguenot rebellion at La Rochelle. Once again the naval administration struggled to equip a fleet and the ports refused to send ships. In February a mob of unpaid sailors rampaged through London and held a rally at Tower Hill, where they resolved to cut off Buckingham's head.

Buckingham pressed on in the face of a supply and manning crisis. The fleet that arrived off La Rochelle in July 1627 was one of the largest in English history. It had set sail with the expenditure of a large amount of political capital: Charles's detested Forced Loan.

Buckingham's plan was to capture the Île de Ré, off La Rochelle. The island would be used as a base controlling the sea approach to the city. The French Protestants would rebel, thereby tying up the French army.

Things got off to a bad start. Once again the amphibious operation was botched. The men did not want to get into the boats; Buckingham was reduced to wielding a cudgel, 'beating some and threatening others' until they boarded.

It took three days to disembark the men. They were the rawest of recruits: once on land they needed to be trained. While the men were given the rudiments of soldiering, the French hunkered down in the citadel. Buckingham marched his men across the island to besiege it, but the chief engineer had been killed during the botched landing and no one knew how to besiege a fort. There were only five heavy guns anyway. Buckingham settled down for a long siege and sent to England for reinforcements and supplies. In the meantime, he trusted to the Navy to blockade the French garrison.

The fiascos robbed the English of the vital element of surprise. That forced Buckingham into a war of attrition – exactly the kind of operation the English could least sustain. The supply lines broke down. The Navy could not prevent the French from breaking the blockade with small boats one September night, bringing food to a citadel that had been on the point of surrender. In October the French managed to reinforce the island with 4,000 men, easily outsailing the English Navy.

Buckingham now had to take the citadel or face defeat. When the ladders thudded against the thick walls of the citadel the discovery was made that they were too short. The game was up.

Retreat turned into rout. As the men fled along a thin causeway to their ships on the other side of the island the French attacked. Rout turned into slaughter. Buckingham returned with 3,000 men from an army of 8,000.

That was the background to the disasters of 1628, with which this chapter began. After the defeat at the Île de Ré Buckingham was detested even more by sailors, soldiers, parliamentarians and the public. Yet still he determined on relieving La Rochelle and winning glory. Parliament was ranged against him, hostile as ever; unpaid sailors rioted outside York House, his London home, threatening to dismantle it brick by brick.

On the other side of town, in Fleet Lane, a young man named John Felton slipped into depression. Today it would be called post-traumatic stress disorder. He had joined the Cadiz expedition and at Île de Ré he had been in the midst of the carnage. When he slept he dreamed of the horror he had seen. When he was awake he said little, but read much. Once of the things he studied was parliament's Remonstrance against Buckingham.

On 22 August Buckingham arrived at Portsmouth to take command of the fleet. Once there he was obliged to herd a mass of mutinous sailors back onto their ships at the head of a troop of cavalry. That night he lodged at the Greyhound Inn. The next morning, as the Lord Admiral made his way through a throng of officers he stopped to greet one of his colonels. The colonel bowed. Felton lunged over the inclined body of the officer, plunging his dagger into Buckingham's chest. Later he said that reading parliament's Remonstrance had convinced him that by 'killing the Duke he should do his country great service'.

It did not stop the expedition from sailing. By then it was too late. As Charles's Navy hovered off La Rochelle, wondering what to do, the starving inhabitants began to negotiate surrender. Charles sent orders to attack the French at all costs. On the third attempt to break through the powerful blockade the ships veered off: 'the sailors were cowed by the batteries on shore, and no good was done'. La Rochelle fell to Louis XIII. It was a disaster for England, for it gave the French full control of their seaboard.

England was reduced to a laughing stock as a naval power. 'Such a rotten, miserable fleet set out to sea no man ever saw,' said one witness. 'Our enemies seeing it may scoff at our nation.'[17]

The truth was that Charles could not afford war. England was not the power it had been in the 1590s. Parliament refused to co-operate in foolhardy ventures. The private shipowners of the realm were not prepared to risk costly merchant ships any more. And worse still, the mariners of England had been treated like dirt. A captain in the Channel Fleet complained: 'Foul winter weather, wasted bodies, and empty bellies make the men voice the king's service worse than a galley slave.'

Without the consent of his seafarers and merchants Charles could not mount offensive operations. Yet he tried again and again in the face of repeated disaster and with empty coffers. Why? Perhaps it was because England's naval heritage carried with it a certain magic. Charles and Buckingham expected great things of the Navy. It blinded them to its administrative weakness. It also blinded them to the sort of Navy they had.

The Navy reconstructed by Coke after 1618 was in essence defensive, completely unsuited to operating far from home for long periods. It was designed with economy in mind and relied on private shipping taking up the strain. In the 1620s there was a fatal mismatch between strategy and capability.

There was no glory in having a defensive Navy, but such a maritime force would have reflected England's weakness and poverty; it could have protected merchant shipping and defended the seas against pirates. It has been estimated that between 1622 and 1642 300 ships and more than 7,000 people were captured by pirates from North Africa. That was not the only source of danger.[18] In 1627 alone the Dunkirk pirates took 150

Dutch and English ships; the next year they took 245. The defence of home waters was subordinated to vainglorious dreams.

The result was that England became vulnerable to the swarms of pirates from North Africa. The Navy was hardly in a state to defend the coast. It was a bitter draught to swallow for a country that had come to define itself as a maritime superpower. The reality was that normal service had been resumed after the dizzy heights of 1588: England was a third-rate naval power, destined to be buffeted by waves of pirates and subordinated to the great naval powers of Europe. As so often in English history, the sea washed danger onto the land. In Charles I's time this meant instability caused by rampaging sailors, resistant taxpayers and truculent parliaments.

The Navy tried its utmost on limited resources. An exasperated Navy official assured Edward Nicholas, the secretary to the Admiralty: 'All shall be done that can be done without the earthly first mover – money, money, money.'

CHAPTER 17

SOVEREIGN OF THE SEAS
1629–1642

It is not our conquests, but our commerce, it is not our swords, but our sails, that first spread the English name in Barbary, and thence came into Turkey, Armenia, Moscovia, Arabia, Persia, India, China, and indeed over and about the world.

Lewis Roberts, *Treasure of Traffic*, 1641

On 8 September 1639 a Spanish Armada carrying 24,000 troops entered the Downs. The Armada of 1588 had failed to reach this most sensitive and strategically vital of English waters.

The Armada was not sent against England, however. Its destination was Flanders, where it was to relieve the Spanish army. It had been chased into the English anchorage by a small but powerful Dutch fleet. Throughout October the Dutch admirals Maarten Tromp and Witte de With blockaded the Armada in the Downs, reinforcing their fleet with so many ships that the Spanish grumbled that it must rain ships in Holland. Eventually, on 11 October, the Dutch attacked.

Charles I was neutral in the war between the Dutch and the Spanish. A squadron under Admiral Sir John Pennington was in the Downs, but it was unable to stop foreign ships entering English waters, let alone to enforce English neutrality. Pennington was an experienced naval commander, long used to making the best of impossible demands from his Stuart masters. His job in 1639, before the Spanish appeared in the Downs, was to enforce England's sovereignty against the Dutch, who had been searching English ships with impunity at sea and even in their home ports.

On 11 October it was Pennington's duty to protect the Spanish once Tromp launched his attack. But he could not get to windward of the Dutch on the morning of the battle. Indeed Tromp sent de With with a force of thirty ships to head off the Royal Navy. The English sailors on their ships and the large crowd of gawkers gathered on the shore could only watch as Tromp brilliantly used the prevailing winds and caught the

Spanish in a trap. The Dutch entered the Downs from the south with the wind behind them. The only way of escape was to the north-east, through the Gull Stream. This is a narrow, shallow, dangerous channel, subject to constant alteration in the shifting sandbanks and shoal patches. Large ships have to take their time leaving. The Spanish could not get out before the Dutch were upon them. They were comprehensively defeated. 'Kill them! Kill them!'[1] shouted the English sailors in encouragement when Tromp's ships opened fire on the old enemy.

There was little Pennington could do in such a situation. He later claimed he had chased the Dutch out of the Downs. It was bravado familiar to many a schoolboy; in reality the Dutch were pursuing the remnants of the Armada, blithely unconcerned about the English huffing and puffing behind them. Pennington did manage to capture two Dutch vessels, but he had to return them with the laughable excuse that 'they were no considerable satisfaction for his majesty for the affront done unto him'.

In reality the Royal Navy was cowed by the best navy in the world, which was lying in English waters basking in one of the greatest victories at sea. Pennington did not dare keep those ships. The incident blew apart an idea that had grown throughout the 1630s that England had recovered her strength at sea.

If in the 1620s England had fatally overreached herself, all but wrecking the Navy in the process, in the next decade Charles took a more realistic view of his sea forces. Now he would stay out of ruinously expensive wars, using a rejuvenated Royal Navy to gain control of the seas around Britain. The naval decline of his father's reign showed that warships could not be mothballed without cost. The reformed state Navy would have to be used, even in peacetime, so that officers and sailors kept up to scratch and the ships remained serviceable.

Sir John Coke was heartened in 1630 when Charles asked for the Navy's accounts from the previous year, hoping it was the beginning of 'better government in sea affairs'.[2] Charles, and officials such as Coke and Edward Nicholas, were convinced by painful experience that the Navy had to be re-established on a new footing, radically different from everything that had gone before.

What was clear was that England's rivals were developing state navies, very different from the naval institutions familiar from the past. In a speech to the Privy Council, Sir John Coke told the councillors and the king that a decline in English sea power meant the decline of 'our ancient reputation and respect'.[3] The French were so far advanced in shipping that 'they threaten to dispute with us the sovereignty of the Narrow

Seas',[4] while the Dutch had grown as powerful and dangerous to England as Spain had once been. From Constantinople to Moscow, from the Mediterranean to the Narrow Seas, England faced repeated embarrassments. Coke urged the Council and the king to 'consider of some speedy and powerful means to redeem us from this contumely and contempt'.[5]

This was the period of Charles's personal rule, the period between 1629 and 1640 when he ruled without calling a parliament. Charles had to find new ways of funding his Royal Navy. Edward Nicholas advised that the Navy should be free of Treasury control. Coke and Nicholas bore the scars of battling the Treasury in the 1620s for money; when it came it was often long-delayed and measly. Charles's decision to impose Ship Money on his people solved these problems. From time immemorial the Crown had been able to call upon the mass of private shipping in the realm. It had, however, also asked for financial contributions. Elizabeth asked for voluntary ship money from coastal regions. In 1634, in the face of renewed threats from pirates and other European navies, Charles asked the ports for ships. The levy was too much for the ports: they could not comply with the orders for large ships.

This seems to have been both anticipated and desired by the king. If the ports could not lend him ships, he would 'lend' them his own ships so that they could fulfil their customary duty and contribute to his fleet. In effect this meant the ports had to victual, man and arm the king's ships. Technically this was still a ship levy. In reality the ports had coughed up £80,000 to pay for the Navy's summer operations. The ports paid for a fleet of nineteen royal ships that put to sea in 1635 under the earl of Lindsey.

The Ship Money fleet of 1635 was considered a success. In recent years the Navy had become the laughing stock of Europe. There was barely enough money to keep it going. The assurgent French navy even compelled English ships to salute *them* in the Channel – perhaps the greatest insult they could have inflicted. Dutch and Spanish ships fought in English waters. Moroccan, Algerine and Dunkirk pirates continued their depredations. The Navy had only four ships available for patrol. Sometimes it did not manage even that – in 1633 it could not mount a winter guard.

Lindsey's patrol of 1635 demonstrated the return of England to naval health. The Navy won no victory and captured no ships, but its very presence did the work. It prevented the Dutch and French fleets from linking up and closing the sea route between Spain and the Spanish Netherlands. Pennington, Admiral of the Narrow Seas, wrote to Coke: 'though my Lord of Lindsey do no more than sail up and down, yet the very setting of our best fleet out to sea is the greatest service that I believe hath been done the king these many years'.[6]

It encouraged Charles to extend Ship Money to the inland shires. Charles was eager to state the seriousness of his case. This was the king's 'great business', a sacred responsibility to protect British waters in a dangerous world. There was an upsurge in piracy from Morocco and Algiers. The French navy was contesting for dominance of the Channel. English trade was suffering around the world. The war between Spain and the Dutch Republic was spilling over into English waters. Dutch herring busses were plying English fisheries. Charles had to reclaim sovereignty of the seas – not just for his own dignity but for the good of all his subjects, in Lowestoft as much as Leicester, who depended on international trade for their prosperity.

In 1635 the intellectual and legal scholar John Selden published his book *Mare Clausum*. It was a rejoinder to the Dutch jurist Hugo Grotius's book *Mare Liberum*, which asserted the freedom of the seas. Selden's book, whose title means 'The Closed Sea', trawled through the historical records to assert that English kings held sway over British waters. It was a logical nonsense: Grotius's doctrine of the freedom of the seas was right when applied to the Portuguese or Spanish claims to exclusive rights over the Indian Ocean, the Pacific or the West Indies, quite wrong when it came to the Narrow Seas. It all started with Edgar, who had, so Selden argued, been recognised as *Rex Marium*, the sovereign of the seas. For centuries, therefore, the 'utmost limits' of an English king's sovereignty were 'the shores of the neighbouring countries'.

The appeal to national pride and self-interest was successful. The English believed that the Ship Money rate was to meet a specific threat to the safety of the realm and that it was temporary. In 1635 the Crown assessed the national rate at £200,000 and it collected over 97 per cent of it – an extraordinarily high figure for the time. Over the next five years the rate would bring in £800,000. Its success reflected England's desire to be a great naval power.

Ship Money represented a definite break with the past, a step towards a permanent, professional, maritime fighting force with a guaranteed revenue stream and a defined role. The view from the White Cliffs of Dover seemed rosy. Regular winter and summer patrols involving sizeable numbers of ships meant that the officers and men were prepared and the ships kept in good order. New ships were added to the fleet every year – a series of big, imposing vessels that culminated in the *Sovereign of the Seas* in 1639, the symbol of England's restored naval power.

The *Sovereign* carried 102 guns on three decks, more than had ever been mounted on a warship. Each gun was engraved with the motto *Carolus Edgari sceptrum stabilivit aquarum* – 'Charles has grasped Edgar's sceptre of the waters'. She was the largest, most imposing ship in the world, and she looked the part. Out of a whopping £65,856 total cost, £6,691 had been spent on the glistening gilded carvings that shone on her stern and bows against a black background.

The stern was a riot of bling. There were golden carvings of Mercury and Neptune. Aeolus, god of the wind, soared on an eagle. In the upper centre of the stern was an enormous representation of Victory. Her right hand pointed to Jason, brandishing an oar and the Golden Fleece; her left to Hercules with his club. One arm was encircled by a crown, emblem of wealth and power, and the other by a laurel wreath, emblem of honour. At one end of the taffrail was a lion, at the other a unicorn; in the middle was a golden lantern so big that it could hold ten men. Just below the taffrail was the motto *Soli Deo Gloria:* Glory Only to God. Other carvings showed Tudor greyhounds, Welsh dragons, Scottish unicorns and the English lion. There were numerous royal arms, the Prince of Wales's three feathers and the monograms *CR* (Charles Rex) and *HM* (Henrietta Maria) everywhere. On the beakhead bulkhead stood a line of golden statues, six twice-life-size women. These were Counsel, Carefulness, Industry, Strength, Valour and Victory. Joining them was Cupid leading a bridled lion, which alluded to Charles's mercy. The figurehead itself was an enormous golden effigy of a mounted King Edgar trampling lesser monarchs.

It was a floating illustration of Selden's *Mare Clausum*. This ship existed to affirm Charles's rights to the British seas.

Ship Money was raised on the plea of imminent disaster – threats such as were readily apparent to Englishmen in the mid-1630s. But ships like the *Sovereign* were not designed to chase pirates around. They were built to enhance the reputation of the Crown. In 1636 the Ship Money fleet was sent to make the Dutch herring busses take out licences for fishing in English waters. The mighty fleet returned with just £500 in fees from the Dutch. In 1637 one requisitioned merchantman was sent to make the Dutch take out licences. It found about 700 vessels guarded by twenty-three Dutch warships. No money was collected that year.

The Ship Money fleet was not used for the things demanded by Charles's subjects. The king needed a fleet for something other than warding off pirates and making Dutch herring fishermen pay for licences. Charles did not want to go to war; he could not afford it. But his Navy was, it seemed, powerful enough to tip the balance between the giants of Europe, the

Dutch Republic and Spain. In 1638 and 1639 they were fighting for control of the Narrow Seas. Charles remained neutral, but his naval power in the Narrow Seas was for hire. English ships helped the Spanish to run the Dutch navy's blockade of Dunkirk. They carried Spanish troops and gold from the Indies. The Dutch were furious at this duplicity and violation of neutrality. It was a dangerous game, but Charles felt he could play it now that he had a formidable Navy. If the Spanish proved intransigent, he could play them off against the French.

But it was not to be. Once again war raised its head. This time it was internal. In 1638 Scotland rebelled against Charles's rule and the Ship Money fleet was ordered to blockade the Firth of Forth. Lords Lieutenant were ordered to raise 30,000 men. For the first time since 1382 a war was being fought without parliament. It was a dismal failure. Once again it proved possible to mobilise, but impossible to sustain a campaign. Food and supplies ran out; the men went unpaid. What should have been a swift strike against a nervous opposition turned into a hesitant, sluggish campaign that plunged the state into administrative chaos and the Crown into bankruptcy. The Royal Navy ships proved too large to closely blockade Scottish ports and too slow to chase enemy ships. 'It seems,' said one official, 'the king's ships do little good upon the coast of Scotland. It will be more credit to His Majesty to recall his ships than suffer them to remain there to be laughed at as they are.'[7]

The fragility of the Royal Navy was exposed to England's rivals. Just as Charles was trying to organise a war, the collection of Ship Money met resistance from the English people. In 1639 less than a third of the money demanded had been raised. Pennington's Narrow Seas fleet was treated as a virtual irrelevance by Tromp.

The collapse of Ship Money was sudden. In 1637 everything seemed fine. The English ambassador in Paris was informed by a correspondent that the rate was so well accepted that it would likely become permanent. Indeed 'if men would consider the great levies of money in foreign parts for the service of the state, these impositions would appear but little burdens'.[8]

But there was a big difference between England and other states. The Crown relied upon co-operation with the people to fight a war. Ship Money was regarded as unconstitutional, so Charles met resistance. Compare this with France, where the Crown could exact large amounts of tax without resistance – large enough to build up a fleet in a short amount of time.

But most instructive in explaining the weakness of the English state and Navy was the way the Dutch had transformed themselves into a commercial–military state.

The United Provinces of the Netherlands had emerged from rebellion and war.[9] They were a decentralised federal republic made up of independent provinces, states and cities. Dutch cities had long dominated the north European shipping business, making a fortune from the carrying trade from the Baltic to Iberia. The cities were the economic and industrial hub of Europe, and the Dutch ports perfectly situated to trade between the Baltic and Spain and between central Europe and the rest of the world.

For a long time the English believed they had the edge over the Dutch. While the Royal Navy declined in the early seventeenth century, the merchant navy flourished. Virginia, Massachusetts, Bermuda and Newfoundland were colonised in the first decade of the century and Barbados, the Leeward Islands and Rhode Island in the 1620s and 1630s. This was done by private effort. Voyages to the East Indies began on a small scale at the beginning of the century, but within a few years the East India Company (EIC) was returning a high dividend to its shareholders. While the English state remained committed to peace, the East India Company's fleets took on the Portuguese in the Indian Ocean. The Company's ships defeated the Portuguese in 1612 and 1615 and gained a hold on Surat and the Red Sea trades.

English investors were interested in quick returns, which they got in the early years of the Company's life.[10] Indeed, members of the Company and investors scoffed at their Dutch rival, the Vereenigde Oost-Indische Compagnie (VOC). While the English distributed their profits, the Dutch seemed to sell their investors short by ploughing their profits into fortified bases throughout the Indian Ocean.

This difference in attitudes and organisation would have profound implications for the future of both companies. The VOC and the Dutch States General were bound together in a mutually profitable embrace. The VOC was a creation of the state and it reflected the state. Like the Republic it was federated into regional chambers. Although funded by private capital, the major investors and directors were the regents of states and the burgomasters of town councils. This meant that the VOC was bound up with the state, without being dominated by it. The company was able to innovate and perfect business skills in freedom from the state, but it could conduct diplomacy in the name of the Dutch States General. The government of Holland gave the company weapons and gunpowder from its arsenal; it was exempt from paying customs; and it benefited from the extremely low Dutch lending rate.

The result was a true world commercial and political force. Jan van Oldenbarnevelt, Advocate of Holland, encouraged the VOC to fortify bases throughout Asia and build up its naval strength. In 1614 the States General loaned the VOC five warships and gave it 200,000 guilders. The creation of the Wisselbank – the first public bank in Europe outside Italy – gave the Dutch traders financial clout. Throughout the Dutch trading network, local rulers and merchants were tied into credit agreements. The result was that the VOC achieved astonishing success in Asia as a military and trading organisation. By 1617 it had forty fighting ships and twenty fortresses that stretched from Persia to the Moluccas.

The English East India Company was completely overshadowed by the VOC from the 1610s. The VOC's investment in fortresses and warships paid off. By 1618 the EIC and the VOC were engaged in an unofficial naval war for control of the trade of Java and the Banda Islands. The English were completely outmatched, losing their trade and ships to the commercio-military Dutch machine. The dispute was solved by diplomatic means in Europe, but it was a compromise typical of the English government, which lacked the commercial sophistication of its rivals across the Narrow Seas. The treaties left the EIC at the mercy of the Dutch. In return for a third share of the spice trade the English had to pay a third of the VOC's defence costs. With the full force of the state behind it, the VOC could dictate terms to the English. The EIC was on the back foot in Asia, barely able to compete with its rivals, with whom it was locked into an unequal and humiliating alliance.

The EIC needed royal support, but the directors were aware that too close an association with the English Crown would be fatal to their independence. If they gave the king too much power the Company could become an unprofitable adjunct of the state. A centralised monarchy was very different from a federal republic.

Nonetheless, the Company believed it had a right to state support when its very existence was threatened. In 1623 ten Company men at the trading post at Amboina in Indonesia were executed by the Dutch for conspiracy. The Company demanded retribution for what it regarded as a massacre. James, however, refused to allow the Navy to intervene against the VOC in the Narrow Seas. The EIC was shocked. It told the king that it was on the point of giving up trade entirely because it received no protection. When the EIC defeated the Portuguese in a sea battle in 1622 and captured the strategically invaluable island of Hormuz, which guards the entrance to the Persian Gulf, the Lord High Admiral, the duke of Buckingham, exacted a staggering £10,000 from the Company as his share of the prizes and James demanded, and got, the same. A significant English naval victory was undermined by the Crown. The Dutch did things differently.

In the Netherlands trade, defended and advanced by warships, paid for the navy. There was no Dutch navy as such. There were five independent admiralties: Amsterdam, Rotterdam, Friesland, Noorderkwartier and Zeeland. The great companies, such as the VOC and the West India Company, had their own fleets and some of the towns provided warships for convoy duty. The extent of Dutch trade and the state's many enemies gave its ships and sailors a wealth of experience navigating and fighting around the world. Continual service against the ships of the Spanish Netherlands was the backbone of naval power; it kept ships in continual service and was a training ground for men of all ranks.

Admirals such as Maarten Harpertszoon Tromp and Witte Corneliszoon de With perfected their skills serving the Dutch companies and states around the world. Both men came from humble backgrounds and had gone to sea as boys. Tromp was enslaved by Barbary corsairs twice before he was twenty-four. It was as a slave in Tunis that he mastered the art of naval gunnery, impressing Yusuf Reis, one of the most famous Barbary corsairs, also known as John 'Birdy' Ward, a deserter from the Royal Navy. Tromp was freed and was decorated several times as a squadron commander fighting Dunkirk pirates.

De With first served as a cabin boy with the VOC fleet. He worked his way up the ranks of the merchant navy and the Admiralty of Rotterdam. Like other officers he moved between the various Dutch navies throughout his career. He fought Barbary corsairs and captained ships on convoy duties in the Baltic and with the VOC. He was a flag officer on a spectacular circumnavigation of the world in 1623–26, attacking Spanish colonies and ships on the western coast of the Americas. He then served as Piet Hein's flag captain on the voyage to the West Indies that resulted in the capture of the *flota*. Closer to home he was a commodore in the fishing fleet's protection squadron.

English officers did not have anything like the experience or training enjoyed by their rivals. In the United Provinces there was true cooperation between private individuals and the state in developing naval power; that had once prevailed in England, but by the 1630s the joint enterprise had withered. James and Charles were quite prepared to subordinate the interests of their countrymen's trade to the demands of foreign policy and dynastic ambition.

There was one exception. An expedition led by William Rainborow blockaded the corsair stronghold of Sallee, forced the Moroccans into a treaty of peace and returned with 350 freed English slaves. But in the main the Navy was not used to further trade. In the 1630s Charles began to undermine the East India Company. He encouraged others to make voyages to Asia and break the Company's monopoly. In so-called British waters the Dutch continued to draw a rich fortune from the North Sea fisheries – which were considered the Republic's version of the Spanish gold mines in America. Dutch fishermen knew they could count on their navy – there was a specialist and permanent fisheries protection squadron. English fishermen and traders were, by comparison, let down by their Navy, which was powerless against the pirates and, from 1638, the Dutch. In 1639 pirates from Dunkirk captured four herring busses and, in mockery of the English, anchored in the Downs after the act.

In the 1630s this did not seem to matter. English shippers were profiting spectacularly from the war between Spain and the Dutch, taking over much of European trade. London was emerging as a world emporium comparable to Amsterdam. But any wise observer would realise that this prosperity was held on shaky tenure. Once peace returned the Dutch would be back in full force. 'Our great trade depends upon the trouble of our neighbours.' Signs for the future of English trading supremacy were ominous at the end of the decade.

Maarten Tromp and the Dutch navy met little opposition as they scoured the Narrow Seas for English ships carrying Spanish gold, men and materiel in 1638/9. Tromp conducted his searches at sea and also in English ports. It was a further reminder to English merchants that the Dutch were the dominant power in the Channel. Pennington's task was to defend merchant shipping from Tromp, but as he said, 'before we seek reparations of that which is so ill resented, it behoves us to have a mastering strength for fear of a greater loss and dishonour, for they are very strong here in the Narrow Seas at present'.[11]

Tromp's reply to Pennington's demands was a succinct way of pricking English pretensions to sovereignty: 'My advice was that no-one could command at sea further than his guns can reach.'[12]

At the Battle of the Downs, therefore, Pennington was facing the greatest navy in the world with just ten Navy ships and ten lacklustre requisitioned merchant ships. He was wise enough to know he had no chance. The Lord Admiral privately told him to make 'as handsome a retreat as you can in so unlucky a business'. The only person who failed to see the bleakness of the situation was Charles, who had the gall to ask the Spanish for £150,000 in return for protecting their Armada. It was a fantasy vision of what the Navy could achieve. Pennington could only watch with envy as Tromp's ships devastated the Spanish.

The Dutch lesson was clear. Great navies were the product of flourishing trade. They could not be conjured into existence by taxation. Trading networks around the world provided officers and men with excellent seamanship and fighting skills. Money from trade paid for warships, and warships helped increase trade. That was why the Dutch had the best navy in the world, one that made a mockery of the Royal Navy. The *Sovereign of the Seas* looked like some absurd joke, a mad boast that could never be fulfilled.

English naval officers knew this all too well. Sir John Pennington's career in the Navy had been thwarted by foolish strategies, poor organisation and lack of money. In 1642 he was given a new task by his Stuart master. He was ordered to travel from York to the Downs and take over command of the fleet from the Lord Admiral, the earl of Warwick.

Pennington was unsure of the reception he would receive from the Navy. The country was dissolving into civil war. He sent word to a brother officer, Sir Henry Palmer, who lived nearby to go out to the fleet and signal to him when it was safe to board. But unbeknown to Pennington, Palmer claimed he was ill and refused to go on so risky a mission. Meanwhile the captains waited with 'great duty and submission' for Pennington. Warwick was also nearby, 'making merry' ashore. When he heard what was happening he abandoned his feasting and went out to the ships. He was racked by a dilemma: the king had ordered him to give up his office, parliament told him to seize the fleet. 'I was in a great strait between these two commands that had so great power over me.'[13]

It was a race between Pennington and Warwick. Would the Navy remain royal, or would it be parliamentarian?

Warwick won the race. He had made his decision by the time he reached his flagship. He summoned the captains, and those who refused to serve him as parliament's admiral were taken prisoner by their own crews. The mood among the sailors was firmly in favour of parliament. Memories of the betrayals of the 1620s ran deep. In 1641 parliament had taken control of naval finance and vetted all officers. Charles was shaken to the core by the ease with which parliament took his Navy in 1642, on the eve of the Civil War.

Edward Hyde, first earl of Clarendon, witnessed these events as a young MP and adviser to Charles. In his great history of the turmoil of the mid-seventeenth century he wrote that it was 'a loss of unspeakable ill consequence to the King's affairs which greatly affected his position in the eyes of other princes who saw him at one stroke deprived of his sovereignty of the sea'.

PART 6: FORGED IN THE FIRE

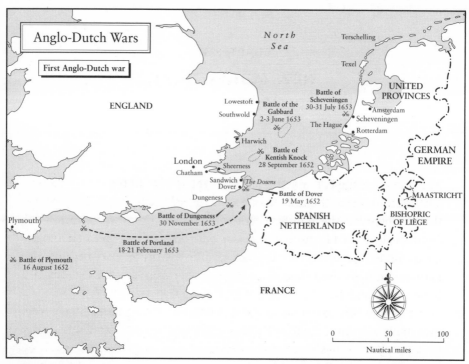

Anglo-Dutch Wars

First Anglo-Dutch war

North Sea

Terschelling

Texel

ENGLAND

UNITED PROVINCES

Lowestoft
Southwold

Battle of the Gabbard
2-3 June 1653

Battle of Scheveningen
30-31 July 1653

Amsterdam
Scheveningen

The Hague

Rotterdam

Harwich

Battle of Kentish Knock
28 September 1652

GERMAN EMPIRE

London
Chatham

Sheerness

Sandwich
Dover

The Downs

MAASTRICHT

Battle of Dover
19 May 1652

Dungeness

BISHOPRIC OF LIÈGE

Plymouth

Battle of Dungeness
30 November 1653

SPANISH NETHERLANDS

Battle of Portland
18-21 February 1653

Battle of Plymouth
16 August 1652

FRANCE

N

0   50   100

Nautical miles

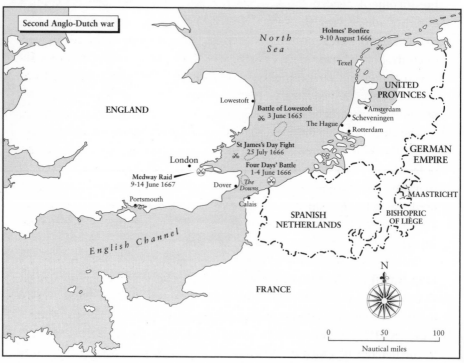

Second Anglo-Dutch war

North Sea

Holmes' Bonfire
9-10 August 1666

Texel

ENGLAND

UNITED PROVINCES

Lowestoft

Battle of Lowestoft
3 June 1665

Amsterdam
Scheveningen

The Hague

Rotterdam

St James's Day Fight
25 July 1666

GERMAN EMPIRE

London

Four Days' Battle
1-4 June 1666

Medway Raid
9-14 June 1667

Dover

The Downs

MAASTRICHT

Portsmouth

Calais

BISHOPRIC OF LIÈGE

SPANISH NETHERLANDS

English Channel

FRANCE

N

0   50   100

Nautical miles

CHAPTER 18

NEW MODEL NAVY
1642–1652

At Lyme Regis the Parliamentarians had their backs to the wall. The Royalists outnumbered them six to one and commanded the hills from which they bombarded the poorly defended port. But the town held out for eight weeks in 1644, through incessant artillery attacks and periodic infantry raids. Lyme survived against Charles's army in part because the Parliamentarians used their unassailable superiority at sea to supply the besieged townsfolk.

Sea power was marginal to the English Civil War: its influence was essentially negative. Charles I was deprived of mobility and the means to supply his armies over great distances. Parliament derived much of the income it needed to prosecute the war from duties levied on ships entering and leaving the capital, but Charles lacked the naval resources to blockade the great port of London. Parliament enjoyed the advantages of control of the seas on easy terms. The Navy transported munitions, relieved armies and garrisons and cut off supplies destined for the king from abroad. It also helped isolated towns such as Lyme that were besieged by overwhelming force from land.

The siege of Lyme does not merely illustrate the utility of naval power in a Civil War unremarkable for the contribution of navies. It was an object lesson in leadership. The people of Lyme were roused to defend their town by the energies of a hitherto obscure army officer. Robert Blake fired the defenders up with a sense of the righteousness of their cause. When the town seemed doomed the men of Lyme took the fight to the superior enemy in a raid on the Royalist guns.

Robert Blake won fame at another besieged town. This time it was a long way from the sea. Taunton came under siege three times between October 1644 and June 1645. It held out thanks to Blake's extraordinary qualities as a leader. He summoned all the men of the town to the church and made them sign the Solemn League and Covenant. This tied everyone to the defence of Taunton; no one could claim to have been pro-Royalist or neutral if the enemy prevailed. Blake signalled to the town and the Royalists that this was a fight to the finish. He enthused the townsmen with his example – he promised to eat three of his four boots before he surrendered – and worked them hard at providing makeshift defences for their poorly defended town. Like all great military commanders Blake knew that the best form of defence in a hopeless situation was attack. As at Lyme, the forlorn garrison at Taunton made frequent sallies against their more numerous enemy. It worked. Taunton did not fall.

There was nothing in Robert Blake's background to suggest he would thrive as an army officer. His origins were in the gentry, and after a stab at academia he drifted into trade. He was successful enough to sit as the burgess MP for Bridgwater, his home town, in the parliament called in 1640. It was the Civil War and the religious and political passions it unleashed that transformed Blake the middling merchant into Blake the heroic leader. The descent into civil strife, and the explosion of ideas and discussion in the 1640s, awoke a republicanism that had lain dormant since his university days. But most importantly he was an avowed enemy of the Church of England and a committed Puritan. Religious zeal helped him rally, and bind, people to a cause. Blake was always at his best when he was in a losing position; he had the power to impose order on a rabble, turn resistance into offence and convert lost causes into victories.

That was why in 1649 the 51-year-old Robert Blake was chosen to be one of three generals-at-sea. Few could have expected that he would become one of the greatest admirals in English history.

His army background was key to his success. Parliament's army had been 'new modelled' in 1645. The regional armies were amalgamated into a national force and given a new leadership structure. It was funded by an unprecedented flow of cash which allowed it to sustain longer campaigns. Between 1642 and 1645 parliament spent £35,671 a month on its armies; between 1645 and 1651 the sum rose to £90,416 per month. The New Model Army became, in a short space of time, one of the greatest military forces in Europe, renowned for its leadership and rigid discipline.

The Navy, by contrast, seemed rooted in the past. During the Civil War it did its duty adequately. It was presided over by men who had participated in England's colonial ventures in the 1620s and 1630s. In many ways they were throwbacks to the era of Hawkins and Drake. The Lord Admiral, Warwick, was an enthusiastic privateer and colonial promoter. The members of the Board were similarly inclined: they were long-distance traders and colonisers. Their strategic vision for the Navy was also rooted in the Elizabethan heritage. John Hawkins would have been at home in the Navy of the 1640s; unlike the army, very little seemed to have changed. Large ships like the *Sovereign* were laid up and smaller, swifter ships hired from the merchant community. This was a new type of small, nimble warship known as a frigate, ideal for intercepting royalist vessels, privateering and operating near coastlines and in ports. The most famous of its kind was the *Constant Warwick*.

The Navy was politically moderate and Elizabethan in its outlook. The army, in contrast, became more radical as the war went on. Charles became parliament's prisoner in 1647. When parliament tried to come to terms with Charles and disband the army, the troops mutinied and occupied London. The revolt was led by the radical religious and political elements in it, the Independents and Levellers, who were opposed to the moderate views of most MPs. They did not want a settlement with Charles. In 1647 the army radicals demanded universal male suffrage and religious freedom. The army was the most powerful force in the country.

The army began to dictate terms to parliament. The country did not like what was happening, and nor did the Navy.[1] Later in 1647 the commander of the fleet, William Batten, was bullied out of office. He was replaced by the ultra-radical Colonel Thomas Rainborow. In May 1648 one of the most serious mutinies in the Navy's history swept through the fleet.

The Navy was challenging the army's assumption of supreme power in the state. Kent joined the Navy's rebellion. Upnor Castle, which guarded the Medway, was seized by the rebels. The officers, men and dockyard officials at Chatham allowed this to happen, and surrendered their ships, including the mighty *Sovereign of the Seas* and the *Prince Royal*. Batten took control of the mutinous fleet.

For a brief moment the Navy had power over the future of the nation. There were plans to blockade London and free Charles from his imprisonment on the Isle of Wight. But the army quickly seized the initiative. The earl of Warwick, who was very popular in the Navy, rallied the remainder of the fleet and pursued Batten to the Netherlands. Batten put his portion of the fleet in the hands of Charles, Prince of Wales. The Royalists were now a force at sea, led by Charles I's nephew, Prince Rupert of the Rhine.

Shortly after, in December, the army struck against its enemies in England. Parliament was purged, reducing it to a rump. In January Charles I was tried and executed. The government was in the hands of a military dictatorship, detested alike at home and abroad.

Diplomatically, militarily and economically, the Commonwealth was fighting for its life. Suddenly the Navy became very important to the new regime. But it also posed a problem. The Navy sucked up money, its administration was corrupt and it showed every sign of being disloyal to the Commonwealth as it had been to Charles. Attempts to create a state Navy by the king and by parliament had failed. The ancient vices were deep rooted. England had a thoroughly modern army. Could the Navy, which was seemingly impervious to reform, be revolutionised in the same way?

Robert Blake was one of the men chosen by the army to bring the Navy to heel. Meanwhile a committee of sixteen Regulators scrutinised the political sympathies and religious convictions of every man in the Navy, from dockyard carpenters to captains. Many of the experienced officers and men were politically and religiously conservative. They were purged.

Ships with royal connotations were renamed to celebrate England's delivery from ungodly tyranny: *Charles* became *Liberty*, the *Prince Royal* was now *Resolution*. The massive, bedizened *Sovereign of the Sea* was called simply *Sovereign*, no doubt because in the post-monarchical, republican era sovereignty could mean only one thing – jurisdiction over the sea. New ships got names like *Naseby* or *Worcester* to commemorate great victories over the Stuarts or generals such as *Fairfax*. Few could be in doubt that this was the army revelling in its control over the Navy. Gaudy royal decorations were stripped off and replaced with gaudy republican decorations. Royal standards were substituted with a flag bearing the cross of St George and a harp. The sailors were deluged with patriotic republican propaganda.

Once the Navy was remodelled the generals led it, in three squadrons, to the Irish coast where Prince Rupert had based the Royalist sea forces. Blake was put in charge of blockading the prince in Kinsale.

It was an onerous task. From May until October Blake kept his men motivated and disciplined. Just like the defenders of Lyme and Taunton, they fell under the spell of this gruff, driven, demanding man. Rupert could not stir from Kinsale to prevent Cromwell moving his army to Ireland or to pillage English traders. It was only when an autumn storm blew the Commonwealth's ships off station that the prince managed to escape. He made for Portugal.

Blake went in pursuit. For eleven months he remained at sea. First he blockaded Rupert at Lisbon. The Portuguese king would not allow the English republicans to attack the English Royalists in his waters. Blake had to put pressure on Portugal and keep an eye on Rupert. If English naval history was a guide it would suggest that Blake was doomed to failure. He was a long way from home and he faced the hostility of both Rupert and the Portuguese. Perhaps because he was not a sailor with the weight of

Robert Blake, General-at-Sea

naval history on his shoulders Blake held firm. The supply lines were kept open and the ardours of a blockade survived. The Portuguese were bullied into reluctant compliance when Blake captured the returning Brazilian convoy.

Rupert had to make his escape, and Blake allowed it. He was behind the prince as he entered the Mediterranean. Rupert set about attacking English shipping, but when Blake's squadron arrived the Royalists knew the game was up. One ship surrendered without resisting, one was driven ashore and the remaining four scampered into Cartagena. They were wrecked as they tried to slip out.

This was Blake's apprenticeship as a naval commander. He acquitted himself superbly. His achievements far surpassed any previous English admiral. Robert Blake may have had to turn to professional naval officers for technical advice, but his experience of soldiering gave him the confidence and skills to lead men and shape tactics. He brought fresh thinking to naval warfare. For almost a year the fleet was kept at sea in good fighting shape. Blake had learnt his soldiering during the ardours of withstanding sieges. Those qualities of mental fortitude, physical resilience, unflagging patience and morale-boosting leadership he now brought to the Navy and imposed upon the most gruelling and unrewarding aspect of maritime warfare – blockade. But he could unleash his aggression as well when the occasion served. When he returned to English waters Blake staged a series of superbly orchestrated amphibious operations that gave the Commonwealth control over the Scillies and the Channel Islands.

Unlike his predecessors Blake fought for God, not glory and gold. For that reason he was prepared to stick to his tasks, not seek a quick result. Difficult or complex situations did not daunt him; in fact he seemed to relish them. If one word describes him it is dogged.

While Blake was active in distant waters, the Navy also took part in the reduction of Ireland and Scotland and took the fight to pirates in British waters. A squadron led by Sir George Ayscue forced Barbados to submit to the new regime. Another squadron was sent to bring Virginia and Maryland into obedience to the Commonwealth. In addition to this, the Navy organised convoys for merchantmen in the Mediterranean from 1651 and English warships attacked hostile French ships in the Atlantic. For the first time the Navy was capable of simultaneous operations around the world. While Blake was pursuing Rupert and blockading Lisbon the Admiralty had been able to send him food and ammunition on chartered merchant ships. When Blake left a fresh squadron under William Penn replaced him.

Just twenty-six years earlier Charles I's Navy had headed off to disaster at Cadiz. That and the disasters at La Rochelle had revealed a service that was incapable of operating effectively beyond sight of its own shores for more than a couple a weeks. These debacles were well within living memory, but the contrast between the fiasco at Cadiz in 1625 and Blake's year-long vigil in Iberian waters made it seem like a different age. The Commonwealth possessed the political will, born out of fear, to organise and fund a Navy. Where the Crown and parliament had failed a military dictatorship had succeeded. At first the priority was defensive – to eliminate the Royalists as a threat to the new state. The success of this led to offensive operations, designed to further English commerce and prestige.

The rest of Europe had to sit up and acknowledge a new force in the world. Once they saw the extent of the Commonwealth's naval mastery, Portugal, then Spain, then France, then Venice had to swallow their distaste and recognise the Commonwealth. Thanks to Blake's campaign in Iberian waters the Portuguese colonies were opened to English traders and the Spanish made available their ports in Iberia, Italy and Sicily, which provided essential supply bases for military and commercial operations in the Mediterranean.

The new English government had been defined by its successes on land. That was how it achieved hegemony in the British Isles. After 1651 it became a serious naval power. There was only one other country strong enough to stand up to the assurgent England.

In 1652 the two great admirals of their age came face to face. In May Admiral Maarten Tromp led a squadron into the Channel to protect incoming Dutch trading ships. The seas were rough, so Tromp sought refuge for his forty-two warships in the Downs. Not only did he treat the English roadstead as his own property (as he had done so often in the past) but he refused to strike his colours to Dover Castle. The next day Blake approached from Rye. Blake had just twelve ships, but he ordered the Dutch to strike sail in salute. Tromp replied with a red flag of war and a tremendous broadside. Then battle began.

Despite their overwhelming superiority, the Dutch failed to sink or capture a ship; the English, however, took one Dutch ship and crippled another. It was a good old-fashioned melee; neither Blake nor Tromp had any sophisticated tactics to offer. This five-hour confrontation is known as the Battle of Goodwin Sands, the sandbank that protects the site of Tromp's greatest triumph and England's deepest shame – the Downs.

The English and the Dutch had been squaring up to each other for months. In July they were at war.

The Anglo-Dutch wars of the seventeenth century do not take up much space in the present-day national historical consciousness. But the effect of this titanic struggle was to transform the Navy and British history.

There was plenty that bound the English and the Dutch. There was the shared religion, the long-standing English admiration for Dutch political and financial institutions. Both countries had trade routes that criss-crossed the world. Many of the leading figures in the English government believed that the future of the English state was as a republican mercantile oligarchy, similar to their neighbours across the Narrow Seas. Flourishing overseas trade, imperialism and enterprise would lay the basis for remod-elling English society, making it more like the Netherlands.

One thing stood in the way: the Dutch themselves. Amsterdam was the European entrepôt; Dutch shippers dominated the carrying trade; and the VOC overshadowed the English in the Far East. The States General had made life easy for their traders, wresting the concession from the Danes that Dutch ships could pass into the Baltic without paying tolls. By the early 1650s English ships were all but ousted from the Baltic and they were falling behind the Dutch in the Iberian, Asian and American trades. England was in an economic slump. It wanted to be more like the Netherlands, but how could it ever begin to compete?

And most worryingly for the Commonwealth, the House of Orange supported the exiled Stuarts, providing a refuge for them in the Netherlands and running arms to Scotland. The Dutch must be won over to the new republican government. In 1651 talks began to forge an Anglo-Dutch political and economic union.

It would have been a true world force – a military–commercial superpower. But it was not to be. The Dutch came up with a counter-proposal for a system of free trade. This was unacceptable to the English – the better-organised Dutch would simply take over their existing trade.

If you could not join the Dutch you had to beat them. That was the feeling among English radicals. They believed with burning intensity that England's God-given destiny was to become the pre-eminent world power. Control of the seas must be wrested from the Dutch by main force.

The naval campaign to bring the American and Caribbean colonies to submission was aimed as much against the Dutch as the Royalists. During the Civil War and its aftermath the Dutch had gained a foothold in the English colonies, trading between them and Europe. This was welcomed by the colonists: the Dutch had ensured their economic well-being. When the Commonwealth reasserted control over the colonies it was determined to exclude the Dutch. The Rump Parliament passed the Navigation Act in 1651 in retaliation for the breakdown in talks with them. Henceforth all imports to England and its colonies must be carried on English ships or ships belonging to the country where the goods originated. The Act was aimed against the Dutch, who were the major European carriers, but the impact on them was slight – English trade was a small part of their economy. It did however have a harmful effect on English importers and exporters who had benefited from the low shipping charges offered by the Dutch. The intention was to benefit English shippers. But there were too few English merchant ships to take up the slack.

The Navigation Act was not a major cause of war. More important were ideological and religious motivations. The Act signalled England's ambitions. Its desire to become a great maritime power, at the expense of the Dutch, was evident to the world.

It was the same old England, desperate to muscle in on someone else's trade and take it for herself.

Throughout the world the Navy was displaying this bellicosity. Ayscue's squadron, which had compelled the submission of Barbados, also captured a number of Dutch ships. English warships and privateers stopped and searched many Dutch ships in the belief – or on the pretext – that they were carrying arms and money for Royalists or Scottish and Irish rebels. There were well-founded accusations of torture carried out during these searches. Even more worrying for the Dutch was the Commonwealth leadership's desire to revive the ancient doctrine of the sovereignty of the seas.

This kingly pretension had not died with Charles I. In fact it had grown even more outrageous. English warships insisted that foreigners salute in honour of the Commonwealth. This had always been the case in 'British' waters. Now the definition of British waters was stretched to extraordinary lengths. Admiral William Penn made Dutch ships salute him in the Strait of Gibraltar. An English frigate fired a broadside at three Dutch warships off the Barbary coast because they had not dipped their sails. The Venetian ambassador believed that the Commonwealth was going to 'lay claim to absolute sovereignty' over the Atlantic.

English pretensions met resistance from Dutch captains; violence begat violence. Outrage at Dutch high-handedness was whipped up in England just as horror at English belligerence swept through the Netherlands. England was an insignificant trading nation as far as the Dutch were concerned, and the Navigation Act was irrelevant to them. But it was a violent, predatory island, inconveniently located. As it was said, England's long coastline was like an eagle with its wings outstretched, poised over the busiest shipping lane in the world, ready to swoop on rich Dutch cargoes. England had nothing to lose; the stakes could not have been higher for the Dutch, who were utterly dependent on international trade.

In 1652 the States General ordered an additional 150 ships to augment their navy and provide convoys for merchant ships coming up the Channel. Their navy was now in excess of 220 ships. The intention was to scare off the English. But it only served to convince them that the Dutch were about to strike the first blow of a by now inevitable war.

Tensions were high when Blake ordered Tromp to salute off the Downs in May. The Dutch admiral was under strict instructions from his political masters to comply with English orders to honour their flag, but Tromp was evidently sick of the humiliation. Even after the Battle of Goodwin Sands the States General were eager to prevent war. But the Commonwealth was wise to Dutch prevaricatory tactics. It was set on war. 'The English are going to attack a mountain of gold,' said the Grand Pensionary, the political leader of the States General; 'we have to face a mountain of iron.'[2]

The mountain of iron was the republican Navy. In three years it had undergone a revolution.

It was of a size and strength beyond the wildest dreams of English monarchs. In 1649 the Navy consisted of forty-five ships commanded and manned by men of questionable loyalty to the new regime. In 1650 the number of ships stood at seventy-two. In 1654 the state fleet comprised 200 ships, including the most heavily armed and technologically advanced warships in the world, from the monstrous 100-gun *Sovereign* to brand-new frigates. It had regular funding from unprecedentedly high direct taxation and increased customs dues. It was highly disciplined, well led, and had fought in a variety of locations.

The mountain of gold was the Dutch seaborne trade. The navy had to protect its merchant fleets or the republic would be crippled. Unlike England, the United Provinces were dependent upon imports to feed themselves. The English could therefore fight an offensive war, while the Dutch were on the defensive from the very start. Their vulnerability was made worse because the fortunes of the opposing navies were travelling in different directions. The Dutch had been the dominant naval power for decades, but after the Thirty Years War their navy was in decline. Although still regarded as the best in the world, it was, despite its increased size in 1652, only so on paper. Only Tromp's flagship, *Brederode*, carried over fifty guns; two thirds of his fleet comprised ships with between twenty and thirty guns. The English had five ships with fifty guns or more and half the Navy's ships had over forty guns. The English Navy therefore consisted of big ships with immense firepower. Tromp said that his best ship was inferior to fifty English ships. The Dutch were constrained in their arms race with the English by nature itself: they needed ships with a shallow draught to negotiate the shoals on their coast. Tromp's primary task was defending the mountain of gold – convoying the merchant fleet and warding off the English who had little of value to defend.

Ayscue was the first naval commander to set about pillaging the seaborne wealth of the Netherlands. With his fleet of ten ships, recently returned from the West Indies, he attacked thirty merchantmen homeward bound from Portugal. He captured seven and sank three. He was lying low in the Downs when Tromp and de With came in pursuit with 102 warships. It could have been a repeat of 1639 for the two Dutch admirals, but this time the shoals and tides of the Downs played against them. At first it was too calm for large warships to enter the anchorage. Then, when the wind did blow, it was in the wrong direction. Tromp took the wind and entered the North Sea to meet a more deadly threat.

Robert Blake was off Shetland, lying in wait to intercept the incoming fleets of the VOC and the Dutch West India Company, which were taking the north-about route to avoid the Narrow Seas. He had also taken the opportunity to attack the herring busses and exact the 10 per cent tax that the English claimed as their right. Tromp went in pursuit. He located Blake near Fair Isle. Before battle could be joined the wind reached gale force. A Dutch writer described the horrors:

> The fleet being as it were buried by the sea in the most horrible abysses, rose out of them, only to be tossed up to the clouds; here the masts were beaten down into the sea, there the deck was overflowed with the prevailing waves; the tempest was so much mistress of the ships they could be governed no longer, and on every side appeared all the forerunners of dismal wrecks.[3]

The Dutch ships were blown towards the forbidding Sumburgh Head, the rocky southern cape of Shetland. Any thought of fleet discipline broke down as every captain strained to save his ship from destruction on the rocks. Three days later, when the wind abated, Tromp found he had just thirty-four ships out of the hundred or so he had led to those perilous waters. Some had fled to the fjords of Norway; many more scurried away to hide from Blake and the weather among the islands of Shetland; ten warships were wrecked and six sank. The East and West India ships also suffered as they approached the rendezvous at Fair Isle; a few met their fate on the Shetland rocks and some managed to join Tromp before he fled for home with his reduced fleet.

Geography and the weather had done Blake's work for him. A large portion of the Dutch fleet was scattered across the North Sea and the ships took months to make it home. Tromp was dismissed as supreme admiral of the Dutch navies and replaced by de With.

But then the course of the war changed again. Admiral Ayscue, with a force of thirty-eight Navy ships and conscripted merchantmen, was monitoring the movements of vice commodore Michiel de Ruyter, who with thirty warships was convoying merchantmen along the Channel. For a long time Ayscue hesitated. It was clear to de Ruyter that the English admiral had his eye on the merchantmen and was not interested in a profitless naval engagement. At last, on 16 August, Ayscue led his squadron in a charge into the midst of the Dutch convoy. In doing so he nullified his advantage – superior firepower. Ayscue's ships found themselves out of formation and surrounded. Once again the Dutch displayed their superior tactics against the gung-ho English.

The Battle of Plymouth was deeply depressing for the English. Although they lost no ships, Ayscue was forced to retreat to Plymouth and ceded de Ruyter temporary control of the Channel. After two major engagements in the war it was honours even. But as it turned out the battle had unintended consequences. The States General now believed that the English Navy was badly damaged, its leadership feeble and its ships, for all their firepower, poor performers. It encouraged them to order de With to seek out the English fleet in the Downs for a repeat performance of their great victory against the Spanish thirteen years earlier.

The English Navy was about to fight its first fleet action since 1588.

CHAPTER 19

LINE OF BATTLE
1652–1653

> The very heavens were obscured by smoke, the air rent with
> the thundering noise, the sea all in a breach with the shot that
> fell, the ship ever trembling, and we hearing everywhere the
> messengers of death flying.
>
> Captain Thomas Cubitt of the Battle of Scheveningen

The Dutch called her 'the Golden Devil'. She was the most imposing warship in the world, with 102 guns mounted on three gun decks. The lavish
gilding must have made her glisten like a jewel box in the sun. Such ships,
the first-rates of the English Navy, spent most of their lives moored in the
dockyards with their masts removed. It was not until late in the afternoon
on 28 September 1652 that *Sovereign* sailed into her first battle, thirteen
years after she was launched.

Her stately, intimidating progress was halted when she and the *James*
ran aground on the Kentish Knock, a sandbank that stands eighteen miles
out to sea from the mouth of the Thames Estuary. It must have seemed
that she had joined the list of large English warships – *Grace Dieu* and
Mary Rose among them – that were costly, showy failures.

The Dutch States General were alarmed by the situation in the Channel. A queue of over 200 merchantmen was waiting for safe passage to
clear the Strait of Dover. Robert Blake and the English fleet were in the
Downs, waiting to strike. The States General ordered the commander of
the Dutch navy, Admiral de With, to attack and defeat Blake so that the
mainstream of commerce could flow once more.

On 25 September news reached Blake that de With was at sea. The
next day he led the fleet out of the Downs and into the North Sea. First
out was Blake's squadron, then came the division under William Penn,
and last were the ships under Rear Admiral Nehemiah Bourne. It is hard
to get large ships out of the Downs, so Blake and Penn were far ahead of
Bourne. The wind that carried the English through the Gull Stream made

it difficult for the Dutch fleet to ride in open sea, and it was with some difficulty that de With got it into battle formation.

Blake, followed by Penn, made for the Dutch. It was then that *Sovereign* and *James* ran aground on Kentish Knock. Penn was aboard *James*. He watched as Blake's ships streamed past him to engage the Dutch with just a small proportion of his fleet. But as he reached them the Dutch took the south-east tack. It brought them past the stranded Penn and onto a direct course with Bourne's rearguard, which was in disarray after struggling to exit the Downs.

What seemed like a brilliant piece of seamanship turned into a disaster for the Dutch. *Sovereign* and *James* were quickly towed off the shoal, meaning that Penn was in the perfect position to change course and catch the Dutch strung out on their tack.

Into the Dutch formation sailed the *Sovereign*. The Golden Devil, once freed, was burning for an orgy of destruction. The twenty Dutch ships that took her on came under a terrifying bombardment. The massive warship turned the sea red around her.

It was a similar story with the other big English ships. The Dutch fought best when their ships were close together, so that they could join to immobilise isolated enemy ships by aiming their cannon into the sails and rigging and sweeping the decks with musket fire, before boarding. But as the Dutch fleet tacked towards Bourne the wind fell off, leaving the ships at some distance from each other. And it was not just the weather that had weakened the Dutch.

After the Battle of Plymouth the States General believed that they could easily defeat the English. De With shared this ebullient mood. His officers and men, however, did not. The navy was below strength: many of its ships had not returned or were not fit after the storm off the Shetlands. The men were unpaid and on the point of mutiny; they detested de With, a stern disciplinarian, and wanted to serve under Tromp. Just before the battle de With, when he was within a mile of Blake, decided to transfer to Tromp's former flagship, *Brederode*. He flourished his commission from the States General from the boat, but the men in *Brederode* jeered and refused to let him board. At the crucial moment he was an admiral with a rowing boat for a flagship. At last he got on board a VOC ship, and found the captain and officers drunk and the crew untrained. From this unpromising flagship he tried to lead the fleet into the battle.

It meant that the Dutch were in chaos as they began to manoeuvre. Many of the captains held off from battle. The big English ships sailed among the dispersed enemy and wreaked carnage with their heavy guns.

These large ships were all but impervious to return fire. De With later reported that the English could keep up a heavy rate of fire during battle and even the modest guns on their frigates carried further than the best Dutch cannon. But it was too late in the day for a long battle. At dawn the next morning, thoroughly disturbed by English firepower, a significant number of Dutch ships deserted. To de With's fury his officers refused to fight on. The Dutch scrambled for home 'like a flock of sheep fleeing the wolves'.

The Dutch lost three ships. It was a victory for the English, but in the circumstances a disappointing one. The Dutch could have been knocked out of the war in a single encounter had Blake not rushed into battle too close to sunset. De With was astonished; he was expecting total annihilation.

Tromp was recalled and a major programme of shipbuilding was begun. In a fit of complacency after the Battle of Kentish Knock, the English let their fleet run down. Blake was in the Downs with only forty-two ships. And these were low on ammunition and under-victualled and the men had not been paid. Twenty ships were dispatched to the Mediterranean. The English believed they had destroyed the Dutch navy. Intelligence reports to the contrary were ignored.

Finally, on Monday 29 November, Blake was informed that the Dutch were off North Foreland. There were 500 ships, eighty-eight of them warships. Blake knew he had to leave the Downs, or he would be trapped as surely as the Spanish in 1639. He was under orders to avoid a battle at all costs.

Blake's ships spent the night off Dover; the Dutch were six miles out to sea. The next morning Tromp prepared to attack. At first the two fleets were separated by shoals, the Varne Bank which lies in the middle of the Channel. Blake went south-west, landward of the shoals, towards Dungeness Point, with the Dutch racing with him to seaward. As he reached the end of the shoals he was exposed to Tromp's ships, which broke the English line, detaching Blake's *Triumph* from the small fleet. The Navy was unable to manoeuvre because of its proximity to Dungeness Point.

Blake had entered a trap of his own making. Suddenly he found himself deserted by half his fleet. The captains who remained to fight were dismayed at their admiral's folly. But Blake had not been lured into battle. He had not blundered. He *wanted* to fight, even though he was outnumbered and outmanoeuvred. This was the kind of fighting he relished, the kind he had experienced at Lyme and Taunton. He trusted to God's favour, personal courage and big English guns.

The English were lucky, like the Dutch at Kentish Knock, because the battle began late in the day. That's all the luck they had. By nightfall, the English had lost five ships. Blake and the badly mauled survivors made it back to the safety of the Downs. The Dutch were in complete control of the Channel. Tromp had the chance to make good his victory. After he got the merchant fleet on its way he turned back to find Blake, who had fallen back to Long Sands Head in the outer Thames Estuary. Tromp was about to inflict the worst possible defeat on England.

Not for the first time in the war an admiral chose the least risky option. Tromp decided not to enter the dangerous waters of the Thames Estuary.

It was the turn of the English to panic. Four captains, including Blake's brother, were made scapegoats. Blame lay elsewhere. The defeat exposed Blake as a poor naval strategist. The captains had warned him against the course of action that had made battle – and defeat – inevitable. Blake saw things differently. He believed that he lost only because his captains had not shown the requisite bloody-mindedness. There were dark hints that at heart the Navy was still politically suspect, that it harboured crypto-Royalists and pro-Dutch traitors.

Reforms were brought in. It was reported that Blake had been badly let down by twenty merchant ships because the captains were unwilling to endanger their employers' investments. Henceforth merchant auxiliaries would be captained by Navy officers, who did not have any financial tie to the ships. Fresh Articles of War were issued which defined the duties of officers and men and increased Blake's authority over the fleet. Blake could punish officers who disobeyed him by convening courts martial. There were twenty-five offences that carried the death penalty. The effect was to reduce the influence of the council of war and place ultimate authority in the hands of the admiral. At the same time pay was increased for the men. And most importantly the state pledged itself to find even more money for the Navy from increased taxation.

The situation was critical. The Dutch navy was rampant. It had control of the Channel, and in March it took control of the Mediterranean after defeating the Navy at the Battle of Leghorn. Throughout the winter the government raced to equip the fleet with ammunition, victuals and new ships. Thirty new frigates were ordered. The dockyards were enlarged and given the infrastructure to process and preserve large amounts of food and beer. There were new bakehouses, slaughterhouses and breweries. Hospitals were built at Dover and Southampton. Wages were increased. The state found 20,000 men to man the fleet.

The administrative backbone of the Navy was strengthened as new ways were improvised to oversee the dramatic increase in work. In 1652 the Council increased taxation from £90,000 per month to £120,000. The Navy also had the ability to borrow in anticipation of revenue. Suppliers advanced services even before their old bills were paid, something unheard of before. The fact that the Admiralty was prompt to pay its debts gave it a mighty advantage over previous administrations.

The Navy rethought its tactics. From now on the fleet would be divided into three squadrons – Red, White and Blue. The aim was to make real the new hierarchy established in the reforms. The generals would command the Red squadron, the Blue would be led by the vice admiral, and the White by the rear admiral. Within each squadron there would be a vice and a rear admiral.

From February the English Navy spread itself along the Channel, waiting for Tromp to bring in the incoming convoy, which was assembling at the Île de Ré. What Blake neglected to do was to post scout ships. It must have been an odd sight for the experienced Tromp when he neared Portland Bill on 18 February. To his south was Penn with a handful of ships; there was a similar group to the east; and Blake and Dean, the generals-at-sea on board *Triumph*, were to the north-west with just a few ships. The rest of the fleet was with the inexperienced third general, George Monck, several miles away to the east. Rather than surprising Tromp, the English now found themselves in disarray. Tromp knew he stood a good chance of a handsome victory.

Tromp's squadron made straight for *Triumph* to resume his duel with Blake. Other Dutch ships got between Blake and Penn. De Ruyter sailed

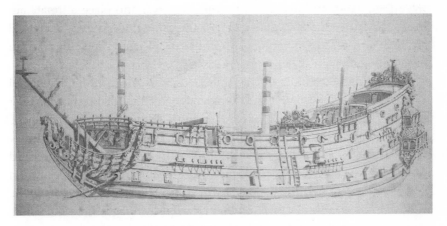

The *Triumph* by Willem van de Velde, an example of the English ships of the First Anglo-Dutch War.

into Penn's formation, and his men boarded the English ships *Oak*, *Assistance* and *Prosperous*. Blake's ship was in serious trouble, encircled by Dutch ships and bombarded by his enemy's flagship.

It was a furious battle that day. One English ship was lost and several severely damaged. Eighty men died or were wounded on *Triumph*. That list included its captain and Robert Blake himself. The two generals-at-sea were standing together amid the bombardment. A piece of shot cut through Deane's coat and breeches and hit Blake above the knee. Blake showed no pain and continued to command. Other talented captains in the English fleet were killed or wounded and on all ships the casualty list was dismally high. Tromp was preparing to board *Triumph* and, at a stroke, decapitate the English Navy.

The day was saved by the enterprise of John Lawson, vice admiral of the Red squadron. He could have come to Blake's aid at once, but that would have put him in the melee. Instead he took the starboard tack, passing south of the battle. Once he was to the west he took the larboard tack and entered the battle at the crucial moment from the south-west with the wind behind him. The Dutch boarders on the three English ships were repulsed and the Dutch vessels encircling *Triumph* beaten back. Over a hundred men died or were wounded on Lawson's ship, *Fairfax*, and the vessel was badly damaged. But Lawson had made a brilliant tactical assessment – showing better strategic awareness than the generals-at-sea.

Lawson, unlike the generals, was a seaman through and through.[1] He came from the hardest school in the English maritime world, the north-east coast. During the Civil War he had captained *Centurion*, in which he had a part share, and did valuable work for the Parliamentary cause. He brought essential supplies into Hull, which was under siege by the Royalists; he helped blockade his home town of Scarborough, which was under the king's control; and he scored notable successes capturing his enemy's ships. It was seafarers like Lawson whom the Admiralty needed to bring into the Navy when many of its experienced officers were dismissed on political grounds. Lawson was also a God-fearing man and a committed republican. Above all he was brave. When the Dutch stole one of Scarborough's colliers in 1650 he sailed into the estuary of the Elbe, under the guns on the fort of Glückstadt, and reclaimed her.

After their reprieve Blake, Penn and Lawson led their ships westwards, inflicting serious damage on the Dutch. During the bloody opening stages of the battle Monck had been beating westwards with the main English fleet. It took him hours to arrive. His men-of-war took on the Dutch squadron under Johan Evertsen, while his frigates sped towards the merchant convoy.

Tromp had to go in support of the convoy. In his haste he left behind his damaged ships. Four were sunk; one blew up; two were captured. A commodore and twelve captains were killed during the furious cannonades that battered the Dutch ships that afternoon. Those of their warships that were captured by the English were described as 'much dyed with blood, their masts and tackle being moiled with brains, hair, pieces of skulls; dreadful sights, though glorious, as being a signal token of the Lord's goodness to the nation'.[2]

The English remember it as the Battle of Portland. More appropriate is the Dutch name for the battle: the Channel Fight. It resumed at 13.00 the next day. By then Tromp had managed to realign his warships into a protective crescent formation around the merchant ships. He tried his best to shepherd them homeward along the Channel. The English frigates screamed into battle, followed by the big ships. By sunset the Dutch had lost three warships and many more were hulled below the waterline. De Ruyter had to be towed to safety when his ship lost its mainmast. And as well as repelling the English, the Dutch warships had to try and keep panicky merchantmen from deserting to French ports. The next day, 20 February, Blake was able to harry the Dutch at will. Tromp's fleet was now in full flight, unable to fire back. Only thirty-five warships were serviceable and they had dwindling stocks of shot and powder. To make matters worse, the English frigates had raced ahead to the Strait of Dover. Once in the Strait, Tromp knew his convoy would come under sustained attack. He brought his beleaguered fleet into the shallow waters off Cap Gris Nez, halfway between Boulogne and Calais, to wait out the night.

Tromp was facing complete destruction. One more attack from Blake and it would all be over.

When the sun rose on the 21st the exultant English were astonished to find that the sea off Cap Gris Nez was empty. Unaccountably, Blake had veered off at the end of the third day. The wound was troubling him and he was gripped with fever. He should have handed over command, but that was far from his nature. During the night the shallow-draught Dutch ships and their expert seamen had negotiated the shoals off the cape. It was risky, but the only hope Tromp had of salvation. He was as amazed as anyone that the English had failed to finish him off. Blake sank seventeen Dutch men-of-war and captured forty merchantmen, but once again the killer blow had not been struck.

Now the English had control of the Channel. Dutch convoys were forced to take the north-about route. Tromp was at sea, convoying the merchant fleets. The English, led by Deane and Monck in Blake's convalescent absence, were also out in force, contesting for control of the North Sea and, with it, complete maritime dominance.

In May the English fleet was off Aberdeen; throughout the rest of the month they scoured the seas, up to Shetland, down to the Scheldt estuary and then Sole Bay. On 1 June the generals at last got news of Tromp's location.

The Battle of the Gabbard – a shoal about thirty miles east of Harwich – was fought on 2 and 3 June. It was one of the most important battles in British naval history.

Both fleets were parallel to each other, both arranged in three squadrons and both on a line of bearing. What happened next was either a well executed tactic or a brilliant improvisation. The wind died away before the English could redeploy. The fleet was left in a long line, the ships nose to tail. From this position they pummelled the Dutch with broadside after broadside, subjecting the enemy ships to terrible damage and huge loss of life. The Dutch attempted to break the English line, but the lack of wind hampered their progress. Under intense fire their boats endeavoured to tow the ships into battle to fight at close quarters. But the English still held the wind gage and they prevented the Dutch getting anywhere near them.

The Dutch liked to get in among English formations. By fighting like this they isolated the bigger English ships and used their superior seamanship to bring their guns to bear at close range on the enemy's sails and rigging and to sweep their decks. That would be the prelude to boarding crippled English ships.

Blake (and many other officers) favoured bloody-minded determination above subtle tactics. Such a way of fighting at sea came naturally to men in the seventeenth century. Captains and crews plunged into battle with one thing on their minds: plunder from captured enemy prizes. Once the red mist of war descended on captains' minds and the blanket of gunpowder smoke covered the site of battle, tactical considerations tended to go out of the window. The idea of organising a fleet to work as a single entity rather than a loose collection of individual sea warriors was considered unrealistic. The result was that at battles such as Plymouth and Dungeness and during the opening stages of the Battle of Portland the English played into the hands of the Dutch by charging pell-mell into battle.

But by forming a tight line on 2 June the English prevented the Dutch breaking into their formation. Instead the Dutch came up against a wooden wall bristling with English guns. The line allowed the English fleet to make ultimate use of its broadside. The Dutch could not manoeuvre past them and fire at their lightly defended bows and sterns. They could not get close enough to board.

If it was not a new line-ahead tactic, it was a fine display of the discipline that Blake and Monck had imposed upon the Navy. After the disaster at Dungeness, Blake and the Navy Commissioners had been pushed into reform, improving logistics and centralising the command structure. Although the Battle of Portland had ended in triumph for the English, the opening stages had exposed their poor seamanship. Immediately after, Blake and Monck issued new Sailing and Fighting Instructions. They provided a set of flag signals so that orders could be better transmitted. They included rules for keeping the fleet together in storms, strong winds and at night. When tacking, the highest-ranked officer should go to windward, followed by his captains in order of seniority. This order was strictly enforced. Speedier ships tended to race ahead. Now a captain violating the hierarchy would lose a month's worth of pay. Do it a second time and he would lose four months' pay. A third offence would get him cashiered.

The intention of the Instructions was to make it easier for the generals to handle the fleet. Once the red flag of battle was run up on the mizzen-mast of the admiral's ship then it was up to each squadron to engage the enemy 'nearest unto them'. Each ship should 'endeavour' to keep in line with its squadron commander.

These new orders did not invent line-ahead tactics. What Blake and Monck intended was for every captain to aid his senior officer. Brave, gung-ho captains had a tendency to charge off into ship-to-ship duels. There were also plenty of captains who took advantage of the melee-type battle to skulk on the outskirts of the action, using the fog of war to conceal their cowardice. Now both types of captain – the adrenaline-fuelled hero and the sneaky coward – were required to keep close to their squadron commanders and go in aid of their fellows. The intention was to make the English ships fight in cohesive groups. Nowhere in the Instructions is there mention of the whole fleet forming one single line.

On 2 June 1653 the weather conditions meant that the English found themselves in a long line. The captains held their positions with their divisional commanders, in accordance with the new Instructions, and kept the Dutch at bay. The smaller, faster frigates remained out of the action as the big ships bombarded the enemy. They were finally unleashed on the second day when the Dutch gave way and fled. They sailed among the damaged Dutch vessels, capturing and sinking enemy ships that had been pulverised by almost two days of bombardment in which 6,000 barrels of gunpowder were used to propel a deadly tempest of iron at them.

Tromp and seventy-four warships managed to reach the safety of the Texel. Eleven warships and two hoys were captured; six men-of-war were sunk, two blew up and one was lost in an accident. Dutch casualty figures are unknown, but they would have run to the thousands. For weeks after the battle 'the tide ever brings in abundance of arms and legs, and dismembered bodies'[3] on to the Suffolk shoreline. Not many of them were English: only 236 were wounded and 126 were killed. One of the first to die was General-at-Sea Richard Deane, who was struck by a cannonball as he stood next to his fellow general, George Monck. Monck quietly and calmly covered his colleague with his cloak and the battle continued. It would not do to dishearten the men with the news. As it was, the English fought with discipline and good order. This was a major development – and it proved deadly effective.

General-at-Sea George Monck had sailed with Charles I's fleet to Cadiz in 1625. He served on the Île de Ré and went with the fleet that failed to relieve La Rochelle in 1628. Monck was a soldier in these disasters, but he had seen at first hand the muddle and indiscipline displayed by the Navy. He had had a long, distinguished military career when he was appointed general-at-sea in November 1652 at the age of forty-five. Like Blake he was a hard-working and diligent army officer. But, in contrast to Blake, his experience as an artillery commander had given him a superb grip of formal battlefield tactics.

This was seen at the Gabbard, where the deployment of the fleet gave English guns and ships the best chance to display their advantages. After Deane's death Monck, the gunnery specialist, was in sole command. The 'discovery' of the line of battle might have been the result of a freak of weather, but it provided a perfect illustration of its possibilities. It became orthodoxy in following years. Battles would be determined by the abilities of opposing fleets to hold their line and batter their opponents to smithereens. It sounds simple enough, but in the age of sail it was a complicated manoeuvre. Keeping station in a line was exceptionally difficult. Ships performed very differently from each other, and collisions were always a risk when they were in close proximity. Carefully formed lines had the tendency to be bent out of shape by wind and tide and broken down by the chaos of conflict.

Despite this, the line of battle became, after the Gabbard, the holy grail of naval tacticians. Hitherto admirals could control the run-up to battle, but not the monstrous chaos of a sea fight. The line gave them the possibility of planning and directing battles. It called upon a new kind of vessel – the ship of the line – that was strong enough to hold its position and wreak carnage on the enemy.

The immediate effect of the Gabbard was the complete blockade of the Netherlands and the economic collapse of the Dutch Republic. Grass grew in the once bustling streets of Amsterdam. On 24 July Tromp led out the fleet to break the blockade. At stake was the very survival of the Republic.

The English Navy was under the command of Monck, with Penn in command of the White squadron and Lawson leading the Blue. During the night of 30 July Tromp managed to get to windward of the English near the town of Scheveningen. Early the next morning Monck attacked first. He beat towards the Dutch fleet and tried to break through it to gain the wind. The course of the battle was set by Monck's determination to get in the position he had enjoyed at the Gabbard, and Tromp's desperation to avoid it.

It was an exceptionally hard-fought battle. As usual the English ships made the most of superior firepower, relentlessly battering the enemy. Among the many Dutch sailors killed was the great Admiral Tromp. He was a hero to his men, and his death from the bullet of an English sharpshooter sent them into despondency. De With took over, but there was little he could do to prevent his ships being pounded to destruction. The English claimed they sank between twenty and thirty enemy ships.

Thousands of Dutch citizens watched the battle from the shore. It was a scene of carnage, the seas strewn with wreckage and drowning men, the ships hidden amid acrid clouds of smoke. Most dramatic of all would have been the raging fires. The English lost *Oak* to Dutch fireships; *Worcester*, *Triumph* and *Andrew* were seriously damaged by them. James Peacock, vice admiral of the Red squadron, died of burns sustained while putting out fires on his flagship, the doughty *Triumph*. Deaths amounted to 250 men, including five captains and two admirals. The damage they had inflicted on the Dutch was, for the third time that year, overwhelming. It is noteworthy that no Dutch ships were captured. This was because the new Instructions forbade the taking of prizes in battle. In the past, formations had been disrupted by ships towing prizes away. Now the emphasis was on keeping the line at all costs, which meant that enemy ships must be destroyed. At the Battle of Scheveningen 1,300 Dutch sailors were captured, most of them rescued from the waves.

The Dutch could not fight again. Lawson resumed the blockade. De With told the States General that the English were the masters of the sea.

They had to sue for peace. Cromwell, for his part, read aloud the account of Edgar's maritime dominance to the Dutch ambassador.

England won the major battles in the last phase of the war, but it lost the peace. In the negotiations with the Dutch it was Cromwell who began to make concessions. The Dutch agreed to respect the Navigation Act. They also promised to salute the English flag, something they would do with sarcastic zeal.

The Navy might beat the Dutch in the Narrow Seas, but everywhere else the Dutch maintained their advantages. They defeated the English in the Mediterranean and made life hard for traders in the Persian Gulf and in the Far East. They could close the Baltic when they chose.

The war might have been a costly adventure for the state, but for the Navy it was a triumph. The Navy that conquered at Scheveningen was very different from the one that prevailed at Kentish Knock. Blake had imposed rigid discipline on the fleet; Monck had built upon that to develop battle tactics.

Once the pressures of war had overwhelmed the English Navy; now they honed it.

CHAPTER 20

DUTY
1653–1660

Is there no one to sit at the helm of the ship of our poor Commonwealth, but an army of rude, unruly and contentious soldiers?[1]

Rev. Oliver Heywood

'Tis not for us to mind state affairs, but to keep the foreigners from fooling us.[2]

Robert Blake

Oliver Cromwell took in the awesome sight of the English fleet at sea – some 160 vessels. 'God,' he said, 'has not brought us hither where we are but to consider the work that we may do in the world.'[3]

The figurehead of the eighty-gun *Naseby*, the newest and greatest ship in the Navy, depicted Cromwell on horseback trampling six vanquished nations – the Netherlands, Ireland, Scotland, Spain, France and England. It resembled the beakhead emblem on the *Sovereign*, which had depicted Edgar trampling his vassal kingdoms.

During the Dutch war the English government had changed twice. In 1653, midway between the battles of Portland and the Gabbard, the Rump Parliament was dissolved in an army *coup d'état* orchestrated by Cromwell. In its place came the Barebones Parliament, its members nominated from the army or on the grounds of religious conformity to the new regime.

In 1648 the Navy had almost frustrated the army's plans. In 1653 it was much stronger. Would it accept the army's pretensions?

Cromwell could count on the personal loyalty of Deane, Monck and Blake. They consulted the Navy's senior officers soon after the coup. The mood among the captains was that winning the war took priority over politics.

In December Cromwell went a step further and became Lord Protector.

By then the war at sea had wound down. The fleet was riven with conflicting opinions and divided loyalties. Some, including Blake and Monck, welcomed Cromwell's assumption of ultimate power. Many tolerated it. But there was a sizeable contingent of seamen who, like many of their countrymen, saw the Protectorate as a new tyranny. Sailors on active duty at Spithead wrote and sent a petition calling upon parliament to stand up for the liberties of free-born Englishmen. Rear Admiral John Lawson, in command of the Channel squadron, encouraged his men to express their opinions. The virus of free thought spread through the rest of the fleet. The nose was shaved off the effigy of Cromwell that adorned *Naseby*.

An inactive fleet was a dangerous one. In any case Cromwell had high ambitions to further England's glory. The victorious Navy was his tool to make England a global power. In 1655 Blake was dispatched to the Mediterranean with a powerful fleet. It had an immediate impact on the region's turbulent political life. The duke of Tuscany trembled that Blake would punish him for not helping the English at the Battle of Leghorn. The Venetians fretted that Blake would seize a naval base. Even the pope worried that the zealous Cromwell was going to sack Rome.

Rulers and officials in Spain and Italy tried to fête the famous English admiral, but the old warrior retained his air of mystique, preferring the rough austerity of his cabin to the luxuries offered by Catholic grandees. The Commonwealth's ornate, heavily armed ships must have looked terrifying as they lay in the limpid seas. Worse still was the thought of the men who crewed them: Protestant ruffians, in the Catholic imagination, bent on mischief and iconoclasm.

But Blake was in the region for other reasons. The problem of the Barbary corsairs, which had menaced English lives and trade in the reigns of James I and Charles I, was rearing its head again. Blake was to intimidate the North African regents, forcing them to free slaves, return captured ships and pay compensation. He met resistance from the Dey of Tunis, an autonomous regent of the sultan of the Ottoman Empire. Blake claimed that the Tunisians had broken their agreement with England by seizing a merchant ship called the *Princess*. The Dey said that it had been taken because an English captain contracted to transport Turkish soldiers to Smyrna had sold the men into slavery instead. Negotiations dragged on.

Blake determined to display the full extent of English naval power. In the bay of Porto Farina, near Tunis, were nine Ottoman warships and the *Princess*. They lay in a shallow bay defended by shore batteries.

This was fighting as Blake understood and liked it: black and white in military and moral terms. He was going straight into the cannon's mouth.

Chastising the Dey of Tunis was secondary to his purposes. He aimed to prevent the Ottoman Empire wresting Crete from the Venetians by destroying their ships. That would be doing God's work.

First Blake sailed for Sicily. Then he came back for more negotiations. Then he departed again. The Dey was smugly satisfied that Blake was powerless to do him harm and the ships were safe in the impregnable Porto Farina. At 04.00 on 4 April Blake's ships sailed towards Porto Farina on the morning sea breeze; they stopped short and dropped anchor. Then they continued into the bay, paying out their long anchor ropes. First came the frigates and smaller ships. They were covered by the larger ships, which bombarded the shore batteries.

The cannonade was devastating against the onshore artillery. Any further resistance was made nigh impossible by the resulting smoke, which enveloped the ships. Boatloads of English sailors and marines made for the enemy ships. The boarding parties were under strict instructions not to take any prizes and not to dally, but to set fire to the ships and return. The bay was small. The danger was that it would become overcrowded and the English would not be able to get out against the wind. At the time of withdrawing the English faced an added danger. No longer under bombardment from the men-of-war the shore batteries would be able to assail the frigates, and once the smoke cleared the Ottoman gunners could open fire. But Blake's men were unencumbered by prizes. To the amazement of the defenders they got out swiftly. The men heaved on the capstans, the cables stretched taut, and the ships were hauled back to their anchors with astonishing speed.

It was a brilliantly conceived and executed plan, and it served to demonstrate the discipline and power of the English Navy. The whole of Europe took note.

Blake's next task was to station himself off Cadiz. England and Spain were at peace, but there were rumours flying around that Cromwell was about to provoke a war. While Blake was in the Mediterranean Admiral William Penn led a fleet of thirty-eight ships to the Caribbean. They carried 3,000 soldiers under the command of Colonel Robert Venables. The goal was the capture of Hispaniola.

Blake's orders were to prevent a Spanish fleet going to the defence of the empire. This placed him in an intolerable position. War had not been declared, and in any case he could not anticipate where Spanish ships were bound. He very nearly engaged a Spanish fleet after two months off Cadiz. He was abreast of his opponents off Lagos and ready to haul the red battle flag up his mizzen when he was called down to the gun deck.

There he was shown that the seas were running so high that the lower tier of guns could not be run out. The next day he was ready to fight, but at the last moment he learnt that the Spanish ships were sailing out to escort home the *flota*. He believed that it would exceed his orders to attack it. He was back in the Downs in October 1655.

A month earlier Penn had returned from the Western Design. The operation had been a fiasco. Venables and Penn could not agree on strategy. The army was decimated by disease in Hispaniola and was beaten back by a scratch force of Spanish volunteers. They did manage to take Jamaica, but the island was considered worthless. After a frustrating campaign Penn headed home, where he was sent to the Tower for his pains. Blake was spared punishment, even though Cromwell was disappointed that he had failed to destroy the Spanish fleet.

Over the winter Blake put together a fleet and in March 1656 it sailed for the coast of Spain. Just as it was about to leave, political dissension flared up again. Lawson resigned as vice admiral, claiming the expedition was not ready. But that was a pretext. Behind it lay politics. Lawson would never be reconciled to the new regime and, worse still, he was alarmed that one of Cromwell's protégés, the 31-year-old Edward Montagu, had been preferred as Blake's co-general.

A number of officers were then arrested for expressing their reluctance to fight. For them the war against Spain was an affront. It could not be justified by Spanish aggression. It could not even be dressed up as commercial: the City saw the whole thing as ruinous to the European economy. Many of the officers and men felt they were going to fight for the vanity of Cromwell. Lawson intended to derail the war. He failed. Blake and Montagu re-established order in the Navy. The fleet was impressive and ably led. But not for the first time its aims were uncertain. Politicians wanted Blake and Montagu to capture the *flota*. As history showed, that was easier said than done.

In fact the treasure fleet had already arrived in Spain. Blake and Montagu decided to blockade Cadiz and wait for another treasure convoy. The most obvious problem was the lack of a supply base. That was solved when King João of Portugal was intimidated into a treaty in which he allowed English merchants access to Brazil and, most crucially in the circumstances, gave English warships permission to use Portuguese ports.

The blockade was kept up through the spring and summer, notwithstanding Atlantic storms. Everyone involved must have been heartily sick of the whole enterprise. In August Blake divided the fleet into three. The first, commanded by Blake, cruised off Cape St Vincent. Montagu took the second to Tripoli and Sallee to negotiate treaties. And the third, commanded by Captain Richard Stayner and consisting of eight of the best frigates, remained in Cadiz Bay. Blake presently left to help Montagu in Sallee. On 8 September Stayner's squadron beat away from land to escape the dangers of a lee shore in a stiff westerly.

From Cadiz it looked as though the English had given up. That's what the admiral of the *flota* believed. He headed for Cadiz. When he spotted the small English frigates he assumed they were fishing boats. He got the shock of his life when Stayner fired a broadside at the leading ships and then took on the most powerful ship. Three ships were captured, one was burnt, and two more were forced on shore.

After over a century of being tantalised by stories of the wealth of the Indies, the English had finally secured the fabled *flota*.

It was a massive anticlimax. A small ship ignored by the English had carried the most treasure. The one that carried the second-biggest haul had been set on fire. One of the captured ships carried treasure, but the others were disappointingly light of precious metal; one carried only hides. The proceeds from the dazzling victory were modest – nowhere near enough to fund the war. Montagu returned home with the loot, such as it was, and Blake was left to ride out the winter off Cape St Vincent. There he remained, plagued by the pain in his thigh from the wound inflicted at the Battle of Portland and tortured by kidney stones and the dropsy. He lived off jellies and broths.

It was not until the following spring that he received intelligence that the *flota* was at sea. Excitement spread around the weary fleet. Stayner and some of the other captains were all for departing at once. Blake put paid to any such a suggestion. He would not desert the blockade. The captains were ordered back to their numbing duties. Two months later, on 12 April, the news Blake had craved arrived. The *flota* was anchored at Tenerife, too terrified to proceed lest they meet the English Navy. And, Blake now learnt, the Spanish ships in Cadiz were not ready to put to sea.

Blake left the scene of his yearlong vigil on 14 April 1657. On 18 April Tenerife was sighted and the next day he was off Santa Cruz de Tenerife.

Santa Cruz was one of the most forbidding ports in the world for would-be looters. The rocky coastline prevented an amphibious landing. The crescent bay was defended by the fort of St Philip. Between St Philip to the north of the town and the fort of St Juan to the south were shore batteries. Connecting the harbour fortifications were three lines of earthworks behind which were stationed musketeers. Seven great galleons lay end to end sealing off the harbour mouth, broadsides facing the sea, and nine smaller armed ships were close to the shore. The Spanish were impregnable.

But not for Blake. Porto Farina had been his dress rehearsal. Once again he forbade his men to take prizes. It is hard to think of another admiral of the time who would give this order with the *flota* sitting before him – or one who would be obeyed if he did. But Blake had absolutely no greed for money, and every one of his captains feared his explosive rage, which had been smouldering during his illness.

Stayner led the frigates into battle, standing on the forecastle of his ship, *Speaker*, to negotiate her way into the harbour. He gave only one verbal command to the captains of the other frigates: they were to follow him and do exactly as he did. There could not have been a better choice to spearhead this lightning attack. Stayner was one of the rising stars of the Navy. He had gone to sea as a boy with the Newfoundland fishing fleet and got his first command in the Navy in 1649, when he was twenty-four. He captained frigates with success during the Dutch War. He knew what Blake was about: he had fought at Porto Farina.

From his position on the forecastle Stayner spotted a gap between the two largest Spanish galleons and led his squadron through it. All this was done in eerie silence. Blake had forbidden his men to open fire until they were in position. Once the guns fired the smoke would make the delicate manoeuvres almost impossible. The frigates withstood the salvos fired from the great galleons as they followed Stayner through the gap. They moored themselves alongside the galleons at 09.00. Once there, the frigates opened fire.

Meanwhile the large English warships fired so much shot into the forts that they were rendered powerless. The gunners fled in terror. The shore batteries were also useless, as Blake had foreseen, because the treasure ships in the inner harbour blocked their line of fire. The sea breeze blew the smoke of battle into the musketeers' eyes, obscuring the English boarding parties as they rowed towards the Spanish ships and clambered aboard them. The sailors went about their orgy of destruction in a pall of protective smoke. The big ships entered the harbour to finish off the galleons. At 14.00 the Spanish admiral's flagship exploded, followed straight after by the vice admiral's ship.

Every time a Spanish ship sank it opened up a gap for the shore batteries to aim at the English. The battle grew hotter the longer it went on. Under renewed bombardment some of the English officers got over-enthusiastic. Vice Admiral Bourne, Rear Admiral Stayner and three other captains tried to secure prizes. This would have complicated the operation, especially the all-important escape. Blake had to repeat his order three times before it was obeyed. As at Porto Farina, his ships made a speedy exit by warping.

Stayner led the attack at 08.00 on *Speaker*. She was the last ship to leave, at 19.00, so crippled that she had nine feet of water in her hold, she had lost her masts and had to be towed to safety. Blake lost no ships in the action. He might not have treasure to show for it, but he had destroyed the entire *flota* at negligible cost to his own fleet. Casualties amounted to just fifty. He had struck a blow at the most sensitive part of the Spanish empire. And, most importantly, he ensured that the treasure lay idle in Santa Cruz when it was badly needed to sustain the Spanish war effort in Flanders.

Once again all Europe was abuzz with news of the extraordinary prowess of the English Navy. 'The whole action was so miraculous that all men who knew the place concluded that no sober men, with what courage soever endued, would ever undertake it.' So wrote Clarendon, who went on to say that the Spanish concluded they had been set upon by devils, not men. As the Venetian ambassador noted, it was England's greatest victory since the defeat of the Armada, and it was celebrated accordingly.

In July Blake set sail for home, leaving a smaller squadron to maintain the blockade. He wanted to set foot on English soil one last time. As he approached Plymouth Sound he gave his final order: his ships left on duty off Cadiz must be resupplied. He died just as his flagship, *George*, was sailing into Plymouth on 7 August 1657.

That Blake is not better remembered is perhaps because none of the battles he fought were in defence of his country. Indeed, his major victories came in wars in which England was the aggressor. But his contribution should not be underrated. Blake's ruthless imposition of discipline and organisation shaped the Navy during its formative years; it had never known the like. A poor tactician in fleet engagements he may have been, but he was at his best in a scrap, facing impossible odds. In addition, Blake possessed the patience and virtues of leadership that allowed the Navy to conduct blockades for long periods of time, a model of unshakeable determination that would resonate down the generations. Interspersed in the months and years of watching and waiting were operations of breathtaking audacity, as at Porto Farina and Santa Cruz, which were the result of meticulous planning and observation. He was feared throughout Europe. Clarendon said of Cromwell: 'His greatness at home was but a shadow of the glory he had abroad.' That was largely due to Robert Blake.

He was buried at Westminster Abbey on 4 September 1657. Three hundred and sixty-four days later Oliver Cromwell was dead as well. Under

Blake the Navy had remained politically neutral in a time of turmoil, willing to mutter in opposition but loath to intervene in the political whirligig of Interregnum England. That was about to change.

Cromwell had a son, an inoffensive fellow called Richard. He became Lord Protector in succession to his father. He was supported by parliament and the council. But to the army he was 'Queen Dick', a milksop who had no experience fighting the godly cause. The senior officers found him unacceptable as commander-in-chief and, just as ominous, the state's finances were in disarray and the men were owed pay. The answer was to cut spending on the military. That would mean the end of the army's political dominance.

The Navy supported Richard. In part that was thanks to Edward Montagu, general-at-sea and firm supporter of the new Protector. The two arms of the military were at odds, general-at-sea pitted against the land generals. In March 1659 Montagu led a fleet of forty ships to the Sound of Denmark. The army seized its chance. Richard was deposed and the Rump Parliament restored.

The army mistrusted Montagu. They believed that he favoured restoring Charles Stuart. Admiral John Lawson was brought out of retirement and given command of the Channel Fleet. Lawson was a committed republican; unlike Blake and other officers he was never prepared to hold his nose and support regimes he detested. He was loved by his men as a fighting admiral and because he had stood up to Cromwell. The aim was to divide and rule the Navy; if Montagu threatened the regime Lawson would strike.

Montagu was forced into retirement, but it did not end the threat to the Rump Parliament. Both army and Navy seethed with discontent. The men had not been paid for months, in some cases years. The volatile situation came to a head in October when soldiers locked the doors to the Palace of Westminster and stationed troops around it. Now the army governed England.

For the first and only time in English history the Navy staged a coup. On 13 December Lawson entered the Thames with twenty-two ships. The Navy, a creation of the army, had its hand on the throat of the army. London was under blockade in the midst of winter. The City was in uproar and the people were facing starvation and, with no coal ships able to enter the Thames, freezing conditions. On Christmas Day the generals threw in the towel. The Rump was restored.

An admiral was the arbiter of England.[4] Already the City was making demands for the restoration of Charles Stuart. That was unacceptable to

Lawson. His ships and their guns stood against the junta, but also against the City and the Royalists.

But the Navy could not long hold the balance. Only a week later, General George Monck led his army across the Tweed and into England. As he marched towards London he gauged the feeling in the country. People were fed up with tumult. The desire was for parliamentary elections. In the interim the MPs who had been purged in 1648 were readmitted.

This scenario was alarming to Lawson. The restored MPs were conservative and there was a risk that a newly elected parliament would be Royalist. The admiral had a choice. He could use the fleet to join other die-hard republicans, risking civil war. Or he could work with Monck for the sake of stability, even if that meant the inevitable dusk of his political ideals. In the end he chose the latter. Lawson stood aside, allowing Monck and Montagu to lead the Navy as generals-at-sea. The problem was that the Navy had been bent and hammered into a shape determined by its political masters. There were plenty of officers who would not compromise as their admiral had done.

It was with great trepidation that Samuel Pepys boarded *Swiftsure* at the Tower on 23 March 1660.[5] He was there as Montagu's secretary when the general took command of the Navy for the summer patrol. The ship sailed down to Tilbury to meet up with Lawson.

Lawson and Montagu had history. On the eve of the expedition to Cadiz Lawson had attempted to undermine the young general by resigning. Montagu knew he had entered a nest of vipers. And sure enough Pepys began to hear whispers that Lawson's officers were not prepared to accept Montagu this time either. By now elections were under way for a Convention to determine England's future. People were talking openly of Charles Stuart coming home to rule the country. Monck and Montagu were in secret talks with the Stuart court-in-exile, advising how he might negotiate his return.

All plans were dependent on the Navy. No one was sure what it would do.

Montagu and Pepys transferred to *Naseby* and sailed for the Downs. When they entered the anchorage Pepys took note of the wrecks and wave-beaten masts that protruded above the waves, casualties of the treacherous sandbanks which now provided navigation markers for sailors. They sailed on to join the rest of the summer guard under the shelter of Deal Castle. There was a tremendous salute which produced so much smoke that Pepys lost sight not only of the other ships but even of men on deck.

Pepys found life on board a warship a pleasant experience. There was plenty of opportunity to take wine with the officers. He began to learn the rudiments of ships and sailing from some of them, the start of a genuine interest in seafaring rare among civilian officials. He gambled at ninepins with Montagu, the officers and the men. There was much music played on board, and singing, particularly of satirical songs directed at the government. He experienced the pangs of anxiety about his wife, familiar to most sailors, and the monotony of life aboard a ship. He let off steam on a brief visit to the taverns of Deal and in a drunken mock fight late at night with the younger officers; 'after that', he wrote in his diary, 'to bed very late – with drink enough in my head'.

The fleet lay in the Downs through April. Montagu had begun purging the officers in March. This delicate filleting continued while he was in the Downs. Pepys had intelligence about the loyalties of the officers. The most radical were sent ashore; others were dispatched on convoy duty or their ships were paid off. Yet still Montagu doubted the loyalty of the captains. This was particularly worrying for him because he was using his position in the Downs to conduct secret negotiations with the Stuarts across the water in Holland. The secret was all but open to the men on the ships, with messengers and dignitaries scuttling to and from *Naseby* from the shores of England or the Netherlands.

The captains did not like what they saw or heard, but they were now leaderless. Lawson had been approached by the Royalists. With one eye on the state of the Navy and the other on his immediate future, he agreed not to stand in the way of the king's return.

On 1 May 1660, after weeks of negotiations between Monck and Charles, the king-in-exile's Declaration of Breda, spelling out the concessions he was prepared to make, was read to the Convention Parliament. The next day the Convention replied, stating that monarchy was the natural government of England. On 3 May Montagu summoned his officers to a council of war aboard *Naseby* and showed them copies of both documents. The atmosphere was tense, but there was precious little chance to discuss matters. Pepys had already drafted their unanimous agreement. 'Not one man seemed to say no to it,' Pepys wrote, 'though I am confident many in their hearts were against it.'[6]

It was a different story above deck. The officers went out to the quarterdeck, Pepys read aloud the Declaration of Breda to the crew and, 'with the greatest joy imaginable', they shouted 'God bless King Charles'. Pepys then went from ship to ship and read out the document. When they heard it the sailors threw their hats into the air and 'loud *Vive le Roy*'s echoed from one ship's company to another'.

The captains may have been stony-faced and reluctant to have any part in the Restoration. After all they had been groomed to obey their political masters, and a good part of their service had involved sealing off England from Royalist agents; now they were not merely acquiescing in the restoration of the monarchy but were instrumental to it. They would lose their commands. But the men on the ships, like people on land, were eager for things to be settled. Whatever their political views they were united by one concern. They would be paid when the country got stable government. No wonder they cheered the king. Unlike the officers they had nothing to lose. Any further resistance was washed away with the gift to each sailor of a pint of wine.

This was the feeling of the fleet that arrived off Scheveningen on 13 May. The monstrous effigy of Cromwell had been removed from *Naseby*; the royal arms were painted on to the ships; the harp emblem of the Commonwealth was cut out of the flags and replaced with yellow cloth hastily cut to resemble a crown and the letters *CR* – Carolus (Charles) Rex. The royal party kept the fleet waiting. Montagu and Pepys whiled away the time playing ninepins. On 22 May the Lord High Admiral of England, James Stuart, duke of York – the king's brother – paid a visit. He had held the post since he was four; only now, aged twenty-seven, did it have any meaning. The next day the king boarded *Naseby*, which was immediately renamed *Royal Charles*.

The fleet returned to Dover with the royal family. The cannon fired in celebration all the way. Charles entertained the assembled company, including an entranced Pepys, with tales of his escape from the Commonwealth's army in 1651. The Navy was Royal once again.

The Navy had made England feared and respected around the world. It achieved a level of success that exceeded the defeat of the Armada. The deeds of this period of naval history are not well known now, but they were celebrated as a golden age long into the eighteenth century. Under republican government and Cromwell's Protectorship the Navy had come of age.

It had been floated on the money that a ruthless military government had extorted from the people of England. Money had lubricated the administrative system, making it work with unprecedented efficiency. Money had transformed it from a force of forty mainly large ships to one of 130, from enormous first-rates to the indispensable frigate. Money manned the fleet and, when it lasted, kept it loyal. 'Money, money, money' – that's what was said to be the first mover of the Navy back in

1628. But the revenue had dried up and in 1660 the Navy had debts in excess of £1,250,000.

It looked as if it might be the millstone that sank the restored monarchy. To an observer it would seem that traditional government, with its creaky revenue-raising mechanisms and antiquated administrative system, would turn the Navy's glory days into a flash in the pan, a deviation from the historical norm.

But in fact the Restoration did not stop the process of revolution that had gripped the Navy. It spurred it on.

PART 7: SONS OF THE SEA

CHAPTER 21

CLUB MED

When sailors get good wine,

They think themselves in heaven for the time.

John Baltharpe

Cadiz. Tangier. Malaga. Alicante. Genoa. Leghorn. Naples. Messina. Gallipoli. Zante. Constantinople. Smyrna. Scanderoon. These were exotic names, enough to set the pulse of an English sailor racing. As ships entered Mediterranean harbours they were frequently greeted by boats full of prostitutes, promises of delights awaiting. 'There's many a lad in the navy gets a clap before the ship's moored.[1]'

Shore leave meant respite from the routine and privations on board. Sailors were notorious for rowdiness and drunkenness in towns; they were eager customers at brothels in England and elsewhere. A Christianised Turk living at Leghorn reverted to Islam when he witnessed English sailors on the rampage. It was said that a sailor's annual wages could be blown in a matter of hours. These were pleasures that were clung to until the last bitter moment. When he left England on a warship for the Mediterranean the chaplain Henry Teonge recorded in his diary the activities of the crew and the women they had brought with them to spend the last night in home waters: 'You would have wondered to see here a man and a woman creep into a hammock, the women's legs to the hams hanging over the sides or out the end of it. Another couple sleeping on a chest; others kissing and clipping; half drunk, half sober or rather half asleep.'

It was a similar scene in every Navy ship departing at the beginning of summer.[2] Their destinations varied. In 1680, for example, six ships were stationed in the Soundings, the western approaches to the Channel. During their time in that station they might convoy merchant ships going south, as far as Tangier, the Biscayan coast, Portugal, the Canaries and Malaga, or north to Iceland. Two warships went with the Newfoundland fishing fleet and convoyed them back across the Atlantic, bound for the lucrative Iberian and Italian fish markets. Two ships went to the eastern Mediterranean guarding the Levant Company fleet. Two ships were to begin the season protecting the herring fleet off Yarmouth as they ploughed the seas before convoying them to the Mediterranean. Another two escorted the merchants trading to Iberia and Italy. Less lucky crews were dispatched to patrol Irish waters (two ships); Jersey, Guernsey, Portsmouth, Sheerness, the Leeward Islands, Barbados and Jamaica were assigned one guard ship each. Ten ships patrolled the Strait of Gibraltar, and one was stationed at the English naval base, Tangier, which – with Bombay – had been the dowry of Charles II's Portuguese bride.

This last group, the Mediterranean squadron, was the core of English naval strength in the region. It varied in size. In 1679, when Algerine piracy was particularly rife, there were thirty-five ships patrolling the Strait. Their primary role was to take on the corsairs, keeping station off the enemy coast or cruising the seas searching for predators. But during their time in the area they might be dispatched to convoy merchantmen anywhere between English waters and Scanderoon (modern-day Iskenderun in Syria). Ships in need of repair and resupply went to Leghorn.

The women Teonge records spending the last nights with their men were with the ship from the Thames Estuary to the Downs, where they had to return ashore. There were always tearful partings when that moment came. The men sang, to the sounds of trumpets, the traditional sailor's ballad 'Loath to Depart'.

John Baltharpe, a petty officer in the Royal Navy, wrote a long piece of doggerel verse about a voyage to the Mediterranean in the 1670s on board St David, which with forty-six guns and a crew of 240 was one of the largest frigates in the Mediterranean. It is rich in detail of the thoughts and feelings of the men on a tough cruise, particularly their thoughts and feelings regarding sex and alcohol. He recounted his parting from home: 'On deck I stood, and by moonlight, / Of England that same night lost sight; / Farewell fair England, thrice farewell.'

Cry they might as they left England; as soon as they reached a foreign port these lachrymose tars made haste to the brothels or entertained women on board. When Montagu left Lisbon in 1661 thirty-seven men, from a crew of 300, had to be treated for venereal disease. Prostitutes who took a boat out to greet an English ship could be sure of business.

There would be others waiting for those ships. Mediterranean ports were the temporary homes of sailors, and many wanted berths to take them onwards or back to England. The Navy needed between 3,000 and 4,000 men a year to crew between twenty and forty ships, most of which were fourth, fifth and sixth rates, and a handful third rates.* In peacetime the service had little trouble manning its ships. And in peacetime the Mediterranean was the hub of the Navy's activities.

For the mass of seamen a stint on a warship was but one aspect of a life at sea. Edward Coxere was fluent in four languages, the result of the harum-scarum life of a mariner. He served several masters in the Civil Wars. Afterwards he fought for the Spanish against the French, then the Dutch against the English. Then he served the English against the Dutch. He was captured by Barbary corsairs and made to attack ships from all nations. He was rescued from slavery and put into an English warship to fight the Spanish. Then he was captured by the Spanish. He escaped, returned home and sailed for Newfoundland.

Not all sailors were buffeted as far and wide as Coxere, but most drifted between merchantmen and Navy ships, securing their pay and moving on. For many a sailor, the Navy represented a means of transport, a stepping stone in a perpetual hunt for lucre, not a career. These men were able to survive a brutal and capricious lifestyle. When they joined one of the king's ships at Yarmouth or Leghorn, Portsmouth or Messina they entered a world they knew, a structured life.

The ship's bell struck the hour, every hour. Every fourth hour the bell rang eight times. That was the signal for the rotation of the watch. The routine never changed while the ship was at sea. When the men joined the ship they were assigned one of two watches, the starboard or the larboard. For four hours one watch was on duty, while the members of the alternate watch slept or relaxed. At eight bells the off duty men got out of their hammocks or roused themselves and took up their allotted station. The youngest, nimblest seamen, known as 'topmen' went aloft, high on the steepling masts and out on the yards, to handle the sails, keep lookout and repair the miles of rigging. The 'waisters' down below in the waist of the ship comprised older sailors, no longer capable of working aloft. These men were experienced, and their task was to assist the boatswain with the headsails and other specialised tasks. The least experienced of all, the ordinary seamen, spent the watch with the waisters in the waist, on the quarterdeck or as forecastlemen, hauling on ropes, a job which required

* Rate	Guns	Crew	Number in 1660	in 1688
1st	86–100	430–815	4	9
2nd	54–90	270–660	11	11
3rd	52–74	210–470	15	39
4th	32–26	115–280	45	43
5th	26–32	80–135	35	12
6th	4–18	18–85	20	8
			130	122

little skill or dexterity but a lot of sweat. For topmen, waisters and ordinary seamen it was four hours of hard, repetitive toil; every manoeuvre in a ship at sea required the united backbreaking labour of dozens of men.

There were men exempt from the remorseless cycle of the watch. These were known as 'idlers' because they slept at night and worked during the day. They were the specialists and craftsmen, a distinct sort from the men who kept watch, who were known as 'seamen'. Idlers might do skilled work for the ship's carpenter, the sailmaker, the gunner, the blacksmith and other small crews which did vital daily work separate from the present business of the ship. At times, such as when the vessel tacked or was buffeted by storms or sighted a hostile ship, the whole crew—including the idlers and men off duty—might be piped urgently to their stations to contribute their muscle power. This obligation to muck in at odd hours would have been common for an English sailor in the Mediterranean in the 1660s and 1670s because their frigates had smaller crews compared to a line of battle ship.

A sailor over the age of twenty and who had five years' worth of experience at sea was rated an able seaman, deemed 'fit for helm, lead, top and yards' – that is, steering the ship, taking the soundings and working aloft. He was paid twenty-four shillings a month. Ordinary seamen did more menial tasks and were paid less. In addition to the able and ordinary seamen and the idlers were other groups. Every ship carried trumpeters who transmitted orders throughout the ship. Also among the ship's company would be a large number of boys, many of them officers' servants on board to learn the ways of the sea. The loblolly boys assisted the surgeon. The youngest topmen worked on the highest yards, where the sails were lighter. Edward Barlow, a boy from Prestwich, joined the *Naseby* as apprentice to the chief master's mate in 1659. In 1661–62 he went to the Mediterranean. His journal informs much of what we know about life in the Restoration Navy.

We are lucky that Edward Barlow kept a journal in which he detailed the horrors, as well as the respites, of life in the Royal Navy. He wrote about how after only half an hour's worth of sleep he and his fellows were

> forced to go up into the maintop or foretop to take in our topsails, half
> awake and half asleep, with one shoe on and the other off, not having
> time to put it on; always sleeping in our clothes for readiness; and in
> stormy weather, when the ship rolled and tumbled as though some great
> millstone were rolling up one hill and down another, we had much ado
> to hold ourselves fast by the small ropes from falling by the board; and

being gotten up into the tops, there we must heave and pull to make fast
the sail, seeing nothing but air above us and water beneath us, and that
as raging as though every wave would make a grave for us: and many
times in night so dark that we could not see one another, and blowing
so hard that we could not hear one another speak.

The daily tasks involved in keeping a ship in good shape were legion.

And there were other major jobs, which did not occur daily. Raising
the great anchors with the capstan or recovering one of the ship's boats
might involve hours of toil. After weeks at sea or after battles with the
corsairs the men had to repair leaks, damage from cannonballs and mend
broken masts and yards. Ships also had to be careened—beached and laid
over to repair the hull below the waterline and scrape off the barnacles
and weeds—and tallowed with animal fat to make them waterproof.

It was part and parcel of life at sea. Baltharpe described the topmen
chatting as they worked high up on the yards: 'pastimes with girlies',
comments on the honesty of the purser and complaints about the officers
forming part of the conversation. As the time at sea wore on, when rumours spread that the ship was bound for a friendly port the talk would
be of wine and of the women awaiting them at Leghorn or Malaga or
some other destination.

When the bell rang eight times again the men coming off duty
retired to their messes on the gun deck. Each mess contained between
four and eight sailors, half of whom belonged to the starboard watch and
the other half to the larboard, so that those relaxing and sleeping might
have a bit of space while their fellows worked. The mess centred on a
table between two guns. Here a sailor had to get what rest and privacy he
could and store his few personal possessions. Here too would be stowed
the sailors' hammocks and pewter plates. No natural light penetrated the
gundeck, and, because the gunports were shut while at sea, the air was far
from fresh.

At seven every night the men took their plates to the galley, situated
in the forecastle, collected their food and returned to their mess table.
Regulations stated that the men should be given fish, pork or beef every
day, and a gallon of beer. This was the most sociable time of the day.
Tales were told, songs sung, money hazarded on games. Many of those
who recorded the sights and sounds of life on seventeenth-century ships
noted the universal fondness for dancing and bawdy songs. Baltharpe said
that his fellow crew members danced to the tune of a fiddle; sometimes
they would just 'hop about'. Bulstrode Whitelocke, when he travelled to

Before Britain could be defended from the sea, the island's rivers had to be secure. The importance of rivers in the medieval period is highlighted in Matthew Paris's map of Britain, c.1250

Deadly elegance: the Gokstad ship at the Viking Ship Museum, Oslo.

The Battle of Sluys, 24 June 1340. Fighting at sea was nasty, brutish and short – much like combat on land – but in confined spaces and with the added risk of drowning.

Henry Grace à Dieu, also known as the *Great Harry*. This immense floating castle was the pride of Henry VIII's navy and a symbol of his majesty.

English ships clash with the Spanish Armada off Gravelines, 28 July 1588.

A model of Charles I's *Sovereign of the Seas*, launched in 1637. The Dutch called her the 'Golden Devil' because of her outrageously ornate decorations and firepower of 100 guns. Everything about her was designed to awe: ten men could fit into her stern lantern.

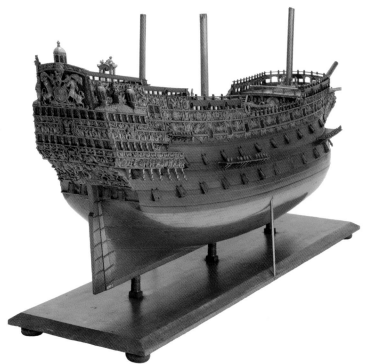

The Navy's disgrace: the mighty *Royal Charles* (formerly the *Naseby*), flagship of Prince James, Duke of York, is sailed out of Chatham by her Dutch captors after the raid on the Medway, 9–14 June 1667

An English frigate in action with Barbary Corsairs, 1680. The campaign against the corsairs in the Mediterranean in the late seventeenth century helped transform the service.

The results of a ruthless operation by the Royal Navy. Twelve French ships of the line were burned by English raiding parties led by Rear Admiral George Rooke on 23–24 May 1692.

Sir Cloudesely Shovell served in the Royal Navy during the time it came of age, between the 1660s and the early eighteenth century. He fought in some of the Navy's most gruesome battles and commanded with distinction in the wars against France between 1689 and his death by shipwreck in 1707.

Few officers left such an enduring mark on the Navy as George Anson. His circumnavigation of the world was the stuff of legend and his victory at the First Battle of Cape Finisterre in 1747 elevated him to the pantheon of great admirals. Anson's reforms, talent for administration and strategic brilliance were instrumental in giving the Royal Navy dominance in every ocean of the world by the end of the Seven Years War.

Britain's yards were the envy of the world, a matter of national pride and the foundation of naval strength. Here, on 21 October 1755, HMS *Cambridge* (80 guns) is being floated out from the dry dock in which she was constructed. HMS *Royal George* (100 guns) rides at anchor in the Thames. Under construction, in the centre of the painting, is one of Anson's new 74-gun third rates.

Chase and kill: the First Battle of Cape Finisterre, 3 May 1747. This crushing victory over the French brought naval warfare out into the Atlantic.

The day after the Battle of Quiberon Bay, 21 November 1759. This was one of the greatest victories in the history of the Royal Navy; the vivid depiction of the ships aground on jagged rocks in rough November seas is a reminder of the risks taken by Admiral Lord Hawke in pursuit of total victory and of the skills of his men.

Sweden as ambassador during the Interregnum, chatted with the sailors and even joined their roughhousing on deck, 'affording them now and then a douse in the neck, or a kick in jest ... which demeanours please those kind of people'.[3]

At other times the men puffed on clay pipes. It was hardly surprising that on a wooden ship, where naked flames were dreaded and continually watched for, this was subject to strict regulations. Smoking took place around a tub of water on the forecastle. While on the theme of material needs, the 'pissdale', the urinal, was on the upper deck; bowels were evacuated into the plunging waves from the 'heads' in the beakhead.

It was well said that 'nothing will poison a sailor'; he had to have 'an invincible stomach, which ostrich-like could near well digest iron'.[4] Fresh food and beer lasted only so long at sea. Then the crew had to fall back on preserved foodstuffs, some of them years old. A shortage of fresh food made diseases, in particular scurvy, inevitable. The West Indies were a veritable graveyard thanks to tropical illnesses such as yellow fever. Typhus swept through places where men were crowded together for prolonged periods in unhygienic conditions. Dysentery was a danger to the health of a ship's company. As a result of repetitive hard labour in cold weather seamen suffered from hernias, rheumatism, ulcers and respiratory complaints.

The ships in the Mediterranean squadron also remained on duty for long periods. A frigate escorting the Newfoundland fishing fleet would take five weeks to cross the Atlantic; it then waited weeks, perhaps months, while the catch was brought in before sailing to and around the Mediterranean, a leg of the voyage which could last six months. As the weeks passed, the stocks of food and beer deteriorated and rations were restricted. Disease proliferated. The ships would be in need of repair. Sailors were put on 'short allowance' – that is to say the rations for four men would have to do for six.

Such hazards were common to all ships, and the Navy provided more plentiful supplies than most merchantmen. The arrival of a ship in a Mediterranean port meant, among other things, a respite from the onboard fare – the black bread and ageing salted beef and pork (nicknamed 'salt junk'). Baltharpe recorded vividly the delights of arriving at Messina. Sailors stocked up in the market, buying ale, cabbages, carrots, turnips, nuts, eggs, lemons, oranges and figs to take back on board. But more enticing were the liquors: Sicilian wine and brandy. The young Barlow, on his maiden voyage to the Mediterranean, recalled his amazement at the goods on sale at Alicante: fruits, figs, oranges, lemons, pomegranates, almonds. Much of this was purchased from bumboats that raced out to meet the frigates.

If there was no money at hand sailors would swap their clothing for alcohol; they came back to ship lacking 'not only coats but also wits'. Pursers sold sailors 'slops', or hard-wearing work clothes, the cost deducted from their pay. There was no uniform as such, but most sailors typically wore red Monmouth caps, blue or white shirts, white kerchiefs, leather jackets and blue waistcoats. Sailors obtained these clothes on credit and exchanged them for food and wine. The more they bought, the less money they claimed on return.

'A merry life and a short!' was the maxim of English sailors. Coxere recalled spending money from a Spanish prize on shore so that for the next leg of the voyage he and his fellows 'had good victuals and good drink often'. It was better to enjoy comforts today than save for the future.

Supplies often ran low or the food became unpalatable. Officers showed paternalistic concern for their men, preferring a harmonious ship to a fractious one. But concern and solidarity only went so far. Edward Barlow believed that the sailor's lot was so brutal and his temperament so cussed that he had to be driven to work. It was an opinion that was becoming more common in the second half of the seventeenth century.

The Naval Discipline Act of 1661 'for the regulating and better Government of His Majesty's Navies' introduced thirty-five articles; ten more orders were added in 1663. The Act stated that offences such as swearing, quarrelling and drunkenness should be punished by a fine (a day's pay) or imprisonment. Sodomy, murder, theft, embezzlement, sleeping on watch, striking an officer, mutiny and desertion could be punished by death. The orders of 1663 allowed captains to impose lesser punishments for offences such as sleeping on watch or theft.

Captains preferred not to resort to the death penalty. The most common punishment was the lash. One of the first recorded instances of miscreants being whipped around the fleet came from a squadron in the Mediterranean in 1654. One sailor was given four lashes on every ship for striking his captain; two men were given three on each ship for the crimes of drunken brawling and theft. By the Restoration this practice had grown common and was harsher. A sailor who abetted the striking of an officer in 1675 was given nineteen lashes on six ships and thirty-one on the flagship. There are hardly any accounts of punishments for homosexuality. Titus Oates, a chaplain on a naval ship and soon to have a major impact on English history, was discharged for sodomy.

Other crimes were dealt with in humiliating and painful ways at the discretion of the officers. On Teonge's ship sailors who swore stood for an hour with marlinspikes forced into their mouths. By long tradition the first sailor caught lying on a Monday was taken to the mainmast while the crew chanted 'A liar, a liar, a liar!' His task for the rest of the week was to scrub the sides of the ship and the chains, directly below the heads. The post of shit-scraper was actually named 'the liar'. On one occasion sailors who stole beef had pieces of beef hung round their necks and were fastened to the mainmast; their fellows then queued up to rub the raw meat into the offenders' mouths. Other punishments included being clapped in bilboes (iron restraints). Sailors returning late from shore leave were ducked from the yardarm.

These were official punishments, intended to be exemplary. In the day-to-day life of the ship discipline was enforced directly. The extent of this varied from ship to ship and officer to officer. The sudden lash of a rope-end or the harsh rap of the boatswain's cudgel could be a daily experience. During the Interregnum Admiralty officials heard complaints from ordinary seamen and sometimes upheld them. After the Restoration those who tried to go above their captains' heads faced the lash.

The harshness of the disciplinary code had to be balanced against other considerations. An aggrieved ship's company was like a powder keg. Most officers had to rely on co-operation with their crew and they put persuasion far above the prescribed punishments as a tool of leadership. And most men knew that a disorderly ship was a dangerous one, that obedience and harmonious relations made for safety and profit from prize money.

The quality of life depended on the character and abilities of the officers. Sailors served with enthusiasm officers they trusted. At the heart of a ship's life were the standing officers – the boatswain, gunner, carpenter, purser and cook. Unlike everyone else on board, these men belonged to the ship, serving at sea and when the ship was laid up 'in ordinary'; as captains and crew members came and went they provided continuity.

The standing officers, like the men they commanded, gained their experience on a variety of ships throughout their careers, be they merchantmen or warships.[5] They rose through the ranks. As they served and gained experience they picked up certificates attesting to their skills and competence. They obtained recommendations from senior figures in the Navy – dockyard officials, captains, flag officers – and were then examined by the Navy Board, which then passed suitable names to the Admiralty. Successful candidates had their names entered in the official lists. When a vacancy on a ship arose there was a fierce scramble. Those chosen to become a standing officer were given a warrant by the Admiralty.

In the daily round of chores and duties the boatswain loomed large in a sailor's life. He and his mate were in charge of the working of the deck and the yards. The bosun was the foreman to the crew. He supervised many of the most common daily tasks: maintaining the ropeworkings of the ship, the sails and anchors. He reigned supreme above deck and directing activities aloft, governing the duties of the crew with a silver whistle round his neck and rope-end in hand.

The gunner's inner sanctum was the powder room and magazine, below the waterline. The ordnance, shot and powder had to be checked constantly, guarded against naked flames and kept in readiness for battle at short notice. During a battle the guns had to be fed with powder. The gunner sent up the explosives to the gun decks in small batches to prevent serious explosions. It was an important job, only to be entrusted to an experienced, meticulous man. A small mistake, such as powder left carelessly in the vicinity of naked flames, could lead to catastrophe; ships' magazines exploded with sickening regularity, obliterating ships and their crews in a moment. During the frequent sharp running duels with North African pirates a frigate's guns had to fire rapidly and accurately. The success of the ship depended on the training the gunner had given to his crews and the state of preparedness of the ship's arsenal; its safety relied on the care taken to isolate gunpowder in small batches so that accidental explosions were limited.

The carpenter had a vital and endless role: wooden sailing ships needed repairs all the time. He had to keep the pumps in order, hunt for and plug leaks, replace spars that had sprung in bad weather, inspect the caulking, maintain the rudder and so ad infinitum as the ship cut through the waves and navigated storms. Every day he reported to the captain how much water the ship was making. These men knew the ships intimately.

Pursers were vital and loathed members of the company. They procured supplies and allocated them to the men; they paid the men and advanced them credit. If they failed to revictual the ship adequately their standing with the crew plummeted. Many a purser filled his pockets by selling raggedy slops at inflated prices to desperate sailors who needed them to swap for food, drink and sex in foreign ports.

The lowest of the ship's standing officers, the cook, was commonly a badly wounded sailor employed as a reward for faithful services. His domain was the galley, located in the forecastle.

The standing officers were a permanent fixture in a fluctuating world. They enjoyed status and regular employment. Less secure, but almost as important, were the petty officers who assisted them – the various mates and lesser rated officers. The mates were qualified to deputise for the master, boatswain, carpenter and gunner and assist them in their work. Other men of this rank included the sailmaker, cooper, armourer, purser's steward, quartermasters and various other craftsmen and mates. Among the crew were men who enjoyed authority but no official status: each mast top and every gun had its 'captain' who oversaw working and fighting. The petty officers were chosen by their senior officers. When the voyage came to an end they sought employment elsewhere.

The petty officers were the backbone of the Navy. A ship was only safe and successful if all its many tasks were performed like clockwork. The vessel was held together by many different teams, who made up the cogs in the mechanism. The petty officers led and managed these teams, kept order below decks and acted as conduits up and down the ship's rigid hierarchy. So much depended on the petty officers. Those who excelled took the step up to mate and then warrant officer.

Promotion for any standing officer meant being transferred to a higher-rate ship. Or they could become master attendants in the dockyards, responsible for the ships of the line kept in ordinary. A carpenter could become a master shipwright. Pursers were drawn from the Navy's onshore bureaucracy and the lucky ones ended up as senior clerks at the Admiralty or Navy Board. Occasionally warrant officers made it to the top. John Berry, for example, joined the Newfoundland fishing fleet when he was a small boy. He became a boatswain in a Royal Navy ship stationed in the West Indies in his mid-twenties. Within two years he was appointed captain of his ship. He eventually rose to the rank of rear admiral.

There were plenty of men prepared to serve on a warship in lesser positions than those they were used to. Midshipmen, in this period, were highly experienced seamen who had worked their way up and hoped one day to receive warrants. But some midshipmen were travelling in the opposite direction: former boatswains, gunners, masters, sometimes even captains seeking employment. They were ready and qualified to take over the duties of running the ship should any of the standing officers become indisposed.

Also appointed on a voyage-by-voyage basis were the non-standing warrant officers. The surgeon was examined at the Barber-Surgeon's Hall and issued with a warrant by the Navy Board. Until 1665 chaplains were picked by the captains; after that they were selected by the Archbishop of Canterbury, and after 1677 by the Bishop of London.

Warrant officers enjoyed several privileges. Not least of these were where they slept and where they defecated – things that, next to food, preoccupied everyone at sea. The boatswain and carpenter had cabins at the quarterdeck bulkhead with easy access to the deck in case of emergency. At the end of the maindeck was the wardroom, where the master and lieutenant and, space permitting, other warrant officers, had cabins. The privilege of sleeping and eating in the wardroom conferred status. The gunroom, the aftermost part of the gundeck, was partitioned off by canvas and provided a small amount of space for the other warrant officers, midshipmen and some mates to sling their hammocks. Most of the petty officers slept under the forecastle. The wardroom officers enjoyed the use of the quarter galleries for the purpose of defecation. The other officers and senior petty officers were allowed to use the two tiny private roundhouses in the head for the same call of nature. Henry Teonge made a lot of his luck in getting hold of a much-used chamber pot. These things mattered.

Of all the warrant officers, the master enjoyed the greatest status and was the most technically qualified. He was responsible for the navigation, steering the ship and trimming the sails. He gave his orders to the boatswain and the quartermasters, the petty officers who steered the ship. Masters were non-standing warrant officers because they were experts in specific geographical locations: they joined the voyage, not the ship. A master gained his qualifications as the result of an exacting examination at Trinity House. He was expected to be expert in all matters of deep-sea and coastal navigation and pilotage. His certificates specified the rate of ship he could command and the geographical area in which he had gained his experience. If a ship was lost or damaged as a result of error the master took the blame.

Officers were every bit as obsessed with food and drink as the men. Teonge recorded over seventy different foodstuffs, including exotic fruits, fish, cheeses, salads and veal. When things went well, he wrote, an officer could have a better life in the Mediterranean, 'where we have good meat, and good drink, and good divertissements, without the least care and sorrow and trouble', than he did at home. At Christmas they had beef, plum pudding, mince pies; on the king's birthday they ate veal, mackerel, lobster, salad and eggs. Off Malta a group of captains ate a meal comprising 'a gallant baked pudding'; a leg of pork and cauliflowers; a dish made up of trotters, two roasted pigs, a turkey, a hog's head and three ducks; a dish made of Cyprus birds; then pistachios and dates; and the whole lot washed down with a 'store of good wines'.

It was a boozy existence. Teonge noted twenty-two different beverages, from Margate ale to chocolate. Meals were washed down with wines, sherry, raki, cider or ale. On Saturdays by custom the officers indulged in endless toasts to wives and absent friends. 'Punch and brandy,' Teonge remarked, '... have run as freely as dishwater'. Officers enjoyed playing and listening to music and singing; some brought musical instruments on board or had servants with musical skills. They read books, many of them spending their time off duty studying navigation, geography and naval history. Sometimes a captain fostered a convivial atmosphere among the entire ship's company. Sir John Harman, for instance, was said by Pepys to be hung over when he appeared before parliament because he had been carousing with his crew the night before. The duke of Grafton was a highly popular captain, described as being on familiar terms with the men under his command; he would often join in the 'rough sports' enjoyed by his crews.[6]

It was a hard, precarious life for everyone on board. Battles with Barbary pirates were savage. In one encounter all the officers on *Rupert*, from the captain down to the boatswain's mate, were killed. But at least the officers enjoyed some small comforts. The sailors who drifted in and out of the Navy had the most to lose. At melancholy intervals on his voyage from the Thames to Scanderoon, Henry Teonge had to bury men who died from accidents and diseases.

The Mediterranean station became, during the reign of Charles II, the most likely destination for an English sailor. Behind this social history lies a very important point not just for the history of the Navy but the history of England. During this time England went from being an exporter of wool and cloth and a bit-part player in the European economy to a major trading nation. In 1660 the total tonnage of English ships stood at 162,000; it had leapt to 340,000 by 1686. That meant more shipwrights, flourishing ports and, crucially, more seafarers. The Mediterranean was the mainstay of the country's booming wealth. This sea would become the most vital region for the Royal Navy until the 1950s; it would be the scene of some of its greatest triumphs. The giant stride for English trade meant a greatly expanded role for the Navy. It also provided the revenue to fund a large permanent marine force. The presence of thousands of English sailors at ports from Tangier to Syria was a testament to this significant development in the country's history. For all the hardships, service in the Royal Navy was no worse and often better than on civilian ships or privateers. Barlow complained that beggars in England led better lives than sailors in the Navy. But that was a ridiculous exaggeration: beggars did not have periodic feasts of fruits or trysts with Mediterranean women. British sailors were well fed and probably enjoyed meat more than their relations on land. Their working life was hard, but so was the lot of many in seventeenth century England. Even compared to other sailors a man in the Navy did well: he ate better and did less work because warships were overmanned compared to merchantmen.

It was a tempting lifestyle, for all the dangers and privations. The complaining Barlow had the chance to go home early from his first Mediterranean cruise, but he moved to another ship so that he could continue. He 'always [had] a mind to see strange countries and fashions'. On a tour of duty men might see smoke rising out of volcanoes; they experienced earthquakes; they saw at first hand places whose names were familiar from the Bible and the classics. The allure of the exotic and the chances of earning a tidy sum in prize money meant that the Navy's berths were always taken. A century and a half later the wanderlust of English sailors had hardly changed: 'such is the love for roaming of our men',[7] wrote Nelson, 'that I am sure they would desert from heaven to hell merely for the sake of change'.

This is the story of the peacetime Navy; war was another matter.

CHAPTER 22

BATTLEFLEET

Of all our navy none should now survive,
But that the ships themselves were taught to dive.

Andrew Marvell

'We did heretofore fight for tickets; now we fight for dollars!'[1] So went the cry from English sailors in the Medway in 1667. For years they had received paper tickets that promised payment at a later date. Now these sailors had coin in their pockets. The problem was that they were prisoners-of-war serving on Dutch ships.

The Dutch raid on the Medway was the worst disaster in English naval history. On 10 June they arrived off the Isle of Sheppey, to find a solitary frigate guarding England's most important estuary. The fleet sailed on down the Medway, encountering the improvised English defences at Gillingham. Peter Pett, scion of the great shipbuilding family and Navy Commissioner at Chatham, had sunk a dozen ships above the defensive chain.

The advance Dutch frigates cleared a channel by removing the scuttled ships. A fireship sailed over the chain and engineers demolished the stages to sink the chain and allow the larger warships to sail over. *Unity* was captured and *Charles V* and *Matthias* burnt. Most spectacularly of all, the mighty *Royal Charles*, flagship of the admiral of the fleet, was captured. This disaster forced the duke of Albemarle (George Monck, as he was in republican days) to give orders to scuttle the rest of the English fleet in Gilliam Reach.

The next day the Dutch frigates opened fire on Upnor Castle, while the fireships made for the Royal Navy's principal ships, which now had holes smashed in their hulls to render them immobile. The small, poorly armed skeleton crews stood no chance against the fiery terror. *Loyal London* (92) was burnt first*; then *Royal James* burst into flames, then *Royal Oak*.

---

* The numbers in brackets after a ship's name here, and hereafter, refer to the number of main armament guns she carried.

The following day Dutch demolition teams rowed back in among the half-submerged English ships. Then the Dutch withdrew and began to harry the east coast. The whole of England was tormented by terrible rumours. Samuel Pepys recorded: 'The Dutch fleet are in great squadrons everywhere still about Harwich, and were lately at Portsmouth; and the last letters say at Plymouth, and now gone to Dartmouth to destroy our Strait's fleet ... it was pretty news come the other day so fast, of the Dutch being in so many places, that Sir W Batten at table cried, *By God ... I think the Devil shits Dutchmen.*'[2]

If you go to the Rijksmuseum in Amsterdam you can still see the gigantic coat of arms taken from the transom of *Royal Charles*. The ship itself was turned into a tourist attraction for parties of gawpers until 1672 when she was auctioned for scrap.* The Royal Navy lost four of its five flagships. It was stabbed in its vitals, Gillingham Reach, where the bulk of the battlefleet was laid up.

The Medway raid was a disastrous end to what was intended to be a glorious war. Perhaps reigniting the struggle with the Dutch made sense at court back in 1663. The new Lord High Admiral, James, Duke of York, had spent his youth in exile during the 1650s yearning for military glory. He was a soldier through and through.

James had been spoiling for a chance to lead his fleet. For personal, patriotic and political reasons the Dutch were the favoured enemy. Political because the Dutch republicans, led by Grand Pensionary Johan de Witt, gave succour to the English republicans. Patriotic because the Dutch were regarded as monopolising world trade. This was an age that believed the commodities of the world to be finite and the Dutch took the lion's share. The personal dimension combined the political and national. James detested the Calvinism of the Dutch Republic. He was also deeply involved in trade and colonialism.

James and his court followers established the Company of Royal Adventurers Trading into Africa, which sent ships commanded by Sir Robert Holmes to the West African coast in search of gold and slaves. This action trenched on the Dutch, who claimed a monopoly in West Africa.

The States General, in retaliation, sent Michiel de Ruyter to Guinea, where he rooted out the Royal Africa Company from its trading stations. He then raided the West Indies and attacked the Newfoundland fishing fleet. In response Sir Thomas Allin, commander-in-chief in the

* The Dutch also took the fourth rate *Unity*, or rather retook her, as she had been captured from them in 1665.

Mediterranean, attacked the homeward-bound Dutch Smyrna convoy. On the other side of the Atlantic Captain Richard Nicholls entered New Amsterdam harbour with four frigates and compelled the surrender of the town. It gave the English control of the eastern seaboard of North America from Virginia to Maine. The town was renamed, in honour of the Lord High Admiral, New York.

A peacetime Navy manned by a maximum of 4,000 sailors swelled into a battlefleet of over 100 battleships and 30,000 men.[3] The Mediterranean Fleet and ships on convoy duty round the world were recalled. English trade was left unprotected. The sailors on the recalled ships were not paid off. Instead they were 'turned over' – transferred to another warship, their pay deferred until they were finally discharged, which could be years hence.

Such men were put on the big floating castles – the first-, second- and third-rate battleships – which had to be brought out of ordinary and made ready. Their masts were raised and their guns brought on board. Finding tens of thousands of seamen willing to serve in them was a daunting task for the naval administration – and a moment of tribulation for the maritime community. There were never enough men willing to take their chances with campaigns of indeterminate, vicious sea battles, disease, the capricious victualling system and the lottery of naval pay.

But men *did* volunteer. A trusted officer with a good record could attract recruits from among those who knew him. The chartered companies, fishermen and Thames watermen were also supposed to provide quotas of sailors. Very often they wriggled out of their obligations with excuses or sent wholly unsuitable mariners – old men and boys. Many sailors volunteered for the battlefleet for one simple reason: when war came they reasoned that if they did join a warship it was better to go as a free man. The alternative was far worse.

The crew on a merchant ship returning from a long voyage on one of the distant trading routes might glimpse the shore of England and anticipate time on home soil after months at sea. Instead they would be met by a small boat and transferred to a warship. Fishermen homeward bound from Newfoundland, members of the herring fleet, men on colliers plying the east coast and foreign sailors got caught up in the Admiralty's dragnet.

The lanes and byways of maritime regions saw sailors fleeing inland when rumours of war became current. Barns and woods became the temporary dwelling places of these men. They picked up spades or helped with the plough – anything to conceal their real trade. They were evading the merciless press.

Any professional sailor was liable to serve in His Majesty's Navy in time of war. Parish constables in the maritime regions were charged with recruiting set numbers of seamen. Press officers and their gangs swept towns such as Portsmouth, Plymouth, Harwich and Yarmouth, searching homes, taverns and ships for sailors. It frequently led to fights – not just between the press gangs and the sailors, but also when sailors' wives intervened.

Edward Coxere was skilled at avoiding press gangs. On one occasion his ship, which had been to Malaga by way of Newfoundland, was searched by the press. Coxere hid on board, then smuggled himself ashore. He took to the back streets of Rotherhithe, hid in an alehouse and borrowed some clothes. He went to Dover, dodging press gangs the whole way, so he could hand over his wages to his parents. Coxere hid in his parents' house, but in the end emerged to volunteer because he was sick of being under self-imposed house arrest. It was hard for a press-master to miss a mariner. A life spent at sea affected the way a man walked, and the bow-legged, rolling gait was a dead giveaway. So were a tanned, weather-beaten face and tattoos.

When Pepys transported impressed men from the London jails to the fleet he was distressed at the miserable sight of landlubbers who had been pressed illegally, trooping off to a fate they could only imagine. Constables were eager to palm off parish nuisances on to the Navy, to the disgust of officers.

An unlucky landsman found himself in an unfamiliar place, in the wooden belly of a ship of the line – one of the sea monsters that were designed to hold their place in the line of battle in the face of murderous onslaughts. They lacked the intimacy of the frigates used in the Mediterranean during peacetime. A sailor on a ship like *Royal Charles* was one of several hundred men, perhaps even close to a thousand. Despite their fairytale looks, the big ships were floating artillery platforms destined to pummel and be pummelled in return at close quarters. Only the veterans of the First Anglo-Dutch war knew the reality of the carnage awaiting them.

Before the war started the second rate *London* exploded in the Thames, the result of an accident in the magazine. Most of the men on board – between three and four hundred – died; twenty-three men and one woman were blown clear and survived. It was a foretaste of what was to come.

War was declared in March. By the beginning of April the battlefleet was at Harwich, a hundred strong and ready for action. The king, an accomplished yachtsman, sailed among the mighty ships reviewing his

Navy from sea level. It sailed on 28 April to blockade the Dutch coast. By early May it was back, in need of food. At last, on 1 June, the Dutch were sighted off Southwold.

The Dutch were at sea to confront the English and remove the threat of blockade. They were led by Jacob van Wassenaer Obdam, a man who had risen without trace to the top of the Dutch navy. He had plenty of theories about fleet actions, but precious little experience. James had a fleet led by veterans of Cromwell's wars, men such as John Lawson, the earl of Sandwich (Montagu), Sir George Ayscue, the duke of Albemarle (George Monck) and other names from the past. Most important, he had William Penn, one of the great fighting sailors of the age, beside him as Captain of the Fleet.

Obdam did not believe that his fleet was up to the task of defeating the English. However he was under strict orders to engage. His plan was to take a defensive position downwind and keep the English at bay, so that he could disengage in good time, satisfying his bellicose political masters but saving his fleet.

For two days the fleets manoeuvred, each trying to gain the gage. Obdam had it at one point but, unaccountably, failed to attack. To the English it looked downright odd. The Dutch supreme commander was nicknamed 'foggy Obdam' for his indecisiveness. It was off Lowestoft that battle was finally joined. James had studied Blake and Monck's tactics and Fighting Instructions intently. What the duke wanted above all was to emulate the line of battle imposed upon the fleet at the Gabbard and Scheveningen. The updated Instructions of 1664 provided a signal to be given by the Admiral for a tack in line ahead to the larboard and starboard. He also ordered captains to hold their fire until they were close to the enemy. On the eve of war in 1665 he added new signals regarding line discipline. Most innovatively of all, he drilled the fleet in gunnery and formation in the run-up to battle.

James was clear on his tactics and aims for the coming battles: he would lead from the centre and he expected every captain to retain his discipline, keeping the fleet in its original cohesive line and firing broadsides at close range, until the enemy line was fractured. The battles he would lead would be formal affairs, fought according to textbook.

The two fleets passed each other, but at a distance, in line ahead. Then James ordered the fleet to tack in unison and engage at close quarters. At this stage in the history of naval warfare signalling in the heat of battle was in its infancy. The Admiral's flag was hoisted too late and there was not enough time to come about as James wished. Two more times the fleets passed each other at medium range, exchanging ineffectual barrages.

Such formalism probably meant little to the tens of thousands of sailors working the ships or waiting with their guns, catching glimpses through the open ports of ships half hidden in gunpowder smoke. It also confused some of the captains, who found it impossible to manoeuvre in unison as James wished. The English line held, even if it became somewhat bunched. Things were worse with the Dutch, who had lost all semblance of fleet discipline. Then the wind turned to the south-west, forcing the Dutch towards the English centre and vanguard. The English rearguard, led by Sandwich, broke out of line and sailed behind the Dutch. The move cut off the Dutch from their intended escape home.

The English centre and part of the van were hotly engaged. The Dutch were encircled and the lines broke down into a confusing melee with opposing ships and detached squadrons engaged in lethal duels. At no other time in history had there been so many heavy guns involved in a battle at sea. If being pressed to work a gigantic ship of the line had been bad enough at first, now it turned into hell.

The sound of the bombardments at the Battle of Lowestoft could be heard in Hyde Park. As ships' timbers were smashed into murderous splinters, chainshot fizzed through the rigging, the monstrous cacophony built and the dense black smoke descended, the cohesion of the fleet collapsed. From the first broadside the toiling gun crews lost sight of their close companions as the gun decks filled with smoke. This was when experience and training were vital, for in the cramped, dank gun decks the crews had to work in darkness, senses disorientated by explosions from all sides and the terrible heat emanating from overworked muzzles. In a way this was a small mercy, as it blotted out the cries of the dying and concealed the viscera slopping along the gun deck. For days after a battle, the survivors of all ranks would be deaf and blackened from the smoke. In the darkness cannonballs that penetrated the oak hull would ricochet around the deck, pulverising skulls and ripping off limbs. Very often guns broke loose from their tackles and caused disruption and injury by crashing up and down the deck. Still worse they might accidentally explode, killing their crews in a trice.

The force of a well-directed broadside was like an earthquake: your whole ship shuddered with the impact, and to the incessant din of the batteries were added the sounds of tearing, crashing and splintering as tons of iron ripped into your ship. Above decks and aloft the boatswain's and carpenter's crews scurried and climbed, making running repairs. They were exposed to the iron rain of cannonballs, small shot and musketballs lashing the decks. The lucky ones dodged the yards and spars that came crashing down onto deck. Aloft a deadly hail of chainshot scythed rigging, slashed sails and atomised masts.

Blood and adrenaline pumped into thousands of minds, not least the captains' who were obliged to follow strict orders and command their ships into the confusion of battle. Keeping together a battle line and directing it from the centre (as James intended) became impossible. For a start the hundred-strong line was so big that most flag officers and captains lost sight of all but the nearest vessels. Squadrons remained as units, but the line of battle disintegrated. For an hour the big English ships fired their broadsides at the Dutch. Obdam's fleet contained bigger and better ships than the ones Blake and Monck faced in the last war. As a result the battle was exceptionally bloody. The Dutch ship *Oranje* fought like a fury against Sandwich's Blue Squadron. Sandwich made for Obdam's flagship, *Eendracht*, but was encircled by Dutch warships. James sailed into the confusion to save the earl.

Into the epicentre sailed *Royal Charles*. The two flagships engaged each other. The battle-hardened William Penn wore a full suit of armour on the quarterdeck of *Royal Charles*. It was a wise choice. The deck and rigging of the ship were swept by chainshot. James was splattered with the brains and blood of the courtiers who stood with him.

This was the true face of naval warfare. The relentless deafening din, the pall of acrid smoke, the cartwheeling shards of wood and ricocheting shot were far from anyone's notion of romance. Obdam was said to have been smashed off his own deck by the force of a cannonball. There were no surviving witnesses in any case: *Eendracht* took a shot to her magazine and exploded, blasting lumps of charred timber over the entire battle site and slaughtering the crew in seconds.

Now the Dutch were leaderless and routed. Morale collapsed as the English mauled the remaining ships and sent in fireships to finish them off. The unflagging *Oranje* had been fighting hard all day, and now she turned on James's flagship. But she was shot to damnation and had lost half her crew of 400. Her brave captain fought on until the last moment. He died within an hour as a prisoner of war and his wreck of a ship was burnt by the English. The Dutch 'began to turn their arses and run'.

Around 300 Englishmen died, a third of them in *Mary*, which had been in the thick of it,* shielding James's flagship from Dutch boarding parties.

---

* HMS *Mary* was used to a mauling: in republican days she was named *Speaker*, the ship that under Stayner had led Blake's light squadron at Santa Cruz, where she bore the brunt of the Spanish counterattack.

That number included all the officers, bar the lieutenant, the master and Captain Jeremiah Smith. Smith was knighted for his bravery during the battle and he was commemorated, along with the admirals, in a series of portraits painted by Sir Peter Lely known as the *Flagmen of Lowestoft*. The only other non-flag officer in the series was Joseph Jordan, who took over command of *Royal Oak* when Lawson was mortally wounded. Jordan found the ship damaged and in disorder, its captain dying and its master dead. He was able to bring her back into the fight, where he did 'brave things', according to Pepys. The Royal Navy lost just one ship, the Dutch seventeen and had nine captured. Death in a sea battle was impartial. On the English side courtiers were decapitated and several captains killed, including the earl of Marlborough. Two flag officers were slain. Around 5,000 Dutchmen were killed or wounded and 2,000 taken prisoner.

If the English formation had not withstood the test of battle, its ships and men had. James had every chance to finish off the disordered Dutch fleet and end the war. James and Penn were exhausted by the day's ordeal; they retired to their cabins, leaving the flag captain, John Harman, in charge. In the middle of the night a courtier, Henry Brouncker, ordered that the fleet's sails be slackened. When James awoke the next morning he found to his horror that the Dutch had evaded him.

Why Brouncker acted as he did is a mystery. It was claimed that he was acting under orders from the duchess of York to keep her husband safe. Perhaps he was shell-shocked from the fight and wished to save the prince from the indiscriminate slaughter of another artillery barrage at close quarters.

Still, James could at last claim to be a valiant warrior. He had kept his cool on a brain-bespattered quarterdeck awash with gore. But it was clearly too dangerous for the heir to the throne to be exposed to such danger and Charles had to remove him from active command.

The months after Lowestoft were not good for England. A wealthy VOC fleet escaped the predatory Navy. The Dutch started to build warships that equalled the English second rates in size and armaments. And most alarmingly, France joined the war. Faulty intelligence suggested that the French navy was heading from the Mediterranean to link up with de Ruyter. The battlefleet was split in two on 29 May. Prince Rupert with twenty ships sailed west to cut off the French. The duke of Albemarle was left in the Downs with fifty-six ships. On the 31st he left the Downs – just in time as it turned out, for de Ruyter was out in force and in position to trap the Navy in its anchorage. Charles sent messages to Rupert to rejoin the main fleet. They did not arrive till 1 June – the day that

Albemarle decided to attack de Ruyter without waiting for reinforcements.

On the first day the Dutch captured four ships after another bloody line battle. During the evening Rear Admiral Harman's ship *Henry* was attacked by two fireships, which singed her sides and sails. The crew began to jump overboard in panic, but Harman rounded on the rest with his sword and forced them to stay on board. *Henry* lost two masts, the spar of one injuring Harman's leg when it crashed down. She was approached by the Dutch vice admiral, Cornelis Evertsen, who asked the English to surrender. 'I'm not up to it yet!' Harman shouted back. He fought off three Dutch fireship attacks and cut through the dispersing Dutch battleships. Evertsen was cut in two by a cannonball fired from the parting *Henry*. She retired to Harwich for repairs and was back with Albemarle the next day.

On 2 June the English sailed down on the enemy line abreast, forming the line of battle when they reached close range. The English kept formation as they manoeuvred, something they had not done at Lowestoft. For ten hours the two fleets passed each other repeatedly on opposite tacks, firing all the while.

By the beginning of the third day both sides had worn each other down after hours of furious fighting and manoeuvring in line. The English were certainly the worse off. Albemarle had begun with fifty-six ships; he commenced the second day with fifty and the third with just twenty-eight. Only a few had been destroyed or captured; the majority had been blasted out of action. One of these, *Antelope*, was described by her lieutenant: 'our ship [was] cruelly shattered, our commander's arm shot off, 55 of our men killed and never so many more wounded, our masts, sails and rigging all in tatters, our deck dyed with blood like a slaughter house!'[4] Albemarle formed his fifteen stoutest ships into line abreast to cover a retreat. What had saved the English was their ability to hold a line and manoeuvre in unison. 'Nothing equalled the good order and discipline of the English,'[5] wrote an admiring Frenchman.

That afternoon the beleaguered duke saw a welcome sight: Prince Rupert and the rest of the fleet.

The two forces sped towards each other. But a hidden danger lurked to hamper their union. The Galloper Shoal – which lies due east of Clacton-on-Sea – was at low tide. *Royal Charles*, *Royal Katherine* and *Prince Royal* ran aground. The Dutch were approaching. The first two ships got free and away, but *Prince Royal*, the doughty survivor of the reign of James I and the second-largest ship in the Navy, was stuck fast. She was the flagship of the luckless George Ayscue, who ordered his men to stand firm and wait for the sea to free them too. But the men were in terror and the rudder was damaged. Ayscue earned the unenviable distinction of being the only English admiral of his rank to surrender. Back in the first war he had been defeated by de Ruyter, unquestionably the best admiral of his age; now he was the Dutchman's prisoner. De Ruyter ordered *Prince Royal* to be burnt. Her loss was a blow to national prestige and left a gaping hole in the line of battle.

The English began the fourth day with fifty-two ships, the Dutch with sixty-nine. Both Rupert and Albemarle broke the Dutch line, but they were beaten back by counterattacks. The English retained their discipline, but they were out of ammunition and demoralised. They lost ten ships, three admirals, ten captains and over 20 per cent of their sailors (4,250 men dead, wounded or captured) over four days of carnage. De Ruyter managed to dismast Rupert's *Royal James*, which had to be towed out of the battle protected by the prince's division, and to press home the attack on Albemarle's flagship and the remaining ships, which had borne the brunt of four days' fighting.

The English were able to flee into a thickening fog. They were second to the Dutch in seamanship and signalling; they could not even count on superiority of firepower any longer. Only fleet discipline saved the Royal Navy from utter defeat. John Evelyn was at Sheerness and 'beheld that sad spectacle, namely more than half of that gallant bulwark of the kingdom miserably shattered, hardly a vessel entire, but appearing rather so many wracks and hulls, so cruelly had the Dutch mangled us'.[6]

The Four Days Battle took place between 1 and 4 June 1666; truly it was 'the most terrible, obstinate and bloodiest battle that ever was fought on the seas'.[7]

Now de Witt was ready to deliver the *coup de grâce*. The English were defeated and he would personally take the Dutch fleet into the Medway and destroy what was left of the Royal Navy. In July de Ruyter was at sea with a large fleet that carried soldiers ready to be landed on English soil.

But, amazingly, the English were ready to fight again. *Antelope*, for example, returned from the Four Days Battle with a starboard side that looked like a sieve and 'a breach that a coach might enter' on the larboard; she had twelve guns broken and every mast, yard, rope and two sets of sails were ruined. Yet after a few weeks of repairs she was fit to fight again. Rupert and Albemarle led out the fleet on 22 July. There were eighty-seven ships in the line of battle, which stretched ten miles; the Dutch had only seventy-two. The two fleets met just east of the Galloper Shoal on the 25th, St James's Day.

The Dutch line came under a vicious barrage from the English line. It

killed 7,000 Dutch sailors, including four admirals. The English lost just
300 men. On 26 July de Ruyter organised a fighting retreat.

Now it was the English who had command of the seas. How best to
exploit it? Albemarle and Rupert resolved to hit a Dutch port. But that
was no easy thing. Dutch ports are inaccessible to attackers. The greatest prize of all, Amsterdam, lay snugly at the end of the bottleneck of
the Zuyderzee, protected from encroachment by ships, guns and shoals.
There was one possible target. The Vlie – a seaway between the islands of
Vlieland and Terschelling – was used as an anchorage for merchantmen.
The British battlefleet proceeded to the Dutch coast and a detachment of
frigates and fireships led by Rear Admiral of the Red Sir Robert Holmes
entered the Vlie.

When he entered the seaway Holmes beheld 150 merchantmen. English fireships destroyed the Dutch frigates guarding them and in all about
130 warships and merchantmen went up in flames. The next day the
English burnt the town of West-Terschelling. 'Holmes's Bonfire' was celebrated throughout England with bonfires.

A more serious burning occurred within weeks. The Great Fire of
London overshadowed all the other events of 1666. Its effect on the Royal
Navy was devastating. Already the ferocity of the battles and the length
of the war had placed strain on the public finances; the Great Fire and
plague derailed the economy. The Navy could no longer afford to pay its
sailors. In some cases the men were barely fed. Ships' companies mutinied
as the situation deteriorated. The battlefleet had to be put into ordinary
and the seamen fobbed off with tickets.

The memory of the vandalism at Terschelling rankled with the Dutch.
The Medway Raid was their retribution on England. Some in England
came to see Holmes's Bonfire as needless provocation rather than a victory. For Pepys the restraint of the Dutch in not pillaging Gillingham was
a sorry contrast with the English at Terschelling, and indeed the English
troops who rushed to the Medway after the Dutch had left and plundered
the deserted town.

The Dutch were able to navigate the unfamiliar river and breach the defences that guarded the beating heart of the Royal Navy. The Navy could
be thankful that the disaster was not much worse: at least the dockyards at
Chatham had been spared. But in reality the Dutch had inflicted a defeat
and humiliation on England far more serious even than the capture and
destruction of its principal ships. The war had cost a fortune and England
gained very little from it. The Dutch could afford to pay for new ships,
repair battle-damaged ones and pay their dockers and sailors even after

crushing defeats. As Batten, said, the devil really did shit Dutch ships. The English could not keep pace, even when they won impressive victories or turned defeats like the Four Days Battle into successes. By the second half of 1666 they could not man, replenish or equip their battlefleet.

The indifference of English sailors to the defeat at the Medway was revealing. These men had been corralled into the fleet, and those who survived the savage battles were kept virtual prisoners – underfed prisoners at that. Their families had been left destitute. When *Royal Charles* was captured the renegade English brandished their tickets and declared that they had now come to be paid. It was revenge for years of pain. 'Indeed,' remarked Pepys, 'the hearts as well as the affections of the seamen are turned away; and in the open streets of Wapping ... the wives have cried publicly *"This comes of your not paying our husbands"*.'[8]

CHAPTER 23

TANGERINES

If it had not pleased God to give us a King and Duke that understood the sea, this nation had 'ere this been quite beaten out of it.

Samuel Pepys

On 14 January 1676 the Mediterranean Fleet was off Tripoli. That night the boats of all the ships were lowered. Then the men collected their weapons and explosive material and boarded the boats.

Lieutenant Cloudesley Shovell of HMS *Harwich* planned and executed the operation. It was an exceptionally dark night, and the boats sneaked into the harbour and captured the guard boat without detection. The men then boarded and burnt four pirate ships and returned to the squadron without a loss. It was a cool, quick, professional operation. Shovell won fame at home and was rewarded with money and a gold medal from Charles II. A year later he got his first command. He was twenty-seven years old.

Cloudesley Shovell was at the forefront of a generation of naval officers who had grown up with the Restoration Navy.[1] He served with distinction from 1663 until his death in a notorious shipwreck in 1707. His career tells us much about the Navy at a time of fundamental change in the second half of the seventeenth century and the beginning of the eighteenth.

Shovell's great good fortune was to be born in the little Norfolk village of Cockthorpe. This was the home of Christopher Myngs, the son of the village shoemaker, who rose to become a captain in the Commonwealth Navy. He gained his early experience in the Mediterranean and took part in the Battle of Scheveningen. But it was in the West Indies, enforcing the Navigation Acts and raiding the Spanish Main, that he perfected the arts of captaincy and, it has to be said, Elizabethan-style pillaging. Despite a reputation as a religious radical, Myngs was retained after the Restoration.

Another Cockthorpe boy, John Narborough, became his cabin boy, and served with Myngs in the Caribbean. In 1663 Narborough became Myngs's lieutenant and the thirteen-year-old Cloudesley Shovell was chosen as the new cabin boy.

There were many boys like Narborough and Shovell who used local and kinship connections to get on the first rung of the ladder that might raise them to lieutenant and then, with luck, captain. But there were various routes to the top in the Stuart Navy.

As ever the process was highly political. In 1660 a Cromwellian–republican Navy had to be turned into a Royal Navy, if not a Royalist Navy. The trouble was that the most experienced officers were veterans of the Dutch War and hence closely associated with the republic and Cromwell. There were a few Cavaliers who had naval experience. In exile the Stuarts had a tiny naval force comprising the squadron that had mutinied in 1648 and that was led by Prince Rupert and a roving band of privateers. In 1660 Thomas Allin was made captain of HMS *Dover*. Allin had captained one of the Royalist ships sunk by Blake off Cartagena in 1650. Robert Holmes also served in Rupert's squadron and then as a privateer; in 1660 he became one of the new Cavalier captains as well. These former followers of Rupert progressed to become flag officers. Sir William Batten, who had defected with a portion of the parliamentary Navy to the Stuarts in 1648, became Surveyor of the Navy.

But they had to serve alongside admirals and captains who had sunk their ships and pursued them for over a decade. William Penn and John Lawson, who had hunted down Royalist privateers in the Mediterranean in the early 1650s, remained admirals. A majority of the captains in the 1660s had been officers in the Interregnum Navy. But the king and Lord High Admiral were under pressure to advance the naval careers of gentlemen and nobles.

It was a dilemma for Charles II and his brother James, duke of York. According to Pepys James 'perceived it must be the old captains that must do the business, and that the new ones would spoil all'.[2] James developed a close working relationship with the professional sea officers of the previous regime, particularly Lawson and Penn. They had a bias towards what were known as 'tarpaulin' officers, named after the protective oiled canvas clothing worn by professional sailors. As the name suggests, such officers were defined as those who had joined ships as boys and had worked their way through the ranks, learning the art of captaincy the hard way. Pepys called them 'sons of the sea'.

Tarpaulins were firmly linked to the merchant marine. Sir John Lawson was the son of a master mariner from Scarborough, and he was an established member of the town's seafaring and maritime community before he joined the Parliamentary Navy in the Civil Wars. Captain Sir Richard Haddock from Leigh-on-Sea could trace a line of seafaring and naval forebears to 1327. He captained merchant ships and Navy ships before and after the Restoration, served as flag captain to both the earl of Sandwich and Prince Rupert, advanced to Comptroller of the Navy and became an admiral. His sons, Richard and Nicholas Haddock, were respectively Comptroller of the Navy (1733–49) and commander-in-chief in the Mediterranean in the later 1730s. Sir Richard Stayner, the hero of Santa Cruz, started out in the Newfoundland fishing fleet and ended his life as rear admiral of the fleet sent to escort Charles II's bride from Portugal to England; he was given responsibility to take possession of Tangier. Throughout the 1650s tarpaulins had been raised to positions of command to lead the expanding Navy. As time went on, captains were chosen from long-serving warrant and petty officers. Such men, with their experience of practical seafaring and the battles of the First Dutch War, were the mainstays of the Navy. Why not simply keep them?

In response to James's preference for tarpaulins, Edward Montagu, now earl of Sandwich, said that there must be a balance between retaining experienced officers and respecting political realities. It was essential to secure the support of the political nation for the Navy. It could not be seen as a hangover of the Commonwealth, a haven for unrepentant rebels. For many it was entirely right and proper that the hereditary warrior class, with their values of honour and unconditional support for the monarchy, should command in military matters. Experience counted for less, in this view, than martial values and instinctive leadership qualities. To say otherwise would be to upset the natural order.

In any case, Sandwich had been propelled to the highest command in the Navy without any prior experience thanks to his position at court – only in his case it was the court of Lord Protector Cromwell. For time out of mind aristocrats and courtiers had led fleets as admirals, relying on the experience of senior flag captains. In the changed circumstances of the Interregnum inexperienced men with the right credentials were given command and fared extremely well – Blake and Monck are the supreme examples. The challenge was how to introduce the nobility and the gentry to the Navy without impairing the quality of the service.

The lieutenancy was a way to fast-track young gentlemen on their way to command ships. The early 1660s saw a number of such gentlemen parachuted into ships as lieutenants. Robert Holmes's younger brother

John became a ship's lieutenant in 1664 at the age of twenty-four. He was made a captain a year later and within ten years he was a flag officer. The Cavalier Walter Strickland was rewarded when his son Roger became lieutenant of *Sapphire* in 1661 at the age of twenty-one. He served as lieutenant on four other ships over the next five years before he gained his first command as temporary commander of a captured prize. He became captain of a naval ship in 1668.

A number of gentlemen were posted into ships as captains before they were ready. Sir Frescheville Holles captained *Antelope* at the age of twenty-three after a brief stint on his own privateer. The earl of Ossory became captain of a ship in 1666 with no prior seafaring experience. In 1673 he became Admiral of the Blue, though he professed his ignorance of seamanship. George Legge, later Lord Dartmouth, became captain of *Pembroke* at the age of twenty. The duke of York remarked that Legge 'was, he knows not how, made a captain after he had been but one voyage at sea'.[3] He owed his appointment to favour: his father was a courtier closely associated with Prince Rupert. Within a month *Pembroke* was lost after colliding with *Fairfax* in Torbay.

The division between 'gentleman' and 'tarpaulin' captains was most apparent in the 1660s and during wartime, when courtiers clamoured for command. James and Charles were well aware of the difficulties. The Navy could not be revolutionised without ruining it. But time could transform it without trauma. Charles II made his feelings clear: 'I am not for employing of men merely for quality, yet when men of quality are fit for the trade they desire to enter into, I think 'tis reasonable they should be encouraged at least equally with others.'[4]

A new generation of professional officers was trained up. From 1661 'king's letter boys' joined ship's companies. They were the sons of gentlemen, their maximum age stipulated at sixteen in 1676, sent to sea to learn the arts of seamanship and navigation and begin the route to promotion. James and Charles wanted gentleman officers to think and act like tarpaulin officers. By the later 1670s many of the older generation of Commonwealth tarpaulins and Royalist gentleman captains had died off or retired. Officers brought into the service at the time of the Restoration began to take over. By then they had their own battle scars.

This brings us back to Cloudesley Shovell. His first experience of the Navy was in the West Indies with Myngs and Lieutenant Narborough, the most gruelling station in the Navy. Myngs was there to prevent the Spanish retaking Jamaica. He raided Santiago de Cuba, from where attacks on the English colony were being mounted, and destroyed the garrison and fortifications. It was in the Second Dutch War that he achieved lasting fame. He was appointed vice admiral of the White squadron at the beginning of the war in 1664. He was killed while serving as vice admiral of the Red at the Four Days Battle in 1666.

Narborough and Shovell had learnt the rudiments of seafaring from a master. Myngs was a naval officer in the model of a Drake or Hawkins. He was fiercely loyal to his men, with whom he illegally shared his loot from the Caribbean. At his funeral Pepys was approached by a group of his former sailors, who begged to serve on a fireship, a dangerous mission 'that shall show our memory of our dead commander and our revenge'.

John Narborough took over Myngs's *Victory* in the heat of the Four Days Battle. He distinguished himself and was raised to captain. Cloudesley Shovell became his cabin boy, and went back to the Caribbean with Narborough in 1667, joining squadrons led by Sir John Harman and John Berry which defeated a Franco-Dutch fleet near Nevis, annihilated a large squadron of French ships at Martinique and captured Cayenne in French Guiana and Paramaribo in Dutch Surinam. Two years later Shovell joined Narborough on a voyage to the southern Pacific. This represented an unrivalled experience in seamanship. By the Third Dutch War such officers were crucial to the success of the Navy. Narborough was brought on board James's flagship, *Royal Prince*, as a lieutenant and Shovell went with him as a midshipman.

In 1670 Charles II concluded a secret treaty with the French. The two countries would ally against the Dutch. By this time the Navy had managed to rebuild and repair the ships lost or scuttled in the Medway raid. Charles had enough money for a short war. The plan was for the English and French navies to defeat the Dutch navy and then land troops in the Netherlands. The French army would simultaneously attack the Republic.

The Dutch Republic was facing annihilation. It was outnumbered on land and at sea. Fortunately for the Dutch they had Michiel Adriaenszoon de Ruyter in command of their navy; his tactical brilliance thwarted the Anglo-French navy at the battles of Solebay, Schooneveld (twice) and the Texel. James called de Ruyter the greatest admiral of any age. It is not hard to see why.* In these four battles in 1672–73 he nullified the enemy's considerable advantages in numbers and guns with superior pilotage, signalling and tactics. Outnumbered by his enemies, de Ruyter launched a

* In 2004 de Ruyter came seventh in a poll of the greatest-ever Dutchmen, 'De Grootste Nederlander', ahead of Anne Frank, Rembrandt and van Gogh in that order. The Royal Netherland Navy has had six ships named HNLMS *De Ruyter* and seven called *De Zeven Provinciën* after his flagship.

surprise attack on the Anglo-French fleet at Solebay. It was an audacious plan, but it did not result in a resounding victory. What it did was to eliminate any chance of a seaborne invasion of the Republic.

De Ruyter developed a policy of decapitation: knock out the English admirals and the fleet would be rendered impotent. At the opening stages of the Battle of Solebay James's flagship was targeted by five enemy ships for about four hours. The rest of the fleet was unable to come to the aid of the heir to the throne because of a dead calm. It was a desperate time. Sir John Cox, the ship's captain, was killed; John Narborough took over. The Dutch guns tortured the magnificent *Prince*. Two hundred men perished, including members of James's household. The topmast came crashing down, damaging the mainsail as it fell and putting many of the guns out of action as it smashed onto the deck.

The Dutch fireships moved in to finish off *Prince* and, in all probability, change the course of history by killing the heir to the thrones of England and Scotland. But Narborough acted fast. He had boats bring the ship's bow about until the remaining sails found a breeze. At long last *Prince* began to move. Just as she neared the safety of her fleet the Dutch brought down her foretopsail yard, rendering the mighty flagship useless. James had escaped just in time. He moved his flag to *St Michael* and, when that ship had been smashed to smithereens, to *London*.

No ship carrying an English admiral was safe. *Royal James*, the 100-gun flagship of the earl of Sandwich, came under similar attention from Dutch warships and fireships. Like *Prince* she was able to keep the Dutch attackers at bay with her guns, even though she had an enemy ship lodged under her bows. At last *Royal James* broke free, but by then her hull had taken a pounding and she was sinking, and her crew numbered few survivors from the appalling onslaught. Eventually a fireship was able to grapple her and set her on fire. By midday the last Englishman had abandoned ship, with the exception of Sandwich. His badly mutilated body was recognisable when it was recovered from the waves only because the ribbon of the Order of the Garter still hung from it. The corpse was not singed, suggesting that at some point the earl had become the last man to abandon ship before he was immolated.

The savagery of the attacks on the flagships is a reminder of the merciless nature of naval war at this time. All officers on *Royal James*, with the exception of Captain Haddock, were killed. *Henry* lost her captain and most of her officers. A significant number of captains and officers were killed along with many high-born courtiers, many of whom were mown down as they stood alongside James. Pity the poor sailor who was forced onto one of the great flagships, magnets for enemy cannonballs. James might have been spared a hideous death, but his regal presence in the battle ensured that the ships from which he flew his standard ran with blood and were pummelled to wrecks.

Yet the presence of the prince in the heart of battle – where he was as much exposed to death as any of his fellows – did make a difference to the history of the Navy. Both Charles and James were accomplished yachtsmen. They cared deeply about the Royal Navy and were the first princes for centuries capable of sailing, navigating and piloting a vessel. Their support for the service in difficult years ensured that it was embraced by the political nation and was elevated to national importance. When a prince fought at sea it was inevitable that aristocrats, courtiers and gentlemen would follow him in pursuit of glory. A naval career was now worthy of the high-born. This had profound implications. The class of men who were called on to pay for the Navy now had a personal, sometimes professional, stake in it.

James was eager to establish the ideal of a seventeenth-century admiral. Narborough recorded him at Solebay in the midst of the carnage:

> His Royal Highness went fore and aft in the ship and cheered up the men to fight, which did encourage them very much. The Duke thought himself never near enough to the enemy ... Presently when Sir John Cox was slain, I commanded as captain, observing his Royal Highness's commands in working the ship, striving to get the wind of the enemy. I do absolutely believe no prince upon the whole earth can compare with his Royal Highness in gallant resolution in fighting his enemy, and with so great conduct and knowledge in navigation as never any general understood before him.[5]

If it was not beneath a prince to learn the arts of navigation and sailing, or to motivate the sailors, then it would attract the greatest in the land to send their teenage boys to sea to learn the ropes and, one day, earn their laurels. Sea service was now an *honourable* profession.

Under the care and attention of Charles and James the Navy prospered as an institution, even if it could not best the Dutch at war. Under their eye talented men such as Pepys took over the administration, which prospered as never before. But their greatest legacy was the creation of a professionalised corps of officers.

It bore fruit in officers such as Shovell. In this age commentators on the Navy and officers themselves liked to make a distinction between

'gentlemen' and 'tarpaulin' officers, but in what camp should we put
Shovell? He came from a landowning not a merchant-shipping family. He
got into the Navy thanks to his connections. But he was a sailor through
and through. Young officers like Shovell, who joined the service as boys
from the early 1660s, blurred the distinction between gentleman and tarpaulin. That was the achievement of Charles and James's reforms.

War gave officers the chance to rise rapidly through the ranks. After the
Battle of Solebay Narborough was given command of the third rate *Fairfax*, which convoyed merchantmen to the Mediterranean. Shovell joined
the ship as master's mate. In the final stages of the Third Dutch War Narborough became Rear Admiral the Earl of Ossory's flag captain in the Blue
squadron. He then hoisted his flag as Rear Admiral of the Red from HMS
Henrietta (50). Shovell joined him as second lieutenant.

The great fleet battles in the North Sea hardened officers, but the true
nursery of English officers was the Mediterranean. In 1674 Narborough
became admiral of the Mediterranean Fleet, flying his flag from HMS *Harwich*. Shovell became the ship's lieutenant after ten very active years at
sea. Experience amassed on voyages to the West Indies, the Pacific, the
Mediterranean and in ships of the line during ferocious fleet battles in
home waters, combined with the mentorship of Myngs and Narborough,
marked Shovell out as a future leader.

Narborough's fleet was one of the most impressive sent to the Mediterranean. It peaked at thirty-five ships, not including the warships entering the Strait on convoy duty. One of his first successes was to buy off
the Tunisians. Narborough then based himself at Leghorn and Malta to
take on the Tripoli corsairs. Shovell may have champed at the bit for a
captaincy in his mentor's large fleet, but Narborough kept his talented
protégé at his side on the *Harwich*. It was a wise choice. Shovell led the
attack on Tripoli. Two months later he was with Narborough when four
more ships were destroyed at sea. These actions forced the Dey of Tripoli
to sign a peace treaty. Later in the year Sallee came to terms as well. That
left only the Algerine menace, and the fleet now operated out of Leghorn,
Minorca and Cadiz.

Shovell took command of *Sapphire* (32). He captained several fourth
rates, but evidently preferred *Sapphire*, as he twice returned to command
her. In 1681 he was given command of *James Galley* (30) and he remained
with her for five years, policing the seas and protecting merchant shipping. By this time Narborough had been replaced by Arthur Herbert as
admiral in the region. Shovell prospered, defeating and capturing two
large Algerine ships, which were added to the Navy. Herbert was the most

successful of the admirals in the Mediterranean. In 1682 he forced Algiers into a treaty, which proved durable. Herbert bore the scars of battle. He had once been shot in the face during a fight with two Algerine corsairs, the bullet remaining lodged under his right eye while he attacked a further ten enemy ships. In 1678, during a particularly harsh battle with a corsair, Herbert was blinded for some weeks after a bandolier (an ammunition belt) exploded in his face and burned the clothes off his back. Herbert was also a notorious womaniser and frequenter of brothels.

Shovell replaced Herbert as commander-in-chief in the Strait, although by this time the number of ships was much reduced, a result of the success of forcing Algiers, Tunis and Tripoli to come to terms. Shovell concentrated his forces against Sallee, the last corsair stronghold.

Shovell was nurtured on frigates, the workhorse of the Navy, and battle-hardened on ships of the line in home waters. Fighting skills and independent command were learnt during battles with North African corsairs. Never before in its history had the Navy served continuously so far from home.

Convoying ships called for a high degree of expertise.[6] During daylight the frigates sailed to windward of the convoy; in the dark hours one ship went ahead and another fell astern. Judgement and initiative were essential. Sometimes the number of merchantmen seeking protection was large; in 1680 two convoys left the Newfoundland fisheries, both containing between sixty and seventy ships bound for southern European markets. A homeward-bound convoy from Leghorn in 1677 started with two frigates and twenty-five merchantmen, including several richly laden Levant Company vessels; this number had grown to four warships and thirty-seven merchantmen by the time they reached Majorca; at Alicante there were fifty ships; ninety-two ships joined them at Cadiz for the last leg to the Downs. It was a high responsibility. Captains had to remain flexible, arranging arrival and departure times with the merchant shipmasters. They had to keep the convoy in order, tactfully keeping wayward or inexperienced merchant captains in line, and engaging predatory vessels without leaving the ships vulnerable. In addition they had to procure supplies in foreign ports, find fresh recruits and keep their ships in good working order – no mean feat for a ship that had voyaged from England to Newfoundland, crossed the Atlantic, plied the Mediterranean and collected up a large homeward-bound convoy.

Fighting predatory corsairs was very different from fighting in fleet battles. It called upon skills of seamanship, leadership and independent judgement. Duels with corsairs made officers famous. Captain John

Kempthorne, for example, fought a two-day battle against seven Algerine corsairs in 1669 and got his convoy safely home. His son Morgan
Kempthorne rivalled that achievement in 1681, fighting off seven Alge-
rines in a twelve-hour running battle. Morgan was one of eight men killed
in the engagement.

A captain abroad represented the king. In 1675 Sir John Berry commanded the Newfoundland convoy and he was dispatched with orders
to force the settlers in Newfoundland to emigrate to other colonies.[7]
The Newfoundlanders were in dispute with the fishing interests, and in
London it was accepted that the settlers were detrimental to the fishing
industry. Berry had begun life as a boy on the Newfoundland ships, but
this did not stop him siding with the settlers when he investigated the situation. Instead of removing them he sent home a report. His intervention
was instrumental in preserving the Newfoundland colony.

Two years later Berry was dispatched from the Mediterranean to Virginia to stabilise its tense political situation after a thwarted rebellion. In
1680–81 he was again on convoy duty in the Mediterranean. He had on
board an eighteen-year-old boy learning the ways of the sea. This was the
duke of Grafton, the king's illegitimate son. Convoy duty was an excellent way to learn the technicalities of naval life. The voyage took Berry
and Grafton from England to Tangier, on to Smyrna, then back westwards
to Alicante, Malaga and the Downs. Two years later the duke was vice admiral of England and commander-in-chief of the Narrow Seas.

Captains were eager to serve in the Mediterranean. They were known
as the 'Tangerines', after the naval headquarters at Tangier. Officers enjoyed the food and the opportunities for tourism, shopping and sex. Captains tried to outdo each other with the quality of their tables. There was
a convivial atmosphere in Tangier, where many officers bought or rented
houses and kept up an active social life. But above all the Mediterranean
offered the chance of promotion, glory and profit. The war against the
corsairs between the 1660s and the 1680s was the apprenticeship for a
generation of captains who learnt at the feet of Narborough, Herbert and
Shovell, and many of whom went on to become the admirals who led
the Navy in the first decades of the eighteenth century. The Tangerines'
world came to an end in 1683 when the Tangier colony and naval base
was evacuated.

Often in the past the Navy had slumped into inactivity during periods of peace. Now it had commitments in different locations around the
world, which provided continuity and training. It was becoming a more
professional service.

The same spirit was evinced on shore. Samuel Pepys excelled as a naval administrator, after a slow start.[8] He acquainted himself with the technicalities of warships by dismantling and reconstructing model ships and in searching conversations with the mate of the *Royal James*. The same petty officer schooled Pepys in basic mathematics and in July 1662 he learnt the multiplication table. From this foundation Mr Secretary Pepys graduated to advanced accounting and a mathematician taught him the secret of measuring timber. Armed with his slide-rule, Pepys augmented his knowledge by questioning leading timber merchants, iron merchants and sailmakers. Mathematics, accounting skills and experience gave him an insight into the tricks played by the Navy's contractors and he was able to stamp out some of the corruption that plagued the service's administration. Pepys was an incredibly diligent servant of the Crown with a talent for enquiring into the tiniest detail; his panoptic view of the Navy was unrivalled in his time. He was not the 'saviour of the Navy', as has been claimed; but he set a standard in administration. His achievements were in no small part due to James and Charles's passion to create a great Navy.

This effort was crowned in 1677. From then on lieutenants had to qualify for their commissions by passing an examination. This was a truly revolutionary move, one that was pressed on the reluctant Admiralty by Charles II himself. Earlier in this chapter the king was quoted as referring to naval service as a 'trade'. It was a revealing word. Throughout English history the Navy had been led by a hereditary warrior elite. And hereditary warrior elites, by definition, do not need to qualify by sitting exams.

The decision to professionalise the Navy in this way marked a turning point in English military history. The army would take a long time to catch up. The examinations laid the foundations for the professional, highly skilled service that emerged in the eighteenth century.

It was the legacy of Charles II and his brother, who lavished so much attention on their Navy. The revolution that began with the Commonwealth was sustained in the Restoration.

CHAPTER 24

MAD PROCEEDINGS
1677–1694

There is not so lawful or commendable a jealousy in the world, as an *Englishman's* of the growing greatness of any prince or state at sea.

The earl of Shaftesbury

James watched with excitement and satisfaction as English frigates fired on the French defences while fireships and boats entered La Hogue and destroyed the twelve ships of the line and troop transports that sheltered there under the nose of a large army. On the same day as the action at La Hogue three large warships were burnt at Cherbourg.

'Ah!' exclaimed James with pride as he watched the flames engulf the French ships at La Hogue. 'None but my brave English could do so brave an action!'[1]

His audience must have shifted uncomfortably. They were a group of French officers; their navy and transport ships, which had been defeated and destroyed by the formidable Anglo-Dutch fleet, had been called into service to invade England to restore James II to the throne he had lost in 1688.

It is no surprise that James took so much pleasure in 'his' Navy, even as it ravaged his dreams. Few other monarchs have identified themselves so much with the Navy. He had a short-lived son whom he named Edgar. Although James fought only two battles – Lowestoft and Solebay – those heroic engagements became bound up with his sense of identity. The Navy that he had shaped, honed and drilled had clocked up another victory; he could not help but take pride.

James was in accord with his countrymen in revelling in the prowess of the Royal Navy, but he was fatally out of step with them in most other respects. In 1673 new legislation – the Test Act – required every official in the employ of the Crown to disavow Catholicism. This was a serious problem for James. At some point in the later 1660s he had converted from Protestantism to Catholicism. Prince or not, he had to obey the law and relinquish the post of Lord High Admiral. Responsibility for the Navy was handed to a commission headed by Prince Rupert.

Being a Catholic in seventeenth-century England was hard enough. Being heir to the throne did not ease things – in fact it exacerbated them. Catholicism was identified as un-English and, above all, tyrannical. The Great Fire of London in 1666 was believed to be the work of an international Catholic conspiracy hell-bent on wrecking the Anglican Church and stamping arbitrary government onto free England. From 1661 Louis XIV (a Catholic of course) aimed to establish Universal Monarchy – or French hegemony – over Europe. In 1677 Titus Oates, a disgraced naval chaplain, told the world of a Catholic conspiracy to assassinate Charles II, an act that would bring James to the throne. It was all fiction, but there followed a wave of hysteria and attempts in parliament to exclude James from the succession. 'I think,' said one MP, 'the sun is not more visible at noon-day, than that the Papists have a design to extirpate our religion ... we have discovered that their weapons are near our throats, so we shall not acquiesce in anything less than may secure us; that so, if possible, we may not fall into the hands of such bloody, merciless people; which must infallibly be the consequence of having a Popish King.'[2]

The knives were out for the Stuarts, but Charles flatly refused to undermine the monarchy by altering the line of succession. Instead he compromised. He surrendered his prerogative power over the Navy to parliament. Parliament had been contesting for power over the Navy throughout Charles's reign. After the disastrous Second Dutch War, parliament set up a Committee for Miscarriages, which combed through every administrative and operational decision made by the admirals and the Navy Board. Another parliamentary committee, the Brooke House Commission, investigated naval finances. Now MPs had control over the Navy.

They were not to have it for long. Charles regained control before his death and elevated Samuel Pepys to a unique role, Secretary for the Affairs of the Admiralty. In 1685 James came to the throne.

On the face of it the Navy had never had it so good. Pepys got a budget of £400,000 a year and a Special Commission to reform the service. By 1688 the fleet numbered 168 ships.

In 1688 the king looked to his beloved Royal Navy for salvation. Throughout his short reign he deeply offended his subjects. James purged local government and secured a slavish parliament. When even this fiercely loyal parliament began to criticise him he dissolved it and ruled alone. He granted toleration for Catholics and opened up careers in the army, Navy and the universities to his co-religionists. Even worse, he raised a standing army, which was stationed menacingly on Hounslow Heath. For Englishmen this was a sure sign of tyranny. They had reason to be fearful. In 1685 Louis XIV revoked the Edict of Nantes, which had protected French Protestants. Thousands of refugees came to England, bringing tales of cruelty and oppression. At the same time Louis was engaged in war against the German and Dutch Protestants. Although England did not support Louis's war against the Dutch, James was careful 'to stand neuter, and to be an idle, unconcerned spectator of the horrid tragedy the French King acts upon the theatre of Europe'.[3] Indifference to the fate of Protestantism shamed the nation and weakened England's power in continental affairs. The violence of Louis against his Protestant subjects showed what James might do in England.

Even so, the English and Scots were prepared to put up with their Catholic king. His heir was Mary, the wife of the fervently Protestant William III of Orange, stadtholder of the Dutch Republic.

One man who refused to acquiesce in James's pro-Catholic policies was Admiral Arthur Herbert. Herbert had a long-standing relationship with James. Herbert commended himself as a young officer in the battles of 1666. James interested himself in Herbert's career, and he served in the Mediterranean and in the Third Dutch War. He became commander-in-chief in the Mediterranean in 1679, where he established himself as the Navy's outstanding admiral. Charles II appointed him Rear Admiral of England and James II made him Master of the Robes.

Herbert was a product of James's Navy and a beneficiary of James's patronage; he was notoriously lax in his morals and untroubled by a political or religious conscience; yet he was one of the first to withdraw his support for the regime on the grounds of principle. He was dismissed from his offices and began to talk to other disaffected men. The most important of these was Edward Russell. Like Herbert, Russell had enjoyed James's support in ascending the ladder of promotion in the Navy and establishing himself at court.

Russell came from a family of noble rebels against royal absolutism. The spirit of opposition flowed in his veins; so did vanity and abrasiveness. In 1687 he was the go-between in the secretive negotiations between leading Whigs and William of Orange. Russell recruited Herbert to the cause.

In July 1688 Herbert donned the tarpaulins of a common sailor and slipped onto a ship bound for the Netherlands. Secreted on his person was an incendiary document. Herbert took it straight to William. It was a letter signed by leading Englishmen inviting the stadtholder to intervene in English affairs. For things had changed dramatically in 1688. The birth of a baby boy to James's second wife, after years of childless marriage, meant that the chance of Mary and William coming to the throne disappeared at a stroke. Many suspected another Catholic conspiracy: the infant had surely been smuggled by wily Jesuits into the queen's bed in a warming pan. A Catholic king would not be a one-off: there would be a line of Catholic monarchs stretching into the future. The fiction that the baby was an imposter was a useful one. It allowed the English grandees to invite William, who had a personal stake in the succession, to sort the mess out.

William needed English help to tip the balance of power in Europe and save the Dutch Republic from annihilation at the hands of the French. He needed his wife to accede to the English throne. Now he would have to secure the succession by force. Arthur Herbert was made Luitenant Admiraal Generaal of Rotterdam.

It was clear that William would invade. Now James turned to the mighty force he had helped to create. The Navy, under the command of the earl of Dartmouth, was sent to the Gunfleet anchorage off Harwich.

James might have been a calamitous politician, but not even his most bitter enemy doubted his courage and resolution. In 1688, however, these qualities deserted him. He was paralysed by indecision and consumed by self-doubt. Intelligence reached James and Pepys that William was assembling a vast invasion fleet. Dartmouth was not an admiral of the first rank, but he at least had a plan: he would take the English battle-fleet to the Dutch coast to destroy or bottle up the Dutch. But James advised caution. He knew that the enemy would have to defeat the Royal Navy before an invasion could be contemplated. The Gunfleet was the ideal anchorage. The Navy could cover the Thames Estuary and the east coast; it was ready to head into the North Sea or south-west to the Channel.

James trusted to his Navy. But it was clear to Dartmouth that there was a 'cabal' of officers who preferred the Protestant William to their Catholic master. He accused Captain Lord Berkeley of Stratton, for example, of spreading 'strange notions into the seamen and a great part of the commanders'. No greater action was taken against him, however, than an order to move his ship closer to Lord Dartmouth so that an eye could be kept on him.

There were only eight captains ready to defect, but they were very senior officers with large followings. They were all Tangerines. Cloudesley Shovell was in communication with Russell. Sir John Berry, rear admiral of the fleet, was plotting with the duke of Grafton to kidnap Dartmouth and turn the fleet over to William.

If James lacked courage, William was prepared to make the boldest strike. James, the professional naval commander, could not take seriously the threat of invasion. Summer was over and the seas were battered by gales. Indeed, William's invasion fleet was prevented from sailing throughout October by storms. It was too late for the Dutch to seek battle. 'I see,' James told Lord Dartmouth, 'that God Almighty continues his Protection to me by bringing the wind westerly again.'⁴

He spoke too soon.

On 3 November Dutch ships were spotted from the English flagship. The wind had changed and the enemy was heading west. But Dartmouth could not weather the dangerous Long Sand Head and Kentish Knock shoals. The Navy was under way the following day, by which time Herbert and the Dutch fleet were proceeding merrily down the Channel. The next day the wind veered. The south-westerly blew William's ships into Torbay and halted the Royal Navy at Beachy Head.

'I take myself for the most unfortunate man living,' Dartmouth lamented when he realised how easy the enemy had made things look. William and Herbert had defied all naval logic. They had not sought a battle at all. Rather their 463 ships, which carried 40,000 men, had set out in the hope that they could evade the Royal Navy. They had only forty-nine warships to protect the flotilla.

Dartmouth called these 'mad proceedings', but fortune favoured the brave. William did not have much time to play with. The French army was tied up in the Rhineland; Louis's navy was bullying the pope in the Mediterranean. Delay any longer and the French would invade the Republic by land and recall their navy to bolster the Royal Navy. It was a once-in-a-lifetime opportunity for the Dutch stadtholder.

In 1588 England had been saved by the 'Protestant Wind', which diverted the Spanish Armada. Now, in 1688, the Protestant Wind saved the Church of England and English liberty by blowing William to Torbay and confounding James's Navy. That was the propaganda anyway. Gilbert Burnet, an English bishop who had defected to William, said: 'now by the immediate hand of heaven, we were masters of the sea without a blow'.⁵ William made landfall on another anniversary auspicious for English Protestants, 5 November.

'A great King with Strong Armies, and mighty Fleets, a vast treasure, and powerful Allies fell all at once: And his whole strength, like a Spider's web, was so irrecoverably broken with a touch, that he was never able to retrieve what for want of judgement he threw up in a day.'[6] In two famous battles James had stood tall and unmovable on the quarterdeck of English ships, with the monstrous cacophony of war thundering in his ears and the brains of his close companions smeared across his clothing. Now, with scarcely a shot being fired in anger, he lost his nerve.

He looked yellow and haggard. He suffered constant nosebleeds. His confidence was chipped away bit by bit. Princess Anne, his second daughter, and John Churchill, his favourite army officer, defected to William. The king fled to France. He intended to return when the English realised that they had wrecked the ancient system of government and opened the door to Dutch intrusion. But others did not see it that way. The pro-William naval captains dispatched a lieutenant named George Byng to meet with the stadtholder and Russell at Sherbourne. Byng returned with a letter from William to Dartmouth promising that if the earl brought the fleet over to the Orangists he would retain his seniority. Matthew Aylmer, a Tangerine, a protégé of Herbert and one of the eight Williamite captains in the fleet, smuggled the letter aboard the flagship, where he left it in Dartmouth's toilet. Dartmouth found it and agreed at once to surrender the fleet to William. Once James made his ill-fated decision to leave the country, even his most loyal supporters such as Dartmouth limply threw in the towel.

William had more resolve. He made it plain that unless he was made king alongside his wife he would leave the English to stew in their own mess. William and Mary became joint monarchs at the behest of a Convention Parliament hastily assembled and placed under a good deal of pressure.

William III was a cold, distant, driven man. He dedicated himself to the House of Orange and defending the Dutch Republic against the predations of Louis XIV. He invaded England only to further his cause. The trappings of monarchy held no special allure for him, and England did not particularly interest him for its own sake. In his mind the English owed *him* for their deliverance.

No longer would England stand 'neuter' in the 'horrid tragedy' of European affairs. It would be propelled into the storm. And spearheading it was one of the greatest naval forces the world had seen. The Royal Navy and the Dutch navy had been forged during their titanic struggles with each other. Now they were united. The majority of the ships were to be English. In return all senior posts were held by English officers. This arrangement greatly offended the Dutch admirals, who were more experienced than their English counterparts. It was typical of the way William worked. He had no inclination for politics or national pride: whatever worked was fine by him.

The Navy had to adjust to a completely altered strategic situation. Under Charles, James and Pepys the battlefleet had been orientated to the Narrow Seas. Now the enemy was France, and it had to look westwards. This was not easy. The Navy had no naval bases in the West Country. Its ships, massive and heavily armed, had been designed to confront the Dutch in the North Sea. Now they had to be deployed in the western Channel and the Atlantic. The *Sovereign*, for instance, had never been further west than the Isle of Wight in her fifty-year service.

Louis had created a fleet fit to compete with the English and Dutch. His highly talented minister Jean-Baptiste Colbert, who served the French king concurrently as Controller-General of Finances and Secretary of State of the Navy, built up a fleet that consisted of just sixteen warships in 1661 into one that by 1783 had 276, of which 125 were extremely large battle-ships. In March 1689 French ships brought James to Ireland to begin his campaign to regain his throne.

The first blood between England and France was spilled off Bantry Bay in May 1689, when Herbert encountered a French fleet engaged in land-ing troops. It was a somewhat desultory battle. The French seized the gage and drove Herbert's ships out to sea. The English were outnumbered and outmanoeuvred and their ships were severely chastised. None were lost, however, and the French admiral was criticised for letting Herbert get away. with it. But Herbert had to return to Portsmouth for repairs, and now the French had unchallenged access to Ireland. James crowed to the French admirals that it was the first time they had scored a success against his Royal Navy, and it had happened only because 'his' sailors were still loyal to him.

The English had suffered a minor defeat. Despite this, William knew that English public opinion had to be kept sweet with the illusion of naval dominance. Defeat was dressed up as victory. Herbert became earl of Tor-rington and Cloudesley Shovell, who had commanded the seventy-gun *Edgar* at Bantry, was knighted.

With effective naval support James could upset all William's plans. But the French navy surrendered the initiative to the English. Louis's fleet remained in home waters and Torrington was ordered to the Western Approaches with the fleet. In May 1690 Louis's navy finally got its act together. The Mediterranean Fleet joined the Brest fleet and entered the Channel. Torrington sighted the seventy-five enemy ships of the line led by Admiral Tourville. Torrington did not want to fight. He only had fifty-five ships and he was convinced he would lose: 'Most men were in fear that the French would invade, but I was always of another opinion, for I always said that whilst we had a fleet in being, they would not make the attempt.'[7]

Torrington's concept of a 'fleet in being' entered the lexicon of naval tactics. The idea was that the mere fact of an opposing fleet's existence would be enough to deter an enemy without the need for a battle. According to Torrington the French would never invade if the Royal Navy remained undefeated. In the present circumstances it was too risky to take on a superior opponent. Torrington's council of war agreed. But back in Whitehall Secretary of State Lord Nottingham and Admiral Edward Russell believed Herbert was timid and disloyal. Queen Mary gave Herbert a direct order to attack Tourville.

Against his better judgement, and outnumbered, Torrington attacked Tourville's fleet off Beachy Head. Torrington had to make the most of a bad job. His Anglo-Dutch fleet was much smaller than the French, so there was a risk that the enemy would envelop his line. He followed orders and attacked; but he wanted to hold back from the French line. However the Dutch vanguard rushed into battle and came under heavy fire. Torrington led the rest of the fleet to extricate them. He then did something remarkable. With their sails still set, he ordered every ship to drop their anchors in unison. The French were taken by surprise and they were pulled helplessly out of the way by a powerful tide.

This manoeuvre allowed Torrington to escape to the Gunfleet. He had lost seven ships. Now the French had command of the Channel.

But no one had bothered to plan for a victory. There was no French army ready to take advantage and invade England. Neither side seemed to know how to conduct a naval war. Nottingham was meddlesome but useless; Torrington lost the support of the king, queen and Council; Russell – full of 'vanity and pride' – detested Torrington.

As a result the French were rampant in the Channel and William and Mary's throne looked under threat. Rear Admiral Sir Cloudesley Shovell was guarding the Irish Sea with just a few ships. He knew full well – as did James – that a decent French squadron would rout him and thereby cut off William's supply lines. But no French ships came in aid of the Jacobites. A few days after the Battle of Beachy Head James was defeated at the Boyne and fled Ireland. Tourville had had it in his power to destroy the allied Navy, but he squandered the chance. Both Torrington and Tourville were sacked after Beachy Head, the first for saving his fleet when others had put it in danger, the other for winning a battle but failing to follow it up.

William and Mary looked vulnerable. Prominent men began to open up lines of communication with the deposed king. One of them was Admiral Russell, an architect of the Revolution and the new commander-in-chief; the Navy, it appeared, was ready to back its former master. James believed the time was ripe. He persuaded Louis to launch an invasion.

The French fleet, led once again by Tourville, entered the Channel in May 1692. It comprised forty-four large warships and it was clearing the way for an invading army. Tourville expected to fight a demoralised, potentially mutinous English fleet roughly the same size as his own. It was led by Russell, who had fallen out with William and was flirting with the Jacobite cause. At dawn on 19 May off Cape Barfleur the French sighted the enemy scattered in the fog; they attacked the English centre at 11.00. Shovell later said that he had never seen ships come so close to their opponents before they opened fire. 'In a trice,' wrote a contemporary, 'we were so buried in fire and smoke, and had such hot service ourselves, that we could not see or mind what others did.'[8]

Too late did Tourville realise that the Anglo-Dutch fleet was nearly double the size of his own. Yet he had a chance. The French had the weather gage and prospered in their initial attack. Tourville's White squadron took on Russell in the centre; here both sides were of equal strength. What he feared above all was the allied fleet doubling – or surrounding – his line. To prevent this he ordered his van division to shadow the Dutch vanguard at the head of the line, but hold back from them and avoid fighting. The allied rearmost squadron under Sir John Ashby was becalmed some way away from the battle. Tourville therefore ordered *his* rear division to spread out northwards of the main battle and keep the weather gage, to prevent Ashby doubling his line. The battle would be decided in the centre, where strength was even.

For two hours the opposing sides maintained their lines, testing each other with tremendous cannonades at point-blank range. Tourville's *Soleil Royal* (104) exchanged broadsides with Russell's *Britannia* (100). The biggest ships in the world were involved in this part of the battle. The *Sovereign* was in Russell's division, along with her heirs: the brand-new *Britannia*, *Royal Prince* (now called *Royal William*) and some of the Navy's best second and third rates. *Soleil Royal* carried the most guns of all the warships in the world and outshone even *Sovereign* with her embellishments.

The French strove to hold their line intact, and several of their ships suffered devastating bombardment. The allies did not get off scot-free; several third and second rates were forced out of the line to make repairs.

Then, at 13.00, the breeze picked up. Shovell, rear admiral of the Red, breached the French line with his *Royal William*.

It was a brilliant manoeuvre, not least because the slight breeze presented only the narrowest of opportunities to take decisive action. Shovell was followed by the ships behind him in the line, *Sandwich* (90), *Oxford* (54), *Cambridge* (70) and *Ruby* (50). *Kent* (70) and *St Albans* (50), ahead of him in the line, saw what Shovell was about and followed. All this was accomplished in the din and confusion of battle. The captain of *Oxford* had no idea what had happened until he saw the French suddenly appear on his other side. Tourville now found his line fired upon from both sides. When the wind picked up again the leading ships of the English rear division joined Shovell. And to make matters worse the Dutch vanguard crossed the head of the French column, forcing the line to bend into a fish hook. Shovell said 'from that moment they [the French] began to run'.[9]

Only a dead calm and fog from about 16.00 gave the French any respite. Russell issued written orders: 'Use all possible means to tow your ships into line of battle during this calm.'[10] He scented an imminent and crushing victory – one that would save England. At about 17.00 the breeze got up and cleared the mist. Tourville used it to fight out of danger. Russell tried to re-engage, but the wind died and the fog descended once again. The entire battle was fought in poor weather conditions. Ships were immobilised for long periods and officers were unable to get a complete picture of the battle. The English Blue division had to be towed into action and Ashby mistakenly headed for the centre of the battle, rather than trying to double the enemy line.

At 18.00 the tide began to turn. The French dropped anchor, their sails still set, imitating the ruse set by Herbert at Beachy Head. Russell fell for it: in the absence of any breeze the power of the flood tide swept his division past the enemy. On the other side of the line Shovell was quicker in reading the tide and ordered the ships under his command to drop anchor. One ship that proved laggardly, the *Sandwich*, was propelled through the French line by the strong current, and as a result took a pummelling that killed her captain and many others. At 19.00 Ashby's Blue division at last entered the fray, but it came into action against the beleaguered French centre rather than completing the circle round the French fleet. Added to that, the tide had turned Shovell's ships, so only their stern chasers could be deployed. At 20.00 Shovell used the tide to send in fireships, but they were ineffectual. Shovell was forced to cross the French line again because his little squadron was the only thing standing between Tourville's entire fleet and the open sea; once the ebb tide came they would find the

French fleet stampeding them. During the night, when the tide turned once again, Tourville ordered the ships' cables to be cut. The French took advantage of the ebb and fled out to sea.

Amazingly for a battle that lasted over twelve hours, no ships were destroyed or captured. Securing an out-and-out victory in fleet battles was impossibly hard, as the Dutch wars showed. Both sides could aver victory – the English because they had put the French to flight and the French because they had entered the battle as underdogs and escaped without loss. Russell could claim, with some justice, to be one of the most unlucky of admirals. The fog and lulls and tides cheated him of a tremendous victory that would have gone down in history as one that saved England. As it is, the Battle of Barfleur is scarcely remembered.

An inconclusive success for the English turned into a brilliant victory over the next few days, when Russell and other admirals made sure they prospered from their advantage. The amphibious actions at Cherbourg and, most famously, La Hogue – led by George Rooke – proved decisive. James found that his hope of returning to reclaim his Crown had drained away. Louis transferred the army stationed in Brittany to Flanders. James retired to a life of contemplation and repentance.

The victory was enthusiastically celebrated in England. And it would be for over a century, until more glorious victories overshadowed it. It was, after all, a rare success in an age of inconclusive battles and timorous commanders. It lifted a very real threat hanging over William and Mary. They had never been secure on their thrones; 1692 was their nadir. The Royal Navy saved them.

The Navy had a new enemy, as formidable as the Dutch had been. But there would be no more great fleet battles to test their strengths. After the Battle of Barfleur–La Hogue the French switched their naval strategy to one of *guerre de course*, or good old-fashioned commerce raiding.

William III was unencumbered by pettifogging concerns about supplies, victuals or other tedious matters. In 1693 he ordered George Rooke to convoy 400 merchantmen from England to the Levant; the main fleet would see them past the French naval base at Brest and on to Iberia before returning. Thanks to William's disregard for trivialities it was all rather hurried and the fleet was underprovisioned. As a result it had to turn for home when the convoy passed Brest. When Rooke and the vast convoy rounded Cape St Vincent they were ambushed by Tourville. Rooke stood little chance against the might of Louis's Atlantic and Mediterranean navies. Over ninety merchant vessels were lost. It was, for the City, a disaster comparable to the Great Fire. And for William it unleashed political crisis. George Rooke said of the debacle: 'I embarked myself in this un-happy expedition contrary to my own inclinations and reason out of a passive obedience to the king's pleasure.'

In the next couple of years French privateers operating out of St Malo and Dunkirk ravaged Dutch and English merchant convoys. In 1694–95 the East India Company suffered losses of £1,500,000 from depredations in home waters. This was warfare as the English had always known it, only now they were the victims.

Since 1649 the Navy had grown stronger and it had taken root in the political life of the nation. In the political revolutions of the 1670s, 1680s and 1690s parliament gained a greater say over tactics and strategy. It set the size and armaments of new ships of the line; it voted the number of sailors required for the fleet. The House of Commons specified in a money bill of 1694 that a set proportion of the land tax would pay for forty-three frigates, in addition to the main fleet, which would be used exclusively for convoying merchantmen and cruising for predators.

England was a major trading nation by the 1690s. The Navy was ex-pected to protect traders around the world and defend the nation. It had become a cherished national institution, vital for the health of England's booming economy. If the Navy came of age in the 1650s it reached matu-rity in the last decade of the century. It was about to embark upon a war the like of which it had never experienced.

PART 8: RULE BRITANNIA

CHAPTER 25

JOINT OPS
1694–1713

... he who has the longest purse will wear the longest sword.[1]

Monitor, September 1755

Sir Cloudesley Shovell's fleet entered the Channel on 21 October 1707. The weather was poor and Shovell's sailing masters found it hard to determine their position. By the next evening conditions had deteriorated. The sailing masters and Shovell believed that the fleet was west of Ushant, on the Breton side of the Channel. At 22.00 rocks loomed into sight out of the dark and gloom and rain. The lookouts shouted; guns were fired frantically in warning. Nineteen ships of the twenty-one in the fleet manoeuvred to safety. *Association*, Shovell's 90-gun flagship, struck the Outer Gilstone Rock. *St George* (90) followed her onto the rocks, then the fireships *Phoenix* and *Firebrand*. The Crim Rocks received *Eagle* (70) and *Romney* (50) hit Bishop Rock.

These were the rocks guarding the western approach to the Scillies: the fleet was a long way from Ushant.

Later the men of *St George* said it took just three or four minutes for *Association* to sink. About 2,000 men died in this, one of the worst non-combative disasters in British naval history. The tragedy led to the Longitude Act of 1714, which sparked the race to discover a way of determining longitude at sea.

Shovell's body was found the next day. He was, with Benbow and Rooke, one of the outstanding officers in a difficult, frustrating era for the Royal Navy. This was not an age of famous battles; what glory there was had to be hard earned. Shovell was a product of the Royal Navy in its most important years of development. He had navigated waters from the Pacific to the North Sea and fought in every theatre in which the Navy operated. He was, by the end, 'a very large, fat, fair man', 'familiar and plain in his conversation', popular with his men, with his fellow officers and with his queen. Shovell was sincerely mourned. He was buried at Westminster Abbey.

A few months earlier the Abbey had seen the celebration of the Act of Union between England and Scotland. Queen Anne had no children. Her direct heirs were Catholic; all these were excluded from the succession before a distant Protestant cousin was alighted upon. By act of parliament, Sophia, Electress of Hanover, would inherit the Crown and it would pass to her son, Georg Ludwig.* But this was the decision of the Westminster parliament; there was nothing to stop James Stuart becoming James VIII of Scotland and menacing England from north of the border.

When Shovell joined the Navy as a cabin boy England was a poor and divided country, isolated on the fringes of Europe. Her ascendance to great-power status occurred when he was old in the service.

It happened with astonishing speed. In large part it was due to the Act of Union. The new United Kingdom of Great Britain was a powerful entity. Kings and queens since Edgar at least had aimed to be hegemon of the British Isles. England's empire at home was the prelude to global empire.

But it was also thanks to two wars into which William III dragged his reluctant subjects. The first of these, the Nine Years War, was called the 'Dutch War', because it was felt that it served only the interests of the king's homeland. The English had to stump up money and men to prosecute the war against Louis XIV's overweening ambitions. By 1709 the army had 69,095 men – an unacceptably high number, it was felt, for a maritime nation. For some admirals and Tory politicians the corrective to William's land war was a naval strategy.

But after the destruction of much of the French fleet at La Hogue there was little chance of mighty fleet actions bringing things to a swift conclusion. The French were fighting an unrelenting campaign targeting allied merchant shipping, a tactic against which the battlefleet was more or less powerless. The idea favoured by opponents of the king was that the war could be prosecuted by the Navy delivering lightning strikes against the enemy, while England's allies did the hard work on land. Against William's instincts the admirals formulated a plan to attack the French Atlantic naval base at Brest in 1694. The amphibious assault was a fiasco, but it did not put a stop to the policy of cowing France from the sea. Far from it.

In 1693 flotillas of new types of naval ships – bomb vessels and so-called 'infernal machines' – attacked St Malo, the home port of the privateers

---

* Sophia was the great-granddaughter of James I. She died before she could inherit the throne, which passed to her son, Georg Ludwig, known in Britain as George I.

who were wreaking such havoc on English and Dutch merchantmen. The bomb boats, rigged as ketches, carried siege mortars that could rain devastation on port towns, while the 'machine' was a fishing smack packed full of explosives, bombs, shards of glass and shrapnel. The use of these weapons depended on a high degree of technical skill and expert navigation. Teams of specialists from the Royal Ordnance worked alongside the Navy's best pilot, John Benbow. In the assault on St Malo Benbow piloted the frigates and bomb vessels into the port, negotiating the numerous rocks, sandbanks and heavily fortified islands that made it such a defensible place. The bombardment continued for three days and was brought to a finale with an exploding fireship, *Vesuvius*, directed at the town's sea walls. It was supposed to level the town, but the machine grounded short of its target, and the explosion rocked the city like an earthquake, smashed all the windows and damaged a large number of roofs.

By 1696 the Channel squadron was reduced to bombarding small towns and islands off Brittany. Attacks on St Malo, Calais and Dieppe had proved unsatisfactory. But the new technical specialism evinced on the part of the Navy in these attacks provided excellent training. Naval bombardments would become an essential weapon in Britain's armoury.

To William's mind, France could only be defeated in Flanders. He did not need the Navy for that. The other theatres of the war were in Spain and Italy. There the Navy could do some good – but in the king's view the Navy was best used in conjunction with land forces. In this way he was at odds with his admirals and many politicians. William was imperious and totally unconcerned about the practicalities of naval management. His plan was to use the Navy to prevent the French from invading Catalonia and taking Barcelona by keeping the French bottled up in their Mediterranean base, Toulon. Edward Russell, splenetic and contemptuous of royal authority as ever, was sent to the Mediterranean with the fleet. Russell knew it was a fool's errand: it was late in the season and he would soon have to return home. But then news arrived from William that he was to winter at Cadiz.

Russell exploded with rage. How was the English fleet (sixty-three ships) to support itself so far from home? He managed to turn Cadiz into a temporary naval base for the winter, but his anger mounted when he received orders to keep the fleet in the Mediterranean until October 1695. For William it was easy to order his fleet around the seas like a chess piece; for Russell it was an administrative ordeal. This was the first time the main English fleet had wintered abroad. The next winter Rooke remained in Cadiz with thirty battleships.

It was not a policy that would lead to glory, but it had a major impact on the war. William needed Savoy to join the Grand Alliance. Savoy could close the Alpine passes to France, but it was a poor country with no incentive to stand up to the French. Thanks to the presence of the Royal Navy, Savoy abandoned France and joined the Grand Alliance. With that William achieved a major goal of his strategy: France was completely encircled. As part of the wider maritime strategy a squadron was kept in the sheltered anchorage of Bertheaume and Camaret bays to keep the French Atlantic fleet in Brest.

The strategy of deterrence worked for as long as there was money to pay for it. The French were kept from Barcelona and Savoy was shielded from French reprisals. The watchful eye over Toulon was removed in 1696 when Rooke's squadron was hastily recalled after an assassination attempt against the king's life sparked fears of an invasion. The French seized their chance and took Barcelona. Savoy was compelled to make unilateral peace with France. By then, however, the war was petering out. The belligerents were bankrupt.

Disappointing and unpopular as it may have been, the Nine Years War was, like all wars, good for the service. The Royal Navy had 173 ships of all kinds in 1689; when the Treaty of Ryswick brought the war to an end in 1697 it had 323. This meant building ships on an industrial scale. A stone dry dock that could accommodate first rates was built at vast expense at Plymouth in 1691; another at Portsmouth. By 1695 there were 48,000 men serving in the Navy.

Peace was short-lived. In contravention of various treaties Louis supported Philip V's claim to the Spanish empire in 1701. Philip was the Sun King's grandson; if they succeeded then France and Spain would one day be united. Europe would be menaced by a French super-empire stretching from Gibraltar to Dunkirk and which included large chunks of Italy. France would control the western Mediterranean, much of the Americas and the Philippines. In the short term as well there was plenty to fear. The Dutch Republic was jeopardised by French troops in the Spanish Netherlands. And they, and the English, found themselves excluded from the Spanish empire.

Once again England was drawn into war on the Continent, in alliance with the Dutch, Germans and Austrians. The naval dimension of the War of the Spanish Succession focused on the western Mediterranean, where the allies wanted to cut Spain off from her Italian possessions, and on the trade route between the silver mines and sugar plantations of South America and Spain. After an interval of half a century the Navy was in familiar waters once again. Now, however, the Spanish treasure ships were under the protection of French warships.

Admiral John Benbow was dispatched to the Caribbean to disrupt the Franco-Spanish convoy. Rooke sailed for Cadiz in October 1702 with the main fleet. The plan was to capture the port and use it as the base from which the Navy would blockade Spain and control the Mediterranean. It was an ambition familiar to Drake, Buckingham and Blake. William III, following on from his wider Mediterranean strategy, made the decision. In the previous war Cadiz had proved a vital base from which to open up the Mediterranean front against France. Now the closest allied naval base to the Gibraltar Strait was Portsmouth.

William died before the plan was attempted. His sister-in-law, Anne, came to the throne. Once again Rooke chose the path of passive obedience. Shovell was left off Ushant with a squadron to keep an eye on the enemy battlefleet at Brest and watch for the *flota*. Rooke led fifty warships and 110 transports that carried 14,000 troops to Iberia.

The attempt on Cadiz joined its predecessors on the list of naval debacles centred on that city. As so often, the men took the opportunity to drink, loot and desecrate churches. On the way home, however, Rooke received intelligence that the treasure convoy had put into Vigo.

Vigo Bay was defended by a boom, shore batteries, forts and French warships. Most of the treasure had been unloaded, but Rooke and his officers resolved to capture or destroy the French warships. At dawn on 23 October 1702 *Torbay* (80) crashed the boom. Meanwhile allied grenadiers stormed the fortifications. Allied ships and fireships followed *Torbay* across the boom. The French sailors set fire to their ships and fled ashore. Their English counterparts raced to secure prizes from the inferno. By the end of the battle ten out of fifteen French ships of the line had been captured and the remainder destroyed.

It was a major victory for the allies. The king of Portugal swapped allegiance from Spain to the allies, fearful of offending the new masters of the Atlantic. A good portion of the commerce of Portugal's overseas empire fell to the English and Dutch. That would be an enormous benefit to the English economy in the future. In the short term it gave the Navy the use of Lisbon.

It was from there that Shovell and then Rooke launched operations into the Mediterranean. Lisbon was hardly satisfactory; it was closer to the Strait than Portsmouth, but still 350 miles from Cadiz. As William had taught, France would be defeated when she was encircled. Success in Bavaria and on the Rhine – the epicentre of the war – would come when the French armies were pulled in different directions. Fronts needed to be opened against Louis in Iberia and Italy. That would only happen when the Navy could enter the Mediterranean and support offensives by England's allies.

It was a long hard slog to achieve these war aims. France was the dominant naval power in the western Mediterranean. If the French Mediterranean and Atlantic fleets could unite then the allied navy would come under serious pressure. From 1702 to 1704 the Royal Navy worked hard to begin its offensive in the region. In 1703 Shovell led a fleet into the Mediterranean and once again Savoy deserted Louis and joined the allies.

Then, in 1704, Rooke's fleet captured Gibraltar. It came in the year of a more significant victory – the duke of Marlborough's crushing victory over the Franco-Bavarian army at Blenheim.

Gibraltar exhibited little promise for the future. Its defences left a lot to be desired and it was not big enough for a fleet to anchor. Even so the Navy was made to fight hard for it. It was a successful amphibious assault. Bomb boats shelled the town while marines stormed the rock. Shortly after it fell a French fleet of fifty ships left Toulon and linked up with the Atlantic fleet. This was the nightmare scenario that had haunted Rooke and Shovell. The opposing sides met near Malaga and fought a line engagement. Like many battles of this time, its ferocity failed to translate into a decisive victory.

Had the French pressed a little harder they might have dislodged the Navy from Gibraltar, for Rooke's ships were low on ammunition after their assault on Gibraltar. Shovell noted that some of the ships in his van squadron were down to just ten cannonballs. Rather than fighting to a bloody conclusion, however, the French claimed merely the honour of victory and retired to Toulon and Brest.

The following year the French and Spanish besieged Gibraltar from land and sea. Admiral Sir John Leake, in command of the naval forces at Lisbon, attacked the French blockade and destroyed five battleships, condemning their crews to die in the waves – a horrendous death and a significant toll of French mariners – and saving Gibraltar. Later in the year Sir Cloudesley Shovell led a successful seaborne attack that resulted in the capture of Barcelona. In 1706 Leake managed to chase away a French fleet supporting the recapture of the city. That day the sun went into eclipse. It was an unhappy omen for Louis XIV, the Sun King. Leake followed up his success with the capture of a string of Spanish ports and islands: Cartagena, Alicante, Ibiza and Majorca. 1706 was also the year in which

Marlborough defeated Louis at Ramillies and drove the French out of the Spanish Netherlands.

The decisive battles of the War of the Spanish Succession were fought on land. Less spectacularly, the Royal Navy made itself master of the Mediterranean bit by bit and regained its reputation. It had done it by a succession of clinical amphibious operations, the skilful co-ordination of battleships, bomb vessels and marines. The gains were then defended by conventional means – by ships of the line fighting off the enemy.

The Navy's contribution to the war was to secure local dominance and then support ground troops, whether it be transporting them to the battlefield or siege, assisting in joint operations, or cutting off the enemy's supply lines. In 1704 an additional 5,000 infantry were raised to act with the fleet. They were not part of the ships' complement; they were on board 'to make impression upon the enemy in proper places'.

What the Navy lacked was a winter base to seal its successes in the Mediterranean. None of its conquests in the region could accommodate a fleet. There was, however, a perfectly good port that could be used. In 1707 the decision was made to take Toulon, the base of the French Mediterranean fleet. Once again the well-honed drill of an amphibious operation would be used. The Navy, led by Shovell, supported an army led by Prince Eugene of Savoy in an attack on the city. The assault from land was half-hearted, but the destruction of several shore defences gave Shovell the opportunity he needed. Anglo-Dutch bomb boats sailed close to the shore and fired their shells over a ridge. For eighteen hours bombs rained down on the French fleet hidden out of view on the other side of the hill, the naval gunners aided by signallers on the ridge. Two French ships of the line were burnt and destroyed. More than forty-six were scuttled lest they fall victim to the fire. These ships were supposed to be raised and repaired when the coast was clear, but no effort had been made to refloat them by the time the war ended. By then they were beyond repair.

Shovell's achievement at Toulon has been written off as a failure, and the admiral himself was disappointed. But the effect of the assault was significant. It gave the allies control of the Mediterranean and eliminated the French as a naval power. The search for a base eluded the Navy for another year. In 1708 Leake captured Port Mahon in Minorca. For almost a century the possession of Minorca would underwrite British dominance in the Mediterranean.

The Tories detested Britain's overseas wars. For the Whigs, Britain's first line of defence was, as it always had been, the Low Countries. France had to be confronted there and contained by alliances with German princes and regional powers in the Mediterranean. The Tories, however, saw Britain's future as a maritime power able to counterbalance European superpowers by building up her colonies in the New World.

The Tories came to power in 1710. A year later they unilaterally pulled Britain out of the war, leaving their allies in the lurch. Britain came out of the war with important gains: Gibraltar, Minorca, St Kitts, a stronger position in North America, and the *Asiento* – the monopoly over trading slaves in the Spanish colonies. Spain's empire was broken up: Savoy got Sicily; Austria got the Spanish Netherlands, Naples and Sardinia; Portugal made gains in the New World.

Great Britain's emergence as a great power was built upon a string of military victories. Many in England felt that William squandered English resources and lives to help the Dutch Republic. Tories and Whigs alike deeply mistrusted the king. As a result he had to haggle for cash and political support. In return for the means to fight his wars, William gave parliament the right to scrutinise public accounts. In 1697 it gained control over revenue raising and expenditure on the army and Navy.

Now it had control over the public finances, parliament was prepared to be generous as never before with its constituents' money. The Nine Years War alone cost an eye-watering £49,320,145. The War of the Spanish Succession cost £93,644,560. Wartime naval strength peaked at 228 ships carrying 9,800 guns and employing 52,393 men.

But most important was a financial revolution closely modelled on Dutch methods and sparked into life by the shock delivered courtesy of the French navy at Beachy Head. In 1694 the Bank of England was founded. It raised £1,200,000 as a loan to the Crown against future revenues from tax. Over half of this sum was spent on the Navy. Secure public finances, based on the consent of the political nation, meant that the state could borrow staggering amounts at favourable rates of interest. This was the beginning of the 'fiscal–military' state that would, in time, turn Britain into a war-waging machine. As it was, even at the outset William and Anne were able to wage war with France on land and at sea, in northern Europe, the Mediterranean, the Atlantic and the Americas from 1689 to 1711 with only a few years' respite.

This was unprecedented. And the reason was that Britain could outspend France – this despite the fact that France had a population of 20 million against England's 6 million. Added to that, the apparently insignificant victory at Vigo Bay had opened up the Portuguese empire to British traders. Revenues from overseas trade swelled. In the wars against the Dutch between 1652 and 1672 the English fought well, but in the end the smaller Dutch Republic could always outspend the English and build more ships. Now that England had been conquered by a Dutchman it had learnt some of those tricks. Its revenue raising was formidable. Now it could be said that the Devil shat English ships.

The 'greatest glory of our reign' was, for Queen Anne, the Act of Union. But there were other glories, and those were purchased at an enormous price. Anne was concerned to put a patriotic complexion on her continental wars in a way William never could. She made it clear to her subjects that the reason for fighting France was to further England's glory and prosperity. 'As I know my own heart to be entirely English,' she told her first parliament, 'I can very sincerely assert that there is not anything you can expect from or desire from me which I shall not be ready to do for the happiness and prosperity of England.' She uttered these patriotic sentiments dressed in an outfit modelled on portraits of Elizabeth. Marlborough's triumphs were celebrated with Elizabethan-style victory services at Wren's new St Paul's Cathedral.

Britain emerged from the War of the Spanish Succession the greatest naval power in Europe. Its rivals had, to a large extent, been eliminated or neutered. The Dutch had sacrificed naval power for self-defence on land; France had been knocked back to the 1660s; and the Iberian and Mediterranean powers were extinct volcanoes.

In Britain, by contrast, the Royal Navy was a beloved national institution. There was an appreciation that the country's financial health depended on the Navy. Through this period Britain's economy, overseas trade, banking and public finance became highly developed. That was a major shift, and it made a large permanent Navy not only possible but vital. Parliament was prepared to fund the Navy, even in times of tranquillity. In 1694 the Commons used a Land Tax Bill to allocate forty-three ships for the exclusive protection of trade. It was bolstered by the Cruizers and Convoys Act of 1708. Parliament's intent was to create a specialised force dedicated to defending British trade. The Navy did not just exist to win battles; it had a vital economic function.

The public was prepared to invest in the Navy. This was literally true. From 1714 the Navy ran its own system of public credit. Investors could purchase Navy Bills, which were freely transferable in the Stock Exchange and which yielded a return of 6 per cent. This paralleled developments in state finance, where issues of government stock allowed the government to spend in excess of annual revenue.

The ability of the Navy to fund itself in this way was unique, in comparison both with rival navies and with its own history. The service could spend its money as it saw fit, independent of Treasury control and parliamentary scrutiny. The Navy prospered under these conditions.

Its blooming health was symbolised by the Admiralty building in Whitehall, constructed in 1699. It was replaced by the building that still stands (known as the Ripley Building and now home of the Cabinet Office) on the same site in 1725. It contained an impressive boardroom, state rooms, offices and apartments. This revealed a new and important fact about the Admiralty. Until 1699 it had no home, but was bound up with the person and household of the Lord High Admiral. From 1709 the office of Lord High Admiral was placed in commission (with the exception of 1826–27, when HRH the duke of Clarence took up the long-dormant post). After 1709 the most important man in the Navy was the head of the Board of Admiralty – its First Lord.

Now the Board of Admiralty had a permanent bureaucracy, an archive of records and, most important of all, a home right in the heart of power. The Admiralty's main business was the appointment and management of the Navy's officers. The Admiralty building was the hub of operations that criss-crossed the globe. But the Admiralty was also the senior of the Navy's boards, the planet around which the Navy Board, the Victualling Office and the Sick and Wounded Board revolved. The junior boards fought (often successfully) for autonomy, but they were now up against the political clout of the Admiralty. The First Lord held a position in cabinet; hence he had a hand on the tiller of grand strategy. In times of war the Admiralty issued orders to the other parts of the Navy's decentralised administrative system. The Admiralty did not run the Navy; it made the decisions and issued the orders. The business of getting things done was left to others.

In the first decades of the eighteenth century the Admiralty grew in experience and power. No other country had this kind of permanence and continuity at the heart of its navy. Between 1714 and 1742 four senior admirals held the post of First Lord of the Admiralty, rather than inexperienced politicians or princes. Members of the Navy Board held their positions for long spans of time, providing comparable experience and continuity.

By 1730, a time of peace, more people worked in the dockyards than at the height of Queen Anne's war. It meant that despite the long peace the British political establishment and public opinion were determined to keep up naval strength. The Navy could have declined in these balmy days. It did not. For that reason this was a breakaway time in the history of the Royal Navy.

If Britannia did not yet rule the waves, she dominated them. The wars of William and Anne took a healthy, moderately successful Navy and transformed it into a well-oiled machine. It was led by a professional band of officers, men epitomised by Cloudesley Shovell. They were not as flashy as their predecessors, but they got the job done. Between 1694 and 1713 the Navy expanded in size and it won a series of victories. Few of them were startling or worthy of major commemoration. Instead a series of clinical operations off Iberia and in the western Mediterranean had secured important bases, won over local allies and aided ground troops. Enemy privateering was beaten back by mobile cruisers detached from main fleet operations. The noose was tightened around France; she became brittle and the army was able to break her. That was how to win a modern war – by patience, organisation and quiet professionalism.

The Navy was more than ever the darling of the nation. It moved to the forefront of national life during a time of unprecedented economic boom. That was a blessing and a curse. It led the British to invest every last ounce of hope in their Navy to achieve the impossible; it came to be seen as invincible. Cloudesley Shovell said: 'The misfortune and vice of our country is to believe ourselves better than other men, which I take to be the reason generally we send too small a force to execute our designs.'[2] That overconfidence identified by the plain-speaking Shovell would be revealed in the years ahead.

CHAPTER 26

HEAVEN'S COMMAND
1713–1744

We are designed by [nature] for a maritime power. Experience sufficiently confirms ... when we endeavour to exert our
strength by sea we become the dread of the world; when by
land the contempt of it.[1]

William Pitt the Elder

At Cliveden House, situated magnificently on the wooded hills that over-
hang the Thames, 'Rule, Britannia!' was first performed on 1 August 1740.
It was part of a masque (later reworked as an opera) called *Alfred*, which
linked the legend of Alfred's triumphs over the Vikings with contemporary visions of global naval supremacy. It was sung in honour of Cliveden's tenant, Frederick, Prince of Wales, and when it was introduced to
the public it became an instant hit.

'Rule, Britannia! rule the waves: Britons never will be slaves,' reads the
original text. Nowadays, and since it was first performed, it has been sung
as 'Rule Britannia! Britannia rules the waves: Britons never, never, never
shall be slaves', which is completely different. The latter sounds like a
statement of fact. In the original it is an exhortation.

In 1740 Britain did not rule the waves. But there was a deep-rooted
belief that she had the God-given right to maritime dominance. Her liberty – hard won, as it was believed, in 1688–89 – depended utterly on
her Navy. 'Nations, not so blest as thee,' goes 'Rule Britannia', 'Must, in
their turns, to tyrants fall', while Britain will 'flourish great and free, / The
dread and envy of them all'.

And the reason that Britons remained free while their neighbours
quailed in bondage, so the thinking went, was her Navy. Standing armies,
so history and experience taught, meant that states inevitably became
tyrannical. Just look at England under Cromwell and contemporary
Europe. Empires propped up by force of arms degenerated into corrupt
despotisms. Britain was blessed. Her empire was an empire of trade and

commerce – seaborne, not territorial. Her defences came by way of the wooden wall that encircled her coast, not from liberty-denying redcoats. And navies, unlike armies, were supposed to be self-funding: gains in trade paid for dockyards, guns and sailors.

Or that was how some politicians, propagandists and princes liked to see Britain's destiny. The truth fell short of the aspiration – and corrupt contemporary politicians should take the blame for that deficiency. One day she would rule, 'by heaven's command', when the right people were in charge. In this vision all that was good and free about Britain was due to her Navy. Romanticised to this extent, naval power becomes a panacea for all political maladies. In the second quarter-century the country had been starved of naval victories.

But now, in 1740, Britain had been swept to war with Spain on a wave of popular enthusiasm, much against the instincts of the prime minister, Robert Walpole. Naval triumphs on the scale of the Elizabethans would, it was believed, knock down the corrupt regime of Walpole and purify the land.

Fought on the high seas, in the Caribbean and the Pacific, it was decidedly the *right* kind of war for Prince Frederick and his political cronies, dissident Whigs known as the 'Patriots' and Tories. The heir to the throne champed at the bit, restricted and excluded as he was by his father, George II. Frederick blamed Walpole and turned instead to the Tories and Patriots. There was a deeply held conviction among these groups that wars fought on the Continent were inherently evil. They nurtured tyranny with their standing armies, high taxes and entanglements with European states.

The leading opposition Whig leader, William Pulteney spelt it out: 'our fleets are sufficient to keep dominion of the ocean and prescribe limits to the commerce of every nation'.[2] He went on to say that if Britain retained 'her natural superiority' at sea and asserted the 'honour of her flag in every climate' then she would be able to influence friends and enemies alike, be they landlocked or maritime countries. There would be no need for an army or alliances with foreigners; Britain's command of the trade of the world would be her sole, mighty weapon that would give her leverage over the whole of Europe and security from invasion.

Maritime wars, therefore, were ideological. Victory in Europe appeared to benefit only Britain's allies, whereas wars at sea meant irreversible gains for the country. 'Like other amphibious animals, we must come occasionally on shore,' wrote the Tory statesman Lord Bolingbroke, 'but the water is more properly our element, and in it like them, as we find our greatest security, so we exert our greatest force.'³

This was to forget the War of the Spanish Succession, when a combination of naval power, continental alliances and land victories had broken France. But that seemed like a long time ago. From 1713 until 1739 Europe was untroubled by a major war. Britain was the only serious naval power in the Mediterranean, where it policed the terms of the Treaty of Utrecht. Its power rested on its powerful ships, disciplined crews and key strategic bases at Gibraltar and Minorca.

Britain's dominance was underlined when Spain tried to retake Sicily in 1718 and its fleet was roundly beaten by Admiral Sir George Byng in the Battle of Cape Passaro, off Messina. Byng did not seek to defeat the Spanish in a formal line engagement; instead he ordered a general chase, unleashing his ships to attack the enemy from either side of their line in a dramatic running battle. The tactic was more than vindicated; thirteen Spanish ships were taken and three burnt. Sicily was saved and the peace of Europe was preserved. British self-confidence and tactical improvisation ensured a famous victory.

The Navy intervened four times in the Baltic between 1719 and 1726. Closer to home it guarded the United Kingdom against foreign attempts to support a Jacobite rebellion. In 1726 Secretary of State Townshend boasted⁴ that while one fleet was containing the burgeoning power of Russia in the Baltic, another was putting pressure on the Austrian Netherlands and a third was blockading Porto Bello in Panama, preventing the export of gold and silver.

And at the same time, it should be added, Britain's expanding trade was protected by cruisers and convoys from Iceland to the coast of West Africa, from the Baltic to the Americas and from Gibraltar to Syria. The First Lord of the Admiralty told the king that Britain was not only stronger than her next rival, but the next two great naval powers combined. A generation of Britons was nurtured on the faith that their country was lord of the seas.

The blockade of Porto Bello in 1726 arose out of the need to safeguard the European settlement. Spain and Austria were uniting to undo their losses at Utrecht. Spain, in particular, would not suffer the indignity of Britain's possession of Gibraltar and Minorca. The Navy had squadrons at Gibraltar and in the West Indies, from where they launched offensives against Spanish bases. Operations in the Caribbean revealed a weakness in England's pretensions to maritime supremacy. While successful blockades were maintained 4,000 sailors and soldiers succumbed to yellow fever. Among the casualties were fifty lieutenants, ten captains, the third in command, the vice admiral and the admiral himself, Francis Hosier. The costly blockade of Porto Bello disrupted, but did not prevent, the export of the treasure; but it did force Spain and Austria to come to terms with Britain.

The Caribbean had always been a place of terror for English mariners; the fate of Hosier's squadron was a reminder that joint operations in that sea were no easy matter. Disease wiped out huge numbers of men; *Teredo navalis*, shipworm, which can grow up to two feet long, bored into hulls. Nonetheless the Navy was committed to maintaining its position there.

There was one thing worth the horrors of yellow fever and the expense of ship worm: sugar. Sugar was the great commodity of the seventeenth and eighteenth centuries. It transformed the European economy and made fortunes in the City. The Caribbean was vital to the interests of Great Britain. In the 1720s naval bases with extensive wharves and storehouses were constructed at Port Royal, Jamaica, and English Harbour, Antigua.

As far as the Spanish were concerned British traders in their empire were smugglers and pirates; the *guardacostas*, the Spanish coast guard, occasionally made swoops on British ships and cargoes.

But why should Britain, the greatest naval power in the world, tolerate Spanish interference? Throughout the 1730s pressure built for a maritime war. Publishers rushed out books detailing centuries' worth of enmity between Spain and England; biographies of Robert Blake began to appear; tales of Spanish cruelties against innocent British sailors flew off the press, the most lurid being the account of Captain Robert Jenkins, whose ear was cut off by the *guardacostas* in 1731. Merchants complained of grievous losses to trade.

Political discourse, in parliament and the press, became overloaded with the language of British liberties and hyperbolic expressions of maritime invincibility. The myths of British sea power – in particular the Elizabethan legends – were revived and contrasted with the present ministry, which had been led by Robert Walpole since 1721. Britain had been dishonoured abroad while her mighty Navy looked impotently on. Who was to blame?

Walpole's ministry was accused of the grossest corruption. He was nicknamed Don Roberto: a maritime war against Spain would not only restore Britain's reputation abroad but it would be a war against the prime minister. Also to blame was the monarchy. George II was king of Great Britain, but he was also Elector of Hanover. For many advocates of Britain's 'Blue Water' strategy this meant that the Crown was pulling in a different direction from the country. While the British wanted to turn their backs on the Continent, the Hanover connection pulled the other way. There was a strong suspicion that George II and Walpole were appeasing France in order to spare the Electorate of Hanover from attack. To the Tories and Patriots this extended to restraining British sea power. 'It is now too apparent that this great, this powerful, this formidable kingdom is considered only a province to a despicable Electorate,' declared William Pitt, a leading 'Patriot'. He spoke for many.

War at sea would, in this view, revive British liberties and bring to power patriotic politicians who would reanimate the national spirit. Lord Bolingbroke argued that Britain was fitted by geography, history and temperament to be a trading nation. The health of the body politick depended upon her mastery of the sea; every patriotic statesman should bend his energies to stimulating trade and maintaining sovereignty over the sea. But, Bolingbroke alleged, this was far from the case. 'For eighteen years, we have tamely suffered continual depredations from the most contemptible maritime power in Europe, that of Spain.'[5]

The patriotic navalist din reached a crescendo. Walpole and his ministers had spent years negotiating with Spain. For them Britain's interests lay in securing alliances in Europe. Now the pressure was for the country to go to war. It would be extremely unpopular in Europe, but that did not seem to bother the patriots. In fact, it spurred them on. The virtue of a maritime war on the far side of the Atlantic, it was felt, was that it bypassed degrading European entanglements.

That was the virtue of maritime war full stop: it freed Britain from the stultifying embrace of Europe in general and Hanover in particular; it could be fought and won without the need to raise liberty-quelling armies; it was self-funding. Britain could be as England was in Good Queen Bess's Day: independent, wealthy and defiant.

The Elizabethan era was all the rage. Few remembered how hard she worked to build alliances on the Continent; few liked to recall that the activities of Drake and Hawkins were sideshows by comparison. That would get in the way of the naval myth. Walpole had no choice but to go to war.

The patriots were vindicated. Almost at once the Royal Navy had a hero to compare with Drake. He was an unlikely adventurer. Edward Vernon started in the Navy as a protégé of Sir Cloudesley Shovell back in 1700. He had served around the world, but his stint as commander-in-chief in the Caribbean impressed him most. He considered Spain's navy to be cowardly and weak and her empire ripe for the plucking. By 1739 Vernon had not served in the Navy for over a decade, but he had been elected to parliament and he subjected the Commons to impassioned, hectoring speeches on Britain's destiny to rule the waves. Most notably he criticised Hosier's blockade of Porto Bello. The town, the headquarters of the *guardacostas* and 'only mart for all the wealth of Peru to come to Europe', he wildly claimed, could be captured by just six ships and 300 men. Admiral Vernon, a committed believer in British liberty and naval power, a tireless critic of Walpole, was the darling of the Patriots. He was plucked out of agreeable retirement in Suffolk and sent to spearhead the war. His plan was to secure dominion over the seas and conquer a string of Spanish colonies.

In November 1739 Vernon captured Porto Bello. As promised, he did so with just six ships.

The news reached London in March 1740. The country and the colonies exploded in celebration.[6] Streets were named Portobello. 'Vernon' was given to a host of places and things, including pubs, but most notably to Mount Vernon in Virginia, the future home of George Washington. The name given to the Washington residence is a reminder that Vernon's victory aroused patriotic enthusiasm for an enlarged British Empire as fervently in the American colonies as in Britain itself. A whole range of British commodities, in particular ceramic wares, depicted scenes of the victory. Ballads were composed and sung everywhere; enthusiastic poems were written and plays performed. People celebrated Vernon's birthday in the streets, in coffeehouses and public houses. His victory was ranked with the greatest naval triumphs of all times. In taking Porto Bello he had apparently revealed the wretched timidity and unpatriotic character of Walpole's regime.

The knives were out for the prime minister. Vernon was lauded as a hero of liberty, the saviour of his nation and the instrument of vengeance against tyrants. He was the admiral who had stood up to Walpole *and* the Spanish empire, enemies of liberty both.

The patriots had promoted the notion of British naval superiority and promised easy victories. Here was the proof. The attack on Porto Bello was the model of a combined amphibious operation. 'Rule, Britannia' indeed – Britain stood on the cusp of naval glory.

Vernon moved on to places familiar to his Elizabethan progenitors: Cartagena, Panama and Cuba. Another Elizabethan-style force was sent under Captain George Anson to the Pacific to raid the Spanish South American colonies, capture the inward-bound Manila galleon and link up with Vernon in Panama. The dream of an amphibious war against Spanish colonies was being realised.

Assaults on Cartagena, Santiago de Cuba and Panama went well from a naval point of view; Vernon's ships were quite capable of knocking out shore defences and landing troops. But the ghost of Admiral Hosier came back to haunt Vernon. Once on land in the rainy season the soldiers were vulnerable to tropical diseases. Of the 10,000 men under Vernon's command, 7,000 died. The Spanish defences at Cartagena were better than anyone expected. Vernon had masses of experience and a domineering personality that he exerted to take full control over land as well as naval operations – something he was not qualified to do. Under these conditions, joint operations – the hallmark of the Royal Navy since the War of the Spanish Succession – were impossible.

Meanwhile, Anson's expedition was faring badly. He set out with *Centurion* (60), *Gloucester* (50), *Severn* (50), *Pearl* (40), *Wager* (28), *Tryal* (8) and two storeships in September 1740. Poor organisation and creaky methods of mobilisation meant that the squadron set sail far too late in the year. It attempted to round Cape Horn in winter in horrendous conditions. Stormy seas raged over the ships; rain or snow fell constantly; and the ships had to battle a strong easterly current in the Magellan Strait. Powerful winds ripped sails from the yards; the ships sprang leaks. *Wager* did not make it; *Severn* and *Pearl* turned back. The remaining two warships left England with crews totalling 961; when they rendezvoused at the Juan Fernández Islands after three months beating their way into the Pacific only 335 had survived scurvy, hunger and exposure. This number was less than the crew required for *Centurion*.

Anson refused to give up. He was a tough, taciturn man in his early forties. Many officers in the eighteenth century came from gentry backgrounds and Anson was a prime example of this kind of recruit. The War of the Spanish Succession had already come to an end when he entered the Navy in 1712 with the wind of favour in his sails: his uncle was Lord Chief Justice and a future Lord Chancellor. The boy was on the old side at fifteen. And in any event forging an officer's career in the early Georgian Navy was no easy thing. Promotion, fame and fortune were attainable in seasons of war; in days of peace the naval officers' lot was not a happy one because the number of ships on active service declined to a bare minimum and the officers who rose in the last war clung on to their commissions long into their old age. The Navy became a gerontocracy. Anson served in the Baltic under Sir John Norris and as a newly appointed lieutenant under Sir George Byng. Battle was a rare thing between 1710 and 1739, but Anson was bloodied at the Battle of Cape Passaro. Byng's dynamic victory, the result of experience and courage, left an impression on the boy.

Anson's first command was a sloop cruising the North Sea. Then he captained a frigate stationed in South Carolina from 1724 until 1730, and again from 1732 to 1735. There he developed a prodigious appetite for alcohol and augmented his income thanks to his proficiency at the card table. Colonial society may have been agreeable enough, but there was no mistaking that this was a backwater as far as the Navy was concerned. Things improved in 1737, after twenty-seven relatively quiet years in the service, when he was given command of *Centurion*, which cruised off the West African coast protecting English slaving and trading ships – a two-year mission.

So when the Admiralty sought an officer to lead a daring raid on the Spanish empire in the Pacific, Anson was an inspired choice. He had spent the bulk of his career in distant waters, dealing with piracy and minor colonial disputes. Unlike many of his well-heeled contemporaries, who spent their careers close to home in the main fleet, Anson had been allotted less than glamorous commands. It allowed him to show that he had the requisite grit, developed in distant corners of the world far from the direct supervision of his superiors, which qualified him to lead an operation to the other side of the globe.

Now he had entered the Pacific he found that few of his objectives were feasible. *Wager* had carried most of his soldiers and artillery. Yet Anson was determined to fight on. The leaky, undermanned *Centurion* and *Gloucester* took some prizes and raided settlements on shore. As Drake had discovered in similar circumstances, the only way home was to keep going round the world. The two warships headed west into the Pacific.

It was a voyage of the darkest nightmares. *Gloucester* was burnt when she lost her mainmast and most of her rigging and sprang a leak. *Centurion* was not much better; her foremast had split and she too had a serious leak – serious enough that Anson himself had to take turns at the pump. As the months wore on things on the floating wreck became desperate. Every day eight to ten men on the stricken warship died from scurvy.

Back in the Caribbean things were getting worse for Vernon. Britain had gone to war without an ally in Europe. In October 1742 Vernon returned from the Caribbean, leaving a squadron of ships. But there were to be no more amphibious operations. Britain was now on the defensive.

She had entered the war determined to show that she ruled the waves; that she could project her power into the Americas, Africa, Asia, the Pacific and southern Europe. Yellow fever, scurvy, shipworm, storms and hunger had shown how hollow that claim was.

Expectations had been raised to a hysterical level. Reality hit hard. But it was not the Navy that was blamed – or even the advocates of maritime war. On the contrary, politicians and the public complained that the only reason the Navy had failed was inadequate support by the government. In the wake of these recriminations and heightened emotions Robert Walpole fell from power in February 1742.

He had been keen to avoid conflict in the first place. The war had not only failed in all its aims; it had, as Walpole feared, left Britain isolated and weakened when Europe was once again descending into war. France was on the march and Spain was gaining power in the Mediterranean. 'It looked last year as if the old world was to be fought for in the new,' said Lord Hardwicke; 'but the tables are turned.'[7]

That was an understatement. Britain was in a parlous situation. France and Spain were at war against Austria. Germany and the Netherlands were under pressure from France; Italy from Spain. Britain had to enter the war. For one thing Hanover was in danger.

A more dire threat was spelled out by Sir William Yonge, the secretary at war.[8] Britain might invest all its rhetoric and strategic thinking in the fact that it was an island with a powerful Navy, he said. The British might count themselves lucky that they could turn to the world and ignore Europe, safe behind the defensive moat of the sea. But it was a neglected and inconvenient fact that British naval superiority depended utterly on her position in Europe. If France won victories by land and retook the Netherlands, Yonge averred, 'she would apply herself with the utmost diligence and application to the increase of her navy'. If France became a major naval power, with bases on the Channel, the Atlantic and the Mediterranean, then Britain could kiss farewell to her security from invasion, not to say her colonial and commercial ambitions. Lord Carteret put it as bluntly: if France successfully invaded the Netherlands 'our commerce will quickly be at an end. We shall lose the dominion of the sea, and all our distant colonies and settlements, and be shut up in our own island.'[9]

In short, the foundations of naval supremacy lay on land, in the heart of Europe.

After the diversion of the maritime war against Spain Britain found her stock in Europe at a very low level. Now, in 1742, Britain had to race to regain the position she had enjoyed in the period 1689–1711, the foundations of her emergence as a great power. She had to assemble an alliance among the German states to shore up Austria, defend the Netherlands, and beat France back.

In 1744 Britain once again had large numbers of troops deployed on the Continent. It was incredibly unpopular. The majority wanted to fight exclusively at sea and saw the new war as a ploy on the part of George II to defend Hanover. Why couldn't the Dutch, Germans and Austrians do the fighting, while Britain waged war at sea? That was the typical attitude – and it went down very badly with Britain's potential allies. The national faith in maritime destiny was extraordinarily durable. It was a potent political force. The ministry, however, knew that the continental war was essential to Britain's success at sea. It was the price Britain had to pay for being a world power.

But in 1744 Britain did not look like a world power. She was facing defeat everywhere.

In collections of the 'great battles of the Royal Navy' it is often only the victories that get mentioned, giving the misleading impression that the service's path to greatness was built on an endless succession of triumphs. But it is often its defeats that had the most profound effect.

On 10 February 1744 the Spanish fleet broke out of Toulon, where it had been blockaded by a fleet under Admiral Thomas Mathews. The Spanish were being escorted by the French navy. It signalled France's entry into the war. In a heavy swell and light breezes the British found it hard to form their line. Mathews signalled for his ships to anchor for the night. He assumed that the vanguard and rear would align themselves with the centre so that, at dawn, the line would be ready to attack the enemy. However, neither did so.

On the morning of the battle, 11 February, the British were strung out, with Richard Lestock, in command of the rear division, far behind. Mathews signalled to Lestock to make sail and close the gap. Lestock responded by slowing down even more. Mathews knew that he could not wait and decided to attack without Lestock. His only chance was to dispense with the formal line of battle and attack as quickly as he could. His attack would be like Byng's at Cape Passaro in 1718, an improvised affair in which each captain used his judgement to harry the Franco-Spanish fleet.

But Byng led captains who knew his plans before the battle began. Mathews had not done the same groundwork. Worse still, his signals belied his intentions; he signalled to attack immediately, but he kept the flag that was ordering line ahead as well. As Mathews abandoned the strictures of the line and led his division to isolate the Spanish ships from the French the bulk of his captains were left pondering which signal took precedence. Many of them were thoroughly confused and froze. Captain John Ambrose of HMS *Rupert* (60) threw a tantrum on his quarterdeck because he had no immediate opponent to fight. 'It's better to be blamed for breaking the line than to lie thus and have no ship to engage,'[10] he frothed as he stamped and swore in frustration. However his officers warned him he would be punished for leaving the line – or, to put it another way, showing his initiative. Ambrose spent the battle in an agony of indecision.

Compare this with Captain Edward Hawke of HMS *Berwick* (70). He scorned the risk of court martial and bore down on the Spanish ship *Poder* (64). He held his fire until he was within pistol shot (twenty yards). The resulting bombardment at close range was devastating. *Poder* lost 200 men; *Berwick* just six. The Spanish ship struck to Hawke. He was not the only captain to use his judgement. Three other captains, who would otherwise have remained idle, spaced themselves out to prevent the British line being doubled by the French squadron.

Meanwhile Lestock had managed to get close to the battle, but rather than attack four isolated Spanish ships at the rear of the enemy line he stuck like a limpet to the letter of the regulations. He held off from intervening and his ships fired a few desultory and ineffectual shots at long range. The Spanish escaped and the French recovered *Poder*.

The Battle of Toulon was a fiasco, an embarrassment to a country that aspired to naval dominance. Things might have been different had not Mathews and Lestock detested each other. Mathews refused to discuss tactics with his second in command. Lestock had no compulsion to hurry into battle and perhaps took satisfaction in seeing his detested boss get into trouble. Victory might have been possible had Mathews discussed tactics with subordinates and if he had been clearer in his signals. As it was, most of his captains were too scared or unimaginative to understand their admiral's intention or to show any initiative. They did not even support their fellows who got into trouble.

In the wake of the battle the Navy was torn apart by a spate of courts martial and parliamentary inquiries. These proceedings were marred by perjury, forgery, professional jealousy, personal rivalries and the taint of political corruption. The three captains who used their judgement to prevent the French surrounding the line were judged in breach of orders and cashiered. Other captains, such as Ambrose, were kicked out of the Navy for failing to fight. Lestock was charged with hanging back from battle.

Lestock defended himself by saying that Mathews had committed a grave crime against the traditions and values of the Navy by charging into battle without waiting for the line to be properly formed. He claimed that he was following the Admiralty's Instructions to the letter. It was as if the rules of the service forbade him making a reasonable military assessment and acting decisively. As one pro-Lestock pamphlet put it: 'A line of battle is the basis and formation of all discipline in sea fights';[11] it had been handed down from generation to generation of naval commanders and had stood the test of time 'pure and unaltered'. These were bizarre proceedings. Some captains were punished for acting like rule-bound automata; others were thrown out for acting expeditiously. One might have assumed the worst offender, Vice Admiral Lestock, would share their fate, but he had powerful political friends and he survived. Mathews was dismissed.

The battle went down in the Navy's collective memory as a thing of shame and dishonour. It revealed the service's backwardness in tactics (which seemed stuck in the days of Blake, Sandwich and James II), its lack of zeal and its bitter divisions. In time memories of the battle and the scandalous courts martial that followed would help drag the Navy into the modern world. Before that happened, however, things got a lot worse.

CHAPTER 27

FALL AND RISE
1744–1748

February 1744 was a month of calamity for the Navy. The Battle of Toulon exposed its conservatism and lack of zeal. Back at home the Channel Fleet was undermanned, its biggest ships unready for action and it was under the command of an 84-year-old admiral.

This was the force that was suddenly confronted with the French Atlantic fleet, which entered the Channel. No one knew what the French were up to. Soon it became clear they were to support an invasion launched from Dunkirk.

Violent gales in the Channel caused damage to the Royal Navy, but they also prevented the invasion. Britain had wriggled off the hook. It was no great cause for celebration. The Navy in 1744 appeared to be in disarray. That year *Northumberland* (64) surrendered to two French warships in the Bay of Biscay and *Solebay* was captured off Cape St Vincent without a fight. The Navy suddenly seemed decidedly rickety – led by irresolute captains and decrepit admirals. The crisis raised a political storm that resulted in the fall of another ministry. The threat of invasion continued to hang over Britain. Ships were recalled from around the world to assist in the defence of the realm.

These disasters dealt a heavy blow to national confidence. It was only partially recovered when *Centurion* arrived at Spithead, with Anson and 188 men from the original crews on board. The ship had survived repeated disasters in the Pacific. It only just made it to an island before the crew starved and the ship fell to pieces. Anson and his officers helped the men ashore, where they were able to eat fresh fruit and vegetables. Anson had waited till last to leave the ship and take his turn on land. Now from the beach he saw the worst sight of his nightmare voyage. The *Centurion* was blown out to sea, out of sight and into the Pacific, with only a skeleton crew on board. The survivors of the horrors of Cape Horn and the Pacific were marooned.

After nineteen long days Anson and his men were overcome with emotion when the *Centurion* reappeared. She had been brought back, re-markably, by the men left on board. A few months later Anson managed to get her to Canton with a tiny crew, a proportion of which had 'turned mad and idiots'. There he persuaded the Chinese authorities to let him make repairs and recruit fresh sailors. Even so the ship had only a third of her usual complement. Then Anson led *Centurion* on a mission to find and capture the Manila galleon. This he accomplished with panache. He hunted down the galleon, on its way from South America laden with gold and silver to trade for the riches of East Asia. She was, said Anson, the 'most desirable prize that was to be met with in any part of the globe'. The haul was 1,313,843 pieces of eight and 35,682 ounces of silver. Anson brought *Centurion* back across the Indian Ocean, up the Atlantic and entered the Channel to find, at the final hurdle, that he was in danger from the French in his own backyard.

There was nothing the British liked better than a tale of survival in extreme situations. Anson's heroic leadership was the stuff of legend. He had rallied his dying men, kept his ship afloat in the vast tracts of the Pacific, and had even managed to bring her into battle. Such adventures against the odds were the basis of the national love affair with the sea. Anson became a celebrity overnight. He claimed captain's pay for three years of £719 and prize money of £91,000. He was, by any standards, stag-geringly wealthy. And the treasure from the galleon – paraded through the streets of London in thirty-two wagons – helped raise morale in a catastrophic year for the Navy.

The following year brought scant consolation. In January four British warships encountered two French warships off Ushant, but the British captains balked at attacking. This was a minor enough incident, but it exemplified everything that was wrong. The two most culpable captains escaped scot-free, thanks to their powerful patrons. The same was true of the officers who had performed so poorly at Toulon: naval cowards seemed always to slither away from punishment. Naval courts martial were undermined by the common law courts, parliament and political grandees, setting at naught naval discipline. In July the Navy failed to intercept the ship that carried Bonnie Prince Charlie to Scotland to ignite a Jacobite uprising. The Jacobite army defeated the English at Prestonpans and fought its way to Derby.

That was not all. Ministers had for a long time known that France wanted to capture Ostend. When that happened, Britain would be under constant threat of invasion. And so it came to pass in 1745. The French were massing an invasion force; Bonnie Prince Charlie was at the head of an army in England; the worst-case scenario had been realised. Britain was paying a high price for refusing to have a sizeable permanent army. The burden of national defence had been placed on the Navy. That was all very well, but it also bore the burden of offensive operations. As far-sighted commentators pointed out, having an army was the first step to maritime supremacy. French military strategists knew that if they threatened the Low Countries or made moves to assemble an invasion force (however token) then Britain would be compelled to recall her ships from around the world.

Looked at in this light, Britain's dominance of the sea in the first half of the eighteenth century was illusory. Peace with France meant that ships could be sent around the world to further British interests. Now, in 1744 and 1745, they had to be recalled in panic. There were barely enough troops to garrison port towns that might any day face a Franco-Spanish invasion.

The gloom was partially lifted when a small squadron led by Commodore Peter Warren helped forces of New Englanders to capture the fortress of Louisbourg on Cape Breton Island in Canada. This fortress protected one of the most valuable fisheries in the world – one that employed a third of French mariners. It also guarded the entry to Canada. The French were determined to take it back. The British – thanks to the work of a force of colonialists and an enterprising naval commander – were equally keen to conquer Canada.

The Navy needed heroes. It needed fresh thinking. Fortunately it had two senior officers who were untainted by the disasters of the last few years. Admiral Vernon was put in charge of forces in the Channel and consulted on strategy by the First Lord of the Admiralty, the duke of Bedford. Another senior member of the Admiralty Board, Lord Sandwich, turned to Captain George Anson, who was promoted rear admiral in 1745 and vice admiral the following year.

Vernon had command of the Channel Fleet in 1745. He was a fiery, often querulous man, convinced of Britain's maritime destiny and ashamed of the Navy's betrayal by timid leaders and ignorant politicians. The printing press was his weapon of choice to further his strategic plans: on several occasions he published his correspondence with his superiors. It was a risky way of doing business. Even more dangerous was his determination in pressing for courts martial and parliamentary inquiries into the failings of the previous years, even if the spotlight fell on his friends. Anson was also associated with the opposition and he, like the more bombastic Vernon, was prepared to confront the shortcomings in the service.

Vernon developed and Anson implemented a plan that was to become the cornerstone of British naval strategy for generations.[1]

It was not so much a tactical insight as a triumph of organisation and political will. Naval strategists, from Drake onwards, had seen the value of keeping a squadron in the Western Approaches. Ships placed far out to sea between Fastnet (the southernmost tip of Ireland) and Finisterre could keep a watch for enemy fleets. They could convoy merchantmen. They would cover Ireland. But they would be offensive as well as defensive: a western squadron could watch French naval bases, attack enemy convoys and intercept ships sailing to and from the New World and Asia. It was the key to Britain's defence and maritime ambitions. Because the French had no bases in the Channel capable of receiving battleships it meant that any Franco-Spanish invasion would have to originate from the south-west. The closest port they had for such an endeavour was Brest.

Vernon reasoned that British naval forces should not be diverted into shepherding merchant ships past the French Atlantic seaboard. Instead the Western Squadron should shadow the French Atlantic fleet or – better still – keep it in Brest. It was a radical idea. If it worked then British merchantmen would be safe while French traders would be under continual menace from the Royal Navy's cruisers. And the advantages did not stop there. By keeping a squadron far out at sea the Navy would pre-empt danger to national security, place France under blockade and make Britain the master of North America.

All this was fine in theory, but from Drake's day onwards it was fraught with practical difficulties. William Penn, Cloudesley Shovell, George Byng and others had all led squadrons in the Western Approaches, but they had encountered the same problems. Large warships could not be kept in those waters for long before they were battered by the elements and their crews became ill and hungry. The Navy's main bases were too far east. The West Country simply could not cope with the demands of a fleet. A cruise of a few weeks with the Western Squadron was reckoned by sailors to be worse than a tour to the West Indies. This was because the lack of fresh vegetables and fruit made one thing inevitable: scurvy.

Vernon's desire to take the squadron west in 1745 had been frustrated by his superiors, who quailed at the thought of removing most of the naval forces from home waters at a time when invasion was an immediate threat. It seemed like a gamble too far to have the bulk of Britain's defences far out at sea. A joint Franco-Spanish fleet could slip past and enter the Channel; that had been the fear in 1588 too. When Anson cruised these waters in 1746 he found that the weather hampered his operations.

French privateers and neutral ships informed the enemy of his presence. And he discovered that he could not react quickly enough to intelligence reports. There was a body of opinion that deemed the strategy unworkable. The bulk of the naval forces should remain in the Channel.

Anson realised that the whole strategy relied on intelligence, secrecy, discipline and supplies. A large force of frigates and privateers had to be constantly at sea, scouting for enemy movements in the 150,000 square miles of water between Fastnet and Finisterre. He could only keep the Squadron cruising at sea for limited periods – revictualling in those waters was impossible and the ships suffered wear and tear. Anson therefore worked on an intelligence network that kept him informed of enemy activity on its seaboard. The Western Squadron needed to be able to respond at once to intelligence and get to sea. It needed a reliable victualling system at Plymouth and dockyards to keep the ships in fighting readiness. Most importantly the Squadron needed tight discipline and a better way of signalling orders.

Anson had a stock of political capital. He was a proven hero and an adept politicker; he was rich and he had powerful patrons. All these were essential for an admiral in an age riven by faction and dominated by grandees. Added to this he had an exceptional talent for organisation. Previously naval forces in home waters had been scattered under various commands. Anson brought them under his control. He worked through the Admiralty to make sure the dockyard at Plymouth could supply the needs of his squadron. The signal book was updated so that it fitted the requirements of a cruising squadron in the Western Approaches.

Admiral Anson was a thoughtful man, not given to many words. Even so he achieved wonders by working face to face with his second in command Peter Warren, the naval commander who captured Louisbourg, and his captains. Together they developed contingency plans for battle situations in which they lost sight of their admiral, or if orders had to be changed at the last minute. The admiral drilled his forces every day, working through the various scenarios of a battle on the high seas. He made it known that no gun on a British ship was to open fire till it was yardarm to yardarm with its opponent. Anson knew that the first lesson to master was the formal line of battle, but he also wanted his captains to use their initiative. That too called for discipline, but of a different order.

'It has ever been my opinion,' said Anson, 'that a person entrusted with command may and ought to exceed his orders and dispense with the common rules of proceeding when extraordinary occasions require.'[2] That was the hallmark of Anson's style of leadership. It contrasted with the stale formalism that had retarded the Navy's tactical development. Above all it was the opposite of the spirit that had reigned at the Battle of Toulon.

By the time he had finished with it, the Western Squadron was the best-organised and most disciplined marine fighting force in the world. The long and harrowing circumnavigation of the globe had been the making of Admiral Anson. He had become a leader of men in extreme circumstances; he kept his crew disciplined and motivated even though they were scorbutic, starving and desperate. On that voyage he had been forced to stint his resources. When he made the decision to take on the Manila galleon he had to find it in an expanse of uncharted water and islands, and had to conceal his intentions and whereabouts. That required using every scrap of intelligence that came his way and every ounce of cunning. All these hard-earned skills he brought to the Western Squadron. Peter Warren paid his chief the greatest of compliments: 'In my life I never served with more pleasure, nor saw half such pains taken to discipline the fleet. While I have the honour to continue in it, I will endeavour to follow his example, however short I may fall of it, and could wish to be commanded by him rather than command myself.'[3]

Warren also said that the squadron was full of good officers, but they were made better by being under Anson's command. George Anson, like all great admirals throughout history, knew that a battle was won long before it was fought.

And like all first-rank admirals, he knew that the only victories worth boasting about were ones in which the enemy was annihilated – a rare thing in warfare at sea. His chance to prove his theories came on 3 May 1747. Thanks to his intelligence system he already knew that an important French convoy would be at sea, and his scouting frigates confirmed that enemy warships were escorting large numbers of West and East Indiamen.

The French formed a line of battle to allow the merchantmen to scatter and flee. Warren wanted to attack at once because the French squadron was inferior and the prizes were disappearing. But Anson insisted that his ships form a line. This took some time, but it was a sound decision because the French squadron, though inferior in numbers, was made up of formidable ships. The French admiral stood his ground, screening the merchant convoy and buying it time. When Anson altered course and made directly for the centre of the French line, the enemy turned into the wind and fled. He then flew a signal for a general chase. The formal order of battle was replaced with an order determined by the sailing qualities of the ships. When he was eighteen years old Anson had witnessed this kind of dynamic leadership. Then he was a lieutenant at the Battle of Cape Passaro. Now he was fifty and an admiral.

In this scenario captains had to act on their own initiative, while remaining part of the team. The faster ships engaged the rearmost French ships, weakened or crippled them, then pressed on with the attack further into the French formation, leaving their undigested prey for the larger, slower ships. Captains were required to press home the attack from the enemy's rear to his van, but resist the urge to engage individual opponents in prolonged duels.

Anson's ships were in pursuit of a fleeing enemy in a running battle that engulfed first the rear, then the centre and then the vanguard of an enemy ill-disposed to turn and fight. What mattered most in the thrill of a chase battle (or 'rolling-up operation' as it is known) were the qualities with which Anson had imbued his squadron: seamanship, gunnery and determination. The speed of the leading British ships and their superiority of fire gave the chasers a tactical advantage. The first ships into action inevitably took a battering as they waited till they were within pistol range (twenty yards) of the enemy till they opened fire; in such a battle their captains and crews had to possess the cool resolve to carry on into the fray. The élan and measured aggression of the squadron contrasted strongly with the state of the Navy in the war. Anson refused to be carried away and charge pell-mell into battle. He was perfectly positioned before he lunged. By the end of the day six enemy warships and three Indiamen were captured. The next day eighteen out of thirty-three merchant ships were chased, attacked and captured. The proceeds from the First Battle of Cape Finisterre, as it was called, were impressive; £200,000 in cash was found along with merchandise and Anson alone netted £63,000 in prize money. The Royal Navy was augmented by some fine French warships. Anson was raised to the peerage.

Anson's tactics and reforms were vindicated. They were fully digested by his officers. Anson had ensured the Western Squadron worked, and it did not need his presence. In October it was led by Rear Admiral Edward Hawke after Warren returned home suffering from scurvy. Hawke, like Anson and Warren, was part of a younger generation of captains frustrated by the ponderous ways of their superiors. In common with many ambitious officers his career had been thwarted by peace. But like many a great naval leader in the Royal Navy, Hawke had made his career in the distant corners of the world on frigates, the Navy's workhorses, which policed British trade and colonies come war or peace. It was on active service in West Africa, the West Indies and North America that he progressed from midshipman, through the three grades of lieutenant to the rank of master, until he was posted captain at the age of twenty-nine in 1734.

The inspired attack and capture of *Poder* during the otherwise calamitous Battle of Toulon made Hawke's name. After the battle he served as a commodore, in command of groups of detached squadrons in the Mediterranean. But the Navy did not seem to value its battling commodore. Political connections were vital for those aspiring to high command, and Hawke, unlike Anson, did not have a powerful patron. In 1746 it looked as though his career in the Navy would represent nothing more than a single forgotten achievement before premature retirement at the age of forty-seven. Hawke was to be promoted to rear admiral as a courtesy, before being edged aside by captains who enjoyed the full force of political preferment.

But Hawke then found a surprising patron. George II refused to allow him to be retired from active service. In July 1747 he was promoted to rear admiral of the White and put in charge of Plymouth dockyard. A month later a very sick Admiral Warren appeared out of the blue at Plymouth. Many years before, Hawke had served, briefly, as third lieutenant on a frigate captained by Warren. Now Warren handed over command of the Western Squadron to Hawke. It was a shrewd choice. Thanks to that decision Hawke's name sits one below Nelson in the top league of British admirals.

Hawke set out to join the Western Squadron off Ushant. Now he had what every admiral craves: sole command of a crack force with no superior breathing down his neck. And better still, the French were preparing a convoy. Out into the expanse of the Western Approaches went Edward Hawke with his battleships, where he made it his priority to stay out of sight of the French while keeping his eye on them. Dozens of ships were stopped and forced to reveal information about the enemy. From them he learnt that a massive convoy was gathering in the Basque Roads off La Rochelle, ready to sail for the West Indies. Hawke kept his ships out of the sight of coastal vessels who might report back to the French navy and, to further confuse the enemy, he convinced scouting French warships and privateers that he was making for the seas off Cape Finisterre. Hawke's deviousness worked; the French were lulled into believing the Bay of Biscay to be clear. Off went the convoy.

The French cleared their coast and headed into the safety of the vast ocean. If they were to be attacked it would most likely be near home. Little did they suspect that a predator lurked, fully aware of their movements, in the deep. Hawke had made an astute conjecture, based on the changing winds and his knowledge of weather patterns in the Atlantic, as to where the enemy convoy would be.

The French convoy was spotted at dawn on 25 October. Hawke signalled for line ahead. The French warships were close hauled in line, guarding their merchant ships. Hawke then signalled for a general chase. The French wanted him to stick to formal battle tactics – the line engagement. Hawke knew this would allow the enemy convoy to escape. He had fourteen ships with him, the French only eight, but the French warships were some of the best in the world. Their largest had 80 guns; there were three with 74 and one with 70. Only two of Hawke's ships had 70 or more guns. The rest of his fleet carried between 44 and 64 guns. Hawke signalled for a general chase and the ships flew off to do battle.

As agreed, no captain was to open fire until he was within pistol shot of his opponent. First upon the enemy were two of the smallest ships, *Lion* (50) and then *Princess Louisa* (60). The *Lion* took a hammering and sustained a high rate of casualties. A 'few minutes after', wrote Captain Charles Watson of the *Princess Louisa*, he 'got within pistol shot of the enemy's sternmost ship of 70 guns'[4] and opened fire. Then, in turn, *Princess Louisa* was seconded by *Monmouth* (64) and Watson continued: 'as I found the rest of our ships coming up, I stretched ahead to engage the other ships'. *Monmouth* also got to windward of the French and exchanged broadsides as she passed the Frenchmen until she attacked the leading enemy ship. This began at 11.30. At 13.30 Hawke's slow and heavily armed flagship *Devonshire* compelled the surrender of the rearmost French ship. She then attacked the enemy flagship and moved on to force two others to strike their flags.

It was a resounding success. The British captains outsailed, outmanoeuvred and outgunned the French. They fought as individuals, but they also came in support of each other at crucial moments. At Toulon the old formalism of the line of battle was shown up as fusty and restrictive; this was a new form of dynamic battle. British ships sustained high casualty rates in the initial assaults as they held fire until they were within pistol range. But it paid off. By the end of the day six French ships of the line were totally dismasted and in British hands.

By sailing close to the French before firing the British made the most of their advantages. The French preferred to fire at musket range and aim at the masts, rigging and sails of their opponent. Gun crews got tired very fast in a battle, and the rate of fire quickly decreased. By holding fire the British were able to get in close to their opponents and then unleash several volleys in quick succession while their crews were still fresh and at the point when their enemy's crews were starting to tire. There was no need to aim precisely. Broadside after broadside smashed into the hulls and masts of the enemy just twenty yards away at most, turning their gun decks into shambles, dismounting guns and terrifying the sailors. To sail in close like this under fire required coolness on the part of the men – but also of the captains, always tempted to engage early as the adrenaline kicked in. Since 1745 daily gun practice had become a requirement on British ships. Sailors became accustomed to a fast rate of fire. Hawke's fleet included some highly talented young captains. Philip de Saumarez, John Bentley and Charles Saunders had learnt their trade the tough way – sailing round the world with Anson. George Brydges Rodney was destined for great things. Well drilled men and motivated captains, confident that they were attuned to their admiral's plan, ensured a handsome victory.

The French lost 4,000 sailors, a significant proportion of their seafaring community. Hawke sent word to Commodore George Pocock in the Leeward Islands that an unescorted French convoy was headed his way. Pocock captured thirty ships from the convoy and privateers snapped up a further ten. More importantly the French oceangoing Navy was, after two battles in the Finisterre meridian, all but destroyed. Hawke's great victory was misleadingly and confusingly called the Second Battle of Finisterre. In reality it was nowhere near Cape Finisterre. Hawke hunted down, intercepted and defeated the enemy 300 miles out at sea, due west of Lorient. Such a thing was unheard of. No battle of this size had taken place so deep in the ocean.

These two victories were, for Britain, a glimmer of light. Otherwise the outlook was bleak. By 1748 France had the better of the war. Flanders was under her control, the nightmare scenario for Britain. At the Treaty of Aix-la-Chapelle Britain had to concede many of its gains in the New World to France in order to restore the European map to its pre-war outline. Cape Breton was given back to France in return for the evacuation of the Netherlands. Temporary dominance of the sea, hard won as it was, meant that Britain had something to bring to the negotiating table; but set against the expectations raised at the beginning of the war it was a somewhat paltry advantage. To the public – long fed on navalist rhetoric – it was offensive to swap a naval triumph so that Austria might regain its lost lands. But Lord Chesterfield admitted: 'We may keep Cape Breton by our fleets, but I fear we and the Dutch together shall never be able to keep Flanders by our armies.'[5] For all the Navy's successes in the Americas or off Finisterre, the French could set them at naught by force of arms on the Continent.

Britain had gone to war with the aim of laying down the law to Europe by becoming master of the seas. In the end she had to make do with the status quo of 1739. Even that was more than she had any right to expect after a disastrous war.

'Rule Britannia' captures one incontrovertible truth. It was an article of faith for the British in the 1740s that they had a right to rule the waves. Even defeat could not dim the fire. In many respects this enthusiasm was dangerous. It placed a burden of expectation on politicians, admirals and administrators that was impossible to fully satisfy. It led to military blunders and unwinnable wars.

But it meant that the Navy possessed a magic unknown in other countries. The nation was prepared to pay for and back its Navy no matter what. The enthusiasm survived the shambles of the 1740s; it emerged from disaster at Toulon stronger and better led. The blend of history, romance and myth that rallied opinion four-square behind the Navy was a very potent force.

When 'Rule Britannia' was first performed at Cliveden in the masque *Alfred* the strains of the music might have been heard down at Sashes Island, nearby on the Thames. That was the site of Alfred's defensive *burh* mentioned at the very beginning of this narrative. Behind the myth of Alfred and the dawn of English sea power lay a truth. Alfred's strategy is called 'defence in depth'. It began on land, in the very centre of the country. Maritime supremacy had to rest on solid foundations. Global power was possible only when the British Isles were safeguarded. That was the lesson of 1744–45. Naval success, in the modern world, depended upon discipline, training and efficient administrative systems.

Exactly a century before, Britain had been a poor and divided country with a second-rate Navy. Between 1649 and 1660 it had risen to become a great European power thanks to an enormous, highly disciplined Navy. The Navy was willed into existence by a strong, highly centralised state that ruthlessly taxed its people. The result was victory over the Dutch and Robert Blake's stunning triumphs in the Mediterranean and the Atlantic.

The military revolution continued under the Stuarts, with Crown and parliament co-operating in spending money on the fleet. Most importantly the Navy became a professionalised service with responsibilities in peacetime to protect burgeoning extra-European English trade. Under William III the state's finances were completely reformed, providing an unprecedented flow of money to the Navy. A by-product of the pan-European wars from 1689 to 1711 was an upsurge in British trade that transformed the economy and made it possible to spend even more on the

Navy. Those wars also sharpened the service. Success depended on logistics and feats of organisation. In the 1620s the Navy could not sustain a foray to Brittany for a few weeks; by the end of the century it campaigned for years on end off Iberia and in the western basin of the Mediterranean, completing an encirclement of France.

A theme of this phase of the history, from 1603 to 1748, has been the way that the British fell in love with their Navy. They revelled in its history and achievements. No other country supported its naval services in this way. The Royal Navy was, as a consequence, well funded and vociferously celebrated. Sometimes this confidence was misdirected. On a number of occasions the Navy fell far short of the expectations heaped upon it.

In 1747–48 the Navy rallied and vindicated itself after a catastrophic few years. It was a resilient institution. Battered by war, her confidence shaken, Britain emerged from defeat with a new way of thinking about naval warfare. A fresh generation of leaders, headed by Admiral Anson and Edward Hawke, had come to the fore.

III

TO GLORY

1748–1805

INTRODUCTION

'Salt junk', the meat and fish preserved in salt for long periods of time, was the bane of every sailor's life. It was taken out of its aged barrel and soaked in fresh water prior to becoming the company's main meal. The cook put the meat into a copper and boiled it. As the water bubbled away the fat separated from the meat and rose to the top to form a thick scum. The cook scraped off this fatty slush. It was useful stuff; it waterproofed the rigging and was used to make candles. The cook sold it and made a handy profit. It was his slush fund.

There are dozens of words and phrases that we use every day that derive their meaning from naval slang. Some, like slush fund, do not contain any clues as to their nautical origin. Phrases such as 'all at sea', 'sailing close to the wind', 'high and dry', 'plain sailing', 'wide berth', 'push the boat out', 'press-ganged', 'taking the wind out of your sails', 'shot across the bows', 'loose cannon', 'shipshape', 'batten down the hatches' belong more obviously to the sea. Others such as 'close quarters', 'cut and run', 'fathoming' something, 'broad in the beam' and the 'cut of your jib' take a moment longer to work out that they derive from seafaring. Most expressions in common usage with a similar parentage are, like slush fund, more obscure.

Many of them are negative in connotation. It is not surprising, given sailors' preoccupation with their bellies and the foulness of the menu, that food is the source of much slang. The meat that came out of the slushy water was tough and chewy; men gathered around their mess tables talked while they tried to digest the tough fare – hence 'chewing the fat'. The meals were served on square plates, giving rise to the phrase 'square meal'. The monotony of shipboard food, routine and discipline was broken by the daily intake of alcohol. The rum ration was introduced by Admiral Vernon during his time in the West Indies between 1739 and 1741, when he gave the men half a pint of the spirit a day each. Vernon wore a black waterproof made of a fabric known as 'grogram', a blend of silk, mohair and wool stiffened with gum. Consequently he was nick-named 'Old Grogram' and rum was called 'grog'. Today grog is an inter-changeable term for all kinds of firewater; the term 'groggy' is even more common.

Words and phrases deriving from discipline and ship routine are equally popular. 'Learning the ropes' is self-explanatory. The phrase 'enough room to swing a cat' comes from the cat-o'nine-tails, which was so large and belowdecks so cramped that it could only be used above deck. In the evening the bosun would sound his pipe, ordering the men to retire below decks and take down their hammocks. If there was any dis-turbance on deck the bosun might 'pipe down' the refractory men. 'Hand over fist' refers to pulling a rope as quickly as possible. A seaman skilled at painting (a necessary task on a ship exposed to the elements) was called a 'dab hand', dab perhaps coming from 'daub' and hand referring to the name given to ratings.

The opposite of a skilled professional is a 'waster'. This derives from 'waister', the name given to unskilled men who hauled on ropes in the 'waist' of the ship, rather than being given specialised jobs to do. A derog-atory word for the work a true waster might accomplish is 'sloppy'. This comes from the rough working clothes, 'slops', sold at the mast by the purser.

There are many more phrases that come from seamanship. A ship that was safely beached on dry land was 'hard and fast'. The 'offing' is the part of the sea that can be seen from land. To 'get under way' derives from a specific nautical term, 'way' meaning the forward movement of a ship under sail. If a ship makes progress 'by and large' it does so against the wind. To 'tide over', in the sense of coping with one problem till another comes along, comes from the practice of using the tide when there was little or no wind. 'To Tide over to a place,' wrote Captain John Smith in 1627, 'is to go over with the tide of ebb or flood, and stop the contrary by anchoring till the next tide.' If a ship is 'taken aback' it means that the wind has unexpectedly changed and is blowing against the wrong side of the sail, putting strain on ropes and masts. If we have been taken aback we are often asked how we are 'bearing up'. That originally meant turning the ship into the wind. A ship 'edging' towards or through something comes from the means by which a ship made progress in bad weather by frequent short tacks. If something went 'by the board' it went over the side.

The mile upon mile of rope on a warship was a fertile breeding ground for evocative phraseology. 'Money for old rope' brings us back to corruption in the dockyards. The inquiries into the Navy in the early seventeenth century found that even though old rope should have been used as oakum to caulk the king's ships, many officials were selling old rope and making money. The anchor cable was fastened to a wooden bitt; when it was paid out to its maximum length the rope was at its 'bitter end'. When all the blocks and tackles used to hoist the sails were used to their limits it was said to be 'chock-a-block', 'chock' meaning full. Rope could be fun as well. A way of letting off steam was to race up the rigging to the masthead and slide back down to deck along the backstays. It was part training and part exercise. Young midshipmen were required to learn the arts of the skilled topmen, and this exercise was a popular form of recreation after dinner. It was called 'skylarking', and the word, with its contraction 'larking', entered general use. While we are on the subject of midshipmen, these boys were nicknamed 'snotties' – a term still in use for annoying boys who can't deal politely with the slime emanating from their nostrils.

Our language is thick with words and phrases taken from the sea. Delving into the origins of slang is like an archaeology of our culture that takes us back to a time when the Navy permeated daily life.

The next phase of the narrative describes the way in which the Navy became a highly efficient, highly motivated war-winning machine. During this time the service won innumerable victories and defended the country from foreign invasion. Artists and journalists scrutinised the inner workings of the Navy as never before. The activities of ships and sailors were detailed in a vast array of literature – historical as well as journalistic. It was often suffused with technical terminology, but it was intended for the eager landlubber as much as the professional seaman. Popular prints and caricatures depicted life below decks for the first time. In the nineteenth century the Navy became the subject of popular fiction. It was a presence in people's lives, be they in Oxford or Orfordness. It is little wonder that during the Navy's path to greatness the distinctive language of the warship seeped into everyday usage.

PART 9: KILLER INSTINCT

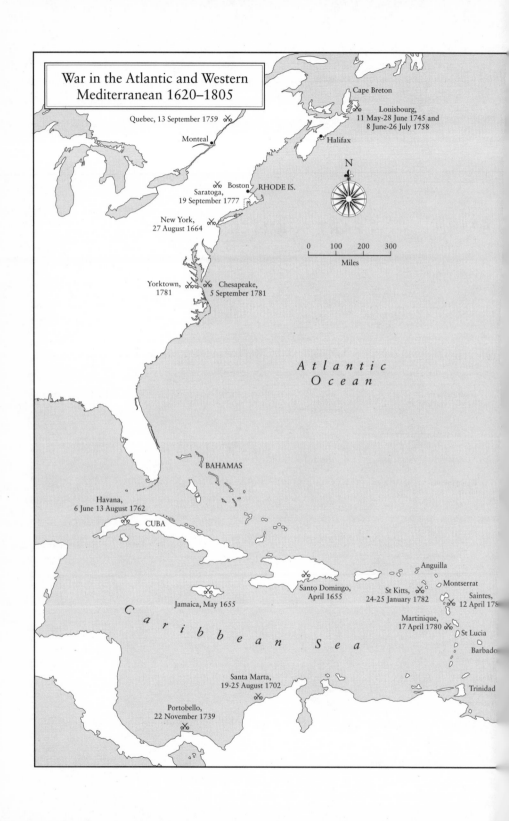

War in the Atlantic and Western Mediterranean 1620–1805

Cape Breton

Louisbourg,
11 May-28 June 1745 and
8 June-26 July 1758

Quebec, 13 September 1759

Monteal

Halifax

N

Boston
RHODE IS.

Saratoga,
19 September 1777

New York,
27 August 1664

0   100   200   300
Miles

Yorktown,
1781

Chesapeake,
5 September 1781

*Atlantic
Ocean*

BAHAMAS

Havana,
6 June 13 August 1762

CUBA

Anguilla

Montserrat

Santo Domingo,
April 1655

St Kitts,
24-25 January 1782

Saintes,
12 April 178

Jamaica, May 1655

Martinique,
17 April 1780

St Lucia

Barbado

Caribbean Sea

Santa Marta,
19-25 August 1702

Trinidad

Portobello,
22 November 1739

N

*Atlantic
Ocean*

*North
Sea*

Copenhagen,
2 April 1801

Camperdown,
11 October
1797

Bantry Bay,
11 May 1689

Kinsale,
(blockade)
1649

London

Plymouth Portsmouth Chatham

Beachy Head, 10 July 1690

Cherbourg, August 1758 Barfleur-la Hogue, 19-24 May 1693

Glorious First of June,
1 June 1794

Battle of Ushant,
27 July 1778

Brest

St Malo, 16 November 1693
and June 1758

Cape Finisterre
(II) 25 October 1747

Quiberon Bay,
20 November 1759

Cape Finisterre
(I) 14 May 1747

Belle Isle,
June 1761

La Rochelle, 1627 and 1628
Rochefort, September 1757

Cape Ortegal,
4 November 1805

*Bay of
Biscay*

Brest, Rochefort,
Quiberon blockade 1759-1763
and 1797-1801

Cape Finisterre
(III) 22 July 1805

Ferrol

Vigo, 23 October 1702

Toulon, 1707,
18 September-18 December
1793

Leghorn,
1653

Brest, Rochefort, Quiberon,
Ferrol, Cadiz, Toulon,
blockade 1803-1815

Barcelona,
1706

22 February 1744,
Hotham's Action,
13-14 March 1795

Lisbon (blockade), 1649

Minorca, 1708,
25 May 1756

Majorca

Port Mahon

Cape St Vincent

Lagos, 18-19 August 1759

Cadiz, 1625
Cadiz (blockade), 1656-7 and 1797-1801
Cadiz, 1702

Alicante

Mediterranean Sea

yrna Convoy,
June 1693
onlight Battle,
January 1780,
Battle of
pe St Vincent,
February 1797

Malaga,
24 August 1704

Cartagena,
28 February 1758

Poto Farina,
14 April 1655

Trafalgar,
21 October
1805

Capture of Gibraltar,
1-3 August 1704

Algiers

Tangier

Algeciras Bay,
6-12 July 1801

0   100   200   300

Miles

CHAPTER 28

BATTLE READY
1748–1757

In this country [Britain] it is thought good to kill an admiral
from time to time, to encourage the others.

Voltaire

The Royal Navy had a lot for which to thank the French.[1] For a country that aspired to be the predominant global naval power of the mid-
eighteenth century, Britain's fleet seemed stuck in the seventeenth.

Naval planners had a fondness for enormous first- and second-rate
ships of the line. These might have been needed for massive fleet battles
in the North Sea, but they were completely unsuited for global conflict.
As the French realised, the face of maritime warfare had changed. What
was needed was a seaworthy ship capable of fighting in all the oceans of
the world and that could take part in amphibious attacks. The first- and
second-rate ships of the Royal Navy performed poorly in bad weather
and could not serve far from home. They were crammed with guns, had
too little room for supplies, and they were unstable. They had too deep
a draught for most ports in the world. The seventy-gun third rates and
sixty-gun fourths had different problems. They were three-deckers, but
they were too small in comparison with their two-deck French rivals and
could not match their weight of armament.

It was an open secret that a British warship could not take on an enemy
ship of equal armament without help.[2] The advantages enjoyed by the
Royal Navy were its sheer number of ships and the seafaring skills of its
officers and men. This could not be expected to last.

All this was known. But the Navy Board of the 1740s was a deeply conservative institution.

The model for reformers was the French ship *Invincible*, a two-decker
carrying seventy-four guns, captured at the First Battle of Finisterre. Experts flocked to study her. Their findings sent shockwaves through naval
circles. She was 50 per cent larger than her British counterparts in terms

of tonnage; she was much longer; and, although she carried the same number of guns, fired a broadside 75 per cent heavier. And despite her greater size, *Invincible* was faster and more seaworthy than the Royal Navy's third rates. She was also less cramped and could stow more supplies for long voyages. The Royal Navy was a long way behind her rival.

Invincible did not represent the breakthrough to a global warship, but she pointed the way. The new generation of French warships were expensive to build, they did not withstand enemy fire very well and they required continual maintenance. Their hull forms were state-of-the-art, but their rigging was inferior to British warships. The dream was a hybrid of a British and French warship – one that combined the speed, manoeuvrability and firepower of *Invincible* with the durability, internal strength and cheapness of the Navy's leviathans.

George Anson was firmly behind the campaign to reform the Navy, but he had to do battle with the immovable conservatism of the Navy Board. Throughout the century the size and shape of ships had been set by the 'Establishments' – rules establishing the exact dimensions of each class of warship. The most recent Establishment of 1745 had attempted to modernise the Navy, but it limited reform in the late 1740s and early 1750s when the lessons gleaned from the prizes taken at the battles of Finisterre were being digested. When the Admiralty wanted to change the size of a warship by even a couple of feet they had to take the matter to the Privy Council. Sir Jacob Ackworth, Surveyor of the Navy for thirty-four years until his death in 1749, and his successor, Sir Joseph Allin, were both men of old-fashioned principles, prepared to block the newfangled ideas proposed by Anson. If anyone ordered them to change the dimension of a ship they could hide behind the Establishment and refuse to budge.

The Royal Navy was wedded to the accustomed way of doing things in other respects as well. Admirals were appointed from the captains' list: senior officers progressed to flag rank by virtue of long service. The dismal wars between 1739 and 1748 showed that many senior officers were elderly, unimaginative and cowardly. Naval discipline was in disarray; in many cases the verdicts of courts martial for cowardice or disobeying orders in the 1740s were undone by civilian courts and politicians.

George Anson was one of a handful of stars the Navy could boast. He was a fighting officer through and through. But he was a canny politician as well, and he was committed to saving the Navy from its debilitating complacency. One of the major problems revealed by the recent war was that after a long peace many flag officers were past their best. Seniority in the upper echelons of the Navy depended on the date an officer was posted captain. When a vacancy for rear admiral was created by death or retirement, the most senior captain automatically ascended, regardless of his abilities or age. Anson wanted to reach down the list and appoint captains in the prime of their careers to positions of leadership. This could not be done overtly because it was considered too radical a step to retire an admiral merely on the grounds of decrepitude, senility or incompetence.

Instead Anson instituted the rank of commodore. The admiralty or commanders-in-chief on foreign stations could appoint the most able captains to command detached squadrons of ships irrespective of where they stood on the list of captains; they could even have authority over captains who were senior to them. The sacred inviolability of the captains' list was left untouched, as the rank of commodore was held temporarily and did not entitle the holder to speedier promotion to flag rank. Superannuated captains at the top of the captains' list were kicked upstairs to become rear admirals in a new and ship-less 'Yellow Squadron', where they could enjoy the honour, trappings and pay of a flag officer while being kept at an arm's length from anything like responsibility.*

It allowed Anson to cull many of the unsuitable captains and promote the best without being accused of provoking a revolution. In Fact, most officers had little to grumble about; they saw the status of their profession rise thanks to Anson's reforms. Hitherto naval ranks carried no precise military definition. When Anson negotiated with the Chinese during his circumnavigation this ambiguity presented serious diplomatic problems. Captains became the equivalent of colonels in the army. The new rank of commodore was regularised and enjoyed the status and authority of a brigadier-general. The intention was to make the profession of naval officer an honourable and dignified office.

Most important in achieving this end was the introduction of a uniform for commissioned officers. It was a blue wool coat with white facings, white waistcoat, white cuffs and white breeches. Depending on rank the coat included embellishments such as lace, gold and metal thread. For some officers the long-awaited uniform was a letdown. It did not look warlike enough and was too close to domestic male fashions. Over time the uniform changed, but it stuck close to the essentials of its prototype. The blue officer's uniform would leave its civilian origins behind and become the ultimate symbol of masculinity and valour. Naval uniform

---

* Ironically one of the first officers marked to be 'yellowed' under Anson's scheme was not a senile admiral at all, but Edward Hawke, who was expected to make way for more politically suitable officers. As it turned out he was promoted to the White Squadron after the intercession of George II. See above p. 304.

began to influence male and female fashions. Midshipmen, the standing warrant officers and their mates would have to wait until 1787, surgeons until 1805, masters and pursers until 1807 and seamen until 1857 until they got uniforms.

In general officers welcomed this development. Uniform conferred status. It established officers – from lieutenants to admirals – as gentlemen. In a service still divided between 'gentlemen and tarpaulins' this recognition of social status meant a lot. A uniform showed that a man was an officer in the king's service.

All this was intended to forge cohesion and an attachment to the service within the brotherhood of officers. Anson also stood up to prime ministers who wanted to appoint relations of their political supporters to captain ships. A lieutenant who had proved himself in battle, Anson said, was preferable every time to one who merely had powerful friends and relations. Throughout his time at the head of the service officers were promoted to captain and flag rank on the basis of experience and merit. That was the carrot. As for the stick, many of Anson's proposed reforms, such as subjecting half-pay officers to martial law, were politically objectionable. He did manage to beef up the legal basis of courts martial and increase the number of fixed penalties for specific offences, including those that were punishable only by death. Disloyalty and cowardice could not now be brushed under the carpet for the sake of political expediency. These changes were in response to the weaknesses highlighted by the Battle of Toulon and the fallout from the courts martial in the last war.

The movement for reform originated from the Admiralty. From the start it was up against some deep-rooted prejudices in its mission to hone the Navy for war. Some of Anson's disciplinary reforms were considered by parliament to smack of despotism and were blocked. Likewise his modest proposal to create a reserve of seamen that could man the fleet in case of a sudden war was defeated. But it was within the Navy that Anson met his greatest opposition.

The Admiralty had always been kept at an arm's distance by the Navy Board, which claimed specialist knowledge in administrative matters. In the 1740s the reforming First Lords Bedford and Sandwich sent the Navy Board repeated requests for information about the running of the Navy. Most commonly the Board simply ignored the requests. In 1749 the First Lord of the Admiralty, Lord Sandwich, took his fellow Lords on a tour of the dockyards. This was unprecedented. Even the Navy Board did not resort to such an outlandish thing. The Lords of the Admiralty came away with first-hand accounts of waste and inefficiency in the yards. For the first time the Admiralty could claim to be better informed on such mat-ters than the Navy Board. There followed a string of orders from the Ad-miralty to the Navy Board about regulating the yards and sharpening up administrative procedures. Predictably the Admiralty came up against a wall of obstruction and hostility to innovation. 'Custom,' wrote Anson, '... is usually a power too mighty for reason to grapple with; and it is the most terrible to those who oppose it ...'[3]

Although he professed that commanding a squadron at sea was his passion, Anson proved an outstanding desk admiral. It was long, slow, frustrating work overcoming the entrenched traditionalism in the Navy. The Navy Board was jealous of its power and continued to stymie the Ad-miralty. The government was making cuts in expenditure, and the Navy must take its share of the pain. In 1751 Anson replaced Sandwich as First Lord. He brought to an end the running battle with the Board and tried to get his way by compromise and co-operation. Anson's main concern was to get the Navy ready for war at short notice, something it was not good at. In 1739, when the much-bruited war against Spain was finally declared, the Navy had only eighty-nine ships ready for service and mo-bilisation took a tortuously long time. By 1753, a time of peace and re-trenchment, the Navy had 129 ships ready for immediate use. Of these sixty-seven were ships of the line, an improvement on the thirty-eight that had been available in 1749.

Anson's campaign was slow and unspectacular, but it was vital. Many of his ambitions to revivify the service and improve its ships remained unfulfilled. 'Patience and perseverance' were said to be Anson's chief vir-tues. He needed them.

But then, after four years of patient waiting, two events gave Anson the chance he needed. French troops entered the Ohio valley in 1754, and a year later Sir Joseph Allin, Surveyor of the Navy, went mad.

The first raised the prospect of war and persuaded the government to spend more money on the Navy. The second allowed Anson to parachute his two favourite shipwrights into the Navy Board as joint acting Survey-ors in 1755.

Appointments to the Navy Board usually came slowly, but Anson's pro-tégés – Thomas Slade and William Batley – took theirs up within days. Three weeks later they began work on a revolutionary new class of 74-gun ships of the line. These ships, much larger and longer than the Establish-ment allowed, were built amid a cloud of secrecy. A few months later the old guard on the Navy Board were shoved out and men acceptable to Anson appointed. This was an internal coup in the Navy.

The new 74s represented 'the greatest breakthrough of British naval shipbuilding in the eighteenth century'.[4] They went against everything traditionalists believed in. The 74 of 1755 was a large ship with two gun decks. It borrowed freely from *Invincible*. It broke many of the rules that had governed shipbuilding for generations. The new ships were not slavish imitations of the French prizes, but they were close enough to offend traditionalists. Anson's Admiralty and his tamed Navy Board had taken the initiative without asking anyone's permission. It was a bold move and Anson was much criticised.

He would be vindicated. In the year after the coup ten new 74s were constructed. In time the new way of building ships would be improved and perfected. They had the speed and firepower of the French 74s and the robustness of traditional British warships. 'The 74 gun ship of the line,' said one naval architect, '... contains the properties of the first rate and the frigate. She will not shrink from an encounter with a first rate, nor abandon the chase of a frigate on account of swiftness.'[5] They could stand their ground in the traditional line of battle *and* they could chase down enemy ships. At the Battle of the Nile thirteen out of Nelson's fourteen ships were 74s. At Trafalgar two thirds of the line of battle would consist of them. Anson and his shipwrights also started work on new classes of 28-, 32- and 36-gun frigates, made to designs based on French frigates and privateers.

1755 is a year of fundamental importance to the history of the Royal Navy. Anson was at last free to make the changes he needed to modernise the Navy. In that year as well the Admiralty took full control over the marines. On Anson's voyage to the Pacific many of the soldiers he brought along had been ageing veterans palmed off by the army. Now the marines could be shaped into an elite force capable of advanced amphibious warfare.

More prosaic, but just as important, Anson tightened his grip on the Navy's administration. In 1755 a vacancy occurred on the Victualling Board. The incident shows Anson at his best. He wanted to appoint an experienced seafarer; the prime minister wanted to advance an inexperienced relative of a political crony. 'His Lordship might as properly have asked to have him made Captain of a Man of War,'[6] Anson told the prime minister, and he insisted that in future 'more people of business should be appointed to the Victualling Board'. This is one instance in a story of a Board – crucial in the history of the Navy – that was growing ever more professional and efficient. Experienced officers marvelled at the change since 1739. Back then a cruiser could not spend much more than a fortnight at sea. By the mid-1750s cruises of three months were commonplace. And it was not only the quantity that had improved: sailors and marines actually appeared to *like* the food.

This revolution was possible because the Victualling Board now produced its own food and beer, rather than relying on private contractors and individual captains and pursers. Functions were centralised, fraud was beaten back and an impressive complex of storehouses, brewhouses, mills, packing centres and the like were established at Deptford, Portsmouth, Plymouth and Gibraltar. This meant that provisions were plentiful, easily available and cheaper.

The reforms that Anson had been pressing on a reluctant Navy for years began to bear fruit in 1755. Yet only a year later he found himself out of office. His Navy had failed the test of war. Once again high hopes of Britain's natural supremacy at sea had met a sorry fate. Hostilities began in the Ohio valley, where the French were extending a line from Louisbourg in Canada down to New Orleans. The Navy struck first. A fleet under Vice Admiral Edward Boscawen was ordered to attack a French fleet carrying troops to Canada. Boscawen did well in thick fog on the St Lawrence River, but nowhere near well enough to win a war before it was declared.

The French did not want war, but they were better prepared for one. The Royal Navy was not ready and the French could subject it to the utmost pressure by simultaneously threatening to invade Britain and capture Minorca. They could only accomplish one of these objectives. But which one?

That was the thought that nagged at Anson in 1756. He threw the bulk of his resources (drained by years of peacetime cuts) at the Western Squadron in order to defend his country. He reasoned that Britain's colonies were so scattered throughout the world that the Navy needed to double in size in order to defend them and the country's shore. But the Navy could make up for its numerical weakness with strategic brilliance. 'The best defence ... for our colonies as well as our coasts,' said Anson, 'is to have such a squadron to the westward as may in all probability either keep the French in port, or give them battle with advantage if they come out.'[7]

The other plank of his strategy was to boost Britain's strength in the Mediterranean. Vice Admiral John Byng – the son of George Byng, the victor of the Battle of Cape Passaro – was belatedly dispatched to defend Minorca with ten ships of the line.

Byng arrived in Gibraltar to discover that the French had already invaded Minorca and St Philip's Castle at Port Mahon was under siege. The admiral lapsed at once into a state of defeatism. The local army

Right: Lord Howe, a flawed genius who did much to transform the Royal Navy in the last third of the eighteenth century.

Below: Admiral Lord George Brydges Rodney. The mercurial Rodney was loathed and admired in equal measures by contemporaries and historians. His great victories were hard to surpass; his failures endangered the service and his country.

HMS *Brunswick* fighting the French ships *Vengeur du Peuple* and *Achille* at the Battle of the First of June, 1794, by Nicholas Pocock. Few paintings capture so well the sickening proximity of warfare in the age of sail, the mess of masts and sails, and the way that gunsmoke enveloped the scene.

The Royal Navy's most famous ship, HMS *Victory*, in all her glory as she leaves the Channel.

The Admiral as hero. Rear Admiral Sir Horatio Nelson leads an attack on a Spanish gunboat during the blockade of Cadiz, 3 July 1797. Nelson had won everlasting fame in February of that year when he led the boarding parties onto two enemy ships during the Battle of Cape St Vincent.

Overleaf: Officers who served at the Battle of Trafalgar commended Nicholas Pocock's painting as a realistic depiction of the confusion and damage that followed the battle.

Above: One of the carronades on HMS *Victory*. This vicious gun gave the Royal Navy the edge in the kind of fighting the service relished the most – at the closest possible quarters.

The gundeck on HMS *Victory* (*above*) and showing hammocks slung (*right*). No sailor would have experienced things quite like this: guns were never run out except when they were to be fired. The rest of the time the men's living area would have been dark and poorly ventilated.

Saturday Night at Sea by George Cruikshank. Sailors carouse at their mess table. The joyousness is typical of Cruikshank, and is no doubt idealised, but he captures well the cramped conditions of life on board, where personal items had to compete for space with military equipment.

HM Brig *Black Joke* engaging the Spanish Slave brig *El Almirante* in the Bight of Benin, 1829. This was one of the most famous pursuits in the Navy's long campaign against slavery on the West African coast.

Old meets new: the state-of-the-art steam warship *Nemesis* destroying Chinese junks in January 1841. Such ships extended the Navy's reach from the oceans to river systems.

Bombardment of the Bomarsund fortress during the Crimean War. The Navy's speciality in coastal bombardment, and the number of modern steam gunboats at its disposal, made it feared around the world in the nineteenth century.

HMS *Warrior*, preserved as a museum ship at Portsmouth.

HMS *Inflexible*. When she was commissioned in 1881 she was the most advanced battleship in the world.

commander told him that St Philip's could not hold out. In fact it was in a good position to do so if Byng could land troops and supplies and cut off the French lines. Instead he left most of his troops at Gibraltar. He fought an inconclusive battle against the French warships that were covering the invasion. Byng then made a fateful decision. He claimed, quite wrongly, that Gibraltar was in danger and decided to return there without pursuing the French, relieving St Philip's or cutting the enemy supply lines.

Thanks to this decision the fortress was compelled to surrender. Byng returned home and was amazed to find himself under arrest. The public response to the fall of Minorca was one of horror and anger. Once again the Navy had let the country down. It was the opinion of most naval experts that had Byng acted more decisively and rallied British forces in the Mediterranean the French would have been driven from Minorca. As it was, the admiral did the thing the French most wanted.

No one was sure who to blame – Byng, the Admiralty or the government. The ministry and Anson were the first victims, faulted for poor strategic planning and for not giving Byng enough ships. Byng managed to attract some sympathy. The government fell and it was replaced by a coalition led by the duke of Newcastle and William Pitt. Pitt's brother-in-law took over from Anson. Then Byng stood trial.

The admiral was convinced that he had nothing to worry about. He had a friendly president at the court martial, he had a good defence, and the whole thing was surely a formality. But he had not counted on the inflexibility of Anson's Articles of War. The Twelfth Article stated that any officer who did not defeat the enemy 'through cowardice, negligence, or disaffection' was guilty. The court found him not guilty of cowardice and disaffection, but he was undoubtedly negligent. Even so Byng believed he would be shown leniency. But the new Articles gave no alternative but the death penalty.

There was an outcry in favour of Byng. No one really wanted him to be executed. Even the French pleaded on his behalf. The Admiralty tried to save him and the court itself recommended clemency. But the public were not in a merciful mood and nor was the king. Byng faced a firing squad on the quarterdeck of his flagship. Voltaire's response is famous. It was an extraordinarily harsh punishment. But its effect really was to 'encourage the others'.

Byng's failure was one of many in the opening years of the war. The army was defeated and Hanover fell to the French. The Western Squadron failed to prevent French convoys leaving for Canada and the West Indies and building up their forces there. Britain was on the back foot in America and after the fall of Minorca a much-reduced power in the Mediterranean. An attempt to launch an amphibious operation against Rochefort miscarried. Similarly an assault on Louisbourg failed. Alarmingly for Britain's security the Austrians gave the French navy free use of Ostend and Nieuwpoort while Russia, Sweden and Austria allied with France. Elsewhere the outlook was grim: the East India Company lost Bengal to Siraj-ud-Daulah; Madras was under threat from the French at Pondicherry.

Pitt confronted the seriousness of the situation: 'The Empire* is no more, the ports of the Netherlands betrayed, the Dutch Barrier Treaty an empty sound, Minorca, and with it the Mediterranean lost, and America itself precarious.'[8]

---

* By 'Empire' Pitt meant the Holy Roman Empire.

CHAPTER 29

COUNTERATTACK
1757–1759

In 1757 Britain seemed to be in the same sorry state as a decade before. Britons flattered themselves that they were a maritime superpower. The reality was different. The bulk of British naval forces were in home waters, ready to defend the country against invasion. Now it looked as if France was the ascendant European, colonial and maritime power.

Britain had to fight back. As usual many spoiled for a naval war. Pitt, the famous Patriot Whig who had made his name insulting Hanover, deprecating Britain's commitments in Europe and advocating a navalist strategy, was at the head of the government. Anson returned as First Lord and was given a seat in the cabinet. Conditions seemed set fair for the Navy to strike back.

To the anger of his many supporters, however, Pitt committed British troops and money to the war in Germany. It looked like the greatest political betrayal imaginable. But the gamble paid off. Britain's new ally, Prince Ferdinand of Brunswick, won a succession of victories in 1758 that drove the French out of Hanover and Westphalia. Frederick the Great of Prussia won important victories against Russia, Sweden and Austria. The Navy had a minor role in the German campaign. Captain Charles Holmes, a man who had risen from able seaman, sailed his frigate into the Prussian port of Emden, which had been captured by the French. The next day the French evacuated. The Navy also landed troops at St Malo and Cherbourg, which restored faith in amphibious operations and tied up French troops that might otherwise have been useful in Germany.

'The way to save America,'[1] Frederick the Great told the British ambassador, 'is not to suffer the French to become masters of Europe.' If France and her allies defeated Hanover and Prussia then France would be free to turn to the sea and devour British colonies. Pitt found that Britain needed continental allies and that Hanover was vitally important. In 1758 he was ready to go on the offensive in the New World.

Pitt had told Anson that he wanted the squadron in Canada to winter at Halifax in 1757 and capture Louisbourg the next spring. It was a daring plan: the eight battleships would be frozen in for the duration. But for all the hardship it meant that the Navy had an advantage when the weather softened. The advance party could ensure that the remote target was already weak before the campaign got under way by preventing French supplies getting through. In June 1758 sixteen ships of the line, gunboats and frigates under Boscawen arrived at Halifax to join the hardy force that had seen out the winter.

But before Boscawen set sail some minor but important victories were scored against the French. Admiral Henry Osborne, commander in the Mediterranean, prevented a fleet sailing from Toulon passing the Strait of Gibraltar. He then destroyed the squadron sent to reinforce it. A couple of months later Admiral Hawke, with eight ships of the Western Squadron, attacked a French convoy of forty merchantmen protected by five battleships and seven frigates. Hawke was annoyed when the enemy scattered and ran, but the actions of Osborne and Hawke prevented French naval forces from linking up to relieve Canada.

The enormous British flotilla rendezvoused at Halifax. Throughout May the army and Navy trained together. In June the British arrived off Louisbourg with twenty-one ships of the line, two 50s, frigates and a flotilla of bomb vessels, landing craft and 150 transports carrying 12,000 soldiers. Attacking the great fortress at Louisbourg was no easy matter – it was the largest building in North America and its harbour was guarded by Lighthouse Point, which was an ideal battery location, and by five battleships. Poor weather delayed the assault. When it began the army had to work hard under heavy fire to secure a beachhead. The division under James Wolfe then stormed Lighthouse Point. It took a further eleven days to land and position the artillery there. Then the British bombarded the fort.

Three days later mortars on Lighthouse Point destroyed three French ships. Boscawen sent in cutting-out parties on the fleet's boats. They burnt another ship and captured the fifth. The fortress fell shortly after. It was as successful a combined amphibious operation as could be imagined. Louisbourg was the gateway to Canada.

By the end of 1758 the tide was beginning to turn. Britain was ready to go on the offensive. Morale and national pride had been restored. Pitt enjoyed public support. Naval and military forces were concentrated for major amphibious operations on the St Lawrence. A large army under James Wolfe began to be assembled. Its vast flotilla – some 20,000 tons of transports – would be convoyed across the Atlantic by fourteen ships of the line, six frigates, three bomb vessels and three fireships. It was to be led by Admiral Charles Saunders, a survivor of Anson's circumnavigation.

Britain was on the rampage against France's colonies and trade. Senegal was in British hands; in December 1758 the French colony of Gorée was taken by Captain Augustus Keppel, who had sailed round the world with Anson as a fifteen-year-old; and in May 1759 the sugar island of Guadeloupe fell to the British.

The leading members of the cabinet met at George Anson's London home on 19 February 1759. Anson laid out the naval strength of the country. There were 275 ships in service and eighty-two in ordinary. Many of these were serving abroad as Britain's war went global. Of 100 ships of the line in the Navy, fifty-nine were serving abroad. Of the forty-one on call for home defence, twenty were under repair. All these ships would be ready by May. By now Anson's 74s and his remodelled frigates were being launched. The size of the Navy was approaching 300 ships. The First Lord could be very proud of what he had achieved in just over a decade of reforms. Behind the array of maritime force lay a sophisticated and efficient administrative system, flourishing dockyards and a motivated officer corps. Britain had the means to challenge the French everywhere in the world.

That was a fact the French knew well. But they also knew that Britain's claim to global naval dominance was precarious. A credible threat of invasion was enough to set all Britain's dispersed forces scampering for home. The members of the cabinet who met at Anson's house knew that France was massing its forces for an invasion of Britain. It was to be a multi-pronged campaign, which, it was hoped, would divide and overwhelm the Royal Navy. Forces from Dunkirk would sail to Ireland. Troops embarked in Brittany would land on the Firth of Clyde and capture Glasgow and Edinburgh. The Channel and Flemish ports would be used for a descent on Maldon, Essex. Their objective was to capture London and bring Britain to a humiliating peace. At the meeting at Anson's house the head of the army reported that there were just 10,000 troops available to defend London and the ports.[2] They would face 50,000 French soldiers. Louis XV feared that if Britain continued to oust France in America the balance of power in Europe would be altered, Britain would 'usurp the commerce of the nations' and she alone would 'remain rich in Europe'. France had to act decisively or lose her possessions in America, the West Indies and her seaborne trade.

Although the Royal Navy far outnumbered the French navy, in European waters they were equal. The defence of the realm depended upon preventing the Toulon and Brest fleets linking up. This was familiar strategic terrain for Anson. It meant that once again the security of the kingdom and the conquest of North America depended upon the efficiency and vigour of the Western Squadron and the Mediterranean Fleet.

It was a risky strategy. Ministers were always uncomfortably aware of the fact that a fleet cruising in the Western Approaches might not spot an enemy fleet. Anson had briefly left his desk to command the Western Squadron in 1758. It was not a happy return. It proved exceptionally hard to victual the fleet at sea. Scurvy ravaged the crews. Anson could only keep the squadron at sea for six weeks at a time. It was a far cry from the glories of 1747. The Navy was also facing a crisis of manpower. There were 71,000 serving in February 1759,[3] the largest number there had ever been. Even so it was not enough to man all the ships. Sailors were desperate to avoid serving. It is not hard to see why. Pay was bad and conditions were awful. Since the beginning of the war just 143 men had died in combat, but 13,000 had perished from illness. As a result the Navy was undermanned and leaking sailors: 12,000 had deserted. It was hard to replace them.

Could the nation trust to the Navy in these circumstances? The Mediterranean Fleet was in disgrace after Byng's failure. The Western Squadron was misfiring. These were nervous days indeed.

Anson appointed his two best officers to the vital commands. Admiral Boscawen was dispatched to Gibraltar in May. His orders were to prevent the Toulon fleet passing the Strait. If they did manage to leave the Mediterranean he was to follow and fight. Admiral Hawke was once again given the Western Squadron. His orders from Anson were to wait off Ushant and keep an eye on Brest. He was to make frequent returns to Torbay to revictual. His frigates and smaller ships of the line were to cruise the seas and disrupt any ships carrying supplies into Brest.

The challenge in 1759 was to keep Hawke's fleet at sea continuously. The prime minister fretted that 'Hawke can't keep that station without often coming in'.[4] In July ministers agreed to Hawke's demand for a rotation of ships, whereby six ships at a time returned to be cleaned and refitted while the rest kept station. But Hawke soon found this was unsatisfactory and weakened his plans. The problem was that Plymouth was inadequate and the work took too long. He complained that the victuals were inferior and demanded that ships returning from rotation should carry as much fresh meat as possible back to the fleet. He also insisted that a senior administrator be sent to Plymouth to oversee the victualling of the fleet. The man in question was Richard Pett – the man Anson had insisted be appointed to the Victualling Board back in 1755 over the head of the prime minister.

In the summer of 1759 the process of revictualling the fleet stepped up a gear. Anson ordered more transport ships. Pett took the inspired decision to send Hawke fresh vegetables. It had always been easier and cheaper to send out preserved foods: saltbeef, stockfish and the like. In other words a recipe for scurvy. In August nine ships delivered live cattle, turnips, carrots, onions, cabbages and beer. The effect of this wholesome menu was instantaneous. Scurvy was no longer a problem; the crews became stronger. Hawke kept them fighting fit with regular gunnery drills.

This was naval organisation on a colossal scale. It was hard work for victualling ships to operate so far from home and in extremely rough waters. They had to beat westwards to Ushant against the prevailing winds. Once there the transfer of live cattle and vegetables in high seas was fraught with difficulty. It was an expensive and tricky business. The contractors found that the wastage and damage to ships caused while victualling at sea in the rough waters off Ushant left them with heavy losses. Hawke had to cajole them into coming out with enough fresh meat and vegetables and offer compensation for damage. But it was worth it. At this time no one knew how to prevent scurvy. The insistence on fresh vegetables supplied the men with enough vitamin C to ward it off. Hawke was obsessively concerned about the technicalities of naval blockade, in particular the need to revictual effectively at sea. When the beer arrived from Plymouth spoiled, Hawke ordered it to be tipped overboard. The Admiralty and the victuallers had to scour the south coast for enough beer to supply the fleet. When that ran short they sent out wine.

Hawke was not a very likeable man. He was prickly and demanding. But thanks to his persistence and refusal to take no for an answer the Western Squadron was able to remain on station for months without having to make trips home. This kind of continuous service at sea had never happened before. The physician James Lind observed with astonishment that 14,000 men pent up in ships for months on end were enjoying better health than people 'on the most healthful spot in the world'. It was, he said, 'an observation ... worthy of record'.[5]

Blockading Brest was not a simple matter, even without the logistical problems of supply. The roadstead is well protected by rocks and reefs. Ships entering and leaving took one of three narrow channels, which made watching the port very difficult as British ships always had to be close enough to observe which one was being used. And it was not just Brest that had to be blockaded. The French army of conquest could not

Admiral Lord Hawke

be embarked at Brest. Troop ships were gathered at Nantes, Rochefort and in the Gulf of Morbihan, a vast, impenetrable inlet off Quiberon Bay, 100 miles south of Brest. The embarkation ports, as well as Brest, needed to be closely watched. But lingering too close to the perilous lee shore, with its jagged rocks, islands and assorted lurking hazards, was all but impossible.

That was why previous attempts by the Western Squadron to keep the Brest fleet under close observation had been at best only partially successful. Battleships could not get close enough to Brest because of the dangers. They had to cruise off Ushant, which meant enemy ships could evade them. When the Squadron was refitting and revictualling at Torbay or Plymouth it could not get back to station in time, even if intelligence reached it quickly. In 1759 the danger of a French fleet slipping out of Brest and escorting the transports was all too real. The French knew that it was merely a matter of time before the Royal Navy was forced away from its vigil by hunger, illness, poor weather and leaky ships. They were prepared to wait it out. That was why Hawke had to exert every ounce of his will to remain off Ushant, battle-ready and fighting fit.

But that solved only half the problem. To answer it fully, Hawke created an inshore squadron, led by a talented young captain named Augustus

Hervey and made up of frigates and a couple of small ships of the line. It was to remain as close to Brest as possible without interruption. This was a dangerous mission, and Hawke gave Hervey assurances that he would take full responsibility for anything that went wrong. A battleship and frigates were also blockading Nantes. Another captain, Robert Duff, was given command of a light squadron stationed in Quiberon Bay and ordered to blockade the transports in the Morbihan.

These light forces were redundant without the main fleet ready to pounce; the main fleet was useless without frigates scouring the waters near Brest and the other Atlantic ports for advance intelligence of enemy movements. At last the components of a successful western cruise were beginning to come together.

Hawke reported that Brest was 'blocked up in the strictest sense'. Hervey wrote to Hawke: 'I think, Sir, you have insulted them [the French] in a manner that they were never before used to, or that history can give account of.'[6] No ship could enter or leave Brest, be it French or neutral. In 1747 Anson and then Hawke had subjected the French to an 'open blockade', whereby it was intended that the enemy would emerge to be beaten in battle. Now, in 1759, Hawke had achieved what was known as 'close blockade'. It was one of the hardest and most gruelling tasks for a navy. The warships at Brest were starved of supplies, which had to be diverted hundreds of miles overland. The French were powerless against the blockade. And this despite the fact that their fleet and Hawke's were the same size. The blockade was, for the French, a national humiliation. For the British it was a triumph of naval planning, organisation and leadership.

In addition to the Western Squadron, the Royal Navy had a squadron watching the Flemish ports, another off Le Havre, ships in the Downs and a force under George Rodney at Spithead. The latter raided Le Havre and burnt a number of invasion craft.

That left Toulon as the only remaining French port. Boscawen was cruising there throughout the summer, keeping the French admiral de la Clue confined to harbour. In August, however, he was obliged to retire to Gibraltar for supplies. The French fleet left the next day. De la Clue's plan was to escape through the Strait by night, hugging the North African coast.

Boscawen was an old hand in matters of blockade and the cat-and-mouse tactics developed by George Anson. He had served in the Navy since 1726. He had been with Anson in the Western Squadron in the 1740s. At the first Battle of Finisterre it was his ship, *Namur*, that had first spotted the French fleet. He was one of the highest-regarded captains in the Navy. After Finisterre he led a squadron to India. In 1751 he was made a lord of the Admiralty. In the present war he had served under Hawke in the Western Squadron and added to his laurels with the much-lauded capture of Louisbourg. He was not an admiral to allow the French to best him.

Boscawen had taken the precaution of leaving frigates to keep watch on de la Clue and the Strait. When the report reached Gibraltar that the French were on the move the ships were unprepared and the men ashore. There followed a 'stampede', and within three hours Boscawen's eleven ships were at sea and in pursuit. It was another dazzling display of the Navy's preparedness, determination and speed.

During the night the rear division of the French fleet detached and entered Cadiz. Boscawen's force sighted de la Clue's ten-ship division of the French fleet at 06.00. 'The wind was strong at east,' Boscawen reported; 'the weather fine, the water smooth; and we soon perceived that we gained exceedingly fast upon the enemy.' At 14.30 the British ships were upon the French. HMS *Culloden* engaged *Centaure*. Then five other Royal Navy ships surrounded the French ship. Boscawen worked *Namur* through the enemy ships towards de la Clue's *Océan*. Olaudah Equiano, then a slave of one of Boscawen's lieutenants, recalled that although *Namur* passed close to the enemy ships 'our admiral would not suffer a gun to be fired at any of them, to my astonishment, but made us lie on our bellies on the deck till we came quite close to the *Océan*, who was ahead of them all; when we had orders to pour the whole three tiers into her at once'.

Namur and *Océan* engaged at 16.00. Both ships took a pounding, but Boscawen's came off the worse. She lost her mainmast and fell back, where she came across *Centaure*, which had bravely suffered herself to be battered to pieces by the British ships, while her consorts escaped. *Océan* and the three 74s, *Redoutable*, *Modeste* and *Téméraire*, sped off together; one ship made for the Canaries and another for Rochefort.

Boscawen transferred to *Newark* (80) and continued the pursuit through the night. When the sun rose de la Clue was entering Lagos Bay. Portugal was not at war, so de la Clue must have fancied he would evade the Royal Navy by claiming the protection of a third power. Boscawen did not call off the chase. *Océan*, one of the finest ships afloat in the world, and *Redoutable* were driven ashore. They were then burnt by the British. *Téméraire* and *Modeste* were captured in the bay, in violation of Portuguese neutrality. Boscawen headed for home, his objective achieved. He left ships to blockade the surviving French ships.

Boscawen was disappointed with the battle. Unlike the great victories at Finisterre his ships had not rolled up the enemy in a running fight. Rather they had swarmed round *Centaure*. It may have been a failure in a tactical sense, but strategically the Battle of Lagos had a major impact.

It made the French invasion plan a lot harder. And so too did the allied victory at Minden, Germany, in the same month. The French had hoped to withdraw men from Germany and use them in the invasion of Britain. That was no longer possible. Meanwhile, Britain had strengthened her position around the globe with a succession of victories. The Royal Navy was in command of the West Indies. The French were repulsed from Madras and their position in India deteriorated. Vice Admiral George Pocock, commander-in-chief of the naval squadron in India, fought a sharp engagement with the French in September. The French abandoned Pondicherry and conceded command of the seas to Pocock.

Over in Canada maritime dominance paid dividends. From the new base at Louisbourg, Vice Admiral Saunders escorted General Wolfe's army down the St Lawrence with twenty-two battleships, thirteen frigates and other naval vessels. Their objective was Quebec. Once there it proved impossible to attack the town from the lower river. Quebec was heavily defended from attack coming up the St Lawrence. Saunders ordered his best captains – including John Jervis and James Cook – to survey the river. He then forced a passage past Quebec and into the upper river. Wolfe's army was landed near a road that took it up to the Plains of Abraham. There the outnumbered British army defeated the French and took Quebec.

Saunders arrived in the Channel in November to learn that France had at last decided to go for broke. Louis XV had been worsted throughout the world. His only chance was to trigger the invasion. The man responsible for the invasion of Scotland, Admiral Marshal Conflans, knew that he could not risk engaging Hawke. He had to evade the Royal Navy, link up with the transports in the Morbihan and escort them to Scotland. On 7 November things began to go his way. A storm blew Hawke off station and blew in the French West Indian fleet.

Hawke and his storm-damaged ships were forced into Torbay. The duke of Newcastle was all for keeping the ships at home to spare them from the winter weather. But Pitt and Hawke were adamant that the danger had not passed. Anson strained the administrative resources of the Navy to breaking point to get more ships to sea. Hawke huffed and puffed at Torbay, itching to get back on station. He got nineteen battleships out on 12 November; they were forced back a day later. Meanwhile the timorous Conflans had at last thrown caution to the winds. The French fleet left Brest on the 14th. Hawke was now under way with twenty-three ships of the line, but it was not until the 16th that he received intelligence from his victualling ships about the French fleet. His rival had twenty-one battleships and was 200 miles in front, heading to rendezvous with the army.

The race was on. Both admirals had one destination in mind: Quiberon Bay. The invasion of England was on.

CHAPTER 30

QUIBERON BAY
1759–1771

All was going Conflans's way. On 16 November he was sixty miles from his destination, Quiberon Bay, with a north-west wind filling his sails, but by evening the waves had built in size and the winds blew hard from the east. The French were carried out into the ocean. By the next day they were 120 miles from their goal. Only on the 18th was Conflans able to get his fleet back on course. It was hard work beating against a north-easterly and the following day he found himself becalmed seventy miles away.

Hawke made up for lost time. By superior seamanship he made better progress in the gales. He was now on a parallel course to Conflans. But the volatile November sea did not help either admiral. On the evening of the 19th the winds reached gale force, preventing Hawke's battleships straying too close to the rock-strewn shore. The British were about forty miles west by north of their objective. The storm hit Conflans later in the night. He was just twenty miles from Morbihan. Only Duff's light squadron stood between him and the army.

Robert Duff had got his frigates out of Quiberon Bay at dawn. He was ready and waiting for the approaching French fleet. He sent half his ships north and the others south. Conflans scented a quick victory. His vanguard went in pursuit of one British division, the centre went after the other; meanwhile the rearguard remained to windward.

Conflans had no idea that Hawke was anywhere near. When he saw the enemy approaching he was compelled to gather up his scattered ships and get them into the safety of Quiberon Bay. He signalled for his fleet to enter the bay. Once there they would form a line of battle. This was by far the best policy. Hawke would not dare enter while the wind was blowing violently from WNW, the seas were high and the weather was deteriorating. He would not dare risk his ships entering a bay littered with uncharted islands, shoals and reefs. An Admiralty memo from 1756[1] noted that if the French ever chose to enter Quiberon Bay 'we dare not follow them'. Conflans could therefore get the army into

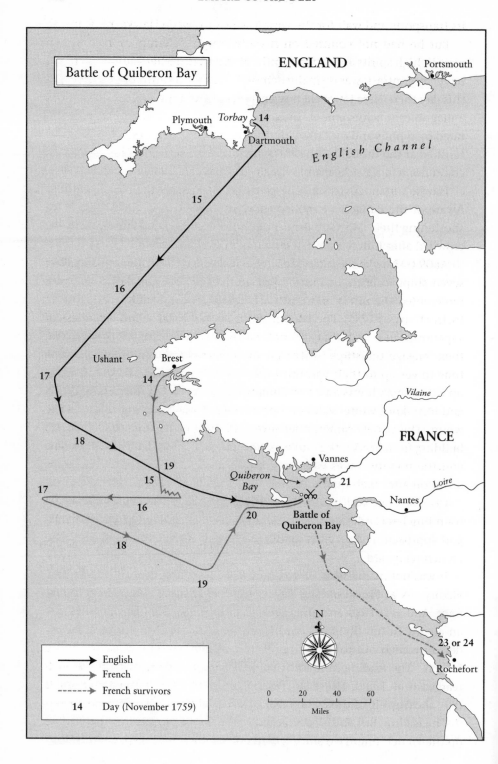

Battle of Quiberon Bay

its transports and wait for the winter winds to sweep Hawke away again.

But he had not counted on his adversary's determination. His men were in high spirits and, after months at sea, were battle-ready. The French navy, by contrast, was dismally demoralised after months of blockade. On this day there were fewer than twenty sick men in the Western Squadron, a magnificent achievement. In contrast, the French fleet had been devastated by typhus and dysentery during the blockade of Brest. Conflans was terrified at the thought of fighting; he knew in his heart of hearts that he could not win a battle against the Royal Navy.

Hawke's manoeuvre was one of the most risky in the Navy's history. Aware of the dangers of the lee shore in a rising gale, the French were shortening their sails. The British did not follow suit; as Hawke wrote 'we crowded after him with every sail our ships could carry'.

At 09.00 Hawke signalled for a general chase. He then signalled the first seven ships to form an impromptu line ahead with full sail. This order represented the ninth and tenth articles of Anson's Additional Fighting Instructions of 1747. The leading ships should form a line regardless of superiority in a way that did not waste a second of time. They should then 'engage the ships in [the enemy's] rear endeavouring at the same time to get up to their van until the rest of [the] ... squadron can come up with them'. It was an exceptionally dangerous thing to do in high seas and forty-knot winter gales on one of the most unforgiving coasts in the world. The vessels came under severe strain. All the time the wind was building from WNW, the rain was whipping in on sudden violent squalls, and the mighty waves were smashing against the rocks. Still the ships drove on after their quarry.

Conflans had not planned for this kind of madness. At 14.30 he was rounding Les Cardinaux, the rocks at the end of the Quiberon peninsula, and approaching safety. As he did so the first British ships fell upon the French rearguard.

It was not madness, however, but brilliant seamanship and hunger for victory. As at Finisterre and Lagos, the French were determined not to fight. And as at Finisterre and Lagos, the British chased down and engaged an enemy in full flight. Richard Howe was leading the vanguard. He ordered his men not to open fire till they were muzzle to muzzle with the French.[2] The leading nine British ships came into battle with the French rearguard at 15.00. Howe on HMS *Magnanime* (74) engaged *Formidable* (80), the flagship of the French rear admiral. HMS *Warspite* (74) joined her.

The leading British ships attacked *Formidable* in turn before moving on up the French line. Two ships, *Dorsetshire* and *Defiance*, kept to windward of the enemy line, fired on but refusing to return fire, until they reached Conflans in the French vanguard. Their intention was to hold on to the enemy's flight until Hawke caught up. *Magnanime* moved up to *Héros* (74). It was a bloody onslaught. By the time *Héros* surrendered 400 men, including all the officers, were dead. Meanwhile Keppel's *Torbay* (70) attacked *Thésée* (74). Both ships were caught in a terrifying swell; both declined to close their maindeck gunports. Keppel manoeuvred into the wind and saved his ship. His opponent was not so skilful: water flooded her gun deck and she capsized. Keppel then sailed alongside *Formidable* and unleashed a double broadside at point-blank range. The French ship, by now battered to the condition of a colander, surrendered to HMS *Resolution* (74).

Here was naval warfare out of the darkest nightmare. Fleet battles were bloody enough; this was conducted in rolling waves, darkening skies and foul squalls. The French ships that fell victim were littered with dead men, broken sails and smashed timber. There was little hope of saving men from the tumultuous waves. Keppel, however, launched boats to rescue enemy sailors from *Thésée*, but recovered only twenty (out of a crew of 650) from the enormous plunging waves. Most ships that foundered lost their entire complements.

It is worth noting that the British ships in the thick of the action – *Torbay*, *Magnanime*, *Dorsetshire*, *Warspite* and *Resolution* – were those 70- or 74-gun ships of the line that Anson had backed as the future of the Navy. They were large enough to take on their French counterparts, stable enough to fight in the heavy seas that day, and fast enough to run down the enemy rearguard and fight through their formation till the bigger ships arrived. Three of the captains on these new ships – Howe, Keppel and Bentley – had served as young officers on Anson's circumnavigation.

Conflans's *Soleil Royal* made it into the bay. He now believed that he was safe. He could form a line of battle and hold Hawke off. The British, he reasoned, would not approach the hidden shoals without pilots. But then Howe's *Magnanime* entered the bay. The French broke ranks and swarmed around her. Then the wind changed, the ebb tide exerted its force, and the French could not go about in the confined space of the bay. They could not manoeuvre with jagged rocks to leeward and British ships to windward. As one French officer recalled, they were trapped in a funnel.

Conflans now had one option: escape from Quiberon Bay. *Soleil Royal* blasted HMS *Swiftsure* out of the way of the exit passage, but just then Hawke's *Royal George* (100) rounded Les Cardinaux, sealing off the open end of the funnel. The admiral spotted his opponent and ordered *Royal George* to be brought alongside *Soleil Royal*. The master argued that such a thing at evening on a rising sea was impossible. 'You have done your duty in apprising me of the danger,' replied Hawke; 'let us next see how you can comply with your orders.' The time was now 16.25. *Royal George* took on *Superbe* (70). Hawke's flagship fired two broadsides; the French ship and all 800 of her crew were lost in the churning waves at 16.41. *Royal George* then went in pursuit of *Soleil Royal*, but *Intrépide* positioned herself between the two flagships and soaked up the fury of the British flagship. *Soleil Royal* fell away from her adversary, and in doing so crashed into two other ships.

Royal George was under attack from seven enemy ships. Could the French turn the tables at the last minute? It might have looked so to a neutral observer, and 'really her situation would have been lamentable if the enemy had preserved any degree of composure, or fired with any direction; but their confusion was so great that, of many hundreds of shot, I do not believe that more than 30 or 40 struck the ship'.[3]

That bore out the warning given by the commander of the French invasion force to the minister of war in August: 'The English outnumber us by only two or three ships. But they are better armed, more battle-worthy, better seamen, and are more aggressive and confident than ours who are incredibly deflated and demoralised.'[4]

It was now dark and the conditions were worse than ever; even Hawke acknowledged it was folly to continue. He ordered an end to proceedings at 17.30. Ships from both sides dropped anchor where they could. They endured a wretched night. The French were facing disaster. The British were not confident of victory. Both sides suffered the worsening weather. HMS *Resolution* and the captured *Héros* were driven onto the Four Shoal.

During the night eight French ships stole out of the bay; seven escaped to Rochefort and one, the badly damaged *Juste* (70), hit rocks and sank with all hands as it tried to enter the Loire. A further seven French ships tried to cross the sandbar into the Villaine river; six made it after they jettisoned all their guns and one sank.

When dawn broke the British line was bereft of an enemy – except one. Conflans found himself anchored in the midst of the enemy fleet, abandoned by his own fleet. *Soleil Royal* was pursued by HMS *Essex*; they both ran aground alongside *Héros* and *Resolution* on the Four Shoal. Conflans deserted the scene and ordered his magnificent flagship to be burnt.

Hawke was almost apologetic about his victory.[5] 'When I consider the season of the year, the hard gales on the day of the action, and the coast they were on,' he reported to the Admiralty, 'I can boldly affirm that all that could be done has been done. As to the loss we have sustained, let it be placed to the account of the necessity I was under of running all risks to break this strong force of the enemy. Had we but two hours more daylight, the whole had been totally destroyed or taken; for we were almost up with their van when night overtook us.' He was bitterly frustrated that so many enemy ships had escaped his maw.

In the cold light of a November morning the victory Hawke had longed for looked decidedly pallid. But that is the way of war.

The Battle of Quiberon Bay is among the most stunning naval victories of all time. It was fought at great risk in appalling conditions. Hawke lost two ships and between three and four hundred men. The French lost seven ships and 2,500 men. It was the culmination of years of painstaking work undertaken by Anson, Hawke, their captains, officers and men. The outcome was momentous.

The battle ended Britain's year of victories, her *annus mirabilis* of 1759 when she defeated France in every theatre of the war. The country was safe from invasion. The French navy was knocked out of the war. The captains who sneaked away during the night found safety at the price of further involvement in the war. The Royal Navy kept up its ruthless blockade of the entire French coast. By 1761 the French minister of the marine found rotten ships, empty stores, exhausted credit and morale at rock bottom.

On New Year's Eve a new song was performed in London:

Come, cheer up, my lads, 'tis to glory we steer,
To add something more to this wonderful year;
To honour we call you, as freemen not slaves,
For who are so free as the sons of the waves.

Heart of oak are our ships, jolly tars are our men,
We always are ready; Steady, boys, steady!
We'll fight and we'll conquer again and again.
We ne'er see our foes but we wish them to stay,
They never see us but they wish us away;
If they run, why we follow, and run them ashore,
For if they won't fight us, what can we do more?

Horace Walpole wrote: 'Our bells are quite worn threadbare with the ringing for victories. Indeed, one is forced to ask, "what victory is there?"

for fear of missing one.'⁶ A new first-rate battleship under construction was named to commemorate the year of triumph, HMS *Victory*. All those stories the British told themselves about their maritime destiny seemed to have been fulfilled.

For Britain was incontestably the master of the seas.

As a new year began the Navy numbered 301 ships and 85,000 men.⁷ The war was effectively won. France was under blockade from Dunkirk to Marseille. Louis was powerless to reverse British gains in Canada, America, the West Indies, Africa and India. The French launched a campaign in Canada in 1760, but it was doomed because there could be no support from France. The British were able to take Montreal. But still peace was not forthcoming because French ambitions were alive in Germany. Newcastle said at the end of the year: 'If we can't make peace, we must try our fate with expeditions ... and beat France into a peace.'⁸

And so 'expeditions' of the naval variety resumed. The following year, 1761, Pondicherry fell to Britain and France was eliminated as a power in India. The great sugar island Martinique and islands in the Lesser Antilles fell after successful amphibious operations. Closer to home, the Navy took Belle Île, off Quiberon Bay. The plan was to use it as a base for blockading France and then, when peace came, exchange it for Minorca.

The amphibious operations against Belle Île and Martinique were tough assignments. Their success – achieved by overwhelming naval superiority – reminded the world of the prowess of the Royal Navy and its ability to mount operations simultaneously anywhere in the world.

In 1762 Spain came into the war on France's side. This represented an opportunity for the Navy. Anson drew up an audacious plan for the capture of Havana. This was no easy task. Hostile ships which approached Cuba from the south had to beat against the prevailing winds, which gave the defenders weeks' worth of notice of an impending assault. The sea in the northern approach to the island offered a faster route for ships sailing with the wind, allowing for a surprise attack; but it was strewn for hundreds of miles with unseen reefs, shoals and tiny low-lying sand islands, or cays. There was a narrow passage through the dangers known as the Old Bahama Channel, but the maps were poor and no one dared hazard their ships by using it.

Anson ordered Vice-Admiral Sir George Pocock to take the Old Bahama Channel. Pocock sent ahead a surveying frigate, which led the squadron of twenty-one ships of the line along with frigates, bomb vessels and 160 troop transports, through the Channel, dropping sailors on the cays to mark the dangers. The narrowest stretches of the Channel were navigated at night, with bonfires lit on the cays. It was a bold plan, skilfully accomplished, and Havana was caught unawares. The sequel was less clear-cut. Cuba fell to the British in August after a protracted and costly siege at Havana. Where Vernon had failed, the modern Navy prevailed. On the other side of the world, Rear Admiral Samuel Cornish and Colonel William Draper launched a spectacular amphibious assault on Manila.

George Anson died in June 1762, Britain's second *annus mirabilis*. He was the architect of the worldwide assault on the Spanish empire, but he did not live long enough to hear of its success. The long war – known as the Seven Years War – came to an end. Britain was the dominant power in North America and India. She kept Canada, but returned Cuba, Manila, Martinique, Guadeloupe, Senegal and Belle Île. France returned Minorca and Spain ceded Florida to Britain. With a string of colonies from Barbados to Labrador Britain was the master of America. She was a global imperial power.

By the end of the war the Royal Navy had 141 ships of the line. Of these thirty-seven were 74s and thirty 64s. Anson's new ships were at the heart of the Navy. And so too was the ethos he instilled in officers and men. Outstanding seamanship had earned Hawke a brilliant victory on 'that dark November day'. The Navy was not just capable of stunning fleet engagements, such as Lagos and Quiberon. It could mount blockades for years on end. It could fight in uncharted waters, such as the St Lawrence, Cuba and the Philippines. It could launch operations simultaneously around the world, while still guarding home waters. Most importantly it had mastered the art of amphibious operations in partnership with the army. French and Spanish colonies and bases in Canada, the West Indies, Europe and Africa had fallen victim to this devastating kind of raid. Behind the thrill of victory lay years of preparation. The British fleet was the best-drilled, -supplied and -administered on the globe.

In the peace that followed Britain was prepared to exert her naval power whenever occasion demanded it. Her rivals had good reason to fear this force. Colonial disputes in Honduras, the Turks Islands, the Gambia and the Newfoundland fisheries were settled by ships of the Royal Navy. In 1770 Lord Hawke, by then First Lord of the Admiralty, ordered the mobilisation of the fleet. The reason was the expulsion of the British garrison on the Falkland Islands by the Spanish. Spain got the support of France, which was spoiling for revenge after the humiliations of the Seven Years War. Merely to mobilise the fleet, however, was enough on its own to force Spain and France to back down. In 1772 Denmark was humiliated by a show of naval power when George III's sister, the queen of Denmark, was charged with treason over an adulterous affair.

It was a lonely business, however, ruling the waves. Now that North America was, in the main, part of a British empire, continental European could be ignored. France had been royally humiliated; resentment burnt in the hearts of all patriotic Frenchmen. The price to pay for the glories of a transatlantic empire was eternal watchfulness on the high seas and a commitment to match the combined strength of the French and Spanish navies. It enraged people all over Europe. If France aspired to universal monarchy on land, Britain was becoming the bully boy of the high seas.

But few really minded in the victor's camp. It was as though the British Isles had detached themselves from the shackles of Europe, free now to pursue dreams of empire. The mood was fully shared by George III. He declared that he gloried in the name of Briton. Unlike his predecessors he had no strong emotional ties to Hanover and continental politics. On the contrary, he was schooled in the ways of Bolingbroke and the Tories, and all that implied in terms of colonial and naval ambitions. Britain, opined Frederick the Great, 'is not interested in anything but naval dominance and her possessions in America ... and ... [will] not pay any attention to Continental European affairs.'[9]

William Pitt was ennobled as earl of Chatham. It was an appropriate choice. Chatham dockyard was one of the wonders of the world. It symbolised the global power of Britain in the eighteenth century. In 1759 the keel of a new ship was laid down at Chatham. The timbers of 6,000 oak, elm, pine and fir trees were used to construct the rest of the ship. After six years of work HMS *Victory* was launched. Before the Industrial Revolution, the Royal Navy's dockyards were the largest and most technically advanced centres in Europe. At the start of the century Daniel Defoe marvelled at the huge buildings at Chatham, its 'great and extensive works', and the 'streets' of warehouses that contained the 'naval treasures' of Britain.

Later in the century one writer described the majesty of Chatham: 'There are large storehouses, one of which is six hundred and sixty-three feet long, and work-rooms, which by their spaciousness, conveys to us a magnificent idea of their vast contents, and the extensive works carried on within them.'[10] People were astonished by the sheer scale of Chatham and writers enjoyed dwelling on the statistics: the sail loft was 209 feet in length, the mast house 263, the rope house 1,140; the smiths shop – where the gigantic anchors were made – had twenty-one fires; there were four deep docks and six slipways 'on which new ships are constantly building'. There was nothing like it in the world.

Equipment, material and victuals that started life at Chatham or one of the other naval bases sustained a fleet that operated around the world. The store establishment was the foundation of the Navy's global reach. It was industrial in scale in an age before industry. The French ambassador was taken on a tour of the yards at Chatham to impress upon him the dangers of taking on so vast a naval power.

PART 10: THE ART OF THE ADMIRAL

CHAPTER 31

THE SCIENCE OF WAR
1772–1779

... the first and greatest sea-officer the world has ever produced.

Nelson on Lord Howe

America. The very name conjured magic in the 1770s. The British were terrified of losing it; the French were convinced that without its colonies their enemy's economy and naval might would be destroyed for ever. From 1776 the French had been supplying the rebellious American colonists.

The stakes were as high as they could be in 1778. The French Toulon fleet of twelve ships of the line under Admiral Comte d'Estaing crossed the Atlantic in May. He was bound for New York, which was defended by a force of small ships commanded by Richard, Earl Howe. A month later Vice Admiral John Byron was dispatched in pursuit with thirteen battleships. Meanwhile the opposing sides were gearing up to contest for control of European waters.

The Royal Navy, led by Augustus Keppel, and the French navy under Comte d'Orvilliers met 150 miles west of Ushant on 27 July. Keppel's thirty ships of the line were more or less equal with d'Orvillier's twenty-nine. Both fleets manoeuvred through heavy squalls until battle became inevitable.

Victory for either side would have had a major impact on the revolt in the colonies, but in poor weather and with near-equal fleets the outcome was always likely to be indecisive. And so it was – but there were lessons for the future. One side got into disarray and became divided when communications broke down. The other manoeuvred markedly better, keeping the fleet together throughout with clear signals, and outgunned its opponent.

'The French behaved more like seamen, and more officerlike than was imagined they would do,' commented a lieutenant on Keppel's flagship, HMS *Victory*, 'their ships were in very high order, well managed, well rigged and ... much more attentive to order than our own.'[1]

It came as the rudest of shocks that the French should outpace the Royal Navy in signalling, fleet tactics, mobility, discipline and gunnery. British tacticians pointed out one glimmer of silver in the lining of a dark cloud: the French had not possessed the killer instinct to finish off Keppel's fleet.

Cue a bout of national soul-searching. Cue disarray and conflict within the Navy. Articles in the newspapers accused the second in command, Sir Hugh Palliser, of ignoring Keppel's signals. Palliser demanded that Keppel sign a letter praising and exonerating him. Keppel refused. So Palliser wanted Keppel court-martialled for acting in a manner unbecoming an officer and leaving the battle with undue haste. It degenerated into a very eighteenth-century squabble. Keppel sat in parliament as a member opposed to the government of Lord North. Palliser was an MP as well, but he sat on the other side of the House and served on the Board of Admiralty. Their dispute dragged officers, MPS and peers into a tangle of conflicting interests, patronage and politics.

Keppel was acquitted; then Palliser demanded a court martial for himself. He was acquitted too. The courts martial and attendant political storm tore open fault lines in the Navy and sent morale plunging. George Rodney, an unemployed admiral, wrote that the sorry affair 'has almost ruined the Navy. Discipline in a very great measure is lost, and that eager willingness of executing orders ... is turned into neglect; and officers presume to find fault and think, when their duty is implicit obedience. Faction and party [are] ... predominant in our Navy.'[2]

The dispute detracted from the real issue. It was an act of almost criminal folly to detach the squadron under Byron, for it reduced the Navy to parity with the enemy and prevented it from overwhelming and destroying the French fleet at the very outset of the war. As it was Byron achieved nothing in a fruitless cruise in the expanse of the western Atlantic and the Navy conceded control of home waters. Britain had been at its strongest in 1747 and again between 1759 and 1762, when the Western Squadron had kept the French fleet in Brest.

Now in 1778 all the lessons taught by Anson and Hawke had been forgotten. The Navy was overstretched, with ships scattered around the world in the defence of empire rather than where they would have been most useful, European waters. It was also under-drilled. The French had spent the peace developing their fleet and learning the arts of battle manoeuvres. Britain had no ally on the Continent to divert her enemies and too few ships to dictate terms to her European enemies.

As a result, in 1779, the unthinkable happened. A joint Franco-Spanish fleet entered the Channel with the goal of capturing Portsmouth. For the first time since the Battle of Beachy Head in 1690 the Royal Navy was outnumbered in Europe. There were thirty-nine ships of the line against an invading fleet of sixty-six. The British Channel Fleet was entrusted to the affable, laid-back and elderly Admiral Sir Charles Hardy. According to his chief of staff, Richard Kempenfelt, Hardy was reluctant to manoeuvre his fleet.

Kempenfelt had some very advanced theoretical notions about deploying a battlefleet.[3] He believed that the French had mastered the science of naval war. It was evident from the Battle of Ushant that French officers had spent the peace studying fleet tactics in academies. They had developed 'regular rules' for manoeuvring their fleet. Kempenfelt wanted to bring the same scientific approach to the Royal Navy. He believed that a fleet should be commanded and controlled from the centre, so that it manoeuvred in unison like soldiers on a parade ground.

But in that summer, with a large enemy fleet approaching, nothing was going right. Even the simplest fleet drill ended in chaos, with the line of battle scattered about higgledy-piggledy. It took a whole day for the fleet to execute the manoeuvre that took them from line ahead to line abreast. At another time Kempenfelt signalled the ships to return their weekly accounts to the flagship. What he really wanted was to order the fleet to manoeuvre by division, but he had muddled up the coloured flags.

It was a far cry from the Navy of Anson or Hawke. The Navy's blushes were spared because the enemy fleet was in even worse trouble. The Spanish were under-provisioned and did not know the Channel. The French ships were unsanitary; when illness swept through their fleet it killed or incapacitated 8,000 sailors. Hardy declined the opportunity to attack a larger fleet that was in disarray, perhaps for the best.

Kempenfelt was a proponent of the aggressive approach. Conventional thinking held that a small fleet could never prevail against a larger in a line engagement. In Kempenfelt's view, however, a creative admiral in command of an inferior force should wait and watch for a favourable opportunity to attack the weak point of his enemy's line. If the chance did not present itself he should gain the upper hand by skilful manoeuvres, endeavouring to keep '[the enemy] at bay, and prevent his attempting to execute anything but at risk and hazard; to command their attention, and oblige them to think of nothing but being on guard against your attack'.[4]

That kind of maritime chess was the dream of every admiral. To accomplish it he would need absolute control over his fleet, secured through long drills, crystal-clear signals and assured leadership. In addition he would have to anticipate every eventuality of a battle fought on the capricious waves and devise a series of signals to direct his fleet at speed during the confusion of a fleet engagement.

Manoeuvring a fleet of sailing ships was one of the hardest problems for the human mind. No ship in a fleet could sail at the same speed or manoeuvre in quite the same way as another. In order for a fleet to change direction it would have to open up so as to give each ship the room it needed to tack or wear, or else they must run foul of each other. In the face of an enemy this would spell disaster as the fleet became dispersed over a vast expanse of ocean. Even keeping a fleet in line – fundamental to naval warfare – bristled with snags. Fast ships had to back sails to slow down; slower vessels had to try and keep up. If this did not happen then a line would bunch at some points and gaps would open up elsewhere, inviting an enemy counter. Sailing in any kind of formation – and this is particularly true of gigantic battleships – involved constant adjustments and never-ending attention in all kinds of weather conditions.[5]

Commanding a diverse assortment of hulking warships on the capricious waves was one thing. Honing it into a fighting force and bringing it into battle was quite another.

In the second half of the eighteenth century battle tactics, manoeuvres and signalling were in a state of fast evolution. Most admirals were competent officers but mediocre tacticians and leaders of men. Part 10 deals with the art of admiralship in the second half of the eighteenth century, told chiefly through the lives and experiences of three British admirals. In their careers Richard Howe, George Rodney and Samuel Hood reached back to the Navy of Vernon, Anson and Hawke and left their mark on the Navy of Nelson.[6]

Early in his career Richard, Earl Howe, was marked for high command. When the ship he commanded fired the first shots of the Seven Years War in the St Lawrence River in 1755 he was twenty-nine years old and had served in the southern Atlantic, the West Indies, the North Sea, the west coast of Africa and Canada. He had achieved the rank of flag captain at the tender age of twenty-two. In the Seven Years War he served under Boscawen and Hawke and memorably led the chase at the Battle of Quiberon Bay. He was a fighting officer through and through; but he was emerging as a tactician.

This was displayed during an assault on the fortress of Île d'Aix off Rochefort back in 1757. The fort seemed impregnable to attack from the sea. It contained many more guns than a British ship. Howe though it could be taken. He ordered every man to lie down on deck, save the pilot, a helmsman and himself, then guided *Magnanime* under heavy fire until it was forty yards away. He dropped anchor. Then *Magnanime* opened fire. The psychological effect on the garrison was worth more than the actual bombardment, which could never hope to seriously damage the fort. The French gunners were spooked by a ship that would sail so close and so silently. When at last the ghostly ship's cannon roared out the fire was concentrated. It seemed worse than it was. The enemy fled and the fort fell. Howe showed how bravura tactics, mind games and concentrated fire could overcome numerical disadvantages.

The young commodore was emerging as a figure of substance in the Navy. Determined to reform the service, he started on his own ship. At this time captains were given wide autonomy to run their ships as they chose. As the Navy swelled in size officers grew ever more distanced from their men and the petty officers. This was a recipe for discontent, poor hygiene, bullying and ill-discipline. It wrecked the code of teamwork and mutual support upon which the Navy depended. Vice Admiral Thomas Smith promoted a divisional system in his ships, by which the crew was divided into teams, each with a midshipman or warrant officer in charge. Officers came to know their men by name and character. Good officers knew that a ship could not be governed by discipline alone; the men needed to be treated fairly and their grievances attended to. They needed incentives more than coercion. Howe seized on the rudiments of this system. He wrote an order book for *Magnanime*. It was displayed on the ship for all to see and established the duties of his lieutenants, warrant officers and midshipmen, especially their obligations to oversee and lead the crew. The importance of the divisional system to the long term success of the Navy cannot be stated too highly. Victory depended upon the bonds of trust established within ships at all levels. The vitality of the Navy's teamwork and leadership was demonstrated most clearly in perilous situations, such as the Battle of Quiberon Bay and the navigation of the Old Bahama Channel. In time it would help give the service the edge over its rivals.

Richard Howe joined a merchant ship when he was nine and the Royal Navy when he was thirteen. To the end of his days his lack of formal education left its mark on his prose style, which was as clear and elegant as pea soup. His premature introduction to life on the ocean waves also left him withdrawn and somewhat odd in manner. Indeed, Howe's biography highlights a problem for the Navy. Bringing young boys into ships fitted them to be sailors. It did, however, stunt the development of other qualities. British officers were not renowned for their social polish or intellectual refinement. The system made for some excellent masters, lieutenants and captains – men who, whatever their social origins, had spent their adolescence clambering up rigging, tying knots, reefing, splicing, hauling and immersing themselves in practical seamanship. But it left the emergence of astute tacticians entirely to chance. Admirals who could think in broad strategic terms were thin on the ground. As Howe told George III many years later, the British officer's unparalleled brilliance at seamanship had been earned at the expense of other skills necessary for an admiral – literacy, mathematics, languages, political acumen and broader military knowledge.

Howe was one young officer determined to overcome the deficiencies in his education. In 1756 he penned an essay on methods of signalling. He put his theories into practice while commanding the blockade of Rochefort between 1760 and 1762.

Howe set his mind to the line of battle. Conventional wisdom held that unless one side possessed numerical advantage, or one admiral made a mistake, the normal outcome of a line battle was stalemate. But Howe believed that if a naval commander was creative enough he could force a result against an equal, or even superior, opponent by decisive and unconventional action. His eleven-ship squadron had two 90-gun ships and his flagship was one of the new, more mobile 74s. In the event of a battle with a superior foe, Howe would place the big hitters at the extremities of the line, rather than the centre as was normal. By concentrating his fire in a part of the enemy line unanticipated by his opposite number he could – as at the Île d'Aix – gain a psychological advantage through shock and awe. By acting fast and unexpectedly he could reverse the disparity of firepower, break an enemy line and induce panic. And if they were outnumbered Howe told his captains that stealth and cunning would aid their cause: 'I may perhaps attempt by studied delays to conceal from them my purpose of bringing them to action, until later in the day, and that opportunity offers of doing it to more advantage.'[7]

This was a game of naval chess of a highly sophisticated and aggressive variety. That is what makes Howe an innovative thinker at this stage. He was prepared to break with customary ideas and experiment. Naval warfare was, for him, a long game.

Howe lost his chance to prove his theories when peace came. The Admiralty did not have much time for tactical experiments or complex manoeuvres – unlike the French, who used the peace to modernise their navy. Over seven months in 1772, for instance, the French navy's

'Evolutionary Squadron' practised manoeuvres at sea. Because the Royal
Navy had no such opportunity for drilling the fleet its admirals and captains were stale after long periods of peace. In 1739 and again in 1755 the
Royal Navy began a war well below par. It failed to win the first fleet battles of three major wars – the battles of Toulon, Minorca and Ushant – not
least because fleet cohesion was impossible to achieve without practice
and experience.* Even more damagingly, it did not have a system that
could retain the best and brightest officers during intervals of peace and
keep their skills finely honed.

The upward-bound elevator of promotion also stalled, leaving many
a midshipman craving a lieutenancy, ageing lieutenants pining for captaincy and captains despairing of ever receiving their flag. Some of these
officers drifted into the merchant navy or joined a foreign navy. Those
who stayed in the Navy grew old together. It took years of conflict before
the bright young things jostled their way to the top and infused the service with energy. For all the Navy's strength and resources in the eighteenth century, this was its Achilles heel.

Howe served as Treasurer of the Navy Board, and would have been
commander-in-chief in the Mediterranean if the Falklands crisis had escalated. In the absence of naval command in the mid-1760s and early 1770s
he, like many a talented officer of his generation, turned to other pursuits.
His choice was politics. Meanwhile his tactical and seafaring abilities were
allowed to stagnate. In 1775 his chance came again. He was named as
commander-in-chief in North America. He arrived in New York in July
1776 just after the Declaration of Independence was signed.

Howe had the command he craved. It came in the most trying of circumstances. The Admiralty could not spare a single ship of the line for
the naval effort in the War of American Independence. Howe was sent
to America with orders to prosecute the war as aggressively as possible,
but also with powers to negotiate. He was charged with blockading the
seaboard of the rebellious colonies, but also with supporting the army –
led, as it happens, by his younger brother, Sir William Howe. Which of
these aims were to take priority was left to Admiral Howe. He counted
as a friend the most renowned of campaigners for American unity and
independence, Benjamin Franklin. The admiral was predisposed to a negotiated settlement.

Howe at last had the chance to implement some of the reforms he had

---

* Before the Battle of Toulon there had been twenty-six years of peace, before Minorca
nine, and before Ushant nineteen.

begun twenty years before. In 1776 he issued 'Instructions and Standing Orders for the General Government and Discipline of Ships of War'. According to Howe's new orders, a ship's company was to be divided into three, with a lieutenant in charge of each, and subdivided into squads led by midshipmen, 'who are respectively to be responsible for the good order and discipline of the men entrusted to their care'.[8] Throughout the American War naval discipline improved notably. In large part this was because the war placed unprecedented strain upon the Navy. Numbers of seamen peaked at a whopping 105,000. This was a burden too great for the maritime community. So thousands of unsuitable landsmen – commonly the dregs of society – were sent out to man the fleets. These unhappy men had to be managed more effectively than the hardened professionals. Dividing the crew into manageable teams watched over by officers meant that landsmen could be trained quickly and the ship worked efficiently.

Care for the great mass of sailors was one crucial aspect of the art of the admiral. Howe's detailed instructions regarding the management of ships under his command freed his men from the negligence of their captains and the capricious brutality of the bosun and his mates. The three-watch system gave sailors longer to sleep or relax between periods on duty. The result of these changes was that 'the men were kept in better temper; and were less harassed and fatigued in their spirits, as well as in their bodies'.[9]

Howe also dispensed with the Admiralty's permanent fighting instructions, which were old-fashioned and inflexible, and distributed his own signal book. It was 'one of the most important documents in the whole history of naval tactics'.[10] Compared to earlier efforts it was commendably logical and concise. Each page was divided into three neat columns: first, the signal number; second, the colour and design of the flag; and third, the position from which the flag would be flown. To make his intentions crystal clear, Howe would have mobile frigates repeat his signals so they could be seen throughout the line. He also designed a system of light signals for frigates on night reconnaissance duty that would be visible to their own fleet, not the enemy. Howe's signal book was accompanied by another book, one of explanatory instructions to help his captains understand his system. The most popular new signal, no doubt, was: 'There will be time for the men to dine [before battle]'.

Throughout his time in American waters, Richard Howe drilled his fleet, consulted his officers and put his mind to constructing an all-embracing tactical system. Howe was at the height of his powers and creativity. He thought through every scenario he might face and issued instructions to his captains accordingly. What Howe lacked was a major maritime war to test his theories.

Things started well enough in 1776. New York was taken in a well-conducted amphibious operation. But by 1777 he was struggling. With seventy ships he had to support his brother's forces, blockade the entire east coast of America and defend strategic locations. Howe did manage to force the Delaware and land troops in a position where they could take Philadelphia, but it made little difference to the war, especially after the American victory at Saratoga. The British were on the defensive.

Then, in 1778, the French entered the fray. Howe got news that the twelve battleships under Admiral Charles Hector d'Estaing that had caused such a flurry in Britain before the Battle of Ushant were heading for America. Howe calculated they would make for New York. He was correct. He was also outnumbered.

This was a situation for which Howe had planned as a young officer. Only by superior tactics could he defend the British position in America. He stationed frigates in the Atlantic. He then positioned his main force inside Sandy Hook, a sand spit projecting from New Jersey into Lower New York Bay. He deployed his ships perfectly. If the large French ships attempted to approach New York they would be raked by the British ships protected behind the bar. D'Estaing waited off New York for eleven days. Then he disappeared. The game was afoot.

Once again Howe read d'Estaing and divined that his next destination was Rhode Island, where the British were under siege. Howe raced to Point Judith, inviting the French admiral to chase him. To the anger of the Americans, who needed naval support, d'Estaing fell for the bait. Howe outmanoeuvred his opponent in a merry dance. Both fleets were then damaged in a storm. Howe returned to New York, d'Estaing to Boston. When the French once again set out for Rhode Island Howe was ready for them.

Howe had reversed the enemy's advantage. Now he was the pursuer; d'Estaing fled for Boston, where he remained for the winter. Howe handed over his command and returned to a Britain beset by invasion fears and plunged into gloom by the failure of the Navy after the Battle of Ushant. The American colonies were as good as lost thanks, in large measure, to the inability on the part of the British to prevent armaments being taken across the Atlantic from France. The country needed a Hawke or an Anson with the strategic sense and application to blockade France. Instead it got bickering naval officers and a service riven along deep political fault lines.

Howe was palpably the man for the occasion. He was offered the post of commander-in-chief in the Channel, but he would only accept this vital post if he was made Treasurer of the Navy and his brother appointed Secretary of State for the American colonies. The price was absurdly high. Howe, the best admiral in the Navy, went into retirement at the age of fifty-two. And, as we have seen, the amiable and ineffective Charles Hardy took over the defence of the realm.

America was effectively lost, but the government was still preoccupied with the Americas. Attention switched to the West Indies. At the end of 1779 a fleet of eighteen ships of the line was dispatched to relieve Gibraltar under Admiral George Brydges Rodney. The majority of the fleet was to return to Britain, while Rodney would cross the Atlantic with four battleships and take over command of the West Indies squadron.

CHAPTER 32

TACTICS
1779–1782

My eye on them had more dread than the enemy's fire, and
they knew it would be more fatal.[1]

Admiral Rodney, speaking about his captains

Rodney was eight years older than Howe. Both had roughly comparable careers. Rodney was captain of HMS *Eagle* at the Second Battle of Finisterre and, like Howe, distinguished himself as a bold young fighting officer in the Seven Years War. He led superb amphibious operations against Le Havre, Martinique, St Lucia, Grenada and St Vincent. Like Howe he had a brilliant record and a questing tactical mind, but he besmirched it with a tyrannical style of leadership, notorious dishonesty when it came to money, and ruinously expensive addictions to gambling and politics.

Rodney managed to dodge his creditors by taking the post of commander of the Jamaica Station. But he had to come home eventually. In 1774 he was driven into exile in France to avoid debtors' gaol. Four years later, when Britain and France declared war, Rodney had to return home, but in order to do so he had to claim his back pay as rear admiral to satisfy his ravenous creditors. The Admiralty, however, would not pay him until an ugly dispute over embezzled funds was resolved. In the end his passage home was smoothed by a generous gift from a French duke.

Rodney's fleet was state-of-the-art. Warships had always suffered from prolonged service in distant waters where there were no facilities for dry-docking. Hulls were weakened by shipworm and speed was reduced over the course of a cruise by the build-up of weeds and barnacles. The solution was to sheathe hulls in copper.

Rodney's squadron consisted entirely of copper-bottomed ships. Not only were the ships more durable, but the copper sheaths considerably increased their speed. Now the biggest, most lumbering three-decker in the Royal Navy could outpace the fastest ship in its enemies' fleets. The possibilities for battle strategy and manoeuvres were therefore endless.

The first part of Rodney's command was brilliantly executed. Gibraltar was under prolonged siege from the Spanish army and needed frequent resupply. Rodney escorted the convoy that relieved Gibraltar. Shortly after he captured sixteen ships from a Spanish convoy. Then, off St Vincent on the afternoon of 16 January, a Spanish squadron of eleven ships of the line and two frigates was sighted. Rodney ordered an immediate chase. It was a risky action, in darkness on a lee shore. By midnight six Spanish ships had been captured and one had blown up. Rodney acted with resolution and aggression, qualities that had earned his appointment in the first place. 'To bring an enemy to action, copper bottom ships are absolutely necessary,'[2] he concluded. The new technology proved its worth in the Moonlight Battle, as it was called.

Rodney arrived at St Lucia in late March and joined forces with Rear Admirals Sir Hyde Parker and Joshua Rowley, bringing British strength in the region to twenty-one battleships. Shortly after, a French force consisting of twenty-three ships of the line under the Comte de Guichen arrived off Martinique with the intention of taking British islands. The two forces sighted each other on 16 April on the leeward side of Martinique. Rodney gave chase and the next morning he had the weather gage. At 04.30 he signalled for line ahead on the starboard tack. At 06.45 he ran up a flag that was half blue and half yellow: the signal that the fleet was to attack de Guichen's rear.

De Guichen was no fool and realised that Rodney was concentrating forces on his rear. He wore his fleet northward, avoiding the British ships. Rodney once more had to manoeuvre for advantage. At 10.00 the fleets were on parallel courses heading in opposing directions. Rodney signalled for the fleet to wear so as to come into the same course as the French, due north. Now the time was ripe for an attack.

Rodney had brilliantly executed his fleet manoeuvres since the early hours of the morning and the French were in disarray – strung out in a long line. At 11.00 he signalled for his fleet to prepare for battle and close in on the French. At 11.50 the vanguard of the British line was opposite de Guichen's central division. Rodney raised the flag that corresponded to Article 21 of his instructions: every ship was to make for her opposing number in the French line. At 11.55 he signalled 'Engage', then 'Come to close engagement'.

Rodney had the French exactly where he wanted them. He was attacking the rear and centre of a straggling French line, twenty of his ships concentrated against twelve. But it was not so clear-cut to his officers. The captains in the van took the order to engage their opposite number to mean that the first ship in the British vanguard should attack the first ship in the French line, and so on. What Rodney really meant was that the British ships should head due west and attack the French ship opposite them *at that moment*. Captain Robert Carkett, in the leading ship, misunderstood, and chased north to engage the head of the enemy line, which was a long way off. He was followed by the second in line and the commander of the van squadron, Hyde Parker, who was so certain he was following Rodney's instructions that he rebuked those captains who had divined their admiral's real intentions.

Meanwhile Rodney cut through the enemy line. His flagship *Sandwich* (90) was alone and took the thunder of the French flagship and two other battleships. By the end of the battle *Sandwich* had taken seventy shots in her hull and had suffered severe damage to her masts and rigging; she had replied with 3,260 shots. While Rodney was heavily engaged, Rowley's rear division wore out of line, headed south, and attacked the French rear division.

As a result Rodney was left abandoned. To say he was furious would be an understatement. Had the vanguard attacked where he wished and the rear supported *Sandwich* the French would have been annihilated. It would have been one of the greatest victories in the history of the Royal Navy.

The whole debacle illustrates the problems admirals faced with co-ordinating a complicated plan of attack. Parker and the ships in the van had acknowledged the signal ordering an attack on the rear. But that was hours earlier and they must have thought that subsequent manoeuvres had cancelled out the earlier instruction. Rodney had not repeated the signal. When they attacked they did so in the traditional manner – the vanguard's job was to contain the enemy vanguard so that it did not double the British line. Those captains could not be blamed for their inability to read Rodney's mind and glimpse his strategic vision.

But blame them Rodney most assuredly did. He raged at 'the dastardly behaviour of a fleet which called themselves British'.[3] There were too many 'delinquents' who were happy to disgrace their admiral even at the expense of victory, he said, for him to regain control during the battle. He called Parker 'a dangerous man with a very bad temper', who was politically suspect, capable of anything 'if he thinks he is within the pale of barely doing his duty' and who was guilty on 17 April of 'palpable disobedience of signals'. Rodney's attack on his rear admiral, Joshua Rowley, summed up his attitude to subordinates in general: 'I don't know which is of the greatest detriment to a State, a designing man or a man without abilities entrusted with command. Had not Mr Rowley presumed to think, when his duty was only obedience, the whole French rear and the centre had certainly been taken.'

Rodney's flag captain, Walter Young, was fully attuned to the revolution in tactics that Howe and others were bringing about. Richard Kempenfelt was much influenced by Howe, and he had issued a new book of signals for the Channel Fleet. This was sent out to Rodney in the West Indies but, as Captain Young reported to the Admiralty, 'I am apprehensive these are books he will pay little attention to ... they may never be looked at or studied.'[4]

But Rodney's failure to mug up on complex modern signals was not the cause of his failure. Indeed, his attempt to control the Battle of Martinique from the centre by signals was at the heart of his problems. The battle occurred little more than two weeks after Rodney arrived on station. He did not know his fleet and they did not know him. Signals only really worked if they directed captains to implement actions already planned. Rodney had a truly original plan, but he kept his own counsel. He did not like captains who thought for themselves, only those who obeyed without troubling their brains. He was an authoritarian leader who aimed to browbeat his captains into compliance.

After the failure of the Battle of Martinique Rodney drilled his fleet. He also developed a new plan. On a given signal the three-deckers and large ships would draw out of their places and regroup at the head of the line. By this he intended to turn his line of battle into a battering ram to smash through the enemy line. But he was cheated of another chance to fight that year. In September he took his fleet to New York to avoid the hurricane season. There his disgraceful behaviour continued. Rodney had always advocated a single command structure for the various Navy stations in North American waters. He had a funny way of realising it. Once in New York he claimed superior rank over the local commander-in-chief, Vice Admiral Mariot Arbuthnot. Rodney seized a share of Arbuthnot's prize money and appointed his followers to captain ships in the American squadron.

Rodney was by now the most unpopular man in the Navy. No one wanted to serve under such a tyrant. In 1781 Lord Sandwich, the First Lord of the Admiralty, looked for an admiral to send as second in command to Rodney. All his candidates refused. And so he turned to Samuel Hood.

'They might as well have sent me an old apple-woman,' Rodney grumbled.[5] Hood was an odd choice. He was fifty-seven and his career had entered the doldrums a long time before. Hood – in contrast to Howe, Rodney and most officers – had gone to sea at the advanced age of sixteen. As a consequence he was better educated than most officers. His career started well. He had excellent mentors as a young officer in the 1740s and developed good connections with members of the government. All seemed to bid fair. Like Howe and Rodney he distinguished himself as an aggressive young captain in the Seven Years War. As captain of *Antelope* (50) he chased and drove onto the rocks a French ship of equal size. Most notably he captured the French frigate *Bellona* after a running battle. But by the 1770s all his political patrons were either dead or out of office; his career stalled.

Hood became captain of the Portsmouth guardship. In 1776 he left the sea and took the posts of Admiralty Commissioner at Portsmouth and Governor of the Naval Academy. He was an extremely efficient naval administrator. During the mobilisation of 1778 George III visited Portsmouth and was impressed at the Commissioner's energy and knowledge about naval matters.

If Hood lacked family connections and political allies he possessed charm and ambition. By sheer hard work he gained the favour of the king. But the role of commissioner was supposed to mark an honourable end to a quiet career. Hood managed, however, to persuade Sandwich that he would not be precluded from promotion. He had done enough to keep his hand in – impressing the king revived his prospects. His chance came at an age when any other officer with a similar record might have settled for tranquil retirement. Hood's career, however, was all before him.

Samuel Hood knew Rodney of old. In 1743 Hood had been midshipman on Captain Rodney's *Ludlow Castle* and in 1759 assisted Rodney in the assault on Le Havre. He knew what was in store for him. Hood set out for the West Indies on the recently coppered *Barfleur* (90).

After years of waiting, Hood's first year as an admiral was a bitter disappointment. The problems started early on. They stemmed from the naval dimension of the American War of Independence. Britain's strategy, as in previous wars, depended upon asserting her belligerent rights in blockading France and America. Essential to this was stopping and searching neutral ships bound for enemy ports and colonies. In particular, the Navy had to stop naval supplies reaching France from the Baltic and arms getting to the rebellious American colonies. In the Seven Years War, Britain had been strong enough to enforce her rights, but now her heavy handedness united the maritime powers against her. Catherine the Great of Russia formed a League of Armed Neutrality in 1780 with Denmark,

Sweden, Prussia, the Holy Roman Empire, Portugal, the Kingdom of the Two Sicilies and the Ottoman Empire to assert the right of free commerce for neutral countries.

Britain was not in a position to defy Europe. But the actions of the Netherlands were another matter. The Dutch colony of St Eustatius in the Caribbean was used as a base to sell arms to the American rebels. By the Treaty of Westminster of 1674 Britain conceded the Dutch the right to trade naval stores freely, even during war. In 1779 the British government repudiated the treaty and began to arrest Dutch ships taking items to French ports. The Dutch responded by organising convoys, but the Royal Navy used force to capture the merchant vessels. The Dutch were enraged and turned to the League of Armed Neutrality for help. Britain declared war.

This was where Rodney came into it. When Rodney heard that the Fourth Anglo-Dutch War had begun he wasted little time in looting the immensely wealthy island of St Eustatius. Throughout his career Rodney was torn between his desire to be a great admiral and his lust for money. The Caribbean was his sweetshop.

It was a fatal diversion. While Rodney was gorging on the wealth of the Dutch island, Hood was dispatched to Martinique. He wanted to stay to windward to ambush reinforcements from Europe. Rodney moved him to leeward to blockade the island to prevent French ships intercepting his booty as it left St Eustatius for Britain. Hence, when the French admiral François de Grasse arrived with twenty ships of the line Hood could not bring him to battle. He was furious that Rodney's greed had deprived him of a fight, but he overlooked his own inexperience. He had not heeded Rodney's order to send one ship at a time to St Lucia for supplies, so that by the time de Grasse appeared his crews were in poor shape.

Rodney and Hood failed to stop de Grasse taking Tobago. The large French fleet was a source of great danger to the British Empire, but not much was done about it. This turned out to be a terrible mistake.

Rodney went home in July and dispatched Hood with fourteen battleships to reinforce Admiral Thomas Graves at New York. Everyone expected de Grasse to return home, so it came as a major shock for Graves when Hood appeared warning him that the French West Indies fleet was bound for Chesapeake Bay. It was in the bay, at Yorktown, that General Cornwallis's army was being besieged by George Washington. Graves did not have enough ships ready. Rodney and Hood are to blame for not forewarning him. Graves's five available battleships joined Hood's squadron and they arrived at the entrance to Chesapeake Bay at dawn on 5 September.

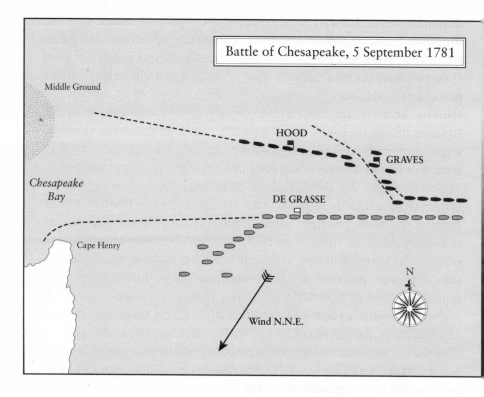

De Grasse used the tide to bring out his fleet. Samuel Hood was an eager analyst of battle tactics. Later he said he would have attacked and overwhelmed the French van as it exited the bay. But Graves suddenly realised he was outnumbered and spent a long time forming a line of battle. By afternoon the two fleets were in line ahead. But the lines were not parallel. The British were at an angle, with the vanguard converging with the head of the French fleet and the centre and rear following in a slanting line. At 16.00 the British van engaged the leading four ships of the French line. The British rear, however, led by Hood, was too far to larboard and out of range. Graves gave two signals simultaneously: one for line ahead, the other for close action.

Graves wanted his ships to turn to starboard simultaneously and bear down individually on the enemy line. Hood saw Graves's signals as contradictory. 'Close action' would mean abandoning line ahead to turn and directly attack the French. He decided that the order to maintain the line took precedence. And so Hood's rear division followed in the wake of the leading ships and did not get into battle at all. As at the Battle of Martinique, confusing signals and poor communication led to failure.

Both these battles illuminate a serious flaw in the Royal Navy. The

Admiralty took a laissez-faire view of tactics. Admirals were expected to introduce their own signals and instructions to the squadrons under their command. At its best this allowed dynamic admirals to weld together a close-knit team of captains well versed in tactics and aware of each other's needs and capabilities. It was a face-to-face concept of leadership and training, whereby officers learnt what to do long before a battle, obviating the need for complex signals in the heat of the moment. But it meant that a squadron was bound to be at its weakest when a new admiral arrived on station or two squadrons joined forces.

Graves simply did not have time to exercise his fleet or explain his system of signals to the new captains. It was a recipe for disaster. A large share of the blame must go to Hood, who was too inexperienced to dare to use his initiative. Hood knew this and he pre-empted blame by firing off some well-written letters home. One of his great gifts was as a politician; in modern parlance, he controlled the narrative. Blame was thrown onto Graves, whose reputation never recovered.

Graves returned to New York. The Franco-American forces took control of Chesapeake Bay, completing the encirclement of Cornwallis. By the time Graves returned with reinforcements Cornwallis had surrendered. It was a dreadful moment for the Navy: French control of the seas helped prise the last remnants of British force out of America.

The colonies were lost for good as a result of the Battle of Chesapeake Bay. The news of Graves and Hood's failure coincided with the death of the great Hawke. Horace Walpole made the connection: 'Lord Hawke is dead and does not seem to have bequeathed his mantle to anybody.'[6]

Hood had achieved nothing and he blamed his superiors for it. Rodney was due back to resume command, but until then Hood was in charge of the fleet and had a last chance to impress. He was not going to squander it. On the way back to the West Indies he drilled his ships continually and held conferences with the captains and lieutenants. He wrote bullishly to the Admiralty: 'I will seek and give battle to the Count de Grasse, be his numbers as they may.'[7]

His opportunity came when he discovered that de Grasse was at the British island of St Kitts, anchored at Frigate Bay with twenty-nine ships of the line. Hood's duty, as he saw it, was to save the colony. He discussed every aspect of his plan with his officers. His tactics were based on instructions issued by Howe for attacking an enemy's rear. Hood's squadron would launch a surprise attack under the cover of darkness on the morning of 24 January. The line would sail into the bay and one by one pummel the rearmost three ships.

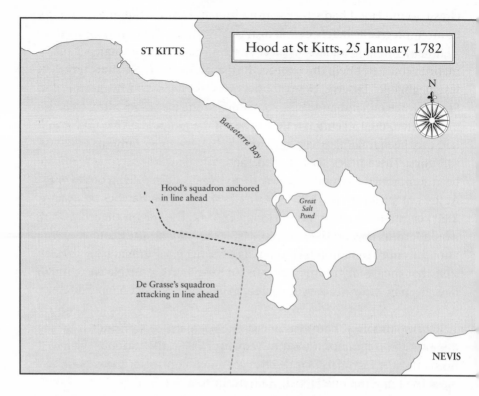

Such an attack relied on a well drilled and well briefed fleet. It miscarried, however, when the leading ship collided with a frigate. The surprise was ruined and de Grasse left his anchorage to annihilate the weaker enemy.

What happened next was one of the finest pieces of manoeuvring conducted by a British admiral.

Hood wrote that his plan relied on the skills and determination of his men. He never doubted them. He sent a frigate to transmit his instructions to every ship. The squadron made a feint, as if accepting de Grasse's offer of a battle, but then raced to Frigate Bay. They anchored in succession, the first ship as close as possible to a small spit of land called Green Point. The rest anchored in a line above an underwater sandbank. Hood calculated this bank could hold fourteen ships. The remainder anchored at a different angle where the water was shallower. Hood's ships were therefore anchored in a bent line, preventing the French ships re-entering the bay and cutting them off from their troops on St Kitts. On every ship, ropes (known as 'springs') were tied to the end of the anchor cable so that the ship could be swung at an angle, giving a greater arc for the broadsides. Having been lured out of Frigate Bay, de

Grasse found Hood had stolen it from him and the curved line proved to be an impregnable defence even against superior forces.

It was a brilliant, audacious piece of seamanship. Unfortunately Hood's marines could not help the besieged British garrison, so the strategic value was negligible. Indeed, Hood found himself in a trap with a powerful French force on land and thirty-two ships of the line blockading him.

But then, on 15 February, de Grasse awoke to find no clue that Hood had ever been in Frigate Bay, save for a line of guttering lanterns attached to buoys. Three times on the 14th the lieutenants of the squadron had been summoned to Hood's *Barfleur* to go through every detail of the plan. At the last meeting – at 21.00 – they had synchronised watches. At exactly 23.00 every ship's cable was cut and a lantern was left on the buoy so it would look as though the ships were still in place. According to one captain, the entire squadron 'sailed out in a line with so little noise or confusion that the enemy did not miss us for four hours after. Nothing could have been more fortunately executed, as not one accident happened from it.'

Rodney arrived at Barbados four days later. Predictably he was dissatisfied that Hood had not fought his way out, but in truth Hood had made his name at St Kitts. His manoeuvres were textbook stuff. It was a masterpiece in miniature. The French were stunned.

CHAPTER 33

BREAKING THE LINE
1782–1792

Hood's brilliance could not conceal the fact that the British were facing disaster in the West Indies. A convoy from France was on its way to reinforce de Grasse, bringing 9,000 troops for an assault on Jamaica. The convoy managed to evade Rodney and Hood and reach de Grasse at Fort Royal, Martinique.

On 8 April 1782 de Grasse, with thirty-six battleships and a huge troop convoy, slipped out. Rodney and Hood went in pursuit with their force of thirty-three ships. On the night of 11 April the French 74 *Zélé* collided with de Grasse's flagship *Ville de Paris* (104). Rodney sent four ships to

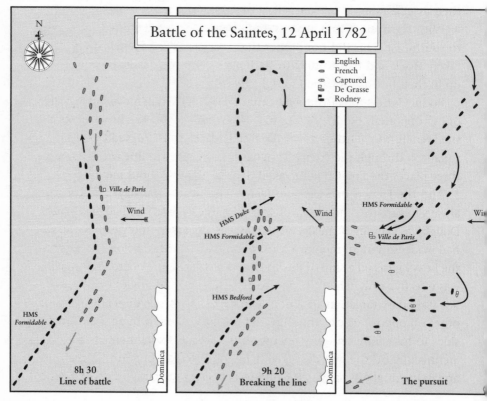

Battle of the Saintes, 12 April 1782

English
French
Captured
De Grasse
Rodney

Ville de Paris

Wind

HMS *Duke*
HMS *Formidable*

Wind

HMS *Formidable*

HMS *Formidable*

Ville de Paris

Wind

HMS *Bedford*

HMS
Formidable

Dominica

8h 30
Line of battle

Dominica

9h 20
Breaking the line

The pursuit

capture the hapless *Zélé* the next day, but de Grasse made the decision to form a line and head off the British predators. Rodney recalled the pursuing ships and formed his own line. The British were heading north and the French south between Guadeloupe and Dominica, near the islands called the Saintes. Rodney raised the signal for close action and altered course to starboard to get closer to the enemy.

HMS *Marlborough*, at the head of the British line, engaged the centre of the enemy line at 07.40. The two fleets passed each other on contrary tacks, exchanging broadsides as they went. They were so close that French sailors could hear orders being given on the opposing ships.

When the British vanguard passed the French rear, it continued north. Meanwhile de Grasse was wary that if his line continued southwards it would end up becalmed under the lee of Dominica. He had to do a U-turn and snake up northwards, parallel once more to the British and on the same course. At 08.15 he signalled for the fleet to wear and put itself on the same tack as the enemy. The signal was ignored. At 08.45 he signalled for his fleet to wear in succession. Once again his captains ignored him. They knew that to bring their ships round in the teeth of the British onslaught would present their fragile bows to the powerful broadsides of their assailants.

With the French line at sixes and sevens, the wind shifted from east to south-east. This did not bother the British, but the French ships were taken aback and had to turn to starboard to fill their sails. Gaps opened up in their line as they tried to right themselves.

Rodney's fleet took instant advantage. HMS *Duke* (90) moved to leeward of her opponent. Rodney's flagship, HMS *Formidable* (98), broke through the French line. Further down the line HMS *Bedford* (74) led Hood's rear squadron through the French vanguard. As the French line was broken in three places the English guns raked their enemies without mercy.

And the French had cause to fear English guns that day. Rodney was always fortunate in his chiefs of staff. In this campaign he had Sir Charles Douglas as captain of the fleet. Douglas was a naval gunnery expert and he had made important modifications to some of the ships. Before his reforms the heavy guns on a ship of the line had a restricted line of fire. A broadside was effective only when the gun barrels were at right angles to a more or less stationary target. In an action such as this, with two lines passing each other on opposite tacks, the ships did not have time to bring their broadsides to bear fully on every enemy ship. Douglas experimented with the architecture on the gun deck, removing obstructive supporting structures and fixing ringbolts bang in the middle between each gunport, so that guns could be secured at an angle. The arc of fire each gun could achieve was now 90°. That meant that a ship could attack several ships simultaneously or several ships could attack a single ship. Douglas also improved the guns themselves, making them safer and quicker to reload and fire.

In this battle, therefore, the French were astonished that British ships were able to pour two broadsides into them before they were able to answer with one. And when the British crashed through the enemy line their firepower was devastating. We only know for sure that *Formidable* (90), *Duke* (90) and *Arrogant* (74) had been modified to allow for the maximum arc of fire. It was no coincidence that all these ships were in the thick of the fighting and that *Formidable* and *Duke* breached the line. When *Arrogant* encountered *Ville de Paris* the men on the French flagship believed they were in the British ship's blind spot, on the bow. They were aghast when *Arrogant* unleashed a broadside. Douglas reckoned that if all the ships had been modified they would have mown down all the masts in de Grasse's fleet.

The element of surprise and the psychological impact of heavy fire at unpredictable angles took its toll. The French line was now sliced into three groups of dazed and damaged ships. When it cut the line *Formidable* was able to rake four enemy ships. In a naval battle, raking an enemy was one of the most devastating forms of attack. 'Raking' meant concentrating your ship's broadside against the lightly defended bows or stern of your enemy. Not only could an enemy ship not respond in kind, but the cannonballs would tear through the pretty gilded backside, mincing the glittering embellishments and blasting out the windows, and then ricochet down the decks of the opposing ship, turning gunroom and gun decks into bloody shambles. When *Formidable* and the four ships in her wake did this to the French ships the battle was all but won.

The English vanguard had sailed out of the battle northwards, but it did not matter. The French were stunned, disorientated and beaten. Both fleets made repairs during a dead calm. When the wind picked up Rodney ordered a chase in line ahead. Then he signalled for his captains to chase and capture the enemy at will. Four French ships surrendered in the afternoon while de Grasse tried to escape with the remnant of his fleet. One of the captured ships was especially valuable, for it carried the siege train designated for the capture of Jamaica. Both sides were shell-shocked after several days of manoeuvring and the carnage of the morning.

At sunset Hood neared de Grasse's flagship, which had been abandoned by the rest of the fleet and was under bombardment from nine British ships. Hood's *Barfleur* raked *Ville de Paris*'s bows. Not until every single gun had been put out of action would the French admiral strike his colours. It was the only occasion in history when a French three-decker ship of the line was taken in battle. The French admiral stood on the ruined quarterdeck, one of a few surviving officers on the ship, waiting for a British officer. Captain Lord Cranstoun boarded *Ville de Paris* to receive the French admiral's sword. As he made his way along the decks his shoes were submerged in gore. De Grasse was now a prisoner of war. When he was brought to London he was cheered by the crowds for his heroism.

Rodney was exhausted and wary of pursuing the enemy through the night. 'Come, come, we have done very handsomely,' he said and signalled for his ships to break off.[1] Hood was hungry for more. Only on 17 April did Rodney allow his second in command to chase the beaten enemy. He managed to further deplete the French West Indies squadron by capturing two battleships, a frigate and a sloop.

When the fleet's physician Sir Gilbert Blane inspected the prizes he was distressed at the poor hygiene of the French ships and the wretched health of the crews.[2] Blane was a fashionable doctor and an extremely important figure in the history of the Navy. Whereas most academic doctors covered themselves in a cloak of classical learning, Blane based his approach on data. Out of raw statistics on morbidity in naval crews gleaned from naval surgeons grew tables and charts. What he came to preach was that 'cleanliness and discipline are the indispensable and fundamental means of health'. Curing a sick sailor was almost impossible; prevention was an attainable goal. Blane made sure that the ships were kept clean and well ventilated, sailors' clothes and bodies were washed regularly and the ships had regular supplies of fresh vegetables and fruit.

It is to Rodney's great credit that he was prepared to bring a young and radical doctor out to the West Indies and back his reforms to the hilt. When Rodney introduced Blane to the fleet in 1780 there were 12,109 men serving and deaths amounted to 1,518 (12.5 per cent). By the time the fleet came into action against de Grasse there were 21,608 men and deaths from disease stood at just twenty-four (1.3 per cent). Thanks to Rodney surgeons now had status in the Navy, and greater authority in areas such as sanitation and diet. At the Battle of the Saintes a crew of healthy and well-nourished British sailors, sailing on clean ships, beat a French fleet hamstrung even before it came into action by disease.

Jamaica was saved, and with it Britain's position in the West Indies. The Battle of the Saintes restored Britain's ailing reputation as a naval power and it was celebrated with unbridled enthusiasm at home. The great Whig statesman and Britain's foreign secretary Charles James Fox hailed it as the greatest naval victory of the century. But Hood was furious. He did not care who knew it. 'Surely there never was an instance before of a great fleet being so *completely beaten* and *routed* and *not pursued*.'[3]

He lambasted Rodney, painting him as a feeble old man who needed a capable man at his elbow. Douglas, Hood added, 'is no more fit for the station he fills than I am to be archbishop'. As always his letters – brilliantly waspish and tactically astute – swayed the mood at home and the judgement of history. If he had been in charge on 12 April, he said, 'I may, without imputation of much vanity, say the flag of England should now have graced the stems of twenty sail of the enemy's line'.[4]

Hood was the man of the moment. After all, the fleet that prevailed at the Saintes had been honed under his stewardship; its officers had participated in his councils; its men had been drilled to their fullest extent. Moreover, de Grasse surrendered to *Barfleur*. Rodney was raised to the peerage. So was Hood. George III called the latter 'the most brilliant officer of this war' and dispatched his son Prince William to Hood as a midshipman. Horatio Nelson, twenty-four and captain of the frigate *Albemarle*, begged to serve under Hood in the West Indies. The admiral was good at talent-spotting and arranged the transfer. 'My situation in Lord Hood's fleet must be in the highest degree flattering to any young man,' wrote Nelson. 'He treats me as if I were his son, and will, I am convinced, give me anything I can ask of him.'[5]

But victories in exotic locations were one thing. Quite another matter was Britain's neglect of home waters. Control of the Western Approaches, absolute dominance of the Channel, the ability to blockade Brest and power over the Strait of Gibraltar had together been the keystone of British imperial power. When they were neglected, the rebellious colonists were flooded with imported munitions, French fleets contested for control of the seas and the country cowered under the threat of invasion.

The Channel Fleet and other home squadrons had been entrusted to a succession of elderly and ineffective admirals. In 1781 Sir Hyde Parker, at the age of sixty-seven, fought an indecisive battle against the Dutch near Dogger Bank. He resigned his commission, telling George III that the Navy needed younger admirals and better ships. In 1782 Howe agreed to lead the Channel Fleet in return for a viscountcy for himself and rewards for his brother. Rarely before had the command been so vital and so difficult. One moment he had to be off the Texel to face a Dutch threat to the Baltic convoys, the next he had to sail westwards with twenty-five battleships to protect merchant convoys from the predations of a forty-strong Franco-Spanish fleet operating out of Brest.

Once again Howe was forced to make up for inferiority of ships by deft manoeuvres. In July he found the enemy fleet to windward forming a line of battle, ready to pounce on a convoy homeward-bound from Jamaica. Howe led his small fleet through the narrow, dangerous channel between Land's End and the Scillies to steal the weather gage and deter the attack. In September he took the Channel Fleet to relieve Gibraltar, which was hanging on against a siege. Howe's great triumph was to escort a relieving convoy into Gibraltar Bay, evading a much larger enemy fleet, and then to bring back the Channel Fleet and the storeships unscathed.

The enemy's control of the Western Approaches was thwarted and Gibraltar saved thanks to Howe's superior tactical skills. That he was reduced to using them for defensive purposes was a measure of how dire the situation was for Britain. The British Navy had been, for long periods, outmatched by the French navy in the West Indies and lost a string of colonies to the enemy's skills at amphibious warfare. The Navy had been put under serious pressure in the East Indies by the brilliant French admiral, Pierre André de Suffren. Indeed, the country was lucky to end the war in 1783 still in possession of India, Canada, its West Indian islands and Gibraltar. The Battle of the Saintes went a long way to redeeming the reputation of the Navy after a disastrous war.

After the battle Rodney returned home, never to serve again. He died in 1792. Rodney is remembered as a trouble-prone and querulous man – one of the Navy's most controversial admirals. Foul to his subordinates and conservative in his approach to signalling he may have been, but unlike his more academic contemporaries he was capable of bold and decisive action that led to results. Even his sternest critic, Samuel Hood, said that if Rodney had been in command at the Battle of Chesapeake the British would have won. 'Within two little years,' Rodney wrote, 'I have taken two Spanish, one French and one Dutch admirals.'[6] It was a remarkable achievement.

Rodney's victory shook up thinking on tactics. It had not gone unnoticed that in most incidents where a line battle had been fought the outcome had been inconclusive. The British Navy had initiated battles, fighting aggressively and with purpose. The French had, for the most part, preferred to fight defensively and deliberately batted for a draw. The Royal Navy often came away with a tactical victory, satisfying no doubt to risk-averse admirals. But it was not enough. The British had most to lose from a draw: at the battles of Toulon, Ushant and Chesapeake, for example, an indecisive result had led to strategic disaster.

The Moonlight Battle taught Rodney an important lesson: 'when the

British fleet take the lee gage, the enemy cannot escape'.[7] Since the 1650s the Navy had been wedded to attacking from windward in a formal line of battle, fought ship to ship in parallel lines. The historical record showed it was costly and unrewarding. For a start it was hard to initiate. Attacking directly from windward meant that your bows would be raked by the enemy line as you approached. Approach at an angle and your vanguard would be mauled while your centre and rear got into range – this was what happened at Chesapeake. On top of that a fleet to leeward had other defensive and offensive advantages. If it was in danger of losing, its damaged ships could slip away downwind and the whole fleet could escape with the wind behind it. On the other hand, if the leeward line was winning, the enemy to windward would find it hard to retreat because it would have to beat against the wind, something that damaged ships would find extremely hard to do. This was the situation de Grasse's ships were in during the first stages at the Saintes; they found it impossible to manoeuvre against the wind in the face of devastating British fire.

Rodney has been criticised for sacrificing this position of strength. He attacked from downwind, but when he broke the French line he resumed the onslaught from to windward, allowing the crippled French ships to scatter out of his clutches with the breeze filling their sails. If he had not cut through de Grasse's fleet the French would have been trapped by the wind.

Whatever the case, it was clear that forcing through the enemy line had led to that rare thing – a decisive result in a line engagement. Rodney had certainly told his captains that the only way to defeat de Grasse was to break his line in several places. At the earlier Battle of Martinique he had intended to turn the orthodoxy of the line engagement on its head by a surprise attack concentrated exclusively on the enemy rear. The effect of this would have been to force the French centre and van to tack or wear in order to come in support of their fellows. This would place them at risk of being raked as they hurried back to rejoin the battle. Unfortunately for Rodney most British captains clung to the good old-fashioned line of battle and were as loath as the French to depart from tactics they had imbibed with their mothers' milk.

The British enjoyed considerable advantages over their enemies – principally superiority of seamanship and gunnery. These seemed to be negated by conventional line tactics. The Royal Navy fought best – as at the two battles of Finisterre, Lagos, Quiberon Bay, the Moonlight Battle and the Saintes – when it managed to disrupt the enemy, induce panic and roll up its opponents in a pell-mell battle. In other words, a British admiral should dispense with formalism and, when the case allowed, break his own line and seek to overwhelm his bewildered enemy in a melee-type engagement.

These ideas were seen as dangerously radical in a service so stubbornly conservative. Lord Howe was First Lord of the Admiralty from 1783 until 1788. In 1790, at the age of sixty-four and ridden by gout, he once more became commander-in-chief of the Channel Fleet. His lifelong crusade to improve signalling climaxed in that year with his 'Signal Book for the Ships of War'. It was described by Brian Tunstall as 'the long-delayed masterpiece for which the more progressive British sea officers had been waiting'.[8] Under this system a coloured flag corresponded to a number. The number referred to an order in Howe's new Signal Book. No longer would combinations of flags be run up and down from the flagship to confuse signal officers and captains in the fleet. The numerical system – long used by the French – was much easier to understand.

The Navy continued to experiment, despite the failures of the American War and the interval of peace that followed. But so too did its rivals. The gap had also closed in terms of raw numbers. By 1790 there were 145 British ships of the line. If the French and Spanish navies combined the numbers would be dead level. But this arms race was a ruinous business. While Britain crowded on sail and lavished taxpayers' money on her Navy, the French and Spanish careered towards the lee shore of bankruptcy. The difference was the sound foundation of finance built up over generations and carefully managed by the prime minister, William Pitt the Younger.

The American wars exposed the Navy's shortcomings. But the service was capable of providing its own remedy. In the 1780s Pitt developed a good working relationship with the Comptroller of the Navy, Rear Admiral Charles Middleton.[9] The Comptroller was a determined reformer. Under his watch the dockyards were brought under closer supervision to eliminate waste and corruption. Middleton grabbed the chaotic naval accounting system by the scruff of the neck and beat it into rational order. Throughout the peace the workforce in the yards was kept at wartime levels. New ships were built and old ones repaired at unprecedented speed. His aim was to have ninety battleships and ninety frigates in readiness at all times. Middleton was the brains behind coppering the fleet. The result was that warships did not have to be repaired so frequently. Longevity of a ship's service was key to the Comptroller's plan. To this end, massive stocks of timber and rope were built up and new docks constructed at Portsmouth and Plymouth.

Great strides were made in the field of naval gunnery as well. A new rapid-fire gun named the carronade was introduced to the forecastles and sterns of ships. The carronade was light, had a short fat muzzle, produced little recoil, used small amounts of gunpowder and was only effective at close range. It was nicknamed the 'smasher'. It could be fired rapidly, battering an enemy at close quarters with extraordinary force. The carronade could also swivel, and when loaded with grapeshot it made mincemeat of enemy sailors and marines on an opposing ship's upper decks.

The carronade was developed by the Carron ironworks in Falkirk; it was a triumph of British industrial innovation. It was taken up by merchant ships and only brought into the Navy at Middleton's insistence. The benefit was immediate. A single blast from a carronade on HMS *Rainbow*'s forecastle was enough to compel the surrender of a stunned French frigate. Carronades were fitted on the upperdecks of battleships and frigates; some smaller vessels were exclusively armed with them. The addition of the smashers did not change the rating of a vessel: a 74, say, still had seventy-four conventional long guns irrespective of the carronades she carried. The British liked to fight at close quarters. The rapid-firing carronade made them even more fearsome.

Long-range guns also saw changes. Under Thomas Blomefield the Ordnance Board greatly improved the performance of naval guns. He subjected every new gun to a test that required it to be fired thirty times before it was accepted. Manufacture was improved. Slowmatches were replaced with gunlocks. Under the old method – a linstock, or slowmatch, held against priming powder – gun captains had to position themselves beside the gun and hope the gunpowder ignited and fired. The new way was safer and more efficient because the gun captain stood back from the gun, aimed it, and, when the time was ripe, yanked on a lanyard that set off a firing mechanism similar to a musket's flintlock. Broadsides were therefore faster and more accurate.*

The French took two decades or more to catch up. The difference was that Britain had an advanced economy and stable parliamentary government. Its industries, both private and state-owned, were improving beyond measure. This was seen in the energy and organisation at every royal dockyard and felt when a broadside was unleashed from state-of-the-art guns.

Middleton wanted to completely reform the ancient and sprawling

---

* Experiments with explosives or combustibles in naval warfare were taboo. When Howe was pressed to use red-hot shot at the relief of Gibraltar in 1782 he said that sea battles were 'quite horrid enough, without having recourse to anything more'.

Navy Board. But he had powerful enemies at the Admiralty – most notably Lord Howe – and his plans were scuppered. Nevertheless, thanks to his administrative zeal and Pitt's willingness to spend money on naval defence, the Navy grew stronger and stronger even in peacetime.

The results were there for all to see. In 1790 the Spanish attempted to exclude British traders from the Pacific coast of North America – the Nootka Sound Crisis. At the same time relations with Russia soured. The naval machinery geared up with consummate ease as Britain mobilised for war. Spain backed down.

Never did war seem so unlikely. After 1789 France was engulfed by the anarchy of revolution. It seemed that France would be knocked out of the great game for global domination by her domestic miseries. By 1792 Pitt felt confident enough to reduce naval expenditure for the first time since the end of the last war.

CHAPTER 34

THE OLD GUARD
1793–1794

No, no, I thank *you* – it is *you* my brave lads, not I, that have conquered.[1]

Admiral Howe, 1 June 1794

At the ripe old age of sixty-nine Admiral Hood pulled off his greatest feat. In 1793 Revolutionary France declared war on Britain. When the people of Toulon rebelled against the Jacobins Hood pounced. He offered immediate military support if the citizens declared for the royalists. Hood occupied the French Mediterranean naval base and took possession of its forts and ships, which Britain would hold in trust until the war was over.

Hood led a team of brilliant young officers. Among his captains were several future stars: Horatio Nelson, Thomas Fremantle, George Keith Elphinstone, Thomas Foley, Thomas Troubridge, Benjamin Hallowell and his young cousin, who was also called Samuel Hood. These men had a brilliant admiral from whom they could learn. Nelson said of his commander: 'he is certainly the best officer I ever saw. Everything is so clear it is impossible to misunderstand him.'[2]

Hood's occupation of Toulon was one of the boldest political moves ever made by an admiral. It infuriated the government, which was not fighting to restore the Bourbons. But Hood had, by his quick decision, taken half the French fleet and given Britain and her allies access to the south of France without a shot being fired. The problem was that there were no available ground troops to exploit the situation.

Yet Hood was aggressive as ever. He used Toulon as his base to extend British power throughout the Mediterranean. As a result Hood had only a third of his squadron in Toulon when a massive Jacobin army (including a young artillery officer named Napoleon Bonaparte) laid siege to the town. It crushed all resistance and in the rapid evacuation Hood could only take away three enemy battleships. Only nine battleships were burnt, leaving the French thirteen. The bright spot was the burning of an enormous stock of timber, whose loss dealt a serious blow to the French navy.

Hood was determined to fight on in the same aggressive, positive manner. His next plan was to capture Corsica. He was successful, but in achieving his ends he alienated the commanders of the army, like many another admiral, by insisting on being supreme commander and meddling in amphibious operations. Similar alacrity on the part of Admiral Sir John Jervis saw the French turfed out of their islands in the West Indies.

Back in home waters, the travails of the Revolutionary government gave Howe the opportunity to test his tactical theories. In May 1794 he was at sea in the Western Approaches with twenty-five ships of the line hunting a convoy bringing badly needed grain from America to famished France. Howe failed to find the grain ships, but on 28 May, over four hundred miles west of Ushant, he located the escorting French fleet, commanded by Louis Thomas Villaret de Joyeuse and consisting of twenty-six ships of the line.

The two fleets ducked and dived for several days. Then, at dawn on 1 June, Howe had the weather gage. From 03.50 he set about ordering his line so that each ship would face a suitable target. At 07.25 he flew signal thirty-four – pass through the enemy line and engage from leeward. At 08.25 he flew signal thirty-six – each ship to steer for its opposite number and engage. At 09.24 both fleets were parallel in line ahead. Howe gave his orders, using repeating frigates to convey his ingenious plan along the line.

Howe wanted to break through the French and then resume the attack from to leeward. This would completely disorientate the enemy and seal off their escape route downwind. By the end of the battle the badly damaged French ships would be too weak to beat into the wind; they would be captured. What made it so radical was that Howe would not drive through the line at opportune points, as Rodney had done at the Saintes. Each of his ships would cut past its opposite number, subjecting its opponent to raking fire as it went. The British line would re-form on the other side of the enemy. The French would be stunned by its daring. Howe's plan combined the advantages of an attack from to windward with the benefits of fighting from downwind. It was brilliant stuff – the endgame of Howe's lifelong study of tactics.

The first ship to break through in the van was HMS *Defence* (74). She was the seventh ship in the British line and she cut between *Mucius* (74 and sixth in the French line) and *Tourville* (74 and seventh), raking both as she went. Then HMS *Marlborough* (74 and sixth in line) did likewise. In the central division Howe's flagship *Queen Charlotte* (100) blasted her way between her opposite number, *Montagne* (118), and *Vengeur du Peuple* (74). Once she had broken the line *Queen Charlotte* engaged *Montagne* at exceptionally close quarters. HMS *Brunswick* (74) pierced the line, raking *Achille* (74) and attacking *Vengeur du Peuple*. But her anchor became entangled with *Vengeur's* rigging and the two ships blasted each other at point-blank range. In the rear *Royal George* (100) and *Glory* (98) cut through.

Only seven ships broke the French line. Some British ships, weakened by the skirmishes of the previous day, became closely engaged but could not cut through. One vessel overshot her place in the line and lost her chance to manoeuvre correctly. Some captains seemed not to have understood Howe's instructions and settled in for a conventional line battle. Others preferred to fight ineffectually at long range. And a few did not even join the action. One captain took his ship to search for his brother, who was captain of *Brunswick*.

The fighting on the Glorious First was exceptionally fierce in some sectors as Howe's battle plan broke down into a free-for-all. Several ships became entangled with each other. *Brunswick* was so tight alongside *Vengeur* that her ports were wedged shut and her guns had to be fired through the closed lids. Ships on both sides were completely dismasted. HMSs *Orion* and *Queen* attacked the French ship *Northumberland* and blasted out her masts. *Queen* then encountered *Jemmapes* and began a vicious duel. By the end of the day *Jemmapes* was totally dismasted and *Queen* had lost her mainmast. The first two British ships to pierce the line, *Defence* and *Marlborough*, ended the battle with no masts between them and under tow. Valiant *Brunswick* had twenty-three of her guns knocked out of action, three serious fires had to be extinguished, she lost her mizzenmast and bowsprit and her mainmast was badly damaged. A ferocious battle took place round *Queen Charlotte*. *Montagne* was battered to a perilous state and she had to disengage. Howe's flagship attacked *Jacobin*, *Républicain* and *Juste*; around her lay twelve French ships, all crippled or dismasted.

Howe had been manoeuvring his fleet and directing the series of battles for five days. He had to be supported by his staff officers to prevent him collapsing onto his quarterdeck. His chief of staff, Sir Roger Curtis, was subsequently blamed for letting some of the badly damaged French ships limp back to the protection of *Montagne*. The British managed to capture seven French battleships. One of them, *Vengeur*, sank after her murderous embrace with *Brunswick*.

By now both fleets were so badly damaged that further action was impossible. Howe was an old man, but everyone must have been as drained as their admiral. The ships had been cleared for action for over three days, during which time all bedding and personal possessions would have been stowed away, livestock thrown overboard and the fires in the galleys extinguished. Sailors and marines may have rested, but food and comfort were in short supply in the long run-up to battle. By the end of the day, as after all battles, the survivors were temporarily deafened by the incessant broadsides, everyone (from Howe downwards) blackened by gunpowder and the ships smashed to smithereens and in need of urgent repairs. The surgeons' cockpits were packed with dying men.

Further action was out of the question. The French counted themselves fortunate that the grain convoy got home and prevented famine in France. The British were delighted at a great victory and the capture of six enemy ships. Around 7,000 French sailors were killed or taken prisoner, against 1,200 killed and wounded in Howe's fleet. The horrors and ferocity of the battle were conveyed to the public in numerous paintings and prints depicting the ruined ships. One of the reasons that confusion reigned in some parts of the British fleet was the high casualty rate among captains in the opening salvos. In the van, two junior admirals were badly wounded; one lost his leg. Other captains were killed or wounded. John Hutt, captain of HMS *Queen* – one of the most heavily engaged – was dying of wounds sustained the day before. Captain John Harvey of HMS *Brunswick* lost his right hand, then a wooden splinter smashed into his back, then his elbow was shattered by roundshot. He remained on deck until the closing stages of the battle and died at Portsmouth.

Howe's plan had gone awry. But he had at least forced a pitched battle from a position of strength after days of manoeuvring for advantage. He had inflicted defeat upon the French by superiority of seamanship and gunnery. All the same, the French had achieved their object – getting the convoy safely to France. And they had extricated some of their ships that they should have lost.

Hood and Howe were old men. The former returned from the Mediterranean and then, when he argued with the Admiralty over reinforcements in his theatre, was dismissed. Howe continued to lead the Channel Fleet for a couple of years until infirmity drove him onto land. The Glorious First of June was his last major battle.

Hood's Mediterranean campaign and Howe's famous victory speak volumes about the possibilities and limitations of naval command in the late eighteenth century. Hood strove all his life to be a bold, imaginative commander. He secured Toulon by taking decisive action, a move so risky that most admirals would have balked at it. He lost it because his available forces were too small to master the huge theatre of operations.

Howe was called a 'scientific' admiral by George III. His ambition was to take a fleet totally responsive to his commands into battle and execute a clinical demolition of the enemy. Naval warfare in the age of sail was not like a game of chess. Howe learnt that on the Glorious First when his beloved signals failed to translate into the perfect manoeuvre. Most of his captains did not, could not, understand the range and subtlety of his grand tactical masterpiece. And if they did, they considered it suicidal: they were not chessmen, to be moved at will. Unlike Hood, and later Nelson, he was incapable of creating a team of inspired officers with whom he could share his vision. He won a famous victory in 1794, but as with Hood at Toulon, it was not enough. It never could be.

Many officers and politicians talked of naval tactics as a 'science' in the late eighteenth century. Kempenfelt, Young, Graves and Howe aspired to match the regularity and precision of the French, who were masters of fleet manoeuvres. It was as if the rationality of the Enlightenment could be imposed on sea battles. Admirals such as Howe tried to apply scientific theory to battle tactics and improve command and control by ever more complex signals.

They were looking in the wrong places. It took an outsider to point it out. Gilbert Blane, Rodney's physician, wrote that the French 'from a spirit of speculative system' developed extensive theories of naval warfare and invented clear, concise forms of signalling. They 'applied the principles of science' to shipbuilding. The result was that their admirals manoeuvred their splendid ships as if they were in a fleet review. But, according to Blane, 'practical seamanship is not suited to their genius. Their ships of war are neither disciplined, commodious, nor even decent; and when the personal exertion and presence of mind, necessary in close action, comes to be called for, I apprehend they are then at a loss.'[3]

Naval warfare was not a science. It could not be taught in academies by armchair tacticians. On the day of battle there were too many factors to upset the best-laid plans. Signal flags might hang limp and unseen. The admiral might become lost to his followers in rain, fog or gunsmoke. The fickle wind would inevitably change direction. Ships damaged in battle became unpredictable things, disrupting the line and deranging manoeuvres. By its very nature, warfare in the age of sail was subject to so many variables that centralised control was a chimera. The admiral of a sailing fleet had to reach down for other qualities to achieve victory. Above all he had to recognise that he was in command of individuals – individual ships, captains, officers and sailors. These individual components of a fleet sailed and fought beyond the direct control of their commander.

An admiral achieved greatness when he found a way to share his tactical vision with his subordinates and motivate them to fight for the same ends. Teamwork, seamanship, training, motivation and initiative were far more valuable in the turmoil of sailing warfare than ingenious plans, crisp manoeuvres and absolute control.

The attempt to impose centralised control over fleets and fight by theory, so prevalent between the 1770s and the 1790s, diverted the Royal Navy from what it did best: getting close to the enemy and fighting hard. Rodney reminded everyone of that advantage at the Saintes when he allowed his captains to fight as they wished, free from the stifling embrace of rigid rules and compulsive signalling. British sailors fought best when they were drilled, motivated, well nourished and in good health. That was Lord Hawke's legacy from the triumphant blockade of Brest in the Seven Years War; it took a long time, and many disasters, to rediscover it.

The three admirals described in this part embodied essential qualities for their task. Rodney was a fearless warrior with natural tactical sense. Hood was a superb leader of men and possessed political courage. Howe was an astute tactician and a man patient enough to grapple with every petty detail of naval work. None was very pleasant. Rodney was volatile and greedy; Hood ruthlessly self-seeking and extraordinarily disloyal to his superiors; Howe cold and aloof from his captains.

All three helped modernise the Navy and set a new standard. Many of the captains who reached prominence in the wars to follow served as midshipmen, lieutenants and junior captains with Rodney in the West Indies, Howe in the Channel Fleet or Hood in the Mediterranean. Nelson compared the last two, men he learnt so much from: 'The Fleet must regret the loss of Lord Hood, the best officer, take him altogether, that England has to boast of. Lord Howe is certainly a great officer in the management of a fleet, but that is all. Lord Hood is equally good in all situations which an Admiral can be placed in.'[4]

But it was Rodney, for all his faults, who was the admiral to surpass.

PART 11: BANDS OF BROTHERS

CHAPTER 35

EGGS AND BACON
1794–1795

I had their huzzas, now I have their hearts.[1]

Admiral Nelson, 1805

The greatest victory in the history of naval warfare was won on 1 August 1798 at Aboukir Bay in Egypt. Firing commenced at 18.15 and continued through the night and into the next morning. At about 22.30 Rear Admiral Sir Horatio Nelson was struck on the forehead by a piece of flying metal. He was forced to retire from the quarterdeck to the cockpit to receive attention from the surgeon. In any case, direction from the flagship became impossible as darkness closed over a scene of carnage.

Nelson raised only nine signals before and during the battle. By the time battle – any battle – commenced it was too late for a commander to have a decisive effect on its outcome. In the years, months, weeks running up to his great battles Nelson formed bonds with his sailors and officers so that when the crucial moment came all knew how to respond. The squadron he commanded in 1798 consisted of the best captains in the Royal Navy. Nelson knew what they were capable of; his captains knew what was expected of them. Within a few hours the French fleet was annihilated, Napoleon's ambitions thwarted, and Britain snatched control over the Mediterranean.

Nelson did not have an elaborate battle plan or a complex system of signals. His officers knew how he wanted to fight and his men were prepared to follow him anywhere. A battle was the culmination of a process that began long before.

Lord Howe said of the Battle of the Nile: 'the most remarkable feature of the transaction consists in the eminently distinguished conduct *of each of* the captains of his [Nelson's] squadron. Perhaps it has never before happened, that every captain had equal opportunity to distinguish himself in the same manner, or took equal advantage of it.'[2] Nelson's flag captain, Edward Berry, wrote that 'upon surveying the situation of the enemy, they [the captains] could ascertain with precision what were the ideas and intentions of their commander, without the aid of further instructions, by which means signals became almost unnecessary'.[3]

But it was not the case that the battle had unique features that allowed individuals to flourish. The captains were liberated to use their initiative because they had a leader of Nelson's calibre. At the time of the Nile the Royal Navy had the best hardware and technology in the world, it was well organised and funded, its men and officers second to none as seamen and fighters. These qualities gave Britain a formidable advantage over her rivals. But it took a man of Nelson's genius to weld them together and extract every ounce of power from the Navy.

To explain the stunning success at the Nile it is necessary to step back four years. In July 1794 Captain Horatio Nelson of HMS *Agamemnon* was spearheading Admiral Hood's assault on Corsica. Nelson was on land directing the siege of Calvi when an enemy cannonball threw up a small shower of pebbles and dust that hit him in the face. Nelson's right eye itself was not damaged; but a piece of rubble ruptured a blood vessel and impaired the optic nerve. The captain lost the sight of his right eye.

In his letter to Hood telling him of his injury Nelson wrote that while he was on the beach he saw how hard the sailors from the transports were labouring bringing stores ashore.[4] Notwithstanding his pain or the responsibilities of command, Nelson ordered that the men be refreshed with wine.

It was a small, inconsequential moment in the war, but it speaks a lot about his style of leadership. The campaign in the Mediterranean was, after the Revolutionaries retook Toulon, arduous and unrewarding. Howe had just beaten the French at the Glorious First. Hood's fleet was engaged in a lengthy struggle. In the absence of victories and prize money the men's morale was beginning to crumble. 'All we get is honour and salt beef.'[5]

The quarterdeck of *Agamemnon* was his stage. From there Captain Nelson crafted his style of leadership. Throughout his time in the Mediterranean Nelson would be offered larger, more prestigious ships. He refused the honour: 'if *Agamemnon* sticks by me I will do the same by her.'[6] He had hand-picked his officers. His three lieutenants and all the officers (bar the surgeon) had served under him in the West Indies in the early 1780s when he was a young frigate captain. He chose his midshipmen from among his Norfolk connections and kinship group. The ship's officers became a cohesive team.

The men were a different matter. Just under half of the company of

Agamemnon were able seamen. That sounds like a low proportion, but it was enough. Half a century earlier when Edward Hawke took command of HMS *Berwick* he reported that his men 'were very little, weakly, puny fellows' most of whom had 'never been at sea, and can be of little or no service'. Yet it took just half a year to transform this crew into the crack unit that distinguished itself at the Battle of Toulon. Good captains had always been able to train unpromising recruits into creditable sailors. Nelson did that on *Agamemnon*.

It was a relatively simple matter to teach landsmen and boys how to work aloft and man the guns. It was much harder – and vital – to teach raw recruits and discontented pressed men to accept the need for the unquestioning obedience that made a ship safe and fit for battle. The Navy's strength relied on ships that each hummed like a well oiled machine, each part contributing to the smooth running of the whole.

This could be achieved by driving the men to work with the help of harsh petty officers and continual threat of punishment. Sometimes it was – but it did not make a ship any better. An able seaman of this period wrote that 'an officer who wins the love of his men will work wonders where a leader of a different stamp will fail'.[7] A captain commented that his duty was 'to blend together and harmonise the jarring elements of the different dispositions and habits of the men who may compose his crew'.[8]

Life on board a warship had not changed greatly since the seventeenth century. The food was still bad and the pay irregular. Sailors messed together on tables strung between the guns on overcrowded decks; they slept in hammocks permitted a width of just fourteen inches.* As with their forebears of a century before, they craved alcohol, fresh food and women; sailors and marines still traded their 'slops' for wine and sex. Twice a day men were issued with their allowance of 'grog' – half a pint of rum per day, watered down. It was a hard, monotonous life, variegated by heady spells ashore, dancing, singing and battle.

In contrast to the crews of the seventeenth century more members of a ship's company wore uniforms. Admirals, captains and lieutenants got uniforms under Anson's reforms. In 1787 midshipmen, warrant officers and their mates also got that privilege. It tied more of the ship's company to the brotherhood of officers, hardening the shipboard hierarchy. There was no prescribed uniform for able-bodied seamen, but there was uniformity. Sailors favoured short blue jackets, coloured waistcoats, check shirts, a

---

* When the two-watch system operated, with the larboard watch 'on' when the starboard was 'off' and vice versa, the available space was twenty-eight inches.

neckcloth, striped or white trousers and round hats or Monmouth caps.

What had changed most markedly since the Navy of Baltharpe and Shovell's days was discipline. Ships were better ordered and more cleanly; existence on board had grown even more regulated. Yet the casual brutality associated with boatswains and their mates was on the decline. Control was still omnipresent, of course, but it took different forms. Ships' companies in the Royal Navy were better trained and more frequently drilled than their counterparts in the seventeenth century and, for that matter, their contemporaries in other navies. Over the course of the eighteenth century the relationships between officers and men had changed. Greater store was placed on leadership; men responded well to officers who commanded by example and they took pride in their ships and their captains.

Ships depended upon teamwork. The ship as a whole was a team, but within it there were many smaller close-knit units. The men were divided in various ways, from messes of six men to divisions up to watches; they were members of a gun crew; they had their accustomed positions aloft; they might serve on one of the ship's boats; some men assisted the specialist craftsmen, such as the carpenter, sailmaker, cooper or gunner. Relations in a ship were hierarchical, from captain down to cabin boy. There were also clusters of hierarchy throughout the ship: every mast and every gun had its 'captain'; each division had a midshipman at its head and a chain of command. Captains were highly competitive: they wanted to show off how quickly their sails were set, how many broadsides their ship could fire in an allotted space of time, how well they could manoeuvre. Within the ship as well the same competitiveness ruled. Each of the teams, however it was constituted, wanted to outdo its rivals.

'Beware of dilatoriness,' said Nelson. 'Expedition ought to be the universal word and deed.'⁹ Captains must keep their crews busy or risk discontent or worse. Frigates were in continual action patrolling, scouting or convoying merchantmen and they had a fair chance of accumulating prize money. They were manned by the best crews and the elite of the officer corps. Motivating men on a ship of the line, which might be engaged on endless blockades or made to hold station for prolonged periods, was a harder proposition. Order was maintained and men kept motivated by routine and drill. Every day the ship was cleaned. The decks were wetted and then 'holystoned' – rubbed with large pieces of sandstone – and then swabbed dry. British warships were famous for their hygiene and orderliness, which was a benefit in itself. But it also helped keep the crew occupied. This was particularly important as warships needed bigger crews than merchantmen because they needed men to fire the guns in battle. Nelson's close friend Cuthbert Collingwood said that it was his aim 'to engage and occupy my men, and to take such care for them that they should have nothing to think of for themselves beyond the current business of the day'.[10]

A well trained crew was expected to work in perfect harmony – and in silence. Only the captain's voice should be heard, and only he (or the senior officer of the watch) gave orders. One sailor remembered that everything happened in silence, 'for all was obedience to a sure design; it was order, precision, exactness and familiarity with the action'. Another recalled that on HMS *Barfleur* 'in working the ship no one was allowed to speak but ... [the captain], and I have seen the *Barfleur* brought to an anchor and the sails furled like magic, without a voice being heard except his own'.[11] Captain Thomas Hardy took things to an extreme, giving orders to a deathly silent *Victory* with only hand signals. For this to happen every man had to know his particular task inside out and co-ordinate it with his fellows. It was the result of endless drill and months of experience. 'By this regular system of duty,' wrote the seaman William Robinson, 'I became inured to the roughness and hardships of a sailor's life. I had made up my mind to be obedient, however irksome to my feelings.'[12]

Every day a drum beat men to their quarters – to battle stations. Francis Spilsbury, a ship's surgeon, left this account of gun drill:

> On the beat of a drum, the men immediately fly to their quarters; and their being so constant in that point of duty, increases their agility, gives them confidence in their own powers, and prevents much of that confusion, which with those less disciplined must necessarily ensue – even the little powder-boy would be ashamed of being reproached by his ship mates, for not knowing his duty. On these occasions a general silence prevails, all attentively listening for the word of command.[13]

Since 1745 every ship in the Navy had been obliged to perform daily gunnery practice. They were not fired every day – that would have been costly – but the men were beaten to quarters and the guns were run out. Sustained fire in battle depended upon brute strength and repetitive, mechanical actions. Throughout the century rates of fire got faster and faster.

A 32-pounder gun on a British ship had a crew of seven men. Its captain was responsible for aiming and adjusting the range. As the gun trucks were run up to the open ports the wheels made the distinctive sound of a ship about to go into battle – an ominous and urgent rumbling. Once a shot was fired the gun, all three tons of it, jerked back and reared up and set the ship trembling. Its backward lurch was halted by thick breech ropes attached to iron rings on either side of the gunport. At that moment the gun crew would have to haul the train tackle taut; this prevented the gun running forward. Then a sponge attached to a stiff rope was rammed down the inside of the barrel to extinguish any sparks. Next the cartridge – gunpowder wrapped in paper – was rammed down the barrel; this was followed by wadding made of old rope; then came the cannonball; and lastly another piece of wadding to prevent the cannonball rolling out. While part of the crew worked at this, at the other end of the gun the captain pushed a quill tube into the touch hole and pierced the cartridge. He poured enough gunpowder into the tube so that once sparked it would ignite the powder in the cartridge. The flintlock was attached above the quill. It was cocked and attached to a lanyard.

The gun was ready again. Now the crew had to haul its three tons to the gunport, sometimes up a wooden slope caused by the roll of the ship. Again the rumbling was heard, perhaps less distinctly than the first portentous sign of battle now that the ship was in action. The gun captain might direct his men to elevate the barrel with a handspike so that wedges (quoins) could be placed under it. Or the gun might need to be traversed left or right. When everything was ready he yanked the lanyard, causing a deafening roar, foul smoke and the crashing recoil. Then the process began again. This laborious work was conducted by men in a crouching position, because the maximum height below decks was five foot six inches, and in crowded conditions. Orders regarding the targets and range were transmitted from the quarterdeck by scurrying midshipmen or directly by a lieutenant stationed on the deck.

Further down, in the safety below the waterline, men without specific tasks and women assisted the gunner's mates in making up new cartridges. Every gun had a boy, a powder monkey, who collected the cartridges as and when they were needed in a cartouche box – a wooden cylinder – from a hatch in the magazine and carried them along the passageways and up to his gun crew. Too much gunpowder on a gun deck would be dangerous, hence the need for powder monkeys to bring cartridges up on demand from the relative safety of the magazines. The cartouche box protected them against any sparks. Cannonballs were kept within reach of the gun.

Aiming a gun was an inexact science. The speed at which a gun fired made the crucial difference to the outcome of a battle. Thanks to regular drill strong British sailors became automata during battles, repeating their actions over and over again even as the roar grew incessant and the heat stifling, while enemy shots penetrated the hull and men fell around them. Once a battle started all the cogs in the great machine of war began turning. What kept the crews working was rhythm. Once in it the men kept up their grim task oblivious to everything else. Benjamin Hallowell, one of Nelson's outstanding captains at the Battle of the Nile, was 'aware of the difficulty of breaking the men off from their guns once they have begun to use them'. At the beginning of an engagement, when the men were still fresh, they could unleash broadsides every minute and a half. That was what made the Royal Navy feared around the world.

The foundation of British naval might was the discipline, order and teamwork shown by thousands of highly trained seamen. Speed of manoeuvre, rate of fire and determination in battle all depended upon these qualities.

No two ships in the Royal Navy were the same. The quality of captains and officers varied from ship to ship. Some governed their men by brutal methods. Nelson's *Agamemnon* was an example of a well-run, happy ship. Sailors sometimes found it hard to pronounce the names of their ships. *Bellerophon* was 'Billy Ruffian'. *Polyphemus* was 'Polly Infamous'. *Agamemnon* was 'Eggs and Bacon'. They had pride in being Eggs and Bacon-men, or Agamemnons as they were properly known.

And Nelson was proud of them. 'My seamen are now what British seamen ought to be ... almost invincible. They really mind shot no more than peas.'[14] The men came to love and respect their captain. 'He was easy of access, and his manner was particularly agreeable and kind. No man was ever afraid of displeasing him, but everybody was afraid of not *pleasing* him.'[15]

When *Agamemnon* left for the Mediterranean Nelson was an experienced, competent captain; there was not much to distinguish him above his peers. The Mediterranean campaign was the making of Nelson as a captain and senior officer. He had been a good scholar all his life, lucky in having a series of mentors to propel him to the next level. The first was his uncle, Maurice Suckling. In 1771 the thirteen-year-old Nelson joined Suckling, who was then captain of the Nore guardship that protected the approach to the Thames Estuary. Suckling knew that the boy's education would be limited in that station, so he dispatched him on a two-year voyage aboard a merchantman to the West Indies. Then he joined a naval expedition to the Arctic as coxswain. After that he spent two years on HMS *Seahorse* in the East Indies. He returned home in 1776 because of illness. It was perfect timing. He arrived to discover that Suckling had become Comptroller of the Navy. Horatio became an acting lieutenant at the age of eighteen. The next year he passed his lieutenant's exam and joined HMS *Lowestoffe* (32) as second lieutenant. *Lowestoffe* sailed for Jamaica in 1777 to assist in the blockade of the American colonies.

Her captain, William Locker, had a profound influence on Nelson. As a young man he had been a protégé of the great Admiral Hawke, and he had been at the Battle of Quiberon Bay. Locker and Nelson became extremely close. In 1778 Nelson transferred to Admiral Peter Parker's flagship. Within a few months he became commander of a brig and a little later, at the age of twenty-one, captain of the frigate *Hinchinbrook* (28).

To be a frigate captain in the West Indies during wartime was, for an aspiring young captain, very heaven. Nelson had imbibed the arts of seamanship and naval discipline from a succession of first-class mentors. Now, as a frigate captain, he had independence. He was sent on convoy duty and engaged in amphibious assaults on Spanish possessions. Frigates were peerless ships for enterprising and ambitious officers to make their names. His next command was *Albemarle* (28), first in North America and then under Hood, the next in his line of mentors, in the West Indies. After the war Nelson again served in the West Indies, this time enforcing the Navigation Acts against American traders. He fell foul of his commander-in-chief, the governor of Antigua and the trading community of the Leeward Islands. From 1787 until 1793 Nelson was stranded in Norfolk, on half-pay and in some measure of disgrace. Hood dropped him.

Nelson's early career had prospered thanks to his influential uncle and the early opportunities that had been placed in his way. He had mastered his trade from some brilliant officers. As the captain of modest-sized frigates detached from the main fleet in dangerous waters he learnt how to discipline and motivate a crew and use his initiative and judgement. In 1793 Nelson was undoubtedly a very fine captain in Hood's Mediterranean Fleet, but there were a number of excellent captains in the Navy, able to motivate a diverse crew on prolonged voyages. Because Nelson had become captain at a relatively early age he stood high on the list of captains relative to his contemporaries. Command of *Agamemnon* would be crucial to his education for high command.

One of the reasons Nelson refused the offer of higher-rated ships was that, with 64 guns, *Agamemnon* was too small to be an effective ship of the line but larger than most frigates. He was more likely, therefore, to be sent away from the watchful eyes of his superiors on detached missions in command of small squadrons of frigates and sloops. While Hood was at Toulon Nelson was sent to Naples, then Tunis. In 1794 he was put in charge of the blockade of Corsica, where he commanded the sieges of Bastia and Calvi. The following winter he cruised off the French Mediterranean coast, using Leghorn as his base.

Agamemnon was kept busy. Her captain was at the forefront of British naval operations. But he thirsted for more. When Hood was dismissed as commander-in-chief in the Mediterranean Vice Admiral William Hotham took over. On 13 and 14 March 1795 his squadron fought a group of French ships that had made a sortie from Toulon. *Agamemnon* was the fastest ship in the British squadron and took the lead in pursuing the enemy. Nelson used the speed and manoeuvrability of his ship to persistently rake the stern of the much larger *Ça Ira* (80). The French ship was devastated; Nelson did not lose a single man. The next day *Ça Ira* and *Censeur* were captured. Nelson went on board Hotham's flagship and urged the admiral to finish off the enemy. Hotham refused. 'My disposition can't bear tame and slow measures,' Nelson fumed. 'Sure I am, had I commanded our fleet on the 14th, that either the whole French fleet would have graced my triumph, or I should have been in a confounded scrape.'[16]

He got a taste of independent command in July, in charge of a squadron supporting Britain's ally Austria in Italy. Genoa was supposedly neutral, but the French were gaining control there. 'Political courage in an officer abroad is as highly necessary as military courage,' wrote the pupil of Admiral Hood. On his own initiative he imposed a tight blockade on Genoa, at the risk of official anger and private prosecution. It was a situation he relished. The small size of *Agamemnon* relative to his seniority as a captain gave him the chance to command a detached force of frigates, thus giving him the opportunity to extend the leadership he had shown as a captain of a ship to a squadron, modest as it might be. He began creating a team of captains on whom he could rely. George Cockburn commended himself to Nelson by his 'zeal, ability and courage'. Another young frigate captain, Thomas Fremantle, had already worked closely with Nelson during the capture of Corsica.

Nelson knew what kind of senior commander he wanted to be. But he chafed under Hotham's caution. Then everything changed for Nelson when a new commander-in-chief arrived.

CHAPTER 36

A SCHOOL FOR YOUNG OFFICERS
1795–1797

It is active young men that are wanted, not drones.[1]

Nelson

Sir John Jervis was an officer of awesome reputation in the Navy. He was to be the last, and most important, of Nelson's teachers. Jervis arrived to find the Mediterranean Fleet in chaos. He set about whipping it into shape.

He started with the vice and rear admirals, who were dispatched home. Then he examined the state of the ships. During almost three years in the Mediterranean standards had slipped. Jervis found that some of the ships were in a 'most undisciplined, disorderly state, the people incessantly drunk'. Plenty of officers were being treated for VD. Many of the ships carried large numbers of women – including Nelson's *Agamemnon*. Leghorn had always been a resort of pleasure and vice for British sailors; now its temptations were threatening to undermine the fleet. Nelson had a mistress there, who was often on board his ship. Even on a well regulated ship like *Agamemnon* drunkenness and desertion were becoming a problem. Jervis intervened to stamp out the twin cankers of indiscipline and idleness.

He sent a number of captains home. The rest were put on notice to improve or meet a similar fate. Jervis restored order on board by stepping up drills and keeping the ships at sea for long periods. He made the fleet practise various complicated manoeuvres and kept men and officers busy at all times. Most importantly he kept them away from the fleshpots of the Mediterranean, especially Leghorn. 'In truth,' he wrote to the First Lord of the Admiralty, 'the war might have been carried into the enemy's country ... but the miserable *crapule* [debauch] which occupied the minds of the chief [Hotham] and another flag officer ... occasioned these dire effects.'[2]

Henceforth all repairs were carried out at sea. The fleet received regular fresh food: 'no price is too great to preserve the health of the fleet'. Soap was purchased for the entire fleet. Medicines, clean clothes and new bedding came from England. Hospitals were set up at Leghorn and Ajaccio and the one at Gibraltar improved. Jervis had a horror of waste and inefficiency. The ships had to make do and mend and captains were urged to impose habits of frugality on their petty officers and men.

By these methods Jervis was able to keep his fleet at sea, blockading Toulon, for twenty-seven weeks.

Jervis set about securing a loyal cadre of captains. The captains at the heart of his reforms included Thomas Fremantle, Thomas Troubridge, George Cockburn, Benjamin Hallowell, Cuthbert Collingwood and Sam Hood. Thanks to his early promotion, Nelson was senior to them all. Indeed, Troubridge had been a midshipman with him on *Seahorse* when they were boys. Illness sent Nelson home to rapid promotion in the American war; Troubridge remained and became lieutenant in 1781 (compared with Nelson in 1775) and captain in 1785, by which time Nelson had seven years' seniority over him. Jervis favoured Troubridge but had to defer to Nelson's position atop the list of captains. He promoted Nelson to commodore.

Jervis was the 'man of business' Nelson had been crying out for since Hood departed.[3] Jervis was autocratic when it came to the management and discipline of his fleet, but he forged an excellent relationship with officers whom he trusted and respected. He took Nelson into his confidence, to the latter's evident delight. Nelson wrote that 'it would appear that he was so well satisfied with my opinion of what is likely to happen ... that he had no reserves with me of his information, opinions and thoughts of what is likely to be done ...'[4]

That was a hallmark of Jervis's style of leadership. He knew his captains and what they were capable of; they knew him and understood his plans inside out. But he was also a fearsome man. No one wanted to be on the wrong end of one of his rollickings, which were legendary in the Navy. A hardened captain quaked when Jervis announced he would visit his ship. Indeed, Jervis enjoyed bullying his subordinates. He once boasted that he had given a group of officers such a dressing down 'that, if it did not bring them to a stool, certainly made them piss and cry'.

So wrote the First Lord, Lord Spencer, to Jervis. The new commander-in-chief knew how to pick and nurture talented young officers. One of these was an American lieutenant on *Victory* named Ralph Miller, who had been passed over for promotion by Hotham. Jervis plucked him out of obscurity and set him on the road to fame. The admiral had a golden generation of officers from which to choose. 'You have established so good a school for young officers, that if a lad has anything in him, it must come out.'[5]

The lieutenants and captains in Jervis's fleet had clocked up experience unparalleled in naval history. Like Nelson they had begun their careers in the American wars, progressing to become lieutenants, commanders and captains under Rodney, Howe and Hood. War meant rapid promotion; it also allowed young officers to put their training to the test. The American wars shaped their education; the wars with Revolutionary France propelled them to ships of the line and flag rank. Officers born in the late 1750s and 1760s rode a tide of opportunity.

Accident of birth was crucial. But there was an added factor in the late eighteenth century. This was an age when more was expected of commissioned officers. It was no longer good enough to be an accomplished seaman and/or well connected. The sons of gentlemen sent to sea at a tender age were treated as ratings, sent aloft to work with the topmen and do menial tasks. They had to learn to splice, reef and knot. One captain sent his well-bred midshipmen to the galley stove to cook for the seamen and understand the conditions in which the men had to live. A midshipman sent by Collingwood to mess with the seamen was at first indignant at the dishonour of sleeping in a hammock on the gun deck, queuing for salt beef and so on. But then he realised what the captain had done for him: 'I am very glad I was so placed, as it gave me a great insight into the character of seamen, and enabled me to govern them as well as their officers ... during those three months I gained more knowledge of the seaman's character, than in all the ships I have since served in'.[6]

'Middies' also had to learn mathematics, astronomy and navigation. Good captains employed a schoolmaster to teach these skills. However a midshipman who wanted to progress to the heights of the Navy was advised to learn more: languages, history, geography, politics, even dancing. As part of their training midshipmen were required to sketch coastlines and map shoals, to help provide the Admiralty with a database of topographical information. When George III sent his son to sea he let it be known that the boy was to be treated like any other aspirant midshipman. The effect was to raise the Navy's social status. The Navy offered riches, titles and honour to those lucky few who made it to the top. Ambitious parents with political or social clout took pains to place their boys with good captains who offered instruction. Frigates were considered an ideal training ground.

William Parker, a frigate captain, had a regulated programme of instruction. On Monday the boys worked on the mizzen topgallant yard.

On Tuesday they practised with pistols, muskets and swords. Marlinspike seamanship – knotting and splicing – took up Wednesday. Thursday was spent on the mizzen topsail and Friday with the gun crews. On Saturday they learnt at the feet of the boatswain. This kind of immersive training was rare. On many a ship a boy would grow up among hard-drinking, foul-mouthed, book-shy officers who cared little about shaping a new generation of leaders.

It was a strange life for a boy of eleven or so, some of whom had never seen the sea before. They had to learn how to be sailors very fast along-side the old hands. They also did their lessons in the schoolroom. At one moment they might be playing marbles on deck or 'skylarking' aloft after dinner; the next leading men in battle. Frederick Chamier led a boat in a landing operation when he was thirteen years old. When he returned from the rush of battle to the ship his captain had these words for him: 'You are fairly a sailor now; been drunk, been aloft, and been in action. Take your hands out of your pockets, youngster, or I shall have the sail-maker stitch them up.'[7]

These boys grew up fast. They were hardened and trained by war. At this time battle tactics were becoming more widely discussed than ever before, with books of theories entering the market or being privately cir-culated. Jervis's star captains Foley, Hood, Miller and Hallowell had been present at the Battle of the Saintes as young officers. These captains and their contemporaries were hungry for glory and promotion. They had tasted battle and they were developing their own opinions on tactics and leadership. Jervis had drawn around him an elite group of officers.

The men he favoured were around Nelson's age or a bit younger; the older generation were sent home. As we have seen with Nelson, he was good at bringing talented officers into his confidence and giving them a chance to shine. Nelson wrote of Jervis: 'his fleet is capable of performing *anything and everything* ... of all the fleets I ever saw I never saw one equal in point of officers and men to our present one, and with a Commander-in-Chief fit to lead them to glory'.[8]

But the great admiral and his first-rate fleet spent 1796 presiding over a deteriorating situation in the Mediterranean. Jervis kept Toulon under close blockade, but Napoleon simply took his army over the Alps into Italy rather than rely on sea power. Jervis was completely overstretched. In addition to the blockade of Toulon he had to protect British trade, defend Corsica, maintain Leghorn as a supply base and assist the Austrian effort against France in Italy and the Adriatic. Nelson was sent with a squadron to help the Austrians in defending the Ligurian coast road.

Things were desperate for Britain. Sardinia ceded Nice and Savoy to France and left the war in April. Napoleon took Milan in May and occupied Piedmont and Lombardy. Leghorn, the most important British base in the region, fell to the French in June. Toulon was still blockaded, but Napoleon had outflanked the Navy. While this was happening *Agamemnon* was reaching the end of her usefulness; she was due an urgent refit at home. Nelson would have to go with her, unless a replacement ship was found. Just in time, however, the captain of HMS *Captain* (74) fell ill. Nelson exchanged places, bringing all the lieutenants from *Agamemnon*, seven midshipmen, the boatswain, the lieutenant of marines and a large number of trusted petty officers, seamen and marines with him. He also transferred two 68-pounder carronades – the murderous big hitters, vital for close-quarters fighting.

Nelson was on the verge of high command, but the admiralty could not promise a rear admiral's flag in the immediate future and HMS *Captain* was obliged to lead the blockade of Leghorn. Napoleon was rampant in Italy. Now, with Leghorn in his hands, the reconquest of Corsica was possible. Throughout 1796 most of the Italian states fell under Napoleon's power. Worse was to come. In August Spain joined France in war against Britain. Elsewhere in the world the Navy was forced on the defensive by a resurgent France. The Leeward Islands were under threat. Closer to home the French were assembling an invasion force at Dunkirk. The Netherlands were under French control, so the Dutch fleet had to be watched. The main fleet was stationed at Spithead, leaving just fifteen battleships to watch Brest, where double that number were preparing to break out and support an invasion of Ireland and Britain.

The Mediterranean had become a French lake. The British government ordered Jervis to evacuate. It was a disaster for Britain's war effort and a calamity for trade. The Navy had to withdraw its ships, hospitals, stores and bases. It also had to get the army out of Corsica and evacuate traders scattered throughout the region. The task became much harder when one of Jervis's rear admirals, in the grip of a nervous breakdown, fled for home bringing a third of the fleet with him. Jervis took the remnants of the fleet to Lisbon. He left Nelson with the delicate task of withdrawing British troops and civilians from a hostile theatre.

Nelson enjoyed every minute of it. Showered with praise by Jervis and the Admiralty, he was left to use his judgement and his own methods. There was no greater testament, however, to his leadership than an incident that occurred in December. Nelson transferred his flag to the best frigate in the fleet, *La Minerve* (38), a French ship that had been given to the talented Nelson protégé George Cockburn. *La Minerve* and HMS *Blanche* (32) re-entered the Mediterranean to bring out the last remnants of the British military from Elba. On the way the two British ships encountered two Spanish frigates. Both enemy ships were captured, but the next day they were attacked by more Spanish ships, including two battleships. *La Minerve* got away, but *Blanche* found herself in the midst of a Spanish convoy and had to fight her way out. When *Blanche* reached Elba, *La Minerve* was already there with a dozen other small British ships. In the words of one of *Blanche*'s crew, 'Nelson came on board and ordered the capt[ain] to beat to quarters, and as we were in a line before our guns, he came round the decks and shook hands with us as he went along and telling us he was rejoiced to find that we had escaped.'[9]

It was an early example of the quality of inspired leadership that would elevate Nelson to the pantheon of the greats. He was not done with *Blanche*.[10] She was sent to scout French movements from Toulon, and when she returned to Elba her crew mutinied. She was a deeply unsettled ship. First her captain quarrelled violently with his officers and had seven of them imprisoned. Nelson believed that he was in the wrong state of mind to command a ship. The captain was court-martialled for homosexual relations with his coxswain, two midshipmen and several seamen. *Blanche* received a temporary captain before Henry Hotham was appointed. When Hotham had his commission read the men protested violently. Then a group of petty officers informed Hotham that the men considered him 'a dam'd tartar' and would not serve under him. The mutineers seized the forecastle carronades, which could sweep the decks with canister shot, and armed themselves with crowbars and other tools.

Hotham and his officers were on a tense standoff above decks on *Blanche*. Nelson had to act. First he sent a lieutenant from *Minerve* who warned the men that if they continued to resist Hotham every third man would be hanged. That only hardened the men in their mutiny. The lieutenant departed and Nelson got ready to face down the revolt.

He let them stew for half an hour. He had developed a personal relationship with the crew, as we have seen. That groundwork allowed him to take the bold decision to confront these angry, desperate men. He boarded *Blanche* and asked the mutineers to explain themselves. When they had done so Nelson, as one of the crew remembered, said: 'Lads, you have the greatest character on b[oar]d the *Blanche* of any frigate's crew in the Navy. You have taken two frigates superior to the frigate you are in, and now to rebel. If Captain Hotham ill treats you, give me a letter and I will support you.'

With that the mutiny was over. It was a remarkable incident, more illuminating than other more famous occasions in Nelson's life.

He was able to command men with his enthusiasm and zeal. Heroic qualities were something he had to cultivate and project, like an actor with a quarterdeck for a stage. But more than that, he took pains to establish enduring bonds with his officers and men. That was the foundation of his style of leadership and it elevated him far above his peers. He knew his men by name, went down to their decks, shook their hands. He won their trust and their hearts in a way unheard of in a high-ranking officer. These qualities burst to the fore in the trying circumstances of Britain's retreat from the Mediterranean.

George Cockburn remembered of this time that Nelson possessed 'powers of high exertions of intrepidity and talent whenever great occasions call for the exertion of the noble qualities'. Added to that, Commodore Nelson was 'blessed with a never failing kindness of heart'.[11]

CHAPTER 37

THE TEST
1797–1798

Never mind manoeuvres, always go at them.[1]

Lord Nelson, to Midshipman Thomas Cochrane

On 13 February 1797 *La Minerve* sighted Jervis's fleet. Nelson had returned from Elba via Toulon and Cartagena. He learnt that the combined enemy fleet was at sea. As he passed the Strait of Gibraltar he was pursued by two enemy battleships. Nelson, along with Lieutenants Culverhouse and Hardy, who had recently been prisoners of war with the Spanish fleet, boarded HMS *Victory*. They were able to tell Sir John Jervis of the size and condition of the Spaniards as well as their destination – Cadiz. Nelson returned to his flagship, HMS *Captain*.

The Spanish fleet led by Admiral Don José de Cordoba consisted of twenty-seven battleships; one of these, *Santisima Trinidad*, had 130 guns, six carried 112 guns, two had 80 and the rest were 74s. It was bound for Brest, to link up with the French fleet. The combined fleet would then launch an invasion of Britain. But first Cordoba had to escort some ships carrying mercury – a vital component in minting silver coins – to Cadiz. Jervis had been reinforced with some ships from the Channel Fleet and his strength stood at fifteen ships of the line.

Jervis was desperate to intercept and destroy the enemy. Cordoba, despite his superior strength, was as eager to avoid battle. He knew that his men were no match for the highly drilled and skilful British sailors.

Valentine's morning was hazy. Jervis's scouting frigates had done better work than their opponents. Cordoba did not know of Jervis's approach until it was too late. Jervis, for his part, did not know how many ships he was opposing. Early in the morning the vast Spanish fleet appeared as a forest of masts; an officer described the huge enemy ships as 'thumpers, looming like Beachy Head in a fog'.[2] 'There are eight sail of the line, Sir John,' the captain of the fleet informed the admiral.

'Very well, Sir,' replied Jervis.

'There are twenty sail of the line, Sir John,' said the captain a little later. 'Very well, Sir.'

'There are twenty-five sail of the line, Sir John.'

'Very well, Sir.'

'There are twenty-seven sail of the line, Sir John.'

'Enough, Sir,' said Jervis, 'no more of that; the die is cast, and if there are fifty sail I will go through them.'

The British were heavily outnumbered. But Jervis knew he had several advantages. He was 'confident in the skill, valour and discipline of the officers and men I had the happiness to command'. He was proud of the 'excellent stock' he led – ships, men and, above all, his elite captains. He also knew that a 'victory to England is very essential at this moment'[3]. In December an attempted invasion of Ireland from Brest had been thwarted by bad weather and the enterprise of Captain Edward Pellew in his 64-gun *Indefatigable*. The blockading squadron was hiding from bad weather at Spithead. Morale at home was low. Jervis would risk everything for victory.

At 10.57 Jervis signalled 'Form line of battle as convenient'. Cordoba was stunned at the speed at which the British achieved this manoeuvre. His sailors were not up to the standards of their British counterparts. It

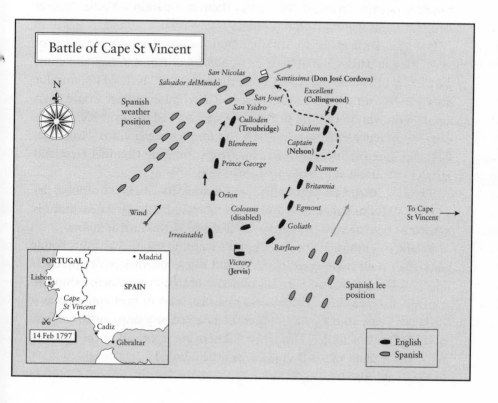

took too long for the Spanish to form their line. As a consequence a gap opened up, with eighteen ships in one disorganised line and nine, led by Joaquin Moreno, in another. At 11.26 Jervis signalled 'The Admiral means to pass through the enemy's line'. Jervis was going to drive through Cordoba's fleet, exploiting the gap to the fullest extent.

It was a dangerous moment. The British were sailing between two sizeable groups of Spanish ships. At the head of the British line at 11.30 Thomas Troubridge in HMS *Culloden* (74) broke through the enemy line and fired on Moreno's squadron to leeward. At 12.08 Jervis signalled to Troubridge to tack and pursue Cordoba's larger group. The rest of the British line would tack in succession, following his ship's wake.

Troubridge anticipated Jervis's order. The reply signal was ready to be hoisted before the order was given. As soon as Jervis's signal lieutenant hoisted the order *Culloden* tacked. It was a pretty smart manoeuvre. 'Look at Troubridge there!' exclaimed Jervis. 'He tacks his ship to battle as if the eyes of England were upon him; and would to God they were! For then they would see him to be, as I know him, and, by heavens Sir, as the Dons will soon feel him.'[4]

HMSs *Blenheim* (90), *Prince George* (90) and *Orion* (74) followed in Troubridge's wake. When it was *Colossus*'s turn to tack she was attacked by Moreno's detached squadron. *Colossus* (74) was knocked out of action by Moreno's 112-gun flagship. This determined action by the Spanish threatened to upset the whole plan. Now it would be the British who had their line cut. But the moment was saved when *Victory* raked Moreno's ship fore and aft. Nonetheless, Moreno's squadron had succeeded in interrupting the British attack. The British line was U-shaped. The port side was heading in pursuit of the enemy; the starboard was parallel to the enemy line, sailing on the opposite tack. But the five leading ships would soon be upon Cordoba's group while their fellows were held up.

At 12.51 Jervis signalled to his rear admiral, Charles Thompson on *Britannia* (100): 'Take suitable stations for mutual support and engage the enemy as coming up in succession.' What he meant was that the rearmost ships should break the line and head directly into battle. The risk was that Cordoba would move to attack the British rear or head east to link up with Moreno. But Thompson failed to understand the situation and the order.

Jervis felt he could fight a battle in such a dare-devil manner because he knew so many of the captains and had spent time discussing the finer points of naval strategy. Most importantly they knew his mind and they understood what was expected of them and how far Jervis wanted them to use their initiative. At the moment Jervis hoisted his signal or moments before (accounts differ), Nelson ordered his flag captain, the New Yorker Ralph Miller, to wear *Captain* out of the line and attack the main Spanish group.

Captain described a wide arc as she left the line. She cut between HMS *Diadem* and *Excellent* and made towards the Spanish. The 74 suddenly looked small as she neared five Spanish monsters, including *Santisima Trinidad*, the largest warship in the world. Nelson came under heavy bombardment. But she was able to reply in kind. According to Ralph Miller *Captain*'s sudden attack had the effect of forcing the Spanish vanguard away from reuniting with Moreno's division.

Just as *Captain* engaged the Spanish ships, Troubridge reached the enemy as well. Then Nelson's old friend Cuthbert Collingwood came into action on HMS *Excellent* (64). The rate of fire from the British ships reversed the superiority the Spanish enjoyed in terms of numbers and size of ships. In three hours of close action Nelson's cherished 68-pounder carronades smashed his opponents every two and half minutes.[5] *Captain*'s 32-pounder cannon poured broadsides into the enemy every four and half minutes.

It was physically demanding to work the guns at that rate. But the men on the British ships had been training and fighting and training again for years. They were prepared for the demands of battle and their ability to fire guns for hours on end gave the British an overwhelming advantage. On the other side, experienced Spanish seamen were a rarity; most were pressed landsmen, at sea for the first time.

Captain and *Culloden* were heavily engaged as they waited for the rest of the fleet to catch up. They were rendered immobile by the big-hitting enemy ships. HMSs *Prince George* and *Orion* pressed on to fight the Spanish vanguard. HMS *Blenheim* relieved *Captain*. At 14.15 Collingwood's *Excellent* (74) got into the action. A series of rapid-fire broadsides from the relatively small ship forced *Salvador del Mundo* (112) to strike her colours. Collingwood pushed on and forced the crippled *San Isidro* (74) to surrender after just ten minutes' fighting at such close quarters that a man could have jumped from one ship to another. He then passed between *Captain* and her two opponents – *San Nicolas* (80) and *San Josef* (112) – and gave the Spanish a taste of her broadside at ten yards' distance. The two enemy ships became entangled. *Excellent* then targeted *Santisima Trinidad*, already under attack from *Orion* and *Blenheim*. The long hours of drill were paying off. Observing from a frigate, the army colonel John Drinkwater remembered how the 'superiority of the British fire over that of the enemy's hulls and sails' was so obvious that it was clear that the Spanish would soon be crushed. A humble British 74 was superior to a 112-gun ship.

Nelson was out of the battle. His extraordinary intervention had helped to hold up the Spanish, but in doing so *Captain* had come under hours of sustained fire from the enemy. Her wheel was out of action, her masts in a bad state, and her rigging, yards and sails torn to pieces. Collingwood's ferocious broadsides offered her a chance. *Captain* rammed the stern of *San Nicolas*, so that her cathead – the wooden beam on her bows – reached the Spanish ship's stern gallery and her bowsprit projected up to the enemy's mizzen. A soldier clambered on to the *San Nicolas*'s gallery and smashed a window. With a cry of 'Death or glory!' Nelson led his marines and sailors into the Spanish warship. They fought their way up to the quarterdeck. They found Lieutenant Edward Berry, who had boarded via the bowsprit, in command of the poop deck.

Nelson then pressed on to *San Nicolas*'s forecastle, which was wedged against the larger *San Josef*. Sailors from the Spanish first rate were shooting down onto the British boarding party. But it was a hopeless case. *San Josef*, already severely damaged and with many of her crew (including the admiral) dead or dying, was under fire from *St George*. When Nelson began to climb up to board her, the Spanish officers surrendered. Nelson arrived on the quarterdeck to receive the sword of every surviving Spanish officer. Later when he went on board *Victory*, with his uniform in tatters and his skin blackened by gunsmoke, 'the Admiral embraced me, said he could not sufficiently thank me, and used every kind expression which could not fail to make me happy'.

It was a remarkable piece of action. No officer of Nelson's rank had boarded an enemy ship in the midst of battle since 1513. Nelson acted with his usual speed and courage. In doing so he won worldwide fame, became the darling of the Navy and secured his place in history. He stole the limelight from the other heroes of the battle, Troubridge, Collingwood and James Saumarez, the captain of *Orion*.

Jervis won a great victory that day at Cape St Vincent. His fleet had defeated one almost twice as big, captured four ships with 3,000 men and killed over 1,000. More important, the Spanish fleet bottled itself up at Cadiz with Jervis – ennobled after the battle as Earl St Vincent – blockading them. Jervis – or St Vincent as he will henceforth be known – had prevailed in spite of a number of tactical mistakes. The most glaring of these was his tardiness in ordering Troubridge to tack. Many of the ships failed to get into action quickly enough.

St Vincent owed his great victory to something other than tactics. He was very different from the 'scientific' admirals of the late eighteenth century who wanted to impose their tactical theories onto the chaos of battle. He once said 'Lord Hawke, when he ran out of the line [at the Battle of Toulon] and took the *Poder* sickened me of tactics'. He contrasted Hawke's aggressive, risk-taking spirit with the staid tactical formalism of his superiors. Under rule-bound admirals the line of battle had ground naval warfare into stalemate. Even forward-thinking, dynamic admirals had overplayed tactics as the decisive aspect of maritime combat.

St Vincent had a once-in-a-lifetime chance and he took it on the wing. He based all his calculations on the excellence of British seamen and the character of his captains and flag officers. The first was a given. The second was less so. St Vincent expected and encouraged his captains to take the initiative. The three outstanding officers at the battle – Troubridge, Nelson and Collingwood* – had served him for a long time. Nelson, in particular, had been given every encouragement and opportunity to act independently during his thirteen months under St Vincent's command. This day was no different. St Vincent could not control the battle, but he trusted his senior officers to anticipate his plans, read the situation, and act decisively. He wanted them to think for themselves and make a judgement based on a common understanding of tactics. His three brilliant commanders exceeded his expectations. What they did was based on discussions, letters and concrete experience of each other's capabilities. It was also based on something that is not tangible – on the bonds and trust built up over a period of time. As tacticians Howe, Hood and Rodney stand head and shoulders above St Vincent; as a fighting admiral St Vincent surpassed them all.

Nelson read the situation superbly. He divined his admiral's intention and acted with resolution and skill. His capture of two enemy ships further demonstrated the fire in his belly and his determination to make every victory a decisive one. It made a legend of the man. Henceforth every sailor who served under him would experience some of the aura of heroism.

Nelson was quick to establish the legend. His account of the battle was the one that dominated the press and gripped the public's imagination. He had learnt how to manage reputation. It added to the magic. Fame, heroism and legend would be key to the next stage of his career.

For the present there was work to perform. Nelson was responsible for returning to Elba with *Captain* and six ships of the line, evacuating the garrison and escorting Fremantle's frigates out of the Mediterranean. He

* St Vincent also singled out the Bostonian Benjamin Hallowell, who was on board *Victory*, James Saumarez and Rear Admiral William Parker.

was now Rear Admiral Sir Horatio Nelson. The mission was accomplished and, for the first time since the Stuarts, there were no British warships in the Middle Sea. He returned to the blockade of Cadiz to find the Navy in crisis.

In April and May 1797 mutinies spread through the Navy's fleets the like of which had not been seen since 1649. In March Lord Howe had received petitions from sailors serving in the Channel Fleet. Rumours of discontent continued through March and into April. On 16 April Admiral Lord Bridport ordered the fleet at Spithead to sea. The companies of every ship refused to weigh anchor. Discontent centred on pay and conditions. Wages had not been raised since 1652. The men also complained about the quality of victuals and the treatment of the sick and wounded. Many officers had considerable sympathy with their men, and the mutiny – in essence more of a strike – was conducted in good enough spirits. On 23 April the men received a royal pardon. Things then soured as legislation ground through parliament. On 7 May a fresh mutiny broke out and Admiral Colpoys ordered the mutineers on HMS *London* to be fired upon. Now the mutineers took control of the entire fleet and expelled over 100 hated officers. The mutiny was being led by the backbone of the Navy, the petty officers who were able to discipline and order their men and present their demands in an articulate and reasonable manner.

On 12 May the ships at the Nore mutinied. Back at Spithead things were reaching a happy resolution. Howe dealt in person with the mutineers' delegates. He entertained them at a banquet on 15 May, having guaranteed that all their demands would be met, including the dismissal of dozens of unpopular officers. The Nore mutiny was more serious. The men had bigger demands: the power of veto over officers, advance pay, longer leave and pardons for all deserters. They were joined by the North Sea Fleet, which was responsible for blockading the Dutch Navy. The ringleaders of this mutiny were far more ruthless. The men were kept away from communication with land. They attempted to blockade the Thames. It only ended in mid-June when a counter-mutiny by frustrated and apprehensive sailors wrested control back from the hard core.

This was a terrifying moment for people in Britain. Edmund Burke wrote at the height of the Spithead Mutiny: 'Our only hope is a submission to the enemy ... as to our Navy, that has already perished with its discipline forever.' Even before the mutiny, in February, three French frigates landed 1,500 men near Fishguard, on the south-west coast of Wales. The French were easily defeated, but the violation of the sacred territory of Britain caused panic. There was a run on the banks. Elsewhere the war was going very badly and the economy was suffering. The subsequent mutinies were a dark and fearful time – one of the worst in modern British history.

From shore it looked as though the Navy had failed the country and its days of greatness were over. It did not look so bad in St Vincent's fleet. Nelson thought the whole thing reflected well on Jack Tar: 'for a *mutiny* … it has been the most manly that I ever heard of, and does the British sailor infinite credit'.[6] The mutiny had spread to St Vincent's fleet when ships from the Channel Fleet joined the blockade of Cadiz. The new ships' crews were fractious and emboldened; their spirit spread around the fleet. The Navy's most valuable asset – its discipline, built up over centuries – was on the verge of collapse.

St Vincent blamed the officers, accusing those on the worst ships of being vice-ridden fops. 'I dread not the men,' he said. It was lax officers he detested. All the same he was not afraid of punishing disobedient men. There were hangings and floggings throughout the fleet. There were other ways of restoring order. HMS *Theseus* was one of the worst ships. The men were openly disobedient, the captain was a feeble man who ringed himself with armed marines, and the first lieutenant ruled the ship by fear. St Vincent sent Nelson and Miller to take control of her. They brought midshipmen from *Captain* and veterans from *Agamemnon*. Within a fortnight discipline had been restored. A letter from the lower decks was left in Nelson's cabin: 'Success attend Admiral Nelson God bless Captain Miller we thank them for the officers they have placed over us. We are happy and comfortable and will shed every drop of blood in our veins to support them, and the name *Theseus* shall be immortalised as high as *Captain*'s ship's company.'[7]

The sure way of restoring discipline was to keep men and officers busy at all times, day and night. That was St Vincent's way. Nelson was put in charge of the inshore squadron, just outside Cadiz. Further out to sea the battleships were kept at manoeuvres. St Vincent knew that trouble had brewed in the Channel Fleet because the men were idle for too long. Even so, morale remained at a low level and every captain was aware of the volatile nature of his crews.

Even in this atmosphere Nelson's star still rose. He led a boat attack on the Spanish gunboats in person and almost lost his life in hand-to-hand fighting. This incident, relatively insignificant as it was, cemented Nelson's status as a hero in the public mind and, most importantly, in the hearts of British tars. In July he was chosen to lead an attack on the Spanish treasure ship hiding at Santa Cruz de Tenerife. The operation failed, but once again Nelson was in the thick of it, among his men. His arm was amputated after it was wounded in the landing operation.

St Vincent continued to rule the fleet by iron discipline and ceaseless activity. Nelson did something different. There was no reason at all why a rear admiral should be fighting in boats or leading amphibious assaults when a lieutenant or midshipman could do the job. But in a fleet demoralised by shaky leadership and low on self-confidence Nelson's decision to lead by example alongside the tars and marines made a difference. He was fast becoming the talisman of the Navy.

Nelson returned to Britain for the first time in over four years. He left a run-of-the-mill captain; he returned a national hero. Glories aside, his battle scars made him one of the most recognisable people in the country.

He returned to the blockade in April 1798 on HMS *Vanguard* (74). The Navy's reputation had been restored by a crushing victory at the Battle of Camperdown. Admiral Lord Duncan's North Sea Fleet, consisting of sixteen ships of the line that had lately mutinied, had been blockading the Dutch at the Texel. The enemy fleet, likewise made up of sixteen battleships, broke out when Duncan was revictualling at Yarmouth. Duncan's ships raced to the Dutch coast, where they found the enemy line attempting to scamper back to their base. The British were to windward, but the direction favoured the Dutch, whose ships had a shallower draught and could evade Duncan by getting among the shoals. 'I made the signal to bear up,' wrote Duncan, 'break the enemy's line, and engage them to leeward, each ship her opponent, by which I got between them and the land, whither they were fast approaching.' He attacked without waiting for all his ships or forming a line. His ships attacked the solid Dutch line in two unevenly sized divisions. They broke the line and sealed off the enemy's escape.

Duncan pulled off the manoeuvre attempted by Howe at the First of June and advocated by armchair theorists. The battle was bloody, but it resulted in the capture of three Dutch admirals, nine battleships and three frigates.

Victories rarely came as complete and heroic as that. It restored the Navy's reputation after the misery and fear of the mutinies. It was the cue for an unprecedented victory service held at St Paul's Cathedral, which celebrated a string of naval triumphs that began with the Glorious First. Redcoated soldiers lined the street, a barrier between multitudes of people and a naval procession that included bands, marching columns of marines and sailors, coaches carrying the admirals and, most impressive of all, artillery carriages mounted with captured French and Dutch flags. The king was led along the nave by the First Lord of the Admiralty bearing the sword of state and the enemy ensigns were ceremonially lodged in the cathedral. The British never really went in for victory parades before, or national pantheons, but the country was thirsty for patriotic thanks-giving and the government felt that it needed to match, and outdo, the pseudo-religious military services pioneered in revolutionary France.

This orgy of patriotic fervour came at a time when Britain's outlook was bleak. Throughout the winter of 1797–98 Napoleon was in northern France organising an invasion of Britain. Austria had left the war and would not re-enter unless the Royal Navy gave her support in the Medi-terranean. Rumours were flying around that a fleet was being readied at Toulon under Admiral François-Paul Brueys. What was Napoleon plan-ning? Was he bound for Ireland? Or England? Would he blast St Vincent's blockade out of the water? Could he even be heading to Greece or, most outlandishly of all, the Levant and thence India? Statesmen at Whitehall were haunted by the myriad possibilities.

Now Britain had a hard choice to make. If ships were sent back into the Middle Sea it would deprive the Channel Fleet of indispensable rein-forcements when France decided to invade. At last it was decided that the country could risk a small squadron in the Mediterranean. Nelson was sent on *Vanguard* (captained by Edward Berry), with *Alexander* (74) under Alexander Ball, *Orion*, commanded by Saumarez, and three frigates. It was a tough assignment. There was no friendly port east of Gibraltar, no base from which to make repairs or resupply. But no one in the Navy knew these waters better than Nelson.

It started badly. *Vanguard* lost all her masts in a storm and was saved from the rocks of Sardinia by the excellent seamanship of Ball's *Alexander*. *Vanguard* had to be repaired in a Sardinian bay. While this was going on Napoleon left Toulon with thirteen battleships and 280 troop transports carrying 48,662 soldiers. Nelson had no idea of this until much later. He had been delayed for too long and he had lost his scouting frigates. On 7 June Thomas Troubridge brought ten 74s and a 50-gun ship to reinforce Nelson.

Nelson now commanded a crack force that included Hood and St Vin-cent's protégés. The captains represented the best of the generation that had cut its teeth in the American wars. The average age was thirty-nine. Seven of the fourteen captains had fought at the Battle of the Saintes. One of them, James Saumarez, had captained HMS *Russell* at that battle. When Rodney breached the line Saumarez, then aged twenty-five, wore his ship out of the line to get to windward of de Grasse's line. His was one

of the ships that helped reduce *Ville de Paris*. Like Nelson at the Battle of
St Vincent, but less dramatically, he acted without orders and on his own
initiative.

Nelson had served with Benjamin Hallowell (*Swiftsure*), Thomas Foley
(*Goliath*) and Davidge Gould (*Audacious*) off Toulon, Corsica and Leghorn.
More recently he had commanded Troubridge (*Culloden*), Sam Hood
(*Zealous*), Thomas Thompson (*Leander* – the only 50) and Miller (*Theseus*)
at Santa Cruz. Saumarez and Ball had been with him from the outset and
had already lived up to their reputations. Nelson did not know the other
captains. Thomas Louis (*Minotaur*) had lots of experience, as did John
Peyton (*Defence*), Henry Darby (*Bellerophon*) and George Westcott (*Majestic*).
St Vincent commended this force to Nelson: 'The whole of these
ships are in excellent order, and so well officered, manned and appointed
I am confident they will perform everything to be expected of them.'

All they had to do was track down the French and defeat them. But
where was Napoleon?

'The smallness of our squadron,' wrote Berry, Nelson's flag captain,
'made it necessary to sail in close order, and therefore the space it covered
was very limited; and as the admiral had no frigates that he could dispatch
to look-out, added to the constant haze of the atmosphere in that climate
our chance of descrying the enemy was very much circumscribed.'[8]

As he sailed south along the coast of Italy Nelson began to hear rumours
that the French had taken Malta, the key to the eastern Mediterranean.
He now believed that Napoleon was aiming either for Sicily or Egypt. The
chance that it was Egypt raised the stakes considerably. If France controlled
Egypt it would enrich itself beyond measure, gain control of the
eastern Mediterranean and make itself irresistible in Europe. It could also
threaten British India. All this played on Nelson's mind. He decided to
take the greatest gamble of his career. He signalled for 'those captains in
whom I placed great confidence' to come aboard *Vanguard*. These were
Saumarez, Troubridge, Darby and Ball. They conferred and Nelson took
the momentous decision to make for Alexandria and destroy the enormous
French flotilla at sea, before it disembarked in Egypt.

Making a decision of this kind placed enormous strain on Nelson. He
was reminded by the British consuls in the Italian states that the fate of
Europe and the safety of Britain were on his shoulders. The weight of
expectation was great as Nelson set out to pursue the elusive French fleet.

On 29 June he arrived for the showdown at Alexandria.

CHAPTER 38

THE NILE
30 June–2 August 1798

Before this time tomorrow I shall have gained a peerage, or
Westminster Abbey.

Nelson, 1 August 1798

Nelson's squadron found Alexandria blissfully unaware of any danger.
There were no French ships and no sign there ever would be. Napoleon
was at large somewhere in the Mediterranean. No one knew where. Nelson
faced ruin for letting him escape.

Nelson weighed anchor on 30 June and set off to hunt for the French.
He scoured the seas off Turkey, Crete and Greece seeking information.
On 20 July he reached Syracuse in Sicily, which Ferdinand IV of Naples
had allowed Nelson to use as a temporary base. It was the one place the
British could use in the Mediterranean. The fleet spent six days taking on
fresh food and water; then it set off to resume the chase. Back went the
squadron to the eastern Mediterranean.

Nelson did not know that Napoleon had arrived at Alexandria on 31
June, the day after he left.

Two days after leaving Syracuse Nelson's fleet put into the Bay of Coron
in Greece. There, finally, he got confirmation that Napoleon was in Egypt.
It was too late: the French army would have disembarked and the battleships returned. All Nelson could hope to achieve was to lock the stable
door and impose a blockade.

Nelson called his force 'the finest squadron that ever graced the
ocean'.[1] 'Unanimity,' wrote Saumarez in his journal, 'I believe greater
never existed in any squadron.'[2] The way Nelson handled his captains
in the summer of 1798 as they hunted Napoleon has been held up as
a model of leadership. Captain Berry wrote that throughout the pursuit Nelson would have all the captains aboard his flagship, 'where he
would fully develop to them his own ideas of the different and best
modes of attack'.[3] According to Berry he communicated his ideas so

effectively that his plans needed no additional instructions.

However there is only one recorded instance when Nelson called all his captains together. It is unlikely that he went so far as to outline his plans in advance to a conference of captains. What he seems to have done was more subtle and much more effective. He had a way of establishing firm bonds with all the men who served under him. With captains he trusted – and most of those with him in 1798 were of the highest quality – he preferred discussion to direct orders. Several captains knew him and his methods. During the cruise he made efforts to get better acquainted with the senior captain, James Saumarez, sometimes spending the whole day with him. He had a lot of time for the talented Alexander Ball.

All the captains, whether they had fought with him before or not, knew him by reputation. They knew what he had done at the Battle of St Vincent, how he had made a judgement and followed it through at great personal and professional risk. They knew from various incidents that he led by example and fought from the front. Hence they knew that aggression, initiative and courage were expected of them all. They also knew that Nelson aimed at complete annihilation of the enemy, not nice tactical victories. 'Death or glory!' he had shouted as he boarded the enemy ship at the Battle of St Vincent. That was the standard of courage.

Through broad discussions of seamanship and tactics they would come to understand Nelson's intent. His predecessors such as Rodney and Howe had tried to micromanage battles. Several of the captains had seen at first hand the limitations of that style of leadership. Nelson did not want to fight in that way; his hallmark as a fleet commander was simplicity of tactics. From William Locker he had learnt that victory came when a British ship got in close to her opponents and let her guns do the talking. He knew that the first moments of battle were crucial, when the enemy was taken by surprise by an act of daring and forced onto the defensive. He knew that most of his captains shared his view. They were the best the service had to offer and they commanded trained and primed crews. All they needed was the courage to extemporise, the freedom to fight as they wished and the confidence that their colleagues were of the same mind.

Nelson did not gather his captains together in order to communicate his intentions. Rather, he would meet them one to one, or in small groups, preferably over dinner. He possessed charm and openness. That counted for a lot. Conversations were informal and conducted on a basis of friendship, mutual respect and equality. Few of Nelson's more illustrious predecessors, it should be said, were pleasant men. Hawke, Rodney, Howe and St Vincent were prickly, difficult and somewhat withdrawn commanders who developed relationships with a few favoured captains. Even successful squadrons and fleets frothed with internal discord and mad jealousies. The result was that all too often talented officers bit their tongues and obeyed mediocre admirals like passive donkeys. Nelson's squadron was unusually cohesive.

Thanks to the recent work of Colin White[4] we now know that Nelson communicated his intentions in other ways. He circulated his 'Public Order Book' from ship to ship among the captains. This contained his thoughts on tactics. The discovery of Captain Darby's Nile Pocket Book sheds light on Nelson's style of leadership. Darby copied out Nelson's instructions and added his own annotations. Personal relationships and detailed written instructions – these were the bedrock of Nelson's leadership.

The squadron arrived at Alexandria on 1 August. The French transports lay there, with their troops disembarked. It was a disappointing sight. Ball and Hallowell proceeded into Alexandria to see what was afoot. Hood and Foley took their ships to scout Aboukir Bay, thirty miles east. At 14.30 they signalled to the rest of the squadron that they had at last sighted their quarry: thirteen French battleships anchored in the bay.

Admiral Brueys had, as a young officer, been at Frigate Bay in St Kitts in 1782 when Hood stole de Grasse's anchorage and defended the bay with his ships at anchor. Now Brueys had the opportunity to emulate Hood's brilliant position. His ships were anchored in a line with the first ship in the vanguard close to shoals; more shoals guarded his larboard flank. The afternoon was advancing towards sunset, so the French admiral could rest content that the British would not attempt anything till the following day. He did not want to fight and, in any case, many of his sailors were foraging on shore.

Nelson did not share Brueys's opinions. He knew it was a tough proposition and he would not have ordered an attack so late in the day 'without knowing the men he had to trust to'. His ships were strung out over ten or twelve miles, but just before 15.00 he signalled for the squadron to turn towards Aboukir Bay.

'The utmost joy, seemed to animate every breast on board the squadron, at sight of the enemy,' Berry remembered.[5] The British ships raced each other into battle. At 16.22 Nelson signalled that every ship should prepare to anchor from its stern. This was an order that Nelson had added to his signal book during the campaign because he had anticipated a battle fought at anchor – just this situation. By hoisting this signal Nelson made it clear to his captains that he wanted them to anchor alongside their opposing ship and fight from that position. The fine details of how

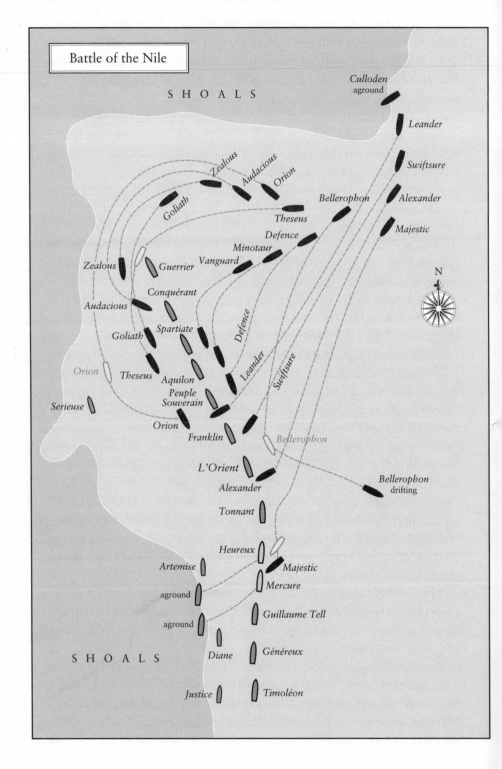

Battle of the Nile

SHOALS

Culloden
aground

Leander

Swiftsure

Alexander

Majestic

Zealous

Audacious

Orion

Bellerophon

Theseus

Defence

Minotaur

Vanguard

Zealous

Guerrier

Conquérant

Audacious

Goliath

Spartiate

Defence

Leander

Swiftsure

Orion

Theseus

Goliath

Aquilon

Peuple

Souverain

Serieuse

Orion

Franklin

Bellerophon

N

Bellerophon
drifting

L'Orient

Alexander

Tonnant

Heureux

Majestic

Artemise

Mercure

aground

Guillaume Tell

aground

Généreux

SHOALS

Diane

Justice

Timoléon

this was to be done were left up to the captains. He had also, at some point, established a system of identifying lanterns so that his ships could fight at night with reduced risk of friendly fire. At 17.30 he signalled for the squadron to form line ahead in the most convenient manner. Foley was winning the race, which was fortunate, as he had an accurate map of the shoals – a French one – in his possession.

As he approached the French, Foley saw that there was room to go round the leading French ship, *Guerrier* (74), and attack from the shore side. He believed that the French would not have prepared their port-side guns because they would not have even considered that the British would risk sailing so close to the shoals. So he followed his instincts. He cut between *Guerrier* and the shoals, raked the French ship as she went by, anchored *Goliath* from the stern opposite the second French ship, *Conquérant* (74), and attacked her undefended side. Next into the attack was Hood in *Zealous*. He feared that he or *Goliath* would run aground any second, but he followed Foley round the head of the French line, raking *Guerrier* as she went. He anchored off the port bow of *Guerrier*. The rest of the British ships came into battle without having to worry about the two leading enemy ships, which were now shattered.

Davidge Gould in *Audacious* was far from audacious, and anchored between *Guerrier* and *Conquérant* on the inshore side. Next came Saumarez in *Orion*. He also crossed around the head of the French line, passed behind Foley and Hood, perilously close to the shore, and sank a French frigate as he went. He then dropped anchor between the stern of *Peuple Souverain* (74) and *Franklin* (80). Then Miller brought *Theseus* inside Foley and Hood's ships. As they passed at a distance of ten yards the men on the British ships cheered each other on. When the French sailors raised a feeble cheer themselves in reply the derisive laughter on the British ships was so loud that it thoroughly demoralised the French, according to one of their captains. Miller anchored between the third and fourth French ships, *Spartiate* (74) and *Aquilon* (74).

By now five British ships had astounded the French by going inshore of their line. Nelson knew it was time to attack from the starboard side, thus doubling the enemy line. *Vanguard* anchored opposite the starboard side of *Spartiate* and *Aquilon*. *Spartiate* became the first French ship to be caught in the crossfire, although this soon came to an end when Miller mistakenly, but generously, left the enemy ship to his admiral and moved down to engage *Aquilon*. Nelson's *Vanguard* was followed by Thomas Louis in *Minotaur*, which passed outside *Vanguard* and anchored in a position from which it could fire upon both *Spartiate* and *Aquilon*. John Peyton's *Defence* overlapped Nelson and Louis and anchored so that she could target *Aquilon* and *Peuple Souverain* (74).

At 19.00, when the sun had just set, Darby's *Bellerophon* got alongside the French flagship, *Orient* (120), the largest ship in the world, and Westcott's *Majestic* took on *Tonnant* (80). These British ships found themselves outgunned and badly positioned. The two British 74s stood a chance against the large French battleships only if they anchored perfectly. Darby should have anchored off the bow of *Orient* so that she could fire upon the enemy without being blasted in return, but he botched his approach and found himself broadside to broadside with the French giant. Westcott mistimed his manoeuvre, sailed past his intended opponent, and *Majestic*'s bowsprit fouled *Heureux* (74). *Bellerophon* was dismasted by *Orient*'s relentless broadsides and she was fired upon by *Franklin* as well; Darby was wounded and had to order his ship's cables to be cut so she could drift out of the teeth of the barrage, which had – remarkably – been withstood for half an hour. *Majestic* was wedged close to *Heureux* and could not bring her guns to bear. Instead she soaked up a lot of punishment, suffering heavy casualties – including her captain – and lost all her masts. HMS *Culloden* had run aground on the shoals before she got into action.

This was a moment of danger for Nelson. Luckily for him at 20.00 in the Egyptian night Alexander Ball and Benjamin Hallowell arrived at Aboukir Bay, having raced back from Alexandria. Hood said that the misfortune that befell *Culloden* was a blessing in disguise, for she became a warning to all other British ships as they came in to battle in the pitch dark. *Alexander* positioned herself off *Orient*'s stern and *Swiftsure* off her bow. Later, at 21.00, Thomas Thompson put *Leander* between *Peuple Souverain* and *Franklin* (80) and from that excellent position was able to rake the stern of *Franklin* while Saumarez moved down to engage her. The varying fortunes of the British ships showed just how complex the task was for each ship and her captain. A team of brawny sailors had to drag the enormous twenty-ton anchor cable from the bow to the stern. Anchoring from the stern meant that a ship sailing before the wind would come to a sudden halt at the right place and hold her course so that she remained broadside-on to her opponent without swinging. The springs attached to the cable allowed the ship to be hauled onto a different angle if need be.

That was hard enough work for the crews. The anchor had to be dropped at exactly the right moment. Simultaneously the topmen had to furl the sails at lightning speed and then rush down to the guns. And all of this in darkness, under enemy fire. The price for making a single mistake was high. *Bellerophon* and *Majestic* failed the test and in return lost masts and a high number of men. Foley had done brilliantly in blazing the trail inshore of the French, but he was unable to anchor at the right moment and found himself between the second and third ship of the French line, not alongside the first as he intended. Gould anchored between the first and second ships at a time when they were virtually beaten.

But those who anchored correctly won an unanswerable advantage over their enemy. Miller positioned his ship beautifully. Thompson found it hard to choose where to place *Leander*. With fifty guns she was no match in an equal contest with the battleships. By anchoring where he did, Thompson was able to rake the bows of *Franklin* so that the cannonballs smashed through the length of the gun decks, blasted out of the stern and hit the bows of *Orient* for good measure.

Benjamin Hallowell was one of the captains who saw what was needed and acted accordingly. He sailed up to *Orient* and anchored in a position off her after-quarter where he could rake both the enemy flagship and *Franklin* without being fired upon in return. His topmen furled the sails and returned to their guns. Opening fire before this was accomplished would lead to disaster: each step must be completed, under enemy fire, before a ship could open her account. Hallowell's *Swiftsure* dropped anchor at 20.03; at 20.05 she began firing.

Only a squadron with trained, highly skilled sailors working in honed teams could hope to pull off tactics like this. As Darby's Pocket Book reveals, Nelson had issued instructions for this kind of scenario, particularly the need to anchor by the stern at the right moment. The Battle of the Nile is the ultimate testament to the seamanship, strength and determination of British seamen. Once the complicated manoeuvres had been completed in the opening phases the men fired their guns without mercy.

The superiority of the British sailor was evident by 22.30. The entire enemy vanguard had been comprehensively beaten within less than two and half hours. *Guerrière*, *Conquérant*, *Spartiate* and *Aquilon* had been dismasted and captured, *Peuple Souverain* had cut her cables and run aground, and *Franklin* was on the point of surrender. The majority of British captains had approached the battle with determination and intelligence. The best among them had positioned their ships so as to rake their opponents. This onslaught devastated the French and flattened their ability to resist. Hence the unprecedented speed at which six enemy ships were overcome. Hood wrote of his attack on *Guerrière*: 'I commenced such a well directed fire into her bow within pistol shot a little after six that her foremast went by the board in about seven minutes, just as the sun was closing the horizon ... And in ten minutes more main and mizzen masts went.'

At 22.30 Nelson was hit on the forehead. He was taken down to the cockpit, believing he was dying. He insisted on waiting in line behind his wounded men before he received the attention of the surgeon. When it was clear that his injury was slight, the concussed and somewhat dazed admiral was taken to the bread room. But it did not matter. This was not a battle that could be directed.

Just before 21.00 someone on *Alexander* managed to throw combustible material through the stern windows of *Orient*. The fire took and spread from the admiral's cabin through the enemy flagship. Efforts to extinguish the fire were hampered by the unrelenting fire from the two English ships. Gunners on *Swiftsure* aimed round- and grapeshot at the places where they saw the fire spreading to keep French fire crews away from the flames. By 21.15 it was obvious that the fires could not be put out. Firing ceased everywhere as the ships prepared for the inevitable shock.

At 21.37 it came. The entire battle site was illuminated for a moment by an apocalyptic explosion. Blackened shards of *Orient*'s timbers rained down on nearby ships. The sound was deafening. But then, for a moment, there was silence. Soon after, the guns resumed.

Ahead of *Orient*'s former position all the French ships had been taken. Astern *Tonnant*, *Heureux* and *Mercure* (74) cut their cables. At around midnight firing ceased again. The men were exhausted and they flopped where they could. Just before dawn Nelson rallied. He sent out boats to the ships that were in good enough condition – *Goliath*, *Theseus*, *Leander* and *Audacious* – to attack the French rear. Only Gould failed to obey. *Tonnant* was dismasted, but refused to surrender. *Heureux*, *Mercure* and *Timoléon* (74) were run aground.

Of the thirteen French battleships only two – *Guillaume Tell* (80) and *Généreux* (74) – escaped. It was a stunning victory, undoubtedly the greatest in British naval history. In the course of one night of carnage the French lost the greatest prize of all – complete control of the Mediterranean. Thanks to Nelson the Royal Navy was back in command of the Middle Sea, with all the strategic and economic advantages it brought. Napoleon and his army were trapped in Egypt.

Victory altered the situation in Europe. France was no longer invincible and its navy's confidence was shattered. The other powers in the Mediterranean – Austria, Russia, Portugal, Naples and Turkey – were emboldened to join Britain in a new coalition against France. Back in Britain people had been nervous all summer as to the fate of Nelson's squadron. Public rejoicing, when news finally reached them, was intense. Nelson was created Baron Nelson of the Nile and became *the* national icon.

In the immediate aftermath Nelson found himself remote from a friendly base and with the pressing need to repair his battered ships and secure his prizes. The day after the battle James Saumarez summoned all the other captains to his ship. They resolved to form a Nile Club and present Nelson with the gift of a sword. It was, they said, in gratitude for his 'prompt decision and intrepid conduct'. In turn Nelson referred to his captains as his 'band of brothers', a quotation from Henry V's speech as rendered by Shakespeare. He commanded the best men in the Navy; they were young (on average a decade younger than their French counterparts), experienced and fired up. His band had, with a few exceptions, done him proud.

The Battle of the Nile exemplified all that was best about the Royal Navy. The captains acted with zeal and good sense. The French fought valiantly in defence of their line, but they could not match the discipline and skills of the British sailors. Nelson did not have much to do during the battle, but, as his captains recognised, his leadership ensured victory. He brought his elite squadron to Aboukir Bay after a gruelling chase that threatened at times to engulf him in anxiety. He had inspired his officers and men throughout. That was evident when the men cheered when they sighted the enemy at anchor and knew that battle was upon them.

At that point most admirals would have considered it too late in the day and waited. Lesser commanders would have been nervous about attacking an enemy at anchor in what appeared to be an impregnable position. Nelson's boldness unlocked the potential of his 'band of brothers' and their men. He trusted them and they wanted to exceed his expectations. They understood the spirit and manner in which he wanted them to fight. He did not overcomplicate matters with detailed orders and endless signals. Surveying the outcome of the battle Nelson wrote: 'Victory is certainly not a name strong enough for such a scene.'

CHAPTER 39

WAR AND PEACE
1798–1803

... our Country will, I believe, sooner forgive an Officer for attacking his Enemy than for letting it alone.

Horatio Nelson

On 15 April 1799 Vice Admiral Eustache Bruix led nineteen ships of the
line out of Brest and into a thick fog. Alexander Hood, Viscount Bridport,
the admiral of the Channel Fleet and brother of the more famous Samuel,
was off Ushant but his blockade was too loose to detect and intercept
Bruix in these conditions. The French squadron was joined by five Spanish battleships off Ferrol and headed south for Cadiz.

Once again the British panicked. Where was Bruix headed? Perhaps he
was going to link up with the main Spanish fleet at Cadiz. Or he could
be headed to cause trouble in the Mediterranean and relieve Napoleon's
forces in Egypt? Worse still, it could be a ruse: Bruix might double back
and invade Ireland or Britain.

Vice Admiral Lord Keith of the Royal Navy was blockading twenty-
eight Spanish warships in Cadiz with fifteen of his own. He was far outnumbered, yet when he heard that Bruix was at large, he formed a line to
prevent the union of the two large fleets. But the French admiral pressed
on and entered the Mediterranean, where he intended to unite with a
large Spanish fleet.

Keith went in pursuit. After the Battle of the Nile, the Royal Navy had
reclaimed its traditional power in the Middle Sea. But it was precariously
held. Napoleon was in Egypt and the French had Malta and much of
Italy. British naval forces were badly overstretched, trying to make the
best of their slight advantage; Bruix's Franco-Spanish fleet left them outnumbered. After the Battle of the Nile, Nelson was the senior officer east
of Minorca. His task since September 1798 had been to aid Ferdinand IV,
king of Naples and Sicily, against the French. Two of his ships of the line
were in Levantine waters helping the Ottomans resist Napoleon's attack

on Syria and a further three were engaged in a long, fraught and expensive blockade of Malta.

The politics and military details of the Mediterranean theatre were devilishly complicated, and Nelson became bogged down in them. Now the British faced the prospect of being swept from the Mediterranean a second time. No one knew what Bruix was up to. He could be destined for Egypt, or to bolster Malta against the British. Or it could be a diversion.

Unbeknown to the British, Bruix headed for Toulon, which he reached on 14 May. Keith got to Minorca, and learnt of Bruix's whereabouts. While Bruix headed back towards Cartagena on 27 May to rendezvous with the Spanish fleet, Keith hurried to Toulon and then searched in vain for the French off Genoa. When the British admiral learnt that Bruix had linked up with the Spanish – bringing the combined strength to forty-three battleships – he turned back to defend Minorca, which he judged to be the likely target.

Keith summoned all the British forces to join him in the defence of Minorca. Nelson refused to obey the order. He considered himself an expert on the Mediterranean and he was, after the battles of Cape St Vincent and the Nile, supremely confident of his own abilities. He was prepared to disobey orders. In the summer of 1799 he judged that his scanty force was most needed off Italy defending Britain's staunch ally Ferdinand IV at Palermo. Even more important to his mind was the fate of Malta. Upon that island hung the fate of the Middle Sea; the blockade of the French on Malta was vital to wider British interests and it could not be abandoned for a minute. He was prepared to launch his few ships at the far larger French fleet in a kind of kamikaze attack rather than let the enemy become mistress of the Mediterranean.

Fortunately for Nelson, Bruix's plans to aid Malta and relieve Napoleon in Egypt were frustrated by the poor state of the Spanish ships and his own trepidation. Bruix led his enormous armada out of the Mediterranean. His aim now was to win control of the Channel. He reached Brest in August, with a frustrated Keith a week behind.

The whole thing was an embarrassment for the Royal Navy. The Franco-Spanish armada had seriously threatened Britain's hard-won position in the Mediterranean and come within an ace of sweeping the home fleet out of the Channel. The First Lord, Lord Spencer, had to regain control, especially now that Brest was crowded with hostile battleships. Spencer had long been determined to tighten up the blockade of the French coast, but he met resistance from within the Navy. The commander of the Channel Fleet, Admiral Lord Bridport, was seventy-three and very hard to manage. He detested the rigours of keeping station off Ushant, maintaining the blockade on Brest and the other French ports – without a doubt the most onerous and unrewarding job in the Navy. Bridport claimed that a close blockade was impossible and during winter months the squadron dwindled in numbers while Bridport stayed in comfort on dry land. The blockade failed to prevent enemy ships coming in and out of Brest. It was not all the aged admiral's fault: the Navy in 1799 was severely overstretched and there was a dire shortage of ships on all stations.

Trouble was brewing throughout the Navy. The Admiralty was chafing about Nelson, who had grown impossible to govern. The hero made a boast of refusing to obey Keith's orders to defend Minorca, claiming he had saved Ferdinand and Malta from the French as a result. Had he been in charge, Nelson claimed, he would have pursued and defeated the entire Franco-Spanish fleet. Things got even worse. Nelson believed that he had earned the right to be made commander-in-chief of the Mediterranean Fleet in succession to St Vincent. Instead Keith got the role and Nelson embarked on a long sulk.

The two were together at the blockade of Malta at the beginning of 1800. Nelson managed to capture *Généreux* (74), one of the two escapees from the Battle of the Nile. A month later, in March, the last of the French ships, *Guillaume Tell*, was taken. Nelson was not there to witness the event: he did not seem to relish time at sea any more, and when he did venture out he brought Sir William and Lady Hamilton, who was pregnant with Nelson's child. His reputation was at a low ebb. Officers and ministers at home were scandalised by his affair with Emma Hamilton and they believed that he was growing slipshod and truculent. Nelson asked Keith for permission to go home. Keith agreed, but did not allow him the honour of returning in a warship. Nelson pulled three battleships away from the blockade of Malta, without orders, and took them to Leghorn, where he took the overland route home, with the Hamiltons as his travelling companions.

A year later the Navy was back in Aboukir Bay. This time it had come as a conquering force. Keith was the master of amphibious operations – a skill Nelson did not possess. The Navy and army had been practising landing operations in Turkey. This was valuable training. The army was embarked in Egypt and comprehensively defeated the French.

Back in home waters Spencer decided that only one man could reverse the bad habits and laxness that had infected the Channel Fleet under Bridport: Earl St Vincent.

The fleet quailed at his impending arrival. A toast was proposed at

Bridport's own table: 'May the discipline of the Mediterranean Fleet never be introduced to the Channel Fleet'.[1] As for St Vincent,he was advised against taking the post of commander-in-chief by his physician, but he said king and country required it and 'the discipline of the British Navy demands it'[2].

Officers and men of the Channel Fleet were accustomed to take leave as and when they felt like it. Admirals and captains frequently passed command to their lieutenants so that they could enjoy hospitality on shore. Of course St Vincent was unpopular: he put a stop to all that. He imposed the iron discipline of the Mediterranean Fleet on them and aimed to blockade Brest as closely as it had been under Hawke, almost forty years before.

To lock down the French Atlantic seaboard required strict order and a regular supply of food, water and alcohol. Ushant was never a pleasant spot at the best of times and the station offered no respite to officers or men. Ships wore out in the hostile waters, men grew ill and grumbled and officers succumbed to disillusion. It is little wonder that few admirals had the stomach for it and sought every opportunity to lead from terra firma. Under St Vincent the squadron was ordered to patrol off the dangerous rocks and shoals of Brest by day and off Ushant at night. There was no rest for anyone, only constant watchfulness and manoeuvring. St Vincent kept his telescope trained on the ships of his fleet to make sure that the captains were present on deck, day or night, when their ships were required to tack in succession. Heaven help a captain who failed to live up to St Vincent's exacting standards.

Ships would be kept at sea for six months at a time and all repairs were carried out there. They were allowed into port only in an emergency and then only for limited periods. St Vincent expected great things of all his men. In return he was attentive to their health. Lemon juice was never allowed to run short. St Vincent used it as a preventative of scurvy, not merely as a curative, as had so often been the case. Damp was kept at bay by scrubbing the lower decks with hot sand (rather than washing with water) and airing bedding. Even more radically, sailors were offered vaccinations.

Between May and September 1800 the fleet brought back only sixteen men needing hospital treatment. The good health of the men, St Vincent said, was his greatest achievement. The Channel Fleet was restored to the state it was in during the days of Lord Hawke. As in the Mediterranean, good officers rose to the challenge, while mediocre ones had their spirits crushed. St Vincent's attitude to weakness was 'Rub out *can't* and put in *try*'.[3] By these means the French and Spanish navies were contained.

It came at a high price. 'For two long, lingering months,' wrote one exasperated officer, 'we had our patience exercised, jogging backwards and forwards like a pig on a string.'[4] Officers were placed under severe strain during months on end when their seamanship was stretched to the limit. Several ships fell victim to the rocks. Gradually the Navy built up accurate knowledge of the French coast by charting and sketching the treacherous coast, and in time accidents declined.

St Vincent had some of the worst captains in the Navy. He also had some of the best, including heroes of the battles of Cape St Vincent and the Nile. Thomas Troubridge – another stern disciplinarian – acted as captain of the fleet. James Saumarez was given command of the eight or so battleships stationed just two miles from Brest harbour. There the squadron commander had to negotiate the reefs and rocks in strong currents and south-westerly winds. It was the toughest job in the Navy, of which few captains were capable. The physical demands reduced Saumarez to looking like a 'shotten herring'.[5] St Vincent wrote that 'with you there I sleep as soundly as if I had the keys of Brest in my pocket'.

For all its strengths the Royal Navy required repeated electric shocks to keep it from slumping into torpor. The methodical Lord Keith restored British power in the Mediterranean. St Vincent revitalised Britain's most important line of defence, the blockade of France. In late 1800 a new threat emerged. The British blockade of French and Spanish ports hurt the Baltic powers, which were deprived of their markets. Denmark attempted to assert her rights as a neutral by dispatching warships on convoy duty. In August 1800 British warships ended the Danish protest with the threat of retaliation. The Danes were no match for the Royal Navy, which was approaching the height of its powers.

But by the end of the year things had changed. Tsar Paul fell out with Britain over the latter's capture of Malta. He put pressure on Denmark, Sweden and Prussia to join a League of Armed Neutrality that would combat British arrogance on the high seas and assert the trading rights of neutrals. Combined their navies had just shy of 100 battleships. This represented a serious threat to Britain. If these powers broke through the British blockade then the French navy would be gorged with vital supplies from the Baltic. Britain's war strategy would crumple in the face of a rejuvenated French navy. Admiral Sir Hyde Parker* was ordered to break up this pact.

---

* Son of the Sir Hyde Parker who commanded the vanguard at Rodney's Battle of Martinique in 1780.

Parker was considered an expert on the Baltic, but he was an old and vacillating man. St Vincent recommended Parker, his second in command in the Channel Fleet, because he wanted to get rid of a flaky senior officer. This rather backfired when St Vincent was suddenly made First Lord and became responsible for Parker again. Lord Nelson, recently promoted to vice admiral, was sent to inject some vitality into this crucial mission. Because of his very public affair with Lady Hamilton and his obvious obsession with her, it was considered that Nelson's attention was fatally diverted; that he had become erratic.

The Navy was ordered to proceed to Copenhagen and either force the Danes into concessions or destroy their fleet. Parker and Nelson were then to attack the Russian navy, and, if need be, intimidate the Swedes as well. The Navy needed to move fast.

When Nelson joined the fleet at Yarmouth on 7 March he was already planning how to defeat the northern league. Parker was planning a ball. The 64-year-old admiral had just married an eighteen-year-old girl and was in no hurry to go to the Baltic. When the expedition did eventually set sail Parker refused to let Nelson see important intelligence. They also disagreed on strategy. The admiral wanted to wait for the enemy to venture out. Nelson wanted to head straight for Kronstadt and strike at the real troublemaker, Russia. Parker thought it too risky. More time was wasted debating whether to enter the Baltic via the Great Belt or the Sound of Denmark. While Parker stalled the Danes built up their defences.

Parker was spooked by the thought of tackling Copenhagen. An attacking force would have to enter the King's Channel, a narrow strip of shallow water that separated a large shoal called Middle Ground from Copenhagen harbour. The city side of the Channel was lined with Danish warships, floating batteries and forts. At last Nelson was given the chance to lead the attack. It was a tougher proposition than the Nile.

'It was my good fortune to command such a very distinguished set of fine fellows,' Nelson remembered of his captains.[6] Thomas Foley served as his flag captain on HMS *Elephant*. His old friends Thomas Fremantle, Thomas Thompson and George Murray were there, with a host of other excellent captains in Nelson's squadron, which consisted of six 74s, three 64s, a 54, a 50, five frigates, four sloops, two fireships, a collection of gun brigs and, most importantly, the seven bomb vessels that would destroy the Danish dockyards once the battleships had broken down the defences. Parker was to retain six of the largest ships and approach Copenhagen from the north.

Nelson had very little time to weld his squadron into a team. On the night of 30 March he went out in a boat to survey the Hollander Deep and leave warning buoys in shallow water. Next day he brought his favourite captains aboard Parker's flagship and outlined his plans. The first ship would enter the channel, anchor opposite a predetermined Danish ship or floating battery of the same size and open fire. The next ship would pass outside the first, anchor alongside the next target and open fire. This would be repeated down the line. The frigates would engage the northern part of the Danish defences while gun brigs and a frigate would rake the southern tip of the enemy line. Once the shore defences were overcome British troops would take the Tre Kroner fortress and the bomb vessels would begin to shell the city and the dockyards. One witness recalled: 'The energy of Lord Nelson's character was remarked; [he] kept pacing the cabin, mortified of everything which savoured either of alarm or irresolution.'[7]

The next day was spent placing more warning buoys to mark dangers. He conferred with his trusted subordinates on board the frigate *Amazon* and then rowed among the ships shouting instructions to each with his 'squeaky' Norfolk drawl.[8] He then dined all his captains, during which he radiated confidence. For the division was very nervous indeed. The pilots and masters did not fancy their chances negotiating the shoals.

Next day bore out their nervousness. The carefully laid plan came unstuck early on when the leading ships into the channel ran aground on the Middle Ground. Nelson had to take personal command, guiding *Elephant* along the middle of the channel. Even so the pilots kept their ships too far away from the Danish ships for Nelson's taste.

By 11.45 all the British ships were engaged (including those aground) and the Danes suffered a pounding, albeit at long range. But it was already clear that resistance was particularly fierce. The floating gun platforms were hard to subdue. The Danes were fighting for something more tangible than the Spanish sailors at St Vincent or the French at the Nile: they were fighting for their families and homes. They could be resupplied and reinforced in the middle of a battle, something not possible in most naval engagements. Nonetheless British naval gunnery began to tell. By 12.45 a number of Danish ships had been knocked out of action by forty British broadsides.

Sir Hyde Parker was five miles away and was fretting at Danish resistance. He raised a signal at 13.15: 'Discontinue the action'. It was later claimed that Parker was afraid that Nelson was in trouble and his signal gave him the chance to retire without fear that he would suffer court martial and disgrace; Nelson was free to obey or ignore it. But that was an excuse. An order was an order, not a suggestion.

The frigates attacking the fortress saw the signal and obeyed. 'What will Nelson think of us?' asked their commander.[9] Nelson's second in command saw it, but concealed the repeating signal behind a sail and kept the signal for close action flying. Nelson saw it and acknowledged it. 'You know Foley,' he said, 'I have only one eye and I have a right to be blind sometimes.' He then placed his telescope to his right eye: 'I really do not see the signal.'

If Nelson had obeyed the signal or if the captains had chosen to obey Parker rather than him, the Battle of Copenhagen would have been re-membered as a naval disaster of the first order. As it was, most of the Danish ships struck by 14.00. Thomas Fremantle wrote that the carnage on board the Danish ships far exceeded anything he had ever seen in naval warfare. Nelson said that it was a massacre: 'It was a sight no real man could have enjoyed.' But Nelson had by no means defeated the Danes. Their batteries were still in operation and were inflicting serious damage on the northernmost British ships. Casualties were high. Moreo-ver Nelson had several ships aground, including his flagship. The advan-tage was with him, but only just.

Nelson then produced one of his most controversial moves. He sent a letter to the Crown Prince of Denmark. 'Lord Nelson has directions to spare Denmark when she is no longer resisting,' he wrote. He went on to say that if the Danes persisted in firing he would have no option but to set fire to the floating batteries without rescuing the Danish prisoners. The Crown Prince agreed to a truce. Nelson wrote again saying that if peace was declared between Denmark and Great Britain it would be 'the greatest victory he had ever gained'.

Nelson's quick thinking extricated him from a sticky situation. He was able to get his damaged ships out of range of the enemy forts. He got his grounded ships afloat. Most importantly he was able to secure the prizes he had taken in the battle. Two enemy ships had been sunk, one had exploded and twelve were taken. Eleven of the prizes were burnt and one used to take wounded men back home. Nelson's senior officers and friends saw his move as a 'masterpiece of policy'. He had reversed a weak position. His bravery was already assured; now he won a name as an astute strategist and a man of political courage. His determination and force of character ensured victory. He had clawed back his reputation.

Parker reinforced his reputation for caution when he sent Nelson ashore to negotiate. When talks stalled bomb vessels were brought within range of Copenhagen. The problem was that the Danes feared retaliation from Russia if they sided with Britain. This threat was lifted within a few days when news arrived that Tsar Paul had been assassinated. That freed the Danes to seek peace. Nelson went in pursuit of the Swedish navy, which hurried back to port. Parker refused to let him push further into the Baltic. The government and St Vincent were by now weary of Parker and ordered him home. Nelson was put in command of the fleet and raised to a viscountcy. But by June it was clear that matters had been settled in Britain's favour. Nelson and the fleet arrived at Yarmouth on 1 July. The Battle of Copenhagen was a messy and cheerless affair, but its importance cannot be denied. Britain needed naval stores for herself from the Baltic as much as she needed to deny them to the French.

At exactly the same time another Nile veteran was showing the mettle of the new generation of British admirals. James Saumarez had been pro- moted to rear admiral and put in charge of the blockade of Cadiz. On 6 July Saumarez, with six battleships, entered the Bay of Algeciras near Gibraltar and attacked three French ships of the line that were sheltering under the guns of Spanish forts. It was an attack imbued with the spirit of Nelson. Saumarez, however, lacked Nelson's luck. The wind and tide turned against him and the attack, known as the First Battle of Algeciras, petered out. The British lost one ship and the remainder were badly dam- aged. Saumarez retired to Gibraltar and set about emergency repair work. On 12 July a Spanish force of five ships of the line (plus an extra French battleship) arrived to escort the French to Cadiz. Once again Saumarez decided to attack against the odds.

In a night engagement subsequently called the Second Battle of Alge- ciras his five battleships took on nine Franco-Spanish battleships. He sent on *Superb* (74), the fastest ship he had, to spearhead the attack. *Superb* caught up with the rear of the enemy squadron and fired three broadsides at *Real Carlos* (112). To the delight of *Superb*'s captain, Richard Keats, *Real Carlos* panicked and opened fire on *San Hermenegildo* (112), which was abreast of her. *Hermenegildo* fired back, believing *Carlos* was the British ship. Then other enemy ships began firing at what they believed to be *Superb*. The real *Superb* had, in fact, moved up the enemy line and cap- tured *San Antonio* (74) after a short fight, leaving the Franco-Spanish ships to shoot at each other in the dark and smoke. *Carlos* caught fire and when *Hermenegildo* moved to rake her stern the two ships became entangled. Both the Spanish sea monsters exploded, with huge loss of life.

Saumarez won a major victory immediately after a defeat. The public expected no less from its Navy. In a range of activities – from months of deadening blockade to glorious, sharp encounters such as at the Second

Battle of Algeciras – the service proved its mettle. The Navy's ruthlessness was displayed at Copenhagen in 1801. After Saumarez's victory the Spanish demanded their ships back from Brest and their relations with France cooled. In October Britain and France began peace negotiations. The Peace of Amiens was signed in March 1802.

The break in hostilities did not last for long. In May 1803 the French swept through Italy. Britain was threatened on several fronts. If Napoleon controlled Italy he could aim at the eastern Mediterranean again and strike at Egypt and India. At the same time Napoleon began gathering an enormous army at Boulogne which would invade England. Britain's admirals were entrusted with the defence of the kingdom. Keith took command of the North Sea Fleet. Lord Cornwallis, an elderly, dour but committed admiral, was put in command of the blockade of Brest. The fleet was every bit as disciplined, efficient and organised as in St Vincent's day. Cornwallis was waiting off Ushant the day before war was declared. Cuthbert Collingwood was put in charge of the onerous inshore duties. Edward Pellew blockaded Ferrol. And Lord Nelson was sent to take command of the Mediterranean Fleet and blockade Toulon.

On paper this was formidable talent arrayed against Napoleon. In reality the Navy had suffered from peace. Earl St Vincent was a great admiral but he was a dreadful administrator, believing the Navy Board to be a sewer of corruption and waste. He thought the same of the dockyards and the men who worked there, and set in train witch hunts against administrators and contractors. Economies were imposed by a First Lord who, like many a military man, believed that civilian administrators knew how to spend money but not what to spend it on. Contracts were torn up with men whom St Vincent viewed as out and out cheats.

The result was that during the peace the Navy's administration was at war with itself and vital work in the yards and stores ground to a halt. When war came again the admirals found that their fleets were short of ships and supplies. And once again the Navy had to be brought up to full strength by impressments and men sent from the county quotas and jails.

Things had got particularly bad in the Mediterranean. When Britain was at peace the fleet there had suffered from neglect. The ships were rotten and in need of urgent repairs; supply lines had broken down; and the men were demoralised, hungry and suffering from illness. This was the fleet Nelson was sent to command in May 1803. Things did not start with a flourish. When he arrived at Portsmouth he found his flagship, HMS *Victory*, in 'a pretty state of confusion'. She was only half-manned and when the numbers were brought to full strength the crew 'consisted of all sorts of persons, some captured by the police, others released from prison etc. In short, there were few men who could either hand, reef or steer'.[10] To make matters worse she might not even be Nelson's flagship for long: Lord Cornwallis had the right of first refusal.

Victory made slow progress to the rendezvous point with Cornwallis, accompanied by HMS *Amphion* (32). To Nelson's intense annoyance there was no sign of the Channel Fleet. Nelson switched to the frigate and hurried on to join his own fleet. When *Victory* located Cornwallis it turned out he did not want her after all and she followed *Amphion*. Nelson wrote an angry letter to the outgoing prime minister saying that he knew how important it was for him to get to the Mediterranean quickly, but 'I can only work with such tools as my superiors give me'.[11]

CHAPTER 40

THE CHASE
1803–1805

Bonaparte has often made his brags, that our fleet would be
worn out by keeping the sea ... but he now finds, I fancy, if
emperors hear truth, that his fleet suffers more in one night,
than ours in one year.[1]

Horatio Nelson, 14 March 1805

When HMS *Victory* caught up with the Mediterranean Fleet on 1 August
1803, Nelson shifted his flag from the cramped frigate *Amphion* and entered the wooden world of the 100-gun ship. He would not leave her for
two years.

Command of the Mediterranean would test Nelson's skills as a leader to
the limits. On the strategic level he had endless tasks nagging at him. The
most important was to keep the French battlefleet blockaded in Toulon
lest it break out to support an invasion of England or a renewed attack
on Egypt. But there were other worries. A massive flotilla of gunboats was
being gathered at Marseille and Genoa. No one knew their target: it could
be Sardinia, Sicily or the Peloponnese. French armies menaced the whole
of Italy and the Balkans and corsairs plagued the seas, disrupting British
trade.

And those were just some of the problems facing the British in the
Mediterranean. To make matters worse for the commander-in-chief the
fleet was unhappy, bedevilled with rotten ships and hungry, unhealthy
men. The fleet that was responsible for establishing British power from
Cadiz to the Levant consisted of eleven ships of the line, several in
poor condition, and about fifteen frigates. The chief task – blockading
Toulon – was made all the more complicated because the only British
bases in the theatre – Gibraltar and Malta – were hundreds of miles
away (Minorca had been returned to Spain in 1802). Supplying the
rickety fleet and keeping it fighting fit was the stuff of administrative
nightmare. Rarely before had the Mediterranean been so important to the

Navy, and governing it had become almost impossible.

Nelson threw himself into solving every problem; the years as commander-in-chief in the Middle Sea show him at his very best. The first priority was to find a base. In that respect the menacing French gunboat flotilla offered a solution. Thanks to surveys made by a British naval officer, Nelson discovered an anchorage in the Maddalena Islands, off Sardinia, which the British called Agincourt Sound. It was two hundred miles from Toulon, but it offered access to regular supplies of water, beef, sheep, poultry, vegetables and onions. Agincourt Sound was to be a regular base for the British fleet. Thanks to the French threat, Sardinia was prepared to let Nelson use it for extended periods, though he had to work hard at diplomacy to keep the deal alive. Without the Sound, Nelson could never have operated anywhere near Toulon.

Agincourt Sound was the first step in establishing the British fleet as a power in the western Mediterranean. The next step meant ceaseless organisation. Nelson knew that the way to a sailor's heart was through his stomach. He took personal oversight of the supply of food to the fleet: 'we must not be economical of good things for our sailors, but only take care that they are faithfully supplied'. Quality, not just quantity, was important for him. He assembled all the masters from the ships and made them sample random selections of Admiralty rations and local produce. The officers had to taste the menus and decide which were the best for the men. Supplies from home were inadequate. Few merchants in the region wanted to be paid in IOUs redeemable in London. Nelson insisted on being sent hard cash to buy provisions.

Even more worrying, local states were under pressure from Napoleon not to do business with the Royal Navy. Nelson got an agent sent out from home to manage the needs of the fleet. His name was Richard Ford and he became indispensable, scouring the Mediterranean for its supplies. Food and naval goods came from the North African coast, the Adriatic, Malta, Syria, and from as far away as the Black Sea. Ford made good use of British agents and merchants based around the region. Store ships scurried between land and the fleet, bringing all manner of supplies to the fleet. Nelson once compared the running of a fleet to the mechanism of a watch: all was well when the parts whirred in harmony, but once the moving parts were disrupted the 'whole machine gets wrong'.[2] He scrutinised ships' accounts to eliminate waste or uneconomical practices. No detail regarding the men's health and comfort was beneath his attention; one moment he could be ordering tens of thousands of oranges from Spain, the next judging the relative merits of different trousers and

Guernsey jackets. 'These things are for the Commander-in-Chief to look to,' he said.

'The great thing in all military service is health,'[3] wrote Nelson to a medical doctor; 'and you will agree with me, that it is easier for an officer to keep men healthy, than for a physician to cure them.' He set up a hospital at Malta and, for good measure, insisted it must have a garden. A cruising squadron was constantly at war with scurvy; between 1803 and 1805 it was repelled and kept at bay, and the thanks go to Nelson, who fought hard to secure citrus fruit wherever it could be found. 'I never experienced anything like the health of this fleet,' he reported after a year. 'We have literally not a real sick man in it.'[4]

A more durable achievement than securing lemons and fresh food was Nelson's attitude to the medical profession. Naval surgeons had long been treated badly by the service; they did not enjoy the distinction of uniform or the status of using the wardroom and they were badly paid. Nelson campaigned for this to be changed and he gave the medical men wide-ranging responsibility for improving health and hygiene. In doing so he won the loyalty of the surgeons and physicians in his fleet. The effects were immediate. 'We are healthy beyond example,' wrote Nelson, 'and in good humour with ourselves and so sharp set that I would not be a French admiral in the way of any of our ships.'[5]

Nelson managed his fleet with care and sensitivity. But what he wanted most was to defeat and destroy the French navy. Every nerve was strained anticipating battle at a moment's notice – yet for now it seemed a distant possibility. Instead Nelson's blockading ships lay in the Gulf of Lion off Toulon and withstood the torture of the mistral and the levanter. As it whips through the valleys and passes of the Alps, the Pyrenees and the Massif Central the north-west wind accelerates until it reaches 60 mph. It is a relentless, dry wind known as the mistral and it is particularly suffered by ships in the Gulf of Lion, which are prey to its gales and sudden storms. The levanter blows in from the east, bringing heavy swells and rain. Over the months Nelson's ships were gradually worn down by the endless gusts and battered by the sudden vicious storms.

The mistral and the levanter made life at sea miserable. It also made close blockade of Toulon impossible. From the hills high above the port lookouts could keep track of the British ships and know when they were blown off station. In any case Nelson did not relish close blockades in the manner of Hawke, St Vincent or Cornwallis. What he wanted most was to draw out the French and then pounce. He must be ready, but be patient too.

As ever drill punctuated the week. But it was a long and tedious job of blockading an enemy who showed no signs of moving. Everyone felt the strain. Nelson endeavoured to break the monotony and the slow agony of the mistral by keeping the fleet on the move. It would hold station off Toulon, its proper base, but it would also move around the western basin of the Mediterranean. Frigates – the eyes of the fleet, Nelson called them – were stationed permanently off Toulon to report on enemy movements. Brief respite could be got at Agincourt Sound.

For his part, Nelson kept himself busy by involving himself in every aspect of the fleet's daily life. He also put his mind to battle tactics. To this end he procured accurate maps of all anchorages in the area and gave them to his captains to study. Once again he anticipated a battle at anchor, perhaps after chasing the Toulon fleet into a bay or sound. He gave orders for this eventuality. But most importantly he kept a daily weather journal. As the blockade passed the twelve-month mark such a compendium of information became valuable. Nelson was learning how to read the Mediterranean.

Nelson paced the quarterdeck, deep in thought or in intimate conversation with his flag captain, Thomas Hardy. He reached out to the officers of the fleet, entertaining them to dinners on *Victory*. They felt the full force of his charm. He got to know the young men serving under him and was able to impart some of his tactical knowledge. Over two years the captains learnt of their admiral's evolving battle plans and his expectations of them.

'I have little to say,' he wrote to Emma Hamilton, ' – one day is so like another, and having long ago given you one day, there is no difference but the arrival of a letter or newspaper, the same faces and almost the same conversation.'[6] Nelson began to be ground down by months of waiting. Everyone was suffering from 'the uniform sameness, day after day, and month after month – gales of wind forever'.[7] Nelson was well aware of the dangers of prolonged shore leave. He did not leave *Victory* once during this time, and the anchorages he chose for refreshment were remote from any fleshpot.

As time wore on the men began to flag. Punishments for the symptoms of boredom – drunkenness, quarrelling and insubordination – multiplied. Life on frigates was, as ever, happier; at least they were kept busy on intelligence-gathering missions, convoy duty or patrolling close to Toulon. It was harder on battleships, which were kept on station and battered by the everlasting winds. To relieve the boredom Nelson instituted various diversions. The band played every day. He also

THE

NAVY & ARMY
ILLUSTRATED.

VOL. 1 —NO. 12]   *FRIDAY, MAY 29th, 1896.*

Admiral John Fisher photographed in a typical insouciant pose. Fisher's flamboyant character and the impact of his reforms on the Royal Navy intrigue historians and split opinions today as much as they did during his heyday.

HMS *Dreadnought*, the ship which changed naval warfare for ever.

Above: HMS *Royal Oak*, one of the new generation of imposing super-dreadnoughts launched between 1910 and 1914. She saw service at the Battle of Jutland and was sunk at Scapa Flow in 1939 by *U-47* in one of the most daring submarine attacks of all time.

Photographs such as this one made Admiral David Beatty a star of the media age during the First World War. The cap placed at a stylish angle, his personalised uniform and aristocratic hauteur broadcast his contempt for authority and determination to do things his own way – preferably with panache.

Above: Battleships stretching into the horizon: the awesome sight of the Grand Fleet's dreadnoughts and escorts en route to Scapa Flow in 1914.

Right: The battlecruiser HMS *Repulse* leads the line of battle during exercises in the 1920s.

HMS *Queen Mary* blowing up at the Battle of Jutland, 31 May 1916, at or shortly after 16.26. To the left is Beatty's flagship HMS *Lion*; around her are pillars of water sent skyward by near misses. Cordite fumes billow from *Lion*'s Q gun turret, destroyed by a salvo fired from SMS *Lützow*.

HMS *Ark Royal* in the 1930s.

The Battle of Cape Spartivento 27 November 1940. Bombs fall astern of HMS *Ark Royal* during an attack by Italian aircraft.

HMS *Ark Royal*, almost lost in the plumes of water thrown up by near misses from enemy bombers off the southern tip of Sardinia.

Johnnie Walker's men drop a pattern of depth charges over a submerged U-boat from the stern of Walker's sloop HMS *Starling*. After a ten-hour hunt Walker's ships raised *U-264*, the sixth kill of the Second Support Group's famous patrol in January and February 1944.

Above: Drama on the bridge of HMS *Starling*. Johnnie Walker takes a bearing on a submerged U-boat after receiving a report from his Asdic operator, 'Echo 180 degrees, 2,000 yards, Sir'. Walker clutches a sandwich in his right hand.

Statue of Captain Frederic John Walker, CB DSO*** by Tom Murphy at Pier Head, Liverpool. It was unveiled by the Duke of Edinburgh in 1998.

British naval power in 1960: HMS *Victorious* leads *Ark Royal* and *Hermes*.

Ships Taken Up From Trade (STUFT) have always been vital for British naval strength. Here a Harrier jump jet lands on *Atlantic Conveyor* during the Falklands War.

The Royal Navy's operations in the twenty-first century are more often than not part of multinational efforts. As seen here, during Operation Enduring Freedom (the war in Afghanistan), it frequently plays a subordinate role. The ships, in four descending columns from left to right, are the Italian frigate *Maestrale*, the French frigate *De Grasse*, the American aircraft carrier *John C. Stennis*, the French carrier *Charles de Gaulle*, the French frigate *Surcouf*, the American guided missile cruiser *Port Royal*, the Royal Navy's amphibious assault ship HMS *Ocean* trailing in the wake of the French flagship, the American carrier *John F. Kennedy*, the Italian destroyer *Durand de la Penne* and the Dutch frigate *Van Amstel*.

encouraged amateur theatricals to keep the men laughing.

In December 1804 the strategic situation changed when Spain finally allied with France. Now Napoleon had 102 battleships at his disposal. The Royal Navy had but eighty-three in serviceable condition. His plan was to deal with Britain once and for all. His huge invasion army was not intended to *conquer* Britain. That was far from his mind. His well-trained hordes would enter London and destroy the dockyards there and on the Medway and at Portsmouth and Plymouth. Britain would be finished as a naval power. Hence she would be ruined as a trading nation. Then his army would return across the Channel, having knocked Britain back to the Middle Ages.

Napoleon's problem was that his ships were in numerous ports and under a British blockade that stretched from Toulon to the North Sea. But recent history had shown that given the right weather conditions French fleets could break out of Brest and Toulon. History also taught that an attack on British sugar islands and colonies would divert the Navy's over-stretched blockading ships. If the components of the French navy could be brought together and concentrated on the Strait of Dover for only a few hours, Napoleon could get his army to Britain.

1805 would be the year when his main enemy would be destroyed.

No one in Britain knew what Napoleon had in mind. Nelson could only guess when, on 19 January 1805, two of his frigates sped to Agincourt Sound to inform him that a large French fleet under Vice Admiral Pierre Charles Villeneuve had left Toulon. Seven days after he heard the news that the French had left Nelson was at Alexandria with his force of eleven ships of the line and accompanying frigates. He made the voyage in extraordinarily quick time, especially as most of his ships were ailing after years of active service in the teeth of the mistral.

What made up for the decrepit ships were Nelson's captains, officers and men. He rated them even higher than his 'Band of Brothers' which had made the same journey back in 1798. The men were at the peak of their training and desperate to fight. The captains were of the first order. They included Benjamin Hallowell and Thomas Hardy, both Nile veterans. Also present was *Superb* and Richard Keats, the ship, captain and crew that had single-handedly tackled the Franco-Spanish squadron in 1801. Nelson's squadron also included William Parker, one of the best frigate captains in the Navy. Over the course of two years Nelson had created his finest team.

There was no sign of the French in the eastern Mediterranean. Nelson had grown fixated on Napoleon's ambitions in the East and so miscalculated. But the French fleet had not gone west either. Only when Nelson arrived back at Sardinia at the end of February did he learn that Villeneuve's inexperienced sailors and poor ships had encountered gales and returned to Toulon. Nelson received reports that Villeneuve was ready to sail. He set his French counterpart a trap. He took his fleet to the waters off Barcelona, then slipped back to Sardinia, leaving frigates to watch the seas. Nelson believed that this would force Villeneuve to sail south to Majorca and fall into his snare. But the ruse was blown by a Ragusan merchantman. Villeneuve went north of Majorca, evading Nelson and his scouting frigates. On 8 April the French fleet passed the Strait of Gibraltar; the next day it picked up the Spanish fleet.

Nelson still believed the enemy would head east. But as April wore on and no news arrived he became very nervous. Villeneuve might be heading for England. These fears plagued Nelson; he slept badly, picked at his food and suffered feverish symptoms. In stormy weather he could be on deck all night, watching out for his fleet and getting soaked through. Then, on 19 April, HMS *Amazon* reported that Villeneuve had been seen leaving the Mediterranean. Nelson was hundreds of miles and a month behind. It took him two agonising weeks to beat to Gibraltar and another to get to Lagos Bay. There he discovered the Franco-Spanish fleet had not sailed north. They must be in the West Indies.

What was Nelson to do? The French fleet could be attacking the British colonies. If so his duty was to pursue them. But what if it was a ruse? Napoleon could be using the Toulon fleet to lure British ships out of home waters so he could launch an invasion. There might well be another British fleet in pursuit of Villeneuve. Nelson had to make a judgement based on what facts he had. He went after Villeneuve. It was eleven British warships against eighteen.

The fleet reached Barbados on 4 June. Now the hunt was on. Relying on poor intelligence it made for Trinidad. On 10 June the British fleet was off Montserrat. Nelson had as good as caught up with his prey, and he relished the prospect of battle. Just 150 miles away, at Anguilla, lay Villeneuve's fleet. The French admiral was alarmed at Nelson's rapid progress. Villeneuve had encountered the Royal Navy many times during his career and he had most commonly been on the losing side. In American waters he had fought with the French royal navy against Rodney at the Battle of Martinique, against Graves at the Battle of Chesapeake, against Hood at St Kitts and Rodney again at the Saintes. While other senior aristocratic officers were purged from the French navy during the Revolution, Villeneuve had proved that he was ideologically sound. He witnessed Nelson's brilliance in August 1798 when he commanded the rear division at the Battle of the Nile. He did not want to meet his scourge again, and set sail for Europe to put into operation Napoleon's grand plan.

The essence of the emperor's strategy was to gather his ships from Toulon, Cadiz, Ferrol, Rochefort and Brest, get them to the Channel and use them to support the invasion of Britain with 140,000 crack troops. Villeneuve was in the West Indies to entice the various British blockading squadrons away. He was supposed to be waiting for the Brest fleet to join him. However the emperor was too clever by half. The new First Lord, Lord Barham (formerly Sir Charles Middleton), called the blockade of Brest 'the mainspring from which all offensive operations must proceed'. He spoke in the spirit of Anson and Hawke: the Navy was at its strongest when it commanded the Western Approaches. The Royal Navy's weary blockading ships held firm and the Brest fleet could not get out. Now Villeneuve was ordered to join with ships at Ferrol and then raise the British blockade at Brest, before heading to Boulogne to escort the emperor and his magnificent force across the Channel.

Nelson led his band of ships back across the Atlantic, bound for Gibraltar. This was the most testing part of the campaign. The winds were faint and provisions running low, but Nelson did not allow spirits to flag. For over two years he had held station off Toulon in weatherbeaten ships; he had led his weary force to Alexandria, then to Sardinia again and across the Atlantic and back to save the West Indies from French predation. It was a triumph of leadership and fleet management.

Nelson sent a sloop to report to the Admiralty. On the way it observed Villeneuve making for Ferrol, not for Cadiz as Nelson had expected. The vital intelligence was brought to the new First Lord, Barham, who grasped the strategic significance at once. The French were not aiming at Egypt after all; they were heading north to link up with the Spanish in the first stage of an invasion of England. He ordered the blockading squadron off Rochefort to join that off Ferrol, where fifteen battleships under Vice Admiral Sir Robert Calder were waiting for Villeneuve. On 22 July Calder intercepted the Franco-Spanish fleet. They fought in fog that afternoon and again the next day. Calder took two Spanish ships and Villeneuve made it into Ferrol. For this inconclusive battle poor Calder was savaged in the press and ordered home to explain himself. Only at this remove in time can we see that Calder played his part in thwarting Napoleon.

For Napoleon banked on secrecy and surprise. Villeneuve was supposed to appear out of the massive expanse of the Atlantic and confound the Royal Navy. He would spring the Brest fleet from their imprisonment, then the imperial navy would carry all before it and screen Napoleon as he raced across the Channel. The problem was that everyone knew where Villeneuve was. Nelson had dogged him across the Atlantic and Calder had diverted him from the push on Brest.

Now Villeneuve awoke to reality. Between him and Napoleon lay the might of the Royal Navy's home fleets. Behind him was Nelson. He knew now that the grand plan was hopeless and made for Cadiz. As he sailed south, Nelson sailed north. They narrowly missed one another. Nelson and Calder's forces joined Cornwallis off Brest. The gateway to Britain was barred and bolted.

On 18 August Nelson returned to a hero's welcome in England. On 23 August Napoleon cursed his navy and left Boulogne. The threat of invasion had lifted.

Nelson spent less than a month in Britain. For over two years he had planned how he would annihilate Napoleon's navy. Now he was ready.

Long before, in 1780, Nelson had contracted a fever in the West Indies. He had been nursed back to health by William Cornwallis. In December 1804 he wrote to Admiral Cornwallis to remind him of their conversations back then: 'I felt that I imbibed from you certain sentiments which have greatly assisted me in my naval career – that we could always beat a Frenchman if we fought him long enough.' It was in that spirit of controlled aggression that he now advised his fleet. It was his duty, he told his captains, to bring the fleet as close to the enemy and as quickly as he could. 'I am sensible beyond this object it is not necessary that I should say a word, being fully assured that the admirals and captains I have the honour to command, will, knowing my precise object, that of a close and decisive battle, supply any deficiency in my not making a signal.'

He was going into more detail in September 1805. On the 10th he outlined his plan with his fingertips on former prime minister Lord Sidmouth's desk. 'Rodney broke the line in one point,' he said; 'I will break it in two.'

It has been assumed that Nelson was referring to the Battle of the Saintes, Rodney's great victory. But this is surely mistaken. Nelson would have known that Rodney broke the line in two places. What Nelson was referring to was Rodney's failure off Martinique in 1780. Rodney had intended to confound the French by concentrating his force on one part of their line. His flagship did pierce the line, but no one followed him. Now, in 1805, Nelson was planning something similar. He would attack the combined Franco-Spanish fleet in two columns. Each would be headed by the biggest hitters in the fleet. The most powerful British ships would mass on key points and smash through the line, passing from to windward to the lee of the enemy fleet in the manner pioneered by Howe at the Glorious First and Duncan at Camperdown.

Nelson explained his plan to Captain Richard Keats. 'Well, what do you think of it?'[8] he asked. Keats was stunned into silence at Nelson's sheer audacity. For a start the first ships in the column would come under devastating fire before they reached the enemy. 'I'll tell you what I think of it,' said Nelson, answering his own question. 'I think it will surprise and confound the enemy. They won't know what I am about. It will bring about a pell-mell battle, and that is what I want.' What he wanted above all was total annihilation of the enemy. He had observed the French and Spanish for years. He knew that once his ships got close to them and prevented escape the Royal Navy's guns would prove overwhelming. He called his plan the 'Nelson Touch'.

He fretted that he would be too late. A squadron of British ships, led by Collingwood and Calder, was watching and waiting off Cadiz. Many of the officers and men were just as impatient. 'Is Lord Nelson coming out to us again?'[9] wrote Edward Codrington, captain of *Orion* (74). 'I anxiously hope he may be; that I may once in my life see a commander-in-chief endeavouring to make a hard and disagreeable service as palatable to those serving under him as circumstance will admit of, and keeping up by example that animation so necessary for such an occasion.'

The fleet Nelson joined off Cadiz was something of an unknown quantity. He knew only a handful of the captains. Thomas Fremantle (*Neptune*, 98), Vice Admiral Collingwood (*Royal Sovereign*, 100), Thomas Louis (*Canopus*, 80) and Edward Berry, in the trusty *Agamemnon*, were friends of old. Three others had been with him in the Mediterranean for the past two years. William Hoste, the captain of *Amphion* (32), had followed Nelson to sea as a midshipman on *Agamemnon* back in 1794. Another frigate captain, Henry Blackwood (*Euryalus*, 36), had greatly impressed Nelson when he hunted down the last French survivor of Aboukir Bay, *Guillaume Tell*, back in 1800. The admiral cherished the young frigate captain as a true Nelsonian, an officer imbued with his fighting spirit and tactical flair.

The other captains were unknown to him and he did not have long to prepare them for battle. As soon as he arrived he withdrew the battleships from the close blockade of Cadiz and left his frigates there, headed by the trusted Henry Blackwood. The fleet relaxed as soon as it left off the rigours of blockade. Boats zipped between the ships. HMS *Victory* became a hub. At the centre was Nelson, eager to meet his new captains and inspire them to destroy the enemy.

Nelson's presence electrified the fleet. Victory was assured. He entertained the captains on his flagship in order to get to know them. George Duff, captain of HMS *Mars* (74), had never met Nelson but was instantly captivated by the little admiral. 'He is so good and pleasant a man, that we all wish to do what he likes, without any kind of orders.'

Nelson's favourite way of communicating was at convivial dinner parties. There were no admirals who could reach out to their men as Nelson did. Nelson's battle plan was received with enthusiasm and emotion by captains who were yearning to deal the final hammer blow to the French navy.

Nelson summarised the general response: 'It was new – it was singular – it was simple!' Simplicity was key. Nelson once said that he did not want a 'Lord Howe victory'. By that he meant that the older generation of admirals had grown obsessed with clever tricks. In short they had overcomplicated battles with unrealistic expectations of how a fleet could be micromanaged in conflict. Howe had done well at the Glorious First of June, but he had failed to fire up his fleet and crush the enemy. In 1805 Nelson was happy to explain the technicalities of the plan, such they were. But he saw that his most important job was to inspire confidence and whet the appetite for battle. He trusted most of his captains and had faith in the men.

It is important to realise that only five captains in Nelson's fleet had ever commanded a ship in a fleet action. The rest needed to be prepared. They could not have had a better guide. The plan would work only if the British ships got into battle quickly. As at the Nile the men would have to work aloft under fire until the last moment. It was up to the captains to keep up discipline on their ships and come to close quarters without opening fire. They needed a cool head, for in the opening moments of a battle the captain stood alone and exposed on the quarterdeck as he brought his ship within twenty yards of the enemy.

Nelson was well aware that in the storm of war there were captains who would panic or freeze with indecision. They would look for their commander-in-chief's signals – often in vain as the smoke clouded the scene. He also knew that some captains were bound to lack the tactical sense to 'read' a battle. For them he had a specific instruction: 'in case signals can neither be seen nor perfectly understood, no captain can do very wrong if he places his ship alongside that of an enemy.'[10]

To make doubly sure that every ship got into action quickly and aggressively Nelson gave secret orders to the frigate captain Henry Blackwood. Blackwood recalled how Nelson gave him the freedom 'of making any use

I pleased of his [Nelson's] name, in ordering any of the sternmost line of battle ships to do what struck me as best'. Nelson was a judicious delegator of power, but he was not indiscriminate. He trusted Blackwood more than some battleship captains to understand the plan and help put it into effect. If Blackwood saw any ships of the line struggling to carry out the orders he was to order them to get quickly into battle by whatever means their captains thought best.

On 19 October Villeneuve obeyed Napoleon's orders to sail for Italy. Nelson received the news from Blackwood and signalled for a general chase. He made south-east for the Strait to cut Villeneuve off from the Mediterranean. The British sailors spent an anxious night, fearful lest the Combined Fleet cheat them of battle by dashing back for Cadiz. This was not withstanding the fact that the British fleet had twenty-seven battleships against thirty-three under Villeneuve.

At dawn Captain Codrington was awoken by the sounds of cheering and men clattering up the hatchways. His men were rushing to see the enemy fleet on the morning of the long-awaited battle. A sailor on *Victory* remembered seeing what looked like a forest on the lee bow. Villeneuve signalled for his captains to form a line of battle.

The result was a shining example of the futility of clever manoeuvres in the face of an enemy. In an ominous Atlantic swell and light breezes the French and Spanish ships found it hard work to get into their allotted order. Things were simpler on the British side. At 06.15 Nelson ordered his fleet to form into two divisions. At 06.30 he signalled to prepare for battle and to bear down on the enemy. The order of the line of battle was the order in which the ships happened to find themselves.

At 08.00 the Combined Fleet had still not completed its manoeuvre. By now the Royal Navy was approaching in two columns. Villeneuve ordered his fleet to wear together and reform on the opposing tack in reverse order. This meant that the rear division would become the vanguard, and the van would take the rear. It also meant that the fleet would be heading for Cadiz and safety. This fresh manoeuvre resulted in disorder. In some parts of the line ships began to bunch; at others inviting gaps for the British began to appear. The line bulged into a crescent.

By now the British were just five miles away. The men cleared the ships for action. Bulkheads were removed and furniture stowed; the men's hammocks were hung along the gunwales for protection; livestock and unnecessary items were tipped off the sides of the ship. The ships' boats were lowered and towed, so that they would not be blasted into lethal splinters during the battle. Men stripped to the waist and wound headbands round their heads to keep the sweat from their eyes and protect their ears.

All this was quite normal before a battle. What was different that morning was the long wait as the fleets edged closer. It was a strange, protracted hiatus which lasted for six hours after the first sighting of the fleets and left enough time for 30,000 men to contemplate at considerable leisure the looming firestorm. Nelson wrote a prayer and his last will and testament. He gave his final orders to his frigate captains and toured *Victory* to encourage his men and urge them to hold their fire until they were close to the enemy.

For the men, after the routine business of preparing the ship, the best solution was to find some form of distraction. There was time to eat a meal of cold meat and wine. Bands played 'Heart of Oak', 'Rule Britannia' and other patriotic naval songs from the poop decks of various British ships. The sailors made their final preparations. On one ship a group of British sailors danced a hornpipe. Villeneuve paraded the imperial eagle around his quarterdeck and conducted a ceremony in which his officers renewed their oath of loyalty to the emperor.

At 10.50 Nelson signalled Collingwood: 'It is my intention to pass through the enemy's line and prevent them getting to Cadiz'. At 11.40 he signalled the fleet using a new system that allowed him to spell out individual words: 'England expects that every man will do his duty'. Shortly after, he raised his favourite signal: 'Engage the enemy more closely'. At 11.50 Blackwood transmitted orders to Fremantle in the third ship in the line; Nelson was going to tack for the enemy vanguard but then change course to starboard and cut Villeneuve's line at the thirteenth or fourteenth ship in the line.

At 11.56 the first shots were fired. The Battle of Trafalgar had begun.

CHAPTER 41

THE BATTLE
21 October 1805

First gain the victory and then make the best use of it you can.

Horatio Nelson

The British ships wore studding sails as they proceeded in two columns towards the Franco-Spanish fleet. These were extra sails hoisted alongside the normal sails, designed to extend the sail area and increase speed in light winds.

Nelson's ships made slow progress even so. The ships at the head of the columns – Nelson's *Victory* and Collingwood's *Royal Sovereign* – bore the brunt of enemy broadsides. *Sovereign* was under attack from seven ships as she crept towards the Franco-Spanish line. The only time she opened fire was to create enough smoke to conceal her exact position.

If we discount the ships and men for a minute, the hours before the battle saw a weight of armament edging inch by inch into fatal proximity. It was a mass of firepower unknown on land. If all the cannons of all the armies at the Battle of Waterloo were lumped together with the guns from the two fleets at Trafalgar, just 7 per cent of the total would be contributed by the land forces.[1] *Victory* alone carried armaments equivalent to 67 per cent of the Duke of Wellington's artillery in 1815.

Collingwood reached the head of the Combined Fleet's rear before Nelson got to Villeneuve in the centre. 'See how that noble fellow Collingwood carries his ship into action,' said Nelson on the quarterdeck of *Victory*.[2] Pierre Servaux, an officer on the French ship *Fougueux* (74), recalled that his ship had fired over 100 rounds at decreasing ranges as *Royal Sovereign* slowly approached. The ship that followed Collingwood, HMS *Belleisle*, had fifty men killed before she opened fire. As she approached all the men lay by their guns in silence. The only words spoken were between the captain and the master.

Collingwood's flagship opened fire only when she was yardarm to yardarm with her prey at 12.10. 'Then she gave us a broadside from

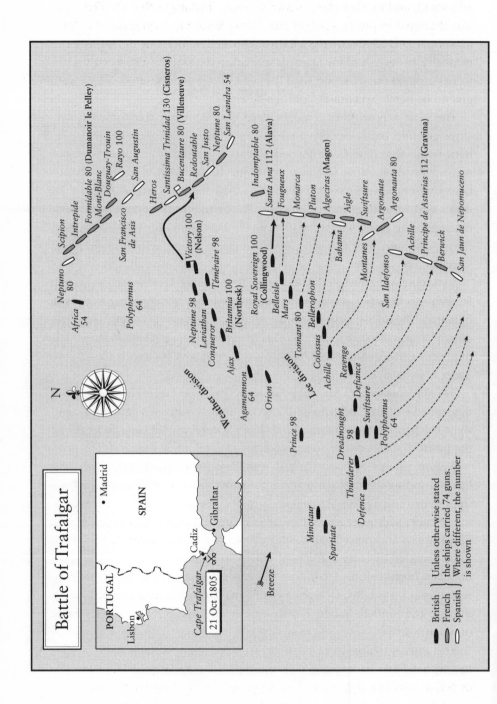

Battle of Trafalgar

21 Oct 1805

PORTUGAL

Lisbon

SPAIN

• Madrid

Cape Trafalgar

Cadiz

Gibraltar

Breeze

N

Weather division

Lee division

British
French
Spanish

Unless otherwise stated
the ships carried 74 guns.
Where different, the number
is shown

Neptuno 80
Scipion
Intrepide
Formidable 80 (Dumanoir le Pelley)
Mont-Blanc
Douguay-Trouin
Rayo 100
San Augustin
San Francisco de Asis
Heros
Santissima Trinidad 130 (Cisneros)
Bucentaure 80 (Villeneuve)
Redoutable
San Justo
Neptune 80
San Leandra 54
Indomptable 80
Santa Ana 112 (Alava)
Fougueux
Monarca
Pluton
Algeciras (Magon)
Bahama
Aigle
Swiftsure
Argonaute
Argonauta 80
Montanes
Achille
Principe de Asturias 112 (Gravina)
San Ildefonso
Berwick
San Juan de Nepomuceno

Africa 54
Polyphemus 64
Victory 100 (Nelson)
Neptune 98
Leviathan
Temeraire 98
Conqueror
Britannia 100 (Northesk)
Ajax
Agamemnon 64
Orion
Royal Sovereign 100 (Collingwood)
Belleisle
Mars
Tonnant 80
Bellerophon
Colossus
Achille
Revenge
Defiance
Swiftsure
Polyphemus 64
Prince 98
Dreadnought 98
Thunderer
Defence
Minotaur
Spartiate

fifty-five guns and carronades, hurtling forth a storm of cannonballs, big and small, and musket shot,' wrote Servaux. 'I thought that the *Fougueux* was shattered to pieces – pulverised.'[3] Next *Royal Sovereign* raked the stern of *Santa Ana* (112) as she passed through the line, blasting dozens of cannonballs the length of the Spanish ship's gun decks. Fourteen enemy guns were slammed out of action with that one broadside. 'What would Nelson give to be here!' exclaimed Collingwood.[4]

The plan was without a doubt bold. But it meant that Nelson's big ships got into battle one by one. This was made more dangerous by the light winds that day. Collingwood was across the line, but once there he was on his own. Now *Fougueux* could get her revenge. Enemy cannonballs smashed into *Sovereign*'s stern, causing carnage on her crowded gun decks and wounding her grievously. The rudder and steering gear were damaged; the mizzenmast went by the board; the hail of shot lacerated the rigging and tore the sails. *Royal Sovereign*'s guns fell silent and she signalled for aid.

Santa Ana was able to reply too after her mauling. Her broadside caused *Sovereign* to heel out of the water and blew away her studding sails and halliards. The British ship was alone on the far side of the enemy line. Five enemy ships crowded round her. Midshipman George Castle looked out of a stern gunport and 'saw nothing but French and Spaniards round [us] firing at us in all directions'.[5]

But *Royal Sovereign*'s tars were hardened fighters. Admiral Collingwood descended into the inferno of the gun decks to rally his men and help sight the guns. After a quarter of an hour *Santa Ana* had been battered to the point of surrender.

Nelson led his division towards the French van then turned to starboard, heading down the line until he found Villeneuve's flagship. Before she opened fire *Victory* was battered by the French vanguard. In twenty minutes her sails were riddled with holes, her masts and yards took heavy punishment and her wheel was blasted to pieces. The gigantic tiller had to be operated by forty seamen labouring in the lower gun deck. The carnage was horrific. John Scott, Nelson's trusty secretary, was cut in two. His replacement was killed straight away. Eight marines were mown down by a single cannonball. When *Victory* opened fire over fifty men were dead or wounded.

The enemy ships were so close together that it looked as if *Victory* would have to ram her way through the line. With her wheel out of action and her rigging and sails cut to pieces, manoeuvring was not going to be easy. It was not until 12.35 that she was able to find her gap astern of Villeneuve's flagship, *Bucentaure* (80).

Victory's 68-pounder forecastle carronade fired a roundshot and 500 musketballs onto *Bucentaure*'s packed quarterdeck. Then *Victory* raked her enemy's stern with a full broadside. The guns had been loaded with double or triple shot. It was a fearsome cannonade, and fired from such close quarters that the officers standing on *Victory*'s quarterdeck were sprayed with splinters from their opponent's stern. This first attack put some four hundred Frenchmen and twenty guns out of action. But then *Victory* found two big French ships waiting for her on the other side of the French line. She was attacked by *Redoutable* (74) and *Neptune* (80). The British flagship became entangled with the former. So closely were they lashed together that *Victory*'s guns were pressed against *Redoutable*'s hull. From point-blank range the British guns, which had been treble-shotted, exploded into the enemy's belly.

Redoutable had one of the best captains and crews in the enemy fleet. Captain Lucas drilled his men in the arts of boarding. The soldiers and sailors were armed to the teeth with muskets, pistols, sabres and grenades. The gunners on the French ship abandoned their positions and massed on deck to board *Victory*, whose upper decks had been swept almost clear of men by enemy fire. Only the vicious forecastle carronade held the boarders at bay.

Royal Sovereign and *Victory* had struck two violent hammer blows at the enemy line. Both ships had suffered to reach that point. Now they had to hold off ferocious attack while they waited for the rest of the ships to come into battle.

Royal Sovereign was alone for fifteen or twenty minutes – although it felt a lot longer to the men in the middle of the fire fight – until the rest of Collingwood's division got into action. HMS *Belleisle* poured broadsides into the hapless *Santa Ana* and then the plucky *Fougueux*. The latter took a terrible pounding from the British ships. After an hour she was draped in the wreckage of her own masts, rigging and sails. Fire broke out and anyone who tried to extinguish it met a hail of shot. *Fougueux* carried on firing, but the British fired faster and decimated her gun crews. As the duel with *Belleisle* neared its close half the crew on the French ship were dead or wounded and the only thing left above deck was the flag flying defiantly.

One by one the leading ships in Collingwood's division entered the fight. HMS *Mars* did not follow *Royal Sovereign*, but cut south. The French ship *Pluton* (74) left her position to engage the British ship. HMS *Tonnant* (80) cut through the resulting gap in the line and attacked *Monarca*

(74) with her port broadside and *Algésiras* (74) with her starboard battery. *Bellerophon* became entangled with *Aigle* (74). *Bellerophon* fired so many broadsides into *Aigle* (74) that the French gunners were driven from the lower decks. As soon as they appeared on the upper decks they found *Bellerophon*'s guns elevated to tear into them. 'When she got clear of us [*Aigle*] did not return a single shot while we raked her; her starboard side was entirely beaten in.'[6] While locked in this tight embrace with *Aigle*, *Bellerophon* was able to fire on *Monarca* as well.

In this part of the battle several British ships were obliged to take on more than one opponent. Within an hour a number of enemy ships were crippled and were suffering heavy casualties. *Bellerophon* fought the 74s *Bahama*, *Montanes*, *Swiftsure* and *Aigle*. HMS *Colossus* (74) engaged *Swiftsure* for an hour and a half and *Bahama* for two. HMS *Revenge* (74) got into action at 12.50. She broke the line more than a mile south from Collingwood's initial incursion. As she did so the Spanish ship *Principe de Asturias* (112) ran her bowsprit over her poop and two hundred Spanish soldiers and sailors prepared to board. *Revenge*'s carronades and a line of marines held them off while the ship's great guns engaged two other enemy ships. Nelson had intended to outnumber and overwhelm the enemy rear, but because of the light winds only a few of Collingwood's division got into action, and it was they who were outnumbered.

Further north *Victory* was saved from the boarding parties on *Redoutable* when *Temeraire* caught up with her. *Temeraire* crossed the line between the French *Neptune* and *Redoutable* and raked *Victory*'s opponent. *Redoutable* was caught between the two powerful British ships and any possibility of boarding vanished. Next was the British *Neptune*, which attacked two enemy ships before targeting *Santisima Trinidad* (130). It was now just after 13.00 and the part of the enemy line either side of Villeneuve's flagship had broken down into a fierce melee.

There was an especially bloody quality to the Battle of Trafalgar. The leading fourteen ships in the two British lines soaked up the enemy's punches. And these ships did the bulk of the fighting outnumbered by their opponents at exceptionally close quarters – so close that oaths and pistol shots could be exchanged through open ports. As Nelson knew, British gunnery would overwhelm its opponents, no matter how bravely the French and Spanish fought or how skilfully they manoeuvred. He also knew that before this advantage could come into play the first British ships would be made to pay an enormous price. At 13.15, half an hour or so after *Victory* broke the line, Nelson was shot through the shoulder by a sharpshooter stationed in the *Redoutable*'s mizzentop.

The admiral was carried to the cockpit. He was conscious for the next few hours and able to follow the course of the battle. 'Oh, *Victory*! *Victory*! How you disturb my poor brain!' he murmured as another broadside exploded and set the ship a-trembling.

Just half an hour after Nelson was taken below the first enemy ship surrendered. It was the prize of all prizes, Villeneuve's flagship *Bucentaure*, smashed into submission by a line of attackers. The British ships then swarmed around *Santisima Trinidad*. At 13.55 brave *Fougueux* finally surrendered. A broadside from *Temeraire* put her last remaining guns out of action.

Nelson put his trust in the Navy's fabled discipline. Even in the early stages of the battle it was clear he was vindicated. The French and Spanish were no pushovers, to be sure. Where the British excelled any other Navy was not just in their discipline but in their ability to retain it amid the terrors of so brutal a battle.

A French sailor later said that the British guns must have been manned by devils, so fast were they reloaded and fired. And the British sailors must have looked like devils as they toiled unceasingly and with grim determination, as sweat streaked down their faces and naked chests. The guns exploded and leapt backwards. In went the sponge to extinguish the sparks. In went the cartridge, cannonball and wadding, rammed home by the crews. They hauled the gun back into position, ready to do its worst. Then the gun would lurch back as another broadside roared.

The French and sailors could not match the rate of fire from their enemy. And the more broadsides a British ship could unleash relative to its opponent the harder it was to reply. The gun crews on the French and Spanish ships were depleted with each thunderous cannonade. And so the next broadside would come that much more slowly. Eventually whole gun crews were slaughtered or disabled; guns were blasted off their trucks. During sustained bombardments from British ships at point-blank range an entire enemy gun deck might be deserted save only for a few wounded wretches.

'Raking' an enemy ship was an appropriate word. A hail of iron entering the unprotected bows or stern of a ship and ricocheting the length of a gun deck was like the harrowing of hell. In a close-range fight the gun captains would reduce the powder in the charge. Too much gunpowder and the ball might pass clean through the enemy ship. Less powder meant the ball had less momentum, but it would smash through the hull of the opposing vessel, and with luck ricochet and cause maximum carnage. The second lieutenant of *Revenge* described the effect on his ship:

The shot entered the 3rd lower deck port from forward on the starboard side and struck the gun (32-pounder) in which it made a large dint, then altering its direction struck the foremast in a vertical position and scooped out a large proportion of the mast, which again altering its direction, it took a horizontal position and after decapitating a young midshipman by the name of Green, it struck the seven men at the foremost tackle of the first gun forward on the starboard side who were running out after loading, and killed the whole of them by severing them nearly in two. It then struck the ship's side in a horizontal position, just above the waterway nearly under the breech of a gun.[7]

The sights and sounds of a pell-mell battle such as Trafalgar haunted men for the rest of their lives. Midshipman Castle wrote that 'it was shocking to see the many brave seamen mangled so, some with their heads half shot away, others with their entrails mashed lying panting on the deck, the greatest slaughter was on the quarter deck and poop'.[8]

For thousands of sailors on both sides the battle was a glimpse into hell. The gun deck turned into a blackened, smoky furnace. Men slipped on the blood and viscera of their messmates as they fought. To continue to man the guns in these conditions required the utmost courage. An officer remarked that the side effects of battle – temporary deafness and the inability to see because of the gun smoke – helped because they blotted out the noise and vision of messmates dying. All the men had to keep them sane and grounded was the mechanical rhythm of loading, hauling, firing, hauling loading ... over and over again.

Before the senses were numbed by the din and the murderous rhythm of war the worst part was the approach into battle. At that point most of the men had nothing to do except wait in silence. Paul Harris Nicolas – a sixteen-year-old lieutenant of marines on HMS *Belleisle* – recalled the utter silence as the ship approached the enemy line.[9] It was punctuated only by shot flying overhead and the shrieks of sailors struck by cannonballs. A man's head was blown off; the captain was prostrated on the deck but got to his feet. 'My eyes were horror struck at the bloody corpses around me,' recalled Nicolas, 'and my ears rang with the shrieks of the wounded and the moans of the dying.' The boy was tempted to lie down, as most of the men were doing. But the example of his senior lieutenant, standing resolutely on the quarterdeck, drove his fears away and made him stand tall as well. 'My experience is an instance of how much depends on the example of those in command when exposed to the fire of the enemy, more particularly in the trying situation in which we were placed for nearly thirty minutes, from not having the power to retaliate.'

The quarterdeck was the most dangerous place on the ship, the target for every sharpshooter and carronade crew. But it was a point of honour for officers – on both sides – to lead their men from that exposed position. They set the tone for the rest of the ship. Other officers stationed in the gun decks were responsible for keeping the men motivated. Collingwood nonchalantly ate an apple on the quarterdeck as his ship broke the line; he rallied his men at a difficult moment in the battle. Good officers sometimes took a hand in the labours of their crews when things were tough.

A bad officer inspired neither courage nor devotion in his men. William Robinson wrote of a midshipman who was just twelve or thirteen. This boy had been in the habit of standing on a gun carriage so that he could kick and beat the seamen under his command. When he was killed on the quarterdeck by grapeshot his body was badly mutilated, 'his entrails being driven and scattered against the larboard side'. The men had little pity: 'Thank God, we are rid of the young tyrant.'[10]

Officers played a part in keeping up morale, and how well they managed to do this depended upon respect they earned long before the moment of conflict. But in the heat of battle other factors came into play. One sailor wrote that the men at the guns remained in place partly in fear of the marines stationed at the hatchway, but mainly because they feared being dubbed a coward by their mates. 'Our only true philosophy ... was to make the best of our situation, by fighting bravely and cheerfully.'[11] Midshipmen sometimes led the men in cheering to keep up spirits. But battle stupefied most of the men. They simply did not register the deaths of their messmates.

There were plenty of instances of individual bravery. On the quarterdeck of *Tonnant* a man working one of the guns was shot through his big toe, so that it hung to his foot by a shred of skin.[12] 'He looked at his toe, and then at his gun, and then at his toe again. At last he took out his pocket knife, gave it to his comrade – "Jack, cut that bit of skin through for me." "No," says the other, "go down to the doctor, man." "Damn it, I'm ashamed of going down to him for this trifle, just whip it off for me, it's only a bit of skin."'

Nelson told his captains that his duty was to bring them to battle in the most advantageous way he could. Timing was everything. Once in the right place at the right time the admiral could trust to the skills, discipline and fortitude that had been built up over generations. The men, as we have seen, were highly trained and regarded discipline as essential to their safety.

But more than that – much more – they knew that they would win. They knew they were better than their enemies. In the horrors of a battle such as Trafalgar that self-confidence translated into power. British sailors had developed a habit of victory. They had traditions, an oral history passed down through generations. They knew the Royal Navy was the best in the world.

Even so the battle was won by a minority of ships. These made up for the deficiencies in the officers in other ships. At Trafalgar some British casualties came from friendly fire. The guilty parties were captains who had a sudden rush of blood to the head as they neared the battle and opened fire indiscriminately. Other ships suffered from poor sailing qualities, took too long to get up to the melee and played little part in the fighting. In Nelson's division HMSs *Victory* and *Temeraire* between them had 282 dead and wounded; the nine ships that followed them into battle had casualties totalling 219. Death and mutilation in Collingwood's division were more fairly spread, for the first eight ships at least – the nine ships astern of HMS *Achille* in the line lost relatively few men.

The French and Spanish sailors fought harder than anyone on the British side had expected. Many ships in the Combined Fleet fought on until they were completely dismasted and could barely fire a gun in anger. Captain Lucas wrote that *Redoutable* 'was so riddled that it no longer represented more than a heap of debris'.[13] Of that ship's crew of 643 men, 300 had been killed and 222 wounded. 'I know of nothing on board that was not cut up by shot,' remembered her captain. By the time she surrendered, the decks were strewn with slaughtered men, the wreckage of masts and splintered timber; all the ship's guns were out of action; four out of six pumps were destroyed and all the internal ladders were in pieces.

Nelson took a great risk at Trafalgar because he attacked in two lines in a light breeze. His ships were exposed to raking broadsides as they inched towards the enemy line. But the admiral knew his enemy all too well. The men of the Combined Fleet were let down by their leadership and their lack of gunnery drill and combat experience told against them. The French and Spanish gunners' aim was poor and they had to use guns fired by old-fashioned slowmatches rather than the flintlock mechanism used by the British. This was important on 21 October 1805. The heavy Atlantic swell caused the ships to roll. The more experienced British gun captains could time their shots so that their guns fired directly into the enemy's hulls or decks. The French and Spanish gunners did not have this kind of control. The slowmatch burnt agonisingly slowly, causing a delay between the decision to fire and the moment the match ignited the cartridge. If the ship was rolling badly then the broadside would pass high into the air or uselessly into the sea. That was bad enough. But it was much worse when two French or Spanish ships were trying to bombard one British ship from opposite sides. Often their shots passed over the British ship and hit a friend by mistake.

After several hours of fighting the leading British ships – those used as the battering ram – had been reduced to floating wrecks. HMS *Mars* had been raked through her stern by a number of enemy ships, killing the captain and taking away the masts. She was left to drift through the battle. Yet in even the most ravaged British ships casualty rates were much lower than in their opposing ships. On *Mars* twenty-nine men had been killed and sixty-nine wounded out of a crew of 615. On ten British ships the casualty rate was between 10 per cent and 20 per cent; only on two was it over 20 per cent;* fifteen ships had rates below 10 per cent.

The comparison with the Combined Fleet is startling. Eighteen ships in Villeneuve's fleet lost over 20 per cent of their crews. Nine of those ships had a third or more killed or injured. Eight captains and two admirals perished, as compared with one British admiral and two captains. The men of the Royal Navy therefore remained in higher spirits and they kept their ships operational. And most importantly they were relieved periodically by the arrival of a fresh ship into the action. The French and Spanish crews became ever more demoralised as the battle degenerated into a melee and their ships lost contact with their colleagues.

The ordinary sailors in the Combined Fleet were also betrayed by the poor tactical sense shown by many of their officers. Villeneuve had anticipated Nelson's battle plan and he sought to counteract it by forming twelve battleships into a Squadron of Observation – a flying reserve that would stand by to reinforce the line wherever it was most threatened.

When it came to it, however, the Squadron of Observation, rather than acting as a dynamic force in the French line, limply joined the rear. Villeneuve, like Nelson, gave his captains the discretion to fight where and how they liked. In the early stages of the battle Villeneuve signalled for ships to come to his aid. This would have had the effect of reversing Nelson's bold strike at the centre by overwhelming *Victory* and the other British ships as they came one by one into battle. He was ignored by his captains who stubbornly held their place in the line. The battle turned

---

* HMS *Bellerophon* lost twenty-eight men and had 127 wounded out of a crew of 522. HMS *Colossus* had forty dead and 160 wounded from a crew of 571. In both cases it was round about a third of the crew. HMS *Victory* had 159 men dead or injured out of 821, about a fifth of her crew.

into a melee. In such a scenario it was always the British who would hold the advantage unless the Combined Fleet managed to co-ordinate some kind of counterattack.

But no captain or admiral in the Combined Fleet showed any tactical awareness of the battle. The French vanguard delayed coming about to help the stricken ships left in their wake. Only at 13.45 did Rear Admiral Dumanoir order his division to turn back. It became another object lesson in why complicated manoeuvres did not work in battle. One ship collided with another and the rest took a long time to come about. It gave the British time to improvise a line of battle with a few available ships to prevent Dumanoir counterattacking the damaged British ships. Dumanoir contented himself by firing at long range at Spanish ships captured by the British.

Villeneuve pointed out a major difference between his fleet and the British: 'To any other nation the loss of Nelson would have been irreparable, but in the British fleet off Cadiz, every captain was a Nelson.'

From his deathbed in the cockpit Nelson heard his sailors cheer. He asked what it meant. He was told they were cheering every time a British ship captured an enemy. When Captain Hardy came down to visit his admiral at 14.35 Nelson rasped: 'Well Hardy, how goes the battle?'

'Very well, my lord,' Hardy replied: 'we have got twelve or fourteen of the enemy's ships in our possession ...'

At 15.25 Hardy reappeared and reported that fourteen or fifteen enemy ships had surrendered 'That is well,' croaked Nelson, 'but I bargained for twenty.'

Nelson died before the final figure was known. His fleet took eighteen of Villeneuve's thirty-three battleships. No British ships had struck or been destroyed. Along with Nelson 458 men were killed and 1,208 wounded. The French had 2,218 dead, 1,155 wounded and 4,000 captured; 1,025 Spaniards died, 1,383 were wounded and 4,000 were taken prisoner.

On 4 November four of the French ships that had escaped with Dumanoir were captured off Cape Ortegal. The Battle of Trafalgar was as decisive a naval battle as they come.

Once the firing came to an end the stupor of battle was lifted. It was a horrible moment. As Captain Codrington recalled: 'The battle after all, as I warned my officers, is nothing compared with the fatigue, the anxiety, the distress of mind which succeeds.'[14] Lieutenant Nicolas described *Belleisle* after the battle: 'The upper deck presented a confused and dreadful appearance: masts, yards, sails, ropes and fragments of wreck were scattered in every direction; nothing could be more horrible than the scene of blood and mangled remains with which every part was covered, and which, from the quantity of splinters, resembled a shipwright's yard strewed with gore.'[15] William Robinson recalled men and officers stumbling round the ship inquiring after their messmates.

Then they had to tip the dead bodies of their comrades overboard. News reached the men that Nelson was dead. Robinson wrote that 'he was adored, and in fighting under him, every man thought himself sure of success'.[16] A seaman on *Royal Sovereign* recalled that he was both sorry and glad he had never seen the great admiral. Sorry because he was a national icon; glad because he could not understand why hardened Jacks should mourn so excessively, like 'soft toads' as he said. He found it creepy: 'God bless you! Chaps that fought like the devil, sit down and cry like a wench!'[17] But he had never been under Nelson's spell.

This was a point when discipline really told. That was especially the case on the evening of 21 October. There was a hurricane brewing. After a welcome measure of rum the shell-shocked, deafened men were set to work to repair their ships. They laboured through the night. When they came to retrieve their hammocks from the netting round the gunwales (where they had been stowed as protection from enemy shot) they found them riddled with holes.

The Battle of Trafalgar set the seal on Britain's absolute dominance of the oceans. It was not the ships that made the Royal Navy great. The Navy was at a low point in 1805, before the battle. After St Vincent's tenure as First Lord there were few ships in commission. Those that were available were in poor condition.

What made the Navy great were the men who manned the fleets, from the admirals down through the ranks to the ships' boys. Once the basics of seamanship and gunnery were mastered everything else followed. The Royal Navy proved invincible at Trafalgar not least because while French and Spanish seamen had languished in port British crews had toiled ceaselessly outside those very ports. Months of duty on blockade had hardened the sailors of the Royal Navy, sharpened their skills and shaped them into crack units. Teamwork, discipline, courage – these set the Navy above any other fighting force in the world. There was no more vivid illustration of this than the recollection of Villeneuve's flag captain:

> The act that astonished me the most was when the action was over. It came on to blow a gale of wind, and the English immediately set to work to shorten sail and reef topsails, with as much regularity and order as if their ships had not been fighting a dreadful battle. We were all

amazement, wondering what the English sailor could be made of. All *our* seamen were either drunk or disabled, and we, the officers, could not get any work out of them. We never witnessed such clever manoeuvres before, and I shall never forget them.[18]

IV
DOMINANCE, DEFIANCE AND DECLINE
1805–2013

INTRODUCTION

'We were getting a bit worried about you, sir,' said a rating to Captain Edward Kinross just after he had been plucked from the sea. Their destroyer had been sunk by the Luftwaffe off Crete in 1941. The ninety survivors had clung to wreckage and rafts for hours, strafed periodically by German planes. Kinross was one of the last to be rescued. 'Nothing like a good swim before breakfast,' remarked Kinross in clipped accent as he passed along the deck to rally his wet and wounded men.

Kinross was the model of the British naval captain – stoical, authoritative, understated and crisply witty. He was, of course, the invention of Noël Coward in his 1942 film *In Which We Serve*. Coward wrote the script and played the part of Kinross, a character based on his intimate friend Captain Lord Louis Mountbatten, whose destroyer was sunk during the Battle of Crete.

Below decks Jack Tar is represented by the cockney Ordinary Seaman 'Shorty' Blake, played by John Mills. After Kinross's rescue one of the ratings comments that they will most likely be taken to Alexandria. 'Join the Navy and see the world,' he snorts. 'Looks to me as if it's going to be the next world,' retorts Shorty cheerfully, as the destroyer comes under renewed aerial bombardment. A little later he expresses his disgust at sitting passive while the ship is bombed. 'Brace up; remember Nelson,' says Chief Petty Officer Walter Hardy in his reassuring West Country burr. 'Yeah, look what happened to him,' replies Shorty, to general laughter.

John Bull is a creature made up of diverse elements. Jack Tar bequeathed him his cheerfulness in adversity and directness of speech. The naval officer gave him his stiff upper lip, calmness in crisis and self-discipline, with a dash of raffishness.

In the midst of a grim struggle for national survival, representations of the Navy's officers and men in films such as *In Which We Serve* were reassuring. The film opens with the line: 'This is the story of a ship ...' But it is about more than that: as Bosley Crowther, film critic of *The New*

York Times, put it, *In Which We Serve* 'is a full and complete expression of national fortitude'. The focus is on the crew of the fictional HMS *Torrin*, but the intent is to recall the entire stirring history of the British Navy and its role as the bulwark of national defence for a beleaguered public. That eternal spirit was recognised by Crowther: 'It catches the "feel" of a destroyer with vibrant intensity – the sweep of her hull through the water, the pounding of pom-pom guns, the co-ordination in battle and the cool, efficient order on her bridge.' He could have been talking, with a slight change of vocabulary, about British sailors at Quiberon Bay or the Nile.

In the midst of total war the Royal Navy was raised high on a pedestal. It symbolised centuries' worth of defiance against the odds and Britain's island independence. This reflexive public support was a boon for the service, but it could also be a burden. It is no exaggeration to say that miracles were expected from the service. This might be called 'Trafalgar syndrome' or the 'Armada miracle' – the faith that the Navy could deliver the decisive knockout blow and rescue the country. In *Ships With Wings*, another navalist propaganda film from the Second World War, a warrant officer dismisses someone who doubts that planes can take off from a bombed British aircraft carrier with the words 'Nelson struck "impossible" out of our signal book'. The magic of Trafalgar affected enemies as well. After the Battle of Jutland in 1916 the great German admiral Reinhard Scheer wrote: 'The English fleet had the advantage of looking back on a hundred years of proud tradition which must have given every man a sense of superiority based on the great deeds of the past.'

It is little wonder that the great writers of naval fiction – Captain Frederick Marryat, C. S. Forester and Patrick O'Brian key among them – focus on the period from 1794 to 1815. All officers who have served since the Napoleonic wars have had to live with the ghosts of a golden generation breathing down their necks. The Battle of Trafalgar also fostered the idea that one great battle and control of the seas by an unchallengeable battle-fleet were the sure ingredients of victory.

It left a lot to live up to. The Navy achieved an aura of invincibility. It was the pillar of national defence and the bedrock of empire. Its officers became an epitome of a certain type of Britishness. As with so many aspects of the national character it was shot through with class. Throughout the nineteenth century officers were drawn from the gentry and upper classes as never before. The identification of the Navy with self-defined national characteristics such as resilience, self-sacrifice and duty attracted generations of princes, from William IV to Prince William. The naval officers of the nineteenth century were a superior, even haughty bunch.

The Navy became fashionable and socially acceptable. Even so, the high professional standards of the service survived its gentrification. Aristocratic insouciance coexisted with uncompromising self-discipline and the clockwork routine long established on British warships. It was an odd mix of values: upper-class yet methodical; urbane but technically competent; individualistic and collegiate at the same time.

In war, particularly a war of national defence, the character of the men who served in the Navy became intertwined with the sense of national identity. That went for ratings as well as officers. Chief Petty Officer Hardy in *In Which We Serve* is, as his name suggests, a pillar of lower middle-class respectability and patriotism.

It was not just the identification of the Navy with history and national greatness that propelled it to the centre of national life. The culture of the Navy also helped make its men standard-bearers of national virtues. The stiff upper lip was, in the Senior Service, an essential requirement. Enduring months at sea, often in bad weather and continual danger, closed men in on themselves. Things that needed to be said in the Navy were said briefly and bluntly. In confined spaces emotions had to be suppressed; during war great achievements and terrible horrors were alike understated. Captains Scott and Oates, Lieutenant Blowers and Petty Officer Evans of the immortal Antarctic Expedition (1910–12) set the highest standards for the service and solidified the legend. The image of the British sailor as a man of few words, grimly determined and able to make the best of a hard job was reassuring when the country had its back to the wall. There were plenty of real examples of courage and self-sacrifice in the world wars that equalled the legends of the past. The representation of calmly authoritative officers and cheery, resilient men connected Britons of 1940 with the best traditions of the service.

It was not the British as they were but as they wished to be. The Navy offered a model of masculinity and patriotism. This was true in time of war. It was truer still during the period of Britain's decline. The Navy was eulogised in a series of films from the 1950s: *Above Us the Waves, The Battle of the River Plate, Cockleshell Heroes, The Cruel Sea, Gift Horse* and *Sink the Bismarck!* The Navy became an emblem of something else in the national sense of self-identity. The image of a ship's company fighting alone far from home with limited resources, relying on their teamwork and ingenuity to see them safe, is a powerful one. If Britain was bankrupt and a diminished world power after 1945 the Navy offered a way of coming to terms with decline. The Senior Service was used to fighting its way out of a hole – a trick the country needed to relearn. This concept of ingenuity and character triumphing over mere money and ostensible strength reached its greatest expression in James Bond, who, bear in mind, is a commander in the Royal Naval Reserve. Like other great naval heroes – both real and imagined – he is a man of few, but well chosen, words.

The Navy once provided a standard of masculinity and conduct. All armed services do, to a certain extent, for the people they protect. But it was the sheer centrality of the Navy to British life in the days of its dominance and defiance that granted it such an impact on the making of the national character. It belongs to a world we have lost.

PART 12: POWER

CHAPTER 42

PERSUASION
1805–1842

Happen what will, England's duty is to take and keep the lead.

Sir Thomas Hardy, First Sea Lord

'Remember Nelson'. So read the signal hoisted by Captain William Hoste on 13 March 1811 as his squadron of four frigates (two 38s and two 32s) came under attack from six French and Venetian frigates (four 40s and two 32s). The British were defending the island of Lissa off Split in Croatia. At stake was control of the Adriatic.

Hoste had gone to sea as a boy with Nelson on HMS *Agamemnon*, one of the best schools for a young officer in the Navy. On this occasion he was facing a far superior French force, packed to the gunwales with troops. With his signal he invoked the spirit of the Royal Navy's presiding deity to put fire into the bellies of his beleaguered men.

The commander of the Franco-Venetian squadron, Bernard Dubourdieu, attacked in true British style. He approached in two columns with the wind behind him. He ordered his ships to hold their fire until they were upon Hoste's ships. He massed his French and Italian troops on the bow of his flagship, *Favorite* (40), which was closing on the stern of Hoste's flagship, HMS *Amphion* (32). Just as the men were about to leap onto the British frigate Hoste ordered a howitzer on *Amphion*'s deck to fire. In it were packed 750 musket balls. With one shot the boarding party was wiped out; Dubourdieu and all his officers died in the blast of shot.

Dubourdieu's plan had been to use his superior firepower to encircle the British. His second in command now took over. But once again Hoste was prepared. His ships suddenly wore together and took the reverse course. The enemy were utterly confounded by this sharp manoeuvre; *Favorite* went onto the rocks and the rest of the Franco-Venetian ships went in pursuit of their prey. *Danaé* (40) attacked HMS *Volage* (22), but despite her superiority the French ship was beaten off by the British carronades.

Hoste's *Amphion* was attacked by the French *Flore* (40) on one side and the Venetian *Bellona* (32) on the other. Hoste was equal to this attack. He darted round *Flore*, so avoiding *Bellona*'s fire. The French ship surrendered after a sharp exchange. Hoste did not slacken: he sped round *Flore* and raked the Venetian, which also surrendered. Elsewhere HMS *Active* (38) forced *Corona* (40) to strike.

Hoste's clever manoeuvres utterly destroyed his enemy. He was one of the most experienced frigate captains in the Royal Navy and he knew the Adriatic well. Since June 1808 he had dominated that beautiful sea with just *Amphion* and a sloop. Between 23 June 1808 and Christmas 1809 he took or destroyed 218 enemy ships on the seas or in cutting-out expeditions. Most of these were trading vessels and gunboats; he also destroyed signals stations along the Dalmatian coast.

The Adriatic was his, a fact underlined at the Battle of Lissa. In 1814 he attacked the French at Cattaro in Montenegro and at Ragusa. In both cases he used the strength and technical expertise of his sailors to haul heavy guns and mortars onto the supposedly inaccessible hills that lour over both cities. The French garrisons were forced to surrender.

A British frigate on its own was enough to terrorise a whole coastline. It could ruin local trade and greatly impair the movements of armies on land. Control of the sea began to pay dividends on land as the war progressed. The British were able to strike at Napoleon's European empire when Spain revolted against French dominance. The Navy could bring in weapons and supplies; it could tie down large numbers of enemy troops with a modest amount of force from the sea. It could choose where to strike.

After Trafalgar the Navy could concentrate on raiding commerce and disrupting enemy communications. It already possessed a quiverful of aggressive, highly skilled frigate captains. The most famous of them all, Captain Lord Cochrane, pursued a career of extraordinary seamanship and cunning that has fed writers from Captain Frederick Marryat (who served with Cochrane) through to C. S. Forester and Patrick O'Brian. Sailing in the sloop *Speedy* (14) and then the frigate *Impérieuse* (40) Cochrane used extraordinary ruses and daring attacks to snap up hundreds of prizes, raid ports and launch cutting-out operations. During the period between 1805 and 1815 the Navy was able to add to Britain's growing empire from the pickings of the French and Dutch empires, key among them Cape Colony, Ceylon, Sierra Leone, Tobago, Trinidad, Java, the Maldives, Mauritius, the Seychelles, Heligoland and Malta.

All this was possible because the French battlefleet had been destroyed at Trafalgar. What battleships remained to Napoleon were confined to port by ruthless blockade. The dominance of the Navy is eloquently expressed in the figures of British losses: of the 317 warships lost between 1803 and 1815, 223 succumbed to the shore and the sea. The weather and the lee shore of the enemy coast were more dangerous than the French Navy. By 1810 Brest was abandoned and Britain had command of the seas. In the absence of an enemy battlefleet her cruisers had the freedom to range the seas. British traders were able to exploit their Navy's dominance of the world's waters. The one area where Napoleon could stymie British maritime advances was in the Baltic with the help of his Danish and Prussian allies. In 1807 the Navy launched an attack on Copenhagen to prevent the Danish navy being used for Napoleon's purposes. Between 2 and 5 September the British fleet bombarded Copenhagen with artillery and Congreve rockets. The city was devastated and the Danes capitulated, surrendering the entire Danish–Norwegian fleet to the British. The verb to 'Copenhagenise' entered the military lexicon to denote a pre-emptive strike against an enemy navy in port.

The Navy had Napoleon's Europe under complete blockade. Napoleon retaliated by forbidding countries under his control from importing goods brought by British merchants. It was called the Continental System and it was intended as a counter-blockade to break the British economy. The British responded by banning any ship trading with European countries unless it flew the Union Flag. Orders in Council allowed the Navy to stop and search any neutral ship it encountered. In 1806 the emperor forced Prussia to close its ports to Britain. The Navy seized 700 Prussian merchantmen. Europe was starved of imports from around the world. Its industries stalled and its economy collapsed. Britain, in contrast, enjoyed an unprecedented commercial and industrial boom. It used the Navy's domination of the seas and coasts of Europe to smuggle in whatever was desired. The British merchant marine took over the trade of Europe.

This was power indeed. It made enemies – the most important was the United States. Britain's high-handedness offended Americans. It pressed her sailors, searched her ships and prevented trade with the Continent of Europe. America faced ruin as a trading nation, just like France, Prussia, the Dutch and the Danes. In 1812 Britain and the United States went to war.

American frigate captains comprehensively outsailed and outfought their British counterparts in the Atlantic, but their success could not prevent the Navy slamming down an embargo on the American Atlantic coast. The War of 1812 was a sideshow in any case for the Navy, which had to concentrate the bulk of its forces in Europe. By 1814 France was broken; her overseas empire was gone and her economy was crippled. 'If anyone wishes to know the history of this war,' said the duke of Wellington, 'I will tell them that it is our maritime supremacy [which] gives me the power of maintaining my army while the enemy is unable to do so.'[1] The Navy had strangled France; the allied armies had smashed Napoleon's empire. As in earlier wars, such as the War of the Spanish Succession, naval supremacy had opened the road to victory; but it was a long march.

On 15 July 1815 Napoleon boarded HMS *Bellerophon*, which was one of the British ships blockading the Aix Roads. The captain was surprised to find himself taking the surrender of the emperor. It was symbolic that Napoleon surrendered to a British warship engaged in the long, unglamorous task of blockading the Atlantic seaboard.

There was no fleet left for the Navy to fight. By 1817 there were only thirteen ships of the line on active duty. Famous battleships such as *Temeraire* and *Bellerophon* were put to other uses: prison hulks, receiving hulks to temporarily house new recruits before they were assigned a ship, as guardships and as victualling depots. The bulk of naval strength consisted of frigates, sloops, gunboats and brigs divided into eight squadrons: North America, South America, the West Indies, the western Mediterranean, the eastern Mediterranean, West Africa, Cape Colony and the East Indies.

Britain stood on the cusp of being a great imperial power. Back in 1763 the British had won a major European war and immediately turned their eyes to constructing a global empire. Back then the rush of confidence had caused the Navy's ships to be sent around the world to guard the colonies. Within two decades the folly of that plan had been exposed. Britain lost her American empire in large measure because the battleships of her continental enemies outnumbered her own in European waters. The Battle of Ushant, indecisive as it was in a tactical sense, may be one of the most significant naval battles in history. For the loss of control of western European waters, which stemmed from the battle, meant that Britain fought the American War of Independence with her enemies' dagger pressed close to her heart. In addition the Navy was unable to prevent the export of arms to North America from Europe and Britain lost her first empire as a result.

It was a hard lesson. In the wars that followed the Navy's sole priority was to safeguard home waters and defeat its rivals in battles close to the European landmass. It is a remarkable fact – and one worth highlighting – that the Battle of the Saintes in 1782 was the last battle fought outside

European and Mediterranean waters by the main British battlefleet until 1944.

Yet between these dates Britain constructed the biggest empire the world had ever seen. The battlefleet remained at all times in European seas so that it could defend Britain from invasion and defeat or intimidate its colonial rivals on their own doorsteps. The successors of William Hoste and Thomas Cochrane – the commanders and captains of widely dispersed frigates, brigs and gunboats – did the hard work of empire-building without the support of fleets of battleships. The ability of the small ships to operate with near-impunity around the world stemmed from maritime dominance in Europe. The savage bombardment of Copenhagen in 1807 also pointed the way to the future. The threat posed by the Navy to flatten major cities and dockyards was one of the most powerful weapons in Britain's arsenal as she went about the business of building her second empire.

The Navy's flexibility as a fighting force gave Britain the power to intervene where statesmen saw fit. In 1816 Edward Pellew, now Admiral Lord Exmouth, bombarded Algiers for seven hours with six battleships, four frigates and a number of bomb vessels in retaliation for the massacre of 200 Christian fishermen. The attack destroyed the entire Algerine fleet. Vice Admiral Edward Codrington intervened in the Greek War of Independence in 1827. His fleet of ten battleships, ten frigates, four brigs and two schooners from the British, Russian and French navies wiped out an Ottoman fleet comprising seventy-eight vessels at the Battle of Navarino. More than a decade later, in 1840, the British Mediterranean Fleet rained 48,000 rounds onto Acre. The enemy on this occasion was Mehemet Ali, the pasha of Egypt, who had taken Syria from the Ottoman Empire. The fierce bombardment ended when the Egyptians' magazine was hit; the resulting explosion killed 1,100 soldiers and destroyed much of the town.

These periodic incidents demonstrated British naval power, lest anyone believed it had withered away in the interim. But they were about more than disciplining errant rulers who offended Britain. British intervention in the Greek fight for independence was necessary to prevent Russia securing a naval base in the Aegean. In 1840 Britain acted to support the Ottoman Empire against Mehemet Ali in part to warn Russia and France off Britain's patch. The Russians had offered the Ottomans help in return for a temporary occupation of Constantinople – which would upset Britain's position in the Mediterranean. The French supported Ali – and the growing influence of the Egyptians was a clear threat to British India.

The defeat of the Egyptians at Acre went far beyond propping up the Ottomans. Lord Palmerston, the foreign secretary, had a blunt warning for his country's friends and foes alike: 'Every country that has towns within cannon shot of deep water will remember the operations of the British Fleet on the coast of Syria in ... 1840, whenever such country has any differences with us.'[2]

This represented an awesome power. The Royal Navy was Britain's instrument in reordering the world in her interests. Sometimes this could be overt, as at Algiers, Navarino and Acre. More often it was subtle. During Latin America's struggle for liberation from Spain and Portugal the Royal Navy's South America Squadron was a potent force. It did not actively intervene, but it prevented Spanish and Portuguese ships from operating freely. 'Only England, mistress of the seas, can protect us against the united force of European reaction,' said Simon Bolivar, the liberator of Latin America. In 1825 British warships in the Tagus helped persuade Portugal to recognise Brazilian independence. The gains in trade were considerable. They also allowed Britain to take the moral high ground: the country favoured liberal, constitutional governments against dictatorships and decrepit empires. The reason was straightforward. States governed by the rule of law and the consent of the people made good trading partners; illiberal, absolutist regimes were unstable and risky for business.

Britain, herself a constitutional monarchy, made herself the champion of freedom – when it suited her. The Royal Navy, with its firepower and worldwide range, enforced the country's diplomatic position. This was seen most clearly between 1831 and 1833 when a small squadron of battleships under Admiral William Parker remained off the Portuguese coast during the struggle for power between the liberal Constitutionalists and the Absolutists.[3]

Parker had been one of Nelson's star frigate captains. He conducted himself off Portugal with tact and diplomatic skill, nudging things Britain's way without having to fire a shot. The mere presence of the Royal Navy off a foreign coast, with its ability to impose crippling blockades or bombard towns to rubble, was enough to affect matters on shore.

Britain wanted a world safe for trade. Compliant, legitimate governments were vital for that end. But Britain was also committed to ending slavery, and it now had the power to achieve it. For centuries the Navy had, like other state navies, protected its country's slave trade. Sugar was the foundation of fabulous wealth and the fuel of industrialisation; slave labour was the engine of the sugar trade. But when Britain abolished slavery in 1807 she also committed herself to stamping out the trade. The

United States banned the importation of slaves in that year as well. In 1810 Britain signed a treaty with Portugal which insisted on a ban. Similar treaties followed with Spain, France, the Netherlands and Sweden. The last country to enforce the ban was Brazil in 1831.

For decades the Navy laboured to end the slave trade on the West African coast. It was a daunting and incredibly expensive task. In 1807, at the height of the war against Napoleon, the Navy could spare only one frigate and a sloop to patrol the West African coast. After 1815 the Preventative Squadron was constituted to uphold the treaties and enforce the ban. From 1819 the squadron was based at Freetown, Sierra Leone, and used Ascension Island and Cape Town as supply bases and hospitals. In 1818 Sir George Collier took over the squadron, starting with two ships, which he built up to six by 1821; a decade later there were still only seven vessels.

But even the most complete blockade of the African coast would not have been enough to stop the trade. Britain might be the sovereign of the seas but no major country would suffer her to exert her power to the maximum and become the unchallengeable policeman of international waters. In times of war a belligerent country claimed the right to stop and search enemy ships and even neutral ships carrying enemy cargoes. That right had been the bedrock of British maritime power, but even in times of hostilities it had enraged neutrals and brought Britain into conflict with other countries, most notably Denmark and Russia in 1801 and the United States in 1812. In times of peace Britain could not act like a belligerent power and search foreign ships at will, even if they were slavers who were breaking their own country's law. It would have been an act of war.

British warships could only stop slavers flying British colours. One answer would have been to declare that slaving ships were pirates under international law, but other countries would not agree to give the Royal Navy arbitrary power to mete out justice on the oceans. Most politicians and rulers of maritime nations believed that Britain's pretensions to sweep away the slave trade were cover for an attempt to rule the waves as sole sovereign. An alternate solution was to sign treaties with other maritime powers which granted each country a mutual right of search in agreed geographical areas and under special circumstances. Britain signed treaties with Portugal and Spain in 1817 (in return for hefty bribes), Sweden in 1824, Brazil in 1826 and with France, Denmark, Sardinia, the Hanse and Naples in 1831.

It was a gruelling, frustrating task. Mosquitoes and tropical diseases plagued the crews. That was just the start of the problems. The ban on the slave trade had made the rewards for smuggling slaves extraordinarily high; a cargo of 800 slaves could net a trader £60,000 pounds. The small Preventative Squadron had to patrol 3,000 miles of coast riddled with inlets, estuaries and swamps. The sheer number of slavers put the Navy at a disadvantage. The slaving vessels were fast and heavily armed. The traders themselves used every legal stratagem and low trick to confound the Navy and bog down captains in endless legal disputes. If a slaver was captured the Navy commander had to take it to Sierra Leone and sit before a court comprising British magistrates and judges from the slaver's country of origin before the ship could be condemned. Most of the countries that Britain compelled to ban the trade were lukewarm in actually enforcing what they had promised on paper. Very often these judges were corrupt. A commander of a Navy ship ran the continual risk of sparking a diplomatic incident or finding himself sued for damages.

The legal difficulties were serious impediments to enforcement. Under the treaties the Royal Navy was only allowed to apprehend and search ships which had slaves on board. Slavers evaded justice by throwing their captives overboard. Ships flying the Stars and Stripes were exempt from search because Britain and the United States could not agree on a treaty of mutual stopping and searching, so slavers took to flying American colours. It was warfare of a kind – but far more complicated and frustrating than outright war.

The Preventative Squadron was the training ground for a new generation of Hostes. Young captains learnt the arts of hunting and pursuing an enemy and developed the cunning and patience of cruiser commanders. The work of beating back the trade required the combination of the doggedness of blockade duty with the intuition and inspiration of a great cruiser captain such as Hoste.

Not all of the captains were ardent Abolitionists. Some were in favour of the slave trade. But all dedicated themselves to the war against slavery with the hallowed professionalism of the service. By necessity their vessels had to be small, swift and lightly armed – two-masted schooners, brigs and brigantines. A frigate would have been far too large to scour the shallow waters in which the slavers lurked to load their captive wretches and too slow to chase them in the open seas. The captains, commanders and lieutenants who led the patrols had to be independently minded and resourceful. This is best illustrated by the story of one remarkable ship and the brave men who sailed her.

In January 1829 HMB *Black Joke* chased the Spanish slaver *El Almirante* for thirty-one hours.[4] The British brig had been a Brazilian slave ship, a Baltimore clipper class named *Henriqueta*,[5] which had taken 3,000 slaves across the Atlantic in six voyages, earning £80,000. She was captured by HMS *Sybille* in September 1827, renamed and brought into service because she was so fast. *Black Joke* mounted an 18-pounder on a pivot and a 12-pounder carronade; she had a crew of fifty-seven. Her opponent in 1829 had fourteen guns and carried eighty men. *Black Joke*'s commander, Lieutenant Henry Downes, pursued the larger and more heavily armed ship through the night. He brought her to battle only when the wind died away and *Black Joke* used her oars to get into range. After eighty minutes fifteen members of *El Almirante*'s crew were dead, including her captain and officers; thirteen were wounded. Downes was able to free 466 slaves.

Between January 1828 and the capture of *Almirante* a year later *Black Joke* pursued and caught three slavers, freeing 1,018 slaves in total. All were much larger ships that carried more guns than the British ship. *Black Joke* was able to hunt down and fight slavers that were too fast for other members of the squadron. In four years she captured twenty-one slavers that carried over 7,000 men, women and children.

Another example (among many) of bravery on the west coast of Africa was HMS *Buzzard*'s capture of *El Formidable*, which had eighteen guns to *Buzzard*'s three. The Navy brig chased under oars the large Spanish slaver for seven hours and fought for three quarters of an hour. The British sailors then boarded the slaver, captured it and freed over 700 slaves. The young lieutenant in command of the brig received high praise. His commanding officer reported to the rear admiral at the Cape of Good Hope: 'The *Formidable* was the crack vessel here and I trust I may be permitted to add, that in no action on this coast has the disparity of force been greater, the resistance more determinedly kept up, or more coolly and gallantly overcome, than in this instance.'[6]

There were careers and fortunes to be made in this kind of active service. But it was a tough station. The men were exposed to diseases and rapacious slavers who would kill to make money. The condition of prisoners in the slave ships was hard for even seasoned sailors to bear. When *Black Joke* chased and boarded *Marinerito* in 1831 many of the captives died in the fight; twenty-six died soon after. The 107 rescued people landed at Fernando Po were 'sick from terror, crowding and privations'; sixty died within a few weeks.

A few months later *Black Joke* and *Fair Rosamond* pursued two slavers into the River Bonny in modern Nigeria. Lieutenant Ramsey reported that 'during the chase they were seen to throw their slaves overboard, by twos shackled together by the ankles, and left in this manner to sink or swim'. Over 150 people were drowned in this way. When the slavers were taken to Sierra Leone the court would not believe they were guilty of trafficking slaves until two survivors gave evidence.

The British public feasted on the exploits of ships such as *Black Joke* and *Buzzard*. Hunting down the slavers required all the cunning, judgement and seamanship displayed by cruiser commanders in Britain's famous naval wars. The officers and men had to board larger enemy ships, cutlasses and pistols in hand, as their forebears had done in the classical age of sailing warfare.

'Set a thief to catch a thief.'[7] That's what naval officers said of ships like *Black Joke*, an American-built clipper that could hunt down other clippers more readily than frigates, sloops and ten-gun brigs. She was called 'the terror of slave dealers and scourge of the oppressors of Africa'.[8] She was ordered to be burnt in 1832 when a survey declared her timbers rotten. This despite the fact that she had beaten two brand-new brigs in a race. She was mourned by the sailors in the squadron and by freed slaves, who petitioned Commodore Frederick Warren to spare her from the flames. Under the previous commodore, Francis Augustus Collier, she had captured five of the ten slavers caught between 1828 and 1830 and took more slaving ships than all the rest of the squadron put together in the two years following.

It was a long, slow and, it must have seemed, unwinnable war. Every year 60,000 people were kidnapped and transported across the Atlantic for a life of forced labour. Against this the Navy's Preventative Squadron – which grew from five ships in 1819 to sixteen in 1832 and twenty-one in 1844 – managed to catch only a handful of slavers. 1829 was a particularly good year; 5,350 were liberated. Between 1810 and 1849 the Navy freed 116,000 slaves; meanwhile a million died on the middle passage or spent the rest of their lives in bondage.

In these circumstances it is even more impressive that the Royal Navy did not give up or put on a token show of preventative action. The campaign against slavery was one of the most glorious in the Navy's history. It was one of the first instances of a nation acting against its interests to snuff out a manifest evil. It was thanks to the doggedness of the Navy, fighting for years on end a battle it could never win, that the struggle was kept alive and other countries pressured into actively enforcing the ban.

Lord Palmerston gave the undaunted men on the front line as much help as he could. In 1835 he forced the other maritime powers to accept that ships found with no slaves on board, but with equipment such as shackles or food in excess of the needs of the crew, could be seized and condemned. It gave the patrols more scope to hunt down slavers and it eliminated the main reason why traders threw their captives overboard when they were about to be apprehended.

Palmerston's active diplomacy was matched by an increase in vessels in the Preventative Squadron. Britain began to use her naval clout more effectively. Many countries, and particularly those whose economies depended on slave labour, were reluctant to take steps to end the trafficking of humans. In 1839 Portugal refused to renew the anti-slavery treaty with Britain. In response Palmerston passed a law indemnifying naval officers for searching, seizing and condemning Portuguese ships. It was a virtual declaration of war said outraged diplomats and MPs. Fine said Palmerston; if Portugal wanted a war she could have one – 'so much the better; there are several of her colonies which would suit us remarkably well'. The Royal Navy would trounce Portugal and the Portuguese knew it.

The main culprit in international slave trade was, by the middle of the century, Brazil, where the majority of enslaved Africans were carried. In 1845 the Prime Minister Robert Peel, passed a bill allowing British warships to stop and search Brazilian ships as if the two countries were at war. That was hostile enough, but four years later Palmerston sent a squadron to Brazilian waters to search and arrest slaving ships. This infuriated the government in Rio de Janeiro; the Navy did not just apprehend slavers at sea but in Brazilian inland waterways as well. Slave ships were ruthlessly hunted down by Rear Admiral Sir Barrington Reynolds and burnt even as they lay in harbour. It was a clear violation of Brazilian sovereignty, a South American version of the bombardment of Acre – a warning that the Royal Navy could operate with impunity. Palmerston said a country rarely gave up something profitable for altruistic reasons: 'Persuasion seldom succeeds unless there is compulsion of some sort ...'[9] He knew that when Britain chose to strike the Brazilians would have to give in. The Royal Navy was an unassailable force in these circumstances: 'the naval operations of our squadron have accomplished in a few weeks what diplomatic notes and negotiations have failed for years to accomplish'.[10]

Only eleven slavers managed to evade the Navy's patrols in Brazil in 1850, and those were later captured. By 1853 Brazil was hardly importing any slaves at all. The Royal Navy bombarded Lagos, a centre of the slave trade. In 1862 Lincoln allowed the Royal Navy to stop and search American ships. The last slave market in the Americas, held at Havana, was closed by British pressure in 1869. From its modest beginnings the Preventative Squadron and British's considerable naval muscle had ended the West African slave trade. The Navy turned its attention to slavery on Africa's east coast.

At the exact time that *Black Joke* was burnt the West Africa squadron received a brand-new warship – HMS *Pluto*, a 365-ton wooden paddle steamer. The Admiralty had been experimenting with steam-powered ships since 1793. It was not until 1821 that a steamship was used by the Navy as a tug. When he was off Portugal during the civil war Admiral Parker was able to keep in touch with the Admiralty with the help of a mail packet steamer. *Pluto* belonged to the first generation of steamships able to be used for warlike purposes. She was big enough to carry four 32-pounders. Paddle steamers were not likely ever to supersede the sailing ship of war. Their twin paddles were twenty-seven feet in diameter; these giant wheels and their sponsons occupied too much room to mount an effective broadside. These ships were under sail for a lot of the time to save on coal. The advantage of *Pluto* to the Preventative Squadron was her ability to negotiate inlets and rivers and to pursue slavers in lulls – feats that no sailing ship could manage.

The engine had arrived. But, in the 1830s and 1840s and for a long time after, this was still a sailing Navy.

Britain's combination of oceanic domination and steam power was, however, transforming the world. The new technology gave the Royal Navy access to the major river systems of the developing world, allowing it a life far from the open ocean. Between 1824 and 1826 the British gun-boats pushed up the Irrawady River in Burma, getting as far as Mandalay.

HMS *Gorgon*, 1837

The Navy's ships were towed up the river by the steam paddle-tug *Diana*. In 1846 Sir Charles Hotham's squadron forced the River Paraná all the way through Argentina to Asunción in landlocked Paraguay in order to open the area for trade. These were feats impossible for sailing ships of war; steam conquered tide, wind and shallows.

The new power was displayed most notoriously during the First Opium War (1839–42). Conflict with China was sparked in 1839 when Lin Zexu, governor of Canton, seized opium worth £2 million, owned by British traders who had illegally imported the drug from India. The British government insisted that the Chinese recompense the traders. Refusal had led to war. It had got bogged down when Admiral William Parker arrived at Macao with two battleships, seven smaller warships, a survey vessel and twenty-two transports.

Parker's flotilla included four steamers. One of these was *Nemesis*, a pioneering iron-hulled paddle frigate built for the East India Company by the Birkenhead Iron Works. She was the world's first iron warship and the first steamship to sail around the Cape of Good Hope. But her main advantage was her shallow draught, which allowed her to navigate the Chinese inland waterways.

This revolutionised naval warfare. Steam opened up the rivers of the world to the Royal Navy. Paddle steamers might not mount impressive firepower, but they could tow the Navy's big-hitting battleships. Before Parker arrived *Nemesis* had shown her awesome potential. In January 1841 the Navy attacked the Bogue (also called the Bocca Tigris), the narrow strait peppered with fortified islands which guarded the waterway between Hong Kong and Canton. In the early months of 1841 the British expeditionary force launched amphibious operations against the Bogue forts.

The first island to be subdued was Chuenpee, which was defended by two forts, one higher than the other. *Nemesis* and another steamer shelled the upper fort while the sailing ships bombarded the lower. Both forts surrendered in under an hour. *Nemesis* then attacked a fleet of fifteen junks with rockets: 'The very first rocket fired from the *Nemesis* was seen to enter the large junk ... and almost the instant afterwards it blew up with a terrific explosion, launching into eternity every soul on board, and pouring forth its blaze like a mighty rush of fire from a volcano.'[11]

Nemesis was a groundbreaking modern weapon; she was a sledgehammer sent to crack a nut. The Chinese could no longer pretend to themselves that they could resist such power. Qishan, the new governor of Guangdon, agreed to open up Canton for trade, pay the British £6 million and cede them Hong Kong. But the emperor refused to acknowledge that he could be beaten by barbarians. Qishan was dismissed and his concessions disavowed. The British resumed the war. This time they would strike at the heart of the Chinese empire.

Naval surveyors charted the waterways. Chinese batteries were overwhelmed by the awesome power of the squadron's guns. The sailors used their brute strength to haul their heavy artillery to outflank Chinese positions – as Hoste had done to command the heights above Cattaro and Ragusa in the 1810s. The Chinese 200-gun battery at Zhoushan was swiped away. The massive defences at Zhenhai were blasted out of existence. Steamships took British and Indian troops to the inland city of Ningbo, which was captured. Ningbo became Parker's base.

The Navy spent the winter surveying the Yangtze. Parker received ten new steamships for the spring campaign. In May 1842 the attackers entered the Yangtze. The steamers were tied alongside the battleships. It was a formidable new weapon, combining the steam power of the new ships with the broadsides of the old; it smashed open the gate to Shanghai. The steamers were able to land troops and marines in key locations, outflanking Chinese positions and destroying shore batteries. Shanghai fell on 19 June. It was as formidable a display of naval bombardment and amphibious attack as could be imagined.

The expedition then proceeded 170 miles up the Yangtze. That warships could penetrate this far inland had been unimaginable. Now it was all too real – although the Chinese court refused to acknowledge the barbarian incursion. On 21 July Parker's forces anchored off Zhenjiang, where the Grand Canal intersected the Yangtze. Zhenjiang was taken after bloody fighting in the streets. Now Parker's path to Nanking – China's capital – was clear. Even more significantly the British squadron lay across the Grand Canal – the great conveyor belt that brought food to the Chinese people. Commerce was paralysed and food stocks would soon be empty. The great empire was about to collapse.

At last the Chinese emperor faced reality. By the terms of the Treaty of Nanking China paid £4.25 million in war reparations. Canton, Fuzhou, Ningbo, Shanghai and Nanking were opened up for trade. Britain got Hong Kong. China was now exposed to the full force of Britain's version of free trade.

The bombardment of Acre had shown that cities close to the sea were not safe from the Navy. The First Opium War brought the Royal Navy inland as well. An early governor of Hong Kong said that the British incursion into China was 'the farthest military enterprise, of the same extent, in the history of the world, surpassing, in that respect, the expeditions of Alexander and Caesar in one hemisphere, and those of Cortes and Pizarro in the other.'[12] Behind this hyperbole lay a truth: the Navy had become, for better or worse, a world-changing force.

CHAPTER 43

MAKING THE WEATHER
1842–1860

The plains of North America and Russia are our corn fields;
Chicago and Odessa our granaries; Canada and the Baltic are
our timber forests; Australia contains our sheep farms, and in
Argentina and on the western prairies are our herds of oxen;
Peru sends her silver, and the gold of South Africa and Australia
flows to London; the Hindus and the Chinese grow tea for us,
and our coffee, sugar and spice plantations are all in the Indies.
Spain and France are our vineyards and the Mediterranean our
fruit garden.[1]

W. S. Jevans

Power. It manifests itself in different guises. Few countries have tasted it
to the extent Britain did in the two decades from 1849. It was not political power in the sense of territorial accumulation or subjected popula-
tions. The empire was a long way from its peak in terms of sheer size; the
same was true of the Royal Navy. The power enjoyed by Britain went far
beyond that.

Britain's trade and colonising had for generations been shielded
behind a thicket. Since time immemorial the seas around Britain had
been claimed as a possession of the sovereign. The Navigation Acts of the
seventeenth century were designed to nurture British trade by excluding
foreign competition from the colonies. Tariffs had been voted by parliament to protect domestic production, in particular agriculture. But all
these had been swept away since the defeat of Napoleon. Britain did not
even insist upon the sacred notion of territorial waters: now she preached
the absolute freedom of *all* seas. In 1805 Britain dispensed with the age-
old, aggressive, insistence that foreigners salute the royal flag in British
waters. In 1849 the Navigation Acts were repealed, exposing the empire
to the full force of unrestrained free trade.

The naval muscle of the country was now used to uphold the absolute freedom of the seas for trade. To make good her word Britain spectacularly renounced one of the foundations of its naval might. In 1854, at the beginning of the Crimean War, Britain and France agreed not to seize neutral vessels carrying enemy goods; nor would they license privateers to capture enemy ships. The bilateral agreement became part of maritime law after the Declaration of Paris in 1856. It was a symbolic moment in the history of British sea power and marked a fundamental change for the Navy. Britain's naval mastery had been made possible by rigorous blockades and the belligerent right of stopping, searching and seizing enemy and neutral shipping. In the Crimean War Britain was more concerned to uphold freedom of trade than exert her power at sea. Moreover after the repeal of the Corn Laws she was dependent on Russian grain: war could not be allowed to get in the way of commerce. The decision brought to an end, for good, the private sea wars that went back for centuries. Britain had built her power at sea on the foundations of privateering; now it could be dispensed with. And more than that: no longer would British captains and crew make dazzling profits cruising the seas, mopping up richly-laden enemy merchantmen. They would have to fight for other reasons – honour, duty, patriotism, pay.

Britain's commercial and maritime reforms were intended to make the seas safe and profitable for everyone. They opened up markets for British goods everywhere and they enabled Britain to import cheap foreign goods – most importantly raw materials and foodstuffs to fuel industrial expansion.

Of course no country would embark upon such a path unless it was confident that the system was loaded in its favour. Britain had become the first industrial powerhouse by the middle of the century – the workshop of the world, as it was constantly said. She was also the world's financier. The City of London was at the centre of the global economy. British loans propped up regimes across the globe, determining the economic fate of millions. Shipping was chartered in London, insurance brokered, currencies floated, and the Stock Exchange traded global commodities. British capital and engineers constructed railways that traversed hitherto impenetrable landmasses and connected remote continents with hundreds of thousands of miles of submarine telegraph lines. Between 1815 and 1880, 80 per cent of capital invested abroad went to countries *outside* the empire. Ships built and owned in Britain carried the produce of the world. British power was bound up with free trade. Who needed formal political authority with this kind of industrial and financial clout?

And then there was the Royal Navy. It was strong enough to make the political weather wherever it went. In the middle of the century Britain did not want new territory to conquer and govern, except for small and conveniently placed naval bases. What it needed above all were markets as an outlet for manufactures and investment. 'All we want is trade,' declared Palmerston, 'and land is not necessary for trade; we can carry on commerce on ground belonging to other people. Possession of land involves civil and military establishments and responsibility.'[2]

British gunboats made all the difference in flattening political barriers to free trade from governments or troublesome officials. It was a power which did not have to be demonstrated very often: the mere fact of British seapower and the proximity of a gunboat was enough to exercise minds. Those whom the British deemed to be pirates could be swept from the seas. Naval hydrographers opened up the uncharted waters of the world to traders; the Navy's gunboats protected them.

The Navy's vigilance gave British merchants and investors in every continent confidence to trade and deterred foreign governments from interfering in their business. No country could stand aloof from Britain's system of free trade: that was the price they paid for independence and non-interference. Countries such as China or Japan which tried to assert their independence in the form of isolation were forced into the global system by the irresistible persuasion of gunboats.

In the middle of the century the Royal Navy had 129 ships stationed outside home waters. Their distribution reflected British interests. Thirty-one were in the most important sea of them all, the Mediterranean. The East Indies and Chinese waters accounted for twenty-five. Anti-slavery patrols required twenty-seven ships; a further ten were stationed in the Cape. The highly valuable South American trade was protected by fourteen warships, while the West Indies had ten. Out in the Pacific there were twelve British ships. The system was supported by the Navy's principal foreign bases: Gibraltar, Malta, Halifax, Bermuda, Antigua, Jamaica, Rio de Janeiro, Buenos Aires, Cape Town, Aden, Mauritius, Trincomalee, Bombay, Singapore, Sydney, Hong Kong, the Sandwich Islands, Valparaiso and stations in between, such as Ascension, St Helena, the Falklands and the Maldives.

With a small number of ships – and small ones at that – the Navy was able to encircle the globe. In Chinese waters and elsewhere the major maritime nations, such as France and the United States, were dependent upon British naval power. British policy in the middle part of the century focused upon using national influence to open up the world to trade, using ships at sea and on waterways rather than boots on the ground. Within these limits the policy was largely successful. The emphasis was on influence rather than coercion; even the violence meted out in China in the 1840s and 1850s and Japan in the 1860s was seen in this light. Rarely was the Navy used for outright coercion, although the ultimate sanction was sometimes hinted at against even powerful countries. In the 1850s Palmerston uttered these intemperate words: 'The United States have no navy of which we need be afraid, and they might be told that if they were to resort to privateering we should, however reluctantly, be obliged to retaliate by burning all their sea coast towns.'[3] At another time he raised the possibility of landing British troops in the Southern states to provoke a slave rebellion. This was just sabre rattling without the slightest intention of being carried out, but it was effective nonetheless. During the American Civil War a US navy ship stopped the British mail-steamer *Trent* and took two Confederate agents travelling in her. In the furore that followed the normally pacific British statesman Richard Cobden had to warn Senator Charles Sumner that 'we, in England, have ready a fleet surpassing in destructive force any naval armament the world ever saw.'[4] Sumner read the letter to Lincoln and the cabinet; the Confederates were released to British custody.

The 'destructive force' of the Royal Navy did not have to be deployed often in order for it to be an effective tool in global politics. In the heyday of British influence it was an often unspoken fact. 'Showing the flag' in distant corners of the planet was among the Navy's most important roles.

Britain's ability to exert its power with impunity around the world had to rest on secure foundations. As ever the key to its success was absolute security at home, in other words complete control of the Channel and the Western Approaches.

This meant mastering the age of steam. In 1845 HMS *Ajax* reached seven knots in trial. *Ajax* had been built as a 74 back in 1809, but now the mature battleship was fitted with an engine that turned a screw propeller. In recent years new frigates had been launched as screw ships; *Ajax* was the first battleship. The screw propeller changed the game where ships of the line were concerned. Paddle steamers could not mount a full broadside and could never be equal in a contest with a good old-fashioned wooden ship of the line. The screw propeller was placed under the water on the stern and did not interfere with the broadside. The space needed for the engine did, however, mean that *Ajax* had to reduce her armament to sixty large-calibre guns. She was also cut down to a single-deck and lost her copper sheathing and masts, which were replaced with a jury rig. *Ajax* was now a blockship: a mobile gun battery used to guard the coast. The Royal Navy retained control of the Channel.

But the Navy's advantage was soon cancelled out. As so often in their eternal rivalry the French navy was superior to the Royal Navy in mastering new technology. In 1847 the French navy ordered *Napoléon* (90), the world's first purpose-built steam-powered battleship. She was launched in May 1850 and commissioned two years later.

And it was not just the proximity of a state-of-the-art warship that started ripples of panic. Relations with France deteriorated in the 1840s. It got worse in 1848 when Napoleon's nephew Louis-Napoleon Bonaparte was elected president of France in 1848. (In 1851 he became dictator in a coup d'état; a year later he became Emperor Napoleon III.) The new Bonaparte had high ambitions to remake Europe and extend French power around the world, to restore *la gloire* of the first Napoleonic era. But before he did this the French navy had to neutralise Britain by exerting the maximum pressure on British home waters. He was off to a good start. In the mid-1840s the French had completed the defences at Cherbourg, making the port its first battleship base in the Channel and an arsenal for an invasion. This was the most serious threat to the security of the realm since 1805 and, as the French hoped, it bedevilled English military planning and profoundly changed the strategic situation. To make matters worse, *Napoléon* superseded sluggish blockships such as the aged *Ajax*. Louis Napoleon, like a good Bonaparte and any good Frenchman, desired nothing more than vengeance on the Royal Navy for centuries of wrong.

The Admiralty had to respond. It was a race it could not afford to lose.

Just three months after *Napoléon* shocked the world the Royal Navy launched HMS *Agamemnon* (91) – note the extra gun. HMS *Duke of Wellington*, launched in 1853, was twice the size of HMS *Victory*, carried 131 guns and had a speed of 10 knots, making her the most powerful battleship in the world. She represented the culmination of the ship of the line.

These ships looked every bit like the proud warships of the days of Hawke, Howe or Nelson. The only difference to a casual observer was the chimney protruding fore of the mainmast and the increased length to make room for the engine. The French built ten new wooden steam battleships and converted twenty-eight old ships. Britain could not be outdone without – it was felt – sacrificing her maritime dominance. The Royal Navy built eighteen and converted forty-one.

The Royal Navy had to be as powerful as the French and Russian navies combined – the so-called 'two power standard'. Most important, it had

HMS *Duke of Wellington*

to reassert control over the Channel. Britain responded to the Cherbourg threat by building up a steam fleet at bases at Portland and Alderney – the British Channel Island right outside Cherbourg – ready to blast the French base out of existence. Elsewhere the Navy had to remain vigilant. During the revolutionary year of 1848 the indefatigable William Parker was in command of the Mediterranean Fleet, charged with defending British interests during months of instability and violence throughout Europe. When his fleet was reinforced it offended the French. 'This is as it should be,' said Parker; 'the presence of our large ships has had the desired effect, and I am quite sure that nothing will tend more to keep our neighbours quiet than a liberal display of three-deckers.'[5]

The danger was that France was in turmoil. The revolution might prompt her to send her navy to intervene in Italy. To keep the French in check, Parker had to look ready to fight at any minute. Above all he had to station his ships to defend British property and trade. That accomplished, he took his fleet to Besika Bay, near the Dardanelles. He was there to prop up the Ottomans against Russia and the Austro-Hungarian Empire. Once again the fleet deterred other powers from interfering with British interests.

Parker achieved his objectives. The next stop in his never-ending tour of British firepower was Salamis Bay. In 1847 a mob of anti-Semites had broken into Don Pacifico's house in Athens and destroyed his property. Don Pacifico was of Jewish origin and at the time he was the Portuguese

consul in Athens. He was also a British citizen. The Greek authorities refused him compensation, but he had the full backing of Lord Palmerston,
who ordered the Navy to seize Greek property to the value of the compensation demanded by Pacifico. Parker's ships blockaded Piraeus and captured Greek warships and merchant vessels. The matter sparked tensions
among the three naval powers. The French and Russian ministers stirred
up opposition to the British.

But in the end the Royal Navy was irresistible. Palmerston came in for
criticism at home and around the world for using the almighty power of
the Navy for trivial ends. Not true, said Palmerston. As a citizen of the
Roman Empire had been free from arbitrary dealings wherever he was in
the world, 'so also a British subject, in whatever land he may be, shall feel
confident that the watchful eye and strong arm of England will protect
him against injustice and wrong'.

It was a breathtaking claim. And with steam gunboats in the Navy's
arsenal it was one that could have some credence. Steam power's great
advantage lay in its ability to bring ships of war close to land, where they
could blockade ports, bombard cities, harbours, roads and forts. This was
a kind of warfare unknown in the age of sail, when wind and tide and the
dangers of a lee shore made station-keeping difficult.

This new way of naval warfare was displayed to the world during the
Crimean War. The war is remembered primarily for the failings and hero-
ism of the army, the compassion of nurses and the blunders of its generals.
But it was a war that profoundly affected the development of the British
Empire. This is best understood when we look at its naval dimension.

The first actions of the war were fought not in the Crimea but in the
Baltic. On 22 June 1854 British steamers bombarded Bomarsund, a fortress in the Åland archipelago. Charles Lucas became the first man to be
awarded the Victoria Cross when he threw overboard a live shell, with its
fuse fizzing away, that had landed on the deck of the steam sloop HMS
Hecla. The British and French returned in July, bombarded the fortress
into submission and had it demolished. It was a taste of things to come.

For this would not be a naval war fought between fleets. In the Black
Sea theatre British gun and rocket boats attacked Odessa. In September the
Navy used twenty steamers to tow fifty-two sailing ships so that 50,000
British soldiers were landed in the Crimea. It was an extraordinary amphibious operation, the first to be conducted by steamships and a demon-
stration not only of the value of steam in transporting armies across the
seas and landing them smoothly but of the vitality of private British sea
power: most of the troop and supply transports were hired merchantmen.

The army marched on Sebastopol. On 17 October the allied navy, led by the new steam battleship HMS *Agamemnon*, attacked the city's port. Many of the old sailing battleships were powered in by paddle steamers lashed to their sides. Although the bombardment was frustrated by Russian ships that had been scuttled, the loss of four Russian three-deckers, twelve 84s and four frigates knocked the Russian Black Sea fleet out of the war.

From now on the naval part of the Crimean War would be dominated by shallow-draught gun- and mortar boats that could steam in close to shore defences and batter them into submission. Back in Britain 156 new gunboats were mass-produced in order to wage this new kind of war. The first batch carried one 69-pounder, one 32-pounder and two 24-pounder howitzers.

Later in the year British and French steam gunboats approached Kerch, which guarded the Sea of Azov. In fear of these vicious weapons the Russians deserted Kerch and the allies entered the Azov. The gunboats terrorised the sea, closing the coastal roads and stopping all shipping. The aim was to seal off the Russian army in the Crimea from supplies sent by way of the River Don. It was a success and Sebastopol was compelled to surrender on 9 September 1855. A month later the Russian forts at Kinburn, on the estuary of the river Dnieper, were attacked by 8,000 troops from land and bombarded from sea by gun- and mortar boats. They were finished off by the battleships, which sailed in and pummelled the forts into submission with the force of their broadsides.

Once again the French were at the forefront of technology. Their navy brought three new types of offensive vessel to the Black Sea. *Lave*, *Tonnante* and *Dévastation* were flat-bottomed, shallow-draught floating batteries. They were towed into position by steamers, where these artillery platforms were used to bombard onshore targets. They were ugly, utilitarian vessels nicknamed 'soapboxes', constructed without regard for sailing qualities. But they were revolutionary. They were the first war vessels to be clad in iron armour. The British ordered five of their own.

Back in the Baltic the great goal was to bombard St Petersburg, but in order to get there the Navy would have to reduce the forts that lay along the Gulf of Finland, culminating in the most formidable of them all, Kronstadt. In preparation for this daunting task the Navy attacked a group of islands called Sveaborg, which guarded the entrance to Helsinki. For two days 1,000 allied guns fired 20,000 shells on the fortress.

The bombardment of Sveaborg was a dress rehearsal for the attack on

Kronstadt by 250 steam gunboats and a hundred other vessels including mortar boats, rocket launches and floating armoured batteries. The projected 'great armament' of 1856 was the harbinger of modern naval warfare. Seaborne shelling of land targets had a long history in the Royal Navy: first Blake and Benbow in the seventeenth century, then Shovell and Vernon in the eighteenth and Nelson and Exmouth in the early nineteenth. Now it had reached its terrifying apogee. Fleet battles had given way to deadly steam-powered assaults on cities and ports. The Russians had tasted this and did not have the appetite any more. Before the great armament reached Kronstadt they brought the war to an end.

On St George's Day 1856 Queen Victoria reviewed the Baltic fleet off Spithead from the royal yacht *Victoria and Albert*. The great armament had not been given the chance to demonstrate its destructive power to the world. This was the next-best thing. The giant three-decker battleships looked as graceful and magnificent as ever, especially garlanded with flags in the bright April sunshine. But everyone's eyes were on the brand-new, state-of-the-art gunboats that steamed among the bedizened leviathans like minnows in a school of whales. The old contrasted with the new. 'The gunboats,' wrote the *Times* correspondent, 'without being models of elegance, move easily through the water, turn deftly, and have a blunt, determined look, with a spice of mischief.'[6]

The royal yacht proceeded along a double line of 278 vessels. The mighty *Duke of Wellington* fired the first salute, followed by the rest. There were twenty-two screw-propelled battleships, twenty screw frigates and corvettes, eighteen paddlewheel ships, four floating batteries, two powder and shell depot ships, one hospital ship, one floating factory, 160 gunboats and fifty mortar boats. There was, in addition, a single, solitary sailing frigate.

This was a modern Navy on display – or at least a portion of it. Utility took precedence over beauty. There could be no dispute at the conclusion of the Crimean War that the age of sail was over as far as battles went (ships continued to use wind power in transit). Gunboats that were built in such profusion for the war against Russia were dispatched around the world. They became the backbone of colonial expansion.

Small gunboats were Britain's key to controlling the world. British military commanders, diplomats, consuls and merchants called upon them to settle local disputes. In 1858 alone gunboats were requested and dispatched to the Newfoundland fisheries, Jamaica, Panama, Honduras, Vera Cruz, Brazil, the Kooria Mooria Islands, Vancouver, Morocco, Alexandria, the Zambezi (at the request of Dr Livingstone), Cyrene (at the behest of

the British Museum, to protect its archaeologists), Sarawak, Borneo and
New Zealand. Gunboats were used against China in the Second Opium
War (1856–60) and to suppress the Indian Mutiny in 1857–58 and the
Jamaica uprising in 1865. The gunboat spearheaded the rapid expansion
of the British Empire from the 1860s. It laid down the law for the world
and policed global trade – on Britain's terms it should be added. In 1863
the Navy's gunboats bombarded Kagoshima as part of an ongoing effort
to force Japan to trade with the West.

An example of a gunboat in action – one of hundreds of such actions
– comes from 1875. The West African squadron were informed that a trading schooner had been captured by pirates on the River Congo and the
crew had been killed. The commodore, Sir William Hewett, transferred to
a gunboat and went up the river. He told the local chiefs to hand over the
murderers. They refused. Hewett said he would return and burn every village forty miles upriver from the mouth of the Congo unless the suspects
were handed over.

Hewett was true to his word. The gunboats shelled a stretch of the
riverbank. Then the marines fired volleys into the bush so that the Navy
Brigade could hack through the vegetation. Eventually a village would be
exposed; then the marines and sailors burnt the settlement and its canoes
and recovered plunder from the merchant ship (which was said to be
found in every village). This was repeated from village to village. Hewett
reached Bomba, where he held a palaver with seven kings, who apparently 'expressed themselves more than pleased with the work that had
been completed, and stated that the commerce of the river was certain to
be increased when it became known that peaceful traders could pass up
and down, without risk to life and property'.[7] Similar stories could be told
throughout Africa and South-East Asia.

Meanwhile cruisers guarded the sea lanes of the world for British traders. They ensured that the arteries that kept the Empire alive were open
at all times. These operations were supported by a string of thirty-eight
naval bases and coaling stations around the world.

By these means Britain's Navy could keep the seas open and draw
weaker nations into the system of global trade. It was power indeed, but
it should be remembered that it had limits: the British army was too small
for major operations and its shortcomings revealed to the world during
the Crimean War. As Palmerston noted in 1865, 'Ships sailing on the sea
cannot stop armies on land'. This might be tautological, but it was something of which Britons, infatuated with their Navy as ever, needed to be
reminded every now and again. Britain's ability to reshape the world by

force of naval arms was limited to the seas and mighty rivers belonging to weak countries; there was little the country could do, even at the height of its powers to assert British interests in the heart of Europe.

But this was an age when oceanic and river-borne trade was in its heyday and Britain's global reach as a naval and trading power was unrivalled. British statesmen and consuls could intervene in a variety of situations to reshape the world in British interests. In 1860, for example, ships of the Royal Navy gave valuable cover for Garibaldi's Red Shirts as they crossed from Genoa to Sicily and then from Sicily to Naples in the campaign to unify Italy.

There were few forces capable of denying this immensity of power. The ability of the fleet's smaller vessels to operate with impunity and such deadly effect – frigates after Trafalgar, brigs in pursuit of the slave trade, gunboats that could devastate an enemy's ports and sail hundreds of miles into great continents* – was dependent upon the existence of an unassailable battlefleet. The Navy could close the seas to its opponents and blockade their ports if it chose. In these circumstances no major power dared risk confrontation with Britain until 1914. The Royal Navy was one of the greatest forces of deterrence the world has ever seen.

At the conclusion of the review the gunboats stunned the thousands of spectators by taking part in a mock assault on Southsea Castle. The review reinforced the Royal Navy's power in the world – and the bombardment of the castle was intended to show France what the Navy could do to Cherbourg if it wished. But it asked some difficult questions. For many observers the dusk of the age of sail heralded the end of Britain's primacy as a naval power. The Royal Navy had enjoyed many advantages over its rivals: a huge pool of manpower to work its enormous fleets; a profusion of state-owned and private dockyards that outpaced rivals in shipbuilding; outstanding seafaring skills; superior battlefleet tactics; mastery of short-range gunnery.

Steam power rendered these advantages pretty much null and void. Wooden battleships were now vulnerable to exploding shells fired from French Paixhans guns. The race was on to keep pace with technological advances and build an iron-armoured battleship. This was a worry for the Royal Navy. As ever the French led the way; it seemed possible that they could use their new ships to form a 'steam bridge' across the Channel.

---

* Gunboats were capable, for example, of going 400 miles or more up the Niger to settle disputes. They could go 500 miles up the Yangtze.

Britain's ports and cities suddenly seemed vulnerable after decades of security.

This worry turned to panic in 1858 when intelligence arrived that the French navy was constructing *La Gloire*, the world's first ironclad battleship. Huge iron plates, 12 centimetres thick, were attached to 43 centimetres of timber and fixed to a wooden hull. She reached a speed of eleven knots. The iron gave her protection against enemy guns and allowed her to mount thirty-six 163 mm guns – the largest naval guns available. *La Gloire* and her sisters – *Invincible* and *Normandie* – gave the French the chance to dominate the Channel and put an end to British naval supremacy.

As so often in the history of modern Britain, military planners and statesmen had to grapple with the problem of maintaining a worldwide empire of the deep while defending the home islands. In 1859 it was believed that Napoleon III was planning an invasion. The ability of the Navy and army, with their global commitments, to defend the realm was in doubt.

One response was to build a ring of coastal fortresses – the so-called 'Palmerston Follies'. Another was to complete a base right under France's nose, at Alderney. But the most valuable was the creation of a permanent reserve of sailors. The naval strength of Britain had always relied on the ability to press men from the vast merchant navy in times of war – a system that, however crude it might have been, gave the country the edge over its rivals. In the nineteenth century naval power rested in part on Britain's industrial might, but also on the large reserve of warships and professional seamen. The Naval Reserve Act of 1859 created the Royal Naval Reserve (RNR). For one month every year sailors and fishermen were given gunnery training on one of the drill ships stationed around the coast. When war was declared members of the RNR would be drafted into the fleet and reserve ships. In 1862 the RNR was expanded to include officers from the merchant navy. The RNR was the enduring, invaluable legacy of the invasion scare of 1859; the follies, apart from being picturesque historical curiosities, served no real purpose. The other response to the French threat was spectacular.

La Gloire was commissioned in August 1860. In December the British riposte appeared. HMS *Warrior* mounted forty heavy guns. She reached 14.3 knots. And if this wasn't enough she was almost twice the size of *Gloire*: 9,180 tons displacement to 5,630, 420 feet in length to 255.5. But *Warrior* really outclassed *Gloire* in her construction. The British battleship, like her French rival, had heavy iron armour – but it was fixed to an iron hull, not wooden as with *La Gloire*. She was the most powerful warship in the world. And she had been constructed at great cost in a stunningly short span of time. She was ordered in May 1859, launched in December 1860 and commissioned in August 1861. In October a section of her armour was fired upon by twenty-nine pieces of shot, weighing up to 200 pounds. The armour passed the test. Britain retained control of the Channel. Her battlefleet remained unchallengeable.

Britain had beaten her two main rivals at sea, the Russians in outright war and France in a long-running design war.

The French might innovate, but the British always bettered the design in a shorter space of time. The Royal Navy accumulated new advantages as it lost its traditional ones. Britain was the richest country in the world and the undisputed leader in manufactures. No one could compete with her iron industry. And, more importantly, her merchant shipbuilding industry was far in advance of any rival; Brunel's *Great Western* (1838), *Great Britain* (1843) and *Great Eastern* (1858) were, when they were launched, the largest and most technologically advanced ships in the world. As ever, the connection between the state of the merchant marine and the health of the Navy was vital. In the last part of the century 80 per cent of ocean-going ships were built in Britain. That industrial might made it impossible that the Navy could ever be superseded.

Money, munitions and iron – these were now the keys to naval power.

CHAPTER 44

ARMS RACE
1860–1899

It is not in the interests of Britain – possessing as she does so
large a navy – to adopt any important changes in ships of war
… until such a course is forced upon her.

Admiral Baldwin Wake Walker

When he boarded HMS *Warrior* as gunnery lieutenant in March 1863
John 'Jackie' Fisher must have known that the most formidable warship
in the world would soon be obsolete. She had been commissioned on 1
August 1861. Almost half a century later his own legacy to naval warfare,
the revolutionary HMS *Dreadnought* of 1908, was superseded by faster,
more powerful battleships by 1914.

This was an age when navies were in fierce competition with each other
and state-of-the-art battleships became irrelevances soon after they were
launched. It was an age when new technologies and a bristling arsenal of
modern weapons left tactics in a state of constant flux. This brave new
world heralded the end of Britain's maritime supremacy.

No one knew these things better than Jackie Fisher. When he became
gunnery lieutenant of *Warrior* he was twenty-two and was one of the
most highly regarded young officers in the service. Nine years before, in
1854, as a thirteen-year-old cadet, he had been posted to HMS *Calcutta*,
an 84-gun ship of the line powered entirely by sails. The boy was recommended by the elderly Admiral William Parker, a veteran of the Glorious
First of June and one of Nelson's protégés. *Calcutta* would have been familiar to sailors from Nelson's Navy, and long before. She was a wooden
warship, with two continuous gun decks where the majority of the 720
crew fought and slept. Flogging was still prevalent and the daily routine
would have changed very little from the seventeenth century. When
Fisher stepped down as First Sea Lord ships were fuelled by oil and submarines and aeroplanes were emerging as major challenges to battlefleets.

Fisher straddles the age of sail and the age of aircraft carriers. He was one of the last generations of boy cadets whose training was conducted entirely at sea in the age-approved manner. He learned the ways of the Navy in the Crimean War on the new screw-propelled ship of the line HMS *Agamemnon* and during the Second Opium War on a steam corvette, a steam frigate and a paddle sloop. In 1861 Fisher sat his lieutenant's exam. He got the top grades in gunnery and seamanship and the highest-ever score for navigation.

Lieutenant Fisher then joined the Navy's main gunnery school, HMS *Excellent* in Portsmouth Harbour, which was testing heavy naval guns for the new ironclads.* From there he went to *Warrior*. But he was back at *Excellent* after a year. This suited his temperament and his interests. Fisher preferred life in harbour to life on the waves. He was an intellectual officer, and he set his mind to contemporary naval problems. Britain did not fight any major wars in the nineteenth century after the Crimean War. There were precious few chances to test new armaments and weapons in the heat of conflict. But other navies did have the experience of war to sharpen their tools. Ironclads fought each other during the American Civil War and at the Battle of Lissa, fought in 1866 between the Italian and Austro-Hungarian navies. The Royal Navy could only watch and learn. As the 1860s wore on and new weapons appeared it was clear that *Warrior's* armour was inadequate. In the absence of the trial of war a greater emphasis had to be placed on experimentation, training and teaching.

During his time as a gunnery instructor on *Excellent* Fisher became a charismatic lecturer, a skill that would prove invaluable as his career progressed. This was what the Navy needed in an age of rapid technological evolution, officers with hungry minds who could communicate their ideas up the chain of command to flag officers and down to new generations of cadets.

What fascinated the young lieutenant was a new form of naval warfare: undersea weaponry. The brand-new ironclads, it now seemed, would be vulnerable to the deadly threat of underwater weapons.

Mines and torpedoes were in their infancy, but other navies were making strides in developing workable weapons. The Russians used remote-detonating mines in the Crimean War, with scant success. The Confederates in the US Civil War had experimented with contact mines and spar torpedoes, which were pushed by small boats or a primitive

* HMS *Excellent* was Fisher's spiritual home; the accommodation ship moored alongside was a blast from the past – it was HMS *Calcutta*, the ship he had joined as a youngster.

submarine (*H. L. Hunley*) against the hulls of enemy ships. Robert Whitehead, an English engineer, was developing a self-propelled torpedo. But he
was working for the Austrian navy in Croatia. In 1869 John Fisher visited
Wilhelmshaven, the Prussian naval base. The Prussians were not noted
for their naval strength, but they were making great strides to become a
force at sea as they emerged as the pre-eminent European power. At Wilhelmshaven work on underwater warfare was far advanced. Fisher wrote
a report for the Admiralty and began work on a paper on the subject of
electrical torpedoes. He was promoted to commander and sent, to his
chagrin, to the China station.

Service at sea was a dull thing for a man with Fisher's active mind. He
described his role as second in command on a ship of the line as akin to
that of an 'upper housemaid' – that is to say, responsible for all kinds of
trivial day-to-day management. Nonetheless, he managed to study and
experiment. He invented and installed an electrical system so that the
gunnery officer could fire the broadside simultaneously with the other
guns. He developed a new gunsight, constructed his own torpedo and
wrote a treatise on the subject. He read the latest works on naval technology. And he cultivated links with senior officers back home by correspondence. For Fisher service far from home on fighting ships was time
wasted. In his study of submarine warfare he had glimpsed the future.
His insight offered no room for complacency: the mainspring of British
power – the battlefleet – would soon be history.

The youthful Jackie Fisher's reputation did not suffer from his absence
in the China Sea. In 1871 the Director of Naval Ordnance recommended
that officers should be taught torpedo management. What was needed
was an instructor 'thoroughly conversant' with the new technology and
who should be able to communicate his knowledge with 'great zeal and
ability'. The only candidate was Commander Fisher, expected back from
the China station. To his delight he was made head of torpedo and mine
training at *Excellent*. In 1872 he secured the hulk of an old ship – *Vernon*,
formerly a fourth rate – as a torpedo-training vessel. He ordered self-
propelled torpedoes from Robert Whitehead and he gave flamboyant
lectures, some of which were attended by senior officers, politicians
and journalists. The HMS *Vernon* training establishment at Portsmouth
became independent of *Excellent* in 1876. The Navy began to acquire torpedo boats, stealthy attack vessels that could launch torpedoes at enemy
battleships at close quarters. In 1874 Fisher was promoted captain. His
name was made in the Navy.

If he was to progress in the service, however, Fisher had to go to sea again. In 1876 he took command of HMS *Bellerophon*, flagship of the North America station. This ship had been launched in 1865, designed to resolve the problems that had become apparent in *Warrior*. *Bellerophon*, like *Warrior*, had a full sail plan and a powerful steam engine. She looked like the prototype British ironclad, but she was shorter, some might say stubbier. But the most important difference was the number of guns and their placement.

This new ship marked the end of the full-length broadside. *Bellerophon* had fewer guns, but they were much heavier and concentrated amidships in an armoured battery. She performed better than *Warrior* at sea, due to her reduced size, and she had thicker armour. *Bellerophon*, like so many ships described in this chapter, was a link in a rapid process of evolution that saw innovative ships rendered obsolete soon after they dazzled the world. The goal of ship designers in the later 1860s was to place extremely heavy guns in armoured gun turrets.

Already USS *Monitor* had mounted the first 360-degree rotating gun turret. But she was not a seagoing vessel. Gun turrets made a ship unstable and few vessels were strong enough to absorb the recoil of heavy guns. The Royal Navy saw the gun turret as essential for coastal bombardment. In 1864 HMS *Royal Sovereign* (121) lost her masts and was cut down to her lower deck. Her hull was strengthened and four gun turrets containing two heavy guns each were placed on the upper deck. This was an experiment and it paved the way for more ships with gun turrets, first HMS *Monarch* and then HMS *Captain*. The latter had an extremely low freeboard, a full sail plan and two turrets. She was a revolutionary ship, born amid much controversy.

In September 1870 she was off Cape Finisterre when waves began crashing over her. *Captain*'s upper deck was not far above the waves at the best of times; in bad weather they engulfed the vessel. Her towering masts and rigging did not help in these conditions; they made the ship unstable. She began to heel dangerously to starboard. The roll increased and just after midnight she capsized. Just eighteen men survived; 480 perished in the stormy waters.

The Navy was not daunted by this tragedy. In 1871 HMS *Devastation* was launched. Like her predecessors she had a low freeboard and two gun turrets. But, significantly, she did not have masts or rigging. She was the first capital ship to go to sea without sails. Once again the Navy had produced a truly revolutionary ship. Both her turrets had two 12-inch guns each weighing thirty-five tons and firing a 700-pound shell. These were the most powerful guns afloat. The armour on her turrets was 14 inches thick. *Devastation* is the iconic ship on 'England's Glory' matchboxes.

Bellerophon was outdated when Fisher took command of her. By necessity the Royal Navy had ships of all shapes and sizes. *Devastation* was launched just ten years after *Warrior*, but she looks as if she came from another age. With change coming so fast the Navy had to retain ships of different eras and capabilities. In the 1870s Fisher captained HMS *Hercules* (launched 1868), HMS *Valorous*, a paddle-wheel frigate dating from 1851, HMS *Pallas* (a centre-battery ironclad, launched in 1865) and HMS *Northampton*, a brand-new armoured cruiser that carried torpedoes.

The Royal Navy was in a state of fast evolution. It is hardly surprising, therefore, that the fleet contained ships of a variety of ages, performance and speeds. Co-ordinating such a motley fleet was becoming exceptionally hard for the service's flag officers, many of whom were bred to the age of sail.* Indeed, it was not just the ships that were in a state of evolution. The men and officers of the Victorian Navy were coming to terms with the shock of the new.

The men who manned the fleet were a different sort from their predecessors. They drank less for a start. The rum allowance was halved in 1825 and cut again in 1850; beer was stopped altogether in 1831. By the middle of the century Jack Tar was portrayed as a bulwark of the nation. In Gilbert and Sullivan's comic operetta *HMS Pinafore* (1878) he is celebrated as a warrior of freedom:

> For a British tar is a soaring soul
> And free as a mountain bird;
> His energetic fist should be ready to resist
> A dictatorial world!

Thanks to tinned meat and vegetables the tars' diet was improved beyond measure. So too were conditions of service. Men were no longer pressed from the merchant navy; recruits were offered better pay in return for ten years' service and a pension after two decades. They got regular shore leave and the disciplinary code was relaxed. Flogging was less common – it was suspended in peacetime in 1871 and in wartime in 1879.

The sailors who manned the fleet served willingly and they were professional Navy personnel. This was signified by the introduction of a

---

* The exceptional admiral who eased the Navy's transition from sail to steam is Geoffrey Hornby. The life of Hornby, the mainstay of the Victorian Navy and a rather neglected figure, is brilliantly told in Andrew Lambert's *Admirals*.

uniform. New recruits received proper training prior to going to sea on one of the Navy's wooden training vessels kept in the home ports. The sailors of the Royal Navy were better nourished, higher paid and more trusted than any of their predecessors. They now seemed less dangerous and depraved. Indeed they became a symbol of the national character – Jolly Jack Tar. A mark of how safe they had grown in the popular imagination was the adoption of the sailor suit for male infants.

The regular officers of the Navy were, in tune with the times, a mixed bunch. Some, like Jackie Fisher, were eager to master new technology and positively revelled in the brave new world of steel and steam. But the majority of the officer class had joined a Navy whose heart and soul yearned for sails and wood, 32-pounder long guns and the sacred line of battle. For these men the 'real' Navy was the one that had been led by Nelson and which held up Collingwood, Hoste, Cochrane and Pellew as models of gentlemanly warriors. The kinds of ships they held in their minds were glorious wooden warships, where everything was as Nelson would have wished: the decks holystoned, the ropes neatly coiled and every last object and person where it should be. The new era could not live up to that age of heroes.

The Navy had changed. It had become a fashionable service. In the nineteenth century prospective officers were drawn from the aristocracy, gentry and upper middle class. William IV had been a career officer; Queen Victoria's son Prince Alfred joined the Navy at the age of fourteen in 1858 and was posted captain in 1866. Prince Louis of Battenberg became First Sea Lord in 1914, as did his son Lord Louis Mountbatten (1954–59), both after conventional careers. Victoria's grandsons Princes Albert Victor and George (later George V) joined HMS *Britannia*, the cadets' training ship. The future king commanded a torpedo boat, a gunboat and a cruiser. His son David (later George VI) was sub-lieutenant in charge of 'A' gun turret on HMS *Collingwood* at the Battle of Jutland.

The officers who served in the long peace between the end of the Crimean War and the beginning of the First World War dreamed of being a Nelson or a Cochrane, but there was little fighting at sea to be had. Those officers who won glory and medals – Fisher, Lord Charles Beresford, Arthur Wilson, John Jellicoe and David Beatty, to name a few – did so fighting on land or in estuaries. Other officers distinguished themselves during one of the myriad gunboat confrontations in isolated outposts of empire. Few of these conflicts called for feats of seamanship.

Most officers in the home, Mediterranean, American, South African and China fleets had little to do but keep their ships spick and span.

Indeed there was a mania for cleanliness in the last decades of the nineteenth century. If they could not compete in the line of battle, officers could compete through the balmy days of peace by having the most spotless, efficient ship. Some captains had the watertight doors taken off their hinges and sent down to the engine room to be burnished. They were reattached gleaming, but no longer watertight. Officers who put a premium on cleanliness did not like the modern Navy; they preferred to move under sail because coal was dirty and they kept gunnery practice to a minimum for the same reason. Somehow the discipline of Hawke and Nelson had mutated into obsessive pernickety concern about paint and brasswork.

Percy Scott sailed on his first voyage as a young midshipman in 1868. He described a new commander who joined the ship in the Indian Ocean.[1] The officer spent ages over his toilette and when he emerged from his cabin he was 'a beautiful sight'. He was spotlessly clean, perfectly groomed and his fingers were dripping with gold rings. He wanted to make the ship look as good as he did. All the blacking was scraped off the masts and spars and they were painted canary-yellow. 'It was customary,' Scott remembered, 'for a commander to spend half his pay in buying paint to adorn Her Majesty's ships as it was the only road to promotion.'[2] The quarterdeck on Scott's ship was a riot of carving and gilt; the coamings that protected the hatchways from water were faced with satin-wood; the gun-carriages were French-polished. To top it all the shells were painted blue with a gold band and white tops. 'Of course we could not have got these shot into the guns had we wanted to fight, but that was nothing.' When a ship was inspected by a flag officer the criteria by which the ship and the officers were judged were cleanliness and order: it was not until 1903 that gunnery was assessed by flag officers. On modern battleships sailors still took part in cutlass drill, as they had done in the days of yore, and modern guns were still aimed by sight along the muzzle as if they were the long guns of Nelson's day. Often gunnery practice consisted of aiming at a cliff a hundred yards away and blasting indiscriminately.

Officers bowed to the rigidity of the service's customs, but they in part mitigated it by cultivating personal eccentricities, the hallmark and privilege of a senior officer in the Royal Navy. In its nineteenth-century heyday many captains set their own dress code. Some liked to adorn their officers in masses of gold braid; others preferred plain austerity. One admiral wore a white billycock hat, another a white topper. When he was captain of the frigate HMS Galatea in 1870 Prince Alfred allowed his lieutenant, Lord Charles Beresford, to keep an elephant on the after-deck.[3]

As commander-in-chief in the Mediterranean, Alfred kept Bruin, a brown bear, on his flagship. Bruin liked to wrestle the young midshipmen and swim over to other ships anchored in harbour so as to startle unsuspecting sailors.

Reading the recollections of officers in the Royal Navy of the late nineteenth century it often seems that many officers believed they were cast adrift in the wrong era. One captain of the old school[4] ordered the sails furled and the anchor to be dropped when his ship had entered harbour; but to his surprise the ship continued ploughing forward, snapping the anchor cable and running aground. He had forgotten to order the engines to be stopped. 'Bless me,' he exclaimed, 'I forgot we *had* engines.' Lord Charles Beresford resented being transferred from the magnificent three-decker HMS *Marlborough* (131), which looked like warships of the golden age, to the ironclad HMS *Defence* in 1863:[5] 'I did not like *Defence*. I thought her a dreadful ship. After the immaculate decks, the glittering perfection, the spirit of fire and pride of *Marlborough*, I was condemned to a slovenly, unhandy tin kettle.' Fisher remembered telling an elderly admiral about torpedoes, only to be met with this response: 'There were no torpedoes when I came to sea and I don't see why the devil there should be any of the beastly things now.'[6]

In 1881 Fisher was appointed to the latest in the list of the Navy's brand-new, revolutionary ships, HMS *Inflexible*.[7] Like Fisher himself, *Inflexible* seemed poised between the old and the new. She had masts and rigging, so looked familiar enough. But in other respects she was hyper-modern. It must have been especially pleasing, given Fisher's interest in electricity and submarine warfare, that she had electric lights (a first for a warship), searchlights and torpedo tubes. At the heart of her defences was a citadel amidships protecting the magazine, boilers and engines. It was 75 feet wide and 110 feet long, protected by 12-inch-thick armour, backed by 11 inches of teak, another 12-inch-thick armour plate and 6 inches of teak. Behind that were layers of shell plating. No other ship in the history of the Royal Navy has had so much armour; no gun then in existence could pierce it.

The emphasis was on buoyancy: *Inflexible* was broader and shorter than most battleships. She packed a massive punch. Her twin turrets housed two 16-inch muzzle-loading rifles, which weighed eighty tons each. They were reloaded outside the turret by hydraulic rams. Her torpedoes were fired from underwater tubes by pistons and propelled under the water by compressed-air motors. This was an inordinately complex ship in which bewildered seamen got lost, and it needed someone of Fisher's technical expertise and understanding of modern warfare to oversee its entry into the world.

Most of the Navy's ironclads never fired their guns in anger. They were intended for deterrence and to maintain Britain's place at the top. Like many of the Royal Navy's innovations, *Inflexible* was launched to counter a specific foreign ship. In this case it was the Italian twins *Caio Duilio* and *Enrico Dandolo*. The British ship was part of the Mediterranean Fleet, intended to display the Navy's power to her numerous rivals in that sea. In 1882 Fisher's ship was responsible for guarding Queen Victoria on a visit to the French Riviera. Later in the year she got a unique chance to fire her guns at an enemy. The target was Alexandria. In 1881 Egyptian nationalists revolted against Western influence over the country. This was unacceptable to the British, who could not countenance losing control over the new Suez Canal. Battleships were detached from the Channel Fleet and sent to join the forces in the Mediterranean. On 11 July 1882 the Navy bombarded Alexandrian shore defences for over ten hours, the only time a British battlefleet went into action between 1856 and 1914. *Inflexible*'s guns performed well, even if their rate of fire was slow.

The bombardment did the job. Modern ironclads, with their low freeboard and heavy guns, were designed for blockade and coastal warfare, but how well would they do in a sea battle? During the assault on Alexandria the accuracy of the British guns was poor. Few officers set much store by gun drills – an abysmal state of affairs for gunnery experts such as Fisher. The big, new, powerful guns on modern battleships were full of sound and fury; but in rough waters in a dynamic battle it was unlikely they could hit anything that was not in front of their noses.

And that was not all that was wrong. In 1884 W. T. Stead, editor of the *Pall Mall Gazette*, published a series of articles entitled 'The Truth About the Navy'.[8] In it he 'revealed' the supposed defects in the service, the result of peacetime defence cuts. The public reaction was ferocious and the furore forced the government to lavish £5.5 million on the Navy.

Stead wrote his sensational exposé as a result of secret conversations with a senior officer. John Fisher left HMS *Inflexible* to take command of his darling HMS *Excellent*. From the Navy's gunnery school, Fisher began to dabble in politics. He presided over a group of young officers concerned about the state of the Navy and the reluctance of the government to spend. Stead was their conduit to the British public, which was as passionately navalist as its forebears.

For years people had taken it for granted that the Royal Navy was invincible. Now they were being told that British naval defences were in a

slump. The Navy linked together the sprawling empire, which had expanded to an extraordinary degree after the Crimean War. It kept open
the sea lanes, defending the system of global commerce that Britain had
established. It also shut the door on Europe, allowing the country to act
as a world power without the historic bugbear of invasion from across the
Channel or Narrow Seas. The choke points of world trade – the Downs,
Gibraltar, the Suez Canal, the Cape of Good Hope and Singapore – were
all under British control. So what was the problem?

With power came fear. Britain was dependent as never before on the
Navy. In 1846 parliament had abolished protective tariffs on corn, which
meant that British farmers had to compete on the world market and labour
moved from the countryside to the booming industrial towns. Without
imports of food the country would starve. Without control of the seas
she would become poor. It was an uncomfortable position to be in – and
people were awaking to the fact that Britain and her empire were vulnerable, perhaps more vulnerable than any country on earth. As Fisher put
it: 'It's not *invasion* we have to fear if our Navy's beaten, it's *starvation*.'[9]
For decades British naval mastery and imperial growth had been possible
not least because Europe was preoccupied with its own internal problems
and there were no serious naval powers there or anywhere else. It was a
balmy situation. But it was coming to an end as other countries bestirred
themselves to accumulate colonies and build warships.

Unless Britain had a crushing superiority of ships over France, Russia
and Germany in northern waters she would lose the security at home that
had allowed her to construct a massive empire. But she also needed to be
the dominant naval power in the Mediterranean, South Africa, the Indian
Ocean, the China Seas and off American waters. Lose any of these and the
whole system would unravel. Britain, it was felt, had to be the dominant
naval power everywhere or she would lose everything.

There was an upsurge in navalist passion not seen for many generations. Fisher got what he wanted; it was a useful lesson in manipulation.

He also knew how to work the Navy's own patronage networks. In
1886 he became Director of Naval Ordnance, where his major contribution was to wrest control over naval armament from the army. He introduced rapid-firing guns to counter torpedo boats and enemy commerce
raiders. For a man passionately interested in new technology and for an
officer happier behind the desk, at a lectern or overseeing experiments,
Fisher was in the right job. And it came at the right time. The *Pall Mall*
controversy was followed by renewed public concern later in the decade
when France and Russia combined their Mediterranean fleets. This sent

ripples of panic throughout the empire where Russia and France most threatened British interests: Turkey, Persia, Afghanistan and China.

The inevitable British response was to initiate an orgy of spending and shipbuilding. The Naval Defence Act of 1889 formally established the 'two power standard': by law the Royal Navy had to maintain a fleet larger than the two largest navies in the world combined – with a margin as well. Work began on ten new battleships that would outgun and outpace any rival battleship in the world. Forty-two new cruisers were constructed to protect trade and communication, and eighteen torpedo gunboats were ordered to defend the fleet. It all cost £21.5 million.

That was the background to Fisher's ascent to flag rank. In 1890 he was promoted to rear admiral; between 1891 and 1892 he was admiral super-intendent at Portsmouth, where he supervised the construction of some of the new battleships ordered after the Naval Defence Review. Thanks to his zeal and grip on detail the new ships were constructed on budget and in record time. The jewel in the crown of his time at Portsmouth was yet another pioneering warship, HMS *Royal Sovereign*. She was large, fast

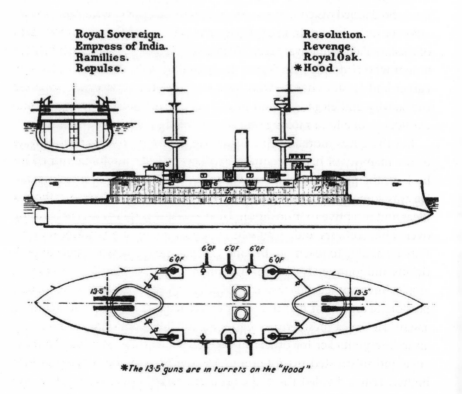

Royal Sovereign class battleships.

and looked more imposing than her recent predecessors owing to her high freeboard. This last quality made the *Royal Sovereign* class high-seas battleships. Most impressive of all were her four massive 13.5-inch guns mounted on babettes – open armoured turntables – placed fore and aft. She also had ten rapid-fire 6-inch guns to combat torpedo boats and cruisers and six torpedo tubes.

Fisher progressed to Third Naval Lord in 1894. Here he was responsible for procurement and equipment – jobs he loved. As so often in his career his mind was fixed on future threats. In the 1890s this meant the danger posed by French torpedo boats, which were being built in great numbers across the Channel. Under his watch the Navy designed and built a new class of vessel, the torpedo-boat destroyer – or destroyer as it became known. Destroyers were fast enough to catch speedy torpedo boats, they were given quick-firing guns to combat them and they had the range to keep company with the fleet they defended.

So far we have considered John Fisher as a technocrat, one of a new breed of officer more concerned with the mechanics of naval hardware than with seamanship or battle tactics. But there is another John Fisher, one who dazzled his contemporaries and has continued to intrigue historians ever since. In certain respects Jackie Fisher was the living embodiment of the late Victorian Royal Navy. He had the panache and zeal that befitted a man who had only one degree of separation from the Navy of Nelson, Parker and Hoste – heroes who overshadowed the service. He possessed the suavity and elegance of an English gentleman and the arrogant self-confidence of a high-ranking official at the height of the British Empire.

But there was more to John Fisher. He was alien in a number of ways to the majority of his contemporary officers. Fisher resolutely turned his back on the past and welcomed the future with the glee of a technocrat. He was something of a maverick in the Navy, unafraid of unorthodox ideas and receptive to innovation. He had learnt early the arts of winning over senior officers and cultivating a following among younger officers. Fisher was able to reach out beyond the Navy and the War Office to politicians and journalists and through them to the public. His performance as a lecturer was legendary and his ability to sustain an informed, logical, passionate argument had the effect of silencing critics and commanding assent. He was a mesmerising figure for his followers – and an intensely annoying politicker for others in the service who detested his flamboyance and mistrusted his intentions for the Navy as he progressed ever higher. Fisher divided the Navy. You either fell under his spell or you hated his guts.

What was not in doubt was his charm.

He was therefore an interesting choice to represent Britain at the first Hague Peace Convention in 1899. Fisher had been knighted in 1894, promoted to vice admiral in 1896 and sent back to sea as commander-in-chief of the North American station. He was recalled to be Britain's naval delegate at the Convention. It had been called by the Russians to try and put a brake on the inordinately expensive arms race among the major powers. We can glimpse something of Fisher's character and modus operandi at the meetings. During the formal meetings he was a fount of knowledge about the latest weapons and technologies. In private he used his charm and force of character for other purposes. Fisher's energy and elegance on the dance floor were famous; he cut a dash in the endless social rounds of the Convention. He was affable in his discussions with the other delegates, but he used his private conversations to impress upon everyone he met things that he would never state boldly in public. Britain was the world's major maritime power, he said, and that was how it would stay; there would be no limits on naval expenditure.

What was at stake was not just Britain's prestige but the very foundation of Fisher's beliefs. He was not a fighting officer and he detested war. He foresaw the horrors involved in a conflict that used the technologies of the twentieth century. He should know: he had been intimately involved with the arms race for forty years and he remained an eager student of all new advances in the science of war.

Only one thing stood between peace and Armageddon: the Royal Navy.

That was at the centre of Fisher's world view. It was shared by many others – in Britain at any rate. The mighty Royal Navy kept the peace because of one powerful thing – deterrence. It was an almost sacred duty. That was why Fisher was so obsessed with winning the arms race. Only by being ahead of everyone else and building up a terrifying arsenal could the Navy continue to police the world and prevent war. Trade, commerce and communication were all dependent upon the Navy's command of the seas; the alternative was anarchy. 'I am not for war, I am for peace!' Fisher told W. T. Stead. 'That is why I am for a supreme Navy.'[10]

CHAPTER 45

THE BRINK
1899–1914

He prowled around with the steady, rhythmical tread of a panther. The quarterdeck shook and all hands shook with it. The word was quickly passed from mouth to mouth when he came on deck. 'Look out, here comes Jack.'[1]

A junior officer on Fisher

Fisher's world was under attack. In 1890 Captain Alfred T. Mahan of the United States Navy published *The Influence of Seapower Upon History: 1660–1783*. Mahan's career in the US Navy had not been entirely happy. He was collision-prone and he hated newfangled steamships. At heart he was an academic, not a naval officer. His career took the right turn in 1885 when he was appointed lecturer at the Naval War College. His famous book was based on his teaching there.

Mahan went deeper than recounting Britain's rise to naval greatness. Behind the narrative lay a grand conceptual theory. He propounded no less than a law of history.

The secret of all great empires in human history, argued Mahan, was control of the sea. The most successful nations had dominated the sea during peace, gaining freedom and security for their trade; in times of war they policed neutral shipping and denied the sea to their enemies. In Mahan's view, Britain's great empire and success as a trading nation sprang from the Navy – and in particular the Navy's mighty battlefleet.

By 1890 there was a growing number of countries that aspired to become colonial powers and assert themselves in the world. Mahan's book told them that, by the 'laws of history', that could only happen when they became serious naval powers. For on the other side of the coin were the great empires that came crashing down. The Spanish and Portuguese empires had had sea power, but when they lost that they lost everything. Carthage and the Napoleonic Empire never had sea power – and they amounted to flashes in the pan. The history of the rise and fall of empires was the natural competition between nations for control of the seas. And it was literally by the force of nature: Britain had risen to domination, but she would in turn lose her primacy and bequeath it to a successor. The contest for maritime power lay, often imperceptibly, behind all human history and determined the fate of nations.

The Influence of Seapower became an international hit. The German Kaiser aspired to learn it by heart. He wanted Germany to become a major world power and in order to do that, he learnt from Mahan, Germany must construct a battlefleet superior to the Royal Navy. By Mahan's law the two countries' navies could not coexist: one had to dominate the other.

The book was no less influential in Japan, which had its own imperial ambitions in Asia. The Japanese already had an excellent fleet. Their battleships and guns were built by British engineers and their officers trained by instructors from the Royal Navy. Mahan's voice was heard in the United States, where calls for overseas expansion were growing louder. In addition to the major navies possessed by Russia, France, Italy, Germany, Austria, Japan and the US were smaller forces built up by Sweden, Turkey, Chile, Argentina and Brazil.

This navalist revival was not all due to Alfred Mahan, but his book gave the drive for naval power intellectual coherence and urgency. He made the acquisition of a navy a matter of a struggle for national survival.

Everywhere it looked the Royal Navy was seeing countries building up navies. It responded by building bigger and better ships. Mahan's book had had its effect on public opinion in Britain too. Already politicians were talking about the inevitable atrophy of the British Empire. The Navy League was formed in 1893 to keep a watchful eye on the nation's greatest asset and prod politicians to keep ahead of rival powers. If Britain did not keep the two power standard, it was believed, she would face disaster: the empire would collapse and the survival of the country would be jeopardised because her food imports would be at the mercy of others.

In 1894 the *Royal Sovereign*-class battleship was superseded by a new bout of shipbuilding. The result was the *Majestic* class, the biggest and most powerful ships in the world. They were powered by triple-expansion steam engines, which gave them a speed of seventeen knots. They were imitated by the emerging naval powers. Britain still led the field. But only just.

Straight after the Hague peace conference Fisher received the plum appointment in the operational Navy: commander-in-chief in the

Mediterranean. He was woefully lacking in sea time, which he needed if he was to progress to the summit of the service.

Like Hood, St Vincent, Nelson, Collingwood and many of his predecessors in this, the most vital foreign station, Fisher knew he had to stamp his identity upon the Mediterranean Fleet straight away. The Navy prided itself on drill and discipline every bit as much as it did in the days of Nelson. Fisher took that for granted. What he expected of his officers was something much more elevated than excellence in routine drill and the all-consuming fad for cleanliness. 'Before his arrival, the topics and arguments of the officers' messes ... were mainly confined to such matters as the cleaning of paint and brasswork ... these were forgotten and replaced by incessant controversies of tactics, strategy, gunnery, torpedo warfare, blockade etc. It was a veritable renaissance and affected every officer in the Navy.'[2]

Fisher instituted a prize for the best essay on tactics. He gave brilliantly compelling lectures and encouraged junior officers to discuss their ideas with him. For many officers Fisher was no doubt a rather forbidding figure, but for young men with the solution to a problem or a piece of fresh thinking he was inspirational. His second in command, Lord Charles Beresford, was an old comrade-in-arms and enjoyed a public profile at least as big, if not bigger, than Fisher's. Both men were fiery, temperamental characters.

For some Fisher was an inspiring leader, brimming with new ideas and receptive to fresh thinking. For others he was a tyrant who had upset the old order. And indeed Fisher was a divisive figure. He had a volcanic temper and he was openly contemptuous of senior officers who did not live up to his standards or who could not keep up with his electric mind. In this aspect of his character Fisher resembled Rodney or St Vincent more than he did Hood or Nelson.

But there was no dispute that Fisher's time in the Mediterranean shook up thinking on naval tactics at the dawn of the twentieth century. At the heart of modern fleet tactics, Fisher believed, should be speed and accurate long-distance gunnery. The two were linked. Advances in torpedo technology meant that their effective range had increased to 3,000 yards – and there were navies experimenting with extending this range. Battleships had to fight beyond their reach. A fleet had to keep mobile and adopt unorthodox formations to avoid becoming sitting targets for torpedo boats and long-distance guns. Stray too close to an enemy fleet and you would be prey to torpedoes; go too far and you could not inflict damage on the enemy. That was the dilemma facing tacticians at the beginning of the century.

It was not enough for the Royal Navy to have bigger and better ships. It needed to demonstrate that its guns could wreak havoc from greater distances than anyone else. This was no easy prospect. The massive 12-inch guns could fire great distances but there was no way to aim them accurately. The smaller guns were fairly accurate to two or three thousand yards, with the use of telescopic sights. By the end of Fisher's time in the Mediterranean they were being tested on moving targets at 5,000 yards – an improvement on the 2,000 yards when he arrived. The ships of the fleet went from steaming at a sedate twelve knots, with plenty of breakdowns, to a normal speed of fifteen knots, with few malfunctions.

Fisher did not just have foreign navies in his sights; he was able to manipulate the press from the Mediterranean. He and Beresford worked through the journalist Arnold White to publicise what they saw as a lack of ships. It was a risky move, but Fisher and Beresford got their way. It boosted Fisher's name as a troublemaker. Then he fell out spectacularly with Beresford. When the latter's ship made a hash of anchoring at Malta Fisher ordered him to go back to sea and return in a 'seamanlike manner'. It was a petty form of public humiliation. Beresford neither forgot nor forgave.

Fisher returned to Britain in 1902. He was now sixty and was concerned that the post of First Sea Lord would elude him. Despite his press campaign against the Admiralty, Fisher was made Second Sea Lord, responsible for the personnel side of the Navy.

Fisher had uneasily bridged the gap between the technical aspect of the modern Navy and its operation side. In the early twentieth century it was a wide gulf. Engineering officers were looked down upon by the sailing officers as lower-class grease monkeys. Fisher determined that that snobbery must end. All officers should have technical training and engineer officers should have the chance to command at sea. Under Fisher's reforms all cadets, whether destined to be engineers or commanding officers, were educated together until they were twenty-two. Future officers would have a grounding in mathematics, engineering, electricity and science as well as the conventional schooling in literature, history, navigation and seamanship.

Cadets began life in the Navy at the age of thirteen at Osborne naval academy. After two years they went to the Navy's training school for another two years. For decades cadets had got their first taste of naval life on an aged, immobile wooden battleship called HMS *Britannia*. But now *Britannia* had become a 'stone ship' – a grand building at Dartmouth. After *Britannia* they would be posted to actual training ships. They would then sit exams. The grades a cadet achieved determined his place on the list of seniority; those who did best would climb the ladder of promotion the quickest.

This was a significant achievement for a man who had dedicated such large portions of his career to training up specialist officers, but it was deeply controversial. Many officers hated the thought that the two branches of the officer corps should be brought together. They would not accept that technology and engineering could hold a candle to traditional officerly accomplishments such as seamanship, navigation, signalling, gunnery and battle tactics. Even more horrifying was the prospect that engineers would one day captain ships and progress to flag rank. But worse than all that was Fisher's reform which allowed warrant officers to qualify to become commissioned officers. It was the victory of middle-class swots over dashing gentlemanly officers who aspired to the mantle of Nelson.

Fisher's magnetic personality attracted as many supporters as it created enemies. Lord Charles Beresford led the camp hostile to Fisher's reforms. Beresford believed he had a claim on becoming First Sea Lord. The only man who stood in his way was his enemy and former boss. But Fisher had powerful friends, the most important being Edward VII. In 1904 Fisher reached the pinnacle of his career, First Sea Lord. He was in a position to fundamentally reshape the Royal Navy, but he was due to retire in 1906. Time was precious.

The new First Lord worked through the 'Fishpond', a group of officers he had collected throughout his career. They were men like him, with hungry minds and aptitude for technological development. He had collected two brilliant officers from his time as captain of the Navy's gunnery school – Percy Scott and John Jellicoe. Scott was the Navy's foremost gunnery expert. In the course of his duties at *Excellent*, on the naval ordnance committee and at sea his inventions had increased the rate of firing and accuracy of ships' guns. Like his boss, Scott was a brilliant but abrasive man. Fisher created the post of Inspector of Target Practice for him. In that job he increased the effective range of naval guns to 10,000 yards. That is a distance of over five and half miles. No gunner could see that far. Therefore Scott invented powerful telescopic rangefinders positioned high up on the skyscraping foremast. Aiming was taken out of the hands of gunners down in the turrets. They would be directed by gunnery officers stationed aloft. These would direct the gun to the target and, when the salvo was fired, adjust the angle of fire based on where the observers saw the shell splashes in the water five miles away. Scott kept hold of the patents for his inventions and made a fortune from Vickers and various admiralties around the world. Jellicoe had been Fisher's assistant at the Naval Ordnance Office. He was an outstanding administrator, gunnery expert and decorated naval hero. Fisher brought him into the Fishpond as Director of Naval Ordnance.

Throughout his tenure at the Admiralty Fisher talent-spotted the best and brightest technical experts in the Navy. The Fishpond was not just stocked from *Excellent*; it included officers who had fallen under Fisher's spell when he encouraged them to speak up and advance their ideas in the Mediterranean. Henry Oliver was a navigation officer on HMS *Majestic* when he was drawn into discussion with Fisher. In 1903 Fisher tasked Oliver with creating a navigation school. Henry Jackson was a pioneer in wireless technology, an expert in torpedoes and electrical equipment and a fellow of the Royal Society. Fisher made him Third Sea Lord. Reginald Bacon impressed Fisher with his technical knowledge of torpedoes when the new First Sea Lord had been commander-in-chief in the Mediterranean. Bacon progressed rapidly to captain and became inspecting captain of the first submarines ordered by the Admiralty.

This was a time of government cuts. Fisher was expected to impose economies on the Navy while maintaining Britain's power. Fisher was ready for the challenge. He had already mapped out the way to transform the Navy.

And he found an international situation in a state of rapid change. Russia lost a naval war with Britain's ally Japan. Britain and France signed the Entente Cordiale. That meant that Britain's two rivals no longer threatened her in the Baltic and Pacific (in the case of Russia), in home waters and Africa (France) or the Mediterranean (Russia and France). Now the threat came from Germany, which was rapidly building up a fleet. Kaiser Wilhelm had long envied the Royal Navy, and he knew at first hand its power: he used to spend his summers with his grandmother, Queen Victoria, at Osborne House on the Isle of Wight, where he fell in love with the swagger and pomp of Britain's senior service. He was made an honorary admiral in his grandmother's Navy. His youthful ardour turned into a desire to outdo, even do down, the British Navy. In 1890 the growth of the Imperial German Navy was assured when Britain ceded Heligoland to Germany in return for Zanzibar. Heligoland had been in British hands since 1814, and its position guarding the main Prussian, later German, naval base of Wilhelmshaven gave it immense strategic value. The Kaiser had ambitions to extend German naval power across the globe, and there were rumours that he had his eyes on acquiring a coaling station in Morocco. In 1905 Germany tried to undermine

French influence there. The two European powers came to the brink of war.

Fisher let it be known that, if it came to it, he would treat the Germans as the Royal Navy had treated the Danes in 1807. He would destroy their fleet in harbour without warning. He dispatched British ships to the Baltic. The German navy was not strong enough to meet this challenge. Fisher declared that 'the best declaration of war would be the sinking of the enemy's fleet!'[3] The king thought Fisher was mad. As so often he used his unpredictability and bullish personality to send out signals of intent. The image he presented to the world was as a pugnacious modern Nelson.

But for Fisher the modern version of a perfectly executed Nelsonian manoeuvre was a highly sophisticated war game. Gaining the technological edge, building ever more impressive ships and displaying them to the world were the crucial moves in modern naval chess. Most importantly, deterrence was workable only if countries went to the brink of war and did not flinch. Fisher ruled the Navy on his principle of 'three Rs and the three Hs': in administration he had to be 'ruthless, relentless and remorseless'[4] and in battle it was imperative to 'hit first, hit hard and keep on hitting'.[5]

At the age of sixty-three Fisher had lost none of his capacity to shock. He immediately sold ninety ships and put sixty-four into reserve. Many of the old vessels were, he said, 'too weak to fight and too slow to run away'. The ships in reserve would be manned by small crews of specialists who would be able to get their ships into service much quicker than any reserve fleet in the past.

Already in 1903 the Royal Naval Volunteer Reserve (RNVR) had been formed to allow men with civilian jobs on shore to train for wartime service with the fleet. The RNR and RNVR provided the Navy with a huge pool of men and officers who could serve in the fleet in time of war. The Royal Fleet Auxiliary (RFA) was formed in 1905 to provide civilian-manned coaling ships to sustain a fleet serving in home waters or abroad. Later, in 1910, the RNR Trawler Section was instituted so that in the case of a European war the fishing fleet would be mobilised for minesweeping duties.

These reforms allowed Fisher to reconfigure the Navy's global commitment. The Mediterranean Fleet was reduced from twelve to eight battleships. The five battleships on the China station were recalled. The South Atlantic squadron was abolished. The North American cruiser squadron was turned into a training squadron. The Channel Fleet was renamed the Atlantic Fleet, given the fastest battleships and cruisers, and moved to Gibraltar. The Home Fleet became the new Channel Fleet. It was a formidable force. It included the Navy's best battleships and destroyers, its new submarines and torpedo boats. It was backed up by the enormous reserve fleet and based at the Nore on the Thames Estuary. In other words, it was aimed at Germany.

Outside home waters the emphasis was on a highly mobile fleet that could be dispatched where it was needed when it was needed. The linchpin of the system was the Atlantic Fleet, which could respond quickly to threats at home, in the Mediterranean or the Western Approaches. Fisher had slimmed the Navy down and readied it for war – a war he believed would be fought in northern Europe unless he deterred it first.

Fisher's assessment of Britain's future as a naval power was radical; it upset many people inside and outside the Navy. His enemies were led by Beresford. Fisher's great rival attacked the scrapping of large numbers of ships, which he believed left trade undefended. He led the angry reaction to the recall of battleships to home waters, which was seen as unbecoming to the world's premier naval power and global policeman. Fisher was typically dismissive of such criticism. Britain still held the Downs, Gibraltar, the Suez Canal, the Cape and Singapore. A ship could not move around the oceans without passing through Britain's maritime gates.

Most galling for Beresford was Fisher's elevation to Admiral of the Fleet in 1905. This promotion allowed Fisher to remain as First Sea Lord beyond retirement age. Now Beresford would never reach the top – unless he could push Fisher out. It also meant that the reforms would go deeper and become permanent.

Fisher was convinced as ever that new technologies had upset all previous thinking on strategy. Jackson and Bacon were responsible for ordering a radical new oceangoing submarine. As far as Fisher was concerned this was more important than developments in gunnery. It was what Fisher had been predicting since he was a whippersnapper. Within a few years, he said in 1905, no battlefleet would be safe in the English Channel or the western Mediterranean because British submarines would send it to the seabed. The First Sea Lord wanted hundreds of submarines, which he would use to dominate the Narrow Seas, just as battleships had always done. Fisher wrote: 'My beloved submarines magnify the naval power of England [sic] seven times more than present.'[6]

'What is the use of battleships as we have hitherto known them?' asked Fisher. 'NONE! Their one and only function – that of ultimate security of defence – is gone – lost!'[7]

But the world, and in particular Britain, was not ready to send its battleships to the scrapyard. Before that happened the Navy needed a battleship that exploited the giant leaps in long-range gunnery and speed. Fisher set up a Committee on Designs, tasked with developing a battleship armed with 12-inch guns and capable of twenty-one knots and a powerful new cruiser, also armed with 12-inch guns but with a speed of twenty-five and a half knots.

HMS *Invincible* and her two sisters *Inflexible* and *Indomitable* were laid down in 1906 and commissioned in 1908. They were the first battlecruisers. They were as large and as heavily armed as battleships, but much faster, intended to counter fast armoured cruisers which, in a war, would be used to attack Britain's extensive trade routes. They answered Fisher's demands for economies: fewer, better, faster battlecruisers rather than lots of small, slow cruisers fanned out around the globe. He called *Invincible* 'my greyhound of the sea'.

But they were overshadowed by the ship with which Fisher's name will always be associated, the most famous warship in the history of naval warfare: HMS *Dreadnought*.

It was clear that battlecruisers would not be enough on their own. Any future war, Fisher understood, would be fought against Germany in the Baltic or North Sea. And the German navy was constructing a powerful battlefleet. Fisher's committee also studied the most recent naval battles, those of the Yellow Sea and Tsushima, fought during the Russo-Japanese War in 1905. In British naval circles the Battle of Tsushima was regarded as the most significant naval battle since Trafalgar, ninety-nine and a half years before. It revealed a new world of technology and tactics. The Imperial Japanese Navy made use of wireless telegraphy and rangefinders, designed and constructed by the Glasgow optical engineering firm Barr and Stroud, to bombard the Russian fleet at 6,000 yards. The Russian navy started the battle with eight battleships, three coastal battleships, eight cruisers and nine destroyers. By the end seven of the battleships and fourteen other vessels had been sunk, seven had been captured and the remaining six disarmed; 4,380 Russian sailors were killed and 5,917 captured. The Japanese lost just three torpedo boats and 117 sailors.

The great Japanese victory showed the world that naval battles would be decided by battleships firing heavy guns at long range. The Royal Navy's observer at the Battle of Tsushima told Fisher's committee that the Japanese 12-inch guns had been accurate and devastating while the 10-inch guns were ineffective. The experts on the Committee on Designs debated and discussed the exact requirements of a modern battleship. The result was HMS *Dreadnought*.

She was laid down on 2 October 1905, launched on 10 February 1906 and sent for sea trials exactly 366 days after work began. That in itself was a breathtaking example of the power of British industry. A key part of British deterrence was the proven ability to outbuild its rivals at short notice. The speed in building the new ship was all the more impressive because it was a leviathan. *Dreadnought*'s immediate predecessor, HMS *Agamemnon*, displaced 17,683 tons and was armed with four 12-inch and ten 9.2-inch guns; she had a speed of eighteen knots. The new ship displaced 18,120 tons. But her most innovative features were her speed and armament. She was the first battleship to be powered by steam turbines, giving her the remarkable speed of 21.6 knots. Her five gun turrets each carried two 12-inch guns that fired armour-piercing shells at a maximum range of 17,990 yards. *Dreadnought* could fire a broadside of eight guns; she could fire six guns aft and four forward. The rate of fire was two rounds per minute. She did not carry any smaller guns, save for a secondary armament of twenty-seven rapid-fire 3-inch guns. She was the world's first ever 'all-big-gun battleship'. That is to say her main battery consisted entirely of 12-inch guns, rather than being a mix of different-sized guns. She could outpace any fleet in the world and blast its ships out of the water.

The awesome battery was useless unless the shells reached their targets. Modern ships moved at great speeds, fought at unprecedented distances, and their guns were capable of rapid fire. It was hard enough determining the position of an enemy ship, but by the time one of *Dreadnought*'s shells had travelled 16,000 yards the target would have moved. There was a legion of variables – the pitch and roll of the ship, the speed and direction of the wind, even the temperature in the magazine. Gunnery officers needed a way to compute the enemy ship's likely range and speed in a fast-changing battle fought over large tracts of ocean. The massive foremast of *Dreadnought* and her successors gave gunnery officers a bird's-eye view of the seas. From high up in the directing tower they used optical rangefinders to glean the data needed to be fed into the ship's computing system.

The data were plotted on a mechanical computer, the Dreyer Fire Control Table, on dreadnoughts from 1912. It was a large iron table, developed by a brilliant young gunnery officer, Commander Frederic Charles Dreyer, and it looked like something imagined by Heath Robinson. It consisted of dials, clocks, gyro-compasses, rotating drums and a typewriter; the moving parts were worked by sliding scales, axles, handles and bicycle chains. It was situated in the transmitting station, buried deep in the belly of the ship, far below the armoured deck. It needed a mass of information, the myriad variables that affected long-range artillery. Some of this came from on-board instruments: the dreadnought's speed and bearing, the direction and speed of the wind, the pitch and roll of the ship and so on. It also needed information about the target ship. The dumaresq (pronounced doomairik) mechanical computer calculated the speed and direction of the enemy from data provided by the lookouts. It was invented by John Saumarez Dumaresq, an Australian who joined HMS *Britannia* as a cadet. The Vickers Range Clock, invented by Percy Scott, calculated the target's range, using data from the dumaresq.

All this information was plotted on the Dreyer Table. It predicted the position of the enemy ship at the time the dreadnought's shells impacted. The Fire Directing Officer took the information and aimed the ship's great guns by sending messages to the gun turrets ordering to what angle the guns should be elevated and trained. He then fired the guns electronically. The men high up on the directing tower reported where the shells landed. If the enemy ship was hit, the system had worked. If not the spotters reported to the Dreyer Table operators where they had seen white plumes of foam thrown up by the shells and the system was corrected accordingly.

Dreadnought was a massive, heavily armed floating computer. It was the most technologically advanced weapon of war in the world. Information buzzed about the ship, from the rangefinder operators and spotters positioned at the summit of *Dreadnought*'s soaring pagoda masts, down to the transmitting station, then to the gun turrets and the magazines below the waterline. Up on the bridge information was processed and the movement of the ship co-ordinated with the guns; deep down below the engine room responded to the orders that pinged around the vessel.

Information also zipped through the fleet; the flagship transmitted orders to the ships regarding their targets. The system called upon teams of specialists. Operators crowded around the Dreyer Table, making their calculations and sending the information where it was needed. The men had to work quickly and while the ship was under bombardment. It was imperfect and in need of constant refinement. Indeed the Dreyer Fire Control Table was severely flawed and it was chosen in preference to a rival analogue computer, the Argo Clock. But the development of such systems was a key moment in the history of naval warfare. The brightest British officers, in partnership with Britain's leading electrical and engineering firms, collaborated on a state-of-the-art weapon. Electronic warfare had arrived.

Dreadnought marked a true revolution in ship design. And she looked the part. She was impressively large and strangely stylish – although she lacked the towering elegance of her immediate successors. She immediately made obsolete every other battleship in the world – so much so that all new big-gun battleships were called dreadnoughts and all the puny ships she left in her wake became retrospectively known as predreadnoughts. The navies of the world ordered their own dreadnoughts. The arms race was reignited.

In 1908 the German navy began work on nine dreadnoughts; the Royal Navy constructed eleven in that year and ordered four more a year later and an additional four the year after that. By 1910 Britain had twenty-two dreadnoughts to Germany's thirteen. The German Naval Law of 1912 envisaged a fleet of thirty-three battleships and battlecruisers. Hungary had four dreadnoughts and Italy four with two under construction.

This was Britain's worst nightmare. It spelled the end of her naval dominance. The Navy might even be outnumbered in home waters, causing her to pull back her forces from around the world. In response to a panicky press and political campaign British dreadnoughts became bigger and faster. The *Orion*-class super-dreadnoughts displaced 22,000 tons and had ten 13.5-inch guns. The *Queen Elizabeth* class ordered in 1912 was 27,500 tons, had eight 15-inch guns and a speed of twenty-four knots. She also carried anti-aircraft guns – a portent of wars to come. By then the German navy had dropped out of the naval arms race. In 1914 the British home fleet numbered twenty-two dreadnoughts, fourteen battlecruisers, twenty-two pre-dreadnoughts and 160 cruisers and destroyers. This was a savage arms race, born out of Britain and Germany's mutual distrust. It pushed the countries to the brink of war. It was made worse by the construction of the Kiel Canal, which would be complete in 1914 and would allow German dreadnoughts from Wilhelmshaven to enter the Baltic, thus evading any British blockade.

The dreadnought and the battlecruiser were not the only new development in Fisher's Navy. British D-class submarines gave the Royal Navy a lead in submarine development. They had diesel engines, electrical engines for when the boat submerged, and wireless radios. This increased their range beyond all precedent, making the submarine an offensive, oceangoing weapon for the first time.

The prototype HMS *D-1* was designed, constructed and launched in strict secrecy. During the annual manoeuvres in 1910 *D-1* left her base at Fort Blockhouse, Gosport, and successfully torpedoed two targets off Colonsay in Scotland. Less well known than *Dreadnought*, *D-1* heralded a new way of war in the twentieth century.

Fisher retired on his sixty-ninth birthday in 1910. A year before he had been raised to the peerage. He revolutionised the Royal Navy. But he divided the service deeper than it had been since the days of Rodney. Beresford had used the press, the Conservative Party and his faction in the Navy to subject Fisher to a barrage of criticism that undermined him and forced his early exit.

Retirement did not blunt his energy or even diminish his power overmuch; he was confidential adviser to the First Lord of the Admiralty, Winston Churchill. Few men have dominated the Navy for so long or changed it so profoundly.

Fisher will always be linked with HMS *Dreadnought*. She was one of the most famous ships ever launched, even if her career was uneventful and she was superseded by new generations of dreadnoughts. *Dreadnought* marked the end of a long tradition of British ships designed to overawe her rivals. That tradition could be said to have begun with Rædwald's Sutton Hoo ship; it included such iconic vessels as Alfred's longboats, Henry V's *Grace Dieu*, Henry VIII's *Great Harry*, the Elizabethan galleon *Dreadnought*, the *Sovereign of the Seas* and HMS *Warrior*. Throughout Fisher's long career in the Navy a succession of state-of-the-art warships had ensured Britain's command of the seas. *Dreadnought* was the culmination of that struggle for primacy.

PART 13: GÖTTERDÄMMERUNG

CHAPTER 46

THE RECKONING
1914–1916

The enemy was a sitting target. Vice Admiral Maximilian von Spee's squadron had enjoyed a successful hunting expedition against British merchantmen and coaling bases. A month earlier he had attacked and sunk two British cruisers commanded by Sir Christopher Cradock at Coronel off the coast of Chile. Spee was returning home when he decided to raid Port Stanley on 8 December. He wanted to destroy the telegraph station and Brunel's once proud SS *Great Britain*, now a miserable hulk moored at Port Stanley which served as a coaling depot for British warships and merchantmen.

The German East Asia squadron steamed towards Stanley on the morning of 8 December 1914. It consisted of two armoured cruisers and three light cruisers. Suddenly shells splashed into the sea; they came from guns over the hill, fired by HMS *Canopus* as it turned out, a pre-dreadnought battleship that had been grounded as an artillery platform. Then Spee's men spotted an even more unwelcome sight: the distinctive steepling masts of British battlecruisers.

Unbeknown to Spee the British squadron – two battlecruisers, three armoured cruisers and two light cruisers – was taking coal on board at Stanley. Spee had no idea that they were anywhere near the south Atlantic. The German ships fled for the open sea. Meanwhile Vice Admiral Doveton Sturdee ordered his men to breakfast while the ships raised steam. HMS *Kent*, one of the armoured cruisers, pursued the Germans. There was no hurry: Sturdee knew that his battlecruisers were fast enough to run down the enemy.

The British left Stanley at 10.00. Sturdee was on the prototype battlecruiser HMS *Invincible*; he also had with him HMS *Inflexible*. In company were two armoured cruisers and a light cruiser. Spee was fifteen miles away. Sturdee began the chase at a leisurely pace – just eighteen knots, so that the smaller ships could keep station. Even so they gained on the German ships, whose engines were worn out from their long time at sea.

At 12.20 Sturdee let slip his battlecruisers. They reached twenty-five knots. At 13.00 *Invincible* opened fire at a range of 16,000 yards. Spee ordered the light cruisers to detach and flee, while he held off the British battlecruisers with his armoured cruisers. Sturdee had anticipated this, so his own armoured cruisers were ready to give chase. Between 13.20 and 14.05 *Invincible* and *Inflexible* bombarded the German armoured cruisers at distances of between 13,000 and 16,000 yards from a parallel course. After that phase smoke obscured the German ships, and the distance widened. Then from 14.45 to 15.30 the opposing ships jockeyed for advantage, the British trying to close in, the Germans attempting to pull away. But during this dance the big British guns struck at ranges of between 10,000 and 15,000 yards. The Germans were unable to inflict comparable damage on their hunters.

Sturdee pressed in for the kill. *Inflexible* steamed out of the smoke and was able to pound the enemy at just 12,000 yards. By 16.04 Spee's flagship SMS *Scharnhorst* had her funnels blasted away and was starting to list; she sank at 16.17. Then the two giant battlecruisers pummelled SMS *Gneisenau* until she went to the bottom at 17.30. Meanwhile the British armoured cruisers had caught up with the remnants of the German squadron. By 21.23 two of the enemy ships were destroyed. Two German ships escaped, the light cruiser SMS *Dresden* and an auxiliary ship.

The four German ships that were sunk had been crewed by 2,086 sailors. *Scharnhorst* was lost with all hands, including Admiral Spee. Just 215 were rescued from the other ships. The British fired 1,174 shells. Only seventy-four found their targets, but that had been enough for total victory. The damage on the British ships was slight and only nineteen sailors died. Fisher's battlecruisers and their fire-control systems proved their worth at the Battle of the Falkland Islands, as Sturdee's triumph is known.

And the architect of the victory was none other than Lord Fisher. He had been recalled as First Sea Lord on 30 October 1914. He rushed to set the trap for Spee. *Invincible* and *Inflexible* had been detached from the home fleet at short notice and sent to hunt down Spee with workmen still aboard, rushing to make them battle-ready. Sturdee had only arrived at the Falklands on 8 December.

To detach the battlecruisers from home defence was a risky move. It was characteristic of John Fisher. As was the pressure he put on the dockyards to get the ships ready for service. The Admiralty had not been a happy place since Fisher left. There had been three First Sea Lords between Fisher's retirement in 1910 and his return in 1914. In large part this was Fisher's fault. He had ruled the Admiralty as his private fiefdom, using a small number of junior officers and members of the Fishpond to carry out his plans. He despised paperwork and kept the Navy's war plans to himself. One of Beresford's main criticisms was that Fisher had not created a naval general staff. The Navy Fisher fashioned seemed like his personal service, a machine only he could control. His successors did not understand his concept of 'flotilla defence' whereby the country would be defended by submarines, destroyers and torpedo boats. It did not help that Winston Churchill took advice from Jackie Fisher during the latter's supposed retirement.

After the first few months of war the public and the government were crying out for an energetic, swashbuckling leader for the Navy after three months of disappointment. The 73-year-old Jackie Fisher was the favoured choice to shake up the Navy with fresh thinking.

For generations the public had been fed on the idea that the Royal Navy was an invincible world power. In the summer and autumn of 1914 it was assumed that the Navy would deliver the death blow to Germany's ambitions before the war escalated. For that to happen there would have to be a decisive battle in the North Sea.

At the very beginning of the war the British Grand Fleet was put under the command of Sir John Jellicoe and moved to its new base, Scapa Flow in the Orkneys. From this eyrie it would keep watch, ready to swoop on the Hochseeflotte (the German High Seas Fleet), which was based at Wilhelmshaven and ports in the Bight of Heligoland. Submarines, destroyers, torpedo boats and light cruisers operating out of Harwich stood ready to intercept the Hochseeflotte if it put to sea. By these means the British Expeditionary Force was safely conducted across the Channel in August and supply lines were kept open thereafter.

The Hochseeflotte would not venture into the Channel. The aim was to break out into the north Atlantic and cause carnage in Britain's vital sea lanes. In order to do that it would have to beat the Royal Navy in the North Sea. Until that happened Germany was under blockade, while the allies were able to receive limitless manpower, materiel and food from their colonies and the wider world.

The Germans made a good start at disrupting Britain's worldwide network. The battlecruiser SMS *Goeben* dented the time-hallowed prestige of the Navy in the Mediterranean by easily evading its forces and entering the safety of the Dardanelles. Following *Goeben*'s success Turkey joined the war on Germany's side. The German cruiser SMS *Emden* enjoyed a career of mayhem in the Indian Ocean. She terrorised British trade routes, bombarded Madras and raided Penang. In September alone *Emden* captured and sank seventeen British merchantmen. SMS *Königsberg* sank HMS *Pegasus* in the Battle of Zanzibar (20 September 1914). The West Indies trade routes and colonies were menaced by SMS *Karlsruhe*. And all this time Spee was at large with his powerful squadron.

Back in home waters both sides were eager for a decisive encounter. For now, the Germans had too few dreadnoughts to risk a battle. They knew that they had to wear down the Royal Navy first, gradually reaching equality by a series of minor actions until they achieved matching firepower. From the start of the war, cruisers, submarines and destroyers from both sides made forays into the North Sea, testing each other's strength.

In August two British officers believed they had discovered a weakness in the German naval defences. Commodore Roger Keyes commanded a submarine patrol and Commodore Reginald Tyrwhitt led a force of destroyers. Both were based at Harwich and operated off the Heligoland Bight, where they saw that German destroyer patrols followed a set routine. Every evening they would be escorted out by cruisers and they were escorted back the next morning. The two British commodores' plan was for submarines to lure the destroyers out to sea, where they would be ambushed by British destroyers and submarines, which would sweep the Bight.

The daring plan was put into effect on 28 August. It was not as simple as it had seemed. The ambush descended into confusion and the German destroyers were reinforced by cruisers. Luckily for the Harwich forces, Jellicoe had detached the Grand Fleet's battlecruiser force, led by David Beatty, to support them at a distance. He stood forty miles off, following proceedings by radio. At 11.30 it became clear that the Harwich boys were in trouble. The mission was not yet over, but the tide was rising, which meant larger German ships could enter the fray.

David Beatty had a decision to make. Supporting the British destroyers and submarines was his priority. But dare he risk some of the Navy's finest battlecruisers off the German coast, which was thick with submarines, mines, torpedo boats and, possibly, dreadnoughts? An officer on a British destroyer in the centre of the action described what happened next: 'There straight ahead of us in lovely procession, like elephants walking through a pack of dogs came *Lion* [Beatty's flagship], *Queen Mary*, *Princess Royal*, *Invincible* and *New Zealand* ... How solid they looked, how utterly earthquaking.'[1]

Beatty saved the day. The Germans lost three light cruisers, two torpedo boats and one destroyer; 712 sailors were killed and several ships badly damaged. The Navy did not lose a ship and only thirty-five men died. The Battle of Heligoland Bight was celebrated as a major victory won under the very nose of the Hochseeflotte. The daring of it shocked the Kaiserliche Marine (Imperial German Navy) and reminded everyone of the élan of the Royal Navy. The Kaiser was badly shaken.

In reality it was poorly planned. It was a huge risk that didn't miscarry only because Beatty made the bold decision to intervene. The battle showed that the Navy's intelligence of the enemy was flawed and its fighting ability below par. Things began to get worse. In September German U-boats and minelayers went on the offensive. On 22 September the British ships *Aboukir*, *Hogue* and *Cressy* were sunk by *U-9* off the Netherlands. Jellicoe was forced to move the Grand Fleet to Ireland while submarine defences at Scapa Flow were improved. On 27 October the super-dreadnought HMS *Audacious* was blown up by a German mine off Donegal. British naval strength was being whittled away. Confidence in the service – and within the service – began to crumble in the face of the lurking, unseen menace of U-boats and mines. The Navy descended from the height of complacency to a nervy, risk-averse service.

Emboldened by its successes the German battlecruiser squadron – the First Scouting Group – became more active in the North Sea. It tried to lure out elements of the Grand Fleet for a battle on its terms by bombarding Yarmouth on 3 November. Faith in the Royal Navy began to plummet.

The government and the public thirsted for another Trafalgar. John Fisher was the man to deliver it. As ever he brimmed with ideas. The first part of his strategy was to make the oceans of the world safe again for British ships. By the end of the year that was largely complete. As we have seen, his actions set in train the elimination of the main threat, Spee's East Asia Squadron, at the Battle of the Falklands. The strikingly successful predator *Emden* was sunk by the Australian cruiser HMAS *Sydney*. *Königsberg* was blockaded in the Rufiji River in Tanganyika by British ships, which she kept at bay with her big guns. Eventually the British resorted to towing out two monitors, HMSs *Mersey* and *Severn*. Monitors were a new type of small, unseaworthy, shallow-draught warships which mounted exceptionally heavy long-range guns stripped from battleships. *Mersey* and *Severn* were able to get close enough to *Königsberg*, but beyond the range of the German ship's main armament, and bombard her with the help of a spotting plane. *Königsberg*'s captain scuttled his stricken ship. *Karlsruhe* was destroyed in an internal explosion as she steamed to raid Barbados. The last survivor of the Falklands, *Dresden*, was scuttled off the Chilean island Más a Tierra when she was cornered by two British light cruisers.

Before 1914 ended the British had Germany confined to the North Sea. It was time to act.

Fisher was experienced enough to know that a decisive battle that would hasten the end of the war was unlikely. Victories such as Quiberon Bay or Trafalgar came at the end of long, hard slogs. Sea battles on their own, however crushing they might be, rarely settled major land wars. After all, Napoleon's final defeat came ten years after Nelson's great victory.

The Grand Fleet was best deployed in the northern North Sea, where it could blockade the Kaiserliche Marine. To seek battle in the southern North Sea would be to enter a thicket of mines and submarines – traps laid to prevent the Royal Navy imposing a close blockade. That much was evident from the quixotic Battle of Heligoland.

Fisher had something other than a major fleet battle in mind. As soon as he resumed the office of First Sea Lord he ordered 596 new vessels. These included five battlecruisers, fifty-six destroyers and sixty-five submarines. Less showy were the minesweepers, forty-five monitors and 260 landing craft. But these were a clue as to Fisher's plan. This enormous flotilla would be used to attack the heart of German naval power: the Baltic. The Grand Fleet would not have to be used at all except as a passive force to terrorise the Kaiserliche Marine and keep it in port. The Baltic was the only place where the Navy could have a decisive effect on Germany.

It was impressive. It was unconventional. But it would not be quick and it might not even happen at all. As ever Fisher was playing games. The dangling carrot of a major naval operation also kept Churchill happy, restraining the trigger-happy First Lord from hazarding the Navy with his own rash adventures.

Did Fisher really intend that the Navy should force its way into the Baltic? It seems unlikely. The steady build-up of flotilla craft to be used in the Baltic would place a heavy burden on German naval strategists. It might force them to make a mistake or act rashly in an effort to pre-empt the British flotilla. That was part of Fisher's bigger game. 'Make the German fleet fight and you win the war!' he declared. 'How can you make the German fleet fight? By undertaking on a huge scale, with an immense armada of rapidly-built craft, an operation that threatens the German Fleet's existence!'[2]

And when the German fleet came out to fight, the Navy would be one step ahead. This was thanks to a major intelligence coup. The vital clues came from a German cruiser that was searched by the Russians after it ran aground in the Baltic, a destroyer in the Channel and a merchant ship captured in Australia. These yielded the Kaiserliche Marine's codebooks and maps. They were passed to the Admiralty's signals intelligence department, based in Room 40 at the Admiralty.

In the Admiralty building Room 40 was on the same corridor as Fisher's office and the boardroom. It was tucked away, notoriously hard to find, and its windows overlooked the internal courtyard. Only a few people knew what went on in Room 40. There a small band of Naval Intelligence officers, linguists and decryption experts used the codebooks and intercepted radio messages to break the German cipher. The experts at Room 40 also made use of direction-finding radio equipment to track the movements of enemy ships, submarines and zeppelins.

This intelligence breakthrough scored its first success in December. Room 40 knew that the German First Scouting Group was preparing to leave port on the 14th for the English north-east coast. The Navy was ready for the enemy battlecruiser squadron. Tyrwhitt's destroyers and Keyes's submarines left Harwich. David Beatty's battlecruisers, a light cruiser squadron commanded by Commodore William Goodenough and a force of six dreadnoughts under Admiral Sir George Warrender were detached from Scapa Flow.

The Germans raided Scarborough, Hartlepool and Whitby as they intended. But little did they know that the Navy would be waiting for them off Dogger Bank, sealing off their escape route.

The whole clever trick nearly blew up in the Navy's face. The British thought they were dealing with the German Scouting Group. In fact their intelligence had been good, but dangerous because not complete: the Hochseeflotte itself was at Dogger Bank, supporting the raid with the full force of its dreadnoughts. Against the might of the German high seas fleet were just ten British capital ships.

The Navy was saved from disaster by the excessive caution of the German admiral. Had the Hochseeflotte attacked it would have crushed the small British force and, at a stroke, reduced the Royal Navy to parity. Admiral Friedrich von Ingenohl thought that the entire Grand Fleet might be about to attack. He turned and fled. The Scouting Group and its attendant destroyers were left to face the Royal Navy.

The tables had turned in favour of Britain. Unfortunately the Royal Navy proved as confused as its enemy. Poor signalling, inadequate scouting and misty conditions prevented Beatty's battlecruiser force from engaging the German battlecruiser squadron led by Franz von Hipper. Hipper's ships managed to evade the British submarines covering the Heligoland Bight.

What price, in these circumstances, a decisive battle?

If it was to come, the Navy had a new naval hero in whom to invest its hopes. David Beatty was held up as a modern Nelson. He was forty-three years old in 1914 and he had a reputation for bravery and leadership won during the Sudan Campaign (1897–99) and the Boxer Rebellion. From cadetship onward Beatty had never distinguished himself as a bright spark or shown much aptitude for technical matters. This put him at a disadvantage in the new technocratic Navy: good exams results placed aspiring officers higher up the promotion list.

But Beatty was an old-fashioned fighting officer. In the end he leapfrogged the swots because he distinguished himself in the rare combat situations in the late-Victorian and Edwardian age. He was the scion of an Irish gentry family and he was well connected. That helped too. He was a dashing young officer and also a wealthy one, thanks to his marriage to a beautiful American heiress. He became a captain at twenty-nine. That propelled him a generation beyond his peers. He was promoted to rear admiral at the age of thirty-nine – the average age of an appointment to captain was forty-two. Beatty was the youngest flag officer since Nelson.

Beatty wore his uniform with aristocratic swagger: cap at a careless angle, hands half in pockets. He sported a jacket of his own design, which had three buttons rather than the four stated in regulations. He projected effortless superiority. Rules were for other people.

But beneath his nonchalant demeanour Beatty was a tough, experienced officer and an excellent leader of men. He encouraged initiative and aggression in his officers in the manner of the best of his predecessors. In 1913 his qualities were recognised when he was placed in command of the First Battlecruiser Squadron. This post suited his temperament. The squadron was responsible for hunting down the enemy fleet and drawing it into the path of the British battlefeet. Unlike the plodding battlefleet, the battlecruiser force depended on its guile, high speed and firepower; it needed a quick-thinking, dashing commander and inspired officers. In an encounter with the Hochseeflotte it would be the First Battlecruiser Squadron that would make the opening moves, fire the first shots and set up the decisive encounter. It would pursue the remnants of the defeated quarry after they had been mauled by the main fleet and finish them off. It was a command tailor-made for a swaggering, fox-hunting young admiral who modelled himself on Nelson. The battlecruiser squadron was where heroes would be made. Beatty wanted to be a hero.

Beatty's squadron was moved to Rosyth, in the middle of the North Sea, so that it could respond to enemy movements in the central North Sea quickly. Beatty was now outside the direct supervision of the more circumspect Jellicoe. On 23 January 1915 Beatty's battlecruiser squadron was scrambled when intercepts indicated that the German battlecruiser force was making a sortie to Dogger Bank to destroy the British fishing fleet, which German naval intelligence blamed for warning the Navy of the raid on Scarborough. Beatty linked up with Tyrwhitt's light forces from Harwich in a position to ambush Admiral Franz Hipper.

It worked. Hipper and his three battlecruisers and one powerful cruiser turned and fled as soon as they entered the trap. Beatty's five faster battlecruisers were steaming on a parallel course. Beatty's flagship, HMS *Lion*, opened fire and crippled SMS *Blücher*, the German armoured cruiser in the rear. Next in the German line was *Derfflinger*, then *Moltke*, and in the lead Hipper's flagship *Seydlitz*. Beatty intended that after the opening salvos his two rearmost ships, *New Zealand* and *Indomitable*, should finish off *Blücher* while the next in the line, *Princess Royal*, took on her opposite number, *Derfflinger*. Then *Tiger* would take on *Moltke*, leaving Beatty's flagship to engage Hipper. The battlecruiser would roll up the Germans as Anson, Hawke and Rodney had hunted down and annihilated their opponents. It started well. HMS *Lion* caused serious damage to *Seydlitz*, sparking a fire that put two turrets out of action and threatened to destroy the ship.

But then things went awry. The captain of *Tiger* ignored *Moltke* and joined *Lion* in the attack on the German flagship. Even worse, *Tiger's* guns failed to hit their target. This left *Lion* to bear the brunt of bombardment from the three German battlecruisers. Just as Beatty was about to deal the death blow to *Seydlitz*, *Lion's* engines gave out and her electricity failed. Beatty wanted the rest of his squadron to continue the chase, knock the German Scouting Group out of the war and reduce the Hochseeflotte to paralysis. With the electricity out, he gave orders for the signal to be given by flag.

Lieutenant Commander Ralph Seymour was well bred, but that did not help him when it came to doing his job as signal officer. Beatty liked his officers to be aristocratic; with Seymour his snobbishness was his undoing. Seymour had made a mess of the signals when Beatty went after Hipper following the raid on Scarborough. Now he made a complete hash of the flag signals at Dogger Bank. Seymour flew the order 'Engage the enemy's rear' and 'Course NE'. Beatty's second in command believed Beatty was ordering him to finish off *Blücher*, which lay to the north-east. The British ships massed on the single German ship, leaving the rest of the squadron. Hipper was spared a terrible defeat. He was able to scamper for home.

Blücher put up a stout defence before she was sunk. The Battle of Dogger

Bank would have taught the Royal Navy some hard lessons if anyone had been prepared to study it. For a start the German ships were much more strongly armoured than was realised. And the German sailors put up a stubborn fight. By contrast the British gunners were underprepared for combat and they were badly let down by their fire-control systems, which were inferior to those of the Germans. *Lion* took sixteen hits from the enemy and *Tiger* six. The British registered just seven hits on the German ships, if *Blücher* is discounted. And those shells that did hit were often ineffective because their ballistic properties were not as good as those of the Germans' armour-piercing shells. This was all the more worrying because the British battlecruisers had been exposed as being vulnerable against enemy fire – their armour was markedly inferior, meaning that their hulls could not withstand tightly grouped enemy salvos very well.

Few of these lessons were absorbed, however. Instead of practising greater accuracy, Beatty had the battlecruiser gunners improve their rate of fire. That caused fresh problems. The cordite propellant used by the Royal Navy to fire its huge shells was made up of 65 per cent nitrocellulose, 30 per cent nitroglycerine and 5 per cent petroleum jelly. It was highly explosive and was easily ignited by enemy fire, which would be concentrated on the gun turrets. To guard against a chain-reaction of cordite fires, which might lead back to the magazine and cause a massive explosion, the cordite charges were brought up from the safety of the magazine to the turrets one by one. The charges were isolated from each other by anti-flash precautions – a series of safety doors, hatches and hoists – which would localise a flash fire.

The process of bringing up the charges one by one was too slow for the kind of barrage Beatty had in mind. Safety measures were ignored, interlocking doors were left open and cordite charges were stocked near the guns or kept in stages between the magazine and the turrets. British battlecruisers might fire their guns quickly, but they were floating powder kegs with inadequate safety systems and poor armour.

Beatty kept up his Nelsonian demeanour in public; in private he was disheartened by his failure at Dogger Bank. In true Nelsonian fashion he declared that his objective was 'complete destruction of the enemy'.[3] He added that his signals were intended for guidance but 'not rigid obedience if they tend to hinder the destruction of the enemy'. This was the language of Nelson, but Beatty laid blame with the vituperation of Rodney. He had not created a 'band of brothers'. Like Rodney he castigated his subordinates, in particular his rear admiral, for failing to read his mind. The press gave Beatty a good ride. He was perfect for the media age: his defiant pose and heroic bearing captured the camera. It helped that the press was heavily censored and fervently patriotic. Beatty's equivocal achievements were magnified into significant victories, promises of glories to come.

Beatty waited for the chance to live up to all the expectations that had been heaped upon him. In May came worse news. Fisher resigned.

The First Sea Lord had been a firm supporter of his protégé Jellicoe and Beatty, a kindred spirit. During his months as head of the Navy his relations with Churchill had grown strained. The two men were uncomfortably alike. Both were domineering and mercurial, but Churchill was desperate for some kind of naval breakthrough that would harvest untold glory and shorten the war.

Churchill developed a plan to attack the Dardanelles, the narrow channel that separates the Aegean from the Sea of Marmara. Once taken, Britain would control entry to the Black Sea. Fisher strongly resisted the plan. It was too dangerous, he said, for warships to take on the fortifications that controlled the strait. Most importantly the Turkish adventure would drain vital resources from the Channel and North Sea. But Churchill prevailed. In February 1915 the Navy attempted to force the strait.

As Fisher predicted it was a disaster. Three antiquated battleships were sunk, two of them by mines. Other ships were badly damaged. The attack was a failure and it led directly to the doomed Gallipoli landings in April. In May two British battleships were sunk by German U-boats. The Navy then had to devote itself to sustaining the beleaguered troops and, eventually, evacuating the survivors in January 1916.

Fisher took no responsibility for the defeat. He blamed Churchill and was determined to save the Navy from the politician. His resignation brought Churchill down, to the relief of Jellicoe and most of the Navy.

Fisher believed that he would be recalled to lead the Navy to glory in the war. It was not to be. He was shunted off to chair the Board of Invention and Research. For all his faults, Fisher had been an enormous force in the direction of the war. No one else matched his zest or powers of imagination. It left Jellicoe and Beatty as the leading men in the Navy. Could they do any better?

CHAPTER 47

JUTLAND
31 May–1 June 1916

It all seemed very cold-blooded and mechanical, no chance
here of seeing red, merely a case of cool scientific calculation
and deliberate gunfire. Everyone seemed cool enough, too, in
the control position, all sitting quietly at their instruments
waiting for the fight to commence.[1]

An officer in HMS New Zealand, 31 May 1916

The distinction of being 'the only man on either side who could have
lost the war in an afternoon' belonged to Admiral Sir John Jellicoe. Not
since Charles, Lord Howard of Effingham had one admiral shouldered the
burden of protecting the country from invasion.

Jellicoe was a quiet, self-controlled, undistinguished-looking man. He
inherited the Navy's strategy from Fisher and he set his methodical mind
to sorting out the details of so vast a system of naval defence. As the
months turned into years he spent his time in the remoteness of Scapa
Flow organising and training his fleet and working out the Grand Fleet's
battle orders – a mammoth, highly detailed set of instructions. The one
thing Jellicoe did not do was underestimate the power of the Kaiserliche
Marine.

David Beatty could not have differed more from his boss. In contrast
to the centralising and systematic Jellicoe, he was inclined to extemporise
tactics and give his subordinates their head. Where Jellicoe was a compulsive micromanager, Beatty had no patience for details. His mind embraced the big picture, the overall strategic situation; he focused on action
rather than meticulous preparation.

The raffish image Beatty created grew more marked as the war went
on. He enjoyed great fame in the press. If Jellicoe could lose the war,
Beatty had the chance of shortening it if he lured the German fleet to
destruction.

The Battlecruiser Squadron was much more relaxed than the rest of the Grand Fleet. Beatty was based at Rosyth, comfortably close to civilised Edinburgh. The battlefleet was kept in austere seclusion in the Orkneys. Jellicoe and Beatty hardly ever met; they lost touch with each other's way of thinking. Over the long months of waiting for battle Beatty's tactics began to diverge from Jellicoe's methods.

Beatty desired nothing more than to resume his duel with Franz Hipper. In May 1916 he would have his chance.

After months in port the Kaiserliche Marine had rediscovered its aggression and developed a plan. At the end of April Hipper's squadron bombarded Lowestoft and Yarmouth. In response a force of four extremely fast *Queen Elizabeth*-class battleships under Rear Admiral Hugh Evan-Thomas was sent to the Firth of Forth to join Beatty's squadron. This agile and hard-hitting unit would act as a rapid-response force to intercept German sorties.

This was what the new German commander-in-chief wanted. Admiral Reinhard Scheer had developed a plan to divide the Grand Fleet and then defeat its various portions one by one. First to be consumed was Beatty. The gung-ho British admiral wanted revenge against Hipper. Therefore Hipper would make himself a juicy quarry for Beatty's enlarged squadron. The British would speed off in pursuit, their blood up. But they would be ambushed by U-boats stationed in the Firth of Forth. If that did not work Hipper would lead Beatty straight into the path of the entire Hochseeflotte.

Jellicoe would then leave Scapa Flow to save Beatty. Instead he would be drawn into the path of U-boats lurking in the Pentland Firth.

Unfortunately for Scheer Room 40 got wind that the Hochseeflotte was planning something major for 31 May. In response to whatever Scheer was planning, Jellicoe planned to bring the Grand Fleet out of Scapa Flow and rendezvous with Beatty at the Skagerrak, the area of sea between Norway and Denmark. There they would block any attempt by Scheer to break out into the Atlantic or the Baltic.

No British ship was damaged by any of the prowling U-boats. Visibility was poor and the U-boat commanders sent reports back to Scheer that the Grand Fleet had broken off into several parts, each heading in different directions. That was exactly what Scheer had longed for. In fact the fleet was together, but it was taking a zigzag course to avoid submarines.

Intelligence reports were only a little better on the British side. Room 40 was aware that the Germans had sailed, but when the Director of Operations asked for the source of Scheer's call sign DK the Room 40 staff said it was still transmitting from Wilhelmshaven. It was Admiralty policy to prevent Room 40 staffers from interpreting intelligence. The drawbacks of this were not yet clear. Scheer used call sign DK only when he was in port. He used a different one when at sea, where he now was. Room 40 had answered a straightforward question. Unfortunately it was the wrong question.

David Beatty proceeded to the rendezvous with characteristic insouciance. He did not expect to meet the enemy and so he saw no need to brief Rear Admiral Evan-Thomas. Evan-Thomas and his force of super-dreadnoughts had trained with Jellicoe. He had no idea about Beatty's approach, which was radically different from Jellicoe's tightly disciplined and centrally controlled fleet.

To make matters worse Beatty received the faulty Admiralty intelligence that Scheer and the main Hochseeflotte was in port. Now he expected only his arch-enemy Hipper. He moved Evan-Thomas and the dreadnoughts north-west, well out of the way of the enemy. He would have Hipper to himself. Beatty's ships would attack the German Scouting Group, cutting it off from its retreat home. Little did he know that this was what Scheer hoped. It would bring Beatty between Hipper and the Hochseeflotte. He would be crushed.

At 14.40 on 31 May 1916 Beatty's flagship *Lion* received the signal from a scouting cruiser: 'Enemy in sight'. Twelve minutes later Ralph Seymour signalled by flag for all the ships under Beatty's command to turn SSE and cut off Hipper's Scouting Group. Evan-Thomas's officer of the watch was too far away to make out the flags clearly. He assumed it was the signal for the squadron to zigzag. Evan-Thomas's flagship HMS *Barham* and the three other dreadnoughts turned two points west. This group of the world's most powerful ships had been drilled by Jellicoe to obey instructions to the letter. They had not imbibed Beatty's ethos that common sense and judgement should override orders in such circumstances. By the time Evan-Thomas realised his mistake, his ships were ten miles away from Beatty.

The model for Beatty's style of command was Nelson. The great admiral famously communicated his plans to his subordinates long before battle and trusted his captains to use their initiative. Beatty reached out to his officers in this way, with a relaxed style of command and the force of personal example. But Nelson's battle leadership was the pinnacle of a vast pyramid of preparation and organisation. Beatty was not a man to get bogged down in details. As a result important things were neglected. It had already meant that Evan-Thomas took the wrong turn. It would have catastrophic consequences as the battle went on.

At 15.30 the so-called Run to the South began. It looked as if Hipper was trying to escape. In reality he was leading Beatty towards Scheer. The Battle of Jutland began at 15.48. At the last minute Beatty ordered his battlecruisers to move into line. He therefore squandered the precious moments when his ships' guns could reach Hipper without being fired upon in return. The result was that they were still manoeuvring when firing began and it was impossible for the gunners to get a good aim. The Germans got the better of the opening salvos, scoring hits on three British battlecruisers. Beatty's ships took longer to find their targets while they came under fearful bombardment.

As the squadron pressed on the men began to notice the first casualties of the battle, large groups of fish floating on the surface killed by the shells that smacked into the water. On board the turrets and even the director towers were drenched with water thrown up in 100-foot columns of foam. Each ship was peppered with fragments of shell that ricocheted from the sea. The pieces whistled and sobbed overhead; some crumped into the hulls and superstructure. 'I remember seeing the enemy line on the horizon with red specks coming out of them,' a young midshipman remembered, 'which I tried to realise were the cause of the projectiles landing around us, continually covering us with spray, but the fact refused to sink into my brain.'[2]

At 16.02 HMS *Indefatigable* blundered out of line and began to list to port. She had received three shells from SMS *Von der Tann* in her stern, which caused a magazine explosion. The German ship then rained eleven shells onto *Indefatigable*'s foremost gun turret, igniting the forward magazine. *Indefatigable* blew up. Only two men survived from her crew of 1,019.

Beatty's flagship HMS *Lion* almost followed *Indefatigable* to the seabed when Hipper's *Lützow* disabled her midship gun turret. The turret commander, Major Francis Harvey of the Royal Marines, was mortally wounded, but even so he saw that the shell hoist was jammed open in the blast. This meant that the flash fire would spread down into the chambers and working room and thence to the magazine. Harvey had lost both his legs and he knew he would soon be dead; even so he gave orders down the voice pipe for the magazine doors to be closed and the magazine compartments to be flooded.

He saved the ship. The flash spread down into the chambers below the turret, which was littered with cordite charges. The massive explosion killed everyone in the vicinity and blasted as high as *Lion*'s masthead and down as far as the main magazine, whose doors buckled inwards. They would have been smashed entirely, to ignite the magazine in a gigantic ball of flame and blow the ship in two, had not the water pressure in the magazine prevented it. Harvey was posthumously awarded the Victoria Cross. He had saved the lives of over a thousand men, including Beatty's.

In these opening minutes HMS *Queen Mary* had done good work against Hipper's squadron. But when HMS *Lion* temporarily fell out of line, *Queen Mary* was left to bear the brunt of salvos fired from *Derfflinger* and *Seydlitz*.

'At about 4.35,' wrote an officer high aloft on the control position of HMS *New Zealand*, 'the stern of a ship projecting 70 feet out of the water with the propellers revolving slowly, drifted into the field of my glasses ... on her stern I read *Queen Mary*.'[3] A tremendous series of explosions had broken *Queen Mary* in two. Once again flash fires had started in the turrets and ignited the magazines; 1,266 men died. HMS *Tiger* was caught in a shower of debris. Beatty had gone into battle with six battlecruisers and four battleships against Hipper's five battlecruisers. Before the dreadnoughts had managed to catch up his once proud squadron was reduced to four.

Just as the explosion that sank *Queen Mary* died away Beatty was told that HMS *Princess Royal* had blown up as well. 'Chatfield,' Beatty said to his flag captain, 'there seems to be something wrong with our bloody ships today.'

It was one of the most famous cases of a workman blaming his tools. Two British ships and thousands of lives had been lost because of explosions similar to the one Harvey contained on *Lion*. German ships took similar damage to their turrets, but their magazines were better protected from flash. The British battlecruisers were at their best blowing inferior opponents out of the water – as at the Falklands. They were vulnerable against superior or equal ships thanks to their Achilles heel.

When the spray and smoke cleared everyone could see *Princess Royal* was safe after all. And better still, Evan-Thomas had managed to get within range of Hipper. Now the tables had turned and the Germans were suffering the full force of the super-dreadnoughts. In the open sea between the capital ships dozens of destroyers from each side fought furiously with each other, trying all the while to aim torpedoes at the big ships. The battlecruisers had to dodge the barrage of torpedoes; only *Seydlitz* was hit, but she managed to carry on.

Things were beginning to go Beatty's way at last, but shortly before 16.40 the light cruiser HMS *Southampton* brought him an alarming piece of news. She had sighted 'an apparently endless procession of ships'[4] coming from the south: sixteen dreadnoughts and six pre-dreadnoughts with light cruisers and 'masses of destroyers'. The British had been drawn into a trap. Scheer was at sea after all.

Now it was Beatty's turn to flee. His four surviving battlecruisers turned 180 degrees and began to race back towards Jellicoe. Once again he failed to make his intentions clear to Evan-Thomas. His flags were too far away to be read by the battleships. While Beatty's ships raced away from the Hochseeflotte, the super-dreadnoughts steamed towards it. The Executive Officer on HMS *Warspite* suddenly saw the whole of the Hochseeflotte,[5] or rather on the horizon he 'saw masts, funnels and an endless ripple of orange flashes all down the line'. For a few horrible minutes the British battleships were engaged by Hipper's force and the main German fleet. Despite numerous hits the dreadnoughts screened the damaged battle-cruisers as they retreated towards Jellicoe.

In modern naval warfare very few men knew what was going on im-mediately beyond their station. Salvos fired from over eleven miles away plunged into the seas around the ship or crashed down onto the vessel. Sailors and marines had no way of knowing if the ship was hit. If they heard the almighty thud and explosion of an impacting shell, they would have no idea if their ship was going the way of *Indefatigable* until the last moment. Only the sound and tremor of the ship's own guns reassured them that they were still in with a chance.

Parts of a ship, including whole gun turrets, were blasted out of action. Men peering into the huge optical rangefinders high up on the foretop were shaken backwards and forwards as the foremast swayed like a tree in a gale. Down below inside the steel hull, sailors heard explosions at close proximity and were knocked to the ground by the aftershock; 'the worst of it,' said one officer, 'was one knew *nothing*'.[6]

Sailors had no idea what was happening with their ship, let alone the fleets. But the local scene was bad enough. A midshipman on HMS *Malaya* entered the 6-inch gun battery, which had lost its electricity. He could smell burning human flesh. Then the lights came on and the boy beheld a terrible sight: 'everything burnt black and bare from the fire; the galley, canteen and drying-room bulkheads blown and twisted into the most gro-tesque shapes, and the whole deck covered by about six inches of water and dreadful debris; and permeating everywhere the awful stench of cord-ite fumes.'[7]

Commander Humphrey Walwyn, Executive Officer of *Warspite*, de-scribed his ship as it fled the Hochseeflotte. Ordered by his captain to inspect damage to the battleship's stern, he took a short cut over the top of the gun turrets and along the deck. The shells were falling 'pretty thick' and *Warspite*'s own guns were blazing, which made his route rather unpleasant. As he got aft a German shell exploded near him: 'I put up my coat collar and ran like a stag, feeling in the deuce of a funk.'[8]

Walwyn got below decks. His tour of the ship under constant bombardment was like entering the bowels of hell. At first everything was fine. He saw no damage aft and moved along the mess deck, cheering up the ammunition supply teams. He got to the foc'sle mess deck and was continuing forward when a 12-inch shell smashed into the boys' mess deck. It exploded with a 'terrific sheet of golden flame'; the mess was filled with fire, stench and impenetrable dust; 'everything seemed to be falling everywhere with an appalling noise'. When the smoke and dust cleared Walwyn saw big chunks of armour plate flung across the mess deck. The fire brigade crews were sick from the stench of cordite.

Walwyn went aft again, to the admiral's cabin, which was flooding. He inspected the captain's lobby, but as he was going up the hatch he was called back and told that a shell had exploded there. He returned and found a large hole and his own cabin blasted open to the elements and covered in burning debris. Throughout the whole of the captain's lobby everything was 'in a filthy state of indescribable wreckage'. Water was pouring into the ship at various points, including the captain's cabin and the sergeants' mess. Walwyn organised men to prevent water reaching the engine room. He then went to the port side of the mess deck and telephoned the captain. He lit a cigarette, but while he tried to enjoy that respite a 12-inch shell exploded nearby in the galley. A stoker came alongside Commander Walwyn and said: 'There goes my ******* dinner'.*

The commander continued forward, but was called aft to inspect a new hit, this time to the engineers' office. The men who were trying to plug the hole were swept back by tons of water. The hole was eventually plugged with 600 hammocks.

Walwyn ran about the battered *Warspite* as it was buffeted by hit after hit. When he got up to the superstructure he found it ablaze; it looked like a gutted factory. Everything above deck was spattered with holes and the hull was pierced in many places. As he rushed through the ship the men asked for news, 'which I couldn't give, as I hadn't the faintest idea what was happening'. In the midst of the inferno a group of marines were happily playing cards on the deck. If the hypermodern ship took on the appearance of a ruined industrial unit, the attitudes and behaviour of the men were identical to their forebears from time out of mind.

* Expletive deleted in original.

Admiral Sir John Jellicoe climbing onto the forward superstructure
of HMS *Iron Duke*, 1916.

As this chaos was unfolding Jellicoe was nervously awaiting reports.
Now battle was inevitable. The Hochseeflotte was unaware that it was
being led into a trap. It was crucial that Jellicoe make the most of this situation. Beatty's job as leader of the Grand Fleet's scouting force was to keep
Jellicoe informed as to the strength and course of the enemy fleet. But
Beatty had become so caught up in the storm of battle that he neglected
to inform his admiral. Jellicoe needed information and time to deploy
his line of battle in this, the long-anticipated Trafalgar of the twentieth
century.

While Jellicoe agonised Beatty and Evan-Thomas resumed their battle
with Hipper. Beatty wanted to occupy the Scouting Group, and prevent
it reporting Jellicoe's presence. At 17.35 the British Third Battlecruiser
Squadron, made up of three battlecruisers led by Rear Admiral Horace
Hood – descendant of Admiral Viscount Hood – joined the fray. This

intervention greatly helped Beatty's cause. Hipper fell back to join the Hochseeflotte. Scheer lost his eyes. He pushed relentlessly on, unaware of the danger.

From about 18.05 Jellicoe could see Beatty, Evan-Thomas and Hood firing furiously at the unseen enemy and being fired on in return. Battle was upon him, but still no news from Beatty. The fleet was in cruising formation in three columns. It had to be brought into a single line, with one of the columns designated to form the vanguard of the line of battle. Jellicoe had to act and made the decision to order the port column to lead the line.

With tortuous slowness the twenty-four leviathan dreadnoughts began to manoeuvre into line behind the port column. Around this evolving line the sea became congested with destroyers seeking their proper stations. Things were complicated when Beatty steamed up and crossed the bows of the Grand Fleet so that he could lead the reunited British fleet from the vanguard. The smoke from the ships obscured Jellicoe's view. Simultaneously Rear Admiral Sir Robert Arbuthnot's cruiser squadron cut across Beatty's bows, almost causing a collision with *Lion* and forcing Beatty's flagship off course when she was firing on Hipper's ships. Arbuthnot was dashing recklessly into the killing ground between the two fleets, apparently in pursuit of a crippled German cruiser. Arbuthnot's four armoured cruisers – his flagship *Defence*, *Warrior*, *Black Prince* and *Duke of Edinburgh* – became targets for the entire Hochseeflotte. HMS *Defence* was blown up, with the loss of 900 men, including Arbuthnot.

While this was happening Evan-Thomas led his ships to their allotted place in the line of battle. As he did so *Warspite*'s rudder jammed. The invaluable fast battleship went helplessly round and round in circles, presenting a tasty target for every German ship. As the shells rained down in the seas around her and on *Warspite* herself Walwyn and everyone else on the ship thought they were goners. They fired back on the enemy 'lustily' from their smashed-up ship. Luckily the Germans thought that *Warspite* had been sunk and ceased firing; in reality she was lost in a tempest of spray and smoke. She was eventually brought under control and limped back to Rosyth.

Undeterred by this mayhem, Beatty and Hood continued their duel with Hipper. The German battlecruisers took a pounding, but once again it was a British battlecruiser that succumbed to the fire fight. *Lützow and Derflinger* bombarded *Invincible*. For the third time that day a flash fire in a turret caused a fatal magazine explosion. *Invincible* was blown in two. Hood and 1,025 men died. Only six survived.

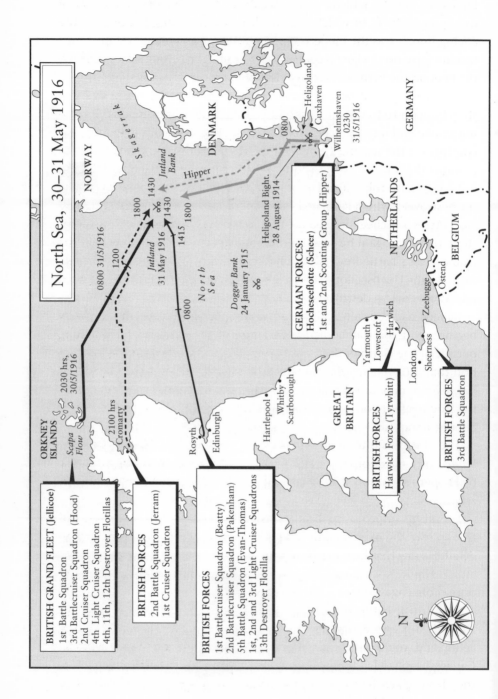

North Sea, 30–31 May 1916

NORWAY

DENMARK

Skagerrak

Jutland Bank

Hipper

Heligoland
Cuxhaven
0800

Wilhelmshaven
0230
31/5/1916

GERMANY

1800
1430
1430
1415
1800

Jutland
31 May 1916

0800 31/5/1916

1200

0800

North
Sea

Dogger Bank
24 January 1915

Heligoland Bight,
28 August 1914

NETHERLANDS

BELGIUM

Ostend

Zeebugge

GERMAN FORCES:
Hochseeflotte (Scheer)
1st and 2nd Scouting Group (Hipper)

2030 hrs,
30/5/1916

Scapa
Flow

ORKNEY
ISLANDS

2100 hrs
Cromarty

Rosyth
Edinburgh

Hartlepool
Whitby
Scarborough

GREAT
BRITAIN

Yarmouth
Lowestoft
Harwich

London
Sheerness

BRITISH FORCES
Harwich Force (Tyrwhitt)

BRITISH FORCES
3rd Battle Squadron

BRITISH GRAND FLEET (Jellicoe)
1st Battle Squadron
3rd Battlecruiser Squadron (Hood)
2nd Cruiser Squadron
4th Light Cruiser Squadron
4th, 11th, 12th Destroyer Flotillas

BRITISH FORCES
2nd Battle Squadron (Jerram)
1st Cruiser Squadron

BRITISH FORCES
1st Battlecruiser Squadron (Beatty)
2nd Battlecruiser Squadron (Pakenham)
5th Battle Squadron (Evan-Thomas)
1st, 2nd and 3rd Light Cruiser Squadrons
13th Destroyer Flotilla

N

Hood succeeded in capturing the attention of the Germans. Unbeknown to Scheer, Jellicoe's line was about to 'cross the T'. This was a deadly manoeuvre in which the attacker steamed along the head of the enemy line. It was the modern version of raking an enemy. While the attacking force on the lateral course poured its full broadside into its enemy, the fleet on the vertical course could only reply with its forward guns.

Scheer wrote that he was suddenly confronted by a crescent of flame stretching north to east, although he could see no ships through the swirling smoke and mist. Jellicoe's flagship *Iron Duke* opened fire, scoring several hits on the leading German ship. Then his dreadnoughts began to pummel the startled Hochseeflotte. Within minutes the Germans were in full retreat with the British fast at their heels. Their retreat was covered by the destroyers, which launched waves of torpedoes at the pursuing Grand Fleet. At 18.55 Scheer ordered the fleet to turn east to throw Jellicoe off his stern, but once again he found himself unexpectedly face to face with the Grand Fleet's battle line. Jellicoe had crossed the T for the second time. At 19.17 the Hochseeflotte did an about-turn again, its perfectly executed retreat covered by destroyers.

Jellicoe had not, after all, been pursuing Scheer's rear. From the very beginning of the war he had been aware of the dangers of a headlong pursuit of the German fleet. His battle plan had worked on the assumption that if the enemy fled before battle their intention would be to lead him over a mine or submarine trap. His plan had always been to pursue the Hochseeflotte on a parallel course out of range. His prudence almost became a trap for Scheer.

The Hochseeflotte disappeared into a smokescreen, its rearguard defended by a mass torpedo attack fired from destroyers and a brave charge by Hipper's squadron. A little later, at 20.23, the tireless Beatty once more attacked.

For all his impetuosity, Beatty was undoubtedly a brave man. He was able to read the overall battle situation while others got bogged down in detail. He saw that he had a chance to divert Scheer further west by a bold attack. Hipper's Scouting Group was leading the Hochseeflotte and Beatty once more engaged it.

The British battlecruisers, for all their damage, were still formidable. Hipper's ships were floating wrecks. The flagship SMS *Lützow* was out of action and would later be abandoned. The rest of the squadron was ailing. Carelessness had led to the destruction of three British battlecruisers. Had they been given better flash protection they might have defeated their opponents. At this stage of the battle Hipper's ships had to move out of range of Beatty's guns. They exposed a group of pre-dreadnoughts. Beatty called upon Vice Admiral Jerram, leading the British vanguard, to join him in an attack on these vulnerable German ships. Jerram refused to act without orders from Jellicoe.

Darkness was falling and Beatty's last charge petered out. Jellicoe put his fleet into night formation. His main fleet was to continue south, to cut off Scheer's escape route. To his rear he placed a screen of destroyers and cruisers.

Jellicoe was not the first admiral in the history of naval warfare to discover at daybreak that his quarry had vanished.

During the night the sounds of battle had been heard on *Iron Duke*, but Jellicoe's staff had received no reports from the flag officers or captains that the Hochseeflotte was breaking through the defensive screen behind the battlefleet. Thomas-Evans's Fifth Battle Squadron saw the German fleet pass astern of it, but failed to report. Throughout the night British destroyers and cruisers fought furious battles with the German ships and suffered severe punishment. Five British destroyers and one armoured cruiser were sunk. The Germans lost one pre-dreadnought and other ships in directionless chaos illuminated by sweeping searchlights. The Navy's captains failed to report in to Jellicoe either because they assumed the commander could see what was going on or because they feared that their radio signals would give away their positions. Everyone thought that someone else had told Jellicoe. To make matters worse, German signals and positions intercepted by Room 40 were not passed on to Jellicoe.

The Hochseeflotte received an ecstatic welcome home. The Germans celebrated a world-changing victory. They had set sail with ninety-nine ships against the Navy's 151. The Hochseeflotte lost 2,551 men and eleven ships, including one pre-dreadnought and a battlecruiser, totalling 62,300 tons. The British lost 6,094 men and 113,300 tons of shipping. The fourteen ships sunk were three battlecruisers, three armoured cruisers and eight destroyers.

Raw figures are no basis to claim a victory, however. Both sides managed to lose the Battle of Jutland. The Royal Navy suffered its worst day since the Medway raid in 1667. The battle revealed serious shortcomings in the service. Thousands of men and three powerful battlecruisers fell victim to poor cordite management and inadequate safety procedures. The fire-control system was clearly not working; just 3 per cent of British shells hit their targets. There was a serious problem with communications and, most glaringly, with naval intelligence. Beatty confused both his subordinates and his commander-in-chief. A potential victory was thrown away during the night, when a great number of captains were too afraid to use their initiative to inform Jellicoe of the situation. The Navy's Operations Division appeared to hold Room 40 in contempt; the result was that vital intercepted information was not passed on to Jellicoe in time or, in some cases, at all.

In contrast the Germans displayed their superior gunnery, better armour protection, prowess in battle and superior tactical sense. Hipper far outclassed Beatty (again) and Scheer manoeuvred his fleet brilliantly. But that could not disguise the fact that the Germans had been forced to retreat very quickly when they realised they had been trapped. The Battle of Jutland was a reminder that the Germans could not defeat the Royal Navy in battle. Never again would they risk their fleet in an encounter with the British. After Jutland the Grand Fleet was reinforced with new or repaired dreadnoughts. It was stronger than before the battle. Jellicoe had twenty-four dreadnoughts; Scheer could muster only ten.

The tarnished, demoralised Royal Navy was, after the Battle of Jutland, even more the master of the North Sea than it had been before.

CHAPTER 48

TO END ALL WARS
1916–1922

What is it that the coming of the submarine really means? It means that the whole foundation of our traditional naval strategy, which served us so well in the past, has been broken down! The foundation of that strategy was blockade. The fleet did not exist merely to win battles – that was the means not the end. The ultimate purpose of the fleet was to make blockade possible for us and impossible for our enemy.[1]

Admiralty memo, 1912

In 1653 a battle in the North Sea fought between hundreds of ships had profound effects on naval tactics. The line of battle emerged as the most important aspect of naval warfare after the Battle of the Gabbard. Now another titanic battle in the North Sea had brought history full circle.

The Battle of Jutland was the last major battle fought between fleets of battleships. The sacred line of battle was defunct. This was not immediately clear in 1916. It was obvious, however, that the naval war in the North Sea had ground to stalemate. When the Hochseeflotte tried to lure the Grand Fleet onto a submarine trap in August 1916 it fled when zeppelin reconnaissance misreported the Harwich light ships as battleships. The Royal Navy would not venture into the mesh of submarines and minefields in the southern North Sea to seek battle.

With conventional surface warfare no longer possible both sides sought ways to steal the advantage. The last great fleet battle pointed to the future even as it closed the door on the past. During the Battle of Jutland HMS *Engadine* launched seaplanes that reconnoitred the German fleet. *Engadine* had already distinguished herself on Christmas Day 1914 when she launched seaplanes in the Heligoland Bight that bombed the German zeppelin base at Cuxhaven – the first seaborne airstrike.

Launching aircraft from ships was an extension of naval bombardment in an age when minefields and torpedoes closed large portions of sea to

HMS *Argus*, the first aircraft carrier with a full-length flight deck, with dazzle camouflage to disrupt accurate range-finding by enemy ships. She is seen in company with a battlecruiser.

surface craft. In the First World War aerial warfare was in its infancy. *Engadine* and similar ships lowered the seaplanes into the sea and recovered them after their missions. Another seaplane carrier, HMS *Ark Royal*, had an experimental launch platform. In 1917, a year after Jutland, HMS *Furious* was fitted with a split flight deck. Aircraft could take off, but it was extremely dangerous to land. The Grand Fleet invested time and resources during the remainder of the war to experiment with aircraft carriers. On 7 July 1918 seven Sopwith Camels launched from *Furious* bombed the German zeppelin base at Tondern. Just before the war ended HMS *Argus*, a converted liner, went into service as the world's first aircraft carrier with a full-length flight deck on which planes could take off and land. The emergence of the aircraft carrier was a direct consequence of the war. It did not have an impact, but it pointed the way to the future.

Beatty wanted the Admiralty to go on the offensive with aircraft carriers and bring the war to the German fleet as it lay snugly in harbour. His plan for an attack by torpedo bombers on Wilhelmshaven in 1917 was turned down. It would have been Pearl Harbor twenty-four years early.

Going above the enemy was one solution. Going beneath them was a surer way of breaking the stalemate.

Back in November 1914 the British declared the North Sea a war zone. Any ship bringing 'contraband of war' to Germany was in danger, even if it carried food. In retaliation the Germans declared the waters around the British Isles to be a war zone. All merchant vessels would be subject to attack without warning, even neutral shipping. U-boat warfare gave the Germans the chance to blockade the allies and bring the British Empire to its knees without first winning control of the seas by a conventional battle. It also introduced a new and terrifying form of commerce raiding. No battlefleet in the world, however strong and invincible, could contain it. It was a revolutionary moment in the history of naval warfare and of the Royal Navy.

In May 1915 alone 120,058 tons of shipping were sunk by U-boats. That was the month that the Cunard liner *Lusitania* was torpedoed off Kinsale with the loss of 1,198 passengers and crew. Of this number 128 were American citizens. In August 185,866 tons of shipping were sunk, including the White Star liner *Arabic*. Only three Americans lost their lives, but after the *Lusitania* outrage the United States government was in no mood to tolerate U-boat attacks. In fear of America entering the war, indiscriminate U-boat activity in the Atlantic was restrained from 18 September. In November a U-boat sank an Italian passenger ship, killing 200 people; nine of them were US citizens. Such incidents forced the Germans to abandon its kill-without-warning policy.

For all the success of the German U-boats and the terror they spread to merchant seamen, fishermen and passengers the campaign had not, by 1916, caused serious damage to the allies' war effort. The main effect had been to antagonise neutrals.

The Royal Navy did not have an answer to the U-boat menace. It was unprepared for this kind of warfare. The Navy was losing control of the seas around the British Isles; German U-boats passed the Strait of Dover with impunity. In November 1916 Jellicoe was appointed First Lord of the Admiralty and Beatty was promoted to command the Grand Fleet. Jellicoe's primary task was to wage war against the submarines. It was a hard assignment. Attempts to seal the Strait of Dover with boom nets and minefields proved next to useless. Patrols conducted by British submarines did not work either. Merchant ships, trawlers and liners were provided with guns to defend themselves against U-boats when they surfaced to attack. The Royal Navy put hundreds of so-called 'Q-ships' to sea – heavily armed ships disguised as tramp steamers or trawlers, which would lure U-boats to surface and then blast them out of the water. Q-ships drew away a lot of skilled Navy personnel for little gain. One of their effects was to encourage U-boat commanders to attack without warning. Depth charges were developed and first used in January 1916 with very limited success.

The problem got worse and worse. The attacks accelerated after Jutland, when it became clear that the Kaiserliche Marine could never defeat the Grand Fleet. The German economy was suffering from the blockade. Hopes for a naval breakthrough switched to submarines. In June 1916 U-boats sank 118,215 tons of shipping. The figures leapt month by month for the rest of the year; in December 355,139 tons were sunk.

In that month the Kaiserliche Marine had made the momentous decision to resume unrestricted submarine warfare. It was the Germans' last hope of bringing Britain to its knees. For that to happen they needed to destroy at least 600,000 tons of incoming supplies a month. In March 1917 that target was almost reached when 500,000 tons of shipping went down. This changed the game. A quarter of British-bound ships were being sunk. In April 881,027 tons was destroyed.

This was a new and ruthless form of warfare unleashed by a desperate Germany. As Beatty observed: 'The real crux lies in whether we blockade the enemy to his knees, or whether he does the same to us.' The Germans had found a way to really harm the allies: U-boats had the power to win the war. Beatty urged Prime Minister Lloyd George to go on the offensive against the U-boats and regain control over that area of sea upon which the fate of Britain and its empire had always depended – the Western Approaches.

Convoys make up a major part of the Royal Navy's history, but in the early twentieth century that technique had grown rusty. Jellicoe and the Admiralty knew that convoying was no easy matter and there had been resistance within the Navy against the whole concept. Officers despaired at the thought of marshalling and shepherding hordes of chaotic private ships. Most naval officers did not believe that merchant captains and their unwieldy vessels could keep station as a convoy zigzagged through the ocean. It would be like trying to herd flocks of panicky sheep.

'What is the Navy doing?' That was the question that dogged the service during the war. There had to be some kind of response to the unrestricted and unopposed use of U-boats in the Western Approaches. Jellicoe moved slowly and methodically in establishing a system to beat the enemy. Convoying was trialled on the French and Scandinavian coal routes early in 1917, then in April between Gibraltar and Britain.

These modest responses coincided with the remorseless success of the

U-boats in the Atlantic. It rattled the politicians. Lloyd George suspected that the Admiralty was poorly organised and the Navy was hidebound by its traditions. This was total war, and the functions of the state had enlarged to encompass almost every aspect of economic and industrial life. Lloyd George understood the all-embracing nature of the conflict and he had posted business men into civil service positions to transform a free economy into a centralised war-winning machine. The most prominent was the self-made Scottish businessman Sir Eric Geddes, who had taken the munitions industry by the scruff of its neck and reorganised transport networks with a kind of brutal efficiency unknown in laissez-faire Britain. Army officers and civil servants resented this civilian intruder's relentless drive and unorthodox methods.

In May 1917 the Navy got to experience those methods. Sir Eric became a vice-admiral and was appointed Comptroller of the Navy, in charge of procurement and shipbuilding. But still Lloyd George thought the Navy sluggish and obstructive to the new Comptroller's plans, so in July Geddes became First Lord of the Admiralty. His task was to ensure that the Navy organised itself into an efficient anti-submarine force that made convoying a priority.

In May the first transatlantic convoy departed from Hampton Roads, Virginia. One armoured cruiser and eight destroyers conveyed merchantmen across the ocean. Other trials took place that summer. In every case the ships under protection crossed the Atlantic safely. Only the stragglers were sunk. The merchantmen responded well to the Navy's orders. The sickening fear that had built up to the panic of spring 1917 began to subside.

The campaign was transformed by a crucial addition to the allies. In January 1917 Room 40 intercepted a message from Arthur Zimmermann, foreign secretary of Germany, to the German ambassador in Mexico. The telegram stated that in the event of the United States entering the war as a result of unrestricted submarine warfare the ambassador should propose that Mexico invade the US to reclaim Texas, New Mexico and Arizona with German support. The intercepted telegram was shown to the US ambassador in London on 19 February; on 2 April the United States joined the allies.

In May the first American destroyers and small, speedy sub-chasers joined the Royal Navy in the Western Approaches.

Convoys became routine. It was a daunting administrative task – one of the biggest the Navy had ever faced. All of a sudden Britain's entire transoceanic trade had to be regulated. The Admiralty created the Convoy

Section and the Mercantile Movements Division which worked with the Ministry of Shipping and Naval Intelligence to schedule rendezvous and convoys. They were supported by the Anti-Submarine Division, the Direction Finding Section and Room 40. The campaign inspired a rush of technological improvements. Fisher's Board of Invention and Research began top-secret experiments to develop a workable underwater sound-detection system – hydrophones, which detected underwater sound, and a prototype form of sonar. By the end of the war the Navy was about to put to sea the R-class submarine, a hunter-killer vessel designed with the sole purpose of detecting and attacking enemy U-boats.

Jellicoe could not thrive in an Admiralty under the pressure of total war. He felt the need to control everything from the centre, but the Navy in 1917 had transformed into a leviathan department with daunting responsibilities in various theatres of war. Under Geddes the Admiralty was undergoing the shock treatment of administrative revolution. The job of First Sea Lord was too big for one man – but Jellicoe was not the kind of officer to delegate and his instinctive caution meant that convoy measures were proceeding too slowly. Worse still, the First Sea Lord stuck up for his old friend Sir Reginald Bacon, admiral in command of the Dover patrol, who was proving resistant to Geddes's plan to establish a barrage across the Strait to prevent U-boats taking the quick route from their bases at Ostend and Zeebrugge to the Western Approaches. Geddes resolved that both Jellicoe and Bacon had to go. At 18.00 on Christmas Eve 1917 Geddes risked earning the undying enmity of the Navy and sacked Jellicoe.

His successor, Sir Rosslyn Wemyss, took over a Navy that was stretched in terms of manpower, hardware and administrative responsibility beyond all precedent. The service was also reeling from Geddes's sacking of Jellicoe. Up at Scapa Flow Beatty had to continue his vigil against Scheer, but by now his fleet was all but hamstrung by the loss of escort vessels to the convoys and battleships to foreign stations. Down in the Mediterranean the situation was chaotic. The Navy had, in defiance of its own history, bequeathed control to the French navy at the beginning of the war, believing that the decisive battle would be won in the North Sea. By 1917 however it was clear that the Mediterranean was as vital to Britain's interests as ever. Naval cover was required to support ground operations in Italy, the Balkans and the Middle East, but even more pressing was the damage being done to merchant shipping and supply vessels by enemy U-boats. Admiral Sir Somerset Gough Calthorpe took command in the Mediterranean, where he had to establish authority over the allied navies and co-ordinate them, against their will, to mount an effective anti-submarine campaign. American and Japanese destroyers had to be drafted in to help. Everywhere there were pressing demands and a shortage of ships.

But the effort was paying off, extemporised as it was. The Germans needed to sink 600,000 tons a month to win the war. They had more than achieved that target in April 1917. In July U-boats sank 557,988 tons. In January 1918 it was down to just over 300,000 tons. The convoys were the Navy's great success of the war. Between May 1917 and 11 November 1918 16,539 ships crossed the Atlantic; just 138 were lost to the enemy. Before February 1917 only forty-eight German U-boats had been lost; in the remaining eleven months of that year sixty-one were sunk, and sixty-nine between January and November 1918.

The campaign was not won because the Navy learnt how to destroy submarines. It was won because the Navy dared U-boats to approach its ships and take their chances. When a U-boat attacked shipping it had to come in close and surface. This was all very well against lightly armed merchantmen; warships manned by professionals were another matter. U-boats were slow – they could not outdistance a destroyer – and they became sitting targets when they surfaced. It was notable that not one battleship of the Grand Fleet had been harmed by a U-boat, despite the prevalence of German subs in the North Sea. It was protected by a screen of destroyers; now the techniques that had defended the main fleet could be used in the Atlantic and the Mediterranean. Suddenly U-boat commanders saw through their periscopes a cordon of destroyers and other armed vessels – including trawlers and yachts – separating them from their prey. It was better not to try against such odds.

The problem for the U-boats was increased by the unanticipated fact that convoys are harder to find in a vast expanse of ocean than a stream of individual ships scattered far and wide. Zigzagging convoys could evade hunting U-boats completely. The Germans' only chance was against stragglers. Tonnage loss stayed high, but it was not enough to offset the numbers of ships being built in allied yards and it was certainly below the level needed to cripple the allied war effort. Germany's chance to win the war was at an end.

The lacklustre Reginald Bacon was sacked as vice admiral at Dover at the beginning of 1918 and replaced with Roger Keyes, who immediately implemented a scheme whereby small craft patrolled the Strait at night, using flares and searchlights to force U-boats to dive. The fleeing U-boat would find itself trapped in the middle of a deep minefield. It was dangerous work for the Dover patrol: when the darkness was lit up it became a sitting target for retaliatory strikes. But the plan worked; U-boat losses in the Channel mounted and their free passage was restricted. In April Keyes launched Operation Z–O, a daring night raid on Zeebrugge and Ostend to block the canals that led to the U-boat pens at Bruges. The Belgian ports were heavily fortified, and the British attack was remarkably courageous – eleven VCs were awarded. They were not successful, however, but the boost to morale at home and within the beleaguered Navy was much needed. The firepower of the Navy was deployed in other ways as well. Unwieldy little monitors, with their huge guns, shelled German positions in Belgium throughout the war, aiding allied offensives on the Somme and at Ypres and confining enemy ships to their bases. In September 1918 this form of gunboat onslaught, which had its roots in Benbow's coastal bombardments in the 1690s, reached its climax when HMS *General Wolfe* shelled targets at a range of twenty miles with her 18-inch gun. It was the largest gun in the Navy's history.

The convoys, the Dover Patrol and the raids put the Royal Navy on the offensive after years of frustration. The Navy had got its victory – but it looked and tasted very different from the triumph it had expected. There was no climactic fleet battle, no final showdown, just a long hard slog in partnership with other countries' navies, the most important being that of the United States.

As on so many previous occasions the Navy had begun the war full of hope and brimming with confidence. And as in other wars in its history it had failed to live up to expectation, instead thriving in unexpected circumstances after long periods of hard graft and active service. By the end of the war it had sixty-one battleships, 129 cruisers, 443 destroyers and 147 submarines; there were 37,000 officers and 400,000 men, all of whom had carried a heavy burden. The Navy was augmented at the end of 1917 by some 7,000 women serving in the newly created Women's Royal Naval Service (WRNS). The Navy was the first British armed service to accept women, and the recruits worked as clerks, telegraphists, dispatch riders, intelligence experts, electricians and cooks. They did not serve on the waves, hence the WRNS' motto in the First World War 'Never at Sea'. The service as a whole was hardened by the demands of modern war.

Up at Rosyth David Beatty had done the valuable job of motivating the Grand Fleet through its months and years of passive duty. For all his faults Beatty remained a commanding figure and an inspiration for his force.

His rival had not fared as well. Hipper succeeded Scheer as commander-in-chief of the Hochseeflotte. In April 1918 he took his fleet out into the North Sea to overhaul an allied convoy bound for Scandinavia. He turned for home before Beatty could catch the Hochseeflotte and win the glory he had craved for so long. The German fleet was in a poor state compared with Beatty's crack force. German morale had hit the seabed and the ships had suffered from their long confinement.

In October Hipper attempted one last sortie to bring Beatty to battle. The great German admiral wanted to fight for the honour of the German fleet, a last moment of hopeless glory. But he never left port. His sailors staged a mutiny off Wilhelmshaven. At the beginning of November the mutiny turned into full-scale revolt. Germany was falling apart; the people were hungry and broken. The blockade had, after four long years, succeeded.

The next time the Hochseeflotte entered the North Sea it was 21 November and the war was over. Beatty insisted that the enemy fleet surrender unconditionally. The once mighty fleet was escorted to Scotland by a British light cruiser. It looked to an observer like a minnow leading a school of leviathans. Hipper watched with a broken heart. The Hochseeflotte was in British hands. In addition the German U-boats surrendered to Reginald Tyrwhitt at Harwich. It was a bitter-sweet moment for Beatty and the Grand Fleet, a let-down after years waiting for the war-winning battle.

Beatty stage-managed the German surrender with his usual flair. The German battleships arrived at the Firth of Forth and they were anchored between the lines of the Grand Fleet. He then signalled: 'The German flag will be hauled down at sunset today, Thursday, and will not be hoisted again without permission.'² The ships were taken to Scapa Flow two days later.

David Beatty was the last of the Navy's cavaliers – at least the last to rise so high. He had not, after all, found his place in history as a great naval warrior. His command of the Grand Fleet after Jellicoe's promotion had been a study in patience and restraint as he stuck to his old boss's plan. Beatty's self-created image as a *Boy's Own*-style young admiral had helped sustain his fleet and give his country confidence. He was the embodiment of British resistance and naval pluck in a media age. He lost none of his swagger. But Beatty's greatest challenge lay ahead of him. He became the youngest-ever admiral of the fleet at the age of forty-eight in April 1919. He was raised to the peerage as Earl Beatty. In September he became First Sea Lord, a post he was to hold for eight years. He had a new battle to fight. It would be waged in Whitehall on behalf of his beloved Navy.

Beatty believed that Britain's centuries-long command of the seas was about to be thrown away in the democratic age. He was ready to fight to retain it. And he would use every trick and stratagem to get his way.

Age had not transformed Beatty into an administrator. The detail of running a Navy was left to his devoted staff. Beatty assumed a political role, using his quick intelligence, strategic mind and force of personality to do battle with the Treasury. He proved to be gifted with the dark arts of political manipulation. This was an age of economic misery and savage cuts. It was also an age that had turned its back on war – for ever, it was hoped. From 1919 the government insisted on the 'Ten Year Rule': all military planning should assume there would not be a war for ten years. Beatty stood out against this attitude, reminding a succession of cabinet ministers from coalition, Conservative and Labour governments that command of the seas was vital for the survival of the country.

Beatty's first hope was that Germany's superior battleships would be added to the Royal Navy as the fruits of victory. That plan came to an end when the German sailors scuttled their interned ships at Scapa Flow on 21 June 1919. It was a sorry coda to the war for the Navy whose prestige had been tarnished by the Great War.

Beatty countered demands for swingeing cuts by making sure the Navy was run as cheaply and efficiently as possible. He built support in all the main political parties and in the press. At the heart of his political crusade was the idea that Britain could only remain the world's major naval power if she continued to build ships. Not only did the country need to keep ahead of its rivals, but it had to keep its shipbuilding industries in a healthy state. If construction ceased for a long period it would be very hard to revive it when new crises emerged. Beatty got his way and four new 45,000-ton battlecruisers were ordered.

There was a major constraint on shipbuilding, however, which went beyond financial belt-tightening. It was ideological. In 1922 Britain, the United States, Japan, France and Italy signed the Washington Treaty. The world's naval powers agreed to limit warship construction. Battleships and battlecruisers were restricted to 35,000 tons displacement, aircraft carriers to 27,000 and all other ships to 10,000. More importantly, new ship construction was restrained by agreed maximums that each navy could have in use. France and Italy were allowed 175,000 tons' worth of capital ships each; Japan had 315,000; Britain and the United States could have no more than 525,000 each. Beatty's battlecruisers were cancelled. The Navy had prevailed in the First World War with the help of allied ships. After the Washington Treaty this dependence became an irreversible fact.

This was a turning point in British and world history. The Royal Navy's supremacy came to an end in 1922.

CHAPTER 49

LEAN DAYS
1922–1939

... we cannot foresee the time when our defence forces will be
strong enough to safeguard our trade, territory and vital interests against Germany, Italy and Japan at the same time ...[1]

The Chiefs of Staff, 1937

According to the plan a force of 121 aircraft would have taken off from
eight aircraft carriers and launched waves of torpedoes on the German
fleet at Wilhelmshaven. Beatty's idea, formulated in 1917, was audacious.
It would have been an epochal event in naval history.

It was a venture typical of a Navy that was the pioneer of a new form of
warfare – naval aviation. Between 1914 and 1918 it had made great strides
in developing aircraft carriers and deploying planes in battle. By the end
of the war it had four carriers, 3,000 aircraft and 55,000 men in its air
force. Admiral Reginald Hall said that battleships were a thing of the past:
'The attack of the future will be by clouds of planes at dusk, early morning
or moonlight on the ships before they go to sea.'[2]

In 1924 the Navy commissioned HMS *Hermes*. She was laid down
during the war as the first purpose-built, full-length-flight-deck aircraft
carrier. She was also the first to take on the appearance of a modern carrier
with a starboard control tower. It would seem that the Navy's eagerness to
stay in the vanguard of naval air power was undimmed.

In 1933 the Navy's once powerful air force had declined to just 160
aircraft and a few ageing carriers. Meanwhile the Japanese and American navies picked up the baton discarded by Britain. The navies of both
those countries experimented with this new form of naval warfare; they
developed aircraft, vessels, pilots and crew specifically for use at sea. Most
galling of all, the Japanese naval air service was worked up to the pitch of
efficiency and fitness by British flying aces training Japanese naval pilots
on planes built by British engineers working in a British factory. Beatty
was a great supporter of naval aviation during the war, but despite his best

HMS *Hermes*

efforts he presided over its decline as First Sea Lord. He and his successors asked for four new aircraft carriers to stay at the forefront of this new way of war. The government stalled them.

The problem went back to 1 April 1918 and the foundation of the Royal Air Force. The Navy ceded control of its aviation to the infant service. Out went the pioneering Royal Naval Air Service, along with its planes and highly experienced pilots, who joined the RAF.

For the Navy the decision was calamitous. As Beatty saw it the Navy needed pilots and engineers it had trained and aircraft designed specifically for naval operations. The new RAF was far too independent and unwilling to trot at the heels of a naval master. In 1923 he asked the government for full Admiralty control over planes and pilots in naval service. He was turned down. The Fleet Air Arm was governed jointly by the Admiralty and the RAF.

It was the neglected child with two squabbling parents. It was underfunded, underdeveloped and directionless.

The Navy's aircraft carriers were stuck in the past, its planes were inadequate and it had too few pilots. Fatally there was no strategy for an offensive carrier task force; the Navy came to regard maritime air power as a mere auxiliary. Things would have been different if the Navy had been allowed to hone its own specialist air force and if the Naval Air Service had survived to act as a counterweight to traditionally-minded admirals. As it was the Air Ministry was more concerned with air defence and strategic bombing and the Admiralty fixated on big guns. The Navy had blazed the trail in naval aviation during the First World War. It had helped shape a weapon that would dominate naval warfare in the twentieth century. Its slump was painful to behold. It would have dire consequences.

The decline, almost eradication, of innovation in naval aviation was mirrored throughout the Navy in the 1920s. Expenditure on the Navy shrank from £356 million in 1918–19 to just £52 million in 1923; in 1933 it was still only £53 million. The only new battleships built between 1913 and 1936 were HMSs *Rodney* and *Nelson* – so-called 'Treaty Ships' because they conformed to the strictures of the Washington Treaty. The irreparable harm done to British shipbuilding and naval armaments industries was only partly mitigated by orders for new cruisers, submarines and destroyers. And even that was paltry. While other navies built newer and better warships to meet their treaty limits, the Navy had to make do with a fleet constructed, in the main, between 1909 and 1913.

It was not just the hardware that rusted. The men shouldered the burden as well. In 1919 there were 400,000 men and women in the Navy and 37,000 officers. The presence of women in the Navy did not last two years; the WRNS was disbanded at the close of the war. By 1932 there were just 90,000 men in the service and the peace had not treated them kindly. Recruits who joined the service after 1925 were paid less than ratings who had signed up before then. This dent to the unity of the service was followed by a fresh insult six years later when the National Government reduced the wages of all public service workers by 10 per cent and reset the pay of older sailors to the rate of 1925; this meant a pay cut for some of 25 per cent.

That was too much for the ratings. On 11 September 1931 the Atlantic Fleet returned to its base at Invergordon on the Cromarty Firth. The men learnt of the savage pay cuts for the first time from the newspapers. Discontent brewed. Protests burgeoned into a fleet-wide mutiny. In reality it was a strike. The men refused to take the fleet back to sea, but remained friendly and respectful towards their officers. The Invergordon Mutiny ended when the cabinet agreed to reconsider the swingeing cuts to sailors on the pre-1925 rates. The ringleaders were jailed and 200 men in the Atlantic Fleet were discharged.

The financial pressure was felt throughout the service. Beatty fought hard for every penny to ensure that the reduced Navy remained a world power and met its manifold commitments. But the political force that had propelled the Navy to world supremacy was sapped: the public accepted, even demanded, cuts for the senior service. However hard Beatty hectored, coaxed and horse-traded, the trend was downhill; the government had other needs to meet and the Navy was one claimant among many. His successors were genuinely afraid of what might happen if the Navy was called upon to go to war. Plans to turn Singapore into a well defended base were repeatedly stalled. Indeed, all of the British naval bases, including Scapa Flow, had slipped below standard. In 1931 the Admiralty reported that British sea power would be unable 'to keep our sea communications open in the event of our being drawn into war'.[3] There simply were not enough ships.

But this was, in its way, an idealistic age. Many believed that the Great War had ended all wars, and peace would be guaranteed by the League of Nations. The London Naval Treaty of 1930 regulated submarine warfare and limited naval shipbuilding again. It was signed by Britain, the US, France, Japan and Italy. But the attempt to limit the growth of rival navies soon hit the buffers. Italy and Japan renounced the Washington and London naval agreements by 1935. Throughout the Thirties the Imperial Japanese Navy began building new carriers, cruisers, destroyers and submarines. In 1937 work commenced on a series of three truly monstrous battleships, the *Yamato* class. *Yamato* displaced over 70,000 tons and carried nine 18.1-inch guns.

Britain was powerless to stop acts of aggression throughout the world. In 1931 Japan invaded Manchuria. The Royal Navy stood neutered in Asian waters and the Admiralty could not afford to deplete the home fleet by dispatching warships to intervene. The British did not close the Suez Canal to Mussolini's forces participating in the invasion of Abyssinia in 1935. In the same year the British government cravenly signed a treaty with Hitler allowing limited, but significant, German naval rearmament.

Appeasement could not be relied upon completely. Beatty's former flag captain and assistant chief of staff at the Admiralty, Sir Alfred Chatfield, was lucky to become First Sea Lord in 1933. In that year the Ten Year Rule was abandoned and rearmament began. Expenditure on the Navy rose from £53 million in 1933 to £81 million in 1936 and £127.2 million in 1938.

Chatfield had the chance to design a new Navy. But what sort of Navy should it be? Naval policy was pulled in a multitude of directions in the 1930s. The service had commitments across the globe and competing strategic priorities. Britain had been able to build a global empire because its battlefleet dominated the North Sea, Channel, Western Approaches and the Mediterranean. British battleships kept the country's colonial rivals – which were all European – at bay in home waters; cruisers and gunboats policed the wider empire and the trading links that held it together. But although the British Empire was at its greatest territorial extent in the interwar decades the Navy surveyed an altogether different world.

Japan menaced the British Empire and its trade in Asia and Australasia. Mussolini's powerful battleships, submarines and air bases threatened Britain's dominance in the Mediterranean. Hitler's new navy, the Kriegsmarine, forced the Navy to keep its strength in home waters. Although the funding tap had been turned back on, there were still strict budgetary limits; Chatfield and his staff were forced to make hard choices. Should the Navy concentrate on threats to national survival posed by submarines? Were aircraft carriers the key to command of the seas in the twentieth century? Did Britain's claim to world-power status rest on her battlefleet? One thing was certain: the Navy could not intervene against Japan in Asian waters if there was the slightest chance that Britain was threatened in Europe.

Chatfield was clear that a first-rank modern Navy needed to make aviation a priority. Aircraft carriers were essential for frontline work of all kinds: they would play a vital role in scouting, fleet battles, hunter-killer patrols, convoy protection, amphibious landings and raids on foreign ports. In 1934 work began on *Ark Royal*, the Navy's repeatedly postponed modern aircraft carrier. In 1937 four new carriers – *Illustrious*, *Victorious*, *Formidable* and *Indomitable* – were laid down. More importantly Chatfield resumed Beatty's campaign for control over the Fleet Air Arm. He won the argument in 1937, but the Admiralty did not gain full control of naval planes and pilots until 1939. Even so the damage wrought by the abolition of the Naval Air Service had long-lasting implications. Many in the Navy took a view from the quarterdeck: they believed that carrier-borne planes were there for reconnaissance and to aid battleship gunners in adjusting their aim. The service might have more carriers than its rivals, but the planes and pilots lagged behind, hamstrung by a lack of clear insight into their offensive capability in modern warfare.

Battleships continued to command the Admiralty's attention. In the 1930s it was still held that Britain's position in Europe and the world remained dependent on the battlefleet. The great steel leviathans gave Britain the ability to blockade European enemies. It was still a powerful deterrent against would-be foes around the globe.

The line of battle might seem antiquated, but battleships decidedly were not. Chatfield got five new ones in 1936–37: the *George V* class. After such a long drought the shipyards found it difficult to fulfil the orders. *George V* was not commissioned until December 1940 and the last in the class, HMS *Howe*, was completed in August 1942. The carrier *Illustrious* was ordered in 1937 and completed in May 1940. It was a far cry from the industry that shocked the world by building *Dreadnought* in a year and a day.

There could never be enough ships to defend Britain's global commitments. The First World War had taught that lesson. Chatfield's priority was to make the most of the myriad problems assailing the Navy and get a balanced fleet. The service had continued to order cruisers even during its lean years in the 1920s. From 1933 the pace was stepped up.* The same was true of destroyers – a trickle in the Twenties, a steady stream in the Thirties. By the beginning of 1939 the Royal Navy had sixty-two cruisers and 159 destroyers. Submarines were a different story. Britain was not an enthusiastic builder of submarines in the interwar years. She was keener on banning them by treaty and developing sonar and depth charges to render them obsolete. Nonetheless the Navy began ordering more boats in response to threats from Germany, Italy and Japan.

The Navy in the late 1930s was substantial and balanced, as the table shows:

	GB[†]	USA	Japan	France	Italy	Germany
Capital ships	15 (9)[‡]	15	9 (4)	6 (4)	4 (2)	5 (11)
Aircraft carriers	7	5	5	1		
Cruisers	66	37	39	18	21	6
Destroyers	184	127	84	78	48	7
Submarines	60	58	58	76	104	57
Other[§]	76	20	48	48	103	55

These figures confirm the fact that although the Navy was still the biggest in the world it was outnumbered in every ocean and sea where it had to operate. It could not fight a war without regional allies. They also show that the battlefleet remained at the heart of the Navy. During the process of rearmament loud voices in the Navy called for greater emphasis to be put on convoy escorts. The lessons of 1917, when the country was almost brought to its knees by U-boat warfare, ran deep. Britain depended upon imports and an enemy could strangle the country by constricting

* One of the ten Town-class cruisers begun in 1936 was HMS *Belfast*, now a fixture of the London riverscape.
† Includes capital ships in Commonwealth navies.
‡ Figures in brackets refer to ships under construction (capital ships only).
§ This includes torpedo boats, escort vessels and gunboats.

her sea lanes. During the anti-submarine campaign of 1917–18 the Navy had restricted losses at sea to 300,000 tons a month with 443 of its own destroyers and significant numbers of American vessels. During the Great War, Britain and the dominions had been dependent on Japanese escort vessels to convoy troop ships coming from Australasia and Asia and to hold the ring in the Mediterranean. Even at its peak, the Navy could not on its own guarantee food imports and defend the empire.

The new carriers, cruisers and destroyers were not, however, intended for convoy duties come another war. Most of them were designated for the battlefleet. The cruisers earmarked for trade protection were equipped to ward off surface raiders, not U-boats.

Does this suggest that the conservative" cheerleaders for battleships won out over prescient naval thinkers who foresaw carnage in the Atlantic? It was not as simple as that. The victory of the Royal Navy and USN over the German U-boats between 1917 and 1918 had, it was hoped, shown the futility of submarine warfare on merchant shipping. Moreover the Navy had developed depth charges and Asdic* – anti-submarine sound detection systems, known now as sonar – which many convinced themselves made submarine warfare obsolete. Even more importantly the threat was assumed not to exist as a clear and present danger. Germany did not possess any submarines at all until 1935 and only a small number thereafter; the threat to merchant shipping was believed to come from German pocket battleships, designed to range the oceans for prey. The burden of close convoy duty would fall – if it was needed – on a few very small armed vessels. The Navy ordered a modest number of sloops in the mid-1930s for this purpose.

But that was not the kind of war envisaged by Chatfield and the Admiralty. The Royal Navy might be less powerful in relative terms. It might be cash-strapped and overstretched. But it was still a mighty force.

Sir Frederick Leith-Ross had faith in it as a war-winning machine.[4] Leith-Ross was a civil servant whose career straddled the Treasury and the military. He was also well travelled: he spent long periods on supranational bodies that wrestled with questions of international finance, reparations and war debts. In 1932 Leith-Ross became chief economic adviser to the government. Come another war with Germany, he believed, Britain could tighten the screws on Germany with a stringent blockade.

The key to this power was the Royal Navy. If another war began the

---

* ASDIC was alleged to stand for Anti-Submarine Detection Investigation Committee, although this derivation is in doubt.

Navy should be ready to seal off Germany from the world and patrol the seas around Europe to prevent contraband reaching the enemy. Germany would be starved of raw materials and food. But it was not just the ability of the battlefleet to clamp down a blockade on German ports at short notice: Europe's long coastline needed to be policed as well.

The problem was that neutral shippers could simply bring war materiel to a neutral country – such as Portugal, Spain, Italy or Sweden – where it would be transported overland to Germany. There were six areas that controlled the sea approaches to Western Europe: Weymouth, the Downs, the Orkneys, Gibraltar, Haifa and Aden. All of these were under British control. Any neutral ship that had not been searched by a British official and issued with a 'Navicert' (Navigational Certificate) in its port of origin would be stopped by a British naval Contraband Control ship in one of these six crossroads of world trade.

The girdle of steel the Navy threw around the world gave Britain an extra lever. The trading nations of the world were dependent on the good offices of the Navy. The refuelling stations that connected the shipping lanes and choke points such as the Suez Canal could be closed to unfriendly nations or companies. British banks, manufacturers and shippers could also use the power of money to put pressure on neutrals to comply. Unco-operative shipping companies or exporters ran the risk of losing valuable business.

Leith-Ross had a further weapon at his disposal. Britain's sea power and financial clout allowed him to construct a huge intelligence network around the globe. He built up a picture of which companies were supplying Germany and their trade routes. This allowed Britain to put diplomatic pressure on the relevant countries or intercept ships at sea. The network of informers – from international bankers to stevedores in ports including New York, Rio de Janeiro, Buenos Aires and Tokyo – reported on suspicious activity. They would inform the Navy if a chemical ostensibly being sent from, say, Rio to Sweden was in fact destined for Germany. Contraband Control patrols would gain prior notice of what was being smuggled and on what ship.

Naval power meant much more than the size and strength of the Navy. Numbers of ships and submarines were crude indicators of a country's true strength. The entire infrastructure of British trade and shipping – its refuelling stations, banks, commercial connections, international treaties and so on – was a weight to put alongside the new aircraft carriers and cruisers. The battlefleet underwrote the entire system. The Navy could not hope to defeat the combined naval power of Germany, Italy and Japan in a war. But it could defend Britain, gain local superiority with the help of allies such as France in the Mediterranean and the United States in the Pacific, and then detach formidable battle groups to devour its enemies as they were encountered. It was pointless, many felt, for the emphasis to be put on small convoy escorts; that would have been too defensive. Only a powerful battlefleet could intimidate rivals and overmaster enemy navies around the world.

It was no wonder that admirals such as Chatfield were prepared to invest in it. The core of battleships, cruisers, carriers and destroyers was the mainspring of blockade and imperial defence that had its frontline in ports such as Buenos Aires or choke points like Gibraltar and stretched all the way to German waters.

It was believed that British sea power – represented by the battlefleet based at Scapa Flow, Gibraltar and Malta – could dominate the waters and reduce any European country to hunger and industrial paralysis. That was the Navy's primary duty in time of war. How well it could manage such a Herculean task depended on the state of its men, ships and equipment.

The officers who led the Navy were overshadowed by the living memory of Britain's pre-eminence – an unchallengeable supremacy that had now vanished. The men who had led the Navy at its meridian were no longer there to see the revamped Navy of the 1930s. The great John Fisher died of cancer in July 1920. He had lived through the zenith of Britain's global power and felt the first chill of twilight.

His two most famous successors had joined the Navy as boys when Britannia unquestionably ruled the waves and lived on to see the harsh realities of the twentieth century. John Jellicoe caught a cold during the Armistice commemorations in 1935. He died two weeks later aged seventy-six. By that time David Beatty was a sick man. His taste for fast living had caught up with him. He fractured his breastbone in a motor-car accident in 1922; his passion for the chase had resulted in numerous broken bones and a shattered jaw. At the age of sixty-five he suffered from severe respiratory problems and heart strain. Even so he insisted on being a pallbearer at Jellicoe's funeral. A few weeks later, in January 1936, he hauled his shattered frame out again to act as pallbearer to another former naval officer, King George V. It was all too much; he caught pneumonia. Within weeks Beatty was dead too.

Their passing was a reminder of past glories. But it is important to stress that the Navy of the 1930s was no less disciplined or led or manned than the Navy of Nelson or Fisher.

In the 1880s Alfred Mahan had eulogised the Royal Navy. He had influenced rulers, strategists and public opinion around the world with his theories about the connection between sea power and national success. But even as he was writing, the pendulum of economic power was swinging from oceanic 'empires of the deep' towards continental empires of wheat and steel, such as Soviet Russia, Germany and the United States.

Mahan had stated that sea power was a precondition of national greatness. That was less clear in the 1930s. A country such as Britain with a fearsome, unbeaten Navy was in relative economic decline while other countries that had not established maritime dominance had become industrial powerhouses and war-waging machines. The United States and Germany might be counted in that category. Russia would rise in the next decade. Britain, in contrast, suddenly looked decidedly weak. Unlike her main rivals she was dependent on the sea lanes for survival. She was vulnerable to any power, whether it had a large fleet or not, that could strangle seaborne routes. The last time the sea had meant danger rather than opportunity was at the beginning of the seventeenth century.

The Royal Navy found itself facing new rivals. It had not lost the race by negligence or stagnation: history had caught up with it. The Navy's heyday had been an aberration, not a stage in a historical process as Mahan had claimed. It had enjoyed its brief time in the sun because other countries were out of it: Russia was in internal crisis, France was reeling from defeat at the hands of Prussia, the United States was consolidating after the Civil War and Japan was emerging from self-imposed isolation.

In the 1930s, therefore, naval planners had to wrestle with a situation that would have been normal to their predecessors in the generations before Trafalgar. Throughout history several nations had shared or contested maritime power in any one era; it was unusual for one nation to monopolise that power for any length of time. Now, three decades into the twentieth century, Britain was one of a number of naval powers.

History taught another vital lesson. The history of the Royal Navy was one of rises and falls, not an even progress to world domination via a series of victories. At the outset of every major war the Royal Navy had been hamstrung by ageing officers, sluggish administrative systems and ships unfit for purpose and in any case too few in number. Sea power was entirely notional until tested by the exigencies of war. Time and again the Navy had been compelled to reclaim its mantle in battle, often after serious disasters. The trouble was that history tended to magnify the victories to such a glaring extent that the debacles and defeats – which carried within them more profound lessons – were obscured. Only war revealed the kind of Navy that was needed. In the interval, senior officers had to haggle for cash. Nelson said as he was departing for the Mediterranean in 1803: 'I can only work with such tools as my superiors give me.'

The admirals and officers of the interwar period might not have always made the best decisions regarding strategy or hardware, but the point is that they were forced to make hard decisions in a fraught international situation and a time of unprecedented economic failure. The empire, built in a period of naval supremacy, was in danger of extinction in a new age. Senior officers knew that the empire and trading links east of Suez were doomed if Britain had to fight Germany, Italy and Japan simultaneously: there was no way the battlefleet could leave home waters. It was the bleakest outlook in the Navy's history.

The units of the Royal Navy scattered around the globe remained as taut, highly drilled and motivated as ever. While politicians appeased Germany, Japan and Italy they developed war plans to confront the enemy and trained their men accordingly. In 1939 the Mediterranean Fleet had a brilliant commander-in-chief in Admiral Andrew Cunningham. Cunningham came from a small-ships background; he was an excellent destroyer captain in the First World War. His second in command was Vice Admiral John Tovey, also a resourceful destroyer captain. They drove their men hard and created excellent teams. Britain could not have asked for better leaders in the vital Middle Sea.

All the same the Royal Navy had to confront a new, harsh and irreversible truth. It had, for the first time, lost its monopoly on national defence. This was a significant moment in its history and it was particularly relevant for an island people in the nervous 1930s. It was best encapsulated in Stanley Baldwin's words: 'The bomber will always get through.'

PART 14: LAST STAND

CHAPTER 50

THE *ARK*
1939–1940

HMS *Ark Royal* was in Britain's most strategically vital waters – the Western Approaches. It was September 1939. War had been declared on the third day of the month. The aircraft carrier was at the centre of a 'hunter-killer' group of destroyers seeking out U-boats that had started preying on British ships within hours of the start of the war.

Aircraft launched from *Ark Royal* were used to widen the search area for U-boats. On 14 September the group received distress calls from SS *Fanad Head*, which was being pursued by a U-boat 230 miles away. Aircraft from the carrier flew off to aid the merchantman. As they did so another German submarine, *U-39*, was lurking and watching undetected by the destroyers' sonar. *U-39* fired off two torpedoes at the massive exposed target in front of her.

Fortunately the lookouts on *Ark Royal* were alert that day. They spotted the torpedo tracks. The British carrier turned into the direction of the attack, so that the torpedoes sped past on either side. *U-39* was forced to the surface by depth charges dropped by *Ark Royal*'s accompanying destroyers. Some of her crew were saved before the boat sank.

U-39 was the first U-boat sunk in the war, but if naval strategists thought they had discovered a new way of combating the U-boat menace in the Atlantic they were soon disabused of that idea. *Ark Royal* was lucky to get away unscathed. Three days after her brush with death another carrier, HMS *Courageous*, was sunk off the coast of Ireland by a U-boat. Just over a week later the German press celebrated the sinking of *Ark Royal*. The carrier, along with *Nelson* and *Rodney*, had been dispatched to the Horns Reef to rescue the submarine *Spearfish*, which had been subjected to a sustained depth-charge attack. On the way home the British ships were approached by three Luftwaffe Dornier seaplanes. One Dornier was shot down by a Blackburn Skua launched from *Ark Royal*; it was the first German plane shot down in the war.

But then the planes were recalled to ship and taken down to the hangars. This illustrated another problem – one that went back to the end of the First World War when the Navy lost its air service. In the inter-war years officers not versed in naval aviation assumed that aircraft car-riers would defend themselves like battleships. British carriers therefore were built with extensive armour – which reduced the space for aircraft and made the vessels slow. In battle, the planes were to be brought into the armoured hangars and the enemy aircraft would be fought off by AA guns. By contrast the US and Japanese navies built faster, more capacious carriers, trusting the ship's defence to its planes rather than armour. Few things illustrate better the Navy's attitude to naval aviation in the inter-war years.

Now, off the Horns Reef, *Ark Royal* was under attack from five Heinkel bombers. They probably could not believe their luck when they encoun-tered no defending aircraft, and they were not deterred by the AA guns. The fifth plane dropped a 1,000 kg bomb directly onto the ship. The last thing the Luftwaffe crew saw was *Ark Royal* heeling to starboard; then the carrier was lost in a plume of water and a cloud of smoke. Later a recon-naissance plane reported seeing the two British battleships and no aircraft carrier.

It was a major victory for the Germans. Before the war was a month old they had destroyed two of Britain's most important ships. The Nazi propaganda machine disseminated illustrations of *Ark Royal* exploding and asked repeatedly: 'Where is *Ark Royal*?' The United States ambassador to Great Britain could answer that: he was taken by Winston Churchill, the recently appointed First Lord of the Admiralty, to see *Ark Royal*. Her captain had heeled the ship and the bomb had narrowly missed the ex-pansive target of the flight deck. The ship had eventually righted itself and got home.

'This is the story of a ship.' So begins the wartime celebration of the Royal Navy *In Which We Serve*, written by and starring Noel Coward. This chapter, and the next, is the story of a ship – *Ark Royal*. Or rather, it is the story of the first years of the Second World War told through the British carrier.

Ark Royal was one of the most awe-inspiring ships afloat. Her great flat flight deck was 800 feet long and gave the carrier her distinctive over-hang at bow and stern, and on either side. The 'island' superstructure towered over the flat surface and AA guns jutted out just below the flight deck. Three lifts carried up to seventy-two aircraft from the hangars below up to the great deck. The hangars were the armoured cavity of the ship, the leviathan's *raison d'être*. They shielded the aircraft from attack and provided a haven where they could be repaired and refuelled between sorties. Around the hangars were workshops, storehouses and offices where the aircraft could be kept in fighting fitness.

The crew of over 1,500 included officers and sailors, pilots, mechanics, engineers, marines, electricians, cooks and medics. It was like a great cavernous floating airbase. Traditionalists saw the *Ark* as ugly and faddish, but for many more it possessed grandeur and beauty. Down below, in the monster's steel belly, the men lived and worked by the glare of artificial light. 'It is easy to get lost,' wrote William Jameson, who served on the *Ark*. 'Mess deck after mess deck where the ratings live, all much alike, with their scrubbed wood tables, polished lockers and crowds of men – eating, sleeping, talking, reading – hundreds of yards of passages, with watertight doors at regular intervals. It was worst at night, when hammocks were slung everywhere; only eighteen inches apart, so that you must bend almost double to pass below the khaki-coloured sausages, swinging gently to the motion of the ship.'[1]

Ark Royal's two near-misses were risks too far for a Navy short of ships. The three carriers *Courageous*, *Hermes* and *Ark Royal* were dispatched to the Western Approaches to patrol for U-boats because the Admiralty was taken by surprise by the Kriegsmarine's early initiative. The Royal Navy simply did not have the capacity to provide convoy protection for incoming ships. An emergency order was placed for corvettes – a small, slow vessel based on a whaling vessel, which could escort convoys. Merchant ships were given weapons and equipped with Asdic. In the meantime the carriers were deployed with near-fatal consequences.

The opening phases of the Second World War were fought in the economic sphere and at sea. Just before war was declared between Britain and Germany, U-boats were dispatched to the Atlantic to raid allied commerce. The day after war was declared on 3 September 1939, Leith-Ross's plan was put into operation. The Navy's main fleet moved back to Scapa Flow to enforce the blockade. All shipping bound for Europe had to present itself for rigorous searches at one of the six Contraband Control Ports.

A neutral ship putting into one of these ports was boarded by parties of British customs officials and sailors who checked the cargo against the manifest. The cargo inventory was sent to the Ministry of Economic Warfare in London by teleprinter. The Ministry then told the Contraband Control officers whether the ship might proceed or whether parts of the cargo should be confiscated. Ships were also stopped at sea and searched. In addition ports around the world were clogged with German merchantmen that did not dare put to sea.

The German response was to unleash their U-boats. By the end of the first week of the war 65,000 tons of shipping had been sunk. But when the Navy managed to provide escorts this fell to 46,000 tons in the second week and 21,000 by the third. Meanwhile the Navy stopped and searched at least 1,525 ships and confiscated 289,000 tons of contraband; the French took 100,000. After fifteen weeks the French and British navies had confiscated 870,000 tons. This included 28 million gallons of petrol and substantial quantities of vital industrial material: sulphur, copper, rubber, resins, ores, phosphates, bauxite and other chemicals and minerals. It also included raw materials for clothing, such as textiles, animal hides, wool, silk and jute; natural oils and fats; fodder, foodstuff and tobacco. The seizures more than made up for the ships lost during 1939 to U-boats and magnetic mines. Germany was placed under severe strain, with food shortages and reduced industrial output. In December the Navy enforced a ban on German exports.

The Germans had expected this and they were ready to hit back. Indeed the Germany navy – renamed the Kriegsmarine in 1935 – hit the Royal Navy hard in the opening stages of the war. In addition to the sinking of the carrier *Courageous* the British lost HMS *Royal Oak* when *U-47* infiltrated Scapa Flow and torpedoed the doughty old battleship. It was a brilliant attack, and an ominous sign that the Kriegsmarine was more than ready for total war.

Before the war began the German pocket battleships *Admiral Graf Spee* and *Deutschland* had left Wilhelmshaven. The former was bound for the South Atlantic, the latter for the seas around Greenland. On 26 September the two ships received orders to begin raiding allied shipping. They were perfectly designed for the task. *Graf Spee* and *Deutschland* were fast and heavily armed with six 11-inch and eight 6-inch guns. Their orders were to stay as far away as possible from allied warships. The lesson of the First World War was that surface cruisers were highly effective when concealed in the great emptiness of water with unlucky, unescorted wayfarers to prey upon.

Up in the north this constraint placed *Deutschland* at a disadvantage. There were too many allied battleships within striking distance. The German pocket battleship returned home. The South Atlantic offered juicy morsels, however. From the end of September *Graf Spee* enjoyed considerable success hunting and destroying unsuspecting allied merchant ships and tankers in the South Atlantic and Indian Ocean. Her captain, Hans Langsdorff, was gentlemanly enough to remove the crews of ships he was about to sink. In November the German battleships

Gneisenau and *Scharnhorst* left Germany for the north Atlantic.

The French and British navies sent task forces to hunt the German raiders down. Once again the aircraft carriers were detached from the fleet and sent to search the open seas. HMS *Eagle* went to the Indian Ocean with two cruisers; HMS *Glorious* was also part of another task force dispatched there. HMS *Hermes* joined a French battleship and scoured the mid-Atlantic. Meanwhile the carrier HMS *Furious* searched for *Gneisenau* off Norway.

Ark Royal formed Force K with the veteran battlecruiser *Renown* and a number of destroyers to patrol the South Atlantic. It seemed now that the muscle of the Royal Navy was being dispersed to search endless tracts of ocean for single ships. *Ark Royal* and her task force were refuelling at Simonstown in South Africa when they received a distress call from a merchantman off the Namibian coast. Shortly after a distress call came from another steamer south-west from the first kill. *Graf Spee*'s course seemed to be towards the rich hunting grounds off the South American coast. The most likely destination was the estuary of the River Plate, between Argentina and Uruguay. Force K steamed off in pursuit.

Force G was already patrolling off the South American coast. The hunting group did not have any capital ships – it consisted of the heavy cruiser HMS *Exeter* and two light cruisers, *Ajax* and *Achilles*. A fourth ship, the heavy cruiser *Cumberland*, was refitting at the Falkland Islands. These ships would be no match for a battleship such as *Graf Spee*, with its long-range guns and powerful broadside.

Graf Spee spotted the masts of the British ships off Montevideo at dawn on 13 December. Langsdorff identified *Exeter*, but assumed the other two cruisers were destroyers. He believed they were escorts for a convoy – a plum target. Instead of attacking at long range, where *Graf Spee* would be beyond the reach of the British squadron, Langsdorff closed on the British at 24 knots.

The commanding officer of the squadron, Commodore Henry Harwood, had already developed a battle plan for his encounter with the pocket battleship. The only hope the cruisers had against *Graf Spee* was to draw her fire away from one particular target. Accordingly *Exeter* turned north-west, *Ajax* and *Achilles* turned north-east. The bigger British ship attacked from starboard of *Graf Spee*; the other two aimed to cross their enemy's bows and engage her from the other flank.

Graf Spee opened fire on *Exeter* at 06.18 at 19,000 yards. The British ship took agonising punishment from typically accurate German gunnery. One shell raked *Exeter* and another exploded a gun turret. Shrapnel

from this hit blasted into the bridge, causing extensive damage and killing everyone present except the captain and one other. Shortly afterwards
two shells hit the forward part of the ship. The seaplane, which was ready
to take off and spot for the guns, was put out of action.

She was spared further punishment from 06.30 when *Ajax* and *Achilles* managed to close to 13,000 yards and caused serious damage to the
German ship's secondary armament. *Graf Spee* now had to target all three
ships. She began firing on the two light cruisers. Then *Exeter* fired torpedoes from the opposing flank. Langsdorff was forced to turn his ship
north-west and move his heavy guns back to *Exeter*. The British ship took
still further blows. Her midships turret was knocked out, as were her
fire-control and compass communications.

Now it was a duel between the two small cruisers and the large German
ship. Both sides manoeuvred for advantage. *Ajax* received heavy blows,
which knocked out two turrets. Harwood's flagship replied with torpedoes and closed the gap to 8,000 yards. It was a furious fight. By the
end *Ajax* had lost all but three guns and her mast had been shot away,
depriving her of radio communication. *Exeter* had suffered even worse.
Sixty-one members of the crew were killed in the explosions or by shrapnel that swept her decks. There were fires burning throughout *Exeter* and
she began to list. Her communications had been down from early on;
messages were passed through the stricken ship by a chain of sailors. At
07.30 her only remaining turret was out of action.

But things on *Graf Spee* were as bad. Shells fired by *Exeter* had penetrated her decks and damaged her water-purification plant. Other hits
from the British ships had damaged her galley and bakery. Damage to
the hull had made movement in heavy seas impossible. And most importantly her oil-purification system was out of action. This was vital for the
running of her diesel engines. She could not return home now without
major repairs. Langsdorff feared that Harwood's squadron would soon be
reinforced. To the surprise of the British – who could see that the German
ship's deadly guns were still operational – *Graf Spee* raced to Montevideo
with *Ajax* and *Achilles* in pursuit.

Both sides faced a dilemma. They wanted more time. Langsdorff
wanted fifteen days to make repairs. Under international rules *Graf Spee*
could not stay in a neutral port for more than twenty-four hours. At first
the British pressed the Uruguayan government to expel *Graf Spee* quickly.
But the Navy also needed time: *Ajax* and *Achilles* were in no state to take
on the German ship. *Cumberland* was speeding from the Falklands; *Ark
Royal* and *Renown* were steaming to the River Plate. They would arrive on

19 December. The British had to stall. The international rules on the use of neutral ports also stated that a warship had to wait twenty-four hours to depart if a merchantman belonging to its enemy left port. Therefore the British made one of their merchant ships leave, so that the Uruguayans would have to delay Langsdorff's departure until 17 December.

Meanwhile an order was placed for fuel for *Ark Royal* at Buenos Aires. In fact the carrier was thirty-six hours away. Langsdorff fell for the ruse. He believed that some of the Navy's most powerful ships were waiting for him. Langsdorff cared deeply for his crew. He did not want to end their lives for the sake of glory. On the evening of 17 December *Graf Spee* left Montevideo. Harwood prepared for a last, desperate battle. But the German ship anchored, the crew were evacuated and at 22.00 Harwood was informed that *Graf Spee* had been blown up by her own crew. His aggression and determination had won one of the most famous victories in modern naval history.

The role of *Ark Royal* in this battle was limited. It was one part of the intense pressure that was applied to Langsdorff in the final days. Naval air power was yet to make its mark on the war. It would soon move to centre stage. This time it would be in chill northern waters.

On 9 April the British Home Fleet moved towards the Norwegian coast to prevent the Kriegsmarine entering the Atlantic. Instead it met the full force of a bomber attack. The Germans were actually engaged in a lightning invasion of Norway via her numerous ports. This might have been madness, given the overwhelming superiority of the Royal Navy. But they had an irresistible weapon: the Luftwaffe, and in particular Fliegerkorps X, a specialist anti-shipping force.

The commander-in-chief of the Home Fleet, Admiral Sir Charles Forbes, brought the carrier HMS *Furious* with him. But she did not carry fighter planes. This was the corrosive legacy of the fight for control of the Fleet Air Arm between the Navy and the RAF. The Navy was not ready for aerial warfare. It fatally underestimated the effectiveness of bombers against warships. The Admiralty believed that AA guns were more effectual than fighter planes and that battleships were impervious to bomber attack. On 9 April Forbes was fortunate to get away with the loss of just one destroyer. Nonetheless he was thoroughly unsettled by this new and deadly form of naval warfare. The fleet was kept away from German bomber range. British naval supremacy in the region was set at naught. It was the terrible legacy of the Navy's neglect of maritime aviation.

The next day British Skua dive bombers operating from the Orkneys sank the German cruiser *Königsberg* in Bergen. It was the first large warship destroyed by aerial attack and one of a few isolated successes. The Navy caused carnage with the Kriegsmarine in areas of Norway where the Luftwaffe had not yet reached. But those areas were disappearing fast. British forces in Norway came under intense bombardment from Fliegerkorps X. When the cruiser *Suffolk* was sent to shell a German airfield near Trondheim it was beaten back to Scapa Flow by Stuka dive bombers. It was little more than a floating wreck.

Ark Royal and *Glorious* were recalled from exercises in the Mediterranean to supply air cover for the beleaguered forces clinging on in Norway and the ships operating in those dangerous waters. The carriers had to remain 120 miles out to sea to try to avoid the Luftwaffe. Even so the British squadron was plagued by German bombers. To make matters worse the *Ark* did not have radar. She had to rely on her accompanying destroyers' radar systems to scramble her fighters in good time. But the destroyers had to signal *Ark Royal* the good old-fashioned way with flags and lights to avoid breaking radio silence. The British carriers became high-value targets for German bombers operating from Norway. *Ark Royal* came under fierce attack as she covered the allied evacuation from southern Norway. Those in the great steel bowels of the massive carrier heard but could not see the monstrous cacophony of the aerial attacks outside.

The Junkers bombers dived towards the *Ark* and dropped their screeching bombs, hoping to penetrate the massive, inviting flight deck. The men in the hangars and engine rooms heard each dive-bomb attack and the bellow of the *Ark*'s anti-aircraft guns firing barrage after barrage up into the sky. Then there would be an almighty thud as the sea erupted in a gigantic plume of water that rose twice as high into the sky as the *Ark*'s soaring control tower. Any minute a 1,000 kg bomb might penetrate the flight deck and explode in the confines of the armoured hangar. But the men of *Ark Royal* simply went about their business or slept in a corner.

The Norwegian campaign highlighted the Navy's weakness in aviation. But the campaign also showed that the Navy had lost none of its fighting spirit. In early April Commodore Bernard Warburton-Lee had led five destroyers in a spectacular Nelsonian assault on German transports at Narvik. Just before the attack the commodore heard that the fjord was defended by six German destroyers. Warburton-Lee attacked in the dark through fog and snow and sank two destroyers and eleven cargo ships. As the British destroyers were leaving they were attacked by five more German destroyers. Warburton-Lee hoisted the signal 'Continue to engage the enemy'. Just then a 5-inch shell hit the bridge. The commodore's secretary, Geoffrey Stanning, was blasted off his feet. When he came to

Stanning found that his left leg was useless and he had shrapnel down his back. He also saw that he was the only man left standing on the ruined bridge and the ship was heading fast towards a rocky shore. Although a mere purser, Stanning took command of the stricken destroyer and ran her safely aground. Warburton-Lee died of his wounds before they made shore; he was awarded a posthumous VC and Stanning received the DSO. Later in the month another assault on Narvik resulted in British forces sinking three destroyers; the Germans scuttled the remaining five.

The Kriegsmarine lost half of its entire force of destroyers. But it was a hollow victory for the Navy. Norway was lost. The fiasco continued for the Navy. The carriers moved up above the Arctic Circle in the middle of May to cover the landing, and subsequent evacuation, at Narvik. On 8 June HMS *Glorious* detached from the squadron. Her captain had been a brave submariner in the Great War, but he was a poor captain of an aircraft carrier. He was also loathed by his officers because he kept trying to sleep with their wives and foisted suicidal tactics on the pilots. When his commander (air) refused to carry out a crazy air attack the captain cracked and determined to head for Scapa to hold a court martial. He left with an inadequate escort of two destroyers. On the way back to Scapa Flow the lonely threesome was sunk by *Scharnhorst* and *Gneisenau*. The carrier went down with the loss of 1,207 lives. The German ships returned to Trondheim fjord.

The Navy was determined to avenge itself for the loss of yet another aircraft carrier. On 13 June fifteen Skuas took off from *Ark Royal*. Their target was *Scharnhorst*. It was a suicidal mission. Skuas were poor fighter planes and Trondheim was thick with Messerschmitt 109 fighters. Only seven Skuas returned. The rest were shot down by German fighters or AA fire as they flew low to drop their loads on *Scharnhorst*. Their bombs missed or harmlessly bounced off *Scharnhorst*'s armour.

That was the finale to the Navy's Norwegian catastrophe. The Admiralty did not understand aerial combat and its carriers were poorly equipped to meet the challenges of this new kind of warfare. The German conquest of Norway and Denmark was a strategic disaster for the Navy. The Kriegsmarine had outflanked it, gaining access to the North Atlantic. As a result of the catastrophe Neville Chamberlain fell from office. He was replaced by the First Lord of the Admiralty, Winston Churchill.

The fall of Norway was one of a regiment of problems assailing Britain in June 1940. The evacuations from Dunkirk and other French ports need no retelling here, save to dwell on the bravery and resilience of the British merchant marine. Without the prompt action of hundreds of sailors, fishermen and owners of small boats Britain would have lost the war in the early summer of 1940.

The Navy's role in the Dunkirk evacuations was one of improvisation. The service was lucky that it had a miracle-worker in charge at Dover – Admiral Bertram Ramsay. Ramsay was a brilliant organiser, an unorthodox thinker and a bold leader. He far exceeded the original hope of bringing back 45,000 soldiers in two days. By organising the 'little ships' and using destroyers to evacuate the troops directly he ensured that 338,266 men got home. The Navy lost six destroyers to aerial and U-boat attack.

On 10 June Italy declared war on Britain. That, combined with the fall of France, transformed the strategic situation for the Navy. *Ark Royal* was redeployed to the Mediterranean. It was about to enter the inferno.

CHAPTER 51

INFERNO
1940–1941

The Nazi 'Atlantic Wall' stretched from the Arctic Circle to the Bay of Biscay. U-boats could operate from French ports, giving them easy access to the Western Approaches. French and Italian naval bases and North African colonies encircled the western Mediterranean. British control over the Suez Canal and access to Middle East oil was under threat. The French navy – the fourth most powerful in the world – was in danger of falling into Nazi hands. It was suspected that Spain was about to join the Axis powers, making Gibraltar untenable. The Mediterranean had been vital to Britain's interests since the seventeenth century. The First Sea Lord, Sir Dudley Pound, was all for abandoning it. Churchill overruled him. Could the Navy hold?

On 22 June the French Vichy government signed an armistice with Germany. On the 23rd *Ark Royal* arrived at Gibraltar. She was the nucleus of Force H, a British squadron sent under the command of Vice Admiral Sir James Somerville to make up for the loss of French naval power in the western Mediterranean. It was a formidable force: in addition to the carrier was Somerville's flagship, the powerful battlecruiser HMS *Hood*, the battleships *Nelson*, *Resolution* and *Valiant*, two cruisers and eleven destroyers. It showed that the British meant business. Churchill wrote to Somerville: 'You are charged with one of the most disagreeable tasks that a British Admiral has ever been faced with, but we have complete confidence in you and rely on you to carry it out relentlessly.'[1]

The 'disagreeable task' was the order to neutralise the French fleet stationed at Mers-el-Kébir in Algeria. The order did not rule out destroying the French ships if their admiral refused to hand them over to the Royal Navy. Somerville had won a DSO during the Dardanelles Campaign and had risen through the Navy, alternating sea service with periods at the Imperial Defence College and the Admiralty. He was as experienced and tough a leader as they came. He had commanded the Navy's destroyers in the Mediterranean between 1936 and 1938 and been commander-in-chief in the East Indies between 1938 and 1939. The new captain of *Ark Royal*, Cedric Holland, had been naval attaché in Paris, which gave him insight into the new Vichy government and the French navy. Both men detested the thought of attacking the French ships. That opinion was shared throughout the Navy.

Captain Holland negotiated with the French. Meanwhile planes from *Ark Royal* dropped mines outside the harbour to add pressure. But it soon became clear that the French were not going to give up their fleet. Somerville was ordered to attack. On the evening of 3 July the great guns of the British battleships roared out. The battleship *Bretagne* was hit and exploded with huge loss of life. Planes from the *Ark* circled above the French ships, helping the gunners perfect their aim. Other planes were out at sea, patrolling for submarines and Italian warships. When the French battleship *Strasbourg* broke out of Mers Swordfish torpedo planes were sent after her. But the attempted pursuit merely demonstrated the unreliability of the Swordfish. The plane was too slow. *Strasbourg* escaped unmolested to Toulon.

The next day bombers were sent over Mers to finish off the damaged ships. In total 1,297 French sailors died. A few days later aircraft from HMS *Hermes* attacked French ships at Dakar. Other vessels at Alexandria were blockaded.

The attack on Mers-el-Kébir was the source of long-standing ill-will between France and Britain. Somerville wrote that 'we all felt thoroughly dirty and ashamed that the first time we should have been in action was an affair like this'.[2] He said it was 'the biggest political blunder of modern times'. In November 1942 the Germans attempted to capture the French ships at Toulon. Before that could happen the French scuttled their ships – proof they said that the attack at Mers-el-Kébir had been unnecessary.

Force H's task was now to secure supply lines to Malta. The colony was vitally important if Britain was to hold her position in the Mediterranean. It gave the Navy control over the seas that linked the Axis powers with North Africa and the route to Egypt, Suez, the Middle East and, ultimately, India. Malta was the perfect base for British ships, submarines and bombers to harry Axis convoys to Italian-controlled Libya.

Admiral Sir Andrew Browne Cunningham (known as 'ABC') commanded the British Mediterranean Fleet. He was an old friend of Somerville – they had been classmates at Dartmouth. In October 1939 he had been ordered to move the fleet from Valetta to Alexandria. The island had no air defences worth speaking of; it was considered vulnerable to air raids, amphibious assault and bombardment from the sea. It was not a safe base for the Navy's prime battleships – although the Navy was required to defend and supply it from Egypt. Now the contest was on between the Italian navy and the Royal Navy for control of the narrow waters between Sicily and North Africa. In the middle sat lonely Malta.

Within days of the attack on Mers-el-Kébir Somerville took Force H eastward from Gibraltar. He wanted to attack the Italian airbase at Cagliari on Sardinia. On the afternoon of 8 July the British squadron was taken by surprise when forty Italian aircraft appeared out of nowhere and subjected the ships to waves of bombing. The defending Skuas shot down two Italians and none of the ships were harmed.

This was Somerville's first experience of aerial warfare, and he did not like what he saw. The sorry experience of Norway weighed on his mind and he was not prepared to risk *Ark Royal* so close to shore. He ordered a retreat. His air defences had been poor and the AA gunners ineffectual. Three days later some of his destroyers bungled an attack on an Italian submarine. Somerville saw that Force H was badly in need of training before it faced combat again. He drilled his men and ships for weeks in the waters off Gibraltar, readying them for operations against the Italian air force.

The day after Somerville's first encounter with the Italian planes, Cunningham and the main fleet fought the Italian battlefleet off Calabria. British and Italian surface naval strength in the Mediterranean was comparable, although the Italians had more submarines and aircraft. The battle was indecisive, although Cunningham had a warning for the Italians. The battleship *Warspite* knocked out the boilers on the Italian battleship *Giulio Cesare* with a shell fired at the enormous distance of 26,000 yards. Mussolini's fleet was forced to withdraw. An attack by 126 Italian planes did little damage. The Swordfish bombers launched from the British carrier *Eagle* were likewise ineffective.

The inexperienced Italian navy had been nervous about contesting control of the Mediterranean with the Royal Navy. The Battle of Calabria did not whet their appetite.

Back in the western Mediterranean Somerville had worked up Force H to a state of readiness. Its objective this time was to deliver Hawker Hurricanes to Malta, to give the island protection against the Italian air force. The Hurricanes were carried on an aged carrier, HMS *Argus*; *Ark Royal's* job was to launch diversionary attacks on the Italian air force at Cagliari en route and to screen the squadron from air attack. The operation was a success. Confidence in the ability of *Ark Royal* to deter air attack – which had been in short supply – was restored. Most importantly Somerville saw with his own eyes how effective naval air power could be.

Ark Royal's next mission was even more ambitious. She provided diversionary attacks and defended an even bigger convoy that brought more supplies to Malta, tanks to General Wavell in North Africa and ships for Cunningham's fleet in Alexandria. Once again the British ships had safe passage through the Mediterranean. Fighters and bombers from the *Ark* and the brand-new carrier HMS *Illustrious* deterred the Italians. Bit by bit the Navy was learning the arts of naval air defence and offence. With Somerville based in the west and Cunningham in Alexandria, the British remained firmly in control of the Mediterranean.

The presence of *Ark Royal* in the west and another carrier, *Eagle*, in the east had made this possible. Now Cunningham had *Illustrious* as well. The aircraft carriers were links in a chain that reached from Britain to Alexandria.

In October *Ark Royal* returned to Britain to refit in Liverpool. The city, like the rest of the county, was under attack from the air. It was the first time for centuries that mainland Britain was placed in the firing line. In all those years Britain could count on the Royal Navy to seal off the country from danger. That was no longer true. The bomber did always get through and only the RAF was capable of downing it.

However, the Navy remained an effective deterrent against seaborne invasion. With a German army encamped across the Narrow Seas an assault was a serious proposition from the summer of 1940. But the Wehrmacht, like Parma's Army of Flanders and Napoleon's Grande Armée, would have to embark on landing craft and take its chances against the Royal Navy in the open seas. In addition to the Home Fleet at Scapa Flow there were 700 small craft watching and waiting in the waters between the Wash and the Isle of Wight. There were also numbers of cruisers and destroyers based in ports between the Humber and Portsmouth. Invasion was as impossible as it had been in 1588, 1745, 1759 and 1805. The Germans would have been blasted out of the water.

Within a month *Ark Royal* was on its way back to Gibraltar. The war in the Mediterranean escalated when Italy invaded Greece. It gave Cunningham the chance to go on the offensive against the Italian navy. Between 4 and 11 November 1940 he put into operation Plan MB8.

The Italian navy had preferred to use its 'fleet in being' as a passive threat to the Royal Navy rather than confronting Cunningham and Somerville's powerful ships again. The bulk of its capital ships were tucked away at Taranto, which was impossible to attack from the sea. Plan MB8 involved using regular supply convoys to Malta as a cover for an assault on Italian assets. *Ark Royal*, fresh from its refit at Liverpool, took part in the first phase, Operation Coat, a reinforcement convoy bound for Malta. *Ark Royal*'s Swordfish bombers detached and launched a surprise attack on Cagliari. Meanwhile warships that had been escorting a convoy from Alexandria to Greece re-formed as Force-X and attacked and destroyed an unsuspecting Italian convoy in the Adriatic.

But the centrepiece of Plan MB8 was the attack on the Italian naval base at Taranto. Cunningham wanted to establish British naval superiority over the Italians once and for all. On 6 November *Illustrious* and two heavy cruisers, two light cruisers and four destroyers left Alexandria under Rear Admiral Lumley Lyster, ostensibly guarding a convoy bound for Malta. At 21.00 on 11 November a wave of twelve Swordfish bombers took off from *Illustrious* and flew 170 miles to Taranto. They arrived at their target and met intense AA fire. Two planes detached and dropped flares to light up the harbour. These two then dropped bombs on the Italian fleet's oil storage depot. Meanwhile six torpedo bombers attacked the enemy ships from seaward. The remaining four dive-bombed ships in the inner harbour. The aircraft left at 23.35. Twenty minutes later the second wave of aircraft from *Illustrious* arrived and carried out their strike.

Two Swordfish bombers were lost in the raid. The Italians lost one battleship and two were sunk and put out of action for six months. The Battle of Taranto was a further indication of the future of naval warfare. It was the most daring and successful use of an aircraft carrier in offensive operations to date.

But it did not stop the Italian navy. Just six days after the raid on Taranto the Italian battleships *Vittorio Veneto* and *Giulio Cesare* with heavy cruisers and destroyers attacked Force H as it was taking another delivery of Hurricanes to Malta. Somerville became aware of the Italians and the Hurricanes took off to fly the remaining 400 miles to Malta. The two naval squadrons fought at long range and it was an uneventful fracas called the Battle of Cape Spartivento. *Ark Royal*'s Swordfish torpedo bombers once again proved useless at attacking moving battleships. The Hurricanes could not make it to Malta; all of them ditched in the sea.

Nonetheless Cunningham had control of the central Mediterranean. From his base at Malta he harried Italian convoys to Libya. He was also able to give support to the British army in North Africa. The Italians were on the run. In January *Ark Royal* escorted yet another convoy taking ammunition, aircraft and supplies to Malta and Alexandria. It was business as usual: the *Ark*'s planes mounted patrols against enemy aircraft and submarines. All went well, and Force H handed over the convoy to HMS *Illustrious* off Sicily.

So far so uneventful. On 10 January 1941 *Illustrious*'s patrolling fighters were drawn down to sea level by ten Italian torpedo bombers. It was a decoy. Suddenly *Illustrious* came under sustained dive-bomber attack. In six minutes the carrier was pelted with six 1,000 kg bombs. Two of them dropped with unerring accuracy down the aircraft lift. The explosions in the confines of the armoured hangar caused enormous damage to the aircraft and their crews; they ignited fuel and ammunition. A third bomb penetrated the armoured deck and exploded inside the ship. Over a hundred men died, including many of the heroes of Taranto. *Illustrious* survived this attack and further attempts made on her while under repair at Grand Harbour, Valetta, but she was knocked out of the war for a year and had to undergo repairs in America. This was a different order of aerial bombardment. 'We were watching complete experts,' said Cunningham.[3]

He was not wrong. These were Ju 87 Stuka bombers, and they were part of Fliegerkorps X, the deadly anti-shipping force which had beaten the Navy out of Norwegian waters a year before. The next day they destroyed the cruiser HMS *Southampton*.

The Luftwaffe had arrived in Sicily. It changed everything. Just as it was winning the war in the Mediterranean and North Africa, the Navy was about to lose air control, and with it command of the seas.

Cunningham was diverted from his successful attack on Axis convoys. He was ordered to escort 58,000 troops to Greece in March. The Germans responded by forcing the Italians to send out their remaining warships to try to intercept the British invasion. The result was Cunningham's crushing victory over the Italians at the Battle of Matapan, fought between 27 and 29 March 1941. It was, as it turned out, the Navy's last major fleet battle, and it emerged victorious. The Italians lost three heavy cruisers and two destroyers; the battleship *Vittorio Veneto* was knocked out of service for five months. The Italians lost 2,300 sailors, the Royal Navy just three. From then on the Axis powers could not compete with the Navy in terms of surface shipping. The battle was a reminder of the fighting spirit of the Royal Navy and its dominance at sea.

But the Luftwaffe rendered the Navy's superiority redundant. In April Cunningham's hard-pressed ships had to evacuate the army from Greece to Crete. They might have thought themselves safe on the island – the Germans and Italians had no chance of getting through the Royal Navy. Instead the Germans parachuted their troops into Crete. Cunningham was hamstrung by his lack of air power. The loss of *Illustrious* was a crippling blow. His other carrier, *Formidable*, fell victim to Stuka bombers as well.

These were dark days for the Navy as it attempted to evacuate as many allied soldiers as it could from Crete. The Germans bombed the British ships as they carried the defeated troops to Alexandria. Cunningham was adamant that the 'Navy must not let the Army down'.[4]

Without air cover the ships were juicy targets for dive bombers from the Royal Navy's nemesis, Fliegerkorps X. The Luftwaffe took a heavy toll: the Navy lost three cruisers and six destroyers; many more were seriously damaged, including three battleships, six cruisers and the carrier. It took an effort of heroic leadership to rally the shattered fleet's spirits as it came under sustained attack from the air. Cunningham reminded his stunned and exhausted men of the mantle they had inherited. 'It takes three years to build a ship,' declared ABC defiantly, 'it takes three centuries to build a tradition'.[5]

It was one of the Navy's worst experiences of combat in its history. But the officers and men rallied to ABC's call.

Meanwhile the British army was being forced into retreat in North Africa by Rommel's Afrika Korps. The Luftwaffe controlled the narrow channel between Sicily and North Africa, enabling supplies to pass unchallenged. After the carnage at Crete, the British Mediterranean Fleet was inferior to the Italian fleet. Malta came under intense bombardment. Convoys to Wavell's army had to take the long route round southern Africa and up to the Suez Canal. For the first time since 1798 the British had lost control of the Mediterranean.

By April it was clear that Wavell needed urgent supplies. The decision was taken to mount Operation Tiger: 307 tanks (known as the tiger cubs), forty-three Hurricanes, plus other materiel and supplies would run the gauntlet of the Luftwaffe and resupply Malta, Wavell and Cunningham the quick way, via Gibraltar. They would be escorted in this perilous voyage by the battlecruiser *Renown*, the battleship *Queen Elizabeth*, four cruisers and a protective screen of destroyers. Air cover would be provided by the dauntless *Ark Royal*. They ventured into the Mediterranean, making for what were now the most dangerous waters in the world: the central Mediterranean with its gatekeepers – Fliegerkorps X.

The size, speed and direction of the convoy were made known to the Italians and Germans just three days out of Gibraltar. They were determined to destroy it. *Ark Royal*'s aircrews and the AA gunners in the warships were about to face their sternest test.

On 8 May 1941 the convoy came under attack from Italian torpedo bombers. The *Ark* had to dodge torpedoes while her fighters fought bravely in the sky for an hour. One Fulmar fighter was lost and four damaged. That left five operational fighters to fend off several other waves of attack that day. Three of them were kept in the air at any time, circling high above the ships and coming in only to refuel. Then the convoy neared Sicily, where the Luftwaffe awaited.

At dusk it came under attack from fifteen Stukas and six Messerschmitts. They were joined by additional bombers and fighters. Though completely outnumbered and outgunned, the *Ark*'s handful of available Fulmars drove them away again and again. 'Once a screening destroyer saw ... a single Fulmar persistently attacking a large group of enemy aircraft and eventually forcing them to break their formation and retire.'[6] Not one Stuka was able to make a dive on the convoy. Meanwhile a group of torpedo bombers used the dogfights far above as cover for a raid on the carrier. *Ark Royal* once again had to swerve out of the way of incoming torpedoes.

Thanks to the bravery of the airmen and the crews of the warships the vital convoy made it, despite the odds stacked against it. The defence of the convoy by a handful of brave young pilots and the gunners on the ships was truly remarkable. Only one merchant ship was lost, and that to a mine. It was one of the most outstanding performances in the naval war. *Ark Royal* came under attack on her way back to Gibraltar. Then it was time to turn around again and steam back through the danger zone, this time with a load of Hurricanes to maintain Malta's air defences.

The success of Operation Tiger was one glimmer in a disastrous situation for the Navy, and it may have had an unintended consequence. Somerville believed that many in Whitehall saw the success as proof that the Navy had been exaggerating the dangers of the Mediterranean. And it had a sad conclusion for so much bravery: many of the 'tiger cubs' were squandered in a futile operation ordered by Churchill.

At the same time as the Battle of Crete and Operation Tiger strained the Navy's nerves to the limit, the German battleship *Bismarck* and the cruiser *Prinz Eugen* exited the Baltic. Their mission was to hunt the Atlantic for merchant shipping. The Navy gained intelligence of their movements. A group of powerful ships was moved into the seas between Greenland and the British Isles: the battleship *George V*, the battlecruiser *Renown*, the aircraft carrier *Victorious* and three light cruisers. A group comprising the Navy's pride and joy HMS *Hood* and the battleship *Prince of Wales* was sent into the Denmark Strait between Greenland and Iceland.

Bismarck was one of the most powerful ships in the world, and the largest warship in any European navy. She was a formidable opponent for any British battleship. HMS *Hood* had been commissioned twenty-one years before; when she entered service she was the largest warship in the world and, despite the appearance of mightier American and Japanese ships (not to mention *Bismarck*), she remained the jewel in the Navy's crown. HMS *Prince of Wales* was a brand-new *George V*-class battleship, as powerful as *Bismarck*, but she had been rushed into service and her crew were inexperienced.

On 23 May the cruisers *Norfolk* and *Suffolk* identified the two enemy ships in the Denmark Strait and began to shadow them, using their radars to keep track because *Bismarck* and her consort were cloaked by foul weather. At 05.52 the next morning *Hood* opened fire on *Prinz Eugen*, in the mistaken belief that it was *Bismarck*. Just after 06.00 *Hood* erupted in a huge fireball. Shells fired from *Bismarck* had penetrated her magazines. Huge chunks of molten metal sprayed into the air and rained down around her, some hitting *Prince of Wales*, half a mile away. *Hood* sank at once, with the loss of 1,415 men.

It was one of the worst moments in the entire history of the Navy. Losing a ship was bad enough, but HMS *Hood* was one of the most famous and beloved ships in the Navy's history; she was the service's talisman. She had been British naval power made visible in her heyday, when she had been the greatest ship afloat. This elegant ship had toured the world in the 1920s, a last reminder of Britain's claim to sovereignty of the seas. The service and the public at large were appalled.

The Navy had to avenge the loss. Every available warship was called upon to join the search for just two enemy vessels. The battleships *Ramillies* and *Rodney* and several cruisers were pulled out of convoy duties in the Atlantic and set on the trail of the German ships. *Norfolk*, *Suffolk* and *Prince of Wales* continued to shadow the enemy. On the evening after the Battle of the Denmark Strait *Bismarck* came under attack from Swordfish bombers from *Victorious*. The raid did little damage. The next day *Bismarck* evaded her stalkers and disappeared into the Atlantic.

Unbeknown to the Navy *Bismarck* was heading for Brest. She had been damaged by *Prince of Wales* and she was leaking fuel. It was a time of anxiety for the British; *Bismarck* was slipping out of their grasp. But then her destination was revealed by an intercepted radio message. HMS *George V*, however, miscalculated the *Bismarck*'s position and headed too far north. The next day, 26 May, a reconnaissance aircraft at last got eyes on the German battleship. The race was now on. It looked as though *Bismarck* would make it to French waters, where she would be shielded by the Luftwaffe, before any British battleships caught up with her.

The only hope for the British was Force H, which had been ordered out of Gibraltar. On the evening of 26 May, in appalling conditions, Swordfish from *Ark Royal* launched their attack. Unfortunately they had mistaken HMS *Sheffield* for the *Bismarck*. However the mistake did no damage because the magnetic torpedoes failed. The aeroplanes returned to *Ark Royal*, where new torpedoes were fitted. The planes took off again, as the sun was setting.

This time their radars took them straight to *Bismarck*. They swooped down and launched their torpedoes. The one dropped by John Moffat hit the enemy ship's rudder. It could not have been better timed or targeted. *Bismarck* began steaming round in circles. The crew managed to get her under some sort of control, but the state of the ship meant that more and more British ships caught up with her. The captain of *Bismarck* signalled the German base: 'Ship unmanoeuvrable. We will fight to the last shell. Long live the Führer.'

Through the night *Bismarck* was subjected to torpedo attacks from the British destroyers *Cossack*, *Sikh*, *Maori* and *Zulu* and a Polish destroyer. The next day she was bombarded by the heavy destroyers *Norfolk* and *Dorsetshire* and by the big battleships *Rodney* and *George V*. The *Bismarck's* upperworks were battered down during this withering attack. Still she refused to surrender. Eventually her own crew scuttled her. She sank just after 10.30 on 27 May. From a crew of 2,200 just 110 men were saved.

Ark Royal had started the month ensuring the safety of Operation Tiger. She ended it the hero of the sinking of the *Bismarck*, one of the most famous naval actions of the war. At last bombers working from a British carrier had struck a decisive blow against a moving enemy battleship. Moffat's torpedo scored a vital hit for the Royal Navy, removing a deadly threat from the Atlantic and sparing its blushes.

Then it was back to convoy runs in the Mediterranean. Force H was Malta's lifeline and *Ark Royal* provided the shield. In July, for example, Operation Substance brought much-needed supplies to Malta. Operation Halberd in September delivered 85,000 tons of supplies brought on nine merchant ships. Through the summer of 1941 great stocks of supplies were built up on Malta. Air strength was improved with significant numbers of fighters and bombers. The Navy was so successful in resupplying Malta so that it could withstand a prolonged siege because the Luftwaffe had been pulled out of the Mediterranean to take part in Operation Barbarossa, the invasion of Soviet Russia, launched on 22 June 1941. The Navy had to deal with the Italians, who were markedly reluctant to take it on. The convoys still came under attack from the air and from torpedoes, but Force H – and *Ark Royal* in particular – were now experts in shepherding convoys through the Mediterranean.

It was vital work. In the summer of 1941 the Navy and the RAF were able to go on the offensive from Malta. Between June and September submarines, the Fleet Air Arm and the RAF sank 108 Axis ships that were carrying supplies for Rommel. In November 79,208 tons were sent to the Axis armies in Africa; just 30,000 tons got through. This hit Rommel hard: a lot of fuel was lost in the Mediterranean. From October surface ships began to operate out of Malta. Force K and Force B comprised the Navy's Malta strike force; each force had four cruisers. In November Force K sank every member of a five-strong Axis convoy that was ferrying vehicles, munitions, fuel and troops to Libya.

When Malta was spared attack it was capable of functioning as a base that could eliminate 60 per cent of enemy convoys and place the Libyan ports under virtual blockade. Its value was incalculably high. The Royal Navy was resurgent.

But then on 13 November *Ark Royal* was torpedoed. After so many near-misses and death-defying runs to Malta she must have seemed invincible. As she was returning to Gibraltar from yet another convoy run she was hit amidships by a torpedo fired by the German U-boat *U-81*. On impact the entire carrier shuddered violently and ominously. Water ran in through the hole in her starboard side, flooding the starboard boiler room, oil tanks and main switchboard. The *Ark* began to list.

Captain Maund ordered his men to abandon ship. He was mindful

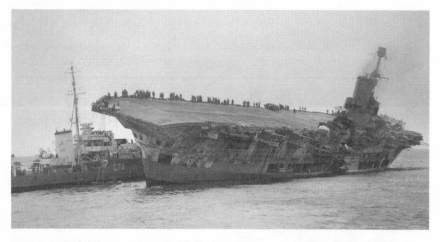

HMS *Ark Royal* listing to starboard after being torpedoed. The destroyer HMS *Legion* is moving alongside to take off members of the crew.

that aircraft carriers sank very quickly when they were holed. In his hurry to spare his sailors and air crews from drowning he neglected to give the order for fire-control procedures, such as closing hatches to localise flooding, to be put in place. Water began to spread through the ship, passing through open doors and hatches in the lower decks. It spread into the central boiler room. It was too late to save the *Ark*, despite last-minute efforts. The list became more extreme, before she toppled over slowly, like a baby. She broke in two and disappeared beneath the waves.

CHAPTER 52

ARMAGEDDON
1942

The sinking of *Ark Royal* marked the beginning of the bleakest period in the Navy's history. Within days the battleship *Barham* was sent to the seabed by *U-331* off the north-west coast of Egypt. A few days after that the Battle of Taranto was made to look like a minor raid when six aircraft carriers of the Imperial Japanese Navy (IJN) attacked the US fleet at Pearl Harbor.

Each IJN carrier carried twice the number of planes of its British counterpart. And those planes were faster and better than the outdated Swordfish. The Japanese had mastered the art of offensive naval aviation. They made British efforts over the first years of the war – valiant as they may have been – look distinctly puny.

Three days later, on 10 December 1941, the Royal Navy faced the full force of Japanese naval air and torpedo attack. A small but powerful force had been sent to deter Japanese attempts to seize British and Dutch colonies. Churchill believed that the mere presence of British battleships in the Indian Ocean would have their traditional effect – they would paralyse all enemies, including the Japanese. At stake was Britain's pre-eminence in South-East Asia. Admiral Sir Tom Phillips was off the coast of Malaya, attempting to disrupt Japanese landings. Fatally he did not request air cover from Singapore.

Now he faced the most formidable maritime air force the world had ever seen. The battleship *Repulse* was attacked by waves of Mitsubishi bombers. She skilfully manoeuvred to avoid swarms of torpedoes, but after the fourth wave of bombers she succumbed to five direct hits and sank with the loss of 508 men. HMS *Prince of Wales* sank in the same attack.

The news of this defeat reached London in the middle of the night. Churchill was awoken and told. 'In all the war, I never received a more direct shock,' he recalled. '... As I turned over and twisted in bed the full horror of the news sank in upon me. There were no British or American ships in the Indian Ocean or the Pacific except the American survivors of

Pearl Harbor, who were hastening back to California. Over all this vast expanse of waters Japan was supreme, and we everywhere were weak and naked.'[1]

Five days after that terrible shock the Navy lost a cruiser to a U-boat off Alexandria; four days after that Forces K and B ran into a minefield while chasing an Italian convoy; a cruiser and a destroyer were sunk and one cruiser badly damaged. The Malta strike force was out of the war. On the same day Italian frogmen steered 'maiale' manned torpedoes into Alexandria harbour and attached limpet mines to Queen Elizabeth and Valiant. These ships were the last two British battleships in the Mediterranean. Now they were grounded forlornly in Alexandria harbour, their superstructures and serviceable great guns protruding above the waterline as visual evidence of Britain's fall.

The Italians had secured naval supremacy in the central Mediterranean. In December the Luftwaffe returned to the Mediterranean. Its bases ringed the western and eastern approaches to Malta. Axis convoys made it to Africa; with negligible naval strength, British convoys to the island became almost impossible. Italian ships harried the convoys and German bomber attack meant that as little as 20 per cent of the supplies got through. Malta had to tough out one of the most terrible sieges of modern history – a truly apocalyptic series of bombing raids.

In February 1942 the most important British base east of Suez fell. Singapore had been at the heart of naval strategy; now it was in Japanese hands. The allies were comprehensively beaten at the Battle of the Java Sea in the same month. HMS Exeter, she of the gallant victory in the River Plate, was lost along with other ships. Sir James Somerville was transferred to command a British fleet of five aged battleships and three carriers in the Indian Ocean. There they faced the might of the IJN aircraft carriers and state-of-the-art fast battleships. Somerville's three carriers between them had ninety planes; they confronted 300 IJN aircraft and their highly trained crews.

It was, as Churchill said, 'the most dangerous moment of the war'. The Navy could not afford any more defeats. Somerville avoided a direct encounter with the IJN. All the same he lost Hermes, the first modern aircraft carrier in history, and two cruisers.

In that month as well the pride of the Royal Navy was seriously dented when the two German battleships Scharnhorst and Gneisenau and the cruiser Prinz Eugen broke out of Brest and proceeded up the Channel to their home ports. They managed to evade the Navy, hundreds of RAF planes and shore batteries. The Times mordantly commented: 'Nothing more mortifying to the pride of seapower has happened in home waters since the seventeenth century.'[2]

It was more significant than a snub to British naval history. The Kriegsmarine needed its ships to disrupt the Arctic convoys that had been carrying vast amounts of war materiel from Britain, Canada and the United States to Archangel and Murmansk since the summer of 1941. The supplies of aircraft, tanks and other warlike supplies were essential for the all-important campaign in Russia. Ships such as *Scharnhorst* and *Bismarck*'s sister *Tirpitz* were needed by the Kriegsmarine to disrupt the supply route to Russia. The presence of the Kriegsmarine's Battle Group I in Norway placed the Navy under enormous strain. The Arctic convoys could not just be escorted by cruisers, destroyers and corvettes. Because of the German battleships lurking in Norwegian fjords the Navy had to detach precious battleships and a carrier from the main fleet to protect the thousands of tanks, planes, munitions and trucks bound for the Soviet Union.*

The first convoys were completed without serious loss. From the beginning of 1942 the Kriegsmarine and Luftwaffe felt they could no longer let the allies get away with these operations. Losses mounted from March 1942, when the Arctic day began to lengthen. Battle raged in the icy Arctic waters. With regular bomber attacks and freezing conditions, the Arctic convoy was the worst job in the Navy – and that was saying something in 1942. Five merchantmen out of nineteen and an escorting whaler were lost from convoy PQ13. From then on the convoys were on the receiving end of persistent attacks from U-boats and bombers. Eight ships were lost from PQ16 in May.

But a worse fate befell convoy PQ17 in June. This was the largest of the Arctic convoys to date, with thirty-five merchantmen protected by close escorts and an Anglo-American covering force. The convoy battled through repeated attacks from U-boats and aircraft until 4 July when Swedish intelligence informed the Admiralty that *Tirpitz* and the heavy cruiser *Admiral Hipper* had sortied from Trondheim while the heavy cruisers *Lützow* and *Admiral Scheer* had left Narvik. The British and American escorts – including the battleships HMS *Duke of York* and USS *Washington*, the carrier *Victorious* and forty other warships – were ordered back to Scapa Flow. The convoy was told to scatter.

Only eleven ships made it to Russia. Twenty-two merchant ships were

---

* A bright spot was the air raid on Kiel on the night of 26/27 February that rendered *Gneisenau* unusable.

sunk by planes and subs. It was an unqualified disaster for the Navy, which was left diminished in the eyes of Washington and Moscow. It was an undeserved victory for the Kriegsmarine – it seemed that merely the threat of a surface strike was enough to panic and disperse allied ships, leaving them easy prey for the Luftwaffe and U-boats. The Arctic convoys were suspended until September. Churchill called it 'one of the most melancholy naval episodes in the whole of the war'.[3]

Out in the Atlantic the U-boat wolfpacks were enjoying a second 'happy time'. The Atlantic convoys had enjoyed some respite when U-boats were diverted to the Mediterranean to target ships such as *Ark Royal*. America's entry into the war in December 1941 gave U-boat commanders thousands of new, juicy, unprotected targets which had hitherto been off limits. Between January and August 1942 U-boats sank 609 ships and with them 6 million tons. U-boat losses amounted to just twenty-two in this period. They were made up for by significant increases in U-boat numbers: ninety-one in January, 140 by April and 196 in October. The problem was compounded in February when the Kriegsmarine upgraded its Enigma enciphering machines and introduced TRITON, a new key. It was now impossible to locate German wolfpacks in the Atlantic.

In July 1942 the U-boats left their happy hunting ground off the American east coast and returned to the mid-Atlantic to attack convoys between Canada and Britain. Losses began to mount. There were food and fuel shortages in Britain. The year 1942 was a golden one for the U-boat arm of the Kriegsmarine; it was disastrous for Britain and the Navy.

The Japanese were rampant in eastern waters. In the Mediterranean, the Atlantic and Arctic the vital supply chains came under sustained attack. This was a fight to the finish for economic survival. With America and Russia now in the war the fate of Europe depended upon keeping open the sea lanes to Britain. In 1942 everything hung in the balance. The Navy was stretched to its limits. Everywhere it was under pressure and it experienced the unfamiliar taste of defeat. Even so, in its darkest hour, the country depended upon it as never before. As Churchill later said: 'The Battle of the Atlantic was the dominating factor all through the war. Never for one moment could we forget that everything happening elsewhere, on land, at sea or in the air depended ultimately on its outcome.'

CHAPTER 53

THE WESTERN APPROACHES
1942–1943

> For us, the Battle of the Atlantic was becoming a private war.
> If you were in it, you knew all about it. You knew how to keep
> watch on filthy nights and how to go without sleep; how to
> bury the dead and how to die without wasting anyone's time.
>
> *The Cruel Sea*, 1953 film

His statue captures the restless energy and continual watchfulness. His taut, lined face gazes out to sea from its position at Pier Head, Liverpool; his oversized binoculars have just been pulled down from his watchful eyes, and will be clamped back within seconds; his right hand is ready to pick up a radio and bark a terse order. His feet are poised like a boxer's.

Captain Frederic 'Johnnie' Walker's statue is far more realistic and dramatic than those of most naval heroes. He looks more like a trawlerman than an officer in George VI's Navy, with his thick jumper, body warmer, combat trousers and sturdy boots. But it was a characteristic pose as he directed the ships under his command from the wind-whipped, wave-smashed open bridge of HMS *Stork*, hunting U-boats in the vastness of the Atlantic. Indeed from the photographs it seems as though his uniform diminished Walker, extenuating his gaunt, careworn appearance. He looked ten years younger directing a 'creeping' attack on a U-boat.

Johnnie Walker was the greatest U-boat hunter of the war. He personified the skill, grit and tenacity of the Royal Navy in its moment of greatest peril.

Before 1941 Walker had been just another mediocre officer, seemingly destined to serve out his time in the Navy in some backwater. He was born in 1896 into a military family. He joined the Royal Naval College at Osborne in 1909 and entered Dartmouth in 1911, where he won the King's Medal for his term. He served on various ships in the First World War and was promoted to lieutenant in 1918. Three years later he trained at HMS *Osprey*, the Navy's anti-submarine warfare (ASW) school at Portland. He

was one of the first ASW specialists in the service and he served succes-
sively as ASW officer of the Atlantic and Mediterranean fleets.

But the interwar Navy had little interest in anti-submarine techniques
and little appreciation for Walker's passion. He was not promoted to
commander until he was thirty-five. In the Thirties he was shunted off
to the commander-in-chief's yacht in the China station. He then served
as executive officer on the battleship *Valiant*, where his captain reported
him lacking powers of leadership. Walker's career in command of ships
was over; he was seen as a prickly character and he found out in 1938
he would never be promoted to captain. He was like many, many other
officers in the Navy: perfectly competent, but destined to eke out their
days as bursars of boys' boarding schools or something similar. Between
1937 and 1940 he was back at *Osprey*, developing ASW methods. At the
beginning of the war he became Staff Officer (Operations) on the staff of
Admiral Bertram Ramsay, the commanding officer at Dover. Walker's job
was to close the Channel to U-boats while the British Expeditionary Force
was in France. He distinguished himself during the Dunkirk evacuation,
when he was mentioned in dispatches. Walker yearned to command at
sea, but his pleas were met with repeated refusals from the Admiralty. He
spent the summer of 1940 turning trawlers and drifters and their crews
into patrol vessels. These small craft would sound the first warning of an
invasion.

But then in October 1941, at the advanced age of forty-five, Commander Walker was whisked away from his desk. An old comrade had
remembered Walker's specialism in ASW and recommended him to Sir
Percy Nobel, admiral in charge of Western Approaches Command at Liverpool. He was put in charge of the 36th Escort Group (EG36), with the
little sloop HMS *Stork* as his flagship. The group consisted of two sloops
and six corvettes.

Permanent escort groups had been formed earlier in the year in response to the U-boat onslaught in the summer and autumn of 1940 –
what the U-boat commanders called the 'First Happy Time'. Between June
and October 270 allied ships were sunk. After that things became even
more scary when the U-boats began to hunt in packs. It was the brainchild of Admiral Karl Dönitz, the head of the U-boat service. Dönitz joins
a list of the most deadly enemies of the Royal Navy, standing alongside
Tromp, de Ruyter, de Tourville, de Grasse, Scheer, Hipper, Fliegerkorps X
and the Treasury.

In October the slow convoy SC7 was set upon by a wolfpack. Twenty
cargo ships were lost from the thirty-five that set sail. The escorts were

utterly unco-ordinated in the face of this kind of group attack. The next day five U-boats attacked convoy HX79 and made a mockery of the large escort. In this battle twelve merchantmen were sunk from a convoy of forty-nine. Once again the Navy floundered. From January 1940 until March 1941 the Navy sank just fifteen U-boats.

The Navy had started the war completely unprepared for this kind of attack, notwithstanding the experience of the First World War. It had relegated experts like Johnnie Walker and it did not have nearly enough destroyers or escort vessels. After the Nazi occupations of Norway, the Low Countries and France many destroyers were pulled back to defend the British coast. Churchill procured fifty aged destroyers from the United States in return for rent-free leases on British bases in Newfoundland, Bermuda and the Caribbean. Shipyards in Britain and Canada raced to build small corvettes. There were not enough available aircraft to provide protection. In any case the RAF was quick to requisition every available plane, including the few long-range land-based American B-24 Liberators that would have given the convoys some air cover. Sir Arthur 'Bomber' Harris was dismissive of the Navy's plight: 'It was a continual fight against the Navy to stop them pinching everything.' The U-boats relished the area of sea outside the range of allied aircraft – the 'Atlantic gap' – where they hunted with relative safety.

During the interwar years naval planners had faith that Asdic (sonar) technology and depth charges would remove the threat of submarine predators. But they had not lived up to expectation. Asdic worked by sending sound waves into the water; when and if it met an object it would ping – or echo – back, allowing an experienced Asdic operator to determine the range and location of the object by the frequency of the pings. The echo could come from wreckage, large fish or air bubbles as much as a U-boat; it took a skilled operator to read the deep from the pings. Asdic was suitable for calm waters and speeds of fifteen knots or slower. Its greatest flaw, however, was that depth charges were released from the stern of a ship while Asdic searched forward of the vessel. This meant that as a ship approached its target it would have to pass above the submerged submarine in order to launch the depth charge, meaning that it lost Asdic contact in the last crucial seconds. Experienced U-boat commanders simply tracked the enemy destroyer's course from the pings hitting the sub and moved at the last moment. U-boats also submerged much deeper than the British subs that the destroyers used for practice. Once one of Dönitz's boats disappeared into the Atlantic deep it was more than capable of outwitting allied destroyers.

The Royal Navy and the Royal Canadian Navy had too few ships to make inroads into the German U-boat arm. Escort vessels could at best ward off attack; they were useless at destroying U-boats. Many convoys made it through unscathed – but that had more to do with the fact that the Germans could not produce enough U-boats to sink the 700,000 tons a month they needed to reduce Britain to surrender.

The psychological effect of the Battle of the Atlantic was profound. Everyone, from Churchill down, had reason to fear the U-boats, especially because they sank more ships as the war went on, not fewer.

By the time Johnnie Walker returned to sea in late 1941 the Navy had learnt to organise escort groups. These groups were trained to combat wolfpack assault. They were better co-ordinated and led than the ad hoc escorts of earlier in the war. They were also beginning to benefit from the breaking of the Enigma code. In May the destroyer HMS *Bulldog* recovered the code books and Enigma keys from the stricken *U-110*. From the late summer of 1941 Western Approaches Command at Liverpool received accurate information about U-boat patrols from Enigma intercepts deciphered at Bletchley Park. Convoys could be rerouted to safety. The U-boat refuelling ships were located and destroyed, undermining the German attempt to extend their campaign into distant waters.

In that year Western Approaches Command took over control of Coastal Command aircraft and supplied its ships and aircraft with new radar systems. The Navy became better at deterring U-boat attacks. It did not manage to sink many, however.

On 14 December 1941 convoy HG76 with thirty-two cargo ships set sail from Gibraltar bound for Liverpool under the command of a retired vice admiral.[1] Protection was provided by a new convoy aircraft carrier, HMS *Audacity* (which had been converted from a captured German cargo ship), and by EG36, led by Commander Johnnie Walker.

It was a vital convoy and the Admiralty knew that it would come under sustained attack from bombers and U-boats, which were out in force off Iberia and in the Bay of Biscay. It was a dangerous mission. But Walker had a few things on his side. He had the benefit of air cover and one of the strongest forces yet sent to guard a convoy in the Atlantic. Walker used the aircraft to patrol the seas for U-boats and fend off the German Kondor long-range reconnaissance planes that were used to guide U-boats to their targets. He also used information sent from Bletchley Park via the Admiralty to map out the positions of the U-boat patrols. He led a team that he had trained up to fighting efficiency. Walker kept his corvettes in a ring around the cargo ships and carrier; this allowed him to detach his sloops and destroyers to hunt down the wolfpacks before they struck.

With Walker in control the Navy's ships were now hunting in packs themselves. He had outlined his plan before the mission. According to his orders, once a U-boat was located the group should illuminate the area with flares and plaster the sea with depth-charges so that the enemy would be forced to dive (U-boats preferred to escape slower allied escorts on the surface). Then the escorts would go in determined pursuit, harrying the boat until she was forced to the surface and destroyed. Walker wanted to abandon the defensive measures hitherto accepted as orthodox, and go on the offensive. He briefed the captains under his command that once a U-boat was sighted they were to attack it continuously without waiting for orders. 'I wish to impress on all officers,' he wrote in the group's Operational Instructions 'that, although I shall take charge in the majority of operations, I consider it essential for themselves to act instantly without waiting for orders in situations of which I may be unaware or imperfectly informed.'[2]

On 15 December the Australian destroyer *Nestor* sank a U-boat off Cape St Vincent. In the early hours of 17 December an aircraft spotted *U-131* stalking the convoy at a distance of twenty-two miles and waiting for a wolfpack to form. Walker went in pursuit with his sloop HMS *Stork*, taking with him three destroyers and a corvette; the rest of the group remained with the convoy. The ships swept the sea a mile apart from each other in line abreast, the Asdic operators detecting then losing their elusive quarry. The U-boat was forced to the surface eventually by a barrage of depth charges. She was just seven miles from her pursuers. Walker's pack descended on her, firing their guns; *U-131* was scuttled by her crew.

At first light next day *U-434* was spotted on the surface ten miles from the convoy. Once again the faster British ships detached from the screen defending the convoy. The destroyer *Stanley* dropped depth charges over the U-boat's diving position, preventing her from resurfacing. While this was happening *Blankney* got Asdic contact and hoisted the black flag: the signal that she was going in to attack. In doing so she lost Asdic contact, but dropped five depth charges in a pattern. She then regained Asdic contact and guided *Stanley* into position. *Stanley* dropped her depth charges and returned the baton to *Blankney*, which dropped more explosives into the water. *U-434* was forced to surface a mile ahead of the British destroyers. As she did so she keeled over in the water. The British ships moved up in the oily waters to pick up survivors.

When *U-574* was forced to the surface she was in no mood to surrender or scuttle. Walker's sloop raced in to attack; *U-574* turned sharply to port, which she continued to do as HMS *Stork* wheeled round and round at top speed. So close were the opposing vessels that *Stork*'s 4-inch guns could not be depressed far enough to target the sub and the gun crews were reduced to cursing and shaking fists at the U-boat, which was a few feet under their noses. Eventually Walker sent *U-574* to the seabed by good old-fashioned means: he rammed her.

Dönitz had lost four U-boats from his pack of seven. But during that night U-boats sank HMS *Stanley*. In panic the merchantmen fired 'snow-flake' rockets, which lit up the entire scene like a fireworks display. It gave a U-boat the chance to sink one of the cargo ships. Two British destroyers then had to turn back for Gibraltar to refuel. Walker's *Stork* had lost her Asdic when she rammed *U-574*, rendering her blind. To make matters worse Dönitz unleashed more wolves to stalk the convoy.

Around the British ships lurked unseen and uncounted U-boats, waiting and watching for a moment to strike. On the night of the 21st Walker attempted a ruse. While the convoy went one way he would take his fast escorts another and stage a mock battle; it would draw off the wolves, which would wrongly believe that one of their own had tasted blood. Unfortunately the sailors on the merchantmen had not been let in on the plan; they were spooked by the dread sounds of battle and fired off their snowflakes. In the bright light a U-boat got a clear aim and torpedoed a merchantman. Later that night the captain of HMS *Audacity* decided to take the carrier out of the convoy and beyond Walker's defensive screen. The lone carrier was set upon and sunk.

Meanwhile Walker's ships kept the wolfpack at bay, tormenting them with depth charges. In the attack *U-567*, the boat captained by the U-boat ace Engelbert Endrass, was sunk. In the mayhem, however, HMS *Deptford* collided with *Stork*. Now both ships were without Asdic and there was no air cover. The morning of 22 December was not a happy one. The convoy battle had raged for almost a week. No one had got much sleep. The strains of such an operation put a toll on all the men. Up on the bridge men scanned the seas for signs of U-boats.

Just when it seemed as if it had all been in vain, a Liberator plane was spotted flying in to protect the convoy on its final leg. At last the U-boat wolfpack gave up. The convoy reached Liverpool with the loss of two merchantmen, a destroyer and the improvised carrier – losses made up for by the sinking of five U-boats. The vice admiral signalled Walker as the convoy approached Liverpool: 'You have won a great victory.'[3]

Walker returned to Western Approaches Command to a rapturous welcome; he was awarded a DSO. The convoy battle was highly significant.

For the first time the U-boats encountered stiff and organised resistance. Walker used air power in conjunction with a dynamic support group to hold off several fearsome U-boat packs. The Germans were shocked. Five boats were a damaging loss.

Most importantly, Walker had taught the Navy how to resist. He had developed a methodical way of protecting a convoy and inflicting harm on the Navy's tormentors. He advised the Admiralty that aircraft were invaluable for ASW; that convoys should be protected by an inner and outer screen, one for defence the other for attacks; and that during daylight *all* escorts should be 'used as striking forces for offensive lunges' at U-boats detected as far as thirty miles from the convoy.[4] But Walker met resistance and suspicion; his ideas were too radical.

In the first months of 1942 Walker protected several convoys. None of them was attacked and no more U-boats were sunk. In April his force was reduced to his flagship *Stork* and four corvettes. There had been little U-boat activity in the western Atlantic: most German submarines were enjoying their 'happy time' in American waters where juicy cargo ships and tankers went unprotected. EG36's task was to escort sixteen ships to Gibraltar.[5] This job gets us closer to Walker's evolving methods.

On 14 April at 21.30 Walker received intelligence from the Admiralty that there was a U-boat nearby. *Stork* was behind the convoy; the corvette *Vetch* was sweeping the seas ahead. Shortly after receipt of the report *Vetch* picked up activity on her radar, suggesting that something was between her and the convoy. The little corvette turned back and fired starshell into the night sky to illuminate the waters. The men saw what they had suspected: a U-boat heading into the convoy. It fired two torpedoes, which narrowly missed *Vetch*, and dived. Twenty minutes later the boat surfaced; *Vetch* caught her in her spotlight and charged towards the German sub, firing furiously with her 4-inch guns. *Stork* did likewise. At 22.39 the U-boat was forced to dive.

Three minutes later *Vetch* dropped depth charges. Between 22.42 and 23.11 *Vetch* and *Stork* between them dropped fifty depth charges in five alternating attacks. The Asdic and hydrophone crews and the depth-charge crews had to carefully co-ordinate with each other to make the onslaught tell. The crews in charge of the highly specialised equipment had to listen and interpret the echoes that pinged back. These men learnt how to read the inky blackness of the deep.

After the last attack Petty Officer Darby Kelly, who'd had earphones clamped to his ears throughout, reported to Walker that the Asdic echo suggested wreckage. 'I was tolerably certain that the Boche had been poleaxed,' reported Walker, 'as indeed it had. Wreckage boiled to the surface and in high delight I lowered a boat to investigate.'[6]

The beaten quarry was *U-252*. Her sinking had an impact on Dönitz. He believed that the Navy had discovered a new way of hunting down his subs and forbade U-boats to attack convoys in the Western Approaches. They were to head straight for American waters. In June, however, they were back. The target was convoys bound for Gibraltar, where the allies were building up their strength again for an assault in the Mediterranean. In June Walker's EG36 was put in charge of escorting convoy HG84 home from Gibraltar.[7] There were twenty-three merchantmen in the convoy. Walker had *Stork* and just three corvettes. He was facing a pack of nine U-boats.*

During the voyage *U-552* sank five merchantmen. Walker did not destroy a single U-boat. But once again raw figures are deceptive. During the passage of HG84 Walker kept his tiny escorting group constantly at work. The four British ships spent days and nights hunting the U-boats and keeping them away. Of the nine-strong wolfpack seven U-boats never managed to get close enough to the convoy to open fire. Walker worked his men and ships to the limits, knowing all the while that he was surrounded by a ravening pack that far outnumbered his little group. He prevented an all-out slaughter of the convoy by keeping up the pressure on the U-boats at all times. Walker was unlucky that the commander of *U-552*, Erich Topp, was the third most successful U-boat *Experte* (ace). He sank thirty-four ships totalling 185,434 tons during the war; five of that tally came against HG84. The other U-boats were driven off by Walker. Dönitz was shocked at the energy and success of EG36. Once again U-boats were ordered to keep themselves submerged in the Western Approaches. It was a significant victory.

The war against the U-boats would never be easy or simple. During the Battle of the Atlantic both sides developed new tactics in response to each other. The fortunes of both sides ebbed and flowed. But before December 1941 the direction had been all one way. Walker's convoy battle of HG76 marked a turning point in the campaign: it was the first time the allies could claim a victory.

Walker's escort group had sunk five U-boats in the Western Approaches in a few months. It saved many ships and their crews. The success rate was testament to Walker's power of leadership – something he had been told

---

* The wolfpack was codenamed 'Endrass' by the U-boat command, in honour of Engelbert Endrass, who had been killed in action with Walker's group.

he did not have. Johnnie Walker took a group of boys and welded them together into an elite unit. Like all great leaders in the Navy's history he established strong relationships with his crews, the overwhelming majority of whom were very raw recruits to the RNVR rather than hardened Navy personnel. Through long periods of drill, group manoeuvres and anti-submarine exercises he communicated to his men his ideas about hunting U-boats – ideas he had been working on since he was as young as the crews he was now commanding.

In the moment of attack there was no time to give orders or waste precious seconds with signals*. 'It should seldom, if ever, be necessary to conclude a signalled report with the words: "Request instruction",' stated Walker's standing orders.[8] A successful kill could happen only if each captain knew exactly where he should be. Like Hawke or Nelson, Walker knew that the battle was won long before it took place. Hunting down and killing a U-boat in the dead of night required patience, cunning and excellent seamanship. Everyone on board had to know his duty when the moment came. Walker's first great success – when he destroyed four U-boats in December 1941 – was marred by confusion in the dark of night. The vanquishing of *U-252* was a more clinical operation. His most recent achievement in sparing convoy HG84 from out-and-out carnage was a triumph of organisation and leadership.

An anti-submarine commander had to think like an individual but act in concert with a group, for hunting down a submarine was a team effort. In the battle of convoy HG84 Walker had deployed the rudiments of what he called a 'creeping attack'.[9] This involved two or more ships and it overcame the problem whereby an attacking ship lost Asdic contact with the enemy at the crucial moment of attack. During a creeping attack Walker would position his ship in optimal Asdic range – 1,000–2,000 yards away from the submerged U-boat. His star Asdic operator – Darby Kelly – would keep the U-boat under observation. Meanwhile a second ship would cut its speed and turn off its Asdic system. Walker would direct the attacking ship into place. She would 'creep' in slowly so that the U-boat hydrophone operators would have no idea she was there and the commander would not resort to evasive tactics before hell was unleashed from above. Once the attacking ship had dropped twenty-six depth charges in a pattern, Walker's ship would speed in and drop another twenty-two depth charges primed to explode at a variety of depths in an

* During the attack on *U-252* Walker exchanged eight signals with *Vetch*, totalling twenty-five words.

'E' pattern over the last point of contact with the U-boat.

That might sound simple enough. But it took practice and training to work. Walker spent long days simulating group attacks on U-boats. The skippers of the ships in the Escort Group had to know Walker's intentions and have the confidence to implement them in the heat of combat with only minimal direction. It tested seamanship to the limit. The commanding officers of the squadron and the crews they led had to develop mutual understanding and an instinctive bond with each other. There could be no faff or discussion when one was hunting in the dead of night. Walker's authoritative manner and single-minded dedication to killing U-boats inspired the twenty-something-year-olds under his command to push themselves to the utmost. 'No officer will ever be blamed by me for getting on with the job in hand,' read one of Walker's instructions.

Most escorting ships acted under orders which stated that their primary role was to get ships safely to their destination. Walker put the emphasis squarely on sinking the enemy. He lived for the thrill of the chase and his single-minded dedication left a deep impression on his men. 'He made it very clear that our task was to destroy U-boats,' wrote his gunnery officer, Alan Burn, 'and all that we did from then onwards was directed to this end.'[10] Walker had one supreme doctrine: 'Hit them as quickly and as often as possible before they had time to think and work out evasive action.'[11]

Walker's men fell under his spell. A young midshipman recalled a quiet man who nonetheless had a 'tremendous presence through his sheer commitment, professionalism and devotion to the task ... One knew he was in total control, with a sure grasp of tactics, strategy and the minutiae of the operation. Everyone knew what was expected of them – and dreaded letting him down by not doing it.'[12] He trusted the men under his command – and they gave everything to live up to his trust. Walker gave credit to those officers and men who had played a conspicuous effort; he took all the blame upon himself when things went wrong. When Sir Percy Noble, C-in-C of Western Approaches Command, visited Walker's flagship he reported: 'That crowd in *Stork* are an amazingly efficient team. They can run and fight their ship blindfold. And every one of them adores Walker. I could see they would follow him without question anywhere he chose to lead.'[13]

Walker was obsessive in his task. He hunted U-boats with passion and the highest degree of skill. He analysed as many pursuits of U-boats as he could – the rare successes and the many frustrations – to learn the myriad tricks U-boat commanders used to get out of trouble. Few other men developed so sharp a sixth sense for the whereabouts and wiles of German subs as Walker did. Few others enjoyed the cat-and-mouse game of U-boat hunting as much as him; it was like a sport, played for survival. The German submariners represented, for him, the greatest danger to his country; he despised them. All that passion and single-mindedness communicated itself to his men. Peter Eustace, a nineteen-year-old radio operator who served under Walker, remembered the sheer elation of sinking a U-boat: 'We had the feeling we were almost invincible.'[14]

Above all Walker owed his success as a leader to the fact that he had reconnected his men with the historic strengths of the Royal Navy. All officers and ratings in the service longed to live up to the example set by generations of British seafarers going back to the days of Drake and Hawkins and beyond. Not many sailors had the chance to test their seamanship or take on the enemy face to face in protracted battles of wits. That kind of naval combat seemed to belong to another age. In the twentieth century sailors no longer fought when they saw the whites of their opponents' eyes; fighting took place beyond the horizon (as at Jutland) or against swooping Stuka bombers. This was naval warfare in all its rawness and immediacy, very different to the classical age of sail but close enough in its essentials. Walker revived one naval tradition: after a kill he gave the signal 'splice the mainbrace', an order for every man to receive an extra tot of rum.

Walker was promoted to captain (d)* in June 1942. In October, to his great frustration, he was pulled back on shore to work at Western Approaches Command.

He had not invented the concept of support groups, nor was he the first to hunt down and kill U-boats. But Walker took those things to a new level. Morale in the U-boat arm began to sink. Thanks to officers like him confidence in the Navy's power to hit back at the enemy was restored.

And the Navy had lost none of its resolve. In August it hurled a crucial convoy through the Mediterranean to beleaguered Malta in Operation Pedestal. The fourteen merchant ships were escorted by two battleships, seven cruisers, twenty-four destroyers and three fleet aircraft carriers. It was a measure of how dangerous the Mediterranean had become that only five merchantmen got through and one carrier and two cruisers were sunk. It was a price worth paying. Malta survived to defy the Axis. The Navy's ability to fight back against the odds was in no doubt. The massive effort to resupply the island in the teeth of relentless attacks from U-boats

---

* Captain (d) means a captain in charge of a flotilla of destroyers.

British aircraft carriers in line ahead: HMSs *Indomitable* and *Eagle* seen from HMS *Victorious* taking part in Operation Pedestal, August 1942.

and the Luftwaffe in the end paid dividends. Thanks to Pedestal the British were able to resume attacks on Axis supply lines to Africa. In September Rommel was left short of fuel in the crucial moment in the campaign.

A month later the tide of the war turned when Rommel was defeated at the Battle of El Alamein. The retreat of the Axis armies meant the withdrawal of Luftwaffe bases on the North African coast. It opened the way for Operation Stoneage, the last opposed convoy to Malta, in November. Force K was able to return to Malta as a result and recommence raids on Axis shipping. In the same month 160 British warships landed over 100,000 troops in Morocco and Algeria. It was the first of the great amphibious landings of the war. Meanwhile the Arctic convoys resumed in September. Now they were protected by a British aircraft carrier. In December allied ships drove off a concerted attack by German surface ships in the Battle of the Barents Sea. It was a major blow to the Kriegsmarine. Hitler lost faith in his navy and Erich Raeder, supreme commander of the Kriegsmarine, resigned. He was replaced by the fearsome Karl Dönitz.

The situation at the beginning of 1943 was a good deal more encouraging than the bleak despondency twelve months before. The exception was in the Atlantic, where U-boat numbers were rising, and with them losses to allied shipping. There were so many U-boats in the Atlantic that convoys could no longer count on evading the German submarines in the open seas. Britain's fuel supplies were running dangerously low. There was talk of abandoning convoys altogether. The Battle of the Atlantic was reaching its climax.

CHAPTER 54

METHODICAL ELIMINATION
1943–1944

> Sink, burn, destroy. Let nothing past.
>
> Admiral Andrew Cunningham

HMS *Campbeltown* signalled to the shore batteries that she was a friendly ship. Twice the guns opened fire, and twice *Campbeltown* silenced them with her reassuring signals. When the aged British destroyer was 2,000 yards from the harbour the shore batteries began firing in earnest.

Campbeltown was not approaching a friendly port. She was heading directly for the gates of the gigantic dry dock at St Nazaire, in the Loire estuary in France. It was one o'clock in the morning of 28 March 1942. The ship faced a blizzard of shells and bullets in her suicidal charge at the gates. The helmsman was killed and his replacement seriously wounded as the ship was peppered by everything the defending forces could throw at her.

The destroyer was carrying commandos. Her bow was packed with 4.5 tons of high explosives encased in concrete. Lieutenant-commander Stephen Beattie took his ship on through the storm of shells and bullets, blinded by the glare of searchlights. At the crucial moment he spotted that his ship was heading for the wrong part of the harbour. Beattie displayed magnificent seamanship and cool-headedness as he swerved out of the way of the harbour jetties and located his target. All the while the enemy fire was becoming more intense as he sailed into the maelstrom. At 01.34 he rammed *Campbeltown* into the dock gates. The old destroyer crashed thirty-three feet over the great gates. Beattie turned to the men on the bridge and said: 'Well there you are, four minutes late' – words in the Navy's high laconic tradition.

The commando raiding parties disembarked. *Campbeltown* was scuttled by her crew. The commandos smashed up the working parts of the dock – the pumping and winding houses in particular. The next day *Campbeltown* detonated. The dry dock was destroyed and put out of action for a decade. It was the 'greatest raid of the war', and the most spectacular in the long line of amphibious landings conducted by the Royal Navy and the army. Five VCs were awarded. Naval officers got three of them – Beattie, Commander Robert Ryder, who risked his life evacuating commandos, and Able Seaman William Savage, killed while firing the forward 2-pounder on the last motor gunboat to withdraw.

The dry dock had been intended for the immense German battleship *Tirpitz* so that she could join the U-boats and decimate allied shipping in the Atlantic from the west coast of France. It was a triumph won at enormous cost. Only 228 men got back home; 168 men died (of whom 105 were from the Navy) and 215 were captured (109 commandos and 106 sailors). Many of the motor launches that were supposed to ferry the commandos and crew of *Campbeltown* back to the destroyers were sunk.

The raid on St Nazaire – Operation Chariot – took place in March 1942. On 7 December an equally stunning raid took place. The sub HMS *Tuna* surfaced outside the mouth of the Gironde estuary. Under the cover of a dark winter's evening five Cockle Mk II canoes were disembarked. Ten marines climbed aboard them and began their seventy-mile journey to the port of Bordeaux. They had to steal past thirty-two German ships before they reached their destination.

Operation Frankton was the brainchild of Major Herbert 'Blondie' Hasler, who was leading ten marines from his Royal Marine Boom Patrol Detachment. Their target was twelve merchant ships, moored in the safety of Bordeaux harbour. The audacious attempt met immediate difficulties. One canoe disappeared in the strong tides and winds that night. Another capsized soon after. The remaining three paddled on, covering between nine and twenty-two miles a night for the next four nights. Two marines were captured as they lay low during the day near Pointe de Grave.

That left Hasler and three other marines in two canoes to carry out one of the most heroic raids in naval history. On the night of 11/12 December they paddled among the German ships and placed limpet mines on six ships. The four marines sank their canoes and began their overland escape to Spain.

Of the ten marines who set out from *Tuna*, two died of hypothermia and six were captured and executed by the Germans. Major Hasler and Marine Bill Sparks made it to Spain and returned home. All these men went down in history as among the greatest heroes of the war. Their bravery has been deservedly commemorated in France and Britain.

These two extraordinary operations were among a series of almost sixty raids on the Atlantic Wall between 1940 and 1944. The examples cited here had clear naval objectives. Both were intended to remind the enemy of Britain's overlordship of the Western Approaches. Operation Chariot aimed to prevent German battleships inflicting carnage on shipping in the Atlantic. The destruction of the dry dock at St Nazaire was essential to maintain the blockade of the Kriegsmarine. Operation Frankton was launched to enforce the economic blockade of Germany by whatever means possible.

The twelve ships targeted by Hasler and his marines were blockade runners. They had brought in cargoes of high industrial–military value sent by the Japanese from East Asia. By December 1942 some fifteen small ships had broken through the Navy's wall of steel. Operation Frankton was intended to show that the Navy would stop at nothing in sealing Germany off from the world. The service did not always need mighty ships or aircraft carriers to enforce its will. Sometimes canoes and determined men were enough.

It went to show how fiercely the economic war was being fought. On the German side the effort to strangle Britain into submission was reaching its climax.

'The Germans never came so near to disrupting communications between the New World and the Old as in the first twenty days of March 1943,' stated a report for the Navy. U-boats sank 120 ships in that month. The Navy came close to abandoning convoys completely in the face of 240 operational U-boats. Things in Britain were dire. There were food and fuel shortages. If the U-boats kept it up the build-up for D-Day would take years. Britain might even be forced out of the war.

In 'Black May', however, forty-three U-boats were destroyed and just fifty-eight allied ships were sunk.

The numbers of U-boats might have soared, but the Navy had become much stronger as well. There were more escort vessels and destroyers at sea. And they were armed with new weapons. The Hedgehog was a forward-firing contact mortar. Because it was projected forward it allowed the ship to retain Asdic contact with the U-boat throughout the attack. More escort vessels were fitted with high-frequency direction-finding (HF/DF, or 'Huff-Duff') equipment, which allowed them to triangulate the positions of U-boat patrols based on their radio transmissions.

Most importantly the Atlantic gap was closed by late spring 1943. Long-range aircraft and escort carriers entered service to provide air cover for the entire routes of convoys. These planes were equipped with their own radar systems and the Leigh Light, a spotlight that was linked to the radar. And, most vital of all, Alan Turing had broken

TRITON, allowing Bletchley Park to decrypt Enigma again.

In May the U-boats encountered an allied defensive network that knitted together air power, convoy escorts and new support groups. In November 1942 Admiral Sir Max Horton took over Western Approaches Command. Horton was a former submarine commander and he was receptive to innovative ideas. He was particularly impressed by new plans proposed by Captain Johnnie Walker.

Horton was similar to Walker in a number of ways. In his submarine days in the First World War Horton instituted the tradition whereby a British submarine returning to its home base after a kill flew the Jolly Roger. Walker liked to play 'A Hunting We Will Go' over his ship's tannoy when it came into Liverpool after a successful hunt. Walker suggested to his new chief the idea of sending to sea numbers of support groups. These elite striking forces would act like a kind of maritime cavalry, swooping down upon and destroying U-boats. It was based on Walker's methods at SG36 and the conviction that ships of the Royal Navy should seek and destroy the enemy rather than cling to the fringes of convoys. Horton took up the proposal and Walker went back to sea in command of the Second Support Group (2SG) in 1943, which comprised his flagship HMS *Starling* and six other sloops of war, all named after birds.

The Navy had plenty of new tricks up its sleeve. Walker was its pioneer.

On 1 June 1943 at 09.30 the Huff-Duff operator on *Starling* reported a U-boat transmission twenty miles away. The alarms sounded on Walker's ships and *U-202* was located.[1] Her commander, Gunter Poser, ordered his boat to dive to 500 feet. He was relaxed about the whole thing. On this patrol alone he had been attacked six times by convoy escorts.

Walker's six sloops began a co-ordinated attack. Beneath the waves Poser ducked and weaved, deploying every trick to evade the patterns of depth charges. The group lost Asdic contact, then located the U-boat again. Walker fell into deep conversation with his hydrophone and Asdic operators, his trusted colleagues of old. 'There was something uncanny in the conversation of these three specialists as they worked out their plans of attack from the front of the open bridge,'[2] remembered Walker's gunnery officer (and later biographer) Alan Burn.

The next attack was known by Walker's men as the 'boss's special'; it was more properly called a 'barrage attack'.[3] This was an assault by three ships in line abreast, each dropping depth charges at five-second intervals so that the U-boat could have no chance of dodging to left or right.

But still *U-202* survived.

Walker then directed a creeping attack, using two sloops simulanteously.

This continued through the day. It was a contest between two masters. Walker paced the bridge as night fell. His adversary was a wily operator. And more to the point, it was clear that U-boats could dive deeper than the range of depth charges. Poser had taken his boat down to 820 feet, to the consternation of his men who feared that the vessel would buckle under the pressure at any moment. Poser kept his cool and ordered his men to use up as little energy as possible; he set a good example by reading in his bunk as depth charges churned the sea above and Asdic pulses pinged off his boat. Meanwhile Walker kept *U-202* in Asdic contact and grew frustrated that his attacks were not paying off; he could have no idea that Poser had dived to such a depth. He played various games to force his adversary to use up his batteries. He simulated attacks to try and make the U-boat change position. He ordered one sloop to drop depth charges further away to give the impression that the group was heading off on a false trail. Poser had his own tricks. The submarine ejected a canister which released a stream of hydrogen bubbles: these Submarine Target Bubbles acted as a sonar decoy. Walker had to keep contact with Poser and wait until he ran out of air and surfaced under the cover of darkness to dash away in the dark. It came down to a battle of cunning and patience; the odds were on Poser slithering away.

But Walker's Asdic operators were not fooled by the bubbles and kept contact with Poser's boat all the while. Walker's analysis of U-boat activity paid off again; he predicted that his quarry would have to surface at midnight at the latest. Sure enough, at 00.02 the eagle-eyed signalman on *Starling* spotted *U-202* on the surface. The sky was lit up by starshell and every ship in the group began firing. Walker ordered *Starling* to try to ram, but then changed his mind. He ordered shallow depth charges to be hurled at the boat instead. That finished off *U-202*. Poser had resisted well during a fourteen-hour hunt. Walker commented laconically: 'I am most grateful to *Kapitänleutnant* Poser for an excellent bit of group training.'[4] Admiral Horton was more fulsome: 'I wish to congratulate your Asdic team on the most outstanding performance of the war.'[5]

That was an exaggeration, of course. But the excited praise highlights the fact that Walker's tactics and training were paying off and having a decisive effect on the Battle of the Atlantic. U-boats were no longer fended off and allowed to escape; they were ruthlessly hunted down and destroyed. In June the Navy went on the attack. Two support groups and aircraft from Coastal Command would dedicate themselves to U-boats coming to and from their bases in the Bay of Biscay.

In other words the enemy were to be blockaded in their ports on the western seaboard of France. Walker was joining such illustrious names as Hawke, St Vincent and Cornwallis in the ages-old task of making the Western Approaches British. The fate of the country depended, now as always, on mastering these waters. Walker told his group: 'The Boche ... must be made to realise that the Royal Navy considers the Bay of Biscay a happy hunting ground and will stamp out any attempt to restrict the free and rightful passage of Allied shipping. When we meet him we will destroy him.'[6]

On 24 June Walker caught *U-119* unawares, forced her to the surface and rammed her. It was straight out of the U-boat hunter's textbook. *Starling* was damaged in the attack, and she became a sitting target for another U-boat out for revenge. Walker transferred to *Wild Goose* to resume command over his group. From there he directed another stunning creeping attack, which outwitted and destroyed *U-449*. On 30 July 2SG and planes from Coastal Command working in conjunction with Walker's group sank *U-454*, *U-461*, *U-462* and *U-504*. In the hunt for the latter Walker developed yet another technique. He called it 'holding the ring',[7] this one a pugilistic term. Three sloops were positioned around the search area, while the enemy sub was held in Asdic contact. Walker then guided in another sloop to a creeping attack. If the U-boat tried to sneak out of the kill zone she would meet one of the other three sloops. It was emblematic of the new ruthless spirit in the Battle of the Atlantic – what Alan Burn called 'methodical elimination'.[8] On 2 August Dönitz suspended sailings from Biscayan ports.

The allies were winning the Battle of the Atlantic. For the first time the Germans were losing more U-boats than they would replace. The British now had hunting patrols in the Bay of Biscay and the U-boats had to cling to the French and Spanish coasts before dashing out into the Atlantic. It was the result, like all great naval victories, of a long hard slog conducted by determined men such as Johnnie Walker.

Elsewhere news was equally encouraging for the allies. In April the Italians lost 100 merchant ships that were trying to resupply the Axis armies in North Africa. In May Admiral Cunningham launched the appropriately named Operation Retribution with the terse order: 'Sink, burn and destroy: Let nothing pass.' The Axis army was trapped in North Africa.

Now the Royal Navy was the dominant force in the Mediterranean again. In July six British battleships and two aircraft carriers, along with the US Eighth Fleet, supported the allied invasion of Sicily and then Italy. The entire Italian fleet surrendered at Malta. It was a satisfying moment of long-delayed revenge. Up in the frozen Arctic convoys had been suspended for the summer because the Navy was simply too overstretched to meet all its commitments. But they resumed in November. On Boxing Day the Kriegsmarine Battle Group I, led by *Scharnhorst*, left its Norwegian base to attack the outward-bound Convoy JW55B and the homeward-bound RA55A. The German battleship was on her own. The mighty *Tirpitz* had been knocked out of action in September. Six British X-class midget submarines had crept into Kafjord and caused great damage to the battleship. It was another of the legendary raids conducted by the Navy.

Dönitz was desperate. It was the last throw of the dice. The enemy of the Kriegsmarine, in this case, was Adolf Hitler who had finally lost patience with his surface fleet and was threatening to abolish it. The Kriegsmarine needed one great victory to win back the faith of the Führer.

Instead the detached *Scharnhorst* encountered the Navy's escorting force, comprising the battleship HMS *Duke of York*, a heavy cruiser, three light cruisers and nine destroyers. The first hit on the German battleship put her radar out of action. From then on *Scharnhorst* was fighting blind in a snowstorm. She fought on bravely for the rest of the day, but the British had her in radar contact throughout. '*Scharnhorst* sunk,' Admiral Bruce Fraser signalled to the Admiralty in the evening. 'Grand, well done,' came the reply.

'Gentlemen,' Fraser told his officers, 'the battle against *Scharnhorst* has ended in victory for us. I hope that if any of you are ever called upon to lead a ship into action against an opponent many times superior, you will command your ship as gallantly as *Scharnhorst* was commanded today.' The sinking ended the threat the Kriegsmarine posed the Royal Navy in the Arctic.* The Battle of the North Cape was also the very last time in the Royal Navy's history that a British battleship engaged an enemy battleship.

Back in the Atlantic the convoys and support groups were tussling with the winter seas. 'The little ships battened down, battling continually with the great rolling walls of green seas. Salt spray whipped across the decks and the bridge in cutting, stinging sheets.'[9] Walker's 2SG worked with an escort carrier, HMS *Tracker*, far out in the mid-Atlantic, where the U-boats were working now that the Western Approaches were a danger zone for them. Through the long days and nights of storms the U-boats remained submerged. In a respite from the bad weather, on 6 November 2SG hunted down and sank another two U-boats. The little sloops could

---

* *Tirpitz* was subjected to numerous bombing raids by the RAF. She was finished off on 12 November 1944.

not withstand these kinds of gales for long. The group went first to New-foundland and then back to Liverpool for much-needed repairs and rest.

Walker and his group, along with two escort carriers headed to the area of the Atlantic south-west of Ireland. Dönitz had ordered his U-boats there, so that they could benefit from cover provided by the Luftwaffe. The Second Support group had to protect the convoys and carriers from both air and submarine attack; it also had to hunt for U-boats. On 31 January Walker sent *U-592* to the briny bottom. The U-boats then tried to move south-west to avoid Walker's obsessive attentions. On the night of Febuary 8/9 the group sank U-boats *238*, *734* and *762* in a succession of creeping attacks over the course of eight hours. Two days later 2SG re-corded its fifth success with the sinking of *U-424*. On 19 February Walker fought a long duel with the German U-boat commander Hartwig Looks. It took ten hours to raise Looks's *U-264*.

The 25-year-old commander took every evasive action he could, but the explosions of 200 depth charges battered his boat beyond repair. The crew were ankle-deep in water and a fire broke out in the engine room. Looks ordered his boat to the surface. There he found himself in the middle of a ring of Walker's sloops. The submariners jumped ship. Looks found himself being hauled out of the sea by a British tar, with the words 'Come on, sailor!'[10] He was taken on board HMS *Woodpecker* where an of-ficer looked at him and said with the appreciation of a connoisseur: 'That was a very, very clever fight.'

When the Second Support Group entered Liverpool harbour it was led into Gladstone Dock by *Starling*, 'A Hunting We Will Go' blaring out of her loudspeakers. Alongside the dock and on the flight deck of the car-rier HMS *Victorious* were hundreds of people and two bands to welcome home Johnnie Walker and his men from the most successful of all anti-submarine patrols. Also present were Admiral Horton and the First Lord of the Admiralty. The First Lord gave a speech in which he proclaimed 'one of the greatest cruises – the greatest cruise perhaps – ever undertaken in this war by an escort group'.[11] He hailed Walker as 'our leading submarine ace'. Churchill and the War Cabinet's congratulations had reached the group as they neared home. Walker had sunk eighteen U-boats in the war; more important than the numbers was the effect it had on demoralising the U-boat crews and altering Dönitz's tactics. As a reward his promo-tion to captain was backdated, which meant that he was now in line to become an admiral. He had three DSOs and he was a Companion of the Order of the Bath. He was now a much-photographed national figure. The Western Approaches belonged to the Royal Navy once more.

Walker in HMS *Starling* using VHF inter-ship radio to direct HMS *Woodpecker* during a creeping attack.

Most prominent among the crowds welcoming home 2SG were hundreds of Wrens – officers and ratings of the Women's Royal Naval Service (WRNS). There were 1,000 men in 2SG; many had wives and girlfriends (and in Walker's case a daughter) in the WRNS at Liverpool, who waited anxiously for their return from patrol. And it was thanks to these women that Walker's group could get to sea at all. Wrens kept the Navy going, performing vital onshore work as mechanics and weapons specialists, as electricians, clerks and cooks. At Western Approaches Command they did vital work plotting the course of wolfpacks. They were the backbone of Britain's naval effort in the war. Of the 863,500 people in naval uniform in 1944, 72,000 were Wrens. They were a welcome sight when 2SG returned home.

Walker had become a celebrity. It did not suit his temperament. 'Isn't it funny?' he said to his wife after the rapturous welcome home. 'All this fuss and ceremony and I'm still just the same old Johnnie they didn't think it worthwhile to promote.'[12]

In March the elite group sank *U-653*. Later in the month Walker took his group northwards on an Arctic convoy, during which they sank *U-961*. In May he was back in his stamping ground, the Western Approaches, hunting for *U-473*, which had torpedoed USS *Donnell*. It might have been like looking for a needle in a haystack, had it not been for information from Ultra. On 15 May *Starling* located the U-boat and raised the black flag. It was to be Walker's last hunt.

It took fifteen hours – the longest of Walker's epic battles. The captain tried all of his well-honed tactics. He took delight in the performance of his team. He did not issue one signal or order until the U-boat was destroyed on the surface: 'Cease firing. Gosh what a lovely battle.'[13]

The campaign in the Atlantic was almost over. Walker had one last assignment to fulfil before he was posted to the Pacific as an admiral.

Walker and the group went to the coast of Wales and joined an immense armada of all the ships in the Western Approaches Command – some 200 in all. On the night of 5/6 June this mass of shipping moved out to sea to take part in their most vital task. They formed a screen cutting off the English Channel from the Western Approaches.

These 200 anti-submarine ships were a fraction of the 5,000 vessels deployed in the greatest amphibious landing in history, Operation Neptune – D-Day.

There were no submarine attacks on D-Day. Back in February when Walker attacked *U-264* its commander, Hartwig Looks, had scuttled his boat. He was testing a new piece of kit that he did not want Walker to see. It was a submarine snorkel, a breathing pipe. The snorkel did not just allow the crew to breath indefinitely under water. When a submarine dived it switched power from its diesel engines – which needed air to operate – to electrical power. The batteries only lasted so long; the U-boat had to surface to recharge them. The snorkel therefore allowed U-boats to creep into the Channel undetected by radar and lurk for long periods in shallow waters on the English or French coasts without needing to surface. They could then maraud among the amphibious landing craft destined for Normandy. But the seasoned anti-submarine units pulled an iron chain accross the Channel approach. No U-boats could pass through.

The Royal Navy played a leading role in securing the seas and bombarding enemy positions on the beaches. It was a triumph of military organisation. Credit for that should go to the outstanding admiral of the war, Walker's old boss Admiral Sir Bertram Ramsay. Ramsay had organised the evacuation from Dunkirk in 1940 and the invasion of Italy in 1943. Operation Neptune was his masterpiece. It involved synchronising thousands of ships, from the midget submarines that provided navigation beacons to the big battleships, monitors and cruisers that pounded the shore defences. It also meant careful co-ordination with the armies waiting for embarkation in England and the air forces. In all 113,000 officers, men and women from the Royal Navy took part, 58 per cent of the total naval personnel employed by the allies on D-Day. Neptune required 2,807 warships of all kinds. Covering the western sector of the landing (the American beaches – Utah and Omaha) were 324 warships, of which almost 50 per cent belonged to the Royal Navy. In the eastern sector (the British and Canadian beaches – Gold, Juno and Sword) 306 warships out of 348 were from the Navy. Added to that were 893 Navy landing ships in the east and 147 (out of 644) in the west. It was the biggest armada in history.

Ramsay was smart enough to know that in a combined operation the needs of the army must dictate to the Navy. He knew from the landings at Sicily that the amphibious assault was just the beginning, not the end, of the operation. Once the beachhead was secure the Navy had to work even harder to build up ground forces and supply them in the coming days, weeks and months. Admiral Ramsay had to negotiate a minefield of vested interests and colossal, fragile egos. He had the tact and capacity to organise Operation Neptune. Most importantly he ensured that the armies' supply lines were kept open for the next year.

The long-contested sovereignty of the seas paid off after years of sacrifice and effort. The Kriegsmarine surface fleet was a dead letter. The U-boat arm had been muzzled after the most gruelling naval campaign in history. The masses of troops landed on the beaches were given safe passage to their destination. The devastating artillery from the warships caused serious damage to German defensive positions and prevented the free movement of tanks.

D-Day was the high point of the Royal Navy. It had toughed out the war and it was able to contribute to the endgame in Europe.

Victory came at a steep price. During the war the Navy lost 1,525 vessels and 50,000 men and women. The bedrock of British naval strength – the merchant marine – was badly burned. It lost 30,000 sailors and 2,400 ships.

The invasion of Normandy had been made possible because the allies had been able to keep the sea lanes open. All the while, Germany had been starved of imports. The blockade had not defeated Germany, but it had weakened her, while Britain remained strong. The Battle of the Atlantic had been won by the allies. It was a crucial victory – the most important in the long history of the Royal Navy.

There was no decisive moment of victory. There was no turning point. It was a long, hard slog – a triumph of patience and grim determination. The allies had been able to build more ships than the U-boats could destroy. Try as he might Dönitz could not build enough U-boats to overcome the Navy's defences and the resolve of the shipbuilding industries in Britain, Canada and America. Materiel, food and fuel stockpiled in Britain and the USSR. It was a vital struggle.

The crushing nature of the contest could be read on Johnnie Walker's haggard face. He was not alone in scoring impressive victories over the U-boats – many officers and thousands of sailors scored impressive hits against the enemy and displayed courage and ingenuity. But Walker's story represents the Navy's stormy passage through the war. The service was, in 1939, unprepared for a major conflict. Throughout the war it stuck to its task and found a generation of heroes (many of them now forgotten) that recalled its golden age in the Napoleonic Wars. Walker was emblematic of the service in its greatest triumph. *The Times* reckoned that he had been 'more continuously in contact with the enemy at sea than almost any other officer and man in the Navy'.[14] By 1944 he was bowed down by the weight of warfare with the U-boats.

On 7 July Walker received two signals. The first ordered him to sea the next day. The other confirmed the death of his son in a submarine in the Mediterranean. That evening he was taken to hospital, suffering from a cerebral thrombosis. He died on the 9th. It was believed that he died of overwork. He was forty-eight years old.

Captain Walker got a hero's funeral at Liverpool Cathedral. Admiral Horton told the thousand or so mourners that 'not dust, or the light weight of a stone, but all the sea of the Western Approaches shall be his tomb'.[15] He was buried at sea from a destroyer. 2SG went on to kill eight more U-boats. Johnnie Walker remained an emblematic figure for the Navy. In 1950 the Admiralty said that 'Captain Walker, more than any other, won the Battle of the Atlantic. His methods had amazing success and more than any other factor gave the Royal Navy supremacy.'[16]

But the final word should go to the man himself. In response to such adulation Walker replied: 'I do not think I am an "ace" U-boat killer. This kind of warfare is not the sort that has one man as its ace protagonist ... Every man has his own job to do – I am merely at the head of the affair. So please don't call me U-boat killer number one. That formidable character is 1,000 British tars.'[17]

PART 15: DECLINE

CHAPTER 55

EAST OF SUEZ
1945–1982

Aircraft launched from the Royal Navy's carrier task force struck the first blows in the Battle of Okinawa on 26 March 1945. The planes from the Fleet Air Arm destroyed the Japanese airbases on the Sakishima Islands and then Formosa. After the air raids the warships moved in and bombarded targets on shore. The British Pacific Fleet (BPF) was well suited to fighting the Japanese. Kamikaze attacks crippled American aircraft carriers. The damage from kamikaze attacks was quickly repaired on British carriers, which had armoured flight decks.

The British and Commonwealth carrier task force in the Far East was the most powerful fleet in the Royal Navy's history. The Navy itself had never been stronger than in 1945. This was despite the fact that during the war the service lost nigh on 50 per cent of the warships it possessed in September 1939. It was a testament to the vitality of shipyards in Britain, the United States and the Commonwealth that by the end of the war the Navy had 885 ships in service: 20 battleships, 65 carriers, 101 cruisers, 461 destroyers and 238 submarines. In addition it had a vast stock of escort vessels, patrol boats, amphibious craft and store/repair ships. A large proportion of its warships were with the BPF: eighteen aircraft carriers, four battleships and a vast fleet of cruisers, destroyers, submarines, escort vessels and support ships. It was the first British fleet of this size to operate out of European and Mediterranean waters since Rodney defeated de Grasse at the Battle of the Saintes in 1782.

The BPF fought professionally and bravely at Okinawa and elsewhere in the Pacific theatre. But the Navy had to acknowledge a new master. Despite its unprecedented strength the BPF contributed 20 per cent of allied air power during the battle and brought a modest force to the 1,300-strong armada mobilised by the Americans. Okinawa was one of the bloodiest and hardest-fought battles of the war. The bulk of the work was done by the United States Navy (USN) and ground forces.

This was deliberate. The Americans did not want to share the fruits of victory with anyone and they most certainly did not want to sacrifice blood and treasure to prop up the ailing British Empire. In order to take the credit the US military had to do the heavy lifting and accept the sacrifice. The Royal Navy was deliberately sidelined. For the Americans the Navy's proud BPF was merely Task Force 57, one of many task forces in the campaign. Admiral Ernest King, the American Chief of Naval Operations, detested all things British and reserved a special part of his notorious temper for the Royal Navy. Under his orders the BPF had to look after itself with no help from the USN. In 1945 335 Japanese warships were sunk. The BPF was responsible for just twelve of those. The surrender of the Japanese Empire took place on an American battleship, USS *Missouri*.

The loss of *Prince of Wales* and *Repulse* in the blistering air attack off Kuantan in the South China Sea shattered the Navy's once indomitable position as arbiter of Asian and Pacific waters. During the war in the Pacific the Navy had to accommodate itself to a junior role and accept American leadership. It was something it had to get used to. The United States Navy had indisputably overtaken the Royal Navy as the world's greatest maritime power.

In addition to acknowledging American hegemony the Navy also had to get used to a world in which the battleship was redundant. The last-ever fight between battleships took place at the Battle of Surigao Strait on 25 October between the IJN and the USN. The last shells fired in anger by a British battleship were those propelled by HMS *King George V* at Japanese military installations at Hamamatsu, in central Honshu.

In 1946 the final battleship was commissioned – HMS *Vanguard*. She entered a world that had little need for battleships. The Second World War had shown beyond question that battles fought between the big guns of capital ships belonged to history. Battleships had been at the core of the Royal Navy since the development of the line of battle in the seventeenth century. Now they were all but obsolete in a world of long-range aircraft, guided missiles and atomic bombs. Small ships and submarines could provide greater firepower than one of the majestic leviathans. They were now gigantic sitting targets for the weapons of the Cold War.

HMS *Vanguard* fired her guns for the last time in 1955 in an exercise. She underwent a refit after that and then went into reserve and became a film set. On 4 August 1960 the seafront at Southsea was thronged with people who came to watch the last British battleship being towed out of Portsmouth for the breaker's yard at Faslane. There was no ceremony on the part of the Navy. *Vanguard* did not go gentle into that good night. She ran aground on the mudflats and had to be pulled off by five tugs.

By 1960 most navies in the world had disposed of their battleships or put them in reserve. The exception was the USN, which kept its four *Iowa*-class battleships. They were recommissioned in 1968 and again between 1982 and 1992. In the 1980s they were fitted with Tomahawk missiles. The last time a battleship was used in conflict was during Operation Desert Storm in 1991 when *Wisconsin* and *Missouri* launched Tomahawks and fired their 16-inch guns at shore targets.

Battleships, in their various manifestations, had formed the core of British naval power since the seventeenth century. The ignominious exit of *Vanguard* went without fanfare or much mourning (the news merited only a few unsentimental paragraphs in *The Times*, for example). It nonetheless sealed a long chapter in British history. *Vanguard* was sold for £500,000. The Americans and Japanese have kept a number of their battleships as museum ships. Britain chose to rid herself of her great modern ships, perhaps choosing permanent oblivion to the agony of a visual reminder of vanished glories. A trace of the destructive potential and scale of the ships is to be found at the doors of the Imperial War Museum in London: the iconic two giant 15-inch guns were taken from warships. One came from the battleship HMS *Ramillies*, the other was fitted first to the battleship HMS *Resolution* and then the monitor HMS *Roberts*. Both guns were used during the D-Day landings in 1944. The dreadnoughts that had played so prominent a part in modern history have vanished with scarcely a trace. Thanks to the survival of the *Victory*, the world of the Georgian Navy seems more real to us.

In the year that *Vanguard* was dragged unwillingly to the scrapyard Britain still looked like a major naval power, albeit a shadow of her former glory. The Navy possessed eight carriers, two large amphibious ships, 14 cruisers, 156 destroyers/frigates, 54 submarines and 207 mine and coastal craft. Since 1945 the Navy had performed its traditional tasks well and discovered a new role. Its carrier force and minesweepers distinguished themselves during the Korean War. While those forces were in action in Asia the Navy's Mediterranean Fleet could intervene in the Persian Gulf when Iran nationalised the Anglo-Iranian Oil Company. British warships continued to police the remnants of the British Empire in Africa and East of Suez.

The Navy could also send sixty-six ships, including three carriers, one battleship, three cruisers and seventeen submarines, to participate in Exercise Mainbrace – a gigantic NATO exercise which involved 203 ships from nine navies engaging in simultaneous operations off Norway and Jutland. This gigantic war game was led by a British admiral.

The Navy of the second half of the twentieth century, it appeared, was to fulfil its traditional duties defending British interests while also forging a new role in NATO. The Royal Navy would take the lead in the West's containment of the Soviet Union in the North Atlantic. Simulated naval wars such as Exercise Mainbrace in 1952, Exercise Grand Slam in the Mediterranean in the same year and Exercise Mariner the next year in the Denmark Strait (along with other minor naval exercises that involved minesweeping and convoy protection) demonstrated how powerful were NATO's naval forces. The Royal Navy was a bulwark against Soviet expansionism. In any future war its area of expertise would be the coast of Norway, the Arctic Circle, the North Atlantic and the GIUK Gap – the area of water between Greenland, Iceland and the United Kingdom. Britain was able to operate simultaneously in the Atlantic, the Mediterranean, the Middle East and 'East of Suez'. The commitment to Asian waters continued, despite the loss of the Indian empire in 1947.

Now that battleships were antiquated, Britain's claims to be a major naval power were dependent upon the capital ships of the twentieth century – aircraft carriers. The Royal Navy's carrier force was second only to the USN's. It allowed Britain to project her power around the world. The Korean War and Exercise Mainbrace demonstrated the reality of this power. In 1953 the Coronation fleet review at Spithead included 300 vessels, including five British aircraft carriers and one apiece from Canada and Australia. And that did not include ships and carriers operating in the Mediterranean and East of Suez.

But the mask slipped, as it was bound to do. In 1956 Britain was forced to abandon its naval base at the Canal Zone in Egypt. The Suez Canal was the fulcrum for British naval power, and determined its reach into the Gulf and Asian waters. Lose free access to the Canal, it was held, and Britain would lose its ability to act as a major naval power. As soon as the base was evacuated Colonel Nasser nationalised the Suez Canal.

The Navy's show of force against Nasser was formidable. It included the carriers *Eagle*, *Albion*, *Bulwark*, *Ocean* and *Theseus*. The last two of these were used as launch pads for helicopters that carried commandos ashore. It was the first helicopter amphibious assault in military history. After the crisis *Albion* and *Bulwark* were converted into 'commando carriers' – amphibious assault vessels that could land marines and other ground forces by helicopter in rapid strikes.

The Navy, RAF and army might have performed well, but the illusion of British world power was irrecoverably extinguished when the military action was brought to an end by pressure from the USA and USSR.

The decisive blow was the American threat to withdraw support for the pound, forcing its devaluation.

Suddenly Britain appeared very weak. The Suez Crisis weakened her position in the Middle East and undermined her in the Indian Ocean. The world 'East of Suez' was now divorced from Western waters and would require a different strategy. Britain's claim to be a great power was stripped bare.

The Suez Crisis had serious implications for the Navy. The conflict had shown that Britain's conventional forces, for all their ostensible power, were inadequate in the modern world. Five aircraft carriers were no match for American financial clout. All the naval power in the world could not sail through the quagmire of international politics or overcome distaste for foreign intervention at home. In 1957 the White Paper on Defence produced by the minister of defence, Duncan Sandys, envisaged a new defence policy for Britain. Greater emphasis would be placed on nuclear weapons as a deterrent force. Conscription was abolished and defence spending cut. In future a smaller military establishment would concentrate on surgical strikes conducted by mobile forces. The White Paper signalled doubt about the future of naval power: 'the role of the Navy in Global War is somewhat uncertain'.

The Navy could not afford to sit still and wait for the axe to fall. The First Sea Lord at the time was Lord Mountbatten. He had always been a champion of new technology. Under his leadership the Navy pressed for destroyers to carry the Sea Slug surface-to-air missile. 'Once we can obtain Government agreement to the fact that we are the mobile large-scale rocket carriers of the future then everything will fall into place,' he said. In 1961 Mark I Sea Slugs entered service on the new County-class guided-missile destroyers.

Mountbatten was also determined that the Royal Navy should have nuclear-powered submarines. The main obstacle was Admiral Hyman Rickover, the officer responsible for the USN's nuclear power programme, who did not want to share American technology. Mountbatten won him over. The first British nuclear-powered submarine, the appropriately named HMS *Dreadnought*, was launched by Queen Elizabeth in 1960, two months after *Vanguard* was towed away.

The Navy entered the 1960s a reduced force, but one that was in the process of updating its technologies and remaining a serious world power. But underneath the surface things were far from well.

The Second World War had bequeathed the Navy a vast fleet of ships and a hoard of equipment. The Navy's core strength – its eight carriers

– was a legacy of the war. Most of its ships and submarines were built during the war, or even in the 1930s. The survival of the wartime fleet gave Britain the appearance of a first-rank naval power in the 1950s. In the 1960s the ageing ships came up for replacement. Ships such as the cruiser HMS *Belfast* – now a distinctive feature of the London riverscape as a museum ship – were put in reserve and then decommissioned. A new generation of warships, such as the twenty-six *Leander*-class frigates laid down in the late 1950s and early 1960s, entered service. The vintage carriers were to be replaced with two enormous CVA-01 aircraft carriers, along with modern escorts such as Type 82 destroyers and cruisers specially designed to carry guided missiles and helicopters.

The revamped fleet would be large enough to fulfil Britain's NATO commitments and to maintain Britain's position East of Suez. Things looked to be going the Navy's way. Then it encountered a major enemy – the RAF.

Mountbatten became Chief of the Defence Staff in 1959. His job was to integrate the army, Navy and RAF, abolishing the venerable Board of Admiralty along with the less mature War Office, Air Ministry and the Ministry of Aviation. The new Board of Admiralty would be shorn of its predecessor's magisterial power and become a committee of the Defence Council of the United Kingdom. The Ministry of Defence would take over responsibility for the three services, which would each enjoy an independent existence under the MOD's umbrella. Mountbatten called the aim of the reform 'a functional, closely knit, smoothly working machine'.

It was supposed to prevent inter-service rivalry. Instead the prospect of cuts in 1964 exacerbated it. The Navy and the RAF were locked in conflict. At stake was the future of both services. The key date was 22 December 1962 when President J. F. Kennedy met Harold Macmillan at the Nassau Conference in the Bahamas. The British were dependent upon the Americans for a nuclear deterrent. Under a previous agreement the RAF was to be supplied with American Skybolt nuclear bombs, which would be carried by the Air Force's V-bombers. But the Americans cancelled the Skybolt programme. Instead Kennedy offered Macmillan submarine-based Polaris A3T ballistic missiles.

That was a turning point in the history of the Navy. It was now responsible for Britain's nuclear deterrent. The RAF was furious. It retained the use of nuclear weapons on some of its aircraft for the time being, but the Navy offered continuous deployment of tactical nuclear weapons, and with the monopoly came a vast chunk of the defence budget.

The Navy had not lobbied for nukes. In having the deterrent foisted upon it the service had to change. Money had to be diverted to pay for four new ballistic missile submarines – the *Resolution* class, whose boats were symbolically given old battleship names: *Resolution, Repulse, Renown* and *Revenge*. It had to develop anti-submarine techniques and anti-mine measures to protect the ballistic missile base at Faslane on the Clyde. It found itself on a collision course with the RAF.

The argument for submarine ballistics was that land-based nuclear weapons were vulnerable to attack and aircraft could be shot down en route to their target. This called into question the future of the RAF. In retaliation – and to save itself – the RAF argued that it alone could maintain Britain's East of Suez role. It lobbied the new secretary of state for defence, Denis Healey, to cancel the Navy's vital CVA-01 carrier programme. Instead the RAF would provide strike forces in the Indian Ocean and South-East Asia operating from island and shore bases. The RAF presented the Treasury with a history lesson which purported to demonstrate that the Navy had never managed to conduct aerial warfare as well as the RAF.

Healey was convinced. In his White Paper of 1966 defence expenditure was cut to £2 billion. Healey reconfirmed Britain's obligations to NATO along with its role East of Suez – but it was to be done on the cheap. The CVA-01 programme was cancelled. Britain was to retain its power East of Suez through V-bombers stationed at Singapore and Australia. The White Paper also affirmed that Britain would not go to war without a major ally.

The Navy was furious. This spelt the end of its traditional role. The Labour minister for the Navy, Christopher Mayhew, and the First Sea Lord, Sir David Luce, both resigned in protest. Mayhew argued that Healey had ended Britain's military independence, making it dependent on the United States for all but the most minor intervention. Britain East of Suez, Mayhew said, was acting 'not as a power in its own right, but as an extension of the United States' power – not as allies, but as auxiliaries of the United States'.

But even more detrimentally, the reduced capability of the Royal Navy meant that Britain had renounced its world role. The post-colonial world, it was held, was not hospitable to British bases planted on foreign soil. If local governments forced Britain to leave, the RAF would have little option but to pack up and go. Land bases were also vulnerable to intercontinental missiles.

The Navy, on the other hand, was more flexible, more mobile and less visible. In 1961 marines from 42 Commando were helicoptered from one of the Navy's commando carriers, HMS *Bulwark*, to Kuwait airport to deter Iraq from annexing the emirate. It was the spearhead of Operation

Vantage, which involved a large naval task force including *Bulwark*, the aircraft carrier *Victorious*, destroyers and minesweepers. During the Indonesia–Malaysia confrontation on Borneo between 1962 and 1966 large numbers of warships from the Commonwealth patrolled the coast and two British commando carriers (HMSs *Bulwark* and *Albion*) moved troops, helicopters and aircraft between the British base at Singapore and Borneo. From 1965 the aircraft carrier *Ark Royal* and escorting frigates enforced a blockade against Rhodesia in accord with United Nations Security Council Resolution 217.

Naval air power could be brought where it was needed rather than sitting indefinitely in foreign territory. Permanent bases offended local pride, while naval forces intervened and then vanished. In 1964, for instance, President Julius Nyerere of Tanganyika requested British help against a coup. HMS *Centaur* landed 45 Commando on shore by helicopter. Nyerere was restored. The commandos returned to their amphibious vessel before they could be accused of outstaying their welcome. In its policing role during the breakup of the British Empire the carrier came into its own as an amphibious assault vessel, particularly when it could land ground troops by helicopter. In contrast RAF strikes from distant bases were pretty blunt instruments.

Mayhew and other advocates of naval power argued that the East of Suez strategy was a grave mistake. It tied British forces to insecure land bases and deprived her of the flexibility and balanced force provided by carriers. But that kind of flexibility did not come cheap. The Navy had Polaris. The RAF got its island bases. As Mayhew said, you could not afford to be a world power on £2 billion.

The Navy had, it seemed, accepted a new role but lost its traditional function. The ballistic missile submarines gave the Navy an unprecedented punch, but the price to be paid, many felt, was the end of the Navy as a conventional force. Going into the 1970s it was uncertain of its future and low on morale.

Yet worse was to come. The financial crisis of the late 1960s forced further cuts. In January 1968 Healey signalled the withdrawal of British forces from East of Suez. The RAF's plan was cancelled when Healey announced withdrawal from the Persian Gulf, Aden, the Maldives, Malaya and Singapore. The Navy's aircraft carriers would end their service and not be replaced.

The Navy's fall was precipitous. In just over twenty years from 1945 it had declined from a serious world force to an institution uncertain that it even had a future. It had been assailed by a series of savage cuts. The retreat from East of Suez fundamentally changed the Navy. With no empire to police and no major bases in the post-colonial world the politicians did not believe that the Navy would need to be deployed to intervene far from home or support ground troops in distant corners of the globe.

The Navy faced existential crisis: what was it *for*?

Even to ask that question was a sign of its reduced state. Britain had accepted American military hegemony. She could no longer afford the Navy that once ruled the waves. In any case, what would be the point in a poor country preserving naval power?

Countries desire strong navies for several reasons. To project their power in the world. To underpin their trade networks. To defend their borders. By the late Sixties Britain lacked the money to float a grand fleet to project its power. In any case it had ceded the role as the world's policeman to the United States. It also lacked the political will to carve out a new position in the world and the imagination to develop a new strategy for its Navy. During the financial crisis of the late Sixties the main justification for Britain's continuation as a military power became its contribution to NATO.

For the Navy that meant transforming itself into a small specialist force dedicated to hunting down and destroying Russian submarines in the GIUK Gap if war broke out. In other words, in the post-East of Suez era the Navy would be restricted to an area of sea close to home. Anti-submarine warfare (ASW) was the basis upon which money was given from the Treasury, weapons were developed and new ships were launched. The Royal Marines, for example, survived on this basis because they transformed themselves into experts in amphibious operations in the Arctic Circle, NATO's northern flank.

Britain lost her last full-sized aircraft carriers in the 1970s: HMS *Eagle* was decommissioned in 1972 and *Ark Royal* in 1978. The new generation of carriers heralded the Navy's new role. The three *Invincible*-class carriers ordered in the 1970s were originally intended as the helicopter-carrying cruisers that would have escorted the CVA-01 aircraft carriers. By 1973 the proposed cruisers were enlarged and planned as anti-submarine helicopter carriers to provide the air cover in anti-submarine hunter-killer groups. They would be protected by the new low-cost *Sheffield*-class destroyers that carried new surface-to-air missiles.

Even so the Navy's surface fleet was vulnerable to attack. The RAF claimed to be able to offer air cover in the North Atlantic, but it was far from satisfactory. Outside home waters a British squadron would be vulnerable to air attack. It would seem that the Navy's range of effective operation had shrunk considerably – to an area of sea close to British home waters. But by good luck the Navy's small *Invincible*-class helicopter carriers were just big enough for the new vertical/short take-off and landing (VSTOL) Sea Harrier jet aircraft.

The great weight of budgetary constraints affected all decisions. Ministers permitted expenditure as long as it went to fulfilling the country's NATO commitment to anti-submarine warfare. It was the Navy's skill to meet that obligation and at the same time use the ASW hardware for dual purposes. For the Navy's senior officers were not content to lie back and accept the sharp limitations of the post-East of Suez and ASW era. Sooner or later a crisis or war would emerge that would require the Navy to operate in situations entirely different to the ASW role it trained for.

HMS *Invincible* was a case in point. Her sole justification was as a platform for ASW helicopters, but the introduction of Harriers also allowed her to operate as an amphibious assault vessel and mini-aircraft carrier in all but name if the situation required. She was fitted with a ski-jump so that the VSTOL aircraft could take off from her short flight deck. *Invincible* could not carry many Harriers, but the jump jets could be used to attack enemy ships and they could give aerial support to amphibious landings. The addition of Harriers was a coup for the beleaguered Royal Navy. It allowed the service to make the best of its resources in an age of acute financial and political pressures. It gave the Navy just enough air cover for it to operate away from home.

Other types of ships could be designed for purposes other than ASW. The ASW helicopters carried by frigates and destroyers could also carry anti-ship Sea Skua missiles. The new Type 22 frigates that came into service in the 1970s were the starveling children of the defence cuts of the Sixties and were developed with a primary purpose as a specialist ASW vessel. But they also carried anti-ship Exocet missiles and anti-aircraft missiles. Type 21 frigates were meant to be fast patrol vessels, but they could also be used to bombard shore positions. In part the Navy was unwittingly helped by the Treasury, which decreed that all new ships should be versatile enough to be purchased by foreign navies.

The Navy managed to negotiate a very difficult decade. Thanks to the foresight of its leaders the service was able to remain the third-most powerful Navy in the world. With limited resources they had managed to develop a fleet that was flexible enough to meet the manifold lurking dangers unforeseen by politicians. Despite the best efforts of Westminster the Navy still had to operate East of Suez. The blockade of Rhodesia lasted until 1975. Ships were required in Hong Kong and, from

1980, in the Persian Gulf during the Iran–Iraq War. The Navy also had a role beyond NATO. It helped to evacuate civilians when Turkey invaded North Cyprus in 1974. It assisted in clearing the Suez Canal of mines after the Yom Kippur War in the same year. The last British aircraft carrier, *Ark Royal*, deployed off British Honduras to deter a Guatemalan army invading the British colony. In 1977 a small task force consisting of a hunter-killer submarine and two frigates was sent to the Falkland Islands to pressurise the Argentine government to evacuate the Falkland island of Thule.

The activities of the Navy around the world were a reminder that Britain still had a global role and the Royal Navy was essential to maintaining it. It might have been slender, but it was important nonetheless.

But then came *The Way Forward*, the British government's Defence White Paper of 1981. It is also known as the Nott Review, after the secretary of defence, John Nott. According to the review, the Navy's primary role was as the operator of Britain's nuclear capability. By 1981 Margaret Thatcher's government had negotiated the purchase of Trident to replace the Polaris ballistic missile system. It would cost £8 billion and it would be taken out of the Navy's budget. According to the Nott Review Trident was the jewel in the crown of Britain's defence. It was at the heart of national defence policy and it trumped everything else.

Apart from operating Trident the Navy's activities would be cut back to encompass little more than ASW in the North Atlantic. And even in that regard the burden of anti-submarine operations would fall on Britain's nuclear submarines and the RAF. The carrier HMS *Hermes* would be decommissioned in 1982. HMS *Invincible* was to be sold to the Royal Australian Navy, leaving just two ASW carriers – HMS *Illustrious*, due to be commissioned late in 1982, and *Ark Royal*, which would be in service from 1985. Even then only one of the carriers, with just five Sea Harriers on board, would be available at any one time.

The White Paper all but excluded the Navy's dwindling surface fleet from missions outside the NATO sea area. Amphibious operations would become a thing of the past with the disbandment of the Royal Marines and the sale of the service's two amphibious assault vessels, HMSs *Fearless* and *Intrepid*, which were the cornerstones of Britain's expeditionary capability. According to *The Way Forward* nuclear war and long-range missiles made the use of conventional naval forces redundant. Surface ships were plum targets. That was the justification for the sale of *Invincible* and the assault ships as well as the cutting back of the numbers of frigates and destroyers to just forty-two operational vessels.

This latest buffeting the Navy received from waves of defence cuts threatened to submerge it. The culture of the service, built up over centuries, would change completely as it transformed from a fleet characterised by surface warfare to one that operated mainly under the waves. The *Statement on the Defence Estimates* in 1982 made this clear: 'In the field of anti-submarine warfare, we attach particular importance to increasing the size of the nuclear-powered submarine force as rapidly as resources will permit.'[1] Nott called the nuclear submarine 'the battleship of the future'.[2]

Keith Speed MP followed in the footsteps of Christopher Mayhew, resigning as minister responsible for the Navy in response to the Nott Review. He told the House of Commons that the cuts to the Navy would 'imperil our national security'.[3] It was deeply unfair that the Navy should pick up the tab for Trident when it was a matter of national security, not a service-specific requirement. The bill for the new Trident system impaired the Navy's ability to function.

Speed argued passionately that nuclear submarines were no replacements for a surface fleet that was needed to defend the country and maintain the maritime power upon which Britain depended. Why did it need maritime power in the late twentieth century? Speed answered this by saying that Britain depended on seaborne trade for 96 per cent of its imports and exports. The Navy protected this and defended Britain's interests around the world. The fleet was the mainstay of Britain's global presence and submarines could not take up the slack. The Navy was supposed to aid the nation's allies in war and peace, maintaining the networks of interdependency across the globe. In peacetime it played a vital role in helping after natural disasters – the modern version of power projection.

'That is the great advantage of maritime power,' said Speed. 'On one day one can have a high profile and the fleet can be there on the horizon. On the next day there can be a low profile and the fleet can draw away below the horizon, or it can move in to render first-aid or emergency services ... that is something which, by definition, standing armies and air forces cannot do.'[4]

The feeling within the Navy was just as apprehensive. 'I am quite unable to describe how sad and upset we all were,' wrote Captain Sandy Woodward, who had just left the Ministry of Defence, where he had been Director of Naval Plans. The scaling-down of the surface fleet and the depletion of the carrier and amphibious forces sent a powerful message to countries around the world that the British presence was vanishing.

That was a conclusion, wrote Woodward, which was drawn in Buenos Aires: 'no British carriers means no air cover, no air cover means no British surface ships, no surface ships means no British landing force, no landing force means "No Contest".'[5]

CHAPTER 56

CONCLUSION: SET IN THE SILVER SEA
1982–2013

... the cruel sea which man has made more cruel.

The Cruel Sea, 1953 film

On a rainy, grey Sunday in June 2012 over a thousand boats took part in a pageant on the River Thames in London to celebrate Queen Elizabeth II's Diamond Jubilee. The pageant will probably not go down in history as one of the finest celebrations in British history – or even in 2012 for that matter. It takes us back, in a convoluted sort of a way, to the beginning of this book. Naval power in the British Isles began on its rivers and pushed out to encompass the globe. The pageant was intended to recall the history of the Thames as a conduit of trade and commerce. It was rather underwhelming.

The last time a Diamond Jubilee was celebrated – for Queen Victoria in 1897 – 165 British warships, including twenty-one battleships and fifty-three cruisers, took part in a fleet review at Spithead. The sight was awe-inspiring: a vast accumulation of grey warships draped with flags and bunting. Crowds of pleasure boats bobbed between the great sea monsters. What made it all the more spectacular was the knowledge that not a single ship had been recalled from the Navy's foreign stations.

It would have been too embarrassing to attempt to stage a fleet review in 2012. Lord West, a former First Sea Lord, told the *Daily Telegraph*: 'I suppose now we could get a couple of submarines out and five or six frigates and destroyers, but it would be very small and not very splendid.'[1] The Royal Navy of 2012 had no aircraft carriers; its surface fleet consisted of a helicopter carrier, a single amphibious assault ship, two landing platform docks, thirteen frigates and six guided-missile destroyers. In addition there were fifteen anti-mine ships, twenty-four patrol and four survey vessels. There were ten submarines.

The Diamond Jubilee was a cause of national soul-searching and nagging fears for the safety of Britain. Was that the situation in 2012? Not a bit of it. I am referring to the momentous Spithead fleet review in 1897.

Rudyard Kipling witnessed the grandeur of the review. His response was the poem 'Recessional', one of the most famous intimations of the end of empire: 'Far-called, our navies melt away – / On dune and head-land sinks the fire: / Lo, all our pomp of yesterday/ Is one with Nineveh and Tyre!'

In the 1890s people were acutely aware that the Navy was the lifeline of the empire. They knew all too well that Britain herself was dependent on imported food for her very survival. Way back at the end of the seventeenth century Admiral Sir Cloudesley Shovell said that it was 'number that gains the victory'. He had seen fleets of equal sizes slug it out in line engagements for no victory on either side. 'To fight, beat and chase an enemy of the same strength I have sometimes seen,' he said, 'but I have rarely seen at sea any victory worth boasting when the strength has been near equal.'[2] This realisation that the Royal Navy had to be not just better but much bigger than its opponents had ruled thinking ever since. The security of the nation depended on overmastering every navy in the world. This reached its climax in the period for the six or so decades after 1815. By the 1880s other powers were catching up fast. There was a race on to develop new technologies and ships that could outgun and outpace their rivals. The Royal Navy could only try to keep ahead of the navies of Japan, Germany, Italy, the United States, Russia and France. Already Britain was being overtaken as an industrial power. In 1897 the Royal Navy had sixty-two battleships; between them the primary European naval powers had sixty-six.

'Consider these ships so vast in themselves, yet so small, so easily lost to sight on the surface waters,' wrote Winston Churchill of the ships of the Navy in August 1914, when the Grand Fleet represented the greatest marine force put to sea. 'All our long history built up century after century, all our great affairs in every part of the globe, all the means of livelihood depended upon them.'

The difference between 2012 and 1897 could not be starker. It represents a radical shift in the history of Britain. Britons in the second decade of the twenty-first century could not be more relaxed about their country's dwindling naval power. The reason why can only be explained by events that started exactly twenty years before the Jubilee.

In the spring of 1982 Rear Admiral Sandy Woodward was working up a British flotilla consisting of five destroyers and four frigates in the Mediterranean prior to tactical exercises in the north-east Atlantic. On 19 March the Argentinian flag was raised on South Georgia. It was clearly the build-up for an invasion of the Falkland Islands. Late in the night of 27 March Sir Henry Leach, the First Sea Lord, sought out Margaret Thatcher and John Nott in the House of Commons. It had been assumed that any campaign to retake the Falklands would be doomed. The RAF could not provide air cover to protect the Navy and the army against 220 Argentine fighter jets 8,000 miles away in inhospitable waters. Nott and the USN shared that opinion: the reconquest of the islands was a military impossibility. During a long meeting Leach convinced Thatcher that the Navy could defeat the Argentine navy, fend off their aircraft and land British troops on the Falklands. Leach knew that he was arguing not just for the Falklands but for the future of the Royal Navy, which was still in shock from the Nott Review.

'First Sea Lord,' asked the prime minister,[3] 'what precisely is it you want?'

'Prime Minister,' said Leach, 'I would like your authority to form a Task Force, which would, if you so required, be ready to sail for the South Atlantic at a moment's notice.'

'You have it.'

Leach had to make good his word. He had until the weekend – 3 April. On 29 March the nuclear submarine HMS *Spartan* was detached from Woodward's flotilla and sent south. Another sub, HMS *Splendid*, left Faslane on 1 April, the same day that Woodward was ordered to prepare to sail and the carriers *Invincible* and *Hermes* were put on four hours' notice. On 2 April the Argentines invaded. Woodward's task force was already at sea.

British naval forces at sea were commanded during the war by Woodward. Overall control of the fleet was in the hands of Admiral Sir John Fieldhouse, based at the military headquarters at Northwood. It was a daunting task. The Argentines had a formidable navy and air force. The Navy had to operate 8,000 miles from home and 3,000 miles from the nearest air base. Woodward had only a handful of ships. The Argentines had powerful air defences, ships armed with Exocet and Sea Dart missiles and four submarines, two of which could evade British sonar.

On 4 April the nuclear submarine *Conqueror* left Faslane and the carriers *Hermes* and *Invincible* left Portsmouth carrying between them just twenty-eight Sea Harriers. They were followed by the requisitioned liner *Canberra*, with 3 Commando Brigade on board. At Ascension the task force split into three groups – the Battle Group under Woodward, the Amphibious Group led by Commodore Mike Clapp on HMS *Fearless* (a landing platform dock [LPD] vessel) and the Paraquet Group, a detached force bound for South Georgia. As Admiral Woodward later wrote, they would have until mid-June to secure victory, before the hard southern winter arrived. The first blood in the naval war was drawn by depth charges and torpedoes launched by helicopters from *Antrim* and *Plymouth* against *Santa Fe*, an Argentine submarine at South Georgia, which was crippled and abandoned by her crew. *Antrim* and *Plymouth* bombarded Argentine positions while SAS and Special Boat Service troops stormed the island. South Georgia was under British control on 25 April.

Meanwhile the British nuclear submarines took up position to the west of the Falklands, to watch and wait for the Argentine navy. On 26 April *Splendid* began shadowing the Argentine task group.

On 1 May Woodward's twelve-ship Battle Group went into action to win control of the sea and air around the Falklands. First an RAF Vulcan flew from Ascension and bombed the runway at Port Stanley. Harriers from *Hermes* struck Argentine positions on Goose Green and Stanley. Then the destroyer *Glamorgan* led the frigates *Arrow* and *Alacrity* to a position just three miles from Stanley, where they bombarded the airstrip. Meanwhile *Brilliant* and *Yarmouth* swept for submarines. In the afternoon the Battle Group came under attack from forty Argentine planes.

On the day that the Battle Group went into action the commander of the sub *Conqueror* reported sighting the aged cruiser *General Belgrano* (an ex-American warship, which had survived Pearl Harbor) in company with two Exocet-carrying destroyers to the south of the islands. To the north was another Argentine group, consisting of the aircraft carrier *Veinticinco de Mayo* and her escorts. Woodward knew he was being caught in the pincer of a naval attack.

Woodward requested permission to attack *Belgrano*. On 2 May the Chief of the Defence Staff Admiral Sir Terence Lewin brought the request to the War Cabinet. At 15.00 *Conqueror* launched torpedoes. Two hit the cruiser, one on her port bow and one on her stern, exploding in the aft machine room. *Belgrano*'s power failed, she began to list, then she sank with the loss of 232 men.

On 4 May the carrier group headed towards the islands, with the Type 42 destroyers HMSs *Glasgow*, *Coventry* and *Sheffield* acting as pickets, the outer line of defence. The battle for control of the air had begun in earnest. Argentine pilots were screaming in at fifty feet, below radar level; they would only be briefly visible to the Navy's radar operators in the darkened Ops Rooms when they chose to 'pop up' to scan for British targets. Then, if the blip on the computer terminal was confirmed as an Argentine aircraft, the destroyers had four minutes to put up 'chaff', a radar decoy system, before the Exocet missile impacted.

At 13.56.30 the radars of two Argentine Etendard jets were picked up in the Ops Room of *Glasgow*; the ship fired chaff. Over on *Sheffield* no action was taken. Her Ops Room had not picked up the warning. At 14.03 two officers on the bridge suddenly noticed a trail of smoke. 'MISSILE ATTACK! HIT THE DECK!' shouted Lieutenant Peter Walpole down the microphone.[4]

Five seconds after he spotted the smoke an Exocet tore into the hull amidships. Men in the galley and the computer room were killed instantly. The explosions also broke *Sheffield*'s water main and blasted down the watertight doors. As a result the fires could not be put out and thick smoke spread through the ship. It began to get very, very hot.

Twenty-one members of the crew died. The survivors were evacuated and the vessel burned for days. The whole fleet – and everyone who watched or read the news around the world – now understood the speed with which death came in modern sea war and the vulnerability of warships. There was a serious flaw in the multi-million-pound missile-defence system. The Navy had designed its systems to counter the Soviet threat. Now it was facing weapons designed in the West: French Etendard strike fighters and Exocets, US Skyhawks, Israeli Dagger fighters, British Canberra bombers and so on.

The loss of *Belgrano* and *Sheffield* forced both sides to change tactics. The Argentine navy returned to port for the duration of the war. Woodward had to move his aircraft carriers out of harm's way.

The British Amphibious Group arrived on 17 May. It was led by the two Landing Platform Docks, *Fearless* and *Intrepid*, the spearhead of the landing force. There was also the P&O liner SS *Canberra*, packed to the gunwales with troops, artillery, engineers and a mountain of kit. *Atlantic Conveyor*, a gigantic Cunard container ship, carried four vital Chinook helicopters and fourteen Harriers; she became a makeshift aircraft carrier. These were two of the 'Ships Taken up from Trade' – a mighty armada which recalled the great conglomeration of private ships commandeered for medieval wars. There were five Hull-based trawlers used for mine-sweeping. Forty-five merchant ships carried troops and everything the operation could possibly need 8,000 miles from home. The list of ships included liners, ferries, container ships, freighters, tankers, tugboats, cable ships, salvagers and oilfield support ships. It was a stunning achievement of logistics and improvisation in modifying and equipping dozens of merchant ships for war at short notice. As so often the naval strength of the UK comprised more than just the Navy.

On the night of 21 May the Battle Group moved into position to screen the landings. The Amphibious Group, under the command of Commodore Clapp, consisted of the big amphibious landing ships *Intrepid* and *Fearless*; five RFA landing ships – *Sir Galahad, Sir Geraint, Sir Lancelot, Sir Percivale* and *Sir Tristram*; the enormous *Canberra* and two ferries; and two fleet store ships. They were defended by seven warships: the destroyer *Antrim* and the frigates *Argonaut, Ardent, Plymouth, Yarmouth, Broadsword* and *Brilliant*. These ships, and the Harriers, were to hold off the enemy air force at all costs in the vulnerable moments of landing.

HMS *Antrim*'s helicopters landed SBS marines, who sneaked up to the Argentine outpost high above the entrance to San Carlos Water. Into the bay steamed the destroyer, followed by the amphibious group. When the landing force was assembled the guns of *Antrim* opened fire on the Argentine position. Then the men from SBS stormed it. That was the signal for the landings to begin.

Once the Argentines realised what was happening the air force swung into action. The British warships came under sustained, deadly assault from seventy-two aircraft. The men on the ships answered the attack with everything they had, from surface-to-air missiles to machine guns and even rifles. This was fighting in the raw. Radar was not effective in the narrow confines of the bay. Weapons had to be fired by line of sight at planes that skimmed over the surface of the water or screeched out of the hills, visible against the shades and shadows for milliseconds at a time. The Argentine pilots released their bombs at 150 feet and continued to keep low, 'preferably clipping the mast, where the missiles can't get you',[5] as one of them said. The Sound became known as 'Bomb Alley'.

The surface of Falkland Sound was disrupted by plumes of water sent upwards by bombs missing their targets. But soon they started to find their sights. *Antrim* was hit, but the bomb failed to explode. Two bombs tore into *Argonaut* and stopped her engines.

Then *Ardent* took a pounding. Two bombs hit her aft and cracked her open. More bombs entered the aperture. The explosions and fires killed twenty-four and wounded thirty. *Ardent* continued to defend herself even though she was doomed. By then nothing could stop seven enemy bombs tearing into the poor ship. Commander Alan West was the last man to abandon her, tears of rage streaming down his face.

The British were fortunate that the Argentine pilots chose to target the warships. *Canberra* sat in San Carlos Water, a gleaming 'great white whale' of a target, packed with men and equipment. But she was spared. On Sunday 23 May *Antelope* was hit. The bombs did not explode at first.

HMS *Coventry*, 25 May 1982

When they did they killed a bomb-disposal engineer and wounded other members of the team. The explosion started fires in the engine rooms, which began to spread. Commander Nick Tobin ordered his men to abandon ship; he was the last off and five minutes later the missile magazine exploded. There was a series of catastrophic explosions through the night; the next day *Antelope* broke in half and sank. On Tuesday Argentine planes broke the picket again and dropped three bombs on *Coventry*. One exploded below the computer room and the Operations Room. A second exploded in the forward engine room. The ship began to list. As they waited to be rescued the crew sang 'Always Look on the Bright Side of Life'. Twenty minutes later she sank.

The same day that *Coventry* sank, two Etendards popped up and glimpsed a huge British ship. They fired Exocets and hurried home. They had not hit one of the carriers, as they had thought, but *Atlantic Conveyor*. Twelve crew were killed. The giant container ship had vital supplies including three Chinooks, six Wessex helicopters and tents for 4,000 men. On Sunday 29 May Argentine planes launched an Exocet at HMS *Invincible*. The missile struck home and exploded. In flew Skyhawks and dropped bombs to finish off the carrier. The celebrations were muted when it turned out that the last air-launched Exocet had been squandered on the crippled *Conveyor*.

The Royal Navy was severely chastised in the Battle of San Carlos, but it held the line and refused to be beaten. Officers and men fought with the tenacity and bravery willed to them by centuries of history. It was as desperate a scrap as any the Navy had faced. Up in the sky the Harrier pilots fought bravely to down enemy planes or disrupt their attacks. Down on the surface the sailors fought back at their tormentors and carried on, despite the calamities suffered by *Ardent*, *Antelope* and *Coventry*. But the Argentines fared even worse. They lost a third of their fighters and some of their best pilots. In addition many of their bombs failed to explode. This was because the Harriers, surface-to-air missiles and AA fire forced the pilots to fly too low for the optimum release height of their bombs. If the bombs had been better fused the Navy would have lost many more ships.

What might have happened if the Argentine planes had managed to attack the amphibious assault on 21 May was illustrated on 8 June. By the beginning of the first week in June Argentine air attacks on the landing parties and warships had tailed off. Back at home there was also a determination not to risk the two amphibious assault ships or the warships. Instead *Sir Galahad* and *Sir Tristram* were sent to land troops from the Scots and Welsh guards at Fitzroy, prior to the final assault on Stanley. Such landings had to take place by sea because of the loss of the Chinooks carried by *Conveyor*.

The journey to Fitzroy took longer than expected. When they got there it was discovered that there were not enough landing craft and there was a disagreement as to the correct landing site. Worse still, there were no air defences. Argentine planes bombed the hapless *Sir Galahad*, which was crewed by members of the Royal Naval Reserve and full of Welsh Guardsmen and ammunition. The ship turned into a cooker. Fifty men were killed and 115 wounded, many with horrendous burns. It left the army with a grievance against the Navy for failing to defend the operation, even though the officers and men of the RNR acted with commendable bravery in evacuating the burning ship. The naval war was far from over. On the same day as the tragedy at Fitzroy, HMS *Plymouth* was hit by five bombs. On 12 June a land-based Exocet exploded in *Glamorgan* and killed thirteen. Two days later the horror came to an end. Stanley was retaken and the war was over.

The Falklands War was an extremely close-run thing. The secretary of defence resigned, his vision of the future of the service in tatters. Clearly the country needed a Navy with the ability to function far from home and provide its own air cover. As a result the Navy survived as an expeditionary force, capable of fighting out of the NATO sea area.

This decision was vindicated in the 1990s with the end of the Cold

War. In 1997 the Navy was finally allowed its longed-for aircraft carriers. The government promised two 65,000-ton carriers to replace the three 22,000-ton carriers. The Strategic Defence Review justified the decision: 'the emphasis is now on increased offensive air power, and an ability to operate the largest possible range of aircraft in the widest possible range of roles'.

The modernisation of the Navy included a decision of symbolic and real importance when the WRNS was disbanded in 1993 and women were fully integrated into the service. In 2012 Commander Sarah West became the first woman to command a capital ship, the Type 23 frigate HMS *Portland*. The Navy's commitment to equality and diversity was put in resolute terms, reminiscent of language used by the service through the generations: 'Success requires mutual trust and respect, with each and every team member a valued individual ... Any form of discrimination, harassment or bullying undermines that necessary trust and weakens our effectiveness: the operational case for equality and diversity is therefore undeniable.'[6]

The end of the Cold War deprived the Navy of one role and gave it another. Its ASW specialism was not needed. Instead it once more became an expeditionary force. And the key to that role was air power. In the First Gulf War Royal Navy Lynx helicopters destroyed almost the entire Iraqi navy with their Sea Skua missiles, minesweepers cleared the waters and the destroyers and frigates provided support for the world's last battle-ships, USSs *Missouri* and *Wisconsin*, as they shelled Iraqi ground positions and launched cruise missiles. The Type 42 destroyer HMS *Gloucester* won the first-ever naval missile-to-missile engagement when her Sea Dart shot down an Iraqi Silkworm missile homing in on *Missouri*.

The new world order called upon the Navy to be able to deliver air power abroad and blockade rogue states under international embargo. Between 1993 and 1995 rotating naval task forces led by the carriers *Invincible*, *Illustrious* and *Ark Royal* took part in operations Deny Flight (1993–95), which enforced a no-fly zone over Bosnia, and Deliberate Force (1995), a campaign to undermine the Bosnian Serb army. Between 1991 and 2003 British aircraft carriers and ships also helped enforce the embargo and no-fly zone over Iraq. In 1999 the nuclear submarine HMS *Splendid* fired her Tomahawk cruise missiles on targets in Belgrade, the first British boat to use these weapons in action. It typified the Navy's new role.

For the Navy envisaged for the twenty-first century was not a blue-water navy destined to fight at sea: that kind of fighting seemed long gone. Its new role is encapsulated in a ship that was ordered in 1992, commissioned in 1998 and is still in service as of 2013. HMS *Ocean* is an amphibious assault ship designed to deliver Special Forces to combat targets or to deliver humanitarian aid. *Ocean*'s first task was to provide relief after Hurricane Mitch devastated Honduras in 1998. But her primary function is as a helicopter carrier capable of delivering troops swiftly by air and/or landing craft. In May 2000 the British military intervened to save the government of Sierra Leone from rebel forces. It meant a rapid deployment of aircraft, ground troops and ships. *Illustrious* assisted the RAF with her seven Sea Harriers and six RAF Harriers. *Ocean* carried four commando Sea King helicopters, two Lynxes, two Gazelles and two RAF Chinooks.

This was exactly the kind of operation the Navy was adapting itself to after the Cold War. *Ocean* allowed Britain once again to project her power by conducting assaults simultaneously from air and sea at short notice. In 1996 the Navy ordered two landing platform docks, *Albion* and *Bulwark*. When needed the rear of the vessel opens, flooding an internal dock and floating her landing craft, which disembark marines, armoured personnel carriers, trucks and tanks. *Albion* and *Bulwark* also carry Sea King, Merlin or Chinook helicopters for amphibious assaults. In operations Veritas and Telic – the British contribution to the actions against the Taliban in Afghanistan in 2001 and Saddam Hussein in Iraq in 2003 respectively – the Royal Navy provided support for ground forces. This included amphibious operations, aircraft flown from *Ark Royal* and *Illustrious* and cruise missiles fired from nuclear submarines. Operation Telic included thirty-one ships, the largest concentration of British warships since the Falklands. During the NATO intervention in the Libyan civil war in 2011 the submarines *Turbulent* and *Triumph* launched cruise missiles, *Ocean* provided a platform for Apache attack helicopters and frigates enforced the blockade.

The modern Navy is intended to be a flexible force, responsive to world events. In 2006 HMS *Bulwark* evacuated British nationals from Beirut during the Israel–Lebanon crisis; Britons were also rescued by Chinooks brought by HMS *Illustrious*. In 2010 *Ocean* and other ships were sent to help bring home travellers stranded after a volcanic eruption in Iceland grounded commercial flights. In the same year RFA *Largs Bay* (one of four dock landing ships built in the 2000s) took aid to the survivors of the Haiti earthquake. In July 2012 *Ocean* was stationed at Greenwich to provide rapid-response protection for the London Olympic Games from air and on the Thames; *Bulwark* provided a similar role off Weymouth.

But despite the increased activity the Navy is expected to do more with less. The surface fleet and the submarine force were whittled down with each review in the 1990s and 2000s. Frigates and destroyers were retired from service. Their replacements were fewer in number; but they were bigger and better. The Type 42 destroyer, which dated back to the late Sixties, was superseded by the Type 45 air-defence destroyer. The Type 45 is an ugly but fearsome ship. The Type 42 displaced 4,000 tons; her replacement displaces 8,000. Everything is concealed behind smooth superstructure panels, giving the vessel a futuristic look. One 45 can track and destroy more aircraft than five 42s working together. In the late 1990s the MOD ordered twelve of these ships; by 2008 that number had been cut to just six. The first destroyer entered service two years late, £1.5 billion over budget and not fully operational. The story of the Type 45 destroyer was the story of the Navy in the first decade of the twenty-first century in microcosm.

The new generation of seven nuclear submarines – the *Astute* class – was approved by the MoD in 1991; three were ordered in 1997. It was not until 2010 that the first of the batch, HMS *Astute*, was commissioned – four years late and almost £2 billion over budget. She was trumpeted as the most technologically advanced and stealthy submarine ever built in the UK; 39,000 acoustic panels make her almost invisible to sonar. She was all too visible, however, when she ran aground off the Isle of Skye in October 2010.

The government promised the Navy two new full-sized aircraft carriers to replace the three *Invincible*-class carriers. The new carriers would be the largest warships ever built in the United Kingdom. The first vessel, HMS *Queen Elizabeth*, is due in 2016; the second, *Prince of Wales*, in 2018. In the meantime the Navy had to put up with reduced air cover. In 2005 HMS *Invincible* was retired, leaving two aircraft carriers. At the fleet review to commemorate the two-hundredth anniversary of Trafalgar the largest ship was the aircraft carrier *Charles de Gaulle*, the flagship of the French Marine Nationale. The following year the Sea Harriers were withdrawn from service and replaced with the RAF Harrier. Then in 2010 the new coalition government announced that both *Ark Royal* and the RAF's remaining Harriers would be retired immediately. This left the UK without a fixed-wing carrier strike force for the first time since the advent of naval aviation. Of the two carriers under construction one would be held in a state of extended readiness or sold abroad. Even if *Queen Elizabeth* comes into service on schedule the fantastic super-carrier will have no aircraft until 2019.

The Royal Navy of 2013 is well below the strength recommended by successive defence reviews. The merchant marine and shipbuilding industries are in a worse state. Look at the ships that went to the Falklands in 1982. *Canberra* was built by Harland and Wolff of Belfast; the *QEII* by John Brown of Clydebank; *Atlantic Conveyor* by Swann Hunter of Tyne and Wear. HMS *Coventry* was built by Cammell Laird in Birkenhead, HMS *Argonaut* by Hawthorn Leslie in Hebburn, HMS *Antrim* by Upper Clyde Shipbuilders, HMS *Ardent* by Yarrow Shipbuilders, RFA *Sir Galahad* by Alexander Stephen of Linthouse and HMS *Hermes* by Vickers-Armstrong in Barrow-in-Furness.

The full list of the yards that built the ships – both private and naval – that went to the South Atlantic is a roll-call of some of the great British shipbuilders. Almost all of them have gone now. Many of the world-famous Clydeside yards had closed or had merged to become the Upper Clyde Shipbuilders in 1968. Nine years later the surving shipbuilding industry was nationalised and named British Shipbuilders; it had closed half of its yards by the time of the Falklands War. The warship builders were privatised in the 1980s. HMS *Ocean* was built by the Norwegian company Kvaerner Govan at the former Fairfield shipyard, which had had a history of British shipbuilding going back to 1834. In 1999 Kvaerner's yard was purchased by BAE Systems Surface Fleet Solutions, which now makes all British warships. And the future of the industry is in jeopardy as orders for new warships tail off in the 2010s. During the conflicts of the 1990s and 2000s the government had to charter foreign-owned merchantmen to carry troops and materiel to warzones. In 2012 the government awarded the contract to build four 37,000-ton refuelling tankers for the Navy to Daewoo of South Korea. The British merchant navy has faded away too. In 1975 there were 1,600 merchant ships crewed by 90,000 men and women. By 2010 there were 504 vessels. Yet the UK still conducts over 95 per cent of its trade by sea.

The poor state of the merchant navy, fishing fleet and shipbuilding industry is a hammer blow to Britain's real and potential strength at sea. It is a situation reminiscent of England's weakest period, in the Middle Ages, when the bulk of her imports and exports were carried on foreign-owned ships. Sea power in this country has been dependent upon the vitality of private shipping and the industrial might of the yards. In every major war the country faced at sea, there were never enough ships; it was the ability to produce new ships quickly, and the vast stock of sailors, that tipped the balance against its enemies. The decline of the Royal Navy is reversible, especially given the proven fighting ability of its personnel. But the slump in shipbuilding is irreparable.

The combat experience and skills of the Royal Navy's officers and men are not in doubt in the second decade of the century. But it is a chronically overstretched service, with too few ships for its manifold global commitments. It has been cut to the bone. In 2010 its manpower was reduced to 30,000. There were fifty-one frigates and destroyers in 1991, thirty-five in 1997; by 2012 that figure had fallen to nineteen. By then the fixed-wing aircraft carrier – symbol of a serious naval power – did not grace the list of the ships of the Royal Navy. The Type 45 destroyer was touted as a thoroughly modern ship because it could do the work of five Type 42 destroyers, but that's a politician's sleight of hand; even the miraculous Type 45 cannot be in five places at once. In 2011 the deployment off Libya disrupted routine naval operations, such as anti-narcotics patrols. There was not a single frigate to spare for home defence. The following year the UK did not have enough frigates to commit to the international effort against Somali pirates and the global capability of the Navy was undermined by the recall of *Ocean* and *Bulwark* to protect the Olympics.

This is a tale of steep decline in an age of austerity. Yet there is more to it than the sapping of Britain's power at sea.

Never has Britain been so strong at sea. Ships carrying British commodities traverse the seas in safety. The world's busiest sea lane is, as it always has been, the Strait of Dover, where over 400 ships pass each day. British warships range the world without let or hindrance and intervene in foreign conflicts without fear of reprisal. Somewhere in the world, under the waves, there is a *Vanguard*-class submarine armed with Trident ballistic missiles that can deliver apocalyptic terror anywhere at fifteen minutes' notice. The country does not need an aircraft carrier – how else could it have survived without one for over a decade? Britain does not even need warships in home waters. In 1982 and again during the conflicts in the Gulf and Libya the Royal Navy could dispatch the bulk of its forces abroad without a flicker of fear for the security of the realm.

This represents strength – strength in the sense of security, not power. It is unique in the history of the British Isles. And it goes back only as far as 1990 and the fall of the Soviet Union. Throughout the history detailed in this book the sea was a thing of terror to the people of the islands. It brought looters and invaders; it made traders prey to the waves and to pirates. The history of Britain makes sense only when you consider the sickening fear of the sea.

For most of the timeline of this book, England was a poor and marginal portion of an island off the mainland of Europe. Other countries dominated the sea lanes. English and Scottish sailors could only compete and learn the skills of seafaring by predation; the Crown could barely defend the coast. It was in the middle of the seventeenth century that the state marshalled its resources to create a powerful Navy. The sudden emergence of Britain as a serious trading nation in the late seventeenth century meant that there was something of value to defend on the high seas. The growth of the Royal Navy in the seventeenth and eighteenth centuries is one of the greatest military revolutions in history. It changed the fortunes of the country. The Navy was, in its heyday, the finest offensive and defensive force in the world. It was propelled to greatness by the standards set by generations of officers and men. Its drill and discipline were second to none. It was enthusiastically supported and cherished by the public.

And small wonder. The fortunes won by the British in the eighteenth century rested on fragile foundations. Britain had to fight time and again to prevent herself slipping into irrelevance again. It was on the sea that this battle had to be fought, and refought. But the real threat came from much nearer home: however much British power extended around the world's oceans the forces on the mainland of Europe could never be ignored. The possibility of invasion from the Continent was the nightmare that haunted Britain, even at the height of her maritime supremacy. Somehow the nation could not free herself from the tentacles that reached from the mainland.

Captain Alfred Thayer Mahan's famous book *The Influence of Sea Power Upon History* was published in 1890. Perhaps a rival book should have been published called 'The Limits of Sea Power'. Trafalgar allowed Britain to dominate the seaways for a few decades. She could even turn her back on the Continent and allow Europe to go its own way. The country constructed a system of global free trade and built a gigantic, sprawling empire. But it could not last for ever. The Royal Navy needed to be as big (with a margin) as the two other largest navies in the world combined; that placed an enormous financial burden on the country as other nations began to build navies. It also made the British watchful and nervous of every power that put a ship in the water.

Central to Britishness is the fear that tomorrow everything good will be snatched away; that our present good fortune is on loan and the debts will presently be called in. Perhaps that is the fate of all island dwellers. By Victoria's Diamond Jubilee in 1897 Britain was facing numerous threats to her global position. Britain's long-standing dream of an 'empire of the deep' – a seaborne network of defended sea lanes and island bases held by a Navy rather than by ground troops – had become a far-flung territorial empire. Foreign possessions had long land borders to be guarded. It could not be done by ships. This was put most pithily by the undersecretary at the India Office in 1899: 'It is to be regretted that Canada and India are not islands, but we must recognise the fact, and must modify our diplomacy accordingly.'[7]

There could never be enough ships. By the end of the nineteenth century it was clear that the world could not be run from the sea in the way it had been in 1850. Railways and telegraph lines had made continental powers more cohesive. Not only was Britain slipping behind as an industrial power, but the balmy and historically abnormal situation that faced her with few serious naval rivals was coming to an end as well. The Japanese navy outnumbered the Royal Navy in the Far East; the combined navies of the USA and Latin America reversed Britain's superiority in those waters; and even in Europe the Navy was being pushed hard by her competitors. Britain's predominance in shipbuilding – one of the principal pillars of her strength at sea – was over. In addition the European scramble for empire was upsetting the balance of power. The rise of Germany compelled her to recall her battleships from around the world. The Navy could not defend home waters *and* fan out around the world to guard an empire. Britain and her myriad international interests scattered around the globe suddenly looked very vulnerable. No wonder that Kipling and other witnesses of the Diamond Jubilee fleet review had intimations of terminal decline.

In the hostile world of the twentieth century the blessing of being an island nation with global clout turned into something of a curse. Britain was dependent on the sea for her livelihood, global position, security and very survival. For 111 years after the Battle of Trafalgar an aura of invincibility hung over the Navy. That was the dubious legacy of the most famous battle in naval history: Britons came to believe that the Royal Navy was capable of miracles until the illusion was cruelly dispelled at Jutland. In two world wars the Navy had to strain every effort to defend the vital convoys bringing fuel and food into the country. At the same time the supply lines to far-flung colonies became impossible to maintain. The Navy fought as valiantly as it had ever done in its illustrious history. In the past that fighting spirit delivered the spoils of victory; in the twentieth century the costs of naval supremacy were soaring while the returns diminished.

The lesson for a maritime people was that the pendulum of world power had swung in favour of continental states, which were taking advantage of railways, motorways and airways to unlock and exploit their resources. This affected the ability of a naval power to dent a continental power. The Royal Navy might put Germany under blockade from the sea, and once upon a time it might have been successful; but in an age of ever-expanding overland communication the effect was muted. Even though the Navy had a mighty battlefleet and controlled the five choke points of world trade at the beginning of the war, Britain's very existence could be endangered by aerial onslaught and submarine warfare. The defence of home waters at all costs entailed the loss of empire. The Second World War was the ultimate reminder of how merciless the sea is and how quickly the advantages of being an island can be reversed.

In 1982 Britain did not have to worry about a predatory neighbour. She did not have to fret about an attack on another colony while she threw everything she had at liberating the Falklands. The idea that sea-borne trade would be intercepted would have been laughable. While the Navy fought in distant waters the seas around Britain were protected by the NATO umbrella. The doors were locked tight while the guard dog ventured away. At no other point in history would that have been possible. In 1990 the last remaining threat to the sea lanes of Western Europe disappeared with the end of the Soviet Union. Today the Royal Navy is integrated into an international maritime force that collectively guarantees the security of the seas.

So it is of little surprise that the majority of Britons today cannot get worked up by the steep decline of the Royal Navy. Without the sense of danger continually lapping at the shores the nation's identity as an island has eroded. As the country has become more secure, sea power has declined. Today the Navy is used as an amphibious expeditionary force designed to project national power and police the world; it has become a thing of national prestige, not national defence. Imports and exports come in and go out as routinely and unregarded as the tide at night. The sea is a thing of leisure, not terror. We are fortunate to live at a time in history when this is so.

This brings us full circle. At the beginning of the span of time this book covers the Anglo-Saxons were content to consign their great seafaring past to oblivion and enjoy their green and pleasant land oblivious of the violence that lurked in the deep. History teaches that if the state cannot provide protection, others step in to fill the vacuum. At the beginning of 2013 a consortium based in the City of London launched Typhon Maritime Security, a private naval protection service that provides armed escorts for merchant convoys in the Gulf of Aden, the Arabian Sea and the Indian Ocean. It marks the resumption of a feature of naval warfare which seemingly belonged to the past and is perhaps a harbinger of what is to come.

Island dwellers cannot ignore the sea for ever. The history of Britain shows that the sea's impact on land is unpredictable; in the future the threat is as likely to be environmental as military. Britain, with its shoestring Navy and eviscerated shipbuilding industry, will struggle if the tide turns again. The challenge for government is to retain a flexible, well balanced fleet, suitable for the financial and strategic limitations of the present, but not to squeeze it so hard that it loses touch with its rich store of traditions and skills. The need for a navy will never go away. History has not finished with us.

GLOSSARY

aft	stern of a ship
Asdic	an early type of British sonar for detecting submarines
ashore	close to shore in relation to other ships
astern	behind a ship
ASW	Anti-Submarine Warfare
ballinger	small sea-going vessel with a shallow draught, mast and oars; in use in the later Middle Ages
basilisk	heavy bronze cannon with an exceptionally long barrel; named after the mythological beast which breathed fire and killed with a glance
battleship	derives from 'line of battle ship', used interchangeably with 'ship of the line' in this book, although battleships in the strict sense date from the late nineteenth century
beam	the width of a ship
bear up/down	turn downwind
beat	to tack to windward
bowsprit	spar or short mast projecting over the bows
brig	a relatively small vessel with two square-rigged masts
brigantine	a small vessel with two masts, with only the forward one square-rigged
bulkhead	any vertical panel, partition or wall within the hull of a ship
buss	two-masted fishing vessel
cable	large rope
capital ship	the principal warships of a navy
careen	clean and repair a ship's hull
carvel	method of building a ship from the frame first with planks laid edge to edge to form the hull. Cf. **clinker**
caulk	method of making the seams of a ship watertight
caulking	material used to caulk a ship, usually made from oakum
chaff	a radar countermeasure consisting of small fragments of material spread in the air as a cloud
chase gun	gun mounted astern or pointing ahead
Cinque Ports	Sandwich, Dover, Hythe, New Romney and Hastings

clinker	method of building a ship or boat by overlapping planks; the frame is added later to strengthen the hull
cog	flat-bottomed merchant ship
corsair	another name for a **privateer**, deriving from the French term for a **Letter of Marque**, *Lettre de Course*
corvette	originally a French term for a sloop. The name was revived for small British convoy escort vessels in the Second World War.
cromster	small Dutch warship with a light draught, used for coastal work; the English version was known as a **hoy**
cruiser	medium-sized warship sent on detached missions
culverin	muzzle-loading gun that fired an 18 lb shot
demi-culverin	muzzle-loading gun that fired a 9 lb shot
dogger	small fishing vessel, most common in the North Sea
double	to surround and attack an enemy ship or line from both sides
ebb	falling tide
EIC	East India Company
fire-control system	the sum of all the components used to co-ordinate a ship's guns onto a moving target
flood	rising tide
flota	Spanish treasure fleet
fore and aft rig	a ship in which the sails are set along the line of the keel rather than perpendicular to it. Cf. **square rig**
foul	to become entangled with another ship
freeboard	distance from the waterline to the upper deck
frigate	in the seventeenth century any small fast warship was dubbed a frigate. In the eighteenth century it came to mean a ship with 28 guns or more mounted on the main-deck only. In the Second World War the name was revived for anti-submarine and convoy vessels that were bigger than corvettes and sloops and smaller than destroyers.
full-rigged ship	a ship with three or more masts, all of them square-rigged
gage	see 'weather gage'
galleass	a hybrid ship with oars and sail plan
guerre de course	a tactic of naval warfare involving attacking an enemy's seaborne commerce
heel	movement of ship to either side at an angle
Hochseeflotte	German High Seas Fleet, 1907–18
hoy	a small coastal vessel
IJN	Imperial Japanese Navy
jury rig	temporary masts and yards

Kaiserliche Marine	Imperial German Navy, 1871–1918
ketch	kind of fishing boat, with two masts rigged fore and aft
Kriegsmarine	German navy, 1935–45
larboard	old-fashioned word for port or left-hand side
lateen	triangular sail set at an angle on a mast
lee	the direction to which the wind is blowing relative to a ship or place
lee shore	coast towards which the wind is blowing
Letter of Marque	papers authorising a person or ship to attack and take enemy vessels in time of war or in reprisal
line abreast	formation in which ships of a squadron sail side by side
line ahead	formation in which ships follow a leader
luff	to turn into the wind
Middle Sea	the Mediterranean
mizzen	the mast immediately aft of the main mast
Nore	a sandbank at the mouth of the Thames
oakum	material used for caulking made from old ropes
Ordinary	ships held in reserve
pinnace	small warship (sixteenth century); a ship's boat
privateer	ship or person authorised by **Letters of Marque** to attack enemy and capture ships
reef	to take in sail
RFA	Royal Fleet Auxiliary
RNR	Royal Naval Reserve
RNVR	Royal Naval Volunteer Reserve
roadstead	an area of sea outside a harbour where ships can safely lie at anchor
ship of the line	a capital ship used in the line of battle, term in use from the seventeenth century. See also **battleship**
shorten sail	to reduce the sails set
sloop-of-war	small cruising warship with up to eighteen guns. In the Second World War sloops were convoy-defence and anti-submarine vessels.
SMS	*Seiner Majestäts Schiffe*, His Majesty's Ship: the prefix for ships in the Kaiserliche Marine
sounding	measurement of depth of the water
splice	way of weaving two rope ends together
square rig	a sail and rigging arrangement whereby the sails are carried on horizontal yards set perpendicular to the line of the keel. Cf. **fore and aft rig**
tack	the course of a ship beating to windward
USN	United States Navy
van	vanguard, the leading division of a fleet or squadron

VOC	Vereenigde Oost-Indische Compagnie, the Dutch East India Company
warp	a way of moving a ship against the wind and tide or in a calm by hauling on a line attached to a dropped anchor
wear	to turn before the wind to change tack
weather gage	the windward position in relation to other ships
yard	spar on a mast from which sails are set

SELECT BIBLIOGRAPHY

Abbreviations
EHR: English Historical Review
HJ: Historical Journal
MM: Mariner's Mirror
ODNB: Oxford Dictionary of National Biography

General

E. H. H. Archibald, *The Fighting Ship in the Royal Navy, AD 897–1984* (1984)
J. Black, *The British Seaborne Empire* (2004)
W. Clowes, *The Royal Navy* (7 vols, 1897–1903)
J. B. Hattendorf, R. J. B. Knight, A. W. H. Pearsall, N. A. M. Rodger and G. Till (eds), *British Naval Documents 1204–1960* (1993)
J. R. Hill, *The Oxford Illustrated History of the Royal Navy* (1995)
E. Grove (ed.), *Great Battles of the Royal Navy: as commemorated in the gunroom, Britannia Royal Naval College, Dartmouth* (1994)
P. Kennedy, *The Rise and Fall of British Naval Mastery* (1976)
A. Lambert, *Admirals: the naval commanders who made Britain Great* (2008)
——, *War at Sea in the Age of Sail* (2000)
A. T. Mahan, *The Influence of Sea Power Upon History, 1660–1805* (1890)
R. Natkiel and A. Preston, *Atlas of Maritime History* (1992)
E. L. Rasor, *English/British Naval History to 1815: A Guide to the Literature* (2004)
N. A. M. Rodger, *The Admiralty* (1979)
——, *The Command of the Ocean: A Naval History of Britain, 1649–1815* (2004)
——, *The Safeguard of the Sea: A Naval History of Britain, 660–1649* (1997)
B. Tunstall, *Naval Warfare in the Age of Sail: the evolution of fighting tactics* (ed. N. Tracey, 1990)

Preface

A. W. Beaglehole, *The Life of Captain James Cook* (1974)
J. Blake, *Charts of War: the maps and charts that have informed and illustrated war at sea* (2009)
M. Blewit, *Surveys of the Seas* (1957)
E. H. Burrows, *Captain Owen of the African Survey, 1774–1857* (1979)
D. Cordingly, *Billy Ruffian. The* Bellerophon *and the downfall of Napoleon: the*

biography of a ship of the line, 1782–1836 (2003)

A. Day, *The Admiralty Hydrographic Service, 1795–1919* (1967)

A. Friendly, *Beaufort of the Admiralty: the life of Sir Francis Beaufort, 1774–1857* (1957)

R. D. Keynes, *Charles Darwin's* Beagle *Diary* (Cambridge, 1988)

A. Lambert, *Franklin: tragic hero of polar navigation* (2010)

E. Linklater, *The Voyage of the* Challenger (1974)

C. Lloyd, *Mr Barrow of the Admiralty* (1970)

R. Morris, 'Endeavour, Discovery and Idealism, 1760–1895', in Hill (ed.), *Oxford History*

P. Nichols, *Evolution's Captain: the tragic fate of Robert FitzRoy, the man who sailed Darwin around the world* (2003)

G. S. Ritchie, *The Admiralty Chart: British naval hydrography in the nineteenth century* (1967)

Part 1, chapters 1–4

R. Abels, *Alfred the Great: war, kingship and culture in Anglo-Saxon England* (1998)

——, *Lordship and Military Obligation in Anglo-Saxon England* (1992)

—— and B. Bachrach (eds), *The Normans and their Adversaries at War* (2001)

A. Bang-Andersen, B. Greenhill and E. Harald Grude (eds), *The North Sea: a highway of economic and cultural exchange* (1985)

F. W. Brooks, *The English Naval Forces, 1199–1272* (1962)

R. L. S. Bruce-Mitford, *The Sutton Hoo Ship Burial: a handbook* (1968)

J. Campbell, E. John and P. Wormald, *The Anglo-Saxons* (1982)

——, *Essays in Anglo-Saxon History* (2003)

H. L. Cannon, 'The Battle of Sandwich and Eustace the Monk', *EHR*, 27 (1912)

A. Care Evans, *The Sutton Hoo Ship Burial* (1994)

R. Glover, 'English Warfare in 1066', *EHR*, LXVII (1952)

R. Hamer (ed.), *A Choice of Anglo-Saxon Verse* (2006)

J. Haywood, *Dark Age Naval Power: a re-assessment of Frankish and Anglo-Saxon seafaring activity* (1991)

N. Hooper, 'Some Observations on the Navy in the Late Anglo-Saxon England', in C. Harper-Bill, C. J. Holdsworth and J. Nelson (eds), *Studies in Medieval History presented to R. Allen Brown* (1989)

J. le Patourel, *The Norman Empire* (1976)

J. Pullen-Appleby, *English Sea Power, c. 871–1100* (2005)

D. Scragg (ed.), *The Battle of Maldon AD 991* (2006)

A. P. Smyth, *Alfred the Great* (1995)

Part 2, chapters 5–7

R. C. Anderson, *Oared Fighting Ships* (1976)

J. L. Bolton, *The Medieval English Economy, 1150–1500* (1980)

C. J. Ford, 'Piracy or Policy: The Crisis in the Channel, 1400–1403', *Transactions of the Royal Historical Society*, 5th ser., XXIX (1979)

I. Friel, *The Good Ship: ships, shipbuilding and technology in England, 1200–1520* (1995)

R. Gardiner and R. W. Unger (eds), *Cogs, Caravels and Galleys: the sailing ship, 1000–1650* (1994)

J. Gillingham, 'Richard I, Galley Warfare and Portsmouth: the beginning of a Royal Navy', in M. Prestwich, R. H. Britnell and R. Frame (eds), *Thirteenth Century England* (Proceedings of the Durham Conference 1995, vol. VI, 1997)

G. Hutchinson, *Medieval Ships and Shipping* (1997)

M. K. James, *Studies in the Medieval Wine Trade* (ed. E. M. Veale; introduced by E. M. Carus-Wilson, 1971)

T. H. Lloyd, *England and the German Hanse, 1157–1611* (2002)

——, *The English Wool Trade in the Middle Ages* (1977)

D. M. Loades, 'The King's Ships and the Keeping of the Seas: 1413–1480', *Medieval History*, I (1990)

C. Platt, *Medieval Southampton: the port and trading community, AD 1000–1600* (1973)

E. Power, *The Wool Trade in English Medieval History* (1941)

C. F. Richmond, 'English Naval Power in the fifteenth century', *History*, ns, LII (1967)

——, 'The Keeping of the Seas During the Hundred Years War', *History*, ns, XLIX (1964)

——, 'The War at Sea', in K. Fowler (ed.), *The Hundred Years War* (1971)

S. Rose, *Medieval Naval Warfare, 1000–1500* (2002)

—— (ed.), *The Navy of the Lancastrian Kings: accounts and inventories of William Soper* (1982)

——, 'The Wall of England', in Hill (ed.), *Oxford Illustrated History*

J. Sumption, *Trial by Battle: the Hundred Years War*, vol. 1 (1999)

R. W. Unger, *The Ship in the Medieval Economy, 600–1600* (1980)

R. Ward, *The World of the Medieval Shipmaster: law, business and the sea, c. 1350–1450* (2009)

Parts 3 and 4, chapters 8–15

S. Adams, *The Armada Campaign of 1588* (1988)

——, 'New Light on the "Reformation" of John Hawkins: the Ellesmere naval survey of January 1584', *EHR*, CV (1990)

K. R. Andrews, *Elizabethan Privateering: English privateering during the Spanish War, 1585–1603* (1964)

——, *Trade, Plunder and Settlement: maritime enterprise and the genesis of the British Empire* (1984)

D. Burwash, *English Merchant Shipping, 1460–1540* (1947)

N. Canny (ed.), *The Oxford History of the British Empire*, vol. I, *The Origins of Empire* (1998)

E. M. Carus-Wilson, *Medieval Merchant Venturers: collected studies* (1954)

C. Cipolla, *Guns and Sails in the Early Phase of European Expansion, 1400–1700* (1965)

J. S. Corbett, *Papers Relating to the Navy During the Spanish War, 1585–1587* (1898)

C. S. L. Davies, 'The administration of the royal navy under Henry VIII', *EHR*, LXXX (1965)

J. Guilmartin, *Gunpowder and Galleys: changing technology and Mediterranean warfare at sea* (1974)

H. Kelsey, *Sir John Hawkins: Queen Elizabeth's slave trader* (2003)

——, *Sir Francis Drake: the queen's pirate* (1988)

J. K. Laughton, *State Papers Relating to the Defeat of the Spanish Armada* (2 vols, 1894)

D. M. Loades, *England's Maritime Empire: seapower, commerce and policy, 1490–1690* (2000)

——, 'From the King's Ships to the Royal Navy, 1500–1642', in Hill (ed.), *Oxford Illustrated History*

——, *The Tudor Navy* (1992)

—— and C. S. Knighton, *Letters from the Mary Rose* (2002)

G. J. Marcus, *The Conquest of the North Atlantic* (1980)

C. Martin and G. Parker, *The Spanish Armada* (1999)

J. McDermott, *England and the Spanish Armada: the necessary quarrel* (2005)

P. McGrath, 'Bristol and America, 1480–1631', in K. R. Andrews, N. P. Canny and P. E. H. Hair (eds), *The Westward Enterprise: English activities in Ireland, the Atlantic and America, 1480–1650* (1979)

G. Moorhouse, *Great Harry's Navy: how Henry VIII gave England sea power* (2005)

M. Oppenheim, *A History of the Administration of the Royal Navy and of Merchant Shipping in Relation to the Navy from 1509 to 1660 with an introduction treating of the preceding period* (1896)

——, *The Naval Tracts of Sir William Monson* (5 vols, 1902–14)

G. Parker, 'The Dreadnought Revolution of Tudor England', *MM*, 82 (1996)

D. B. Quinn, *England and the Discovery of America, 1481–1620* (1974)

—— and A. N. Ryan, *England's Sea Empire, 1550–1642* (1983)

N. A. M. Rodger, 'The Development of Broadside Gunnery, 1540–1650', *MM*, 82 (1996)

——, 'Guns and Sails in the First Phase of English Colonisation, 1500–1650', in Canny (ed.), *Oxford History of the British Empire*

——, 'The New Atlantic: naval warfare in the sixteenth century', in J. B. Hattendorf and R. W. Unger (eds), *War at Sea in the Middle Ages and the Renaissance* (2003)

M. J. Rodriguez-Salgado and S. Adams (eds), *England, Spain and the Gran Armada, 1585–1604* (1988)

G. V. Scammell, *The World Encompassed: the first maritime empires, c. 800–1650* (1981)

G. C. Smith, *Forerunners of Drake: a study of trade with Spain in the early Tudor period* (1954)

J. A. Williamson, *Hawkins of Plymouth: a new history of Sir John Hawkins and of the other members of his family prominent in Tudor England* (1969)

——, *The Cabot Voyages and Bristol Discovery Under Henry VII* (1962)

—— (ed.), *The Voyages of the Cabots* (1929)

Parts 5 and 6, chapters 16–20

S. Adams, 'Spain or the Netherlands? The dilemmas of early Stuart foreign policy', in Tomlinson (ed.), *England Before the Civil War*

658 SELECT BIBLIOGRAPHY

K. R. Andrews, *Ships, Money and Politics: seafaring and naval enterprise in the reign of Charles I* (1991)

J. Barratt, *Cromwell's Wars at Sea* (2006)

M. L. Baumber, *General-at-Sea: Robert Blake and the seventeenth-century revolution in naval warfare* (1989)

——, 'Parliamentary Naval Politics 1641–49', *MM*, LXXXII (1996)

C. R. Boxer, *The Journal of Maarten Harpertszoon Tromp, anno 1639* (1930)

M. J. Braddick, 'An English Military Revolution?', *HJ*, 36, 4 (1993)

Robert Brenner, 'The Civil War Politics of London's Merchant Community', *Past and Present*, 58 (1973)

J. R. Bruijn, *The Dutch Navy of the Seventeenth and Eighteenth Centuries* (1993)

B. Capp, *Cromwell's Navy: the fleet and the English Revolution 1648–60* (1989)

K. N. Chaudhuri, *The East India Company: a study of an early joint-stock company, 1600–1640* (1965)

G. N. Clark, *The Colonial Conferences between England and the Netherlands in 1613 and 1615* (2 vols, 1952)

R. Crabtree, 'The Idea of a Protestant Foreign Policy', in I. Roots (ed.), *Cromwell: A Profile* (1973)

J. D. Davies, 'A Permanent Maritime Fighting Force', in Hill (ed.), *Oxford Illustrated History*

A. C. Dewar, 'The Naval Administration of the Interregnum, 1641–59', *MM*, 12 (1926)

W. H. Dixon, *Robert Blake: admiral and general at sea, based on family and state papers* (1852)

M. C. Fissel (ed.), *War and Government in Britain, 1598–1650* (1991)

S. R. Gardiner, *History of England from the Accession of James I to the Outbreak of the Civil War, 1603–1642* (10 vols, 1883–4)

—— and C. T. Atkinson, *Papers Relating to the First Dutch War, 1652–4* (6 vols, 1899–1930)

J. Glanville, *The Voyage to Cadiz in 1625* (1883)

T. Gray, 'Turkish Piracy and Early Stuart Devon', *Transactions of the Devonshire Association*, CXXI (1989)

——, 'Turks, Moors and Cornish Fishermen', *Journal of the Royal Institution of Cornwall*, ns, X (1987–90)

S. Groenveld, 'The English Civil Wars as a Cause of the First Anglo-Dutch Wars', *HJ*, XXX (1987)

R. Harding, *The Evolution of the Sailing Navy, 1509–1815* (1995)

D. D. Hebb, *Piracy and the English Government, 1616–1642* (1994)

J. Israel, *Dutch Primacy in World Trade, 1585–1740* (1991)

J. R. Jones, *The Anglo-Dutch Wars of the Seventeenth Century* (1996)

G. A. Kempthorne, 'Sir John Kempthorne and his sons', *MM*, 12 (1926)

J. S. Kepler, 'Fiscal Aspects of the English Carrying Trade During the Thirty Years War', *Economic History Review*, XXV (1972)

A. Konstam, *Sovereigns of the Sea: the quest to build the perfect Renaissance battleship* (2008)

SELECT BIBLIOGRAPHY 659

R. Lockyer, *Buckingham: the life and political career of George Villiers, first Duke of Buckingham, 1592–1628* (1981)

A. P. McGowan (ed.), *The Jacobean Commissions of Enquiry, 1608 and 1618* (1971)

E. Milford, 'The Navy at Peace: the activities of the early Jacobean Navy, 1603–1618', *MM*, 76 (1990)

M. Oppenheim, 'The Royal Navy Under James I', *EHR*, VII, 27 (1892)

——, 'The Royal Navy Under Charles I', *EHR*, VIII and IX (1893–4)

C. D. Penn, *The Navy Under the Early Stuarts and its Influence on English History* (1913)

J. R. Powell, *Robert Blake: General-at-sea* (1972)

——, *The Navy in the English Civil War* (1962)

G. V. Scammell, 'The Sinews of War: manning and provisioning English fighting ships, c. 1550–1650', *MM*, 73 (1987)

K. Sharpe (ed.), *Faction and Parliament: essays on early Stuart history* (1978)

——, 'The Personal Rule of Charles I', in Tomlinson (ed.), *Before the English Civil War*

R. W. Stewart, 'Arms and Expeditions: the Ordnance Office and the assault on Cadiz (1625) and the Isle of Rhé (1627)', in Fissel (ed.), *War and Government*

H. Taylor, 'Trade, Neutrality and the "English Road", 1630–1648', *EHR*, XXV (1972)

D. Thomas, 'Financial and Administrative Developments', in Tomlinson (ed.), *Before the English Civil War*

A. Thrush, 'Naval Finance and the Origin and Development of Ship Money', in Fissel (ed.), *War and Government*

H. Tomlinson (ed.), *Before the English Civil War: essays on early Stuart politics and government* (1983)

T. Venning, *Cromwell's Foreign Policy* (1995)

J. S. Wheeler, *The Making of a World Power: war and the military revolution in seventeenth-century England* (1999)

M. C. Wren, 'London and the Twenty Ships, 1626–1627', *The American History Review*, 55 (1950)

M. B. Young, *Servility and Service: the life and work of Sir John Coke* (1986)

Part 7, chapters 21–24

R. C. Anderson (ed.), *The Third Dutch War* (1946)

P. Aubrey, *The Defeat of James Stuart's Armada, 1692* (1979)

J. Baltharpe, *Straights Voyage: or, St David's poem*, ed. J. S. Bromley (1959)

E. Barlow, *Journal of his Life at Sea in King's Ships*, transcribed by B. Lubbock (2 vols, 1934)

N. Boteler, *Boteler's Dialogues*, ed. W. G. Perrin (1929)

A. Bryant, *Samuel Pepys: the saviour of the navy* (1947)

G. Burnet, *Bishop Burnet's History of His Own Time* (1725)

J. S. Corbett, *England in the Mediterranean: British power within the straight, 1603–1713* (1904)

——, *Fighting Instructions, 1530-1816* (1905)

E. Coxere, *Adventures by Sea*, ed. E. H. W. Meyerstein (1945)

J. D. Davies, 'The English Navy on the Eve of War 1689', in *Guerres Maritimes, 1688–1713* (1996)

——, *Gentlemen and Tarpaulins: the officers and men of the Restoration navy* (1991)

——, 'The Navy, Parliament and Political Crisis in the Reign of Charles II', *HJ*, vol. 36, no. 2 (Jun. 1993), pp. 271–88

——, *Pepys's Navy: ships, men and organisation 1649–89* (2008)

J. Ehrman, *The Navy in King William's War, 1689–1697* (1953)

F. L. Fox, *A Distant Storm: the Four Days Battle of 1666* (2009)

S. Harris, *Cloudesley Shovell: Stuart admiral* (2001)

S. Hornstein, *The Restoration Navy and English Foreign Trade, 1674–88* (1991)

B. Ingram (ed.), *Three Sea Journals of Stuart Times …* (1936)

C. Knighton, *Pepys and the Navy* (2003)

——, *Samuel Pepys and the Second Dutch War* (1995)

R. Latham (ed.), *Samuel Pepys and the Second Dutch War: Pepys's navy white book and Brooke House papers* (1995)

P. Le Fevre, 'Tangier, the Navy and its Connection with the Glorious Revolution of 1688', *MM*, 73 (1987)

S. C. A. Pincus, 'Popery, Trade and Universal Monarchy: The Ideological Context of the Outbreak of the Second Anglo-Dutch War', *EHR*, 107 (1992)

F. N. L. Poynter (ed.), *The Journal of James Yonge, 1647–1721, Plymouth Surgeon* (1963)

P. G. Rogers, *The Dutch in the Medway* (1970)

J. Smith, *The Seaman's Grammar* (1653)

W. A. Speck, *James II* (2002)

J. R. Tanner (ed.), *A Descriptive Catalogue of the Naval Manuscripts in the Pepysian Library at Magdalene College, Cambridge* (1903–23)

—— (ed.), *Samuel Pepys's Naval Minutes* (1926)

H. Teonge, *Diary of Henry Teonge, chaplain on board HM's ships* Assistance, Bristol *and* Royal Oak, *1675–1679*, ed. E. D. Ross and E. Power (1927)

Parts 8 and 9, chapters 25–30

F. Anderson, *Crucible of War: the Seven Years' War and the fate of the empire in British North America, 1754–1766* (2000)

D. A. Baugh, *British Naval Administration in the Age of Walpole* (1965)

——, 'The Eighteenth Century Navy as a National Institution, 1690–1815', in Hill (ed.), *Oxford Illustrated History*

J. Black, *America or Europe?: British foreign policy, 1739–63* (1998)

——, *British Foreign Policy in the Age of Walpole* (1985)

—— and P. Woodfine, *The British Navy and the Use of Naval Power in the Eighteenth Century* (1988)

Lord Bolingbroke, *Letters on the Spirit of and on the Idea of a Patriot King*, ed. A. Hassall (1926)

J. Brewer, *The Sinews of Power: war, money and the English state, 1688–1783* (1989)

M. Burrows, *The Life of Edward, Lord Hawke* (1883)

J. S. Corbett, *England in the Seven Years War: a study in combined operations* (1907)

M. Duffy (ed.), *Parameters of British Naval Power, 1650–1850* (1992)

——, 'The Establishment of the Western Squadron as the Linchpin of British Naval Strategy', in Duffy (ed.), *Parameters*

J. R. Dull, *The Age of the Ship of the Line: the British and French Navies, 1650–1815* (2009)

D. Erskine (ed.), *Augustus Hervey's Journal* (1953)

J. Gwynn, *An Admiral for America: Sir Peter Warren, Vice Admiral of the Red, 1703–1752* (2004)

R. Harding, *Amphibious Warfare in the Eighteenth Century: The British Expedition to the West Indies 1740–1742* (1991)

——, *The Emergence of Britain's Global Naval Supremacy: the war of 1739–1748* (2010)

——, 'Edward Vernon', in Le Fevre and Harding, *Precursors*

J. B. Hattendorf, *England in the War of Spanish Succession* (1989)

——, 'The Struggle with France, 1690–1815', in Hill (ed.), *Oxford Illustrated History*

G. Jordan and N. Rogers, 'Admirals as Heroes: Patriotism and Liberty in Hanoverian England', *Journal of British Studies*, 28 (1989)

H. Kamen, 'The Destruction of the Spanish Silver Fleet at Vigo in 1702', *Bulletin of the Institute of Historical Research*, 39 (1966)

B. Lavery, *The Ship of the Line*, vol. 1, *The Development of the Battlefleet, 1650–1850* (1983)

P. Le Fevre and R. Harding (eds), *Precursors of Nelson: admirals of the eighteenth century* (2000)

R. Mackay, *Admiral Hawke* (1985)

—— and M. Duffy, *Hawke, Nelson and British Naval Leadership, 1747–1805* (2009)

—— (ed.), *The Hawke Papers: a selection, 1743–1771* (1990)

G. J. Marcus, *Quiberon Bay: the campaign in home waters, 1759* (1960)

P. J. Marshall (ed.), *The Oxford History of the British Empire*, vol. II, *The Eighteenth Century* (1998)

F. McLynn, *1759: The Year Britain Became Master of the World* (2005)

R. D. Merriman (ed.), *Queen Anne's Navy: documents concerning the administration of the navy of Queen Anne, 1702–1714* (1961)

R. Middleton, *The Bells of Victory: the Pitt–Newcastle ministry and the conduct of the Seven Years' War, 1757–1762* (1985)

——, 'British Naval Strategy, 1755–1762: The Western Squadron', *MM*, vol. 75, no. 4 (1989)

A. Miller, *Dressed to Kill: British Naval Uniforms, Masculinity and Contemporary Fashions, 1748–1857* (2007)

G. B. Mundy, *The Life and Correspondence of the Late Admiral Lord Rodney* (2 vols, 1830)

E. Pearce, *Pitt the Elder: man of war* (2010)

H. W. Richmond, *The Navy in the War of 1739–1748* (1920)

——, *Papers Relating to the Loss of Minorca in 1756* (1913)

N. A. M. Rodger, 'George, Lord Anson', in Le Fevre and Harding, *Precursors*

——, 'Sea Power and Empire', in Marshall (ed.), *Oxford History*

——, *The Insatiable Earl: a life of John Montagu, fourth earl of Sandwich* (1993)

——, *Wooden World: an anatomy of the Georgian navy* (1986)

B. Simms, *Three Victories and a Defeat: the rise and fall of the first British Empire, 1714–1783* (2007)

M. T. Smelser, *The Campaign for the Sugar Islands, 1759: a study in amphibious warfare* (1955)

C. P. Stacey, *Quebec, 1759* (1959)

G. Symcox, *The Crisis of French Sea Power, 1688–1697: from guerre d'escadre to guerre de course* (1974)

D. Syrett, *The Royal Navy in American Waters, 1775–1783* (1989)

——, *The Royal Navy in European Waters during the American Revolutionary War* (1998)

G. Williams, *The Prize of All the Oceans: the triumph and tragedy of Anson's voyage round the world* (1999)

S. Willis, *The Admiral Benbow* (2010)

K. Wilson, 'Empire, Trade and Popular Politics in Mid-Hanoverian Britain: The Case of Admiral Vernon', *Past and Present*, 121 (1988)

P. Woodfine, *Britannia's Glories: The Walpole Ministry and the 1739 War with Spain* (1998)

Parts 10 and 11, chapters 31–41

M. Adams, *Admiral Collingwood: Nelson's own hero* (2005)

R. Adkins, *Jack Tar: life in Nelson's navy* (2008)

——, *Trafalgar: the biography of the battle* (2005)

R. and L. Adkins, *The War for all the Oceans: from Nelson at the Nile to Napoleon at Waterloo* (2006)

G. R. Barnes and J. H. Owen (eds), *The Private Papers of John, Earl of Sandwich, First Lord of the Admiralty* (4 vols, 1932–8)

D. A. Baugh, 'Hood, Samuel, first Viscount Hood', *ODNB*

J. Black, *Britain as a Military Power, 1688–1815* (1998)

N. Blake, *Steering to Glory: a day in the life of a ship of the line* (2005)

J. Bourchier (ed.), *Memoir of the Life of Admiral Sir Edward Codrington* (2 vols, 1873)

K. C. Breen, 'Divided command, West Indies and N. America, 1780–81', in Black and Woodfine, *British Navy*

——, 'George Bridges, Lord Rodney', in Le Fevre and Harding, *Precursors*

J. S. Corbett, *The Campaign of Trafalgar* (1910)

P. K. Crimmin, 'John Jervis, Earl of St Vinncent', in Le Fevre and Harding, *Precursors*

J. Davidson, *The Admiral Lord St Vincent: Saint or Tyrant? The life of Sir John Jervis, Nelson's patron* (2006)

D. Davies, *Fighting Ships: ships of the line, 1793–1815* (1996)

A. Deane, *Nelson's Favourite: HMS* Agamemnon *at war, 1781–1809* (1996)

W. H. Dillon, *A Narrative of my Professional Adventures, 1790–1839*, ed. M. A. Lewis (2 vols, 1956)

M. Duffy, 'Samuel Hood, First Viscount Hood', in Le Fevre and Harding, *Precursors*

E. Fraser, *The Enemy at Trafalgar: eye-witness' narratives, dispatches and letters from the French and Spanish fleets* (1906)

——, *The Sailors Whom Nelson Led: their doings described by themselves* (1913)

J. A. Gardner, *Recollections of James Anthony Gardner*, ed. R. V. Hamilton and J. K. Laughton (1906)

D. Goodall, *Salt Water Sketches: being incidents in the life of Daniel Goodall* (1860)

D. Hannay (ed.), *Letters Written by Sir Samuel Hood (Viscount Hood) in 1781–2–3* (1895)

T. A. Heathcote, *Nelson's Trafalgar Captains and Their Battles* (2005)

C. Hibbert, *Nelson: a personal history* (1994)

F. Hoffman, *A Sailor of King George* (1999)

D. Hood, *The Admirals Hood* (1877)

R. Knight, *Nelson: the pursuit of victory* (2005)

——, 'Richard, Earl Howe', in Le Fevre and Harding, *Precursors*

A. Lambert, *Nelson: Britannia's god of war* (2004)

B. Lavery, *Nelson and the Nile: the naval war against Bonaparte, 1798* (1998)

——, *Nelson's Navy: the ships, men and organisation, 1793–1815* (1989)

S. Leech, *Thirty Years From Home: or, a voice from the maindeck* (1844)

C. Lloyd (ed.), *The Health of Seamen: selections from the works of Dr James Lind, Sir Gilbert Blane and Dr Thomas Trotter* (1965)

J. Macdonald, *The British Navy's Victualling Board, 1793–1815* (2010)

——, *Feeding Nelson's Navy: the true story of food at sea in the Georgian era* (2004)

R. Mackay, 'Edward, Lord Hawke', in Le Fevre and Harding, *Precursors*

A. Morrison, *The Hamilton and Nelson Papers* (2 vols, 1893–4)

G. B. Mundy (ed.), *The Life and Correspondence of the Late Admiral Lord Rodney* (2 vols, 1830)

G. P. B. Naish, *Nelson's Letters to His Wife and Other Documents, 1785–1831* (1958)

A. Nicholson, *Men of Honour: Trafalgar and the making of the English hero* (2005)

N. H. Nicolas, *The Dispatches and Letters of Vice Admiral Lord Viscount Nelson* (7 vols, 1844–6)

C. Oman, *Nelson* (1947)

D. Orde, *In the Shadow of Nelson: The Life of Admiral Lord Collingwood* (2008)

P. Padfield, *Maritime Power and the Struggle for Freedom: naval campaigns that shaped the modern world, 1788–1851* (2003)

J. Raigersfeld, *The Life of a Sea Officer* (1840)

W. Robinson, *Jack Nastyface: Memoirs of an English Seaman*, ed. O. Warner (2002)

D. A. B. Ronald, *Young Nelsons: boy sailors during the Napoleonic Wars, 1793–1815* (2009)

J. Scott, *Recollections of a Naval Life* (3 vols, 1834)

W. Spavens, *The Narrative of William Spavens, a Chatham Pensioner* (1796)

F. B. Spilsbury, *Account of a Voyage to the Western Coast of Africa; performed by His Majesty's sloop* Favourite, *in the year 1805* (1807)

D. Spinney, *Rodney* (1969)

J. Sugden, *Nelson: a dream of Glory* (2005)

——, *Nelson: the sword of Albion* (2012)

J. E. Talbott, *The Pen and Ink Sailor: Charles Middleton and the King's Navy, 1778–1813* (1998)

P. Trew, *Rodney and the Breaking of the Line* (2006)

E. Vincent, *Nelson: Love and Fame* (2003)

T. Wareham, *The Star Captains: frigate command in the Napoleonic Wars* (2001)

C. White, *1797: Nelson's Year of Destiny: Cape St Vincent and Santa Cruz de Tenerife* (1998)

——, *The Nelson Encyclopaedia* (2003)

——, *Nelson: the admiral* (2005)

—— (ed.), *Nelson: the new letters* (2005)

S. Willis, *Fighting at Sea in the Eighteenth Century: the art of sailing warfare* (2008)

——, *The Fighting Temeraire: legend of Trafalgar* (2010)

——, *The Glorious First of June: fleet battle in the reign of terror* (2011)

Part 12, chapters 42–45

J. Beeler, *Birth of a Battleship: British capital ship design, 1870–1881* (1991)

G. Bennett, *Charlie B* (1969)

C. Beresford, *Memoirs* (2 vols, 1914)

L. Bethell, *The Abolition of the Brazilian Slave Trade: Britain, Brazil and the slave trade question* (1970)

D. Brown, *Palmerston and the Politics of Foreign Policy, 1846–55* (2002)

D. K. Brown, 'Wood, Sail and Cannonballs to Steel, Steam and Shells, 1815–1895', in Hill (ed.), *Oxford Illustrated History*

——, *Warrior to Dreadnought: warship development, 1860–1905* (2010)

R. A. Burt, *British Battleships, 1889–1904* (1988)

R. Chesneau and E. Kolesnik (eds), *Conway's All the World's Fighting Ships, 1860–1905* (1979)

N. J. Dingle, *British Warships, 1860–1906: a photographic record* (2009)

B. Edwards, *Royal Navy versus the Slave Traders: enforcing abolition at sea, 1808–1898* (2007)

J. A. Fisher, *Memories and Records* (2 vols, 1920)

R. Freeman, *The Great Edwardian Feud: Beresford's vendetta against Fisher* (2009)

R. Gardiner and A. Lambert (eds), *Steam, Steel and Shellfire: the steam warship, 1815–1905* (2001)

G. S. Graham, *The China Station: 1830–1865* (1978)

——, *The Politics of Naval Supremacy* (1965)

B. Greenhill and A. Giffard, *The British Assault on Finland* (1988)

W. H. Hall and W. D. Bernard, *Narrative of the Voyages and Services of the* Nemesis *from 1840 to 1843* (1844)

C. I. Hamilton, *Anglo-French Naval Rivalry, 1840–1870* (1993)

R. C. Howell, *The Royal Navy and the Slave Trade* (1987)

R. Hyam, *Britain's Imperial Century, 1815-1914: a study of empire and expansion* (1976)

A. Lambert, *Battleships in Transition: the creation of the steam battlefleet, 1815–1860* (1984)

——, *The Challenge: America, Britain, and the War of 1812* (2012)

——, *The Crimean War: British Grand Strategy, 1853–56* (1991)

——, *HMS* Warrior *1860: Victoria's ironclad deterrent* (2011)

——, *The Last Sailing Battlefleet: maintaining naval mastery, 1815–1850* (1991)

——, 'The Shield of Empire, 1815–1895', in Hill (ed.), *Oxford Illustrated History*

N. A. Lambert, *Sir John Fisher's Naval Revolution* (1999)

P. Leonard, *Records of a Voyage to the Western Coast of Africa* (1833)

M. Lewis, *The Navy in Transition, 1814–1865* (1965)

C. Lloyd, *The Navy and the Slave Trade* (1949)

R. Mackay, *Fisher of Kilverstone* (1970)

A. J. Marder (ed.), *Fear God and Dread Nought: the correspondence of Admiral of the Fleet Lord Fisher of Kilverstone* (3 vols, 1952–9)

R. Massie, *Dreadnought: Britain, Germany, and the coming of the Great War* (1991)

T. Pocock, *Remember Nelson: the life of Captain Sir William Hoste* (1977)

A. Preston and J. Major, *Send a Gunboat: 150 years of the British gunboat* (2007)

J. Roberts, *The Battleship* Dreadnought (1992)

M. Ryan, 'The Price of Legitimacy in Humanitarian Intervention: Britain, the right of search, and the abolition of the West African slave trade, 1807–1867', in B. Simms and D. J. B. Trim (eds), *Humanitarian Intervention: a history* (2011)

P. Scott, *Fifty Years in the Royal Navy* (1919)

J. T. Sumida, *In Defence of Naval Supremacy: finance, technology and British naval policy, 1889–1914* (1989)

D. G. Tinnie, 'The Slaving Brig *Henriqueta* and her Evil Sisters: a case study in the 19th-century illegal slave trade to Brazil', *The Journal of African American History*, vol. 93 (2008)

S. Willis, *Fighting Ships, 1850–1950* (2008)

J. Winton, 'Life and Education in a Technically Evolving Navy, 1815–1925', in Hill (ed.), *Oxford Illustrated History*

Parts 13, 14 and 15, chapters 46–56

C. Barnett, *Engage the Enemy More Closely: the Royal Navy and the Second World War* (1991)

——, *The Collapse of British Power* (1972)

P. Beesley, *Room 40: British naval intelligence, 1914–1918* (1982)

——, *Very Special Intelligence: the story of the Admiralty's Operational Intelligence Centre, 1939–45* (1977)

G. Bennett, *Naval Battles of the First World War* (2005)

C. Blair, *Hitler's U-Boat War: the hunted, 1942–1945* (1996)

J. Brooks, *Dreadnought Gunnery and the Battle of Jutland: The Question of Fire Control* (2005)

D. Brown, *The Royal Navy and the Falklands War* (1987)

A. Burn, *The Fighting Captain: the story of Frederick Walker, CB, DSO***, RN and the Battle of the Atlantic* (1993)

N. J. M. Campbell, *Jutland: analysis of the fighting* (1986)

W. S. Churchill, *The Second World War* (6 vols, 1948–54)

A. B. Cunningham, *A Sailor's Odyssey* (1957)

B. Edwards, *Dönitz and the Wolf Packs: the U-boats at war* (1999)

H. W. Fawcett and G. W. W. Hooper (eds), *The Fighting at Jutland: the personal experiences of forty-five officers and men of the British fleet* (1921)

A. Finlan, *The Royal Navy in the Falklands and the Gulf War: culture and strategy* (2004)

N. Friedman, *Naval Firepower: battleship guns and gunnery in the Dreadnought era* (2008)

——, 'The Royal Navy and the Post-War Naval Revolution, 1946 to the present', in Hill (ed.), *Oxford Illustrated History*

R. Gardiner, (ed.), *The Eclipse of the Big Gun: The Warship, 1906–45* (1992)

—— and R. Gray (eds), *Conway's All the World's Fighting Ships: 1906–1922* (1984)

J. Goldrick, 'The Battleship Fleet: the test of war, 1895–1919', in Hill (ed.), *Oxford Illustrated History*

A. Gordon, *The Rules of the Game: Jutland and British naval command* (1996)

G. Gordon, *British Seapower and Procurement Between the Wars: a reappraisal of rearmament* (1998)

E. Grove (ed.), *The Defeat of the Enemy Attack on Shipping, 1939–1945* (1997)

——, 'A Service Vindicated, 1939–1946', in Hill (ed.), *Oxford Illustrated History*

——, *Vanguard to Trident* (1987)

A. Hague, *The Allied Convoy System, 1939–1945* (2000)

P. G. Halpern, *A Naval History of World War I* (1994)

J. R. Hill, 'The Realities of Medium Power, 1946 to the present', in Hill (ed.), *Oxford Illustrated History*

D. Hobbs, *The British Pacific Fleet: the Royal Navy's most powerful strike force* (2011)

J. Holland, *Fortress Malta: an island under siege, 1940–1943* (2004)

J. Hood (ed.), *Carrier: a century of first-hand accounts of naval operations in war and peace* (2010)

M. Howard, *The Continental Commitment: the dilemma of British defence policy in the era of the two world wars* (1972)

W. Jameson, *Ark Royal: the life of an aircraft carrier at war, 1939–41* (1957)

N. A. Lambert, 'Admiral Sir John Fisher and the Concept of Flotilla Defence, 1904–1909', *Journal of Military History* (1995)

B. Lavery, *Churchill's Navy: the ships, men and organisation, 1939–1945* (2006)

D. Macintyre, *The Battle of the Atlantic* (1975)

——, *Fighting Admiral: the life of Admiral of the Fleet Sir James Somerville* (1961)

——, *U-Boat Killer: fighting U-boats in the Battle of the Atlantic* (1956)

A. J. Marder, *From the* Dreadnought *to Scapa Flow: the Royal Navy in the Fisher era, 1904–1919* (5 vols, 1961–70)

R. K. Massie, *Castles of Steel: Britain, Germany and the winning of the Great War at sea* (2003)

J. Neidpath, *The Singapore Naval Base and the Defence of Britain's Eastern Empire, 1919–41* (1981)

P. Nitze (ed.), *Securing the Seas* (1979)

S. W. C. Pack, *Cunningham the Commander* (1974)

P. Padfield, *The Battleship Era* (1972)

L. Paterson, *U-Boats in the Mediterranean, 1941–1944* (2007)

G. Peden, *British Rearmament and the Treasury* (1979)

P. Pugh, *The Costs of Seapower* (1986)

B. Ranft (ed.), *The Beatty Papers: selections from the private and official correspondence, 1902–1927* (2 vols, 1993)

T. Robertson, *Walker, R.N.* (1956)

S. W. Roskill, *Admiral of the Fleet Earl Beatty: the last naval hero* (1981)

——, *Naval Policy Between the Wars* (2 vols, 1976)

——, *The War at Sea* (3 vols, 1954–61)

M. Rossiter, Ark Royal: *the life, death and rediscovery of the legendary Second World War aircraft carrier* (2006)

P. C. Smith, *The Battles of Malta Striking Forces* (1974)

——, *Pedestal: the convoy that saved Malta* (1998)

The *Sunday Times* Insight team, *War in the Falklands: the full story* (1982)

D. Thomas, *Malta Convoys* (2000)

G. Till, *Airpower and the Royal Navy* (1979)

——, 'Retrenchment, Rethinking, Revival, 1919–1939', in Hill (ed.), *Oxford Illustrated History*

——, *Maritime Strategy and the Nuclear Age* (1984)

D. Twiston Davies, *The* Daily Telegraph *Book of Naval Obituaries* (2007)

D. Wettern, *Decline of British Sea Power* (1982)

A. Williams, *The Battle of the Atlantic* (2002)

J. Wintern, *The Forgotten Fleet* (1969)

R. Woodman, *Malta Convoys, 1940–1943* (2000)

S. Woodward, *One Hundred and One Days: memoirs of the Falklands battle group commander* (1992)

P. Ziegler, *Mountbatten: the official biography* (1985)

NOTES

Abbreviations

ASC: *Anglo-Saxon Chronicle*
BND: *British Naval Documents*

Preface

[1] Nichols, p. 145
[2] Keynes, pp. 9–10
[3] Cordingly, p. 253

Introduction

[1] *ASC*, 975
[2] J. S. Brewer (ed.), *Letters and Papers, Foreign and Domestic, Henry VIII*, vol. II, no. 1113

1 England 793–878

[1] D. Whitelock (ed.), *English Historical Documents*, I (1979), p. 842
[2] *ASC*, 851

2 Sea Rovers 878–901

[1] See Abels, pp. 195ff.
[2] *ASC*, 897

3 The Key 901–1066

[1] *ASC*, 992
[2] *ASC*, 1002

4 Cross Channel 1066–1221

[1] *ASC*, 1085

5 Merchant Warriors 1221–1335

[1] For the foregoing discussion on the Lex d'Oléron see Ward, Appendix I

[2] James, Appendix I
[3] For Walter le Fleming see Platt, pp. 70ff.
[4] See Lloyd, *England and the German Hanse*
[5] Power, p. 18

6 Keeping the Seas 1336–1399

[1] Lloyd, *English Wool Trade*, pp. 144ff.
[2] *BND*, p. 23
[3] *BND*, p. 10

7 Defence of the Realm 1399–1509

[1] *BND*, pp. 25ff.
[2] The discussion of Henry V's navy is based on Rose, *Navy of the Lancastrian Kings*
[3] *BND*, pp. 30–1
[4] For Warwick and the Hanse see Lloyd, *England and the German Hanse*, pp. 195ff.

8 Home Waters 1509–1530

[1] Knighton and Loades, p. 13
[2] ibid., p. 26
[3] *BND*, pp. 81–2

9 Brave New Worlds 1530–1556

[1] Loades, *Tudor Navy*, pp. 135-6
[2] McDermott, p. 25

10 English Guns 1556–1568

[1] Cipolla, p. 36
[2] Williamson, *Hawkins*, p. 71
[3] ibid., p. 96
[4] ibid., pp. 91–2
[5] ibid., pp. 144–5

[6] ibid.

11 Revolution 1568–1585

[1] McDermott, p. 120
[2] Martin and Parker, p. 109
[3] ibid., pp. 109–10
[4] Quinn and Ryan, pp. 84–5
[5] ibid.
[6] Martin and Parker, p. 102

12 The Great Enterprise 1585–1588

[1] Kelsey, *Hawkins*, p. 174
[2] Corbet, *Papers Relating to the Navy During the Spanish War*, pp. 131ff.
[3] ibid.
[4] ibid., p. 109
[5] ibid., pp. 131ff.
[6] Martin and Parker, pp. 116ff.
[7] Laughton, vol. I, p. 58
[8] ibid., p. 59
[9] ibid.
[10] ibid., pp. 186ff.
[11] ibid., pp. 199ff.
[12] ibid.
[13] ibid., pp. 202ff.
[14] ibid.
[15] ibid., p. 211
[16] ibid., pp. 288ff.

13 Battle 1588

[1] Martin and Parker, p. 28
[2] ibid., pp. 152–3
[3] Laughton, vol. I, pp. 288ff.
[4] ibid., vol. II, pp. 133ff.
[5] ibid., vol. I, pp. 288–9
[6] ibid., p. 341

14 Crisis July–August 1588

[1] Martin and Parker, p. 180
[2] Laughton, vol. I, p. 14
[3] ibid.
[4] Martin and Parker, pp. 183–4
[5] For the description of the Hellburners of Antwerp see J. L. Motley, *History of the United Netherlands* (4 vols, 1860–7), chapter v, part 2
[6] Martin and Parker, p. 190
[7] M. J. Rodriguez-Salgado, 'Pilots, Navigation and Strategy in the Gran Armada', in Rodriguez-Salgado and Adams (eds), p. 159
[8] ibid., p. 158
[9] Laughton, vol. II, pp. 53–4
[10] ibid., pp. 97ff.
[11] ibid., pp. 96–7
[12] ibid.
[13] ibid., p. 159
[14] ibid., pp. 183ff.
[15] ibid., pp. 137ff.

15 Aftermath 1588–1603

[1] Andrews, *Elizabethan Privateering*, p. 164
[2] ibid., p. 182
[3] Loades, *Tudor Navy*, pp. 267–8

16 Fallen Colossus 1603–1628

[1] Young, p. 202
[2] Scammell, 'The Sinews of War', p. 353
[3] Lockyer, p. 444
[4] Penn, p. 46
[5] McGowan (ed.), p. 265
[6] Young, pp. 140ff.
[7] Lockyer, p. 273
[8] Young, pp. 187–8
[9] ibid.
[10] Lockyer, p. 275
[11] Young, p. 159
[12] Gardiner, vol. 6, p. 62
[13] Lockyer, pp. 339–40
[14] ibid., pp. 341–2
[15] ibid., pp. 345–6
[16] Wren, p. 333
[17] Penn, p. 134
[18] Hebb, pp. 138–9

17 Sovereign of the Seas 1629–1642

[1] Boxer, p. 64
[2] Young, p. 207
[3] ibid., pp. 239–40
[4] *BND*, p. 148
[5] Young, pp. 239–40
[6] Hebb, p. 227
[7] Penn, p. 260
[8] Sharpe, 'The Personal Rule', pp. 75–6
[9] The best account of the Dutch rise as a trading and colonial power and its

relationship with the English is Israel, *Dutch Primacy*

10 For the early years of the East India Company see Chaudhuri, *The East India Company*

11 Andrews, pp. 156–7

12 Rodger, *Safeguard*, p. 412

13 Dewar, p. 411

18 New Model Navy 1642–1652

1 The definitive work on the Navy of the late 1640s and 1650s is Capp, *Cromwell's Navy*, which has informed much of this part.

2 Rodger, *Command*, p. 12

3 Gardiner and Atkinson (eds), *Papers*, vol. I, p. 404

19 Line of Battle 1652–1653

1 For details of Lawson's life and career see Capp, *Cromwell's Navy,* and J. Binns, 'Lawson, Sir John', *ODNB*

2 Gardiner and Atkinson (eds), *Papers*, vol. IV, p. 111

3 Capp, p. 81

20 Duty 1653–1660

1 Rev. Oliver Heywood, *The Whole Works of the Rev. Oliver Heywood, B.A.* (5 vols, 1827), vol. I, p. 58

2 Dixon, p. 249

3 Capp, p. 86. Again, I must thank Capp's definitive *Cromwell's Navy*.

4 The best account of the role of the Navy during the political crisis of 1659–60 is in Capp.

5 For a modern account of Pepys's relationship with the Navy see Knighton, *Pepys and the Navy*

6 Pepys, *Diary*, 3 May 1660

21 Club Med

1 Charles Shadwell, *The Fair Quaker of Deal; or the humours of the navy, a comedy* Act II. Shadwell served as an officer in the Navy; he died in 1726.

2 The Navy's activities in the Mediterranean in this period are

covered brilliantly in Hornstein, *The Restoration Navy*.

3 Capp, p. 246

4 ibid., p. 244

5 Capp, pp. 204ff.

6 J. R. Jones, 'Fitzroy, Henry, 1st Duke of Grafton', *ODNB*

7 Sugden, *Nelson: the sword of Albion*, p. 710

22 Battlefleet

1 Pepys, *Diary*, 14 June 1667

2 ibid., 19 July 1667

3 For details of the press see Capp, pp. 262ff; Davies, *Gentlemen and Tarpaulins*, pp. 71ff and Rodger, *Command*, pp. 57ff and 126ff

4 Ingram (ed.), p. 49

5 Corbett, *Fighting Instructions*, pp. 118–19

6 John Evelyn, *Diary*, 17 June 1666

7 Ingram (ed.), p. 48

8 Pepys, *Diary*, 14 June 1667

23 Tangerines

1 The indispensable text for the development of the officer corps under the Stuarts is Davies, *Gentlemen and Tarpaulins*.

2 Rodger, *Command*, p. 114

3 Pepys, *Diary*, 28 January 1668

4 Davis, *Gentlemen and Tarpaulins*

5 Anderson (ed.), pp. 96ff.

6 For the duties of captains on convoy duty see Hornstein, *The Restoration Navy*.

7 Sir John Berry, *Dictionary of Canadian Biography Online*, http://www.biographi.ca/009004-119.01-e.php?&id_nbr=59

8 Knighton, *Pepys and the Navy*, pp. 30ff.

24 Mad Proceedings 1677–1694

1 Aubrey, p. 121

2 *Cobbett's Parliamentary History of England*, vol. IV, p. 1189

3 Anon, *The Designs of France Against England and Holland Discovered*, in *The Harleian Miscellany*, vol. IX, p. 164

4 Speck, p. 75

5 Burnet, *History*, vol. III, p. 1264
6 ibid., p. 1025
7 Ehrman, p. 350
8 Aubrey, pp. 95–6
9 ibid., p. 97
10 ibid., p. 99

25 Joint Ops 1694–1713

1 Black, *America or Europe?*, p. 126
2 *Calendar of State Papers Domestic*, 1702–3, p. 190

26 Heaven's Command 1713–1744

1 M. Peters, 'Pitt, William, first Earl of Chatham', *ODNB*
2 Cobbett, *Parliamentary History*, vol. XII, pp. 178ff.
3 Bolingbroke, pp. 120–2
4 *BND*, pp. 323–4
5 Bolingbroke, pp. 115–17
6 Wilson, 'Empire, Trade and Popular Politics'
7 Black, *British Foreign Policy*, p. 21
8 Simms, p. 307
9 ibid., p. 302
10 Willis, *Fighting at Sea*, p. 92
11 Tunstall, p. 90

27 Fall and Rise 1744–1748

1 Duffy, 'Establishment'; Harding, 'Vernon'; Rodger, 'Sea Power; Rodger, 'Anson'
2 Gwynn, p. 131
3 ibid.
4 Mackay, 'Hawke'
5 Simms, p. 351

28 Battle Ready 1748–1757

1 Lavery, p. 99
2 ibid., p. 99
3 Rodger, 'Anson', p. 184
4 Lavery, p. 97
5 ibid., p. 107
6 Middleton, *Bells*, pp. 110–11
7 Richmond, *Papers Relating*, pp. 94–5
8 John, Earl of Chatham, *Correspondence of William Pitt, Earl of Chatham*, vol. I, p. 251

29 Counterattack 1757–1759

1 Middleton, *Bells*, p. 58
2 ibid., pp. 108ff.
3 ibid., pp. 109–10
4 ibid., p. 122. The foregoing account of Hawke's blockade of Brest is drawn from Middleton, *Bells*, pp. 120–5, 136, 142–5, and Middleton, 'British Naval Strategy'.
5 Lloyd (ed.), *Health of Seamen*, p. 121
6 Middleton, *Bells*, p. 121

30 Quiberon Bay 1759–1771

1 Mackay and Duffy, p. 93
2 Marcus, pp. 146–7
3 Burrows, pp. 406–7
4 Mackay and Duffy, p. 87
5 *BND*, pp. 393ff.
6 P. Toynbee (ed.), *The Letters of Horace Walpole, Fourth Earl of Oxford* (Oxford, 1903), vol. IV, p. 314
7 Middleton, *Bells*, p. 150
8 ibid., p. 176
9 Simms, p. 521
10 E. Hasted, *Hasted's History of Chatham* (1996), p. 197

31 The Science of War 1772–1779

1 Black, *Britain as a Military Power*, p. 179
2 Barnes and Owen (eds), vol. III, pp. 201–2
3 Tunstall, p. 145
4 ibid.
5 Willis, *Fighting at Sea*
6 Duffy, 'Hood'; Breen 'Rodney', Knight, 'Howe'
7 Tunstall, p. 118
8 Knight, 'Howe', pp. 287ff.
9 Rodger, *Command*, p. 403
10 Tunstall, p. 129

32 Tactics 1779–1782

1 Trew, p. 79
2 Barnes and Owen (eds), vol. III, pp. 200–2
3 ibid., pp. 210ff.
4 Tunstall, p. 168
5 Duffy, 'Hood', p. 257

6 Mackay and Duffy, p. 122
7 Duffy, 'Hood', p. 259

33 Breaking the Line 1782–1792

1 Hannay (ed.), pp. 101–7
2 Rodger, *Command*, pp. 399ff.
3 Hannay, pp. 101ff.
4 ibid.
5 Nicolas, vol. I, p. 72
6 Mundy (ed), vol. II, p. 255
7 Barnes and Owen (eds), vol. III, pp. 193–5
8 Tunstall, p. 194
9 Talbot, *Pen and Ink*; R. Morriss, 'Middleton, Charles, first Baron Barham', *ODNB*

34 The Old Guard 1793–1794

1 Tunstall, p. 210
2 Hood, p. 132
3 Tunstall, p. 210
4 Nicolas, vol. II, p. 146

35 Eggs and Bacon 1794–1795

1 Nicolas., vol. VII, p. 13
2 Knight, *Pursuit*, p. 296
3 Nicolas, vol. III, p. 49
4 ibid., vol. I, p. 432
5 Naish, p. 89
6 ibid., p. 105
7 Goodall, p. 65
8 Scott, vol. I, p. 41
9 Naish, p. 145
10 Rodger, *Command*, p. 490
11 Gardner, p. 108
12 Robinson, p. 38
13 Spilsbury, p. 6
14 Naish, p. 105
15 Bourchier, vol. I, p. 125
16 Naish, pp. 199ff.

36 A School for Young Officers 1795–1797

1 Naish, p. 230
2 Knight, *Pursuit*, p. 205
3 Nicolas, vol. II, p. 69
4 Naish, p. 281
5 Knight, *Pursuit*, p. 204

6 Raigersfeld, p. 36
7 Frederick Chamier, *Life of a Sailor* (1850), p. 19
8 Naish, p. 307
9 Knight, *Pursuit*, p. 210
10 ibid., pp. 214–15
11 ibid., p. 218

37 The Test 1797–1798

1 Sugden, *Nelson: sword*, pp. 312–13
2 Rodger, *Command*, p. 439
3 Crimmin, p. 334
4 White, *1797*, p. 69
5 Knight, *Pursuit*, p. 226
6 Rodger, *Command*, p. 450
7 Naish, p. 326
8 Knight, *Pursuit*, pp. 282–3

38 The Nile 30 June–2 August 1798

1 Knight, *Pursuit*, p. 277
2 ibid., p. 286
3 Nicolas, vol. III, p. 49
4 White, *Nelson: the admiral*, pp. 25ff.
5 Nicolas, vol. III, p. 49

39 War and Peace 1798–1803

1 Crimmin, p. 341
2 ibid.
3 Rodger, *Command*, p. 465
4 Hoffman, p. 201
5 A. B. Sainsbury, 'Saumarez, James, first Baron de Saumarez', *ODNB*
6 White, *Nelson: new letters*, no. 288
7 Knight, *Pursuit*, p. 373
8 ibid., p. 374
9 White, *Nelson: the admiral*, p. 69
10 ibid., p. 459
11 Knight, *Pursuit*, pp. 459–60

40 The Chase 1803–1805

1 Nicolas, vol. VI, p. 359
2 Sugden, *Nelson: sword of Albion*, p. 673
3 Nicolas, vol. V, p. 437
4 ibid., vol. V, p. 198
5 Sugden, *Nelson: sword of Albion*, p. 699
6 Morrison, vol. II, p. 234
7 Nicolas, vol. VI, p. 156
8 ibid., vol. VII, p. 241n.

[9] Bourchier, vol. I, p. 43
[10] Nicolas, vol. VII, pp. 90–1

41 The Battle 21 October 1805

[1] Sugden, *Nelson: sword of Albion*, p. 794
[2] Fraser, *Sailors*, p. 249
[3] Fraser, *Enemy*, pp. 213–14
[4] Fraser, *Sailors*, p. 249
[5] *Times*, 21 October 1912
[6] Rodger, *Command*, p. 451
[7] Lieutenant P. J. Pickernoll in *The Nelson Dispatch* (Journal of the Nelson Society), vol. VI, part 10 (April 1999)
[8] *Times*, 21 October 1912
[9] Adkins, *Trafalgar*, pp. 114–15
[10] Robinson, pp. 56–7
[11] Leech, p. 134
[12] Adkins, *Trafalgar*, p. 163
[13] ibid., pp. 150–1
[14] Bourchier, vol. I, pp. 72–3
[15] Adkins, *Trafalgar*, p. 220
[16] Robinson, p. 49
[17] Fraser, *Sailors*, p. 259
[18] Dillon, vol. II, p. 52

42 Persuasion 1805–1842

[1] Davies, *Fighting*, p. 181
[2] Lambert, 'Shield of Empire', p. 171
[3] For Parker see Lambert, *Admirals*
[4] *London Gazette*, 17 April 1829, p. 710
[5] Tinnie, 'Slaving Brig *Henriqueta*'
[6] *United Service Magazine*, vol. 27, 1838, p. 519
[7] Leonard, *Western Coast*, p. 173
[8] ibid., p. 171
[9] Bethell, p. 344
[10] Ryan, 'Price', p. 253
[11] Hall and Bernard, p. 126
[12] Graham, *China Station*, p. viii

43 Making the Weather 1842–1860

[1] W. S. Jevans, *The Coal Question* (1866), p. 331
[2] Hyam, p. 54
[3] ibid., p. 65
[4] Semmel, *Liberalism*, pp. 74ff.
[5] Lambert, *Admirals*, p. 233
[6] *Times*, 24 April 1856
[7] *Grey River Argus*, 4 February 1876

44 Arms Race 1860–1899

[1] Scott, pp. 28ff.
[2] ibid.
[3] Massie, pp. 376–7
[4] Beresford, vol. I, p. 49
[5] ibid., p. 41
[6] Fisher, vol. 1, p. 172
[7] For *Inflexible* see Brown, *Warrior*, pp. 65ff.; Beeler, pp. 122ff.; Padfield, pp. 84ff.; Massie, pp. 419ff.
[8] *BND*, pp. 604ff.
[9] Kennedy, p. 237
[10] Mackay, p. 223

45 The Brink 1899–1914

[1] Marder (ed.), vol. I, p. 102
[2] Mackay, p. 39
[3] ibid., pp. 219–20
[4] ibid., p. 285
[5] Sumida, p. 146
[6] N. A. Lambert, p. 83
[7] ibid., p. 107

46 The Reckoning 1914–1916

[1] Massie, *Castles*, p. 112
[2] Marder, vol. III, p. 465
[3] Ranft (ed.), vol. I, p. 247

47 Jutland 31 May–1 June 1916

[1] Fawcett and Hooper (eds), p. 15
[2] ibid., p. 62
[3] ibid., p. 16
[4] ibid., pp. 36ff.
[5] ibid., p. 67
[6] ibid., p. 72
[7] ibid., pp. 64–5
[8] ibid., pp. 68ff., which include the following quotes from Walwyn

48 To End All Wars 1916–1922

[1] Black, *British Seaborne Empire*, pp. 261–2
[2] Roskill, *War at Sea*, p. 279

49 Lean Days 1922–1939

[1] Howard, pp. 120–1
[2] Padfield, *Battleship*, pp. 252–8

[3] Kennedy, p. 335
[4] *LIFE Magazine*, 15 January 1940

50 The *Ark* 1939–1940

[1] Jameson, p. 17

51 Inferno 1940–1941

[1] Churchill, *Second World War*, vol. II, p. 209
[2] Macintyre, *Fighting Admiral*, p. 69
[3] Cunningham, p. 303
[4] ibid., p.373
[5] Pack, p. 177
[6] Jameson, p. 271

52 Armageddon 1942

[1] Churchill, *Second World War*, vol. III, p. 551
[2] *Times*, 14 February 1942
[3] Churchill, *Second World War*, vol. IV, p. 237

53 The Western Approaches 1942–1943

[1] For the Battle of Convoy HG76 see Burn, pp. 18ff.; Robertson, pp. 42–60; Macintyre, *Battle*, pp. 119ff.
[2] Robertson, pp. 38–9.
[3] ibid., p. 60
[4] ibid., p. 62
[5] Burn, pp. 43ff.
[6] Robertson, p. 67
[7] ibid., pp. 66ff; Burn, 46ff.
[8] Robertson, p. 38
[9] Burn, pp. 89, 187ff.
[10] ibid., p. 68
[11] ibid., p. 26
[12] ibid, p. 177
[13] Robertson, p. 66
[14] Williams, p. 276

54 Methodical Elimination 1943–1944

[1] Robertson, pp. 95ff.; Burn, pp. 74ff.
[2] Burn, p. 76
[3] ibid., pp. 89ff.
[4] ibid., p. 79
[5] ibid., p. 81
[6] Robertson, p. 122

[7] Williams, p. 276
[8] Burn, p. 97
[9] ibid., p. 110
[10] Williams, p. 277
[11] Burn, p. 141
[12] Robertson, p. 184
[13] Burn, p. 158
[14] *Times*, 11 July 1944
[15] Burn, p. 172
[16] Robertson, p. 14. *The Times* 11/7/44 made similar comments
[17] Robertson, p. 163

55 East of Suez 1945–1982

[1] Finlan, p. 51
[2] *Hansard*, 19 May 1981
[3] ibid.
[4] ibid.
[5] Woodward, p. 68

56 Conclusion: Set in the Silver Sea 1982–2013

[1] *Daily Telegraph*, 1 June 2012
[2] *Calendar of State Papers Domestic*, 1702–3, p. 190
[3] Woodward, pp. 72–3
[4] ibid., p. 14
[5] *Sunday Times* Insight team, pp. 216–17
[6] The First Sea Lord's Equality and Diversity Directive, November 2009, http://www.royalnavy.mod.uk/About-the-Royal-Navy/Organisation/Life-in-the-Royal-Navy/Equality-Diversity-and-Inclusion/The-First-Sea-Lords-Equality-and-Diversity-Directive
[7] Kennedy, p. 250

INDEX